Lecture Notes in Computer Science 16186

Founding Editors

Gerhard Goos
Juris Hartmanis

Editorial Board Members

Elisa Bertino, *Purdue University, West Lafayette, IN, USA*
Wen Gao, *Peking University, Beijing, China*
Bernhard Steffen , *TU Dortmund University, Dortmund, Germany*
Moti Yung , *Columbia University, New York, NY, USA*

The series Lecture Notes in Computer Science (LNCS), including its subseries Lecture Notes in Artificial Intelligence (LNAI) and Lecture Notes in Bioinformatics (LNBI), has established itself as a medium for the publication of new developments in computer science and information technology research, teaching, and education.

LNCS enjoys close cooperation with the computer science R & D community, the series counts many renowned academics among its volume editors and paper authors, and collaborates with prestigious societies. Its mission is to serve this international community by providing an invaluable service, mainly focused on the publication of conference and workshop proceedings and postproceedings. LNCS commenced publication in 1973.

Sang Kil Cha · Jeongeun Park
Editors

Information Security

28th International Conference, ISC 2025
Seoul, South Korea, October 20–22, 2025
Proceedings

 Springer

Editors
Sang Kil Cha
KAIST
Daejeon, Korea (Republic of)

Jeongeun Park
NTNU
Trondheim, Norway

ISSN 0302-9743 ISSN 1611-3349 (electronic)
Lecture Notes in Computer Science
ISBN 978-3-032-08123-0 ISBN 978-3-032-08124-7 (eBook)
https://doi.org/10.1007/978-3-032-08124-7

© The Editor(s) (if applicable) and The Author(s), under exclusive license to Springer Nature Switzerland AG 2026

This work is subject to copyright. All rights are solely and exclusively licensed by the Publisher, whether the whole or part of the material is concerned, specifically the rights of translation, reprinting, reuse of illustrations, recitation, broadcasting, reproduction on microfilms or in any other physical way, and transmission or information storage and retrieval, electronic adaptation, computer software, or by similar or dissimilar methodology now known or hereafter developed.
The use of general descriptive names, registered names, trademarks, service marks, etc. in this publication does not imply, even in the absence of a specific statement, that such names are exempt from the relevant protective laws and regulations and therefore free for general use.
The publisher, the authors and the editors are safe to assume that the advice and information in this book are believed to be true and accurate at the date of publication. Neither the publisher nor the authors or the editors give a warranty, expressed or implied, with respect to the material contained herein or for any errors or omissions that may have been made. The publisher remains neutral with regard to jurisdictional claims in published maps and institutional affiliations.

This Springer imprint is published by the registered company Springer Nature Switzerland AG
The registered company address is: Gewerbestrasse 11, 6330 Cham, Switzerland

If disposing of this product, please recycle the paper.

Preface

The 28th Information Security Conference (ISC 2025) was held on October 20–22, 2025, at Sungkyunkwan University, Seoul, South Korea.

We were deeply honored to serve as the Program Committee Co-Chairs of ISC 2025, and we would like to express our sincere gratitude to the authors, the reviewers, the steering committee, and the organizing committee who made this conference a success. Special thanks go to the General Chairs (Hyungjoon Koo and Hojoon Lee), the Publications Chair (Yuseok Jeon), and the Publicity Chair (Hyoungshick Kim). We also thank the publisher, Springer, for sponsoring the Best Paper Awards.

This year, 71 program committee members participated, a number similar to last year. However, the number of submissions decreased significantly from 120 to 77. While this reduced the review workload, it also required careful consideration to maintain a high-quality program with enough papers to present at the conference. To uphold academic standards, we introduced a revision phase. As a result, 21 papers were accepted without revision, and 10 papers were conditionally accepted pending revisions. Of these, 7 papers successfully completed the revision process and were accepted for publication, resulting in a total of 28 accepted papers. The final acceptance rate was 36.4%.

We found that introducing a revision phase greatly improved the review process. This phase gave authors the opportunity to address reviewer feedback and strengthen their papers. We recommend that future program chairs consider including a revision phase, especially if submission numbers are lower than expected. Maintaining the size of the program committee, as suggested by previous chairs, was also helpful. With fewer submissions, committee members could manage the extra revision process without being overwhelmed. Thus, we recommend that future program chairs expand the size of the program committee even further.

We invited a significant number of junior researchers to join the program committee. For those serving for the first time, we offered additional guidance and support. Following the advice of previous program chairs, we also encouraged invitees to suggest other qualified researchers who might be interested in participating. This strategy enabled us to quickly identify and recruit capable reviewers.

Once again, we would like to express our deep gratitude to all the authors and reviewers who made this conference possible.

October 2025   Sang Kil Cha
                                                                                                       Jeongeun Park

Organization

General Chairs

Hyungjoon Koo   Sungkyunkwan University, South Korea
Hojoon Lee   Sungkyunkwan University, South Korea

Program Committee Chairs

Sang Kil Cha   Korea Advanced Institute of Science & Technology, South Korea
Jeongeun Park   Norwegian University of Science and Technology, Norway

Steering Committee

Zhiqiang Lin   Ohio State University, USA
Javier Lopez   University of Málaga, Spain
Masahiro Mambo   Kanazawa University, Japan
Nicky Mouha   Strativia, USA
Eiji Okamoto   University of Tsukuba, Japan
Michalis Polychronakis   Stony Brook University, USA
Willy Susilo   University of Wollongong, Australia
Jianying Zhou   Singapore University of Technology and Design, Singapore

Publications Chair

Yuseok Jeon   Korea University, South Korea

Publicity Chair

Hyoungshick Kim   Sungkyunkwan University, South Korea

Program Committee

Basavesh Ammanaghatta Shivakumar	Virginia Tech, USA
Elena Andreeva	TU Wien, Austria
Amit Singh Bhati	3MI Labs, Belgium
Lennart Braun	Université Paris Cité, CNRS, IRIF, France
Ilaria Chillotti	Desilo, South Korea
Haehyun Cho	Soongsil University, South Korea
Hyunwoo Choi	Sungshin Women's University, South Korea
Wonseok Choi	Daegu Gyeongbuk Institute of Science and Technology, South Korea
Kelong Cong	Zama, France
Bor de Kock	TNO, Netherlands
Gabrielle De Micheli	LG Electronics, USA
Bjorn De Sutter	Ghent University, Belgium
Antreas Dionysiou	Frederick University, Cyprus
Jonathan Komada Eriksen	KU Leuven, Belgium
Antonio Flórez-Gutiérrez	NTT Social Informatics Laboratories, Japan
Clement Fung	Carnegie Mellon University, USA
Seyedhamed Ghavamnia	Bloomberg, USA
Shibam Ghosh	INRIA, Paris, France
Giuseppe Antonio Di Luna	University of Rome Sapienza, Italy
Erin Hales	Optalysys Ltd, UK
Hans Heum	Norwegian University of Science and Technology, Norwaya
Minki Hhan	University of Texas at Austin, USA
Panagiotis Ilia	Cyprus University of Technology, Cyprus
Akiko Inoue	NEC, Japan
Daehee Jang	Kyung Hee University, South Korea
Kangkook Jee	University of Texas at Dallas, USA
Chenglu Jin	CWI Amsterdam, Netherlands
Vasileios Kemerlis	Brown University, USA
Hyungseok Kim	Chungnam National University, South Korea
Seongkwang Kim	Samsung SDS, South Korea
Seulbae Kim	Pohang University of Science and Technology, South Korea
Soomin Kim	Korea Advanced Institute of Science & Technology, South Korea
Yi-Fu Lai	Ruhr University Bochum, Germany
Sangho Lee	Microsoft Research, USA
Keewoo Lee	University of California Berkeley, USA

Dongyoon Lee	Stony Brook University, USA
Hyung Tae Lee	Chung-Ang University, South Korea
Yongwoo Lee	Inha University, South Korea
Hilder Vitor Lima Pereira	University of Campinas, Brazil
Akash Madhusudan	3MI Labs, Belgium
Michele Marazzi	ABB Research, Switzerland
Bart Mennink	Radboud University, Nijmegen, Netherlands
Omid Mir	AIT Austrian Institute of Technology, Austria
Hyungon Moon	Ulsan National Institute of Science and Technology, South Korea
Mustafa A. Mustafa	University of Manchester, UK
Pierrick Méaux	University of Luxembourg, Luxembourg
Tapti Palit	University of California, Davis, USA
Robi Pedersen	Technical University of Denmark, Denmark
Octavio Perez Kempner	NTT Social Informatics Laboratories, Japan
Matthieu Rambaud	Télécom Paris, France
Junghwan Rhee	University of Central Oklahoma, USA
Mahdi Sedaghat	KU Leuven, Belgium
Dongdong She	Hong Kong University of Science and Technology, China
Amit Kumar Sikder	Iowa State University, USA
Chengyu Song	University of California, Riverside, USA
Prashast Srivastava	Columbia University, USA
Natalia Stakhanova	University of Saskatchewan, Canada
Chao Sun	Southeast University, China
Giorgos Vasiliadis	Hellenic Mediterranean University and FORTH, Greece
Emmanouil Vasilomanolakis	Technical University of Denmark, Denmark
Alexios Voulimeneas	TU Delft, Netherlands
Alexandre Wallet	PQShield, France
Yuntao Wang	University of Electro-Communications, Japan
Seunghoon Woo	Korea University, South Korea
Guomin Yang	Singapore Management University, Singapore
Kevin Yeo	Google and Columbia University, USA
Yves Younan	Cisco Talos, USA
Arantxa Zapico	Ethereum Foundation, USA
Runzhi Zeng	University of Kassel, Germany
Yizhuo Zhai	Georgia Institute of Technology, USA
Jianying Zhou	Singapore University of Technology and Design, Singapore

Additional Reviewers

Xinagyu Liu
Awais Yousaf
Eyasu Getahun Chekole
Yan Lin Aung
Artemii Ovchinnikov
Anastasia Safargalieva
Artur Cordeiro
Adina Carapostol
Alessandro Colombo
Kazuki Yamamura
Sundas Tariq
Varesh Mishra

Contents

Cryptanalysis and Cipher Security

Improving the Differential-Linear Attack with Applications
to GIFT-COFB, GIFT-64 and HyENA 3
   Zhongxin Zhang, Yincen Chen, Ling Song, and Yin Lv

Keyless Physical-Layer Cryptography 24
   Senlin Liu, Dongshu Cai, Dongchi Han, Hongbo Liu, and Xianhui Lu

The Multi-user Security of GCM-SST and Further Enhancements 45
   Yusuke Naito, Yu Sasaki, and Takeshi Sugawara

Network Security

SimSeq: A Robust TLS Traffic Classification Method 69
   Jinghui Cheng and Fanping Zeng

EvoFuzz: Enhancing State Space Exploration and Seed Prioritization
in Stateful Protocol Fuzzing Using Evolutionary Game Theory 89
   Chengdong Wang, Bo Yu, and Lin Yang

A Lot of Data and Added Complexity. How Does PQC Affect
the Performance of My TLS Connection? 107
   *Johanna Henrich, Nicolai Schmitt, Nouri Alnahawi,
   and Andreas Heinemann*

Post-quantum Cryptography

Conditional Attribute-Based PRE: Definition and Construction from LWE 131
   *Lisha Yao, Jian Weng, Pengfei Wu, Guofeng Tang, Guomin Yang,
   Haiyang Xue, and Robert H. Deng*

LastRings: Lattice-Based Scalable Threshold Ring Signatures 152
   Sohyun Jeon, Calvin Abou Haidar, and Mehdi Tibouchi

Side-Channel Attacks and Countermeasures

Simulation-Based Software Leakage Evaluation for the RISC-V Platform 175
   Nicolai Schmitt, Jannik Zeitschner, and Andreas Heinemann

GIR-Cache: Mitigating Conflict-Based Cache Side-Channel Attacks
via Global Indirect Replacement 196
   Hao Ma, Zhidong Wang, Da Xie, Ciyan Ouyang, and Wei Song

Inference Attacks on Encrypted Online Voting via Traffic Analysis 216
   Anastasiia Belousova, Francesco Marchiori, and Mauro Conti

AI Security

MSPP-Net: Fine-Grained Image Privacy Identification via Multi-stage
Semantic Perception 239
   Yinglong Li, Bingyuan Chen, Qingyan Jiang, and Tieming Chen

Exploring Backdoor Attacks in Federated Learning Under
Parameter-Efficient Fine-Tuning 258
   Xiaofei Huang, Xiaojie Zhu, and Chi Chen

Spoofing Camera Source Attribution via PRNU Transfer Attacks
on Physical and AI Generated Images 279
   Shahriar Rahman Khan, Tariqul Islam, and Raiful Hasan

Biometric Security

Comparative Evaluation of Lattices for Fuzzy Extractors and Fuzzy
Signatures 303
   Wataru Nakamura, Yusei Suzuki, Masakazu Fujio, and Kenta Takahashi

A New Code-Based Formulation of the *Fuzzy Vault* Scheme 323
   Sara Majbour, Morgan Barbier, and Jean-Marie Le Bars

Malware Analysis

HoneySentry: A High-Fidelity Interactive IoT Honeypot for Advanced
Threat Detection 347
   Yanbing Shen, Hao Sun, Jiacheng Wang, Haitao Xu, Gang Liu, and Fan Zhang

Towards Architecture-Independent Function Call Analysis for IoT Malware ... 367
   Kensei Ma, Chansu Han, Akira Tanaka, Takeshi Takahashi, and Jun'ichi Takeuchi

HGANN-Mal: A Hypergraph Attention Neural Network Approach
for Android Malware Detection 388
   Mohammad Reza Norouzian and Claudia Eckert

Systems Security

A Graph-Based Approach to Alert Contextualisation in Security
Operations Centres 411
 Magnus Wiik Eckhoff, Peter Marius Flydal, Siem Peters, Martin Eian,
 Jonas Halvorsen, Vasileios Mavroeidis, and Gudmund Grov

HYPERSEC: An Extensible Hypervisor-Assisted Framework for Kernel
Rootkit Detection 431
 Lionel Hemmerlé, Guillaume Hiet, Frédéric Tronel, Pierre Wilke,
 and Jean-Christophe Prévotet

BOOTMARKER: UEFI Bootkit Defense via Control-Flow Verification 452
 Jihoon Kwon, Junho Lee, MyeongYeol Lee, HyunA Seo, and Jinho Jung

Ali2Vul: Binary Vulnerability Dataset Expansion via Cross-Modal
Alignment 474
 Xinyu Bai, Yisen Wang, Jiajun Du, Chen Liang, Siyuan Liang,
 and Zirui Jiang

Access Control and Privacy

CryptNyx: Password-Hardened Encryption with Strong Anonymity
Guarantees 497
 Tassos Dimitriou and Shahad Alshaher

Efficient Dynamic Group Signatures with Forward Security 518
 Amin Mohammadali and Riham AlTawy

Zero Trust Continuous Authentication Models and Automated Policy
Formulation 539
 Nikhill Vombatkere and Philip W. L. Fong

Smart Contracts and Blockchain Security

Jakiro: A Cross-Modal Contrastive Learning Framework for Detecting
Vulnerabilities in Smart Contracts 563
 Zixuan Niu, Xiaofeng Li, He Zhao, Tong Zhou, and Haotian Cheng

BLOCKLENS: Detecting Malicious Transactions in Ethereum Using LLM
Techniques 581
 Chi Feng and Lei Fan

Author Index 603

Cryptanalysis and Cipher Security

Improving the Differential-Linear Attack with Applications to GIFT-COFB, GIFT-64 and HyENA

Zhongxin Zhang[1], Yincen Chen[1], Ling Song[1](✉), and Yin Lv[2]

[1] College of Cyber Security, Jinan University, Guangzhou 510632, China
songling.qs@gmail.com
[2] School of Computer Science, South China Normal University, Guangzhou, China
lvyin@scnu.edu.cn

Abstract. Differential-linear cryptanalysis is a well-known cryptanalytic method combining differential and linear cryptanalysis. Since its introduction, it has become one of the most important tools for analyzing block ciphers. This paper focuses on differential-linear key-recovery attacks and presents a more efficient key-recovery algorithm by incorporating the partial-sum technique. This algorithm enables the key recovery attack to be divided into multiple steps, and the time complexity of a differential-linear key-recovery attack can be significantly reduced by carefully treating each step. Using this algorithm, we propose the first 19-round differential-linear key-recovery attacks on the message processing phase of GIFT-COFB and HyENA, which are currently the best-known attacks against these ciphers. Additionally, we extend the differential-linear attack on GIFT-64 to 19 rounds, surpassing the previous differential-linear attack by one round. We note that the attack results in this paper are far from threatening the security of GIFT-COFB, HyENA, and GIFT-64.

Keywords: Symmetric-key cryptography · Differential-linear attack · Partial-sum technique · GIFT-COFB · HyENA · GIFT-64

1 Introduction

In the past few decades, researchers have committed to developing algorithms to efficiently and accurately evaluate the security of block ciphers. Differential cryptanalysis [4] and linear cryptanalysis [19] remain the two most profound techniques for assessing the security of block ciphers. Resistance to these two cryptanalytic techniques has become a central criterion in block cipher design. In 1994, Langford and Hellman [15] showed that a high-probability differential of E_0 and a high-bias linear approximation of E_1 could be combined into a distinguisher for the target cipher $E = E_1 \circ E_0$, which is usually called *differential-linear cryptanalysis* and abbreviated as DL cryptanalysis. However, assuming independence of the two subciphers might lead to inaccurate estimations. In order to take the effects of dependency into account, Bar-On *et al.* [3] introduced a new tool: the Differential-Linear Connectivity Table (DLCT). The decomposition $E = E_1 \circ E_0$ used in the classical DL attack was then replaced by the decomposition $E = E_1 \circ E_m \circ E_0$. The decomposition of E into three subcomponents is pivotal for estimating the data complexity and the success probability in subsequent cryptanalytic stages.

In recent years, considerable research effort has been directed toward differential-linear distinguishers, as exemplified by works presented at EUROCRYPT 2021 [17], CRYPTO 2022 [21], and CRYPTO 2024 [20,22]. Key-recovery methodologies for differential-linear cryptanalysis have received relatively less attention, where a basic guessing technique is used to recover the key [16,26].

In contrast, various key-recovery techniques have been developed for differential cryptanalysis, such as the early abort technique [18], the meet-in-the-middle technique [7], and the pre-guessing technique [23]. Similarly, techniques for linear key recovery attacks include the so-called Algorithm 2 proposed by Matsui [19], the Fast Fourier Transform (FFT) based key recovery [11] and its enhancements [14,27]. The partial-sum technique was first introduced by Ferguson *et al.* to enhance the integral key-recovery attack on AES [13]. Recently, Dunkelman *et al.* [12] show that the partial-sum technique and the FFT-based technique can be combined into a new technique that allows enjoying the merits of both. Although the partial-sum technique is mainly used in integral attacks, it applies to linear attacks as well, acting as the counterpart of the early-abort technique for differential cryptanalysis. Indeed, the same idea as the partial-sum technique has been implicitly employed in a linear key recovery attack on GIFT in [24,25].

The block cipher GIFT, proposed at CHES'2017 [2], is one of the most famous lightweight ciphers and commonly targeted by differential cryptanalysis, linear cryptanalysis, and DL crytanalysis. According to the 64-bit and 128-bit block sizes, GIFT has two versions, GIFT-64 and GIFT-128, with 28 and 40 rounds, respectively. Due to its excellent performance, GIFT was also used to build Authenticated Encryption with Associated Data (AEAD) schemes, such as GIFT-COFB [1] and HyENA [8]. GIFT-COFB is an AEAD scheme that instantiates the COmbined FeedBack (COFB) mode [9] with GIFT-128. HyENA [8] is a Nonce-based Authenticated Encryption with Associated Data(NAEAD) scheme that instantiates the hybrid feedback-based(HyFB) mode with GIFT-128. Both GIFT-based AEAD schemes are candidates for NIST's Lightweight Cryptography Standardization Project: HyENA has been selected as one of the second-round candidates, while GIFT-COFB was chosen as a finalist. GIFT has attracted the attention of many researchers since its publication and has been the subject of many cryptanalyses. Table 1 consolidates state-of-the-art cryptanalytic results for GIFT-COFB, HyENA, and GIFT-64, covering key recovery complexities and success rates in differential, linear, and differential-linear cryptanalysis.

Our Contributions. Inspired by Ferguson *et al.* [13], we propose a DL key-recovery algorithm by integrating the partial-sum technique into DL key-recovery attack, aiming to reduce the time complexity of cryptanalytic procedures and potentially extend the number of attackable rounds. Building upon the founda-

Table 1. Summary of relevant analysis results of GIFT

Cipher	Attack	Round	Time	Data	Memory	Ps	Ref.
GIFT-COFB	Linear	16	$2^{122.80}$	$2^{62.10}$	$2^{47.00}$	80.01%	[25]
	Linear	17	$2^{125.09}$	$2^{62.10}$	$2^{62.10}$	80.00%	[14]
	DL	18	$2^{102.06}$	$2^{64.00}$	$2^{64.00}$†	85.23%	[26]
	DL	**19**	$2^{115.61}$	$2^{64.00}$	$2^{64.00}$	**85.23%**	Sect. 4.1
GIFT-64	Differential	19	$2^{112.00}$	2^{63}	2^{80}	–	[28]
	Differential	21	$2^{107.61}$	2^{64}	2^{96}	–	[10]
	Linear	19	$2^{127.11}$	$2^{62.96}$	2^{60}	60.00%	[24]
	DL	18	$2^{124.61}$	$2^{61.57}$	$2^{61.57}$†	85.07%	[26]
	DL	**19**	$2^{119.45}$	$2^{61.57}$	$2^{61.57}$	**85.07%**	Sect. 4.2
HyENA	Linear	16	$2^{122.00}$	$2^{61.51}$	$2^{52.00}$	80.01%	[25]
	DL	18	$2^{119.00}$	$2^{63.97}$	$2^{63.97}$†	85.21%	[26]
	DL	**19**	$2^{117.75}$	$2^{63.97}$	$2^{63.97}$	**85.21%**	Sect. A

† We have checked the memory complexity calculated in [26]. The attack accesses each plaintext-ciphertext pair multiple times, and thus, storing the data is necessary.

tional framework of step-by-step key guessing, we propose a systematic methodology to determine the optimal selection criteria at each step of the key recovery process. We apply the recovery algorithm to GIFT-COFB, HyENA, and GIFT-64 and obtain 19-round DL attacks for the message processing phase of both GIFT-COFB and HyENA, as well as a 19-round attack on GIFT-64. Thanks to the new algorithm, we can extend the DL key-recovery attacks of these three ciphers by one additional round compared to previous DL attacks. To the best of our knowledge, these results are the best attacks against GIFT-COFB and HyENA so far. The comparison of our attacks with previous works is summarized in Table 1. Note that attacks against GIFT-COFB and HyENA in Table 1 are all targeted at the message processing phase.

Organization of this Paper. The rest of this paper is organized as follows. In Sect. 2, we introduce the specifications of the GIFT family, GIFT-COFB, and HyENA, and recall the DL cryptanalysis and the partial-sum technique. In Sect. 3, we propose a new DL key-recovery algorithm using the partial-sum technique. Then in Sect. 4, we employ the new algorithm on GIFT-COFB and GIFT-64 and propose 19-round DL attacks on each of the ciphers. Finally, we conclude this paper in Sect. 5. The details of the 19-round DL attack on HyENA are given in Appendix A.

2 Preliminary

2.1 Description of GIFT and GIFT-Based Ciphers

Here we mainly introduce the description of GIFT-128, and the similar structure to GIFT-64. For more details, please refer to [2]. Both versions of GIFT use a 128-bit master key.

Round Function. The round function of GIFT-128 consists of three operations. For convenience, we consider the 128-bit round state as 32 4-bit nibbles. The three operations of the round function are as follows:

1. **SubCells**: Nonlinear S-box substitutions are applied to each nibble, as is shown in Table 2.

Table 2. The S-box of GIFT

x	0	1	2	3	4	5	6	7	8	9	a	b	c	d	e	f
$GS(x)$	1	a	4	c	6	f	3	9	2	d	b	7	5	0	8	e

Property 1. Let (x_3, x_2, x_1, x_0) and (y_3, y_2, y_1, y_0) be the input and the output of the S-box of GIFT respectively. Then we have $x_2 = y_0 y_3 \oplus y_0 \oplus y_1 \oplus y_2 \oplus 1$ and $x_3 = y_0 \oplus y_1 y_3 \oplus y_2 \oplus 1$.

2. **PermBits**: We denote b_i as the i_{th} bit of the cipher state. $\forall i \in \{127, ..., 1, 0\}$, linear bit permutation $b_{P(i)} \leftarrow b_i$ is applied. The permutation $P(i)$ is defined as follows.

$$4 \left\lfloor \frac{i}{16} \right\rfloor + 32 \left[3 \left\lfloor \frac{i \bmod 16}{4} \right\rfloor + (i \bmod 16) \right] + (i \bmod 4)$$

3. **AddRoundKey**: This step involves adding the round key and round constants. At each round, a 64-bit round key is obtained from the master key. The 64-bit round key RK is viewed as two 32-bit words, i.e., $RK = U||V = u_{31}, ..., u_0 || v_{31}, ..., v_0$. For each round, U and V are XORed with the cipher state, i.e., $b_{4i+2} \leftarrow b_{4i+2} \oplus u_i, b_{4i+1} \leftarrow b_{4i+1} \oplus v_i, \forall i \in \{31, ..., 0\}$. A single bit "1" and a 6-bit constant $C = c_5 c_4 c_3 c_2 c_1 c_0$ are added to each state at bit position $127, 23, 19, 15, 11, 7, 3$ respectively, i.e., $b_{127} \leftarrow b_{127} \oplus 1, b_{23} \leftarrow b_{23} \oplus c_5, b_{19} \leftarrow b_{19} \oplus c_4, b_{15} \leftarrow b_{15} \oplus c_3, b_{11} \leftarrow b_{11} \oplus c_2, b_7 \leftarrow b_7 \oplus c_1, b_3 \leftarrow b_3 \oplus c_0$.

Key Schedule. A round key is first extracted from the key state before the key state update. For GIFT-128, four 16-bit words of the key state are extracted as the round key $RK = U||V$, where $U \leftarrow k_5 || k_4$ and $V \leftarrow k_1 || k_0$. Then the key state is updated as follows, $k_7 || k_6 || ... || k_1 || k_0 \leftarrow k_1 \ggg 2 || k_0 \ggg 12 || ... || k_3 || k_2$, where $\ggg i$ is an i-bit right rotation within a 16-bit word.

GIFT-COFB and HyENA. The specifications of GIFT-COFB and HyENA are as follows.

1. **Description of GIFT-COFB.** The E_K functions in Fig. 1 are referred to as the cipher GIFT-128. The feedback function $G : \{0,1\}^{128} \to \{0,1\}^{128}$ is defined as $G(Y_0||Y_1) = Y_1 || (Y_0 <<< 1)$, where $Y_0, Y_1 \in \{0,1\}^{64}$. The encryption algorithm takes an encryption key $K \in \{0,1\}^{128}$, a nonce $N \in$

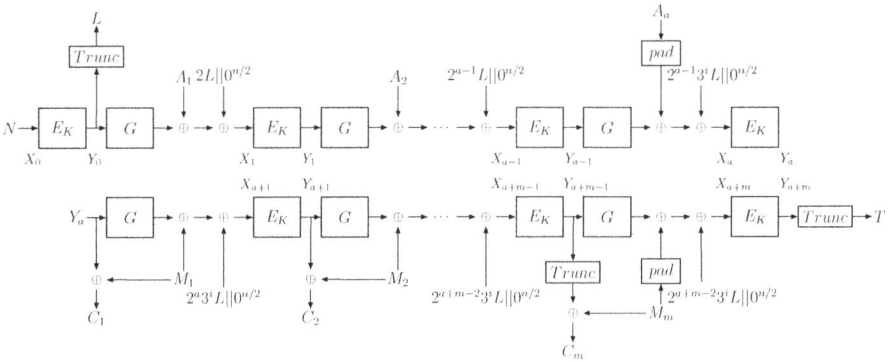

Fig. 1. Encryption of GIFT-COFB.

$\{0,1\}^{128}$ and associated data and message $A, M \in \{0,1\}^*$ as inputs, then outputs a ciphertext $C \in \{0,1\}^{|M|}$ and a tag $T \in \{0,1\}^{128}$. As shown in Fig. 1, the 64-bit value L depends on the values of N and K and thus is unknown. The designers claim that GIFT-COFB achieves 64 bits IND-CPA security under the nonce respecting scenario, thus, the data complexity of valid attacks on GIFT-COFB should be no more than 2^{64}.

2. **Description of HyENA.** The encyption of HyENA [8] is shown in Fig. 2, which takes an encryption key $K \in \{0,1\}^{128}$, a nonce $N \in \{0,1\}^{128}$, and associated data and a message $A, M \in \{0,1\}^*$ as the input and returns a a ciphertext $C \in \{0,1\}^{|M|}$ and a tag $T \in \{0,1\}^{128}$. Similar to the case in GIFT-COFB, HyENA also creates a 64-bit unknown value Δ. The data requirement for a valid attack on HyENA is limited to 2^{64}.

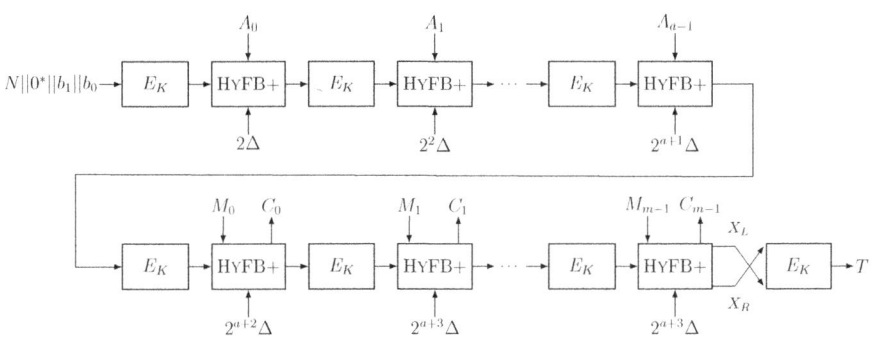

Fig. 2. Encryption of HyENA.

Here we summarize the notations used in our attacks in Table 3.

Table 3. The notations of GIFT

X_i	:The input state of the i-th round, and $X_1 = P$.
Y_i	: The state after *Subcells* transformation of i-th round.
Z_i	: The state after *PermBits* transformation of i-th round.
EY_i	: $PermBits^{-1}(X_{i+1})$.
RK_i	: The round key of i-th round.
EK_i	: $PermBits^{-1}(RK_i)$.
$\mathcal{K}$	:The master key.

2.2 The Differential-Linear Cryptanalysis

In this subsection, we review the general framework of differential-linear cryptanalysis.

Let E be the target block cipher, which can be decomposed as a cascade $E = E_1 \circ E_m \circ E_0$ as illustrated in Fig. 3.

Let Δ_I and Δ_O respectively be the input and output differences of the differential characteristic for E_0, and Γ_I and Γ_O respectively be the input and output masks of the linear characteristic for E_1. Assume that the differential $\Delta_I \xrightarrow{p} \Delta_O$ holds with probability p, and the linear approximation $\Gamma_I \xrightarrow{q} \Gamma_O$ holds with probability $\frac{1}{2} + q$ (or with bias q), and the approximation for the middle part holds with probability $Pr[\Gamma_I \cdot E_m(X_a) = \Gamma_I \cdot E_m(X_b)] = Pr[\Gamma_I \cdot Y_a = \Gamma_I \cdot Y_b] = \frac{1}{2} + r$ (or with correlation r), where "·" denotes the inner product between two vectors. Under the assumption of independence between subciphers, adapting the Piling-up Lemma, the probability of differential-linear approximation can be estimated as: $Pr[\Gamma_O \cdot E(L_a) = \Gamma_O \cdot E(L_a \oplus \Delta_I)] = \frac{1}{2}(1 + prq^2)$ and thus the data complexity is $O(p^{-2}r^{-2}q^{-4})$.

Suppose that N chosen plaintext pairs ($N = O(p^{-2}r^{-2}q^{-4})$) participate in the DL key-recovery attack, with the method in [5], the success probability of the attack can be calculated as

$$P_s = \Phi(2\sqrt{N}|p_{dl} - \frac{1}{2}| - \Phi^{-1}(1 - 2^{-h})),$$

where p_{dl} is the probability of the DL distinguisher and h is the advantage of attack.

2.3 Partial-Sum Technique

The partial-sum technique was first introduced by Ferguson *et al.* to enhance the 6-round integral attack on AES [13]. In the classical integral attack, block ciphers are distinguished based on the integral property (zero-sum) of certain positions, commonly referred to as *balanced positions*. For integral key-recovery attacks, we append a few rounds after the distinguisher. Subsequently, we guess all the involved key bits and verify the integral property on the balanced positions. If the

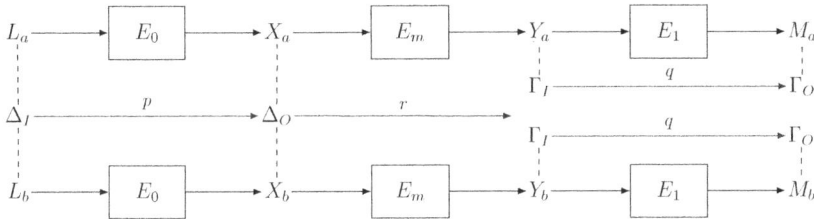

Fig. 3. The differential-linear distinguisher.

sum of these values is zero, we retain the corresponding key guess as a candidate; otherwise, we discard it. Note that the classical integral attack accomplishes the whole task of guessing the involved key bits and verifying the sum value at the end of the distinguisher in one stroke.

The partial-sum technique reduces the time complexity of integral key-recovery attacks by breaking the key guessing process into smaller steps. Rather than guessing all the key bits simultaneously, it allows partial key guessing at each stage and stores the corresponding intermediate values, which enables the verification of integral properties step-by-step. Compared to classical integral attacks, the partial-sum technique distributes the key recovery process, making the time consumption of each step lower than the traditional approach. As a result, the overall time complexity is significantly reduced. For a comprehensive analysis, please refer to [13].

3 A Differential-Linear Key-Recovery Algorithm Utilizing the Partial-Sum Technique

In this section, we review the basic DL key-recovery attack and analyze the time complexity. Then we propose to improve the DL key-recovery attack using the partial-sum technique.

Suppose a DL distinguisher $\Delta_I \to \Gamma_O$ is given and some rounds are added before and after the distinguisher for key recovery attack, as shown in Fig. 4. To facilitate understanding, we define k_b as the subkey bits needed for verifying the differential propagation in the part E_b extended backward from the distinguisher and k_f the subkey bits needed for veifying the linear propagation in the part E_f after the distinguisher. Let $|k_b|$ and $|k_f|$ denote the size of k_b and k_f, respectively, and r_b (resp. r_f) stands for the dimension of the space the plaintext difference Δ'_I (the ciphertext mask Γ'_O) falls in.

3.1 Basic Differential-Linear Key-Recovery Attack

The basic DL key-recovery attack proceeds as follows by guessing the involved key k_b and k_f.

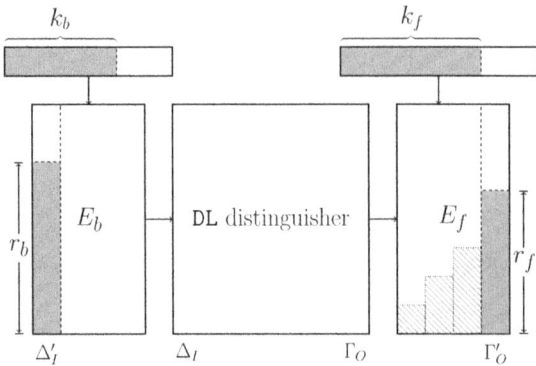

Fig. 4. DL Key-recovery attack

1. Select $D = 2N$ plaintexts, consisting of $y = \frac{D}{2^{r_b}}$ structures, where $N = O(p^{-2}r^{-2}q^{-4})$ as described in Sect. 2.2. Request the ciphertexts of these plaintexts.
2. For all the possible values of k_b:
   a. Partially encrypt the plaintexts in each structure and generate pairs that satisfy the difference Δ_I at the beginning of the distinguisher. The expected number of such plaintext pairs is $y \cdot 2^{r_b-1} = N$. The time complexity of this step is $D \times 2^{|k_b|}$.
   b. For each possible value of k_f:
      * Initialize a counter CT. Partially decrypt each ciphertext pair (C, C') and compute the approximation of $t = \Gamma_O \cdot E_f^{-1}(C, k_f) \oplus \Gamma_O \cdot E_f^{-1}(C', k_f)$, if $t = 0$, then increment the corresponding counter by one.
      * Denote the value of CT as $\mathcal{V}$. If $|\mathcal{V}/N - 0.5| > \theta$, then we accept the key guess as a candidate, where θ refers to a threshold. Set the advantage of attack as h, then with the method in [6], the threshold θ is calculated as: $\theta = \sqrt{\frac{1}{D}} \times \Phi^{-1}(1 - 2^{-(h+1)})$.
      * Exhaustively search for the right key using the candidates.

Complexity Analysis. The data complexity and memory complexity are both equal to D, where $D = 2N$. The time complexity T can be calculated as:

$$T = D \times 2^{|k_b|} + D \times 2^{|k_b|+|k_f|} + 2^{|\mathcal{K}|-h},$$

where $|\mathcal{K}|$ denotes the size of the master key and h is the advantage we set.

3.2 Partial-Sum Technique Used in Differential-Linear Key-Recovery Attack

The basic DL key-recovery attack treats the linear extended part as a whole and obtains the value of $t = \Gamma_O \cdot E_f^{-1}(C, k_f) \oplus \Gamma_O \cdot E_f^{-1}(C', k_f)$ in one step by guessing all the subkey bits k_f involved.

In the partial-sum technique, instead of simultaneously guessing all the subkey bits, we break down the partial decryption into a series of steps. As illustrated by the cyan stepped pattern in Fig. 4, the DL key-recovery process using the partial-sum technique is a gradual progress. In the DL key recovery attack, some rounds may be added before the distinguisher. When we apply the partial-sum technique to the linear extended part, the ciphertexts need to be aggregated to reduce the time complexity. If the partial-sum technique is used when processing the differential extended part, we lose track of the differential propagation of plaintext pairs over E_b. Due to this, we need to guess k_b and handle the E_b first, and then utilize the partial-sum technique for processing E_f.

Suppose processing E_f using the partial-sum technique is divided into ℓ steps, where ℓ is determined according to the concrete situation. Suppose k_{f_i} is the set of subkey bits guessed in Step i of processing E_f, and r_{f_i} refers to the dimension of the space of the intermediate states with uncertain masks after Step i. Step i is equivalent to Step 2b.(i) in the specific description below. Denote z as the XOR value of the intermediate states with mask"1". Similar to Sect. 2.3, at each step, we guess only a portion of the involved key bits and then update the value of z until we reach the output of the distinguisher. For each step, we allocate a counter (list) Cnt_i to record the number of appearances each intermediate state takes, so the size of Cnt_i is $|\mathsf{Cnt}_i| = 2^{r_{f_i}+1}$.

The improved DL key-recovery attack is given as follows.

1. Select $D = 2N$ plaintexts, consisting of $y = \frac{D}{2^{r_b}}$ structures, where $N = O(p^{-2}r^{-2}q^{-4})$ as described in Sect. 2.2. Request the ciphertexts of these plaintexts.
2. For all the possible values of k_b,
   a. Partially encrypt the plaintexts in each structure and generate pairs that satisfy the difference Δ_I at the beginning of the distinguisher. The expected number of such plaintext pairs is $y \cdot 2^{r_b - 1} = N$.
   b. (1) Given those N pairs, allocate a counter list Cnt_1 for each possible value m_1, which includes r_{f_1}-bit value and the value of the target parity z. For each possible value of k_{f_1}, we partially decrypt each ciphertext and compute the value of m_1, then update $\mathsf{Cnt}_1[m_1]$ by $\mathsf{Cnt}_1[m_1] + 1$. The time complexity of this step can be calculated as: $T_1 = D \times 2^{|k_b|+|k_{f_1}|}$.
   (i) For $2 \leq i < l$, allocate a counter list Cnt_i for each possible value m_i, which includes r_{f_i}-bit value and the value of the target parity z. For each possible value of k_{f_i}, perform partial decryption and compute the value of m_i, then update Cnt_i by Cnt_i and Cnt_{i-1}. The time complexity of this step can be calculated as: $T_i = |\mathsf{Cnt}_{i-1}| \times 2^{|k_b|+\sum_{x=1}^{i}|k_{f_x}|}$.

(*l*) In the last step, the value of z is examined to decide if the final-stage counter Cnt_l should be incremented. Denote the value of Cnt_l as $\mathcal{V}$. If $|\mathcal{V}/N - 0.5| > \theta$, then we accept the key guess as a candidate, where θ refers to the threshold. The time complexity of this step can be calculated as: $T_l = |\mathsf{Cnt}_{l-1}| \times 2^{|k_b|+\sum_{x=1}^{l}|k_{f_x}|}$. Then we exhaustively search for the right key using the candidates.

Complexity Analysis. The data complexity is equal to D, where $D = 2N$. The memory complexity is equal to $\max_i\{D, \mathsf{Cnt}_i\} = D$. The time complexity T can be calculated as:

$$\begin{aligned}
T &= D \times 2^{|k_b|} + \sum_{i=1}^{l} T_i + 2^{|\mathcal{K}|-h} \\
&= D \times 2^{|k_b|} + 2^{D+|k_b|+|k_{f_1}|} + \sum_{i=2}^{l} |Cnt_{i-1}| \times 2^{|k_b|+\sum_{x=1}^{i}|k_{f_x}|} + 2^{|\mathcal{K}|-h},
\end{aligned} \quad (1)$$

where $|\mathcal{K}|$ denotes the size of the master key and h is the advantage we set.

Selection Strategy. We aim at optimizing the middle term ($\sum_{i=1}^{l} T_i$) of Eq. (1), thereby reducing the overall time complexity. Thus, the primary criterion for selection is to ensure that the time complexity of each step is balanced as much as possible. The secondary selection strategy is then based on the *greedy algorithm*: we only consider the current step (i) and the immediate next step ($i+1$), which follows two prioritized criteria: 1. the primary objective is to fully exploit the known relationships among keys in order to minimize the number of key bits that need to be guessed at step (i); 2. only when none or multiple selection candidates satisfy the previous criterion do we consider maximizing the difference ($r_{f_{i+1}} - r_{f_i}$) to accelerate the convergence of the search space. The subsequent sections will provide concrete demonstrations of the algorithm's application scenarios.

4 Applications

In Sect. 3, we provide a detailed explanation of how the *partial-sum technique* is applied to differential-linear cryptanalysis. Subsection 4.1 details the algorithm's application in the 19-round differential-linear attack against GIFT-COFB, followed by Subsect. 4.2 showcasing the implementation for the 19-round attack on GIFT-64, and the detailed attack on HyENA will be presented in the Appendix A.

4.1 19-Round Differential-Linear Attack on GIFT-COFB

We target the encryption functions in the message processing phase highlighted in red in Fig. 1 in Sect. 2.1. As shown in the figure, we can get the input X_{a+i} and output Y_{a+i} of E_k, namely GIFT-128. Since L is unknown (depending on nonce N and secret key K), we can not get the value from the most significant 64 bits of the input for E_k. Thus we can propose an attack regarding the underlying primitive GIFT-128 with pairs $(X_{a+i}[63\text{-}0], Y_{a+i})$.

In the following part of this subsection, we give the details of the 19-round DL attack on GIFT-COFB. Our attack is based on a 13-round DL distinguisher from [26]. The correlation of the distinguisher is $2^{-28.78}$ and the active bits in the input difference and the output masks are located at $Z_3[94, 92, 84]$ and $X_{17}[105, 59, 10]$ respectively. As illustrated in Fig. 5, we add three rounds before and three rounds after the 13-round distinguisher. In our attack, the key-recovery attack is broken down into five steps, and we mark S_i ($i \in \{1, \ldots, 5\}$) on the corresponding S-box of step i. The symbol '−' indicates the inactive bits of the state. In the backward extension, '∗' denotes an uncertain bit of difference, and '1' denotes an active bit of difference. In the forward extension, '·' indicates a bit whose value needs to be computed, and '1' indicates a bit linearly involved. Key bits marked with red font in Fig. 5 represent those that have been guessed in the previous steps. The key-recovery attack is detailed with the following steps.

1. Select $D = 2^{64}$ plaintexts, consisting of $y = \frac{D}{2^{r_b}}$ structures, where $r_b = 2^{32}$. Request the ciphertexts of these plaintexts.
2. For all the 2^{22} possible values of k_b,
   a. Partially encrypt the plaintexts in each structure and generate pairs that satisfy the difference Δ_I at the beginning of the distinguisher. The expected number of plaintext pairs is $N = y \cdot 2^{r_b - 1}$.
   b. (1) Given those N pairs, allocate a counter list Cnt_1 for each possible value m_1, which includes r_{f_1}-bit value and the value of the target parity z.

   $$m_1 = EY_{19}[119\text{-}116, 107\text{-}100, 87\text{-}84, 75\text{-}68, 55\text{-}52, 43\text{-}36,$$
   $$23\text{-}20, 11\text{-}4] \| X_{18}[121, 109, 64, 59] \| z,$$

   where $z = X_{18}[97] \oplus X_{18}[76] \oplus X_{18}[14] \oplus X_{18}[2]$. Therefore, the size of Cnt_1 is $|\mathsf{Cnt}_1| = 2^{53}$. For each possible value of k_{f_1}, we decrypt the ciphertexts and compute the value of m_1, then update $\mathsf{Cnt}_1[m_1]$ by $\mathsf{Cnt}_1[m_1] + 1$.

   $$k_{f_1} = RK_1[55\text{-}48, 39\text{-}32] \| RK_2[61, 60, 57, 56, 45, 44] \| EK_{19}[$$
   $$62\text{-}60, 56, 54, 48\text{-}44, 41\text{-}38, 33\text{-}31, 29, 25\text{-}23, 17, 16,$$
   $$13, 8, 0] \| EK_{18}[61, 60, 48, 39, 32, 29, 28]. $$

   Note that there are 19-bit reused subkey bits, $EK_{19}[63, 57, 55, 49, 30, 28, 22, 15, 14, 12, 9, 7, 6, 1]$ and $EK_{18}[55, 54, 49, 38, 33]$, which are also needed in this step. Besides, using Property 1, we can deduce the parity of $X_{18}[14,2]$ without guessing $EK_{18}[7,6,1,0]$. Therefore, we have $|k_{f_1}| = 33$ and the time complexity of this step is: $T_1 = \frac{55}{19 \times 32} \times D \times 2^{|k_b|+|k_{f_1}|} = \frac{55}{19 \times 32} \times 2^{64+22+33} = 2^{115.53}$.

(2) Allocate a counter list Cnt_2 for each possible value m_2, which includes r_{f_2}-bit value and the value of z.

$$m_2 = EY_{19}[119\text{-}116, 103\text{-}100, 87\text{-}84, 71\text{-}68, 55\text{-}52, 39\text{-}36,$$
$$23\text{-}20, 7\text{-}4] \parallel X_{18}[121, 109, 64, 59, 47, 35] \parallel z,$$

z is unchanged in this step. Therefore, the size of Cnt_2 is $|\mathsf{Cnt}_2| = 2^{39}$. For each possible value of k_{f_2}, perform partial decryption and compute the value of m_2, then update Cnt_2 by Cnt_2 and Cnt_1.

$$k_{f_2} = EK_{19}[53, 52, 37, 36, 21, 5] \parallel EK_{18}[23, 22, 17, 16]$$

Note that there are 2-bit reused subkey bits, $EK_{19}[20, 4]$. Therefore, we have $|k_{f_2}| = 10$ and the time complexity of this step is: $T_2 = \frac{6}{19 \times 32} \times |\mathsf{Cnt}_1| \times 2^{|k_b|+\sum_{x=1}^{2}|k_{f_x}|} = \frac{6}{19 \times 32} \times 2^{53+22+43} = 2^{111.34}$.

(3) Allocate a counter list Cnt_3 for each possible value m_3, which includes r_{f_3}-bit value and the value of z.

$$m_3 = EY_{19}[103\text{-}100, 71\text{-}68, 39\text{-}36, 7\text{-}4] \parallel X_{18}[121, 109, 88, 64,$$
$$59, 47, 35] \parallel z,$$

z is unchanged in this step. Therefore, the size of Cnt_3 is $|\mathsf{Cnt}_3| = 2^{24}$. For each possible value of k_{f_3}, perform partial decryption and compute the value of m_3, then update Cnt_3 by Cnt_3 and Cnt_2.

$$k_{f_3} = EK_{19}[59, 58, 43, 42, 27, 26, 11, 10] \parallel EK_{18}[45, 44]$$

Therefore, we have $|k_{f_3}| = 10$ and the time complexity of this step is: $T_3 = \frac{5}{19 \times 32} \times |\mathsf{Cnt}_2| \times 2^{|k_b|+\sum_{x=1}^{3}|k_{f_x}|} = \frac{5}{19 \times 32} \times 2^{39+22+53} = 2^{107.07}$.

(4) Allocate a counter list Cnt_4 for each possible value m_4, which includes r_{f_4}-bit value and the value of z.

$$m_4 = X_{18}[121, 109, 88, 64, 59, 47, 35, 26] \parallel z$$

z is unchanged in this step. Therefore, the size of Cnt_4 is $|\mathsf{Cnt}_4| = 2^9$. For each possible value of k_{f_4}, perform partial decryption and compute the value of m_4, then update Cnt_4 by Cnt_4 and Cnt_3.

$$k_{f_4} = EK_{19}[51, 50, 35, 34, 19, 18, 3, 2] \parallel EK_{18}[13, 12]$$

Therefore, we have $|k_{f_4}| = 10$ and the time complexity of this step is: $T_4 = \frac{5}{19 \times 32} \times |\mathsf{Cnt}_3| \times 2^{|k_b|+\sum_{x=1}^{4}|k_{f_x}|} = \frac{5}{19 \times 32} \times 2^{24+22+63} = 2^{102.07}$.

Fig. 5. 19-round DL Attack on GIFT-COFB.

(5) Allocate a counter Cnt_5 for the target parity z. For each possible value of k_{f_5}, perform partial decryption and compute the value of z, where z can be calculated as follows.

$$z = z \oplus X_{17}[10] \oplus X_{17}[59] \oplus X_{17}[105].$$

If z is equal to 0, then update Cnt_5 by Cnt_5 and Cnt_4. Denote the value of Cnt_5 as $\mathcal{V}$. If $|\mathcal{V}/N - 0.5| > \theta$, then we accept the key guess as a candidate, where θ refers to the threshold. Note that there are 3-bit reused subkey bits, $EK_{17}[53, 52, 28]$, which are also needed in this step. Besides, using Property 1, we can deduce the parity of $X_{17}[59, 10]$ without guessing $EK_{18}[29, 5, 4]$. Therefore, we have $|k_{f_5}| = 0$ and the time complexity of this step is: $T_5 = \frac{3}{19 \times 32} \times |\mathsf{Cnt}_4| \times 2^{|k_b| + \sum_{x=1}^{5} |k_{f_x}|} = \frac{3}{19 \times 32} \times 2^{9+22+63} = 2^{86.34}$. We exhaustively search for the right key using the key candidates.

Complexity Analysis. The data complexity is equal to D, where $D = 2N = 2^{64}$. The memory complexity is equal to $\max_i\{D, \mathsf{Cnt}_i\} = D$. We set the advantage h to 26, then the time complexity T can be calculated as:

$$T = D \times 2^{|k_b|} + \sum_{i=1}^{5} T_i + 2^{|\mathcal{K}|-h} = 2^{115.61},$$

4.2 19-Round Differential-Linear Attack on GIFT-64

We give an 19-round key-recovery attack on GIFT-64 by extending three rounds at the top and appending four rounds at the bottom of a 12-round DL distinguisher from [26]. The correlation of the distinguisher is $2^{-28.61}$ and the active bits in the input difference and the output masks are located at $Z_3[39, 38, 35, 34]$ and $X_{16}[60, 58, 54, 41, 30, 20]$ respectively. We break the key-recovery attack into eight steps, and we mark S_i ($i \in \{1, \ldots, 8\}$) on the corresponding S-box of step i. Key bits marked with red font in Fig. 6 represent those that have been guessed in the previous steps. Table 4 summarizes the k_{f_i} and r_{f_i}-bit value in the i_{th} step, along with the corresponding updates to the target parity z and the time complexity T_i.

Complexity Analysis. The data complexity is equal to D, where $D = 2N = 2^{61.57}$. The memory complexity is equal to $\max_i\{D, \mathsf{Cnt}_i\} = D$. The time complexity T can be calculated as:

$$T = D \times 2^{|k_b|} + \sum_{i=1}^{8} T_i + 2^{|\mathcal{K}|-h} = 2^{119.45},$$

where the advantage h is set to 6.

Table 4. 19-round DL attack procedure table for GIFT-64

Step	r_{f_i}-bit value	k_{f_i}	z	T_i
1	$EY_{18}[63\text{-}32]$ $EY_{18}[23\text{-}20, 7\text{-}4]$ $X_{18}[31, 30, 28, 27, 26, 24]$ $X_{18}[19, 18, 16, 15\text{-}13]$ $X_{18}[11\text{-}9, 3\text{-}1]$	$RK_1[15\text{-}0]$ $RK_2[11\text{-}8, 3\text{-}0]$ $EK_{19}[31\text{-}0]$ $EK_{18}[12, 9, 4, 1]$	z is initialized to zero.	$2^{61.57+24+36} \times \frac{50}{19 \times 32} =$ $2^{117.97}$
2	$EY_{18}[63\text{-}52, 47\text{-}36]$ $EY_{18}[23\text{-}20, 7\text{-}4]$ $X_{18}[48, 35]$ $X_{18}[31, 30, 28, 27, 26, 24]$ $X_{18}[18, 15\text{-}13]$ $X_{18}[11\text{-}9, 1]$ $X_{17}[15, 10]$	$EK_{18}[25, 24, 17, 16]$ $EK_{17}[4]$	$z = X_{17}[14] \oplus X_{17}[13]$	$2^{59+24+41} \times \frac{4}{19 \times 32} =$ $2^{116.75}$
3	$EY_{18}[63\text{-}52, 47\text{-}36]$ $EY_{18}[23\text{-}20, 7\text{-}4]$ $X_{18}[31, 30, 28, 27, 26, 24]$ $X_{18}[15\text{-}13]$ $X_{18}[11\text{-}9]$ $X_{17}[15, 10, 7, 5]$	$EK_{17}[3, 2]$	z is unchanged in this step.	$2^{51+24+43} \times \frac{1}{19 \times 32} =$ $2^{108.75}$
4	$EY_{18}[59\text{-}52, 43\text{-}36]$ $EY_{18}[23\text{-}20, 7\text{-}4]$ $X_{18}[27, 26, 24]$ $X_{18}[11\text{-}9]$ $X_{17}[62, 60, 57, 52]$ $X_{17}[15, 10, 7, 5]$	$EK_{18}[31, 30, 23, 22]$ $EK_{17}[28, 27, 26]$	$z = z \oplus X_{17}[61]$	$2^{49+24+50} \times \frac{5}{19 \times 32} =$ $2^{116.07}$
5	$EY_{18}[55\text{-}52, 39\text{-}36]$ $EY_{18}[23\text{-}20, 7\text{-}4]$ $X_{17}[62, 60, 57, 52]$ $X_{17}[47, 45, 44, 40, 39]$ $X_{17}[15, 10, 7, 5]$	$EK_{18}[29, 28, 21, 20]$ $EK_{17}[20, 19, 18]$	$z = z \oplus X_{17}[37]$	$2^{39+24+57} \times \frac{5}{19 \times 32} =$ $2^{113.07}$
6	$X_{18}[52, 39, 22, 5]$ $X_{17}[62, 60, 57, 52]$ $X_{17}[47, 45, 44, 40, 39]$ $X_{17}[31, 28, 27]$ $X_{17}[15, 10, 7, 5]$	$EK_{18}[27, 26, 19, 18]$ $EK_{18}[11, 10, 3, 2]$ $EK_{17}[12]$	$z = z \oplus X_{17}[30]$	$2^{30+24+66} \times \frac{6}{19 \times 32} =$ $2^{113.34}$
7	$X_{17}[62, 60, 57, 52]$ $X_{17}[47, 45, 44, 40, 39]$ $X_{17}[31, 28, 27, 22, 20]$ $X_{17}[15, 10, 7, 5]$	$EK_{17}[11, 10]$	z is unchanged in this step.	$2^{21+24+68} \times \frac{1}{19 \times 32} =$ $2^{103.75}$
8	\	$EK_{16}[31, 30, 21, 20]$ $EK_{16}[11, 10]$	$z = z \oplus X_{16}[60] \oplus X_{16}[58]$ $\oplus X_{16}[54] \oplus X_{16}[41]$ $\oplus X_{16}[30] \oplus X_{16}[20]$	$2^{19+21+74} \times \frac{0}{19 \times 32} \to$ $2^{110.34}$

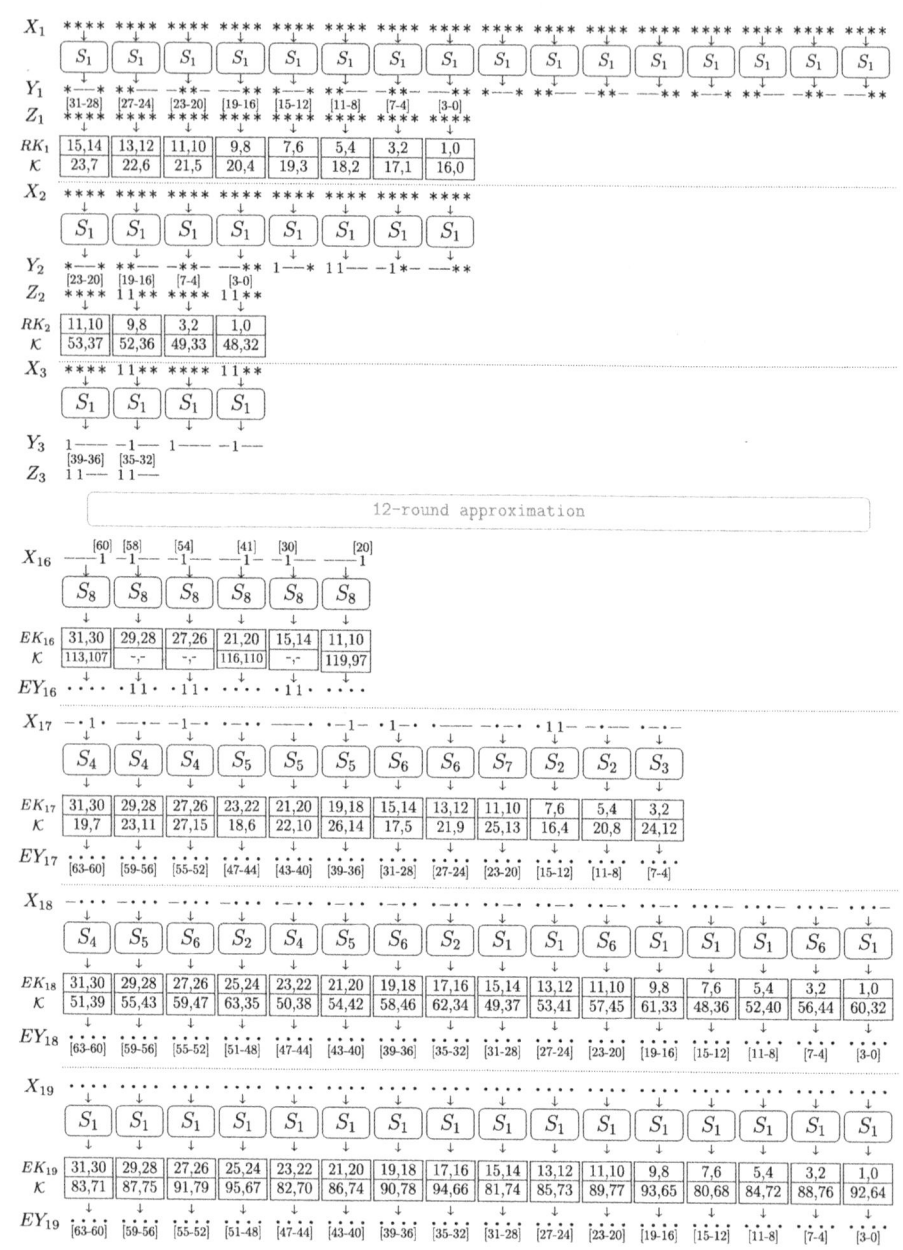

Fig. 6. 19-round DL Attack on GIFT-64.

5 Discussion and Conclusion

In this paper, we showed how to utilize the partial-sum technique in DL key-recovery attack scenarios. To the best of our knowledge, this work represents an initial attempt to adapt the partial-sum technique within the framework of differential-linear cryptanalysis. By applying the partial-sum technique, we propose 19-round DL key-recovery attacks against the message processing phase of GIFT-COFB and HyENA and 19-round DL key-recovery attack against GIFT-64, all of which cover one more round than the previous DL key-recovery attack.

Inspired by [12], we attempted to integrate the FFT-based technique with the partial-sum technique in DL cryptanalysis. In the case of GIFT, applying FFT necessitates fixing the non-XORed state bits with the key, which introduces a bottleneck in optimizing time complexity. Our exploration revealed that FFT-based approaches may be more effective for ciphers that utilize full-state key addition. In future work, it would be worthwhile to explore the application of the partial sum technique to a broader range of cryptographic scenarios.

Acknowledgements. We would like to thank the anonymous reviewers for their helpful comments and useful discussions of the manuscript. The work of this paper was supported by the National Natural Science Foundation of China (Grants 62372213, 62132008) and the Teaching Research and Reform Project of South China Normal University.

A 19-Round DL Attack on HyENA

We target the encryption functions in the message processing phase highlighted in red in Fig. 2 in Sect. 2.1. As shown in the figure, the values of the most significant 64 bits of the input and the full state of the output for the E_k functions (namely GIFT-128) can be obtained.

In the following part of this subsection, we give the details of the 19-round DL attack on HyENA. Based on a 13-round DL distinguisher from [26], a 19-round key-recovery attack is given by adding three rounds at the top and three rounds at the bottom of the distinguisher. The correlation of the distinguisher is $2^{-29.51}$ and the active bits in the input difference and the output masks are located at $Z_3[104, 98, 96]$ and $X_{17}[99, 82, 49]$ respectively. In our attack, the key-recovery attack is broken down into five steps, and we mark S_i ($i \in \{1, \ldots, 5\}$) on the corresponding S-box of step i. Key bits marked with red font in Fig. 7 represent those that have been guessed in the previous steps. In Table 5, the k_{f_i} and r_{f_i}-bit value for each step i are summarized, together with updates to the target parity z and the associated time complexity T_i.

Complexity Analysis. The data complexity is equal to D, where $D = 2N = 2^{63.97}$. The memory complexity is $\max_i\{D, \mathsf{Cnt}_i\} = D$. The time complexity T can be calculated as:

$$T = D \times 2^{|k_b|} + \sum_{i=1}^{5} T_i + 2^{|\mathcal{K}|-h} = 2^{117.75},$$

where the advantage h is set to 9.

Table 5. 19-round DL attack procedure table for HyENA

Step	r_{f_i}-bit value	k_{f_i}	z	T_i
1	$EY_{19}[127\text{-}124, 107\text{-}104]$ $EY_{19}[99\text{-}92, 75\text{-}72]$ $EY_{19}[67\text{-}60, 43\text{-}40]$ $EY_{19}[35\text{-}28, 11\text{-}8]$ $EY_{19}[3\text{-}0]$ $X_{18}[111, 78, 57, 20]$	$RK_1[31\text{-}24, 15\text{-}8]$ $RK_2[19, 18, 7, 6, 3, 2]$ $EK_{19}[61, 60, 59]$ $EK_{19}[57, 55, 54]$ $EK_{19}[51, 44, 41]$ $EK_{19}[39, 38, 28]$ $EK_{19}[26, 25\text{-}22, 18]$ $EK_{19}[13\text{-}6, 3, 2]$ $EK_{18}[55, 54, 39, 38]$ $EK_{18}[28, 27, 12]$	$z = X_{18}[90] \oplus X_{18}[86]$ $X_{18}[53] \oplus X_{18}[24]$	$2^{63.97+22+35} \times \frac{55}{19 \times 32} = 2^{117.50}$
2	$EY_{19}[127\text{-}124]$ $EY_{19}[99\text{-}92]$ $EY_{19}[67\text{-}60]$ $EY_{19}[35\text{-}28]$ $EY_{19}[3\text{-}0]$ $X_{18}[111, 78, 57, 45, 20]$	$EK_{19}[53, 52, 36]$ $EK_{19}[20, 5, 4]$ $EK_{18}[23, 22]$	z is unchanged in this step.	$2^{53+22+43} \times \frac{5}{19 \times 32} = 2^{111.07}$
3	$EY_{19}[127\text{-}124]$ $EY_{19}[95\text{-}92]$ $EY_{19}[63\text{-}60]$ $EY_{19}[31\text{-}28]$ $X_{18}[111, 78, 57, 45, 20, 12]$	$EK_{19}[49, 33, 17, 16]$ $EK_{19}[1, 0]$ $EK_{18}[7, 6]$	z is unchanged in this step.	$2^{38+22+51} \times \frac{5}{19 \times 32} = 2^{104.07}$
4	$X_{18}[123, 119]$ $X_{18}[111, 78, 57, 45, 20, 12]$	$EK_{19}[63, 62, 47, 46]$ $EK_{19}[31, 30, 15, 14]$ $EK_{18}[61-58]$	z is unchanged in this step.	$2^{23+22+63} \times \frac{6}{19 \times 32} = 2^{101.34}$
5	\	\	$z = z \oplus X_{17}[99] \oplus X_{17}[82]$ $\oplus X_{17}[49]$	$2^{9+22+63} \times \frac{3}{19 \times 32} = 2^{90.34}$

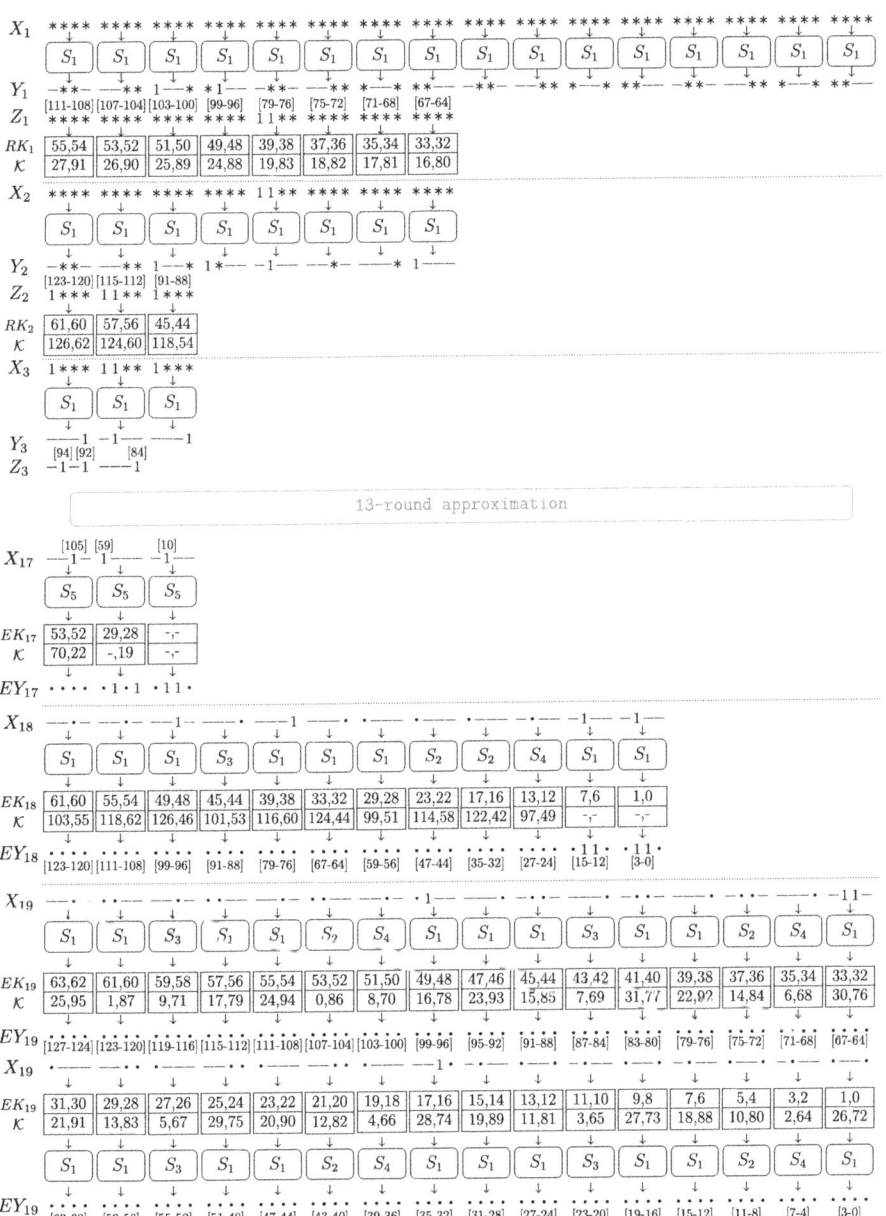

Fig. 7. 19-round DL Attack on HyENA.

References

1. Banik, S., et al.: GIFT-COFB. Cryptology ePrint Archive (2020)
2. Banik, S., Pandey, S.K., Peyrin, T., Sasaki, Yu., Sim, S.M., Todo, Y.: GIFT: a small present. In: Fischer, W., Homma, N. (eds.) CHES 2017. LNCS, vol. 10529, pp. 321–345. Springer, Cham (2017). https://doi.org/10.1007/978-3-319-66787-4_16
3. Bar-On, A., Dunkelman, O., Keller, N., Weizman, A.: DLCT: a new tool for differential-linear cryptanalysis. In: Ishai, Y., Rijmen, V. (eds.) EUROCRYPT 2019. LNCS, vol. 11476, pp. 313–342. Springer, Cham (2019). https://doi.org/10.1007/978-3-030-17653-2_11
4. Biham, E., Shamir, A.: Differential cryptanalysis of DES-like cryptosystems. J. Cryptol. **4**(1), 3–72 (1991). https://doi.org/10.1007/BF00630563
5. Blondeau, C., Leander, G., Nyberg, K.: Differential-linear cryptanalysis revisited. J. Cryptol. **30**, 859–888 (2017)
6. Blondeau, C., Nyberg, K.: Joint data and key distribution of simple, multiple, and multidimensional linear cryptanalysis test statistic and its impact to data complexity. Des. Codes Crypt. **82**, 319–349 (2017)
7. Boura, C., David, N., Derbez, P., Leander, G., Naya-Plasencia, M.: Differential meet-in-the-middle cryptanalysis. In: Handschuh, H., Lysyanskaya, A. (eds.) CRYPTO 2023. LNCS, vol. 14083, pp. 240–272. Springer, Heideleberg (2023). https://doi.org/10.1007/978-3-031-38548-3_9
8. Chakraborti, A., Datta, N., Jha, A., Nandi, M.: HyENA. Submission to the NIST Lightweight Cryptography project (2019)
9. Chakraborti, A., Iwata, T., Minematsu, K., Nandi, M.: Blockcipher-based authenticated encryption: how small can we go? J. Cryptol. **33**(3), 703–741 (2020)
10. Chen, H., Zong, R., Dong, X.: Improved differential attacks on GIFT-64. In: Zhou, J., Luo, X., Shen, Q., Xu, Z. (eds.) ICICS 2019. LNCS, vol. 11999, pp. 447–462. Springer, Cham (2020). https://doi.org/10.1007/978-3-030-41579-2_26
11. Collard, B., Standaert, F.-X., Quisquater, J.-J.: Improving the time complexity of matsui's linear cryptanalysis. In: Nam, K.-H., Rhee, G. (eds.) ICISC 2007. LNCS, vol. 4817, pp. 77–88. Springer, Heidelberg (2007). https://doi.org/10.1007/978-3-540-76788-6_7
12. Dunkelman, O., Ghosh, S., Keller, N., Leurent, G., Marmor, A., Mollimard, V.: Partial sums meet FFT: improved attack on 6-round AES. In: Annual International Conference on the Theory and Applications of Cryptographic Techniques, pp. 128–157. Springer, Heidelberg (2024). https://doi.org/10.1007/978-3-031-58716-0_5
13. Ferguson, N., et al.: Improved Cryptanalysis of Rijndael. In: Goos, G., Hartmanis, J., van Leeuwen, J., Schneier, B. (eds.) FSE 2000. LNCS, vol. 1978, pp. 213–230. Springer, Heidelberg (2001). https://doi.org/10.1007/3-540-44706-7_15
14. Flórez-Gutiérrez, A., Todo, Y.: Improving linear key recovery attacks using Walsh spectrum puncturing. In: Annual International Conference on the Theory and Applications of Cryptographic Techniques, pp. 187–216. Springer, Heidelberg (2024). https://doi.org/10.1007/s00145-025-09554-5
15. Langford, S.K., Hellman, M.E.: Differential-linear cryptanalysis. In: Desmedt, Y.G. (ed.) CRYPTO 1994. LNCS, vol. 839, pp. 17–25. Springer, Heidelberg (1994). https://doi.org/10.1007/3-540-48658-5_3
16. Liu, M., Lu, X., Lin, D.: Differential-linear cryptanalysis from an algebraic perspective. In: Malkin, T., Peikert, C. (eds.) CRYPTO 2021. LNCS, vol. 12827, pp. 247–277. Springer, Cham (2021). https://doi.org/10.1007/978-3-030-84252-9_9

17. Liu, Y., Sun, S., Li, C.: Rotational cryptanalysis from a differential-linear perspective. In: Canteaut, A., Standaert, F.-X. (eds.) EUROCRYPT 2021. LNCS, vol. 12696, pp. 741–770. Springer, Cham (2021). https://doi.org/10.1007/978-3-030-77870-5_26
18. Lu, J., Kim, J., Keller, N., Dunkelman, O.: Improving the efficiency of impossible differential cryptanalysis of reduced camellia and MISTY1. In: Malkin, T. (ed.) CT-RSA 2008. LNCS, vol. 4964, pp. 370–386. Springer, Heidelberg (2008). https://doi.org/10.1007/978-3-540-79263-5_24
19. Matsui, M.: Linear cryptanalysis method for DES cipher. In: Helleseth, T. (ed.) EUROCRYPT 1993. LNCS, vol. 765, pp. 386–397. Springer, Heidelberg (1994). https://doi.org/10.1007/3-540-48285-7_33
20. Niu, Z., Hu, K., Sun, S., Zhang, Z., Wang, M.: Speeding up preimage and key-recovery attacks with highly biased differential-linear approximations. In: Annual International Cryptology Conference, pp. 73–104. Springer, Heidelberg (2024). https://doi.org/10.1007/978-3-031-68385-5_3
21. Niu, Z., Sun, S., Liu, Y., Li, C.: Rotational differential-linear distinguishers of ARX ciphers with arbitrary output linear masks. In: Annual International Cryptology Conference, pp. 3–32. Springer, Heidelberg (2022). https://doi.org/10.1007/978-3-031-15802-5_1
22. Peng, T., Zhang, W., Weng, J., Ding, T.: New approaches for estimating the bias of differential-linear distinguishers. In: Annual International Cryptology Conference, pp. 174–205. Springer, Heidelberg (2024). https://doi.org/10.1007/978-3-031-68385-5_6
23. Song, L., Liu, H., Yang, Q., Chen, Y., Hu, L., Weng, J.: Generic differential key recovery attacks and beyond. In: International Conference on the Theory and Application of Cryptology and Information Security, pp. 361–391. Springer, Heidelberg (2025). https://doi.org/10.1007/978-981-96-0941-3_12
24. Sun, L., Wang, W., Wang, M.: Improved attacks on GIFT-64. In: AlTawy, R., Hülsing, A. (eds.) SAC 2021. LNCS, vol. 13203, pp. 246–265. Springer, Cham (2022). https://doi.org/10.1007/978-3-030-99277-4_12
25. Sun, L., Wang, W., Wang, M.: Addendum to linear cryptanalyses of three aeads with GIFT-128 as underlying primitives. IACR Trans. Symm. Cryptol. **2022**(1), 212–219 (2022)
26. Wang, S., Liu, M., Hou, S., Lin, D.: Differential-linear cryptanalysis of GIFT family and GIFT-based ciphers. IACR Commun. Cryptol. **1**(1) (2024)
27. Wu, W., Li, M., Wang, M.: Improved linear key recovery attacks on PRESENT. IEEE Trans. Inf. Theory (2024)
28. Zhu, B., Dong, X., Yu, H.: MILP-based differential attack on round-reduced GIFT. In: Matsui, M. (ed.) CT-RSA 2019. LNCS, vol. 11405, pp. 372–390. Springer, Cham (2019). https://doi.org/10.1007/978-3-030-12612-4_19

Keyless Physical-Layer Cryptography

Senlin Liu[1,2], Dongshu Cai[1,2], Dongchi Han[1,2], Hongbo Liu[1,2], and Xianhui Lu[1,2(✉)]

[1] State Key Laboratory of Information Security,
Institute of Information Engineering, CAS, Beijing, China
{liusenlin,luxianhui}@iie.ac.cn
[2] School of Cyber Security, University of Chinese Academy of Sciences, Beijing, China

Abstract. We propose a new physical-layer encryption scheme through pilot designs and MIMO techniques. Under formal reduction proofs and informal reliability analysis, we demonstrate that the decoding complexity for the legitimate user grows linearly with the number of antennas, whereas for the eavesdropper, decoding is computationally infeasible. In comparison to traditional wireless physical-layer security schemes, the proposed scheme remains secure even if the eavesdropper has unlimited computing power, infinite antennas, or knows the legitimate channel. Our scheme leverages the physical-layer wireless channel's properties to achieve sophisticated network-layer encryption without a pre-shared key. Additionally, our algorithm involving lattices provides a new approach for secure group communication and can be used to enhance the security of the post-quantum cryptosystem in 6G. Experimental results show that the proposed scheme achieves a bit error rate of approximately 0.5 for the eavesdropper and nearly 0 for the legitimate receiver.

Keywords: Physical layer cryptography · Lattice problems · Channel estimation · MIMO · Wireless security

1 Introduction

Physical layer security (PLS) techniques use the properties of the channel and the inherent uncertainty of noise to prevent eavesdroppers from intercepting confidential information [18]. Compared to traditional cryptography, PLS can reduce the computational complexity of devices and system latency [4]. Furthermore, if eavesdroppers cannot obtain any useful one-bit information in wireless communication, information-theoretic security is achieved [2]. Next, we will review the unreasonable assumptions in traditional PLS and the development process of physical-layer cryptography (PLC).

In recent years, many physical layer security schemes have relied on certain assumptions. Mostafa et al. propose a new beamforming technique to achieve physical layer security and derive the expression of secrecy rates in the wiretap channel model [19]. However, this scheme assumes that the eavesdropper is equipped with only a single antenna. In [23], a low-complexity path tracing algorithm is proposed, which can enhance the secrecy throughput of multiple-input multiple-output (MIMO) wireless communication systems. However, this method also requires restricting the number of eavesdropping antennas. Saad et al. [20] design a new artificial noise algorithm to improve antenna gains, and Zhang et al. [26] propose a layered security approach based on the first-order Taylor algorithm, where these two schemes impose constraints on the computational power of the eavesdropper. In [16] and [22], the authors have demonstrated that the eavesdropper cannot be too close to legitimate users, specifically within half the wavelength of the signal. Otherwise, the security level of these schemes will be compromised.

Furthermore, network-layer cryptography and physical-layer security can be combined to form PLC [12]. In 2013, Dean et al. propose an encryption scheme based on massive MIMO, which utilizes complexity-based security in the cryptography to replace the previously information-theoretic security in the physical layer [5]. The hardness of adversaries' decrypting can be mapped to lattice-based hard problems. Since this encryption scheme is based on the positional differences between legitimate receivers and eavesdroppers, it does not require a key. However, in 2015, authors in [10] and [24] attack this scheme, showing that eavesdroppers can successfully decrypt when the number of eavesdropping antennas is larger than the number of transmitting antennas. Subsequently, in 2017, Dean et al. [6] improve the previous scheme by adjusting security reduction parameters. In 2020, authors in [21] demonstrate that although the new scheme can resist the previous attacks, its correctness is questionable, rendering legitimate receivers unable to decode the signals. These indicate that MIMO-based physical-layer cryptography requires new technologies to achieve the desired security level.

From the above discussion, most of the PLS schemes are based on some unreasonable assumptions, such as limited eavesdropper's antennas, limited eavesdropper's computational power, or far distance between the eavesdropper and the legitimate user. These unreasonable assumptions are not applicable to the security of future 6G. By employing full-duplex and pilot matrix designs, we will present a novel physical layer cryptography scheme that remains secure even if these assumptions do not hold.

2 The MIMO-Lattice Threat Model

2.1 Pilot-Based Channel Estimation

Pilot-based channel estimation involves embedding known pilot sequences into the transmitted data. The receiver then extracts the pilot data and employs suitable channel estimation algorithms to obtain the channel state information (CSI). In Sect. 3, we will assume that the channel estimation is conducted before the formal information transmission. Common channel estimation algorithms include Least Squares (LS) and Minimum Mean Square Error (MMSE).

Next, we will give a toy example to illustrate how to design pilots, which can counter the eavesdropper's channel estimation. Assume a wireless communication system with three legitimate users and one eavesdropper, where the legitimate users have single antennas and the eavesdropper can be equipped with any number of antennas. At the first time, users 1, 2, and 3 transmit pilots x_{11}, x_{21} and x_{31} simultaneously, noting that pilot signals are generally public. At the second time, users 1, 2, and 3 transmit pilots x_{12}, x_{22} and x_{32} simultaneously. At the third time, users transmit pilots $(x_{11} + x_{12})$, $(x_{21} + x_{22})$ and $(x_{31} + x_{32})$ simultaneously.

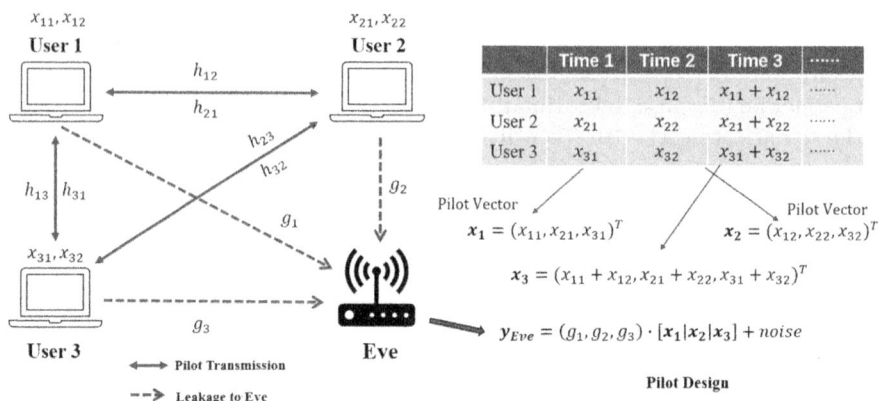

Fig. 1. Pilot Designs at Different Times.

Chosen from any two times, we will demonstrate that the legitimate user can estimate the main channels. For example, if choosing time 1 and time 2, the signals received by user 1 at these two different times are:

$$y_1(1) = h_{21}x_{21} + h_{31}x_{31} + e_1(1)$$
$$y_1(2) = h_{21}x_{22} + h_{31}x_{32} + e_1(2)$$

where $y_1(i)$ and $e_1(i)$ represent the received signals and the channel noises at different times, $i = 1, 2$. Two unknowns h_{21}, h_{31} correspond to two equations, and user 1 can use algorithms like MMSE to estimate the main channels. Similarly, users 2 and 3 can also estimate their own channels. The pilot designs at different times can be seen in Fig. 1.

By using *Data Processing Inequality*, Eve's noise will increase his equivocation of channel estimation. We consider the worst case where the Eve's channel is noiseless and the received signals over the three times are:

$$y_{eve}(1) = g_1 x_{11} + g_2 x_{21} + g_3 x_{31}$$
$$y_{eve}(2) = g_1 x_{12} + g_2 x_{22} + g_3 x_{32}$$
$$y_{eve}(3) = g_1(x_{11} + x_{12}) + g_2(x_{21} + x_{22}) + g_3(x_{31} + x_{32})$$

We can find that: $y_{eve}(1) + y_{eve}(2) = y_{eve}(3)$. There are three unknowns, g_1, g_2, g_3, but only two valid equations exist. In other words, the above eavesdropping channel estimation system is of non-full rank. In theory, even if the eavesdropper has unlimited computational power, he would still be unable to accurately determine the values of g_1, g_2, and g_3. In a later Section, we will prove that the channel estimation error for Eve follows the Gaussian distribution and the formal information transmission can achieve semantic security in the second stage. This idea draws from the theory of secure multi-party computation. In a trivial example, assume User 1, User 2, and User 3 have the private keys sk_1, sk_2, and $(sk_1 + sk_2)$, respectively. It can be observed that any two users can combine to form the master key (sk_1, sk_2) (corresponding to the main channel of the proposed scheme), while the combination of all three users results in a non-full-rank scenario (corresponding to the eavesdropping channel).

Assumptions. For our threat model, we use these assumptions:

1) Different from physical-layer key generation [8], our scheme does not rely on extracting keys from legitimate channels. And, we consider the worst scenario where the eavesdropper can know the legitimate CSI.
2) Different from traditional physical-layer security, our scheme does not require the channel to have a "good" randomness. Even when the secrecy capacity is zero, the proposed scheme can still achieve Shannon's security.
3) Lattice cryptography schemes are provably secure under NP-hard assumptions. Following this, our encryption scheme's security is based on the lattice-based hard problem. However, our scheme doesn't restrict the adversary's computational power and can enable keyless security.
4) Unlike traditional artificial noise methods, the proposed scheme remains secure even when Eve has more antennas than Alice, or even when his antennas are infinite.
5) No assumption is needed about the legitimate channels, because their realizations can be known to all devices, including Eve.
6) The only assumption we need is the passive adversary, which is also a common assumption in physical-layer-cryptography (PLC), as in [6,12,23,25].

Next, we will try to build a bridge between MIMO-based physical-layer security and lattice-based cryptography.

2.2 MIMO-Gaussian Wiretap Model and Lattice Problems

Without loss of generality, suppose both the sender and the receiver are equipped with N antennas, while the eavesdropper is equipped with N_E antennas. Thus, the main channel $\boldsymbol{H}$ and the eavesdropping channel $\boldsymbol{H}_E$ are an $N \times N$ matrix and an $N_E \times N$ matrix, respectively. Each element in the channel matrices follows the complex Gaussian distribution with zero mean and unit variance $\mathcal{CN}(0,1)$. Bob and Eve receive $\boldsymbol{y} = \boldsymbol{H}\boldsymbol{s} + \boldsymbol{e}$ and $\boldsymbol{y}_e = \boldsymbol{H}_E\boldsymbol{s} + \boldsymbol{e}'$, respectively.

On the other hand, if we consider the channel matrix $\boldsymbol{H}$ as a lattice basis, then $\boldsymbol{H}\boldsymbol{s}$ represents the lattice point. Moreover, we can utilize lattice-based techniques to solve the decoding problem in MIMO systems [7]. Next, we will review some lattice-based hardness problems and the relevant theories.

Definition 1. *Covering Radius $\mu(\Lambda)$: the maximum distance from the point $\boldsymbol{x} \in \mathbb{R}^N$ in the N-dimensional space to the lattice $\boldsymbol{L}(\boldsymbol{B})$ is defined as the lattice covering radius: $\mu(\Lambda) = max\ distance(\boldsymbol{x}, \Lambda)$.*

Definition 2. *Approximate Shortest Vector Problem (SVP_γ): given a lattice basis matrix $\boldsymbol{B}$, output a vector $\boldsymbol{v} \in \boldsymbol{L}(\boldsymbol{B})$ such that $\|\boldsymbol{v}\| \leq \gamma\lambda_1(\boldsymbol{L}(\boldsymbol{B}))$, where $\lambda_1(\boldsymbol{L}(\boldsymbol{B}))$ represents the length of the shortest vector in the lattice.*

Definition 3. *Bounded Distance Decoding Problem ($BDD_{L(B),d}$): given a lattice basis matrix B, a vector t and $distance(t, L(B)) < d$, output a vector $v \in L(B)$ such that $\|v - t\| \leq d$.*

It should be noted that when the approximation factor γ is a constant, the SVP is NP-hard [9,17]. In the $BDD_{L(B),d}$, when d is large (e.g., greater than $\lambda_N(L(B))$), the problem is also NP-hard [15]. The security of the lattice-based cryptography relies on these NP-hard problems.

Definition 4. *Denote the encryption algorithm as **Enc** and let m and m' represent the plaintext. An encryption scheme is indistinguishably secure if:*

$$Pr[\textbf{Enc}(m) = c] = Pr[\textbf{Enc}(m') = c]$$

This implies that the adversary's advantage is zero in the attacking game. Usually, indistinguishable security and semantic security are equivalent. We will denote this as IND-secure in Sect. 4.

3 Proposed Physical-Layer Cryptography Scheme

In this section, we will introduce the proposed physical layer lattice-based cryptography scheme which is divided into two stages. In the first stage, each user simultaneously transmits pilot signals for channel estimation through full-duplex. Based on the design of pilot matrices, we will prove that the legitimate users can consistently obtain their CSI. However, at the same time, the scheme can prevent the eavesdropper from estimating the channel correctly. Subsequently, the second stage performs keyless secure transmission among the legitimate users. More specifically, we will prove that Bob's decoding algorithm's complexity is $O(N)$, where N is the number of antennas.

3.1 Anti-eavesdropping Channel Estimation

Considering a system with M legitimate users, each user is equipped with N antennas. And Eve is equipped with N_E antennas. Before private information transmission, each user simultaneously transmits pilot signals for channel estimation. Next, we will discuss how the pilot matrix is designed.

The pilot signals can be derived from the discrete Fourier transform (DFT) matrix [3]. Firstly, the MN-dimensional DFT matrix is defined as:

$$Q_{DFT} = \begin{bmatrix} 1 & 1 & 1 & \cdots & 1 \\ 1 & w & w^2 & \cdots & w^{MN-1} \\ 1 & w^2 & w^4 & \cdots & w^{2(MN-1)} \\ 1 & w^3 & w^6 & \cdots & w^{3(MN-1)} \\ \vdots & \vdots & \vdots & \ddots & \vdots \\ 1 & w^{MN-1} & w^{2(MN-1)} & \cdots & w^{(MN-1)(MN-1)} \end{bmatrix} \quad (1)$$

where $w = e^{(-j2\pi \frac{1}{MN})}$ is the primitive root of unity; j is the imaginary unit.

And then, remove the first column of the matrix $\mathbf{Q_{DFT}}$, the $(M-1)_{th}$ column, and so forth (with an interval of $M-1$ columns). In total, N columns are removed and the remaining matrix is denoted as $\bar{\mathbf{Q}}_\mathbf{0}$.

Secondly, randomly generate an $(M-1)N \times T$ dimensional unitary matrix $\bar{\mathbf{V}}$, where T represents time slot.

Thirdly, multiply the matrix $\bar{\mathbf{Q}}_\mathbf{0}$ by the matrix $\bar{\mathbf{V}}$. To satisfy the Karush-Kuhn-Tucker condition and consider the power constraints of the signal [27], the optimal pilot matrix is:

$$\bar{\boldsymbol{P}} = \sqrt{\frac{E_{pilot}}{N^2(M-1)}} \bar{\boldsymbol{Q}}_0 \bar{\boldsymbol{V}} \in \mathbb{C}^{MN \times T} \quad (2)$$

where E_{pilot} is the total energy of the pilot signal. Obviously, the row rank of the matrix $\bar{\boldsymbol{P}}$ is $(M-1)N$, indicating that the matrix is not full rank.

Fourthly, by using full duplex, all users simultaneously transmit pilots $\bar{\boldsymbol{P}}_j(k)$, where j denotes the user label and k represents the time slot. The pilot transmitted by the user 1 corresponds to rows $1 \sim N$ of the matrix $\bar{\boldsymbol{P}}$, the pilot transmitted by the user 2 corresponds to rows $(N+1) \sim 2N$ of the matrix $\bar{\boldsymbol{P}}$, and so on. Therefore, the pilot transmitted by the user j is:

$$\bar{\boldsymbol{P}}_j = [\bar{\boldsymbol{p}}_j(1), \cdots, \bar{\boldsymbol{p}}_j(T)] \in \mathbb{C}^{N \times T} \quad (3)$$

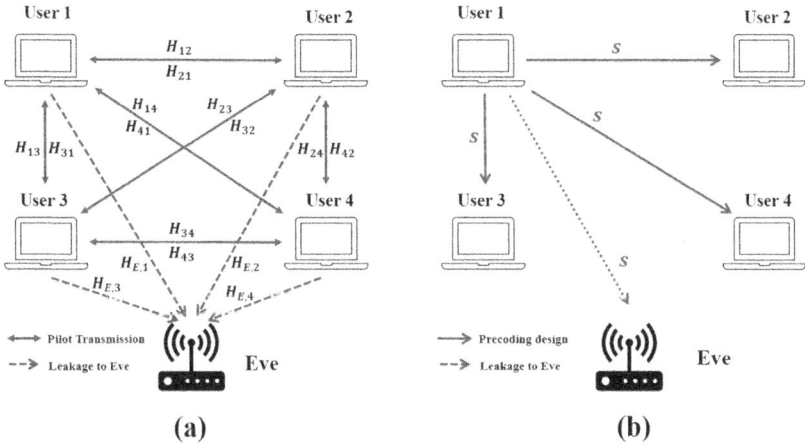

Fig. 2. Two Stages: (a) channel estimation (b) information transmission.

Figure 2(a) depicts the channel estimation process based on full-duplex. And the pilot signal received by the legitimate user i is:

$$Y_i = \sum_{j \neq i}^{M} \boldsymbol{H}_{ij} \bar{\boldsymbol{P}}_j + \boldsymbol{e}_i = \boldsymbol{H}_{(i)} \boldsymbol{P}_{(i)} + \boldsymbol{e}_i \quad (4)$$

where $\boldsymbol{H}_{ij} \in \mathbb{C}^{N \times N}$ represents the channel matrix between the user i and the user j, and $\boldsymbol{e}_i$ represents the additive white Gaussian noise (AWGN). Stack $\boldsymbol{H}_{ij}$ and $\bar{\boldsymbol{P}}_j$ to get $\boldsymbol{H}_{(i)} \in \mathbb{C}^{N \times N(M-1)}$, $\boldsymbol{P}_{(i)} \in \mathbb{C}^{N(M-1) \times T}$ respectively.

Now, the legitimate users can utilize some algorithms such as MMSE, LS and so on to calculate the corresponding CSI. When the pilot's power is infinite [25], the error of channel estimation at the legitimate user can approach 0.

At the same time, the signal received by the eavesdropper is:

$$Y_E = \sum_{i=1}^{M} H_{E,i} \bar{P}_i + e_E = \bar{H}_E \bar{P} + e_E \tag{5}$$

where $\boldsymbol{H}_{E,i} \in \mathbb{C}^{N_E \times N}$ represents the channel matrix between the user i and Eve, $\bar{\boldsymbol{P}}_i$ represents the pilot signal transmitted by the user i, $\boldsymbol{e}_E$ represents the noise. $\bar{\boldsymbol{P}} \in \mathbb{C}^{MN \times T}$ represents the pilot signals from the total of M users and $\bar{\boldsymbol{H}}_E \in \mathbb{C}^{N_E \times MN}$ corresponds to the eavesdropping channel. Now, it is easy to see that the rank of the matrix $\bar{\mathbf{P}}$ is $N(M-1)$, which is not full rank.

Lemma 1: Based on the design of the DFT pilot matrix, Eve's equivalent channel error can be modeled as:

$$\begin{cases} \boldsymbol{H}_E = \boldsymbol{H} + \Delta \boldsymbol{H} \\ \Delta \boldsymbol{H} \sim \mathcal{CN}(0, \frac{P_1 - 1}{1 + MP_1}) \end{cases} \tag{6}$$

where P_1 represents the power of the pilot signal.

Proof: See Appendix A.

Remark 1: Our scheme assumes perfect synchronization mainly to simplify the analysis and to clearly explain the relationship among channel matrices of all parties. In practice, our scheme does not rely on extracting secret keys from the legitimate channel and its realization can be publicly known to all users, including potential eavesdroppers. This is similar to the public parameter in cryptography. Hence, strict synchronization among legitimate users is not required.

3.2 Keyless Secure Transmission

In this subsection, we will introduce a new "interval encoding" to design a physical-layer encryption scheme.

We consider a sequence of L mutually independent messages $\{\boldsymbol{m}_i\}_1^L$ (plaintext in cryptography). As shown in Fig. 2(b), the goal of User 1 with multiple antennas is to securely transmit the plaintext vector to any other legitimate user without relying on a key. The legitimate user 1 (referred to as Alice) maps each $\boldsymbol{m}_i$ to a private vector $\boldsymbol{x}_i \in [ta, ta']^N$, where t is the "interval" of our coding method and a/a' is related to the transmitting power. We don't assume that the channel is relatively constant and the above transmission can be accomplished by L channel uses $\{\boldsymbol{H}_i\}_1^L$. Because $\{\boldsymbol{m}_i\}_1^L$ and $\{\boldsymbol{x}_i\}_1^L$ are mutually independent, from Shannon's secrecy, we just need to demonstrate the security process for one private vector x_i. We will drop the subscript i for convenience.

Alice uses the singular value decomposition (SVD) algorithm to compute:

$$H = U \Sigma V^\dagger \tag{7}$$

where both U and V are unitary matrices, $\Sigma \in C^{N \times N}$ is an diagonal matrix.

Then, Alice transmits the signal $s = Vx$ through the wireless channel, and the legitimate user 2 (referred to as Bob) receives:

$$y = Hs + e = U\Sigma x + e \tag{8}$$

Bob multiplies both sides by the unitary matrix $U^\dagger$:

$$U^\dagger y = U^\dagger U \Sigma x + U^\dagger e = \Sigma x + e_1 \tag{9}$$

where the unitary matrix $U^\dagger$ does not change the magnitude of the noise vector.

Consider the matrix Σ as the lattice-basis of rank N, $\Sigma x + e_1$ corresponds to shifting the lattice Σx by e_1. Bob basically performs eight steps to decode the signal which can be seen in Algorithm 1. Specifically, $U^\dagger y$ belongs to the SVD decoding stage. Then, from Eq. 9, we employ the CVP algorithm to solve for the nearest lattice point, whose complexity scales *linearly* (diagonal basis).

Remark 2: Compared with traditional wiretap codes, our interval code is secure with finite length, making it more practical. For instance, both strong and weak secrecy in prior works rely on the assumption of infinite code length.

Algorithm 1. Decoding Process Based on Lattice

Input: Channel matrix H, received signal y.
Output: Signal x.
1: Use the SVD algorithm to compute: $H = U \Sigma V^\dagger$;
2: Denote each column of the matrix Σ as the orthogonal lattice-basis $\tilde{h}_1 \sim \tilde{h}_N$;
3: Assign $U^\dagger y$ to b: $b \leftarrow U^\dagger y$;
4: Calculate N coefficients $c_j = \lfloor \frac{\langle b, \tilde{h}_j \rangle}{\langle \tilde{h}_j, \tilde{h}_j \rangle} \rceil$, where $j = 1, \cdots, N$;
5: Iteratively calculate from dimension N to dimension 1: $b \leftarrow b - c_j b_j$;
6: Calculate $y_{cvp} = y - b$, which is equal to Σx;
7: Considering Σ as the lattice basis and Σx as the lattice point, then compute x;
8: **return** $\Sigma^{-1} y_{cvp}$, which is equal to x.

Balance Error Rate and Efficiency. According to the theory of the BDD problem, it is necessary to guarantee that the magnitude of the noise satisfies:

$$\|e_1\| \leq \frac{1}{2}\lambda_1 \tag{10}$$

where λ_1 represents the length of the shortest vector in the "Gaussian lattice". According to lattice-based cryptography, the square of λ_1 follows the chi-square distribution [11]. If x is taken from the interval $[ta, ta']^N$, we can obtain:

$$\lambda_1^2 \sim t^2 \chi_N^2 \tag{11}$$

The probability density function of λ_1^2 is given by:

$$f(x) = \begin{cases} \dfrac{t^2}{2^{N/2}\Gamma(N/2)} x^{\frac{N}{2}-1} e^{-\frac{x}{2}} & x > 0 \\ 0 & x \leq 0 \end{cases} \tag{12}$$

where $\Gamma(\cdot)$ denotes the gamma function. In this paper, we use the fact that when $N = 256$ and $t = 8$, the probability of values being less than 128 or greater than 512 is $O(10^{-10})$ (negligible) [11]. Therefore, the lower bound of the length of the shortest vector in the "Gaussian lattice" satisfies:

$$Pr[\lambda_1^2 > 32N] \geq 1 - 10^{-10} \tag{13}$$

Because of $\|e_1\| \leq 1/2\lambda_1$, we can get:

$$\|e_1\|^2 \leq 8N \qquad \frac{\|e_1\|^2}{\sigma_e^2} \sim \chi_N^2 \tag{14}$$

Furthermore, Bob's correct decoding requires that the variance of the noise is less than 4 W. Finally, under this constraint, Bob's error rate of decryption is less than $O(10^{-10})$ by using Algorithm 1.

Remark 3: In practice, the pilot and data can be transmitted together, without the need for a two-phase process as assumed in the above theoretical analysis. The channel estimation and signal detection can be done simultaneously, where the channel may not be constant. Each transmission instance corresponds to a single channel use H_i/H_{Ei}, and hence we do not require a time-invariant channel assumption.

4 Security and Reliability Analysis

The detailed flow diagram of our scheme can be seen in Fig. 3. Specifically, the 16 quadrature amplitude modulation (16-QAM) constellation is illustrated in Fig. 3(1). The channel matrix can be viewed as a lattice basis, and the transmitted vector is the blue lattice point in Fig. 3(2). In a wireless environment, the signal undergoes multiplicative channel and additive noise effects. The distance of the received vector from the lattice point is defined as the bounded error, forming a decoding radius, as shown in Fig. 3(3). Subsequently, the closest vector problem (CVP) algorithm can be utilized to calculate the corresponding lattice point. For User 2, the constellation diagram for 16-QAM demodulation can be seen in Fig. 3(4). For the eavesdropper, the decoding process is similar to that of User 2. Furthermore, if the eavesdropper's equivalent error exceeds the covering radius of the lattice, he will be unable to recover the original lattice point, as illustrated in Fig. 3(5). And, the constellation diagram of the eavesdropper is shown in Fig. 3(6).

Remark 4: Since the modulation type doesn't affect the structure of the channel lattice, our scheme also applies to the phase shift keying (PSK) modulation.

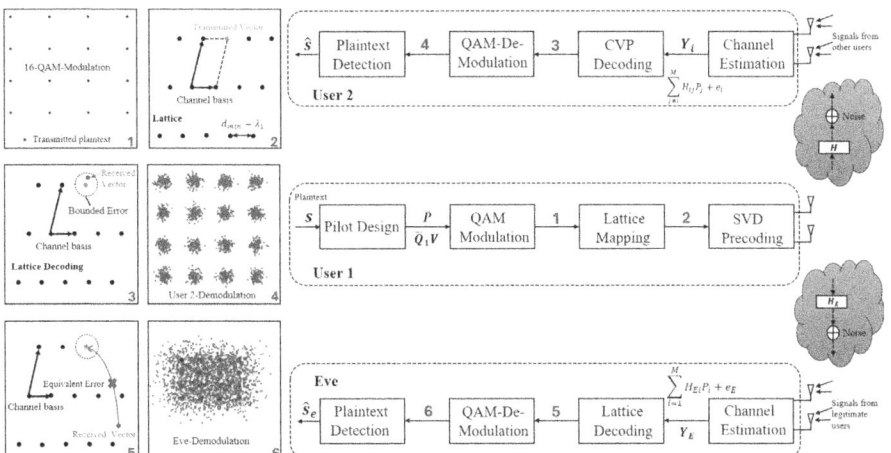

Fig. 3. The block diagram of the proposed keyless physical-layer encryption scheme and the resultant constellations/lattices.

4.1 Security Boundary

By designing the pilot matrix, the eavesdropper's channel estimation process unavoidably incurs errors. From the statistical perspective, Eve receives:

$$\mathbf{y_e} = \mathbf{H_E s} + \mathbf{e}' = \mathbf{Hs} + \mathbf{\Delta Hs} + \mathbf{e}' \tag{15}$$

This MIMO-wiretap channel model is one of the most important instances of the threat model in PLC. Consider the channel matrix $\mathbf{H}$ as the lattice basis, $\mathbf{\Delta Hs} + \mathbf{e}'$ as the equivalent noise term, and $\mathbf{y_e}$ as the ciphertext. Because of $\mathbf{s} = \mathbf{Vx}$, "$\mathbf{s}$" will be considered as the message in the below analysis. The process of recovering the message $\mathbf{s}$ from the ciphertext for Eve is equivalent to solving the BDD problem. When the magnitude of the equivalent noise is larger than the covering radius of the "Gaussian lattice", the BDD problem is NP-hard [15]. Therefore, the hardness boundary can be calculated as:

$$\|\mathbf{e_{BDD}}\| = \|\mathbf{\Delta Hs} + \mathbf{e}'\| \geq \mu(\Lambda) \tag{16}$$

where $\mu(\Lambda)$ represents the covering radius of the lattice (see Sect. 2.2).

In the "Gaussian lattice", when the number of antennas is large, the channel matrix $\mathbf{H}$ is an approximately orthogonal lattice basis. By using $\mathbf{v_1} \sim \mathbf{v_N}$ to represent the lattice vectors, the covering radius satisfies:

$$\mu(\Lambda)^2 = \|\mathbf{v_1} + \cdots + \mathbf{v_N}\|^2 \sim N\chi_N^2 \tag{17}$$

We consider the worst-case scenario: the eavesdropper has an infinite number of antennas, the power of the pilot signal is infinite, and the noise e' is $\mathbf{0}$. Then, from Appendix A and Eq. 17, the equivalent BDD's noise satisfies:

$$\|e_{BDD}\|^2 \sim t^2 a^2 N \frac{P_1 - 1}{1 + MP_1} \chi_N^2 \tag{18}$$

Using the same parameters as in the reliability analysis, we derive the hardness boundary:

$$\begin{cases} \lim_{P_1 \to \infty} \frac{P_1 - 1}{1 + MP_1} = \frac{1}{M} \\ \frac{64a^2 N^2 (\sqrt{1/M})^2}{2} \geq 2N^2 \end{cases} \tag{19}$$

Finally, we can conclude that when the value of parameter "a" exceeds $\sqrt{M}/4$, the eavesdropper's challenge can be reduced to the $BDD_{L(\mathbf{H}),\mu(\Lambda)}$ problem.

4.2 Eve's Equivocation and Secrecy Outage Probability

We further interpret $\mathbf{y}_e = \mathbf{H}\mathbf{s} + \Delta\mathbf{H}\mathbf{s}$ as the encryption process, that is, the plaintext-vector $\mathbf{s}$ is encrypted to the ciphertext $\mathbf{y}_e$. Meanwhile, the message $\mathbf{s}$ can form a complex lattice point from

$$\Lambda_{\mathbb{C}} = \{\mathbf{H}\mathbf{s}, \mathbf{s} \in \mathbb{Z}[i]^N\} \tag{20}$$

where $\mathbb{Z}[i]$ represents Gaussian integers.

Due to limited transmitting power P_t, we define $S_{R_{max}}$ as the maximum sphere centered at $\mathbf{y}_e$ with radius:

$$R_{max}(P_t) = \max_{\|\mathbf{s}\|^2 \leq P_t} \|\Delta\mathbf{H}\mathbf{s}\| = \lambda_{max}\sqrt{P_t} \tag{21}$$

where λ_{max} represents the largest singular value of $\Delta\mathbf{H}$.

As shown in Fig. 3(5), when receiving $\mathbf{y}_e$, Eve will guess the message point. And the total number of guessing lattice points F is:

$$F = |S_{R_{max}} \cap \Lambda_{\mathbb{C}}| \tag{22}$$

where the jth closest BDD lattice point is:

$$S_j = \{\mathbf{H}\mathbf{s} \in \Lambda_{\mathbb{C}} \text{ is the } j^{th} \text{ closest lattice point to } \mathbf{y}_e\} \tag{23}$$

The above signal model uses a one-time pad secret key $\Delta\mathbf{H}$, such that $\mathbf{H}\mathbf{s}$ is the jth closest lattice point to $\mathbf{y}_e$.

Remark 5: We explain the index j as the effective secret key, and the key space is F. Compared with Shannon's one-time pad system, our effective secret key j is no need for Alice and Bob. However, it can fully affect Eve to decode the original plaintext, which motivates our name as *keyless physical layer encryption*.

Obviously, Eve's equivocation $H(s|y_e)$ depends on the value of F. We consider the worst-case scenario where Eve knows the legitimate channel, but Alice doesn't know the eavesdropping channel. Now, F is a function of P_t, $\mathbf{H}$ and $\Delta\mathbf{H}$, while Alice just knows the first two. In this way, Alice can estimate the cumulative distribution function of F:

$$D_F(f, P_t) = Pr\{F < f\} \tag{24}$$

where f is an integer.

Next, we will show that Alice can achieve Shannon's ideal secrecy and perfect secrecy by adjusting our interval encoding and increasing P_t.

1) Shannon's Ideal Secrecy.

Theorem 1: If $P_t > f^{1/N_E} \pi^{-1} \phi^{-2N/N_E} \sigma_1^{-2}$ and $N \to \infty$, for any $f \geq 2$, we have $Pr\{F < f\} \to 0$. And then,

$$H(s|y_e) > 0 \quad \text{(Shannon's ideal secrecy)} \tag{25}$$

where $\phi = [(N_E - N)!/N_E!]^{(2N)^{-1}}$ and $\sigma_1^2 = ((P_1 - 1)/(1 + MP_1))$.

Proof: See Appendix B.

From Theorem 1, no matter how much material is intercepted by Eve, there is not a unique s but many of comparable probability.

2) Secrecy Outage Probability and Shannon's Perfect Secrecy.

Theorem 2: Let $P_t > \rho^{-2/N} f^{1/N_E} \pi^{-1} \phi^{-2N/N_E} \sigma_1^{-2}$, for any given $f \geq 2$ and arbitrarily small $\rho > 0$, the secrecy outage probability satisfies

$$Pr_{sop}(f) \triangleq Pr\{F < f\} < O(\rho) \tag{26}$$

Proof: See Appendix C.

Theorem 2 shows that the secrecy outage probability Pr_{sop} decreases exponentially with the transmitting power P_t. Under this, our scheme can achieve Shannon's perfect secrecy $H(s|y_e) = H(s)$ by using infinite P_t.

4.3 Indistinguishable Security (Semantic Security)

In this part, we explain that the proposed scheme is IND-secure and a new NP-hard problem is defined as:

Problem Formulation 1: MIMO-*Decoding*$_{\mathbf{s},\Delta\mathbf{H}}$: Suppose $\mathbf{s} \in [ta, ta']^N$, $\Delta\mathbf{H} \sim \mathcal{CN}(0, \frac{P_1-1}{1+MP_1})$. Compute $A_{\mathbf{s},\Delta\mathbf{H}} = (\mathbf{H}, \mathbf{y_e} = \mathbf{Hs} + \Delta\mathbf{Hs} + \mathbf{e}')$. The input is a polynomial number of $A_{\mathbf{s},\Delta\mathbf{H}}$. The goal is to output the vector $\mathbf{s}$.

1) Security Reduction. Given the input $(\mathbf{H}, \mathbf{y_e} = \mathbf{Hs} + \mathbf{\Delta Hs} + \mathbf{e'})$, the MIMO-$Decoding_{\mathbf{s},\mathbf{\Delta H}}$ oracle can directly output the message vector $\mathbf{s}$. Next, we will explain the steps of the security reduction:

- Suppose there exists an oracle that can solve the MIMO-$Decoding$ problem;
- Randomly select an N-dimensional lattice basis $\mathbf{H}$ from $\mathcal{CN}(0,1)$;
- Construct the lattice points $\mathbf{Hs}$ by choosing $\mathbf{s}$ from the interval $[ta, ta']^N$, where $a \geq \frac{\sqrt{M}}{4}$ and M is the number of the legitimate users;
- Randomly select a matrix $\mathbf{\Delta H}$ from the Gaussian distribution $\mathcal{CN}(0, \frac{P_1-1}{1+MP_1})$ and the noise vector $\mathbf{e'}$ from the Gaussian distribution $\mathcal{CN}(0,1)$.
- Compute $\mathbf{\Delta Hs}$ and add together to get $\mathbf{\Delta Hs} + \mathbf{e'}$;
- Consider $\mathbf{\Delta Hs} + \mathbf{e'}$ as the equivalent noise term $\mathbf{e_{BDD}}$. And then, compute $\mathbf{y_e} = \mathbf{Hs} + \mathbf{e_{BDD}}$;
- Input the result $\mathbf{y_e}$ into the MIMO-$Decoding_{\mathbf{s},\mathbf{\Delta H}}$ oracle, and we can obtain the message vector $\mathbf{s}$.

Based on this, $\mathbf{y_e}$ can be seen as an instance of the $BDD_{L(\mathbf{H}), \|\mathbf{e_{BDD}}\|}$ problem, where we have proved that $\|\mathbf{e_{BDD}}\| \geq \mu(\Lambda)$. By using the MIMO-$Decoding_{\mathbf{s},\mathbf{\Delta H}}$ oracle, we can find the lattice point $\mathbf{Hs}$. However, based on the below claim, the $BDD_{L(\mathbf{H}), \|\mathbf{e_{BDD}}\|}$ problem is known to be hard, indicating that the MIMO-$Decoding_{\mathbf{s},\mathbf{\Delta H}}$ problem is also hard.

Claim: Even if Eve's computational power is unlimited, there is no algorithm that can solve the $BDD_{L(H),d}$ problem, where $d > \mu(\Lambda)$ [14].

2) The adversarial experiment. The adversarial experiment can be considered as an instance of the BDD problem:

- The adversary $\mathcal{A}$ choose a pair of signals $\mathbf{s_0}, \mathbf{s_1}$ from the interval $[ta, ta']^N$;
- Randomly choose a uniform bit $b \in \{0,1\}$. The ciphertext is calculated as: $c = \mathbf{y_e} = \mathbf{Hs}_b + \mathbf{e}_{BDD}$;
- Give the challenge ciphertext $\mathbf{y_e}$ and channel matrix $\mathbf{H}$ to the adversary $\mathcal{A}$;
- The adversary $\mathcal{A}$ outputs a bit b';
- The output of the experiment is defined to be 0 if $b' \neq b$, and 1 otherwise. If the output of the experiment is 0, we will conclude that $\mathcal{A}$ fails;

More specifically, we can get that the probability of success for the adversary $\mathcal{A}$ is 1/2, which is equivalent to random guessing. In other words, the adversary's advantage is zero. Therefore, the proposed scheme is indistinguishably secure.

5 Implementation and Discussion

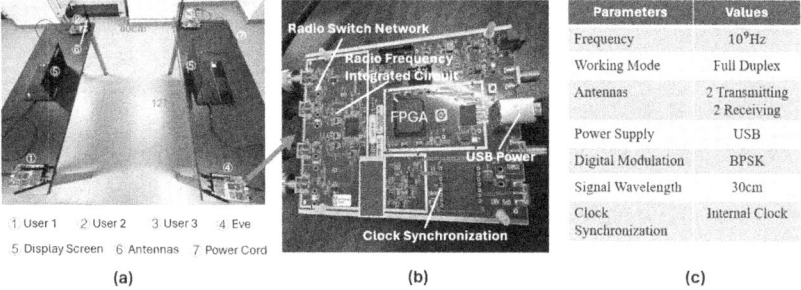

Fig. 4. (a) Laboratory Environment; (b) USRP B210(Users/Eve); (c) Parameters.

This section explains the practicality of the proposed physical layer lattice-based encryption scheme on the universal software radio peripheral (USRP) platform, and the experimental setup can be seen in Fig. 4. The legitimate users simultaneously send our designed pilot signals and perform channel estimation individually which can be seen in Fig. 5. As illustrated in Fig. 6(a), Eve can also try to estimate his channels to User 1. Since both User 1 and Eve are equipped with two antennas, four sub-channels need to be estimated, where the "1-1" in the figure represents the channel between the first antenna of the eavesdropper and the first antenna of User 1. Similarly, the remaining channels can be estimated as shown in Fig. 6(b) and 6(c).

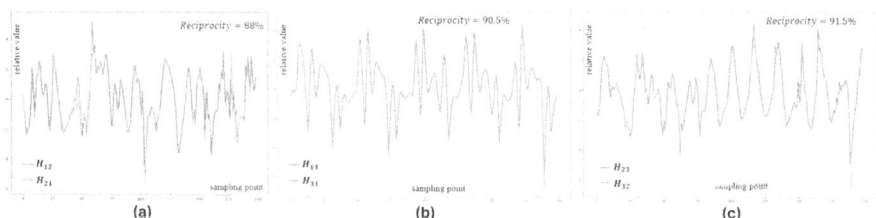

Fig. 5. Channel estimation between: (a) User 1 and 2; (b) User 1 and 3; (c) User 2 and 3.

Remark 6: Our scheme does not rely on extracting secret keys from the legitimate channel and its realization can be publicly known to all users, including potential eavesdroppers. Therefore, it suffices for a single user to estimate the legitimate CSI and transmit it over the public channel, where the channel reciprocity is also not required.

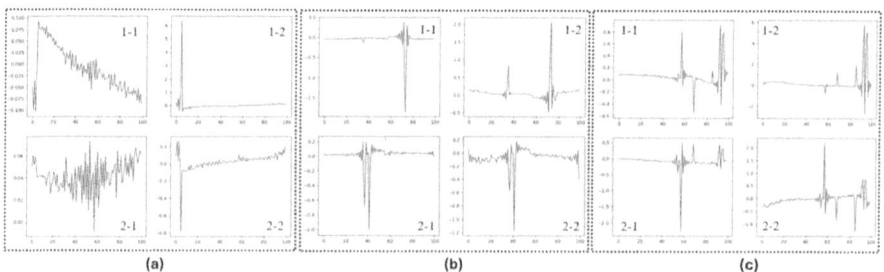

Fig. 6. Channel estimation between Eve and (a) User 1; (b) User 2; (c) User 3. The x-axis and y-axis represent sampling point and relative value, respectively.

Wireless physical layer security's evaluation metrics can be divided into two categories. The first ones are theoretical metrics, including secrecy capacity, secrecy outage probability, ergodic secrecy capacity, and so on. The second ones are practical metrics, including bit error rate (BER), secrecy region, symbol error rate, secrecy rate, and so on. The BER will be used to reflect the security of the proposed scheme in the following paragraphs.

We designate User 1 as Alice, who transmits the signal, and User 2 as Bob, who receives the information. The results in Fig. 7 demonstrate that as the signal-to-noise ratio (SNR) increases from 0 to 17.5, Bob's decoding error probability significantly decreases. In contrast, when the SNR increases from 0 to 17.5, Eve's decoding error probability remains close to 50%. This is because the increase in signal power amplifies the "equivalent error" for the eavesdropper (see Fig. 3). Thus, augmenting the SNR does not reduce Eve's decoding error probability, which aligns with the security analysis presented in Sect. 4.

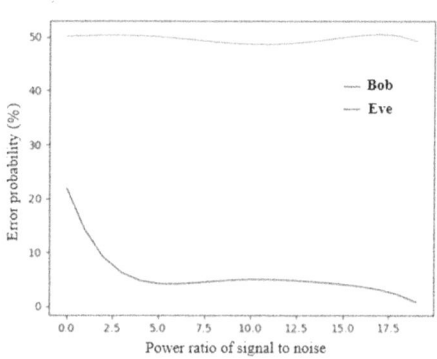

Fig. 7. Decoding bit error probability of Eve and Bob.

Because massive MIMO-devices are prohibitively expensive, only two antennas are used in the experiments. The number of antennas in MIMO-based physical layer security corresponds to the dimension of the lattice-based cryptography (security parameter), thus two antennas are insufficient. Consequently, further simulations are conducted using MATLAB.

The security of the proposed physical layer encryption scheme is not based on the limited eavesdropping antennas, as illustrated in Fig. 8(a). For Bob, the BER decreases from 10^{-1} to nearly 0 as the SNR increases. In contrast, Eve's BER lies between 0.4 and 0.5. Although an increase in the number of eavesdropping antennas from 128 to 512 results in a slight reduction in BER (possibly associated with diversity), the overall BER remains high. The comparison of the four curves reveals that the BER for legitimate users is significantly lower than that of the eavesdropper. Given that the eavesdropper's BER approaches 0.5 (random guessing), it follows that the scheme remains secure when the eavesdropper is equipped with additional antennas. As illustrated in Fig. 8(b), the eavesdropper cannot correctly decode the message under different modulations. In Fig. 8(c), we construct a two-dimensional wiretap channel model, and Eve's positions are gradually closer to the transmitter. Regardless of any distance, the BER for legitimate users is significantly lower than that of the eavesdropper.

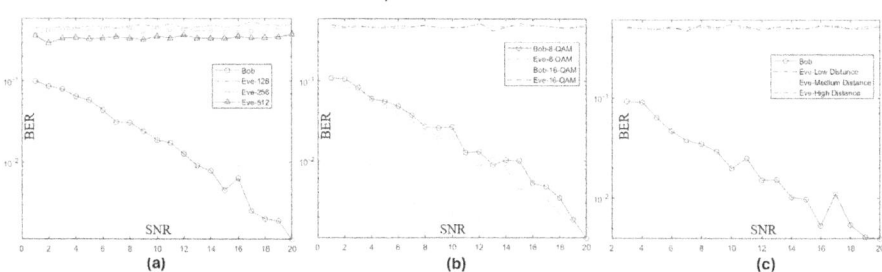

Fig. 8. BER of Eve and Bob: (a) Different Antennas; (b) Different Modulations; (c) Different Distances.

6 Conclusion

We propose a new physical layer lattice-based cryptography scheme which guarantees Shannon's perfect secrecy and ideal secrecy. Based on the pilot designs and multi-party computation, we extend the traditional MIMO detection problem to the new MIMO-$Decoding_{s,\Delta H}$ problem. Then, the newly formulated problem can be reduced to the NP-hard problem in the lattice. If the equivalent error term exceeds the covering radius of the "channel lattice", the eavesdropper will be unable to recover the corresponding lattice point. The proposed scheme is evaluated at both the theoretical and systematic levels. We have conducted the experiment by using the USRP platform to reflect the security of the proposed scheme, where the BER is close to 0.5 at the eavesdropper and almost 0 at the legitimate receiver. For performance, by utilizing full duplex and MIMO, legitimate users can successfully decode the plaintext without incurring additional overhead. For practicality, we demonstrate that the channels between different legitimate users confirm reciprocity. For security, even if the eavesdropper knows the legitimate channel, he still cannot decode the plaintext.

Assuming the MIMO channel is full-duplex, the eavesdropper receives one more pilot matrix than the other transmitters and therefore is less able to estimate the channel fading conditions. To the authors' knowledge, this paper is the first to utilize the received asymmetric pilot matrices to design the MIMO-based physical-layer lattice cryptography scheme. Finally, the proposed scheme has the potential to resist currently known quantum attacks and can be used for enhancing the security of wireless group communication in 6G. That is, we can redesign the simple physical-layer wireless channel's properties to achieve sophisticated application-layer encryption without requiring key sharing. This offers a new approach for designing the post-quantum cryptosystem without keys. Future research will generalize the scheme to active eavesdroppers.

Appendix A Eavesdropper's Equivalent Noise

To clarify Eve's channel estimation, we first decompose the signal, then analyze the equivalent channel error caused by the pilot design. The received pilot signal $\mathbf{Y_E}$ can be transformed into the vector $\mathbf{y_E}$:

$$\mathbf{y_E} = \sum_{i=1}^{M}(\bar{\mathbf{P}}^T \mathbf{G_i}^T \times \mathbf{I_{N_E}})\text{vec}(\mathbf{H_{E,i}}) + \mathbf{e_E} \tag{27}$$

$$= (\bar{\mathbf{P}}^T \times \mathbf{I_{N_E}})\text{vec}(\bar{\mathbf{H}}_E) + \mathbf{e_E} \tag{28}$$

where $\mathbf{G_i} = \mathbf{n_i}^T \times \mathbf{I_N}$; $\mathbf{n_i}$ represents the M-dimensional unit vector; $\text{vec}(\cdot)$ denotes the vectorization of the matrix; "$\times$" represents the cross-product.

The matrix $\bar{\mathbf{P}}$ is not full-rank because of the pilot designs, which leads to Eve being unable to estimate the values of the eavesdropping channel matrix accurately. Following by [1], Eve can take the MMSE channel estimation algorithm to compute:

$$\hat{\mathbf{h}}_{E,i} = K_{\mathbf{h}_{E,i}, \mathbf{y_E}} K_{\mathbf{y_E}}^{-1} \mathbf{y_E} \tag{29}$$

$$= \sigma_{E,i}^2 (\mathbf{G_i}\bar{\mathbf{P}}^* \times \mathbf{I_{N_E}})(\bar{\mathbf{P}}^T \mathbf{\Sigma}_E \bar{\mathbf{P}}^* \times \mathbf{I_{N_E}} + \mathbf{I_{N_E T}})^{-1} \mathbf{y_E} \tag{30}$$

where $\mathbf{\Sigma}_E = diag\{\sigma_{E,1}^2 \mathbf{I_N}, \cdots, \sigma_{E,M}^2 \mathbf{I_N}\}$ and $\mathbf{h}_{E,i} = vec(\mathbf{H}_{E,i})$.

Furthermore, the covariance matrix of $\hat{\mathbf{h}}_{E,i}$ can be calculated as:

$$K_{\hat{\mathbf{h}}_{E,i}} = K_{\mathbf{h}_{E,i}, \mathbf{y_E}} K_{\mathbf{y_E}}^{-1} K_{\mathbf{h}_{E,i}, \mathbf{y_E}}^{\dagger} \tag{31}$$

$$= \sigma_{E,i}^2 (\mathbf{G_i} \mathbf{\Phi} \mathbf{G_i}^T \times \mathbf{I_{N_E}}) = \hat{s}_{E,i} \mathbf{I_{N_E N}} \tag{32}$$

where

$$\mathbf{G_i \Phi G_i^T} = \{1 - (1 + MN\beta\sigma_{E,i}^2)^{-1} - \frac{N\beta(1 + MN\beta\sigma_{E,i}^2)^{-2}\sigma_{E,i}^2}{1 - N\beta\sum_{j=1}^{M}[(1 + MN\beta\sigma_{E,j}^2)^{-1}\sigma_{E,j}^2}]\}\mathbf{I_N} = \frac{\hat{s}_{E,i}}{\sigma_{E,i}^2}\mathbf{I_N} \quad (33)$$

where $\beta = E_{pilot}/[N^2(M-1)]$, E_{pilot} is the total energy of the pilot signal. The covariance matrix of the eavesdropping channel estimation error is:

$$K_{\Delta \mathbf{h_{E,i}}} = K_{\hat{h}_{E,i}} - K_{\mathbf{h_{E,i}}} = (\hat{s}_{E,i} - \sigma_{E,i}^2)\mathbf{I_{N_E N}} \quad (34)$$

Set that the elements in the channel gain matrix follow the Gaussian distribution $\mathcal{CN}(0,1)$, and the time slot T is $(M-1)N$. Then we can get: $\beta = \frac{P_1}{N}$, where P_1 represents the power of the pilot signal. And, the covariance matrix of the eavesdropper's channel estimation is:

$$K_{\hat{\mathbf{h}}_{\mathbf{E,i}}} = \sigma_{E,i}^2(\mathbf{G_i \Phi G_i^T} \times \mathbf{I_{N_E}}) \quad (35)$$

$$= (\frac{MP_1 - P_1}{1 + MP_1})\mathbf{I_{N_E N}} \quad (36)$$

The above estimation process involves three key operations: (1) regularization, (2) channel statistics, and (3) error covariance computation. Under this, even if the number of antennas of the eavesdropper is infinite, its equivalent channel error can still be modeled as:

$$\begin{cases} \mathbf{H}_E = \mathbf{H} + \Delta \mathbf{H} \\ \Delta \mathbf{H} \sim \mathcal{CN}(0, \frac{P_1 - 1}{1 + MP_1}) \end{cases} \quad (37)$$

Appendix B Proof of Theorem 1

To prove the ideal secrecy of the system, we analyze the probability distribution of the equivocation rate F. The key idea is to bound F through geometric properties of the equivalent noise sphere and channel lattice. Now, we begin with the maximum transmitting signal $||s||^2 = P_t$, where the effective secret key is k_0. Therefore

$$D_F(f, P_t) = Pr\{F < f\} \overset{a}{\leq} Pr\{k_0 \leq f\} \quad (38)$$

where (a) holds because of $k_0 \leq F$.

Under channel lattice, let S_R be a sphere centered at $\mathbf{H}s$ with $vol(S_R) = f \cdot vol(\Lambda_\mathbb{C})$, and we have

$$Pr\{k_0 \leq f\} = Pr\{\mathbf{y}_e \in S_R\} \quad (39)$$

Meanwhile, we use the same parameter, i.e., $P_t > f^{1/N_E} \pi^{-1} \phi^{-2N/N_E} \sigma_1^{-2}$ and define another critical volume as:

$$V = (\pi P_t \sigma_1^2)^{N_E} e^{-N} \tag{40}$$

where V defines a threshold which is related to Eve's decoding error probability. Eve's equivalent noise $\tilde{\boldsymbol{n}}_e = \Delta \boldsymbol{H s}$ has i.i.d $\mathcal{CN}(0, P_t \sigma_1^2)$, and we can evaluate

$$Pr\{\boldsymbol{y}_e \in S_R | vol(S_R) \leq V\} \tag{41}$$

$$\leq Pr\{\boldsymbol{y}_e \in S_V\} \overset{a}{=} \int_{S_V} Pr(\tilde{\boldsymbol{n}}_e) \, d\tilde{\boldsymbol{n}}_e$$

$$\overset{b}{\leq} \frac{V}{\pi^{N_E} P_t^{N_E} \sigma_1^{2N_E}} \overset{c}{=} e^{-N} \tag{42}$$

where S_V represents the sphere centered at $\boldsymbol{Hs}$ with $vol(S_V) = V$; (a) comes from the equivalent noise's integral centered at the origin; (b) comes from that its probability density function is less than $1/(\pi^{N_E} P_t^{N_E} \sigma_1^{2N_E})$; (c) comes from the definition of the critical volume.

Finally, we can get

$$D_F(f, P_t) < Pr\{\boldsymbol{y}_e \in S_R\}$$
$$\overset{a}{=} Pr\{\boldsymbol{y}_e \in S_R | vol(S_R) \leq V\} \cdot Pr\{vol(S_R) \leq V\}$$
$$+ Pr\{\boldsymbol{y}_e \in S_R | vol(S_R) > V\} \cdot Pr\{vol(S_R) > V\}$$
$$< Pr\{\boldsymbol{y}_e \in S_R | vol(S_R) \leq V\} + Pr\{vol(S_R) > V\}$$
$$< e^{-N} + Pr\{f \cdot det(\boldsymbol{H}^\dagger \boldsymbol{H}) > \pi^{N_E} P_t^{N_E} \sigma_1^{2N_E} e^{-N}\}$$
$$\overset{b}{<} O(e^{-N}) \tag{43}$$

where (a) comes from the law of total probability; (b) holds due to the Log-Chi-Square distribution and central limit theorem (see [13] Lemma 1).

The above analysis explicitly links the geometric characteristic of V to the secrecy metric $D_F(f, P_t)$, which clarifies exponential decay. Finally, we can get $Pr\{F < f\} \to 0$ and Shannon's ideal secrecy $H(\boldsymbol{s}|\boldsymbol{y}_e) > 0$.

Appendix C Proof of Theorem 2

A connection between Gaussian lattice and secrecy outage probability $Pr_{sop}(f)$ will be established in this appendix. We first define the quality of channel lattice as

$$\Delta(f) = \frac{f \cdot vol(\Lambda_{\mathbb{C}})}{\pi^{N_E} P_t^{N_E}} \tag{44}$$

where it can be regarded as the normalized lattice quality metric and quantifies Eve's decoding capability.

Under the same power constraint $P_t > \rho^{-2/N} f^{1/N_E} \pi^{-1} \phi^{-2N/N_E} \sigma_1^{-2}$ and $N_E \geq N$ in Theorem 2, the above metric $\Delta(f)$ is bounded by Chi-square distribution

$$\Delta(f) \leq \rho^{-2N} \prod_{i=1}^{N} \frac{\chi^2(2N_E - 2i + 2)}{2N_E - 2i + 2} \tag{45}$$

Consequently, we will evaluate the outage event's probability

$$Pr\{\Delta(f) > \rho^{-N}\} \tag{46}$$

$$\leq Pr\{(\prod_{i=1}^{N} \frac{\chi^2(2N_E - 2i + 2)}{2N_E - 2i + 2})^{1/N} > \rho\} \tag{47}$$

$$\overset{a}{\leq} Pr\{\frac{1}{N} \sum_{i=1}^{N} \frac{\chi^2(2N_E - 2i + 2)}{2N_E - 2i + 2} > \rho\} \tag{48}$$

$$\overset{b}{\leq} \sum_{i=1}^{N} Pr\{\chi^2(2N_E - 2i + 2) > 2N(N_E - i + 1)\rho\} \tag{49}$$

$$\overset{c}{\leq} \sum_{i=1}^{N} (e^{1-\rho}\rho)^{N_E - i + 1} \tag{50}$$

where (a) comes from arithmetic-geometric mean; (b) comes from the union boun; (c) comes from the Chi-square tail distribution.

Then, the overall secrecy outage probability is dominated by

$$Pr_{sop}(f) < Pr\{\Delta(f) > \rho^{-N}\} < O(\rho) \tag{51}$$

Combining with Theorem 1's result, we can conclude that Pr_{sop} decreases exponentially with the transmitting power P_t.

References

1. Biguesh, M., Gershman, A.: Training-based mimo channel estimation: a study of estimator tradeoffs and optimal training signals. IEEE Trans. Signal Process. **54**(3), 884–893 (2006)
2. Bloch, M., Barros, J., Rodrigues, M.R.D.: Wireless information-theoretic security. IEEE Trans. Inf. Theory **54**(6), 2515–2534 (2008)
3. Candan, C., Kutay, M., Ozaktas, H.: The discrete fractional fourier transform. IEEE Trans. Signal Process. **48**(5), 1329–1337 (2000)
4. Chen, R., Li, C., Yan, S., Malaney, R., Yuan, J.: Physical layer security for ultra-reliable and low-latency communications. IEEE Wirel. Commun. **26**(5), 6–11 (2019)
5. Dean, T., Goldsmith, A.: Physical-layer cryptography through massive mimo. In: 2013 IEEE Information Theory Workshop (ITW), pp. 1–5 (2013)
6. Dean, T.R., Goldsmith, A.J.: Physical-layer cryptography through massive mimo. IEEE Trans. Inf. Theory **63**(8), 5419–5436 (2017)

7. Gan, Y.H., Ling, C., Mow, W.H.: Complex lattice reduction algorithm for low-complexity full-diversity mimo detection. IEEE Trans. Signal Process. **57**(7), 2701–2710 (2009)
8. Gao, N., Han, Y., Li, N., Jin, S., Matthaiou, M.: When physical layer key generation meets ris: opportunities, challenges, and road ahead. IEEE Wirel. Commun. **31**(3), 355–361 (2024)
9. Khot, S.: Hardness of approximating the shortest vector problem in lattices. J. ACM **52**(5), 789–808 (2005)
10. Korzhik, V., Morales-Luna, G., Tikhonov, S., Yakovlev, V.: Analysis of keyless massive mimo-based cryptosystem security. Cryptology ePrint Archive, Paper 2015/816 (2015). https://eprint.iacr.org/2015/816
11. Lancaster, H.O., Seneta, E.: Chi-Square Distribution. John Wiley & Sons, Ltd., Hoboken (2005)
12. Liu, S., Gao, T., Liu, Y., Lu, X.: Physical-layer public key encryption through massive mimo. In: Proceedings of the 19th ACM Asia Conference on Computer and Communications Security, pp. 353–365 (2024)
13. Liu, S., Hong, Y., Viterbo, E.: Unshared secret key cryptography. IEEE Trans. Wirel. Commun. **13**(12), 6670–6683 (2014)
14. Liu, Y.K., Lyubashevsky, V., Micciancio, D.: On bounded distance decoding for general lattices. In: Approximation, Randomization, and Combinatorial Optimization. Algorithms and Techniques, pp. 450–461 (2006)
15. Lyubashevsky, V., Micciancio, D.: On bounded distance decoding, unique shortest vectors, and the minimum distance problem. In: Halevi, S. (ed.) CRYPTO 2009. LNCS, vol. 5677, pp. 577–594. Springer, Heidelberg (2009). https://doi.org/10.1007/978-3-642-03356-8_34
16. Mathur, S., Reznik, A., Ye, C., Mukherjee, R., Rahman, A., Shah, Y.: Exploiting the physical layer for enhanced security [security and privacy in emerging wireless networks]. IEEE Wirel. Commun. **17**(5), 63–70 (2010)
17. Micciancio, D.: The hardness of the closest vector problem with preprocessing. IEEE Trans. Inf. Theory **47**(3), 1212–1215 (2001)
18. Mitev, M., Chorti, A., Poor, H.V., Fettweis, G.P.: What physical layer security can do for 6g security. IEEE Open J. Veh. Technol. **4**, 375–388 (2023)
19. Mostafa, A., Lampe, L.: Physical-layer security for miso visible light communication channels. IEEE J. Sel. Areas Commun. **33**(9), 1806–1818 (2015)
20. Saad, W., Zhou, X., Han, Z., Poor, H.V.: On the physical layer security of backscatter wireless systems. IEEE Trans. Wirel. Commun. **13**(6), 3442–3451 (2014)
21. Sakzad, A., Steinfeld, R.: Comments on "physical-layer cryptography through massive mimo" (2020). https://arxiv.org/abs/2001.02632
22. Salz, J., Winters, J.: Effect of fading correlation on adaptive arrays in digital mobile radio. IEEE Trans. Veh. Technol. **43**(4), 1049–1057 (1994)
23. Sheng, Z., Tuan, H.D., Duong, T.Q., Poor, H.V.: Beamforming optimization for physical layer security in miso wireless networks. IEEE Trans. Signal Process. **66**(14), 3710–3723 (2018)
24. Steinfeld, R., Sakzad, A.: On massive mimo physical layer cryptosystem. In: 2015 IEEE Information Theory Workshop - Fall (ITW), pp. 292–296 (2015)
25. Wu, S., Hua, Y.: Total secrecy from anti-eavesdropping channel estimation. IEEE Trans. Signal Process. **70**, 1088–1103 (2022)
26. Zhang, W., Chen, J., Kuo, Y., Zhou, Y.: Transmit beamforming for layered physical layer security. IEEE Trans. Veh. Technol. **68**(10), 9747–9760 (2019)
27. Zhu, Q., Wu, S., Hua, Y.: Optimal pilots for anti-eavesdropping channel estimation. IEEE Trans. Signal Process. **68**, 2629–2644 (2020)

The Multi-user Security of GCM-SST and Further Enhancements

Yusuke Naito[1](✉), Yu Sasaki[2,3], and Takeshi Sugawara[4]

[1] Mitsubishi Electric Corporation, Kanagawa, Japan
Naito.Yusuke@ce.MitsubishiElectric.co.jp
[2] NTT Social Informatics Laboratories, Tokyo, Japan
yusk.sasaki@ntt.com
[3] Associate of National Institute of Standards and Technology, Gaithersburg, USA
[4] The University of Electro-Communications, Tokyo, Japan
sugawara@uec.ac.jp

Abstract. GCM with Secure Short Tag (GCM-SST) is a variant of the GCM authenticated encryption mode designed for improved security with short tags, and its standardization is ongoing in various organizations, including 3GPP and IETF. The original design specification was published with informal security claims only, and Inoue et al. then verified them with formal security proofs. They proved that the term regarding tag length t is $\frac{v}{2^t}$ in GCM-SST (cf. $\frac{v\ell}{2^t}$ in GCM), wherein v is the number of decryption queries and the maximum message block length ℓ. However, the proofs were given in the single-user (su) setting only, and its multi-user (mu) security remained an open research problem, which is a significant gap because GCM-SST's specification document explicitly considers mu use cases and even recommends nonce randomization (NR) for improving mu-security. Addressing this issue, this paper proves mu-security of GCM-SST, verifying that the security with short tags stays intact under the mu setting. Moreover, by combining GCM-SST with NR and nonce-based key derivation (NKD), we show that those enhancement methods improve mu-security in the same level as those combined with GCM.

Keywords: Symmetric-key cryptography · Mode · GCM · GCM-SST · Multi-user security · Nonce randomization · Nonce-based key derivation

1 Introduction

Authenticated encryption (AE), which ensures both confidentiality and authenticity, is the major cryptographic technique that protects today's high-volume network traffic. GCM [26] shown in Fig. 1 is an AE based on a block cipher (BC), composed of the counter mode (CTR) and polynomial hash GHASH [26]. It has been a NIST standard since 2007 [13], and its instantiation with AES, namely AES-GCM, has been particularly popular. After 20 years, AES-GCM still provides excellent performance due to wide availability of hardware acceleration, such as the dedicated instructions for AES [15] and carry-less multiplication [16] on Intel

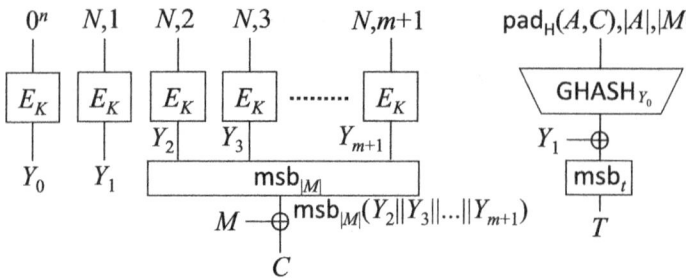

Fig. 1. GCM. N, M, C, and T are respectively a nonce, a plaintext, a ciphertext, and a tag. m is a block length of M. The lengths $|A|$ and $|M|$ are encoded in a single block.

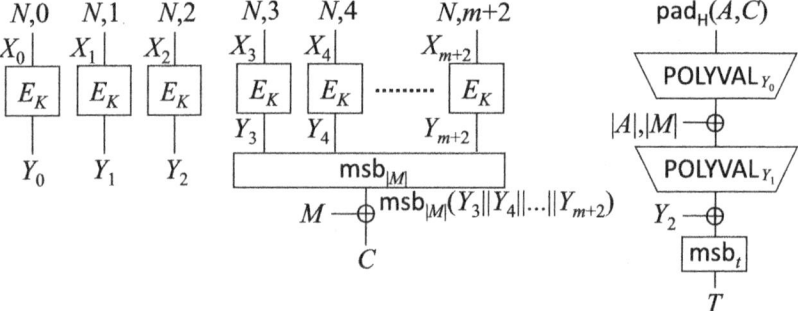

Fig. 2. GCM-SST. pad_H is an injective padding function that returns a data string such that each block is full.

and AMD processors. Meanwhile, researchers have identified several shortcomings of AES-GCM, and its enhancement has been a major research challenge in symmetric-key cryptography [4,17,18,21].

Security with short tags is a major issue in AES-GCM. Ferguson [14] initially raised a concern, and Nyberg et al. [33] presented an attack that work with query complexity $\frac{2^t}{\ell}$ with a t-bit tag and ℓ being the maximum block length per query. Then, Iwata et al. [24] proved the security bound of the GCM mode that includes $\frac{\ell v}{2^t}$ [24], as shown in Table 1, wherein v is the number of decryption queries. When the tag is short, i.e., t is small, this $\frac{\ell v}{2^t}$ term becomes significant and a security bottleneck. Consequently, NIST is revising SP 800-38D [30], the standard document on GCM, to remove support for tags shorter than 96 bits. However, there is strong demand for AEs with short tags in practice, and tag lengths of 32, 64, and 80 bits are included in several industrial standards, such as 5G [1], the Internet of Things and media encryption applications [7]. Therefore, improving GCM to achieve better security with short tags is a significant research challenge.

Addressing the issue, Campagna, Maximov, and Mattsson designed GCM-SST [7]: GCM with secure short tag, as shown in Fig. 2. Following the two-stage MAC construction suggested by Nyberg et al. [33], GCM-SST replaces

Table 1. Provable security bounds of GCM, GCM-SST, and their enhancements using NR and NKD in the su and mu settings. See Sect. 1.1 for details.

Reference	Target	Model	Bound
Iwata et al. [24]	GCM	su[†]	$\frac{\sigma^2}{2^n} + \frac{\ell v}{2^t}$
Hoang et al. [21]	GCM	mu	$\frac{\breve{\sigma}_e \sigma}{2^n} + \frac{\ell v}{2^t} + \frac{up+u^2}{2^k}$
Hoang et al. [21]	GCM w/ NR	mu	$\frac{\breve{\sigma}_e \sigma}{2^n} + \frac{\ell v}{2^t} + \frac{dp}{2^k}$
Bose et al. [6]	GCM w/ NR + NKD	mu	$\frac{\ell_e \sigma}{2^n} + \frac{\ell v}{2^t} + \frac{dp}{2^k}$
Inoue et al. [22]	GCM-SST	su	$\frac{(\sigma_e+\sigma_d)^2+\ell v}{2^n} + \frac{v}{2^t}$
This Work	GCM-SST	su	$\frac{\sigma_e^2+v^2+\ell v}{2^n} + \frac{v}{2^t}$
This Work	GCM-SST	mu	$\frac{\breve{\sigma}_e \sigma_e+(\breve{v}+\ell)v}{2^n} + \frac{v}{2^t} + \frac{up+u^2}{2^k}$
This Work	GCM-SST w/ NR	mu	$\frac{\breve{\sigma}_e \sigma_e+(\breve{v}+\ell)v}{2^n} + \frac{v}{2^t} + \frac{dp}{2^k}$
This Work	GCM-SST w/ NR + NKD	mu	$\frac{\ell_e \sigma_e+\ell v}{2^n} + \frac{v}{2^t} + \frac{dp}{2^k}$

[†]The bound is obtained in the standard model and there is no term regarding k.

GHASH with a cascade of two hash functions with different hash keys derived from a nonce. Moreover, it uses a new hash function POLYVAL [17], a variant of GHASH optimized for dedicated processor instructions [15,16]. The development of GCM-SST started in ETSI SAGE as requested by 3GPP. Then, 3GPP decided to standardize GCM-SST, and further standardization is being discussed in the IETF Internet draft [7].

After the specification of GCM-SST has been released without a formal security proof, Inoue et al. [22] proved that its bound in the single-user (su) setting for a BC with n-bit block is given by $\frac{(\sigma_e+\sigma_d)^2+\ell v}{2^n} + \frac{v}{2^t}$, wherein σ_e and σ_d are the total number of BC calls within encryption and decryption queries, respectively. The bound verifies that GCM-SST improves security with the short tag because it includes $\frac{v}{2^t}$ instead of $\frac{\ell v}{2^t}$.[1] This proof also covers the security in the nonce-misuse setting to capture the improvement by nonce-based hash keys. However, the proof was given in the su setting only, and its multi-user (mu) security remained an open research problem.

Mu-security considers a more realistic setting in which an adversary can access multiple users with their own secret keys, and revisiting the security of popular symmetric-key schemes in the mu setting is a growing research area [4,11,21,25,28,29,38]. TLS, DTLS, and QUIC already determine the rekeying intervals of AES-GCM based on mu-security [35–37], and the other Internet-Draft [20] is discussing the usage limit based on the mu setting in more general cases.

---

[1] A successful forgery requires a collision of the keyed hash functions, and its collision probability increases with the input length GCM-SST enforces the input length of the second t-bit hash function to one block, eliminating the message length ℓ from the 2^t term. Note that GCM-SST processes a message in the first n-bit hash function, and the message length appears in the 2^n term.

Several protocols even implement a countermeasure to improve security in the mu setting. In particular, TLS 1.3 [35] implemented nonce randomization (NR) that masks a nonce with a user-specific random mask, which makes the nonce uncontrollable to the adversary, efficiently improving the offline security. Similarly, nonce-based key derivation (NKD) [18] is proposed to improve online security in the mu setting, which generates a fresh key for each nonce,[2] and NIST [31] is considering to include NKD in revising the standard for GCM (SP800-38D). Consequently, providing provable security for NR or NKD has become a significant research challenge. Bellare and Tackmann [4] first tackled the security proof of NR, and Hoang et al. [21] achieved further improvement by introducing the d-bound model as a generalization of NR, where the number of the same (randomized) nonces between different users is bounded by d. Meanwhile, Bose et al. [6] proved the security of NKD.

The absence of a security bound in the mu setting is a significant limitation because the specification of GCM-SST [7] explicitly discusses use cases in the mu setting and even recommends using GCM-SST with NR. Therefore, we study the mu security of GCM-SST with the following research questions:

– Does GCM-SST improve the security with short tags even in the mu setting?
– Do NR and NKD improve the offline and online mu-security of GCM-SST, in the same way as they are combined with GCM?

1.1 Our Contributions

This paper contains three major contributions that are summarized as follows.

Proving mu Bound of GCM-SST. We prove the mu bound of GCM-SST, while the only su bound was considered in [22]. The target is nonce-respecting setting, as explicitly required in the original design document [7][3]. Let n and k be the block size and the key size of underlying BC, respectively. Our mu bound is $\frac{\breve{\sigma}_e \sigma_e + (\breve{v}+\ell)v}{2^n} + \frac{v}{2^t} + \frac{up+u^2}{2^k}$, where $\breve{\sigma}_e$ is the maximum number of total BC calls in encryption queries for each user, $\breve{v}$ is the maximum number of nonces that are 1) used in decryption, and 2) never used in encryption, for each user, u is the number of users, and p is the number of offline queries.

Most importantly, the second term implies that the original design goal of GCM-SST, having $\frac{v}{2^t}$ instead of $\frac{\ell v}{2^t}$ in the security bound, is achieved not only for the su setting, but also the mu setting. It also implies that the mu bound of GCM-SST is not degraded from that of su security with authenticity.

Regarding the first term, GCM's $\frac{\breve{\sigma}_e \sigma}{2^n}$ is improved to $\frac{\breve{\sigma}_e \sigma_e + (\breve{v}+\ell)v}{2^n}$, namely the term that is composite of encryption queries and decryption queries is removed

---

[2] NKD generates independent keys for each nonce. By reducing the amount of data processed per key, online security is improved. In the case of nonce-respecting setting, since each query has a different nonce, the amount of data processed per key can be significantly reduced, thereby improving online security.

[3] The internet draft by Campagn et al. [7] prohibits misuse of nonces as "For a given key, the nonce MUST NOT be reused under any circumstances.".

in our bound. When $\breve{\sigma}_e \ll 2^{n/2}$, our mu bound implies that GCM-SST ensures beyond-birthday-bound security.

The third term represents offline mu security of GCM-SST, which is the same as that of GCM, i.e. the mu bound is degraded by a factor of u. This is tight due to Biham's attack [5], thus is best possible to achieve.

As a corollary, our bound with $u = 1$ is the su bound of GCM-SST and $\frac{\sigma_e^2 + v^2 + \ell v}{2^n} + \frac{v}{2^t}$ as shown in Table 1. As the mu bound, the birthday term of the su bound of Inoue et al. [22] is improved from $\frac{(\sigma_e + \sigma_d)^2}{2^n}$ to $\frac{\sigma_e^2 + v^2 + \ell v}{2^n}$, ensuring that the su security of GCM-SST is free from the birthday term regarding decryption query complexity $\frac{\sigma_d^2}{2^n}$.

GCM-SST with NR for Higher Offline mu Security. We prove the mu security of GCM-SST when NR is adopted. By using the d-bound model [21], which assumes that the same randomized nonce appears across distinct users at most d times and d is expected to be small like $n/\log_2 n$, we prove that offline mu security of GCM-SST with NR is enhanced to $\frac{dp}{2^k}$, namely, GCM-SST with NR achieves the same offline mu security as GCM with NR.

GCM-SST with NKD for Higher Online mu Security. We prove that mu security of GCM-SST with both NR and NKD achieves the bound of $\frac{\ell_e \sigma_e + \ell v}{2^n} + \frac{v}{2^t} + \frac{dp}{2^k}$. Compared to $\frac{\ell_e \sigma}{2^n} + \frac{\ell v}{2^t} + \frac{dp}{2^k}$ for GCM with NR and NKD, our bound shows that the original goal of GCM-SST achieving $\frac{v}{2^t}$ is preserved even with NR and NKD. Besides, our bound for GCM-SST is advantageous with respect to σ_e vs σ.

Impact of Our Bound in Practical Parameters. Here we show that our improved bound is practically meaningful. The important term in our bound is $\frac{\breve{\sigma}_e \sigma_e}{2^n}$. For the limit per user, the recent NIST's standardization project for accordion specifies that *"NIST expects to limit the total data processed under a single key to 2^{48} bits"* [32], which is 2^{41} 128-bit blocks. Also $\breve{\sigma}_e$ and σ_e in our bound only consider BC calls in encryption, while NIST counts all BC calls in encryption and decryption. By setting $\breve{\sigma}_e < 2^{41}$, NIST's expected case is covered. By specifying $n = 128$ and $\breve{\sigma}_e = 2^{41}$ to $\frac{\breve{\sigma}_e \sigma_e}{2^n}$, the construction is secure up to 2^{87} queries for all the users. This provides sufficient security even when running the system for long time.

1.2 Paper Organization

Section 2 introduces notations. Section 3 defines the specifications of GCM-SST and the enhanced schemes. Section 4 defines the security model. Section 5 shows our bound of GCM-SST and the enhancements, followed by the detailed proof in Sect. 6. Finally, Sect. 7 concludes the paper.

Algorithm 1. GCM-SST

Encryption GCM-SST.Enc$[E_K, \mathsf{H}](N, A, M)$
1: **for** $i \in [0, |M|_n + 2]$ **do** $X_i \leftarrow \mathsf{add}(N, i); Y_i \leftarrow E_K(X_i)$ **end for** ▷ CTR
2: $C \leftarrow M \oplus \mathsf{msb}_{|M|}(Y_3 \| \cdots \| Y_{|M|_n + 2})$
3: $Z_1 \leftarrow \mathsf{H}_{Y_0}(\mathsf{pad}_\mathsf{H}(A, C)); Z_2 \leftarrow \mathsf{H}_{Y_1}(Z_1 \oplus (\mathsf{bin}_{n/2}(|A|) \| \mathsf{bin}_{n/2}(|M|)))$
4: $T \leftarrow \mathsf{msb}_t(Y_0 \oplus Z_2);$ **return** (C, T)

Decryption GCM-SST.Dec$[E_K, \mathsf{H}](N, A, C, T_\mathsf{d})$
1: **for** $i \in [0, |C|_n + 2]$ **do** $X_i \leftarrow \mathsf{add}(IV, i); Y_i \leftarrow E_K(X_i)$ **end for** ▷ CTR
2: $M \leftarrow C \oplus \mathsf{msb}_{|C|}(Y_2 \| \cdots \| Y_{|M|_n + 2})$
3: $Z_1 \leftarrow \mathsf{H}_{Y_0}(\mathsf{pad}_\mathsf{H}(A, C)); Z_2 \leftarrow \mathsf{H}_{Y_1}(Z_1 \oplus (\mathsf{bin}_{n/2}(|A|) \| \mathsf{bin}_{n/2}(|M|)))$
4: $T \leftarrow \mathsf{msb}_t(Y_0 \oplus Z_2);$ **if** $T_\mathsf{d} = T$ **then return** M **else return reject end if**

2 Basic Notations

Let ε be the empty string and $\emptyset$ the empty set. Let $\{0,1\}^i$ be the set of all i-bit strings and $\{0,1\}^0 := \{\varepsilon\}$. Let $\{0,1\}^{n*} := \{X \in \{0,1\}^* \backslash \{\varepsilon\} \mid |X| \bmod n = 0\}$. Let $\mathsf{msb}_i(X)$ be the most significant i bits of a bit string X. Let $\mathsf{bin}_n(i)$ be an n-bit representation of an integer $i \geq 0$. For integers $0 \leq i \leq j$, let $[i, j] := \{i, i+1, \ldots, j\}$, and $[j] := [1, j]$. If $j < i$ then $[i, j] := \emptyset$. Let $|D|_n := \lceil |D|/n \rceil$ be an n-bit block length of D. For a value or a set X, $Y \leftarrow X$ means that X is assigned to Y. For a bit string D and an integer $n \geq 0$, $(D_1, \ldots, D_\ell) \xleftarrow{n} D$ means that D is partitioned into the n-bit strings $D_1, \ldots, D_\ell$ such that $|D_i| = n$ for $i = 1, \ldots, \ell - 1$, $|D_\ell| \leq n$, and $D = D_1 \| \cdots \| D_\ell$. $T \xleftarrow{\$} \mathcal{T}$ means that an element is chosen uniformly at random from a non-empty set $\mathcal{T}$ and assigned to T. For two sets $\mathcal{T}_1$ and $\mathcal{T}_2$, $\mathcal{T}_1 \xleftarrow{\cup} \mathcal{T}_2$ means that $\mathcal{T}_1 \leftarrow \mathcal{T}_1 \cup \mathcal{T}_2$.

3 Specifications of GCM-SST and GCM-SST with NKD

3.1 Primitives

Block Cipher (BC). We fix the key and block sizes of the underlying BCs to k and n. Let $\mathcal{BC}$ be the set of all BC's encryptions with k-bit keys and n-bit blocks. For a key $K \in \{0,1\}^k$ and $E \in \mathcal{BC}$, the encryption is denoted by $E_K(\cdot) = E(K, \cdot)$. The decryption is denoted by E_K^{-1}.

Keyed Hash Function. Let $\{\mathsf{H}_Y\}_{Y \in \{0,1\}^n} : \{0,1\}^{n*} \to \{0,1\}^n$ be a family of keyed hash functions with keys $Y \in \{0,1\}^n$. GCM-SST uses the polynomial hash function POLYVAL [17].

3.2 GCM-SST

GCM-SST is a combination of the CTR mode and two stage keyed hash functions. The specification of GCM-SST is given in Algorithm 1. Let t be a length of tags such that $t \leq n$. Let r be a length of nonces such that $r \leq n$. Let $m_{\max}$ be the maximum n-bit block length of plaintexts. Let add : $\{0,1\}^r \times [0, m_{\max} + 2] \to \{0,1\}^n$ is a function that on an input pair of a nonce and a counter, returns an input block of E_K in CTR such that for any distinct pairs (N, i) and $(N', j) \in \{0,1\}^r \times [0, m_{\max} + 2]$, $\mathsf{add}(N, i) \neq \mathsf{add}(N', j)$. The function add of GCM-SST is realized as $\mathsf{add}(N,i) = N \| \mathsf{bin}_{n-r}(i)$. Let $\mathsf{pad}_\mathsf{H} : \{0,1\}^* \times \{0,1\}^* \to \{0,1\}^{n*}$ be an injective padding function that takes AD $A \in \{0,1\}^*$ and a ciphertext $C \in \{0,1\}^*$ and returns a padded value in $\{0,1\}^{n*}$.

GCM-SST.Enc is an encryption algorithm of GCM-SST that takes an r-bit nonce N, an AD $A \in \{0,1\}^*$, and a plaintext $M \in \{0,1\}^*$, and returns a pair of a ciphertext $C \in \{0,1\}^{|M|}$ and a t-bit tag T. The plaintext is encrypted by using CTR. For authentication, GCM-SST.Enc cascades two keyed hash functions H_{Y_0} and H_{Y_1}, where the hash keys are defined as $Y_0 = E_K(\mathsf{add}(N,0))$ and $Y_1 = E_K(\mathsf{add}(N,1))$. The first hash function H_{Y_0} with a padded value $\mathsf{pad}_\mathsf{H}(A, C)$ is performed, and the hash value is XORed with the lengths $|A|$ and $|C|$, Then, the second hash function H_{Y_1} with the XORed value is performed and a tag is defined by XORing the hash value with the mask value $Y_2 = E_K(\mathsf{add}(N, 2))$ and truncating $n - t$ bits. GCM-SST.Enc is also shown in Fig. 2.

GCM-SST.Dec is a decryption algorithm of GCM-SST that takes an r-bit nonce N, an AD $A \in \{0,1\}^*$, a ciphertext $C \in \{0,1\}^*$, and a t-bit tag T_d. If the tag T defined in the algorithm is equal to T_d, it returns a decrypted plaintext M; otherwise returns an invalid symbol **reject** $\notin \{0,1\}^t$.

3.3 GCM-SST with Nonce-Based Key Derivation (NKD)

Let $F_L : \{0,1\}^r \to \{0,1\}^k$ be a key derivation function (KDF) with an s-bit key L that accepts a nonce and returns a nonce-based key of GCM-SST. The encryption and decryption algorithms of GCM-SST-NKD are defined as follows.

- For an input tuple $(N, A, M) \in \{0,1\}^r \times \{0,1\}^* \times \{0,1\}^*$, the encryption GCM-SST.Enc is defined as

   $\mathsf{GCM\text{-}SST\text{-}NKD.Enc}[F_L, E, \mathsf{H}](N, A, M)$
   $:= \mathsf{GCM\text{-}SST.Enc}[E_{F_L(N)}, \mathsf{H}](N, A, M).$

- For an input tuple $(N, A, C, T_\mathsf{d}) \in \{0,1\}^r \times \{0,1\}^* \times \{0,1\}^* \times \{0,1\}^t$, the decryption GCM-SST-NKD.Dec is defined as

   $\mathsf{GCM\text{-}SST\text{-}NKD.Dec}[F_L, E, \mathsf{H}](N, A, C, T_\mathsf{d})$
   $:= \mathsf{GCM\text{-}SST.Dec}[E_{F_L(N)}, \mathsf{H}](N, A, C, T_\mathsf{d}).$

The KDF can be realized by using SoP [3], EDM [10], CENC [23], or its variants such as [12,19,27]. For example, CENC is defined as $\mathsf{CENC}[E_K](N) := \mathsf{msb}_k\big((Y_0 \oplus Y_1) \| (Y_0 \oplus Y_2)\big)$, where $Y_i := E_K(N\|\mathsf{bin}_{n-r}(i))$. These schemes achieve n-bit (or more) mu-PRF security [8,9,19,25,27].

4 Security Model

We consider distinguishing-type security notions for BCs and GCM-SST. For the security notions, we define the following distinguishing advantage of an adversary **A** that has access to either $\mathcal{O}_1$ or $\mathcal{O}_2$ and returns a decision bit. For $i \in [2]$, let $\mathbf{A}^{\mathcal{O}_i} = 1$ be an event that **A** with $\mathcal{O}_i$ returns 1. The distinguishing advantage of **A** is defined as

$$\mathbf{Adv}^{\mathsf{dist}}_{\mathcal{O}_1,\mathcal{O}_2}(\mathbf{A}) := \Pr\left[\mathbf{A}^{\mathcal{O}_1} = 1\right] - \Pr\left[\mathbf{A}^{\mathcal{O}_2} = 1\right].$$

4.1 Security Models for BCs

We consider two security models for BCs: the standard multi-user-pseudorandom-permutation (mu-PRP) security and the ideal cipher (IC) models.

Standard Model. In the standard model, the underlying BCs are assumed to be mu-PRP secure, where BC instantiations with independent keys are securely replaced with independent random permutations (RPs). Let u be the number of users. In the mu-PRP game, an adversary interacts with either the real-world oracles or the ideal-world oracles. Let $\mathsf{Perm}(n)$ be the set of n-bit permutations.

- The real-world oracles: $(E_{K^{[1]}}, \ldots, E_{K^{[u]}})$ where $\forall \nu \in [u] : K^{[\nu]} \xleftarrow{\$} \{0,1\}^k$.
- The ideal-world oracles: RPs $(\Pi_1, \ldots, \Pi_u)$, where $\forall \nu \in [u] : \Pi_\nu \xleftarrow{\$} \mathsf{Perm}(n)$.

At the end of this game, **A** returns a decision bit in $\{0,1\}$. The mu-PRP advantage function of **A** is defined as

$$\mathbf{Adv}^{\mathsf{mu\text{-}prp}}_E(\mathbf{A}) := \mathbf{Adv}^{\mathsf{dist}}_{(E_{K_1},\ldots,E_{K_u}),(\Pi_1,\ldots,\Pi_u)}(\mathbf{A}).$$

For all possible adversaries **A** that have access to u users, make at most q queries, and run in time t, the maximum advantage is defined as

$$\mathbf{Adv}^{\mathsf{mu\text{-}prp}}_E(u, q, \mathsf{t}) := \max_{\mathbf{A}} \mathbf{Adv}^{\mathsf{mu\text{-}prp}}_E(\mathbf{A}).$$

Ideal Cipher (IC) Model. Let $\mathcal{BC}$ be the set of all encryptions of κ-bit key and n-bit block BCs. An IC is an ideal BC and defined as $E \xleftarrow{\$} \mathcal{BC}$. In the IC model, all parties including AE oracles and adversaries obtain IC's outputs by making offline queries to an IC $E^{\pm} = (E, E^{-1})$.

4.2 Security Models for GCM-SST and GCM-SST-NKD

Multi-user AE (mu-AE) security is the indistinguishability between the real and ideal worlds. Let u be the number of users. Let $\$_\nu$ be a random-bit oracle of the ν-th user that takes an input tuple (N, A, M) of a nonce, an AD, and a plaintext, and returns a pair of a random ciphertext and a random tag defined as $(C, T) \xleftarrow{\$}$

$\{0,1\}^{|\text{GCM-SST.Enc}[E_K](N,A,M)|}$. Let $\perp_\nu$ be a reject oracle that returns **reject** for any query. Let $K^{[1]}, \ldots, K^{[u]}$ be users' keys defined as $\forall \nu \in [u] : K^{[\nu]} \xleftarrow{\$} \{0,1\}^k$. In the mu-AE game in the standard or IC model, an adversary **A** has access to either real-world oracles $\mathcal{O}_{\text{real}}$ or ideal-world oracles $\mathcal{O}_{\text{ideal}}$ defined as follows.

$$\mathcal{O}_{\text{real}} := \Big((\text{GCM-SST.Enc}[E_{K^{[\nu]}}, \mathsf{H}], \text{GCM-SST.Dec}[E_{K^{[\nu]}}, \mathsf{H}])_{\nu \in [u]}, \boxed{E^{\pm}} \Big).$$

$$\mathcal{O}_{\text{ideal}} := \Big((\$_\nu, \perp_\nu)_{\nu \in [u]}, \boxed{E^{\pm}} \Big).$$

In the standard (resp. IC) model, the boxed oracle is removed (resp. included). At the end of this game, **A** return a decision bit in $\{0,1\}$. The mu-AE-security advantage function of **A** is defined as

$$\mathbf{Adv}^{\text{mu-ae}}_{\text{GCM-SST}}(\mathbf{A}) := \mathbf{Adv}^{\text{dist}}_{\mathcal{O}_{\text{real}}, \mathcal{O}_{\text{ideal}}}(\mathbf{A}).$$

Queries to each user are called online queries. Queries to encryption oracles GCM-SST.Enc$[E_{K^{[\nu]}}, \mathsf{H}]$ or $\$_\nu$ (resp. decryption oracles GCM-SST.Dec$[E_{K^{[\nu]}}, \mathsf{H}]$ or $\perp_\nu$) are called encryption (resp. decryption) queries. In the IC model, queries to an IC are called offline queries.

We consider nonce-respecting adversaries where for each user, all nonces in encryption queries are distinct. In this game, making a repeated query and a trivial decryption query is forbidden, where the trivial query (N, A, C, T_d) is such that the query tuple was obtained by some previous encryption query to the same user.

The mu-AE security of GCM-SST-NKD is equal to the above one where GCM-SST is replaced with GCM-SST-NKD.

Adversaries and its Resources. In our proofs, we consider computationally-bounded or computationally-unbounded adversaries. Queries to encryption (resp. decryption) oracles are called encryption (resp. decryption) queries. Let σ_e be the total number of BC calls in encryption queries and $\check{\sigma}_e$ the maximum number of BC calls in encryption queries per user. Let v be the number of decryption queries and $\check{v}$ the maximum number of decryption queries per user. Let ℓ be the maximum block-length of pairs of AD and plaintext in all queries. Let v_n be the number of decryption queries with fresh nonces, i.e., the nonces are different from the other nonces in encryption queries within the same user, and $\check{v}_n$ the maximum number of decryption queries with fresh nonces per user. For computationally-bounded (resp. computationally-unbounded) adversaries, the time resources are expressed by its running time t (resp. the number of offline queries to an IC denoted by p).

4.3 d-Bound Adversaries

In the d-bound model, the number of collisions of nonces in encryption queries across users is bounded by d. Note that there is no collision in nonces in encryption queries within the same user.

Definition 1 (d-bound model). *For $\nu \in [u]$, let $\mathcal{N}^{[\nu]}$ be the set of nonces in encryption queries to the ν-th user. Then, an adversary is d-bound if for any $N \in \{0,1\}^r$, $|\{\nu \in [u] \mid N \in \mathcal{N}^{[\nu]}\}| \leq d$.*

The parameter d can be small by using a random nonce: each original nonce N_{orig} is defined by incrementing 1, i.e., $N_{\text{orig}} \leftarrow N_{\text{orig}} + 1$ (initially $N_{\text{orig}} = 0^n$), and a randomized nonce N is defined as $N = N_{\text{orig}} \oplus R$ with the r-bit original nonce N_{orig} and a user-specific random mask $R \in \{0,1\}^r$. The parameter d is studied in e.g. [28].

4.4 Multi-user PRF (mu-PRF) Assumption

In our proof of GCM-SST-NKD, we assume that the KDF F is mu-PRF secure against computationally-unbounded adversaries, since we consider the security of GCM-SST-NKD in the IC model. Let P_F be an ideal primitive used in the KDF. Let u be the number of users. Let $\mathsf{Func}(r,k)$ be the set of all functions from $\{0,1\}^r$ to $\{0,1\}^k$. In the mu-PRF-security game, an adversary $\mathbf{A}$ has access to either real-world oracles $((F_{L^{[1]}}, \ldots, F_{L^{[u]}}), P_F)$ or ideal-world ones $((\mathcal{R}_1, \ldots, \mathcal{R}_u), P_F)$, where $\forall \nu \in [u] : L^{[\nu]} \xleftarrow{\$} \{0,1\}^s$ and $\mathcal{R}_\nu \xleftarrow{\$} \mathsf{Func}(r,k)$ (i.e., $\mathcal{R}_\nu$ is a random function). At the end of this game, $\mathbf{A}$ return a decision bit. Then, the advantage function of $\mathbf{A}$ is defined as

$$\mathbf{Adv}_F^{\text{mu-prf}}(\mathbf{A}) := \mathbf{Adv}_{((F_{L^{[\nu]}})_{\nu \in [u]}, P_F), ((\mathcal{R}_\nu)_{\nu \in [u]}, P_F)}^{\text{dist}}(\mathbf{A}).$$

For all possible adversaries $\mathbf{A}$ that have access to u users and make at most q queries to the KDFs and p queries to P_F, the maximum advantage is defined as

$$\mathbf{Adv}_F^{\text{mu-prf}}(u,q,p) := \max_{\mathbf{A}} \mathbf{Adv}_F^{\text{mu-prf}}(\mathbf{A}).$$

4.5 Universal Hash Function

In our proofs, we use the following AXU assumption for a family of keyed hash functions $\{H_Y\}_{Y \in \{0,1\}^n}$ of GCM-SST.

Definition 2 (Almost XOR Universal (AXU) Hash). *$\{H_Y\}_{Y \in \{0,1\}^n}$ is said to be ω-AXU if for any $Z \in \{0,1\}^n$ and distinct messages $D, D' \in \{0,1\}^{n*}$,*

$$\Pr[Y \xleftarrow{\$} \{0,1\}^n; H_Y(D) \oplus H_Y(D') = Z] \leq \frac{\omega \max\{|D|_n, |D'|_n\}}{2^n}.$$

Note that the parameter of POLYVAL is $\omega = 1$.

5 Mu-AE Security of GCM-SST

5.1 Mu-AE Security of GCM-SST

Mu-AESecurity in the IC and d-Bound Models. The following theorem shows the mu-AE-security bound of GCM-SST in the IC and d-bound models.

Theorem 1 (Security of GCM-SST-NKD in the IC and d-bound models). *Assume that $\{H_Y\}_{Y\in\{0,1\}^n}$ is ω-AXU and the underlying BC is an IC. For any computationally-unbounded adversary $\mathbf{A}$ with resources in Sect. 4.2, we have*

$$\mathbf{Adv}^{\text{mu-ae}}_{\text{GCM-SST}}(\mathbf{A}) \leq \frac{\max\{2\breve{\sigma}_e\sigma_e, 18\breve{v}_n v_n\}}{2^n} + \frac{\omega \ell v}{2^n} + \frac{\omega v}{2^t} + \frac{(d + \frac{n}{\log_2 n})(p+q)}{2^k}$$
$$+ \left(\frac{6(\log_2 n)(\sigma_e + 3v)}{2^n}\right)^{\frac{n}{\log_2 n}}.$$

The proof is given in Sect. 6.

Regarding the above bound, the first four terms are dominant. Assume that $\omega = 1$. Regarding offline security, the fourth term shows that GCM-SST achieves about k-bit offline security. Regarding online security, since $\breve{v}_n v_n \leq \breve{v} v$, the first three terms shows that GCM-SST is secure as long as $\sigma_e \leq 2^n/\breve{\sigma}_e$ and $v \leq 2^n/\max\{\breve{v}, \ell, 2^{n-t}\}$. Hence, if the parameters of a single user are limited as $\breve{\sigma}_e, \breve{v}, \ell \ll 2^{n/2}$, then GCM-SST achieves beyond-birthday-bound security.

Remark 1. The IC model ensures k-bit offline security when NR is adopted. In contrast, only with the standard mu-SPRP assumption, the security game is defined without NR, i,e, adversaries can choose BC's inputs, and the offline security is degraded to $k - \log_2 u$ bits due to Biham's attack [5]. NR makes BC's inputs for GCM-SST uncontrollable, preventing adversaries from recovering the BC's input-output tuple in the IC model.

Mu-AE Security in the Standard Model. Without the d-bound assumption, an adversary can make the same nonce to each user. Hence, by replacing d with u, removing the user's key collision terms $\frac{(d+\frac{n}{\log_2 n})(p+q)}{2^k}$ and $\left(\frac{6(\log_2 n)(\sigma_e+3v)}{2^n}\right)^{\frac{n}{\log_2 n}}$ and introducing the mu-PRP term $\mathbf{Adv}^{\text{mu-prp}}_E(u, \sigma_e + 3v, \mathbf{t} + O(\sigma))$, we have the following bound of GCM-SST in the standard model. The corresponding bad events of the proof in Sect. 6 are coll_{off}, $\text{coll}_{\neq u}$, and mcoll. In the standard model, the key collision events are considered in the mu-PRP assumption. Note that the bound with $u = 1$ is the su-bound.

Corollary 1 (Security of GCM-SST in the Standard Model). *Assume that $\{H_Y\}_{Y\in\{0,1\}^n}$ is ω-AXU. For any computationally-bounded adversary $\mathbf{A}$ with resources in Sect. 4.2, we have*

$$\mathbf{Adv}^{\text{mu-ae}}_{\text{GCM-SST}}(\mathbf{A}) \leq \frac{\max\{2\breve{\sigma}_e\sigma_e, 18\breve{v}_n v_n\}}{2^n} + \frac{\omega \ell v}{2^n} + \frac{\omega v}{2^t}$$
$$+ \mathbf{Adv}^{\text{mu-prp}}_E(u, \sigma_e + 3v, \mathbf{t} + O(\sigma)).$$

5.2 Mu-AE Security of GCM-SST-NKD in the IC Model

For each nonce, the KDF in GCM-SST-NKD provides a fresh key of GCM-SST under the assumption that F_L is mu-PRF secure. Hence, in the mu-setting, there are at most q keys of GCM-SST via the KDF in GCM-SST-NKD. By using Theorem 1, we obtain the following bound of the mu-AE security of GCM-SST-NKD.

Corollary 2 (Security of GCM-SST-NKD in the IC and d-bound models). *Assume that $\{H_Y\}_{Y\in\{0,1\}^n}$ is ω-AXU and the underlying BC is an IC. For any computationally-unbounded adversary $\mathbf{A}$ with resources in Sect. 4.2, we have*

$$\mathbf{Adv}_{\mathsf{GCM\text{-}SST\text{-}NKD}}^{\mathsf{mu\text{-}ae}}(\mathbf{A}) \leq \frac{\max\{2\ell_e\sigma_e, 18v_n\}}{2^n} + \frac{\omega\ell v}{2^n} + \frac{\omega v}{2^t} + \frac{(d + \frac{n}{\log_2 n})(p+q)}{2^k}$$
$$+ \left(\frac{6(\log_2 n)(\sigma_e + 3v)}{2^n}\right)^{\frac{n}{\log_2 n}} + \mathbf{Adv}_F^{\mathsf{mu\text{-}prf}}(u,q,p).$$

Compared with GCM-SST, by using NKD, the online security is improved: GCM-SST-NKD is secure as long as $\sigma_e \leq \frac{2^n}{\ell_e}$ and $v \leq \frac{2^n}{\max\{\ell, 2^{n-t}\}}$.

6 Proof of Theorem 1

Without loss of generality, we assume that the adversary is deterministic and makes no repeated or trivial query.

6.1 Coefficient-H Technique

We derive the security bound in Theorem 1 by using the coefficient-H technique [34]. A set of values that an adversary obtains in the security game is called a "transcript." Let T_R and T_I be transcripts obtained by random samples of $\mathcal{O}_{\mathsf{real}}$ and $\mathcal{O}_{\mathsf{ideal}}$, respectively. We call a transcript τ *valid* if $\Pr[\mathsf{T}_I = \tau] > 0$. Let $\mathcal{T}$ be the set of all valid transcripts such that $\forall \tau \in \mathcal{T} : \Pr[\mathsf{T}_I = \tau] > \Pr[\mathsf{T}_R = \tau]$. Then, we have

$$\mathbf{Adv}_{\mathsf{GCM\text{-}SST}}^{\mathsf{mu\text{-}ae}}(\mathbf{A}) \leq \mathsf{SD}(\mathsf{T}_R, \mathsf{T}_I) := \sum_{\tau \in \mathcal{T}} (\Pr[\mathsf{T}_I = \tau] - \Pr[\mathsf{T}_R = \tau]).$$

The statistical distance $\mathsf{SD}(\mathsf{T}_R, \mathsf{T}_I)$ can be bounded by using the coefficient-H technique [34].

Lemma 1. *Let $\mathcal{T}_{\mathsf{good}}$ and $\mathcal{T}_{\mathsf{bad}}$ be good and bad transcripts into which $\mathcal{T}$ is partitioned. If $\forall \tau \in \mathcal{T}_{\mathsf{good}} : \frac{\Pr[\mathsf{T}_R = \tau]}{\Pr[\mathsf{T}_I = \tau]} \geq 1 - \varepsilon$ s.t. $0 \leq \varepsilon \leq 1$, then $\mathsf{SD}(\mathsf{T}_R, \mathsf{T}_I) \leq \Pr[\mathsf{T}_I \in \mathcal{T}_{\mathsf{bad}}] + \varepsilon$.*

Hence, we obtain an upper-bound of $\mathbf{Adv}_{\mathsf{GCM\text{-}SST}}^{\mathsf{mu\text{-}ae}}(\mathbf{A})$ by (1) defining good and bad transcripts; (2) upper-bounding $\Pr[\mathsf{T}_I \in \mathcal{T}_{\mathsf{bad}}]$; and (3) lower-bounding $\frac{\Pr[\mathsf{T}_R=\tau]}{\Pr[\mathsf{T}_I=\tau]}$ for $\forall \tau \in \mathcal{T}_{\mathsf{good}}$. The bound of $\Pr[\mathsf{T}_I \in \mathcal{T}_{\mathsf{bad}}]$ is given in Sect. 6.6 and the bound of $\frac{\Pr[\mathsf{T}_R=\tau]}{\Pr[\mathsf{T}_I=\tau]}$ is given in Sect. 6.7.

6.2 Definitions

We call the stage that an adversary makes queries the "query stage" and the stage after the query stage the "decision stage".

For $\beta \in [p]$, the β-th offline query-response tuple is denoted by $(\hat{K}^{(\beta)}, \hat{X}^{(\beta)}, \hat{Y}^{(\beta)})$ where $\hat{Y}^{(\beta)} = E_{\hat{K}^{(\beta)}}(\hat{X}^{(\beta)})$. For $\alpha \in [q]$, values corresponding to the α-th online query are denoted by using the superscript symbol (α), e.g., $M^{(\alpha)}$, $T^{(\alpha)}$, $X_i^{(\alpha)}$, $Y_i^{(\alpha)}$, etc. Let $\mathsf{u}_\alpha \in [u]$ be the user index corresponding to the α-th query, i.e., if the query is to the ν-th user, then $\mathsf{u}_\alpha = \nu$. For $\alpha \in [q]$, let $K^{(\alpha)} := K^{[\mathsf{u}_\alpha]}$. Let $m_\alpha := \lceil |M^{(\alpha)}|/n \rceil$ be the block length of the plaintext $M^{(\alpha)}$. For the plaintext $M^{(\alpha)}$ (resp. ciphertext $C^{(\alpha)}$), let $M_i^{(\alpha)}$ (resp. $C_i^{(\alpha)}$) be the i-th n-bit plaintext (resp. ciphertext) block, i.e., $M^{(\alpha)} = M_1^{(\alpha)} \| \cdots \| M_{m_\alpha}^{(\alpha)}$ and $C^{(\alpha)} = C_1^{(\alpha)} \| \cdots \| C_{m_\alpha}^{(\alpha)}$. Note that the length of the last block is $\leq n$. For $\alpha \in [q]$, let $\mathsf{query}^{(\alpha)}$ be a predicate for the online α-th query: if the α-th query is an encryption one, then $\mathsf{query}^{(\alpha)} := \mathsf{enc}$, and else $\mathsf{query}^{(\alpha)} := \mathsf{dec}$. For $\nu \in [u]$, let $\mathcal{Q}^{[\nu]} := \{\alpha \in [q] \mid \mathsf{u}_\alpha = \nu\}$ be query indexes for the ν-th user. Let $\mathcal{Q}_\mathsf{e}^{[\nu]} := \{\alpha \in \mathcal{Q}^{[\nu]} \mid \mathsf{query}^{(\alpha)} = \mathsf{enc}\}$ and $\mathcal{Q}_\mathsf{d}^{[\nu]} := \{\alpha \in \mathcal{Q}^{[\nu]} \mid \mathsf{query}^{(\alpha)} = \mathsf{dec}\}$. Let $\mathcal{Q}_\mathsf{e} := \cup_{\nu \in [u]} \mathcal{Q}_\mathsf{e}^{[\nu]}$ and $\mathcal{Q}_\mathsf{d} := \cup_{\nu \in [u]} \mathcal{Q}_\mathsf{d}^{[\nu]}$. Let $\mathsf{E}_\mathsf{off} := \{(\hat{K}^{(\beta)}, \hat{X}^{(\beta)}, \hat{Y}^{(\beta)}) \mid \alpha \in [p]\}$ and $\mathsf{E}_\mathsf{on} := \{(K^{(\alpha)}, X_i^{(\alpha)}, Y_i^{(\alpha)}) \mid \alpha \in \mathcal{Q}_\mathsf{e}, i \in [0, m_\alpha + 2]\} \cup \{(K^{(\alpha)}, X_i^{(\alpha)}, Y_i^{(\alpha)}) \mid \alpha \in \mathcal{Q}_\mathsf{d}, i \in [0, 2]\}$.

6.3 Sampling Algorithms

We realize an IC $E^\pm$ by lazy sampling. Let E be a table that is initially empty and keeps query-response tuples of $E^\pm$. Let $\mathsf{E}(\hat{K}, \hat{X}) := \hat{Y}$ if $(\hat{K}, \hat{X}, \hat{Y}) \in \mathsf{E}$; $\mathsf{E}(\hat{K}, \hat{X}) := \varepsilon$ otherwise. Let $\mathsf{E}^{-1}(\hat{K}, \hat{Y}) := \hat{X}$ if $(\hat{K}, \hat{X}, \hat{Y}) \in \mathsf{E}$; $\mathsf{E}^{-1}(\hat{K}, \hat{X}) := \varepsilon$ otherwise. Let $\mathsf{E}(\hat{K}, *) := \{\hat{Y} \mid (\hat{K}, \hat{X}, \hat{Y}) \in \mathsf{E}\}$ and $\mathsf{E}^{-1}(\hat{K}, *) := \{\hat{X} \mid (\hat{K}, \hat{X}, \hat{Y}) \in \mathsf{E}\}$. For a new query $(\hat{K}, \hat{X})$ to E (resp. $(\hat{K}, \hat{Y})$ to E^{-1}), the response is defined as $\hat{Y} \xleftarrow{\$} \{0,1\}^n \setminus \mathsf{E}(\hat{K}, *)$ (resp. $\hat{X} \xleftarrow{\$} \{0,1\}^n \setminus \mathsf{E}^{-1}(\hat{K}, *)$), and $\mathsf{E} \xleftarrow{\cup} \{(\hat{K}, \hat{X}, \hat{Y})\}$. For a query stored in E, the same response is returned.

In the decision stage of the ideal world, we define dummy user's keys $(K^{[\nu]})_{\nu \in [u]}$ and internal pairs of input and output blocks $\{(X_i^{(\alpha)}, Y_i^{(\alpha)}) \mid \alpha \in [q], i \in [0, m_\alpha + 2]\}$ by using Algorithm 2. In this algorithm, the IC table E is updated by the dummy values. For each $\nu \in [u]$, first, dummy hash keys and dummy internal pairs for encryption query indexes $\mathcal{Q}_\mathsf{e}^{[\nu]}$ are defined according the structure of GCM-SST.Enc. For each $\alpha \in \mathcal{Q}_\mathsf{e}^{[\nu]}$, dummy output blocks $Y_0^{(\alpha)}$ and $Y_1^{(\alpha)}$ are chosen uniformly at random from $\{0,1\}^n$. By using the plaintext $M^{(\alpha)}$, the ciphertext $C^{(\alpha)}$, and the tag $T^{(\alpha)}$, the remaining dummy output blocks are defined. Note that if the last plaintext block is not full n bits, then the truncated bits of the output block is chosen uniformly at random from $\{0,1\}^{m_\alpha n - |C^{(\alpha)}|}$. After the sampling for $\mathcal{Q}_\mathsf{e}^{[\nu]}$, dummy internal pairs for decryption query indexes $\mathcal{Q}_\mathsf{d}^{[\nu]}$ are defined according to the structure of GCM-SST.Dec. Note that the algorithm defines only $Y_0^{(\alpha)}, Y_1^{(\alpha)}$ and $Y_2^{(\alpha)}$ for authenticity. With the plaintext $M^{(\alpha)}$, the ciphertext $C^{(\alpha)}$, and these dummy values, we can define a dummy tag $T^{(\alpha)}$ and check if $T^{(\alpha)} = T_\mathsf{d}^{(\alpha)}$.

Algorithm 2. Sampling Algorithm

1: **for** $\alpha \in [q], i \in [0, m_{\max}+2]$ **do** $X_i^{(\alpha)} \leftarrow \mathsf{add}(N^{(\alpha)}, i); Y_i^{(\alpha)} \leftarrow \varepsilon$ **end for**
2: **for** $\nu \in [u]$ **do**
3:    **for** $\alpha \in \mathcal{Q}_{\mathsf{e}}^{[\nu]}$ **do**
4:       $Y_0^{(\alpha)} \xleftarrow{\$} \{0,1\}^n; Y_1^{(\alpha)} \xleftarrow{\$} \{0,1\}^n; \mathsf{H}_0^{(\alpha)} \leftarrow \mathsf{H}_{Y_0^{(\alpha)}}; \mathsf{H}_1^{(\alpha)} \leftarrow \mathsf{H}_{Y_1^{(\alpha)}}$
5:       **for** $i \in [m_\alpha]$ **do** $Y_{i+2}^{(\alpha)} \leftarrow M_i^{(\alpha)} \oplus C_i^{(\alpha)}$ **end for**
6:       $Y_+^{(\alpha)} \xleftarrow{\$} \{0,1\}^{m_\alpha n - |C^{(\alpha)}|}; Y_{m_\alpha}^{(\alpha)} \leftarrow Y_{m_\alpha}^{(\alpha)} \| Y_+^{(\alpha)}$
7:       $Z_1^{(\alpha)} \leftarrow \mathsf{H}_0^{(\alpha)}(\mathsf{pad}_\mathsf{H}(A^{(\alpha)}, C^{(\alpha)}))$
8:       $Z_2^{(\alpha)} \leftarrow \mathsf{H}_1^{(\alpha)}(Z_1^{(\alpha)} \oplus (\mathsf{bin}_{n/2}(|A^{(\alpha)}|)\|\mathsf{bin}_{n/2}(|M^{(\alpha)}|)))$
9:       $T_+^{(\alpha)} \xleftarrow{\$} \{0,1\}^{n-t}; Y_2^{(\alpha)} \leftarrow (T^{(\alpha)}\|T_+^{(\alpha)}) \oplus Z_2^{(\alpha)}$
10:       **for** $i \in [0, m_\alpha+2]$ **do** $\mathsf{E} \xleftarrow{\cup} \{(K^{[\nu]}, X_i^{(\alpha)}, Y_i^{(\alpha)})\}$ **end for**
11:    **end for**
12:    **for** $\alpha \in \mathcal{Q}_{\mathsf{d}}^{[\nu]}$ **do**
13:       $Y_0^{(\alpha)} \xleftarrow{\$} \{0,1\}^n$; **if** $\mathsf{E}(K^{[\nu]}, X_0^{(\alpha)}) \neq \varepsilon$ **then** $Y_0^{(\alpha)} \leftarrow \mathsf{E}(K^{[\nu]}, X_0^{(\alpha)})$ **end if**
14:       $Y_1^{(\alpha)} \xleftarrow{\$} \{0,1\}^n$; **if** $\mathsf{E}(K^{[\nu]}, X_1^{(\alpha)}) \neq \varepsilon$ **then** $Y_1^{(\alpha)} \leftarrow \mathsf{E}(K^{[\nu]}, X_1^{(\alpha)})$ **end if**
15:       $Y_2^{(\alpha)} \xleftarrow{\$} \{0,1\}^n$; **if** $\mathsf{E}(K^{[\nu]}, X_2^{(\alpha)}) \neq \varepsilon$ **then** $Y_2^{(\alpha)} \leftarrow \mathsf{E}(K^{[\nu]}, X_2^{(\alpha)})$ **end if**
16:       $Z_1^{(\alpha)} \leftarrow \mathsf{H}_0^{(\alpha)}(\mathsf{pad}_\mathsf{H}(A^{(\alpha)}, C^{(\alpha)}))$
17:       $Z_2^{(\alpha)} \leftarrow \mathsf{H}_1^{(\alpha)}(Z_1^{(\alpha)} \oplus (\mathsf{bin}_{n/2}(|A^{(\alpha)}|)\|\mathsf{bin}_{n/2}(|M^{(\alpha)}|)))$
18:       $T^{(\alpha)} \leftarrow \mathsf{msb}_t(Y_2^{(\alpha)} \oplus Z_2^{(\alpha)})$
19:       **for** $i \in [0,2]$ **do** $\mathsf{E} \xleftarrow{\cup} \{(K^{[\nu]}, X_i^{(\alpha)}, Y_i^{(\alpha)})\}$ **end for**
20:    **end for**
21: **end for**

6.4 Adversary's View

In the decision stage, all the user's keys and all internal pairs defined for each query are revealed to the adversary **A**. Hence, **A**'s transcript τ consists of user's keys $(K^{[\nu]})_{\nu \in [u]}$, offline tuples $(K^{(\alpha)}, X_i^{(\alpha)}, Y_i^{(\alpha)})_{\alpha \in [q], i \in [0, r_\alpha + 2]}$, online tuples $(N^{(\alpha)}, A^{(\alpha)}, M^{(\alpha)}, C^{(\alpha)}, T^{(\alpha)})_{\alpha \in \mathcal{Q}_\mathsf{e}}$, and $(N^{(\alpha)}, A^{(\alpha)}, M^{(\alpha)}, C^{(\alpha)}, T_\mathsf{d}^{(\alpha)})_{\alpha \in \mathcal{Q}_\mathsf{d}}$.

6.5 Good and Bad Transcripts

We define three conditions on bad transcripts in the following. The set of bad transcripts $\mathcal{T}_{\mathsf{bad}}$ is a subset of $\mathcal{T}$ such that one of the conditions holds. The set of good transcripts is defined as $\mathcal{T}_{\mathsf{good}} := \mathcal{T} \backslash \mathcal{T}_{\mathsf{bad}}$, which is the subset of $\mathcal{T}$ such that no condition holds.

coll$_{\mathsf{off}}$ and coll$_{\neq \mathsf{u}}$. These condition is defined as follows.

$\mathsf{coll}_{\mathsf{off}} \Leftrightarrow \exists \beta \in [p], \alpha \in [q], i \in [0, m_\alpha + 2]$
$\quad$ s.t. $K^{(\alpha)} = \hat{K}^{(\beta)} \wedge (X_i^{(\alpha)} = \hat{X}^{(\beta)} \vee Y_i^{(\alpha)} = \hat{Y}^{(\beta)})$.

$\mathsf{coll}_{\neq \mathsf{u}} \Leftrightarrow \exists \alpha, \beta \in [q], i \in [0, m_\alpha + 2], j \in [0, m_\beta + 2]$
$\quad$ s.t. $\mathsf{u}_\alpha \neq \mathsf{u}_\beta \wedge K^{[\mathsf{u}_\alpha]} = K^{[\mathsf{u}_\beta]} \wedge (X_i^{(\alpha)} = X_j^{(\beta)} \vee Y_i^{(\alpha)} = Y_j^{(\beta)} \neq \varepsilon)$.

coll$_{\text{off}}$ considers a collision in pairs of key and input block (or output block) between online and offline queries. If the event does not occur, the independence of input-output tuples between online and offline queries is ensured. The second event coll$_{\neq u}$ considers a collision in pairs of key and input (or output) block between different users. If the event does not occur, the independence of input-output tuples between distinct users is ensured.

coll$_{=u}$. The condition is defined as

$$\exists \nu \in [u], \alpha, \beta \in \mathcal{Q}^{[\nu]}, i \in [0, m_\alpha + 2], j \in [0, m_\beta + 2]$$
$$\text{s.t. } N^{(\alpha)} \neq N^{(\beta)} \wedge Y_i^{(\alpha)} = Y_j^{(\beta)} \neq \varepsilon.$$

coll$_{=u}$ considers a collision in output blocks within the same user. In the real world, for each user, output blocks in encryption queries are all distinct. Assuming that coll$_{=u}$ does not occur, one can ensure that no output collision occurs in the ideal world.

forge. The condition is defined as

$$\exists \alpha \in [q] \text{ s.t. } \text{query}_\alpha = \text{dec} \wedge T^{(\alpha)} = T_d^{(\beta)}.$$

In the ideal world, for each decryption query, the response is **reject**. Hence, assuming that **forge** does not occur, no forgery occurs in the real world.

mcoll. Let $\mu := \frac{n}{\log_2 n}$. The condition is defined as

$$\exists (\alpha_1, i_1), \ldots, (\alpha_\mu, i_\mu) \in [q] \times [0, m_{\max} + 2] \text{ s.t. } \forall j \in [2, \mu] : Y_{i_1}^{(\alpha_1)} = Y_{i_j}^{(\alpha_j)} \neq \varepsilon$$
$$\wedge (N^{(\alpha_1)}, i_1), \ldots, (N^{(\alpha_\mu)}, i_\mu) \text{ are all distinct.}$$

The condition is a multi-collision one in all output blocks. The multi-collision event is used for evaluating the probabilities of coll$_{\text{off}}$ and coll$_{\neq u}$.

6.6 Upper-Bounding $\Pr[\mathsf{T}_I \in \mathcal{T}_{\text{bad}}]$

Let $\mathbf{C} := \{\text{coll}_{\text{off}}, \text{coll}_{\neq u}, \text{coll}_{=u}, \text{forge}, \text{mcoll}\}$. For $C \in \mathbf{C}$, let $\Pr[C]$ be the probability that C holds before the other conditions in $\mathbf{C}$. We then have

$$\Pr[\mathsf{T}_I \in \mathcal{T}_{\text{bad}}] \leq \Pr[\text{coll}_{\text{off}}] + \Pr[\text{coll}_{\neq u}] + \Pr[\text{coll}_{=u}] + \Pr[\text{forge}] + \Pr[\text{mcoll}]$$
$$\leq \frac{\max\{2\breve{\sigma}_e \sigma_e, 18\breve{v}_n v_n\}}{2^n} + \frac{\omega \ell v}{2^n} + \frac{\omega v}{2^t} + \frac{(d + \frac{n}{\log_2 n})(p + q)}{2^k}$$
$$+ \left(\frac{6(\log_2 n)(\sigma_e + 3v)}{2^n}\right)^{\frac{n}{\log_2 n}}.$$

These bounds are given below.

Evaluation of $\Pr[\text{coll}_{\text{off}}]$. For each $(K^{(\alpha)}, X_i^{(\alpha)}, Y_i^{(\alpha)})$ and $(\hat{K}^{(\beta)}, \hat{X}^{(\beta)}, \hat{Y}^{(\beta)})$, we have $\Pr[K^{(\alpha)} = \hat{K}^{(\beta)}] \leq \frac{1}{2^k}$. For each $(\hat{K}^{(\beta)}, \hat{X}^{(\beta)}, \hat{Y}^{(\beta)})$, the number of users with input blocks $X_i^{(\alpha)}$ such that $X_i^{(\alpha)} = \hat{X}^{(\beta)}$ is at most d, since **A** is a d-bound adversary. Hence, we have

$$\Pr[\exists (K^{(\alpha)}, X_i^{(\alpha)}, Y_i^{(\alpha)}), (\hat{K}^{(\beta)}, \hat{X}^{(\beta)}, \hat{Y}^{(\beta)})$$
$$\text{s.t. } K^{(\alpha)} = \hat{K}^{(\beta)} \wedge X_i^{(\alpha)} = \hat{X}^{(\beta)}] \leq p \cdot \frac{d}{2^k}.$$

For each $(\hat{K}^{(\beta)}, \hat{X}^{(\beta)}, \hat{Y}^{(\beta)}) \in \mathsf{E}_{\text{off}}$, the number of output blocks $Y_i^{(\alpha)}$ such that $Y_i^{(\alpha)} = \hat{Y}^{(\beta)}$ is at most μ by mcoll. Hence, we have

$$\Pr[\exists (K^{(\alpha)}, X_i^{(\alpha)}, Y_i^{(\alpha)}), (\hat{K}^{(\beta)}, \hat{X}^{(\beta)}, \hat{Y}^{(\beta)})$$
$$\text{s.t. } K^{(\alpha)} = \hat{K}^{(\beta)} \wedge Y_i^{(\alpha)} = \hat{Y}^{(\beta)}] \leq p \cdot \frac{\mu}{2^k}.$$

With these bounds, we have

$$\Pr[\mathsf{coll}_{\text{off}}] \leq \frac{(d+\mu)p}{2^k}.$$

Evaluation of $\Pr[\mathsf{coll}_{\neq \mathsf{u}}]$. The evaluation is the same as that of $\Pr[\mathsf{coll}_{\text{off}}]$, where $(\hat{K}^{(\beta)}, \hat{X}^{(\beta)}, \hat{Y}^{(\beta)})$ is replaced with $(K_j^{(\beta)}, X_j^{(\beta)}, X_j^{(\beta)})$ such that $\mathsf{u}_\alpha \neq \mathsf{u}_\beta$. We thus have

$$\Pr[\mathsf{coll}_{\neq \mathsf{u}}] \leq \frac{(d+\mu)q}{2^k}.$$

Evaluation of $\Pr[\mathsf{coll}_{=\mathsf{u}}]$. Let σ_ν be the number of tuples defined in online queries to the ν-th user. Let $\sigma_{\mathsf{e},\nu} := |\{(K^{(\alpha)}, X_i^{(\alpha)}, Y_i^{(\alpha)}) \mid \alpha \in \mathcal{Q}_{\mathsf{e}}^{[\nu]}, i \in [0, m_\alpha + 2]\}|$ be the number of tuples defined in encryption queries to the ν-th user. Let $v_{\mathsf{n},\nu} := |\{\alpha \in \mathcal{Q}_{\mathsf{d}}^{[\nu]} \mid \forall \beta \in \mathcal{Q}_{\mathsf{e}}^{[\nu]} : N^{(\alpha)} \neq N^{(\beta)}\}|$ be the number of decryption queries with fresh nonces of the ν-th user. Note that $\sigma_\nu \leq \sigma_{\mathsf{e},\nu} + 3v_{\mathsf{n},\nu}$. For each distinct tuples $(K^{(\alpha)}, X_i^{(\alpha)}, Y_i^{(\alpha)}), (K^{(\beta)}, X_j^{(\beta)}, Y_j^{(\beta)})$ s.t. $N^{(\alpha)} \neq N^{(\beta)} \wedge \mathsf{u}^{(\alpha)} = \mathsf{u}^{(\beta)}$, the output blocks $Y_i^{(\alpha)}$ and $Y_j^{(\beta)}$ are independently chosen, and thus $\Pr[Y_i^{(\alpha)} = Y_j^{(\beta)}] \leq \frac{1}{2^n}$. With the bound, we have

$$\Pr[\mathsf{coll}_{=\mathsf{u}}] \leq \sum_{\nu \in [u]} \binom{\sigma_\nu}{2} \cdot \frac{1}{2^n} \leq \sum_{\nu \in [u]} \frac{0.5(\sigma_{\mathsf{e},\nu} + 3v_{\mathsf{n},\nu})^2}{2^n}$$
$$\leq \sum_{\nu \in [u]} \frac{0.5 \max\{2\sigma_{\mathsf{e},\nu}, 6v_{\mathsf{n},\nu}\}^2}{2^n} \leq \sum_{\nu \in [u]} \frac{\max\{2\sigma_{\mathsf{e},\nu}^2, 18v_{\mathsf{n},\nu}^2\}}{2^n}$$
$$\leq \frac{\max\{2\breve{\sigma}_{\mathsf{e}}\sigma_{\mathsf{e}}, 18\breve{v}_{\mathsf{n}}v_{\mathsf{n}}\}}{2^n}.$$

Evaluation of Pr[forge]. We first consider the following collision event for input to the second hash function.

$$\mathsf{coll}_{\mathsf{H}_0} \Leftrightarrow \nu \in [u], \alpha \in \mathcal{Q}_\mathsf{e}^{[\nu]}, \beta \in \mathcal{Q}_\mathsf{d}^{[\nu]} \text{ s.t. } N^{(\alpha)} = N^{(\beta)} \wedge$$

$$Z_1^{(\alpha)} \oplus (\mathsf{bin}_{n/2}(|A^{(\alpha)}|)\|\mathsf{bin}_{n/2}(|M^{(\alpha)}|))$$
$$= Z_1^{(\beta)} \oplus (\mathsf{bin}_{n/2}(|A^{(\beta)}|)\|\mathsf{bin}_{n/2}(|M^{(\beta)}|)).$$

Since $\mathsf{pad}_\mathsf{H}(A^{(\alpha)}, C^{(\alpha)}) \neq \mathsf{pad}_\mathsf{H}(A^{(\beta)}, C^{(\beta)})$ or $(|A^{(\alpha)}|, |M^{(\alpha)}|) \neq (|A^{(\beta)}|, |M^{(\beta)}|)$, the AXU hash function ensures that for each $\nu \in [u], \alpha \in \mathcal{Q}_\mathsf{e}^{[\nu]}, \beta \in \mathcal{Q}_\mathsf{d}^{[\nu]}$, the input collision probability is at most $\frac{\omega \max\{|A^{(\alpha)}|_n + |M^{(\alpha)}|_n, |A^{(\beta)}|_n + |M^{(\beta)}|_n\}}{2^n}$. Summing the bound for each ν, α, β, we have

$$\Pr[\mathsf{coll}_{\mathsf{H}_0}] \leq \sum_{\nu, \alpha, \beta} \frac{\omega \max\{|A^{(\alpha)}|_n + |M^{(\alpha)}|_n, |A^{(\beta)}|_n + |M^{(\beta)}|_n\}}{2^n}$$
$$\leq \sum_{\nu, \beta} \frac{\omega \ell}{2^n} = \frac{\omega \ell v}{2^n}.$$

We next evaluate the probability $\Pr[\mathsf{forge} \mid \neg \mathsf{coll}_{\mathsf{H}_0}]$. For each $\nu \in [u]$ and $\beta \in \mathcal{Q}_\mathsf{d}^{[\nu]}$, we consider the following two cases.

- If $\exists \alpha \in \mathcal{Q}_\mathsf{e}^{[\nu]}$ s.t. $N^{(\alpha)} = N^{(\beta)}$, the forgery is equal to the condition $\mathsf{msb}_t(Z_2^{(\beta)} \oplus Z_2^{(\alpha)}) = T_\mathsf{d}^{(\beta)} \oplus T^{(\alpha)}$. By $\neg \mathsf{coll}_{\mathsf{H}_0}$, the inputs to the second hash function are distinct, and thus the AXU hash function ensure that for each ν, α, β s.t. $N^{(\alpha)} = N^{(\beta)}$, we have $\Pr[T^{(\beta)} = T_\mathsf{d}^{(\beta)}] \leq 2^{n-t} \cdot \frac{\omega}{2^n} = \frac{\omega}{2^t}$.
- If $\forall \alpha \in \mathcal{Q}_\mathsf{e}^{[\nu]} : N^{(\alpha)} \neq N^{(\beta)}$, by using the randomness of $Y_2^{(\beta)}$, we have $\Pr[T^{(\beta)} = T_\mathsf{d}^{(\beta)}] \leq \frac{1}{2^t}$.

With the bound, we have

$$\Pr[\mathsf{forge} \mid \neg \mathsf{coll}_{\mathsf{H}_0}] \leq \sum_{\nu, \beta} \frac{\omega}{2^n} \leq \frac{\omega v}{2^n}.$$

By using these bounds, we have

$$\Pr[\mathsf{forge}] \leq \frac{\omega \ell v}{2^n} + \frac{\omega v}{2^t}.$$

Evaluation of Pr[mcoll]. For each $Y \in \{0,1\}^n$ and μ tuples $(K^{(\alpha_j)}, X_{i_j}^{(\alpha_j)}, Y_{i_j}^{(\alpha_j)})_{j \in [\mu]}$ such that $(N^{(\alpha_1)}, i_1), \ldots, (N^{(\alpha_\mu)}, i_\mu)$ are all distinct, $Y_{i_1}^{(\alpha_1)}, \ldots, Y_{i_{\mu-1}}^{(\alpha_{\mu-1})}$, and $Y_{i_\mu}^{(\alpha_\mu)}$ are defined by using independent n-bit values, and we have

$$\Pr[Y_{i_1}^{(\alpha_1)} = \cdots = Y_{i_\mu}^{(\alpha_\mu)} = Y] \leq \left(\frac{1}{2^n}\right)^\mu.$$

Summing the bound for each $Y \in \{0,1\}^n$ and μ tuples and using Stirling's approximation ($x! \geq (x/e)^x$ for any x), we have

$$\Pr[\text{mcoll}] \leq 2^n \cdot \binom{\sigma_e + 3v}{\mu} \cdot \left(\frac{1}{2^n}\right)^\mu \leq 2^n \cdot \left(\frac{e(\sigma_e + 3v)}{\mu 2^n}\right)^\mu$$

$$\leq 2^n \left(\frac{3(\sigma_e + 3v)}{\frac{n}{\log_2 n} \cdot 2^n}\right)^{\frac{n}{\log_2 n}} \leq \left(\frac{6(\log_2 n)(\sigma_e + 3v)}{2^n}\right)^{\frac{n}{\log_2 n}}.$$

6.7 Lower-Bounding $\frac{\Pr[T_R = \tau]}{\Pr[T_I = \tau]}$

For each good transcript τ, we show that $\frac{\Pr[T_R=\tau]}{\Pr[T_I=\tau]} \geq 1$. In this evaluation, we use the symbol "$\star$" for values and sets corresponding to τ. For a set $\mathcal{L}$, let $T_R \vdash \mathcal{L}$ (resp. $T_I \vdash \mathcal{L}$) be an event that T_R (resp. T_I) satisfies all elements in $\mathcal{L}$. Fix a good transcript τ that consists of user's keys $\mathcal{K}^\star = (K^{[u]\star})_{\nu \in [u]}$, primitive query-response tuples $(K^{(\alpha)\star}, X_i^{(\alpha)\star}, Y_i^{(\alpha)\star})_{\alpha \in \mathcal{Q}_e, i \in [0, r_\alpha+2]}$, primitive query-response tuples $\mathsf{E}^\star_{\text{off}} := (\hat{K}^{(\beta)\star}, \hat{X}^{(\beta)\star}, \hat{Y}^{(\beta)\star})_{\beta \in [p]}$, and internal tuples $\mathsf{E}^\star_{\text{on}} := ((K^{(\alpha)\star}, X_i^{(\alpha)\star}, Y_i^{(\alpha)\star})_{\alpha \in \mathcal{Q}_e, i \in [0, r_\alpha+2]}, (K^{(\beta)\star}, X_j^{(\beta)\star}, Y_j^{(\beta)\star})_{\beta \in \mathcal{Q}_d, i \in [0, 2]})$. Note that if the internal tuples are fixed, then responses to online queries are uniquely fixed. Hence, we can omit the responses to online queries in this evaluation.

Evaluation of $\Pr[T_W \vdash \mathcal{K}^\star]$ for $W \in \{R, I\}$. In both real and ideal worlds, each user's key $K^{[\nu]}$ is chosen uniformly at random from $\{0,1\}^n$, and thus

$$\Pr[T_R \vdash \mathcal{K}^\star] = \Pr[T_I \vdash \mathcal{K}^\star].$$

Evaluation of $\Pr[T_W \vdash \mathsf{E}^\star_{\text{off}} \mid T_W \vdash \mathcal{K}^\star]$ for $W \in \{R, I\}$. In both real and ideal worlds, for each offline query, the response is defined by an IC, and thus we have

$$\Pr[T_R \vdash \mathsf{E}^\star_{\text{off}} \mid T_R \vdash \mathcal{K}^\star] = \Pr[T_I \vdash \mathsf{E}^\star_{\text{off}} \mid T_I \vdash \mathcal{K}^\star].$$

Evaluation of $\Pr[T_W \vdash \mathsf{E}^\star_{\text{on}} \mid T_W \vdash \mathcal{K}^\star, \mathsf{E}^\star_{\text{off}}]$ for $W \in \{R, I\}$. Regarding the good transcript, by $\neg$forge, for each $\beta \in \mathcal{Q}_d$, the response is **reject** and $T^{(\beta)\star} \neq T_d^{(\beta)\star}$. By $\neg\text{coll}_{\text{off}}$, $\neg\text{coll}_{\neq u}$, and $\neg\text{coll}_{=u}$, for each distinct input blocks in τ, the output blocks are distinct. Hence, we have $\Pr[T_R \vdash \mathsf{E}^\star_{\text{on}} \mid T_R \vdash \mathcal{K}^\star, \mathsf{E}^\star_{\text{off}}] > 0$. In the real (resp. ideal) world, each output block is defined from 2^n or less elements in $\{0,1\}^n$ (resp. $\{0,1\}^n$). Thus, each output block in the ideal world is defined from the space larger than the real world, and we have

$$\Pr[T_I \vdash \mathsf{E}^\star_{\text{on}} \mid T_I \vdash \mathcal{K}^\star, \mathsf{E}^\star_{\text{off}}] \leq \Pr[T_R \vdash \mathsf{E}^\star_{\text{on}} \mid T_R \vdash \mathcal{K}^\star, \mathsf{E}^\star_{\text{off}}].$$

Deriving the Lower Bound. The above evaluations show that

$$\frac{\Pr[T_R = \tau]}{\Pr[T_I = \tau]} \geq 1.$$

7 Conclusion

This paper studies mu-security of GCM-SST, bridging the gap between the design document [7] and Inoue et al.'s security proof in the su setting. By providing the new security bound of GCM-SST, we verify that its security with short tags is valid under the mu model. We also show that NR and NKD improve offline and online mu-security of GCM-SST, in the same way as combined with GCM. This work focuses on the nonce-respecting setting, as suggested in the design document [7], but GCM-SST provide a certain security improvement from GCM in the nonce-misuse setting because of the nonce-based hash keys. The proof by Inoue et al. [22] captures this property based on the nonce-misuse resilience model of Ashur et al. [2]. Extension of this model to the mu setting, along with the proof of GCM-SST in such an extended model, are outstanding open research problems.

References

1. 3GPP TS 33 501: Security architecture and procedures for 5g system (2024). https://portal.3gpp.org/desktopmodules/Specifications/SpecificationDetails.aspx?specificationId=3169
2. Ashur, T., Dunkelman, O., Luykx, A.: Boosting authenticated encryption robustness with minimal modifications. IACR Cryptol. ePrint Arch. 239 (2017). http://eprint.iacr.org/2017/239
3. Bellare, M., Krovetz, T., Rogaway, P.: Luby-Rackoff backwards: increasing security by making block ciphers non-invertible. In: Nyberg, K. (ed.) EUROCRYPT 1998. LNCS, vol. 1403, pp. 266–280. Springer, Heidelberg (1998). https://doi.org/10.1007/BFb0054132
4. Bellare, M., Tackmann, B.: The multi-user security of authenticated encryption: AES-GCM in TLS 1.3. In: Robshaw, M., Katz, J. (eds.) CRYPTO 2016. LNCS, vol. 9814, pp. 247–276. Springer, Heidelberg (2016). https://doi.org/10.1007/978-3-662-53018-4_10
5. Biham, E.: How to decrypt or even substitute des-encrypted messages in 2^{28} steps. Inf. Process. Lett. **84**(3), 117–124 (2002)
6. Bose, P., Hoang, V.T., Tessaro, S.: Revisiting AES-GCM-SIV: multi-user security, faster key derivation, and better bounds. In: Nielsen, J.B., Rijmen, V. (eds.) EUROCRYPT 2018. LNCS, vol. 10820, pp. 468–499. Springer, Cham (2018). https://doi.org/10.1007/978-3-319-78381-9_18
7. Campagna, M., Maximov, A., Mattsson, J.P.: Galois Counter Mode with Secure Short Tags (GCM-SST). `draft-mattsson-cfrg-aes-gcm-sst-18` (2023). https://datatracker.ietf.org/doc/draft-mattsson-cfrg-aes-gcm-sst/18/
8. Chen, Y.L., Choi, W., Lee, C.: Improved multi-user security using the squared-ratio method. In: CRYPTO 2023. LNCS, vol. 14082, pp. 694–724. Springer, Heidelberg (2023). https://doi.org/10.1007/978-3-031-38545-2_23
9. Choi, W., Kim, H., Lee, J., Lee, Y.: Multi-user security of the sum of truncated random permutations. In: ASIACRYPT 2022. LNCS, vol. 13792, pp. 682–710. Springer, Heidelberg (2022). https://doi.org/10.1007/978-3-031-22966-4_23

10. Cogliati, B., Seurin, Y.: EWCDM: an efficient, beyond-birthday secure, nonce-misuse resistant MAC. In: Robshaw, M., Katz, J. (eds.) CRYPTO 2016. LNCS, vol. 9814, pp. 121–149. Springer, Heidelberg (2016). https://doi.org/10.1007/978-3-662-53018-4_5
11. Degabriele, J.P., Govinden, J., Günther, F., Paterson, K.G.: The security of chacha20-poly1305 in the multi-user setting. In: CCS 2021, pp. 1981–2003. ACM (2021)
12. Dinur, I.: Combining outputs of a random permutation: New constructions and tight security bounds by fourier analysis. In: EUROCRYPT 2025. LNCS, vol. 15601, pp. 244–273. Springer, Heidelberg (2025). https://doi.org/10.1007/978-3-031-91107-1_9
13. Dworkin, M.: NIST Special Publication 800-38D: Recommendation for block cipher modes of operation: Galois/counter mode (GCM) and GMAC (2007). https://csrc.nist.gov/pubs/sp/800/38/d/final
14. Ferguson, N.: Authentication weaknesses in gcm (2005). https://csrc.nist.gov/csrc/media/projects/block-cipher-techniques/documents/bcm/comments/cwc-gcm/ferguson2.pdf
15. Gueron, S.: Intel advanced encryption standard (AES) new instructions set (2010). https://www.intel.com/content/dam/doc/white-paper/advanced-encryption-standard-new-instructions-set-paper.pdf
16. Gueron, S., Kounavis, M.E.: Intel carry-less multiplication instruction and its usage for computing the GCM mode (2014). https://www.intel.com/content/dam/develop/external/us/en/documents/clmul-wp-rev-2-02-2014-04-20.pdf
17. Gueron, S., Langley, A., Lindell, Y.: AES-GCM-SIV: nonce misuse-resistant authenticated encryption. RFC **8452**, 1–42 (2019)
18. Gueron, S., Lindell, Y.: Better bounds for block cipher modes of operation via nonce-based key derivation. In: CCS 2017, pp. 1019–1036. ACM (2017)
19. Gunsing, A., Mennink, B.: The summation-truncation hybrid: reusing discarded bits for free. In: Micciancio, D., Ristenpart, T. (eds.) CRYPTO 2020. LNCS, vol. 12170, pp. 187–217. Springer, Cham (2020). https://doi.org/10.1007/978-3-030-56784-2_7
20. Günther, F., Thomson, M., Wood, C.A.: Usage Limits on AEAD Algorithms (2025). https://datatracker.ietf.org/doc/html/draft-irtf-cfrg-aead-limits-10
21. Hoang, V.T., Tessaro, S., Thiruvengadam, A.: The multi-user security of GCM, revisited: tight bounds for nonce randomization. In: CCS 2018, pp. 1429–1440. ACM (2018)
22. Inoue, A., Jha, A., Mennink, B., Minematsu, K.: Generic security of GCM-SST. Cryptology ePrint Archive, Paper 2024/1928 (2024). https://eprint.iacr.org/2024/1928
23. Iwata, T.: New blockcipher modes of operation with beyond the birthday bound security. IACR Cryptol. ePrint Arch. 188 (2006)
24. Iwata, T., Ohashi, K., Minematsu, K.: Breaking and repairing GCM security proofs. In: Safavi-Naini, R., Canetti, R. (eds.) CRYPTO 2012. LNCS, vol. 7417, pp. 31–49. Springer, Heidelberg (2012). https://doi.org/10.1007/978-3-642-32009-5_3
25. Luykx, A., Mennink, B., Paterson, K.G.: Analyzing multi-key security degradation. In: Takagi, T., Peyrin, T. (eds.) ASIACRYPT 2017. LNCS, vol. 10625, pp. 575–605. Springer, Cham (2017). https://doi.org/10.1007/978-3-319-70697-9_20
26. McGrew, D.A., Viega, J.: The security and performance of the galois/counter mode (GCM) of operation. In: Canteaut, A., Viswanathan, K. (eds.) INDOCRYPT 2004.

LNCS, vol. 3348, pp. 343–355. Springer, Heidelberg (2004). https://doi.org/10.1007/978-3-540-30556-9_27
27. Mennink, B., Neves, S.: Encrypted Davies-Meyer and its dual: towards optimal security using mirror theory. In: Katz, J., Shacham, H. (eds.) CRYPTO 2017. LNCS, vol. 10403, pp. 556–583. Springer, Cham (2017). https://doi.org/10.1007/978-3-319-63697-9_19
28. Naito, Y., Sasaki, Y., Sugawara, T.: Tight multi-user security of CCM and enhancement by tag-based key derivation applied to GCM and CCM. Cryptology ePrint Archive, Paper 2025/953 (2025). https://eprint.iacr.org/2025/953
29. Naito, Y., Sasaki, Y., Sugawara, T., Yasuda, K.: The multi-user security of triple encryption, revisited: exact security, strengthening, and application to TDES. In: CCS 2022. ACM (2022)
30. National Institute of Standards and Technology: Announcement of Proposal to Revise SP 800-38D. Recommendation for Block Cipher Modes of Operation: Galois/Counter Mode (GCM) and GMAC (2023). https://www.nist.gov/news-events/news/2023/08/announcement-proposal-revise-sp-800-38d-recommendation-block-cipher-modes
31. National Institute of Standards and Technology: Pre-Draft Call for Comments: GCM and GMAC Block Cipher Modes of Operation (2025). https://csrc.nist.gov/pubs/sp/800/38/d/r1/iprd
32. National Institute of Standards and Technology: PRE-DRAFT Call for Comments: NIST Launches Development of Cryptographic Accordions. NIST SP 800-197A (Initial Preliminary Draft) (2025). https://csrc.nist.gov/pubs/sp/800/197/a/iprd
33. Nyberg, K., Gilbert, H., Robshaw, M.: Galois MAC with forgery probability close to ideal (2005). https://csrc.nist.gov/csrc/media/projects/block-cipher-techniques/documents/bcm/comments/general-comments/papers/nyberg_gilbert_and_robshaw.pdf
34. Patarin, J.: The "Coefficients H" technique. In: Avanzi, R.M., Keliher, L., Sica, F. (eds.) SAC 2008. LNCS, vol. 5381, pp. 328–345. Springer, Heidelberg (2009). https://doi.org/10.1007/978-3-642-04159-4_21
35. Rescorla, E.: The transport layer security (TLS) protocol version 1.3. RFC **8446**, 1–160 (2018). https://doi.org/10.17487/RFC8446
36. Rescorla, E., Tschofenig, H., Modadugu, N.: The datagram transport layer security (DTLS) protocol version 1.3 – draft-ietf-tls-dtls13-43 (2021). https://tools.ietf.org/html/draft-ietf-tls-dtls13-43
37. Thomson, M., Turner, S.: Using TLS to secure QUIC. RFC **9001**, 1–52 (2021). https://doi.org/10.17487/RFC9001
38. Zhang, X., Shen, Y., Wang, L.: Multi-user security of CCM authenticated encryption mode. In: CCS 2024, pp. 4331–4345. ACM (2024)

Network Security

SimSeq: A Robust TLS Traffic Classification Method

Jinghui Cheng[1] and Fanping Zeng[1,2]($\boxtimes$)

[1] School of Computer Science and Technology, University of Science and Technology of China, Anhui, China
chengjinghui@mail.ustc.edu.cn, billzeng@ustc.edu.cn
[2] Key Laboratory of Wireless-Optical Communications, University of Science and Technology of China, Chinese Academy of Sciences, Beijing, China

Abstract. With the increasing deployment of encrypted protocols such as TLS, traditional deep packet inspection techniques have become ineffective, posing challenges to traffic classification. In this paper, we propose SimSeq, a robust TLS traffic classification method that relies solely on packet length sequences. To simulate real-world network conditions, we design two perturbation scenarios that emulate fast retransmission and timeout retransmission behaviors. Each scenario is configured with multiple packet loss rates, where smaller rates represent mild congestion and larger rates reflect more congested network conditions. We generate perturbation views of packet sequences using reliable transmission logic and leverage a contrastive learning framework to learn robust and discriminative representations. The encoder, composed of a BiLSTM and attention pooling module, is pretrained with a SimCLR-style contrastive loss and then finetuned with scenario-specific classification heads. Experimental results on the CESNET-TLS22 dataset show that SimSeq achieves strong and stable performance under both scenarios, with average F1-scores of 0.88 and 0.93, respectively.

Keywords: TLS traffic classification · Contrastive learning · Packet length sequence · BiLSTM · Robust representation

1 Introduction

In recent years, a large number of websites and applications utilize Transport Layer Security (TLS) technology for privacy protection and secure communication, and with the wide application of TLS, encryption of network traffic has dramatically improved user privacy and data security [11]. However, encrypted traffic also makes traditional Deep Packet Inspection (DPI) techniques, which study packet payload, become largely ineffective [1], bringing new challenges to network management, traffic monitoring and threat detection. Despite the encryption of traffic content, TLS traffic classification is still crucial: it helps network administrators to identify application types, detect malicious behavior (e.g., malware transmissions in encrypted tunnels), and optimize quality of service (QoS).

Machine learning (ML) and deep learning (DL) based methods have made significant progress in encrypted traffic classification by leveraging side channel features such as packet length, timing and flow patterns. However, existing methods still have limitations: for example, classification performance will drop significantly when faced with dynamic network environments, new encryption protocols, or adversarial evasion techniques. many studies [8,12,13] designed various deep learning models to try to automatically extract complex and representative high-level features from the packet length sequence of the flow, which contains rich and discriminative implicit information. In addition, it is convenient and low-cost to measure and obtain the packet length sequence in large-scale networks in the real world, and can even support real-time traffic classification tasks [1].

In this work, we use the metadata of the traffic: the sequence of packet lengths as the only classification basis, and TLS encrypted traffic transmission usually requires the implementation of reliable transmission logic, even if the underlying transmission protocol is not TCP (for example, QUIC internally implements a reliable transmission mechanism similar to TCP to meet the normal working requirements of TLS), that is, TLS always relies on reliable transmission, regardless of whether the underlying protocol is reliable.

Based on this, we developed the SimSeq method. Considering the possible changes in packet length sequences in real network environments, we designed two different scenarios: Scenario α is when the network is not so congested; Scenario β is when the network is more congested. In both scenario, we designed two packet length sequence perturbation algorithms caused by reliable transmission logic based on the topological position of the packet length sequence information sampling point. Then, we used the contrastive learning idea similar to SimCLR to generate two views from the original packet length sequence by two perturbation algorithms in both scenario for contrastive learning to learn the robust representation in each scenario, which is then used for classification. The specific method will be introduced in Sect. 3.

In summary, our contributions can be summarized as follows:

- A TLS encrypted traffic classification method is proposed based entirely on the packet length sequence information of the flow without relying on the encrypted content in the packet payload.
- Two Internet traffic scenarios were constructed. In both scenario, the impact of the real network environment on the packet length sequence was simulated. Two perturbation algorithms were designed to generate two views from the original sequence for comparative learning.
- By contrastive learning, we learn robust representations in packet length sequences and achieve stable and good performance in two scenarios.

The rest of the paper is organized as follows. Section 2 reviews related work. Section 3 introduces the two proposed scenarios, the design of the perturbation algorithms, and the architecture of contrastive learning. In Sect. 4, we evaluate the proposed method. Finally, Sect. 5 concludes the paper.

2 Related Work

Due to the rapid development of Internet encryption technology, the practicality and effectiveness of encrypted traffic classification methods based on ports, deep packet inspection, and machine learning have declined and can no longer meet the requirements of today's traffic classification situation. Deep learning algorithms can partially overcome the limitations of the three methods discussed above, so researchers apply deep learning algorithms to the field of encrypted traffic classification. We elaborate on two key perspectives of the existing work.

2.1 Encryption Traffic Classification

Cao et al. [2] used CNN, LSTM and SDAE employ the packet length sequence of TLS encrypted control traffic to fingerprint software defined networks (SDN). Shen et al. [14] used graph-based neural networks on the packet length sequence of encrypted traffic. Zheng et al. [21] built an autoencoder model to restore the packet length sequence. Lin et al. [7] adopted the bidirectional encoder representations transformer to extract features from payload byte sequence. Liu et al. [8] present Flow Sequence Networks (FS-Net) to learn representations from packet length sequences and achieve accurate encrypted traffic classification. They can achieve high accuracy on encrypted traffic classification with traffic datasets tested in an offline environment. Zou et al. [22] proposed CAD-Net, an encrypted traffic classification model based on channel attention mechanism and deformable convolution. The model is based on ResNet-18 and introduces channel attention mechanism (CAM) to focus on key features. Experiments have shown that CAD-Net outperforms existing methods in both service and application classification tasks.

2.2 Robust Encryption Traffic Classification

Jiang et al. [6] proposed SePeric, a robust network traffic classification method, which explores the association in the packet length sequence and adjusts it to eliminate the influence of abnormal sequence order, while extracting additional features from the byte sequence of the first packet to supplement the insufficient discrimination, in order to solve the performance degradation caused by packet loss, duplication, disorder and insufficient sequence discrimination in early network traffic classification. This method shows higher robustness in actual scenarios. Jenefa et al. [5] proposed a deep learning method combining convolutional neural network (CNN) and recurrent neural network (RNN) for network traffic classification. This method uses CNN to extract features from raw traffic data and then classifies the extracted features through RNN, thereby effectively processing large and complex datasets and achieving a high accuracy of 0.98 on the CIC-IDS 2022 data set, which is better than traditional machine learning methods. Shi et al. [15] observed that the characteristics of traffic data with noisy labels are clean and their true underlying distribution is statistically close to clean data, and designed a robust federated network traffic classification algorithm (RFNTC) to solve this problem. Zhang et al. [20] proposed the EDW-Voting (exponential decay window voting) method, the classification result of the latest traffic have a greater impact on the final decision. Experimental results show that EDW-Voting is superior to the original ML classification results and the fixed-size sliding window voting (FSW-Voting) method in terms of overall accuracy and per-class F-measure. Malekghaini et al. [9] studied the impact of data drift on deep learning encrypted traffic classification. They analyzed real ISP traffic data and found that model performance degraded over time. The study showed that traffic time series features (UW-F) are more robust to drift than TLS handshake byte features (UW-H), and proposed recommendations for architectural adaptability to improve generalization performance.

3 Design of SimSeq

The overall approach consists of the following parts: a packet length sequence perturbation mechanism that relies on reliable transmission logic(to be introduced in 3.1), a pretraining phase(to be introduced in 3.2) and a finetuning phase(to be introduced in 3.3).

3.1 Packet Length Sequence Perturbation Mechanism

To better illustrate how the perturbation mechanism is designed, we construct a simple linear topology as shown in Fig. 1. For ease of understanding, we assume that there is only one-way traffic in this topology (as shown by the direction of the arrow in the figure).

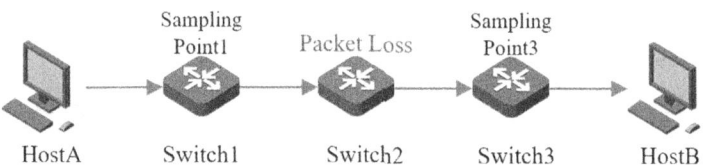

Fig. 1. Causes of packet length sequence changes.

When TLS is used for traffic encryption, it is basically always used in conjunction with reliable transmission logic. Because the core task of TLS is to provide confidentiality, integrity, and identity authentication, but to complete these tasks correctly, the premise is that data needs to be delivered reliably and orderly, so regardless of whether the underlying layer is a reliable transmission protocol, TLS needs a reliable transmission mechanism to work together. The additional reliability mechanism typically includes implementations of timeout retransmission and fast retransmission, so we designed two scenarios. As mentioned above, the first scenario α represents a situation where the network is not so congested, so the perturbation algorithm is designed by simulating the fast retransmission mechanism; the second scenario β represents a situation where the network is more congested, so the perturbation algorithm is designed by simulating the timeout retransmission mechanism. In both scenarios, two perturbation algorithms are designed based on the relative position of the sampling point and the packet loss point(the sampling point is upstream or downstream of the packet loss point), these two perturbation algorithms are used to perturb the original samples to generate two views for subsequent contrastive learning.

So first we need to understand why the sampling point located upstream or downstream of the packet loss point will produce different perturbations to the original data packet length sequence. In fact, the generated perturbations involve subsequence repetition and shifting within the packet length sequence. The reasons will be introduced in detail below.

Algorithm 1: Scenario β Repetition Perturbation

Input: A sequence of packet lengths seq, packet loss rate p, minimum loss packets l_{min}, maximum loss packets l_{max}
Output: Perturbed sequence with retransmissions

1 $retransmitBuffer \leftarrow [\,]$
2 $perturbedSeq \leftarrow [\,]$
3 $i \leftarrow 0$
4 $n \leftarrow length(seq)$
5 **while** $i < n$ **do**
6   **if** $random() < p$ **then**
7          $L \leftarrow randomInteger(l_{min}, l_{max})$
8          $end \leftarrow \min(i + L, n)$
9          $subseq \leftarrow seq[i : end]$
10         $retransmitBuffer$.extend($subseq$)
11         $perturbedSeq$.extend($subseq$)
12         $i \leftarrow end$
13   **end**
14   **else**
15         $perturbedSeq$.append($seq[i]$)
16         $perturbedSeq$.extend($retransmitBuffer$)
17         $retransmitBuffer \leftarrow [\,]$
18         $i \leftarrow i + 1$
19   **end**
20 **end**
21 $perturbedSeq$.extend($retransmitBuffer$)
22 **return** $perturbedSeq$

Subsequence Repetition Perturbation. As shown in Fig. 1, in this perturbation algorithm design, we focus only on sampling point 1. $HostA$ sends data packets to $HostB$. Assume that there are three switches between the two hosts and that packet loss occurs at switch 2. In the two scenarios we constructed, more data packets will be lost and retransmitted in the scenario β where the network is more congested (the number of packet losses is randomly selected within the interval $[2, 5]$), and a single data packet will be lost in the scenario α where the network is not so congested. At this time, the data sampling point is at sampling point 1. Due to the retransmission mechanism (whether fast retransmission or timeout retransmission), $HostA$ will retransmit all lost data packets. In this way, not only are the data packets lost on switch 2 during the original transmission not lost on switch 1, but also switch 1 will receive these data packets again during the retransmission phase, resulting in the subsequence duplication phenomenon. The following Fig. 2 is an illustration of this phenomenon.

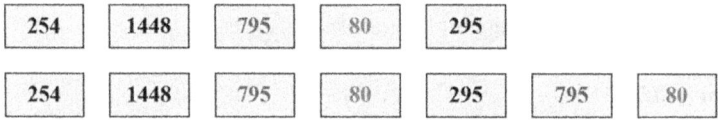

Fig. 2. Packet length subsequence repetition.

In Fig. 2, packets of length 795 and 80 were retransmitted once and received repeatedly by switch 1, which is the phenomenon described above.

Then, the perturbation algorithm designed based on this phenomenon in scenario β is shown in Algorithm 1 (the perturbation algorithm design in scenario α is similar).

Subsequence Shift Perturbation. In the other perturbation algorithm design, similarly, in Fig. 1, we only focus on sampling point 3 this time. $HostA$ sends data packets to $HostB$. Among the three switches, the data packet loss still occurs in switch 2. The difference between the packet loss in the two scenarios has been introduced earlier. Also due to the retransmission mechanism (whether fast retransmission or timeout retransmission), $HostA$ will retransmit all lost data packets. In this case, switch 3 where sampling point 3 is located cannot receive the first sent data packets, but can receive the retransmitted data packets (we assume that the retransmission is successful once), so the subsequence disordering phenomenon occurs. Figure 3 below illustrates this phenomenon.

In Fig. 3, data packets of length 1448, 80, and 295 are retransmitted once, and shifts occur in the data packet length sequence collected at sampling point 3.

Then, the perturbation algorithm designed based on this phenomenon in scenario β is shown in Algorithm 2 (the perturbation algorithm design in scenario α is similar).

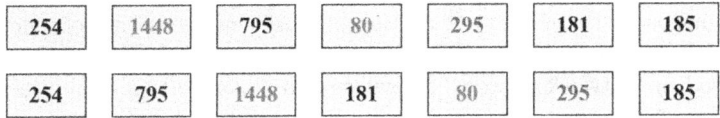

Fig. 3. Packet length subsequence shift.

Algorithm 2: Scenario β Shift Perturbation

Input: A sequence of packet lengths seq, packet loss rate p, minimum loss packets l_{min}, maximum loss packets l_{max}
Output: Perturbed sequence with retransmissions

1 $retransmitBuffer \leftarrow [\,]$
2 $perturbedSeq \leftarrow [\,]$
3 $i \leftarrow 0$
4 $n \leftarrow length(seq)$
5 **while** $i < n$ **do**
6   **if** $random() < p$ **then**
7        $L \leftarrow randomInteger(l_{min}, l_{max})$
8        $L \leftarrow \min(L, n - i)$
9        $subseq \leftarrow seq[i : i + L]$
10       $retransmitBuffer$.extend($subseq$)
11       $i \leftarrow i + L$
12   **end**
13   **else**
14       $perturbedSeq$.append($seq[i]$)
15       $perturbedSeq$.extend($retransmitBuffer$)
16       $retransmitBuffer \leftarrow [\,]$
17       $i \leftarrow i + 1$
18   **end**
19 **end**
20 $perturbedSeq$.extend($retransmitBuffer$)
21 **return** $perturbedSeq$

3.2 Design of Pretraining Phase

The length sequence of data packets is essentially time series data. In order to fully explore the potential time series patterns in the original packet length sequence, we use a self-supervised method based on contrastive learning to pretrain the encoder. This study constructs a contrastive learning framework similar to SimCLR [3]: that is, both construct positive sample pairs (two perturbed views of the same original sample) and negative sample pairs (other samples in the same batch) for unsupervised representation learning, and then use the Normalized Temperature-scaled Cross-Entropy (NT-Xent) loss. The SimCLR method targets images as the data type and uses image enhancement to generate two views; while our method targets packet length sequences and uses perturbation logic based on network protocol knowledge to generate two semantic views at the protocol behavior level. There are precedents for applying this contrastive learning method for image data to time series data [10,18,19].

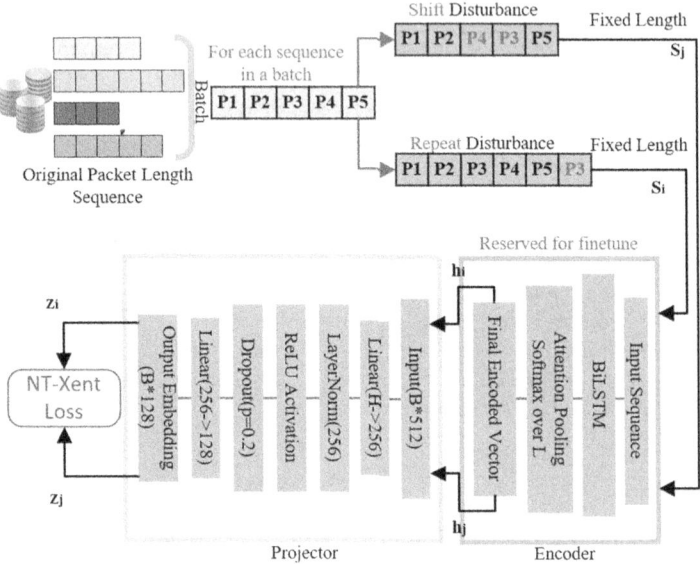

Fig. 4. Framework of SimSeq pretraining.

The pretraining process is shown in Fig. 4. The part of the data perturbation to generate two views has been introduced in 3.1. The rest of the process is mainly related to the pretraining model, which can be divided into three parts as follows.

Encoder. It is composed of a bidirectional long-short-term memory(BiLSTM) network combined with an attention pooling module to extract the global representation of each packet length sequence. The attention mechanism can adaptively assign weights to each time step, thereby enhancing the perception of key features. The two components of the encoder are shown in Fig. 5, Fig. 5(a) is the schematic diagram of BiLSTM, and Fig. 5(b) is the attention pooling structure we designed.

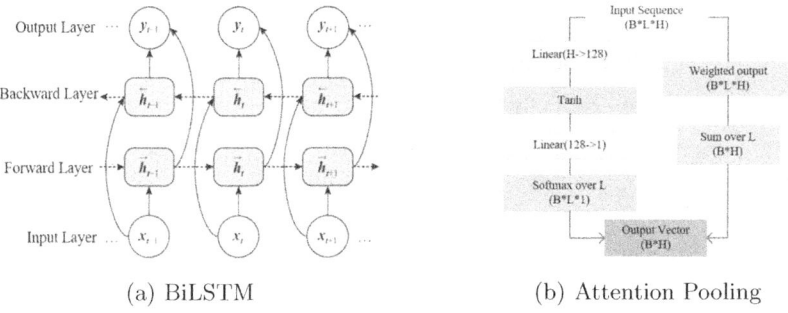

(a) BiLSTM   (b) Attention Pooling

Fig. 5. Components of the encoder.

Given a perturbed sequence of packet length sequence $\mathbf{X} = [\mathbf{x}_1, \mathbf{x}_2, \ldots, \mathbf{x}_T]$, where $\mathbf{x}_t \in \mathbb{R}^d$ denotes the input at time step t, a bidirectional LSTM (BiLSTM) is used to capture temporal dependencies in both forward and backward directions.

$$\overrightarrow{\mathbf{h}}_t, \overleftarrow{\mathbf{h}}_t = \text{BiLSTM}(\mathbf{x}_t), \quad t = 1, \ldots, T \tag{1}$$

The hidden representation at each time step is obtained by concatenating the forward and backward hidden states:

$$\mathbf{h}_t = [\overrightarrow{\mathbf{h}}_t; \overleftarrow{\mathbf{h}}_t] \in \mathbb{R}^{2d_h} \tag{2}$$

To derive a global representation of the sequence, we apply attention pooling over the hidden states $\{\mathbf{h}_1, \ldots, \mathbf{h}_T\}$. The unnormalized attention score at time step t is computed as:

$$e_t = \mathbf{v}^\top \tanh(\mathbf{W}_a \mathbf{h}_t + \mathbf{b}_a) \tag{3}$$

where $\mathbf{W}_a \in \mathbb{R}^{d_a \times 2d_h}$, $\mathbf{v} \in \mathbb{R}^{d_a}$, and $\mathbf{b}_a \in \mathbb{R}^{d_a}$ are learnable parameters. The attention weights are then normalized via the softmax function:

$$\alpha_t = \frac{\exp(e_t)}{\sum_{i=1}^{T} \exp(e_i)} \tag{4}$$

The final sequence representation $\mathbf{z} \in \mathbb{R}^{2d_h}$ is computed as the weighted sum of all hidden states:

$$\mathbf{z} = \sum_{t=1}^{T} \alpha_t \mathbf{h}_t \tag{5}$$

This vector $\mathbf{z}$ serves as a compact, context-aware representation of the input sequence and is subsequently utilized for contrastive learning.

Projector. Its structure is shown in Table 1, which is used to map the encoder output to the embedding space required for contrastive learning.

Table 1. Projector Architecture

Layer	Description
Linear	Fully connected layer: $\mathbb{R}^{d_{in}} \to \mathbb{R}^{d_h}$
LayerNorm	Layer normalization over feature dimension
ReLU	Non-linear activation function
Dropout	Dropout with rate 0.2
Linear	Fully connected layer: $\mathbb{R}^{d_h} \to \mathbb{R}^{d_{out}}$

NT-Xent Loss. In this work, we employ the Normalized Temperature-scaled Cross-Entropy Loss (NT-Xent) as the contrastive loss function. Given a batch containing N positive pairs, totaling $2N$ samples, the loss for a single positive pair $(\mathbf{z}_i, \mathbf{z}_j)$ is defined as:

$$\ell_{i,j} = -\log \frac{\exp(\operatorname{sim}(\mathbf{z}_i, \mathbf{z}_j)/\tau)}{\sum_{k=1}^{2N} \mathbf{1}_{[k \neq i]} \exp(\operatorname{sim}(\mathbf{z}_i, \mathbf{z}_k)/\tau)} \tag{6}$$

where $\mathbf{z}_i$ and $\mathbf{z}_j$ are normalized feature vectors, $\operatorname{sim}(\cdot,\cdot)$ denotes the cosine similarity between two vectors, τ is a temperature hyperparameter controlling the smoothness of the distribution, and $\mathbf{1}_{[k \neq i]}$ excludes the similarity of the sample with itself.

Based on the loss for a single positive pair, the overall NT-Xent loss for the batch is computed by averaging over all positive pairs:

$$\mathcal{L} = \frac{1}{2N} \sum_{k=1}^{N} (\ell_{2k-1,2k} + \ell_{2k,2k-1}) \tag{7}$$

The goal of pretraining is to minimize the distance between two different views generated by the same original sample, while maximizing the distance between other samples in the same batch, so as to learn a more discriminative sequence representation. The detailed experimental design will be introduced in 4.2.

3.3 Design of Finetuning Phase

After completing the pretraining phase, we further finetune the pretrained encoder combined with a classification head to improve its performance on downstream classification tasks. The core goal of the finetuning phase is to use the learned capabilities of the encoder to adapt to the actual multi-category classification task by training task-specific classifiers.

The model structure design in the finetuning phase consists of two parts: a fixed encoder and a trainable classification head. The encoder part loads the model weights obtained from the pretraining phase and remains frozen throughout the finetuning phase to retain its general representation ability. Classification heads have different designs in different scenarios, the details are shown in Table 2.

Table 2. Classification Head under Different Scenario

Under scenario α	Under scenario β
Linear(output_of_encoder → 256)	Linear(output_of_encoder → 256)
–	BatchNorm1d(256)
ReLU	ReLU
–	Dropout(0.3)
Linear(256 → 128)	Linear(256 → 128)
–	BatchNorm1d(128)
ReLU	ReLU
–	Dropout(0.3)
Linear(128 → num_classes)	Linear(128 → num_classes)

In scenario α, due to the relatively light disturbance(the perturbation algorithm is designed with a small packet loss rate setting and only loses one packet at a time), the enhanced data still retains more original features in the time series structure, so the feature representation output by the encoder is of high quality and less noise. To avoid over-modeling, we adopted a simpler classification head structure and removed regularization mechanisms such as normalization and Dropout to fully retain the discriminative information of the input features.

In contrast, in scenario β, due to the large disturbance introduced by the simulated congestion and timeout behavior, it may bring instability to the representation learning. Therefore, we introduced Batch Normalization and Dropout to improve the stability and generalization ability of the model.

4 Experiment and Analysis

In this section, we conduct a series of experiments to evaluate the proposed SimSeq method.

As mentioned above, we designed two different scenarios. Each scenario employs two reliability-aware perturbation algorithms following similar design paradigms. Both mainly use packet loss rate to simulate network congestion levels, thereby creating different degrees of perturbation. Two distinct packet loss rates were configured for each of the two scenarios in our design. They are all packet loss rates that are more in line with the actual network environment in order to explore the robustness of the SimSeq method in a scenario. The details will be introduced below.

4.1 Dataset and Preprocessing

We conducted experiments on the CESNET-TLS22 dataset, which is a large-scale encrypted traffic set collected from a real network environment, the dataset includes both TLS1.2 and 1.3 flows, all CESNET-TLS22 samples were collected over TCP, and labels were derived from CESNET DPI systems. The original dataset contains 11 million TLS flows, covering a wide range of application categories. In order to ensure the quality of labels and alleviate category imbalance, we adopted a downsampling strategy. The original dataset has 21 labels, from which we selected 8 representative, more common and more meaningful labels, the 8 selected categories were chosen based on traffic volume and semantic distinctiveness. The number of samples in a single file of the original dataset corresponding to these 8 labels and the number of samples we finally retained through random downsampling are shown in Table 3.

Table 3. Retained Sample Statistics by Category

Category	Original Count(flows)	Retained Count(flows)
Streaming Media	1,284,276	91,896
Antivirus	798,703	100,948
Instant Messaging	283,150	140,207
Music	500,795	105,490
Advertising	1,373,571	83,552
File Sharing	827,090	124,267
Games	257,400	60,220
Mail	499,124	88,452
Total	5,824,109	795,032

Since the dataset is too large, the available information is given in the form of a CSV file. We directly extract the CATEGORY field as the label and extract the packet length sequences from the PPI field. The length of these sequences is not longer than 30. Then it is divided into a pretraining set and a finetuning set in a ratio of 8 : 1. The finetuning set is further divided into a training set, a validation set, and a test set in a ratio of 8 : 1 : 1. Finally, it is divided by 1460 (the maximum payload length of standard Ethernet) for normalization.

4.2 Pretraining

In the pretraining stage, a batch size of 2048 is used, the initial learning rate is 1×10^{-3}, the optimizer is Adam, and the weight decay is set to 1×10^{-4}. The training is performed for a maximum of 500 epochs, and an early stopping strategy (tolerance epoch is 10) is used to avoid overfitting. The model parameters of the encoder with the lowest loss during the training process are saved.

Table 4. Convergence epochs and final loss under different packet loss rate p settings

	Scenario α		Scenario β	
p	$p=0.01$	$p=0.02$	$p=0.05$	$p=0.1$
Convergence epochs	241	252	356	325
Final loss	0.1412	0.1428	0.2823	0.2927

Table 4 shows the convergence epochs and final losses in different p settings (in all experiments, we use p to control the degree of perturbation). These packet loss rates are typical values selected based on network conditions. We can see that as p increases, the degree of perturbation increases, and the convergence epochs of the contrastive learning model increase. This shows that stronger perturbations weaken the semantic consistency between positive sample pairs, thereby reducing the optimization potential of the contrastive target.

In the same scenario, as the packet loss rate p increases, the number of convergence epochs and the final loss of the model show high stability. This shows that the model has good adaptability to changes in the intensity of perturbations in the scenario, allowing the model to maintain good training performance within a certain range of perturbation.

4.3 Finetuning and Classification

We perform supervised finetuning on the pretrained model to evaluate its performance in downstream classification tasks. Based on the encoder weights obtained from pretraining, we built an end-to-end classification model, which consists of a pretrained feature encoder and a lightweight fully connected layer, which outputs the final multi-class labels as a classifier. During the finetuning stage, the pretrained encoder is frozen and only the classifier is trained.

During training, the cross-entropy loss function serves as the optimization objective, with the Adam optimizer employed for parameter updates. The initial learning rate is set to 1×10^{-3}, and the batch size is set to 128. The early stopping strategy is introduced during the training process and the training is terminated early when the validation accuracy does not improve within 10 consecutive epochs. The training loss, validation loss, and accuracy on the validation set during finetuning are shown in Fig. 6 (taking $p = 0.05$ as an example).

To assess the model's robustness against data perturbations, we use the same packet loss rate parameter p(previously defined for perturbation algorithms and pretraining) to control the perturbation intensity, and the model is fully finetuned under a total of four p settings in two scenarios, all data used in the finetuning stage also need to be perturbed under the same scenario and p setting.

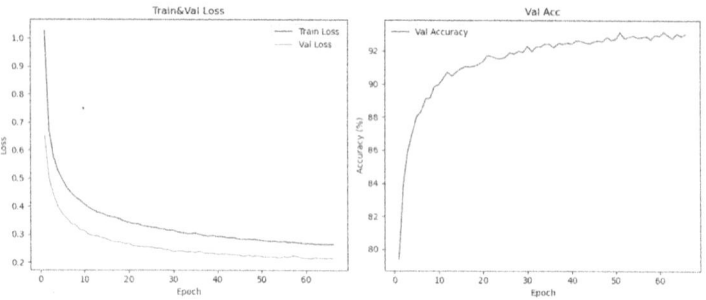

Fig. 6. Finetuning training.

We evaluate the model performance using accuracy and macro-averaged F1-score. Accuracy is defined as the ratio of correctly predicted samples to the total number of samples:

$$\text{Accuracy} = \frac{\sum_{i=1}^{C} TP_i}{\sum_{i=1}^{C}(TP_i + FP_i + FN_i)} \tag{8}$$

where C is the number of classes, TP_i is the number of true positives for class i, FP_i is the number of false positives, and FN_i is the number of false negatives.

The F1-score is the harmonic mean of precision and recall, providing a balanced measure between the two. For a given class i, it is calculated as:

$$\text{F1-score}_i = \frac{2 \times \text{Precision}_i \times \text{Recall}_i}{\text{Precision}_i + \text{Recall}_i} \tag{9}$$

where Precision_i and Recall_i are defined as:

$$\text{Precision}_i = \frac{TP_i}{TP_i + FP_i}, \quad \text{Recall}_i = \frac{TP_i}{TP_i + FN_i} \tag{10}$$

then the macro F1-score is defined as:

$$\text{Macro F1-score} = \frac{1}{C} \sum_{i=1}^{C} \frac{2 \times \text{Precision}_i \times \text{Recall}_i}{\text{Precision}_i + \text{Recall}_i} \tag{11}$$

Macro-averaging treats all classes equally regardless of their support. The following performance description uses macro F1-score.

The results of the finetuning experiment are shown in Table 5 and Table 6. It can be observed that although the high packet loss rate p leads to a slower convergence speed and a slight increase in the final loss during the contrastive learning training process, the model trained with high p values demonstrates better classification performance in the finetuning classification task. This is mainly because the stronger perturbation generates more diverse and challenging training views, prompting the model to learn more robust and generalizable representation features. In contrast, a low perturbation p makes the pretraining

Table 5. F1-score comparison across categories under different scenarios and p values

Category	Scenario α		Scenario β	
	$p=0.01$	$p=0.02$	$p=0.05$	$p=0.10$
Advertising	0.79	0.81	0.89	0.88
Antivirus	0.93	0.93	0.96	0.96
File sharing	0.84	0.86	0.90	0.90
Games	0.83	0.86	0.91	0.91
Instant messaging	0.94	0.94	0.97	0.97
Mail	0.88	0.89	0.93	0.93
Music	0.91	0.93	0.97	0.97
Streaming media	0.81	0.82	0.89	0.89

Table 6. Overall accuracy and macro-averaged F1-score under different scenarios and p values

	Scenario α		Scenario β	
p	$p=0.01$	$p=0.02$	$p=0.05$	$p=0.10$
Accuracy	0.87	0.89	0.93	0.93
Macro F1-score	0.87	0.88	0.93	0.93

task relatively simple, and the model is prone to overfitting simple features, limiting the improvement of the performance of downstream tasks.

In addition, we also compared with other related works. Rosetta [17] uses a similar data perturbation method, but we believe that TLS does not always use TCP as the underlying transmission protocol, so we did not consider the impact of the *Nagle* algorithm, but only considered the impact of the reliable transmission logic of retransmission on the packet length sequence. Rosetta did not mention the data processing method; therefore, we used our own dataset to experiment with this method. The results are shown in the Table 7, the percentages in the table are the comparison between our method and Rosetta.

To prove that the performance does not rely solely on the classification head, we apply the same perturbation to the original data and use a linear layer instead of the encoder to map the perturbed data to the same output dimension as the encoder, and then input the same classifier for supervised training. The results are also shown in Table 7 in the `Only Linear` row, a more intuitive diagram is shown in Fig. 7.

We also used two other data perturbation methods, Random Mask [4] and Random Swap [16], the former simulates packet loss by randomly setting some packet lengths to zero, and the latter simulates disorder by randomly swapping packet positions. These two methods cannot set the packet loss rate, but rather a perturbation probability, so we only replaced our perturbation logic with these two to get the overall performance, The macro F1-score is 0.68 and 0.71, respec-

Table 7. Accuracy and F1-score comparison across methods under different scenarios and p values

	Scenario α				Scenario β			
	$p = 0.01$		$p = 0.02$		$p = 0.05$		$p = 0.10$	
	AC	F1	AC	F1	AC	F1	AC	F1
Rosetta [17]	0.89	0.89	0.85	0.84	0.86	0.85	0.82	0.82
Ours	0.87	0.87	0.89	0.88	0.93	0.93	0.93	0.93
	(2.2%↓)	(2.2%↓)	(4.7%↑)	(4.8%↑)	(8.1%↑)	(9.4%↑)	(13.4%↑)	(13.4%↑)
Only Linear	0.65	0.66	0.63	0.64	0.54	0.53	0.51	0.51

tively, such performance clearly cannot match the results achieved by contrastive learning using perturbation methods related to TLS traffic characteristics.

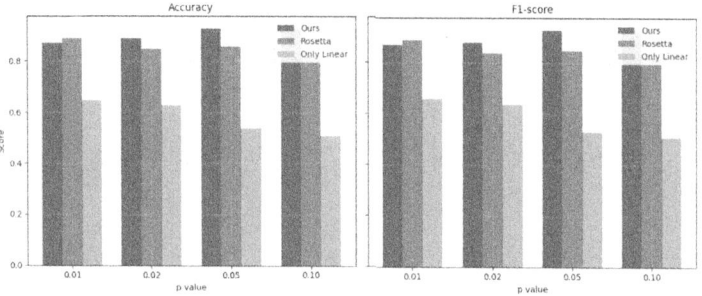

Fig. 7. Accuracy and F1-score comparison under different p values.

4.4 Additional Robustness Verification

In order to further verify the validity and robustness of this perturbation algorithm based on reliable transmission logic design and whether the classification performance on non-TCP-based TLS-encrypted traffic is as we envisioned when designing the perturbation algorithm, we extended the experiment to the QUIC protocol, which also uses TLS as its encryption protocol. However, for the QUIC protocol, the underlying transmission uses UDP instead of TCP. In protocols like QUIC (TLS over UDP), reliable delivery is implemented at the application layer. Thus, retransmission effects remain the dominant factor affecting packet length sequences, while fragmentation plays a minimal role. Therefore, we believe that the designed method is applicable to this type of traffic.

We use CESNET-QUIC22 dataset for the verification, we process the CESNET-QUIC22 dataset in the same way as we process the CESNET-TLS22 dataset. We select the same eight labels as before and retain up to 100,000 samples for each category (if there are less than 100,000 samples, we retain all of them). However, the samples extracted during the downsampling process will be tested to see if they are valid flows, so the number of traffic samples obtained in the end is as shown in the Table 8.

Table 8. Retained Sample Statistics by Category on CESNET-QUIC22

Category	Original Count(flows)	Retained Count(flows)
Streaming Media	1,870,334	94,882
Antivirus	258,091	99,501
Instant Messaging	225,334	99,116
Music	296,179	97,447
Advertising	778,450	96,216
File Sharing	121,395	99,367
Games	63,076	61,141
Mail	95,641	29,214
Total	5,824,109	795,032

We then used exactly the same experimental process as the previous experiment to conduct the experiment and obtained the following classification results in Table 9 and Table 10.

Table 9. F1-score comparison across categories under different scenarios and p values

	Scenario α		Scenario β	
Category	$p = 0.01$	$p = 0.02$	$p = 0.05$	$p = 0.10$
Advertising	0.79	0.81	0.91	0.91
Antivirus	0.94	0.93	0.97	0.96
File sharing	0.90	0.92	0.94	0.94
Games	0.88	0.89	0.95	0.95
Instant messaging	0.93	0.94	0.96	0.97
Mail	0.97	0.97	1.00	0.99
Music	0.95	0.93	0.97	0.97
Streaming media	0.80	0.82	0.90	0.89

It can be found that the performance of the classification on the traffic encrypted by the QUIC protocol based on the underlying UDP transport layer protocol with the help of the application layer to achieve reliable transmission mechanism is quite close to the performance obtained by the previous experiment on the TCP-based TLS traffic dataset, and the performance is also stable, which is in line with our assumptions above.

Table 10. Overall accuracy and macro-averaged F1-score under different scenarios and p values

	Scenario α		Scenario β	
p	$p=0.01$	$p=0.02$	$p=0.05$	$p=0.10$
Accuracy	0.89	0.91	0.94	0.94
Macro F1-score	0.90	0.91	0.95	0.95

4.5 Analysis

Our method performs significantly better than Rosetta at high packet loss rates $p \geq 0.05$, indicating that it is more robust to extreme network noise, but it is slightly inferior to Rosetta at low packet loss rates $p \leq 0.02$, probably because Rosetta's enhancement strategy is more suitable for slightly disturbed scenarios. The overall disadvantage of Only Linear verifies the necessity of extracting nonlinear features through contrastive learning. The remaining two perturbation methods fail to incorporate TLS traffic characteristics, consequently disrupting critical timing patterns and leading to degraded performance.

5 Conclusion

In this paper, we proposed SimSeq, a robust TLS traffic classification method that leverages packet length sequences and contrastive learning to address the challenges posed by dynamic network conditions. By designing reliability-transmission-aware perturbation algorithms to simulate fast retransmission(scenario α) and timeout retransmission(scenario β) behaviors, we generated perturbed views that preserve the semantic consistency of TLS flows under varying packet loss rates. The BiLSTM-based encoder with attention pooling effectively captured temporal dependencies, while the SimCLR-style contrastive learning framework enabled the model to learn discriminative and noise-resistant representations.

Experimental results on the CESNET-TLS22 dataset demonstrated that SimSeq achieves strong performance across both scenarios, outperforming baseline methods like Rosetta under high packet loss rates. Notably, our method exhibited superior robustness to extreme network noise, while maintaining stability in mildly congested environments.

Future work could explore adaptive perturbation strategies for hybrid network conditions and extend the framework to other encrypted protocols or apply it to the classification of malicious traffic using TLS encryption, in addition, our current design prioritizes performance optimization (e.g., adding regularization) for high-congestion scenario over deployment versatility, we will focus on developing adaptive unified classification heads afterwards. SimSeq's reliance on lightweight packet metadata ensures practical applicability for real-world deployment, providing a scalable solution for encrypted traffic analysis without compromising privacy.

References

1. Barradas, D., Santos, N., Rodrigues, L., Signorello, S., Ramos, F.M., Madeira, A.: Flowlens: enabling efficient flow classification for ml-based network security applications. In: NDSS (2021)
2. Cao, J., Yang, Z., Sun, K., Li, Q., Xu, M., Han, P.: Fingerprinting {SDN} applications via encrypted control traffic. In: 22nd International Symposium on Research in Attacks, Intrusions and Defenses (RAID 2019), pp. 501–515 (2019)
3. Chen, T., Kornblith, S., Norouzi, M., Hinton, G.: A simple framework for contrastive learning of visual representations. In: International Conference on Machine Learning, pp. 1597–1607. PmLR (2020)
4. Devlin, J., Chang, M.W., Lee, K., Toutanova, K.: Bert: pre-training of deep bidirectional transformers for language understanding. In: Proceedings of the 2019 Conference of the North American chapter of the Association for Computational Linguistics: Human Language Technologies, vol. 1 (long and short papers), pp. 4171–4186 (2019)
5. Jenefa, A., et al.: A robust deep learning-based approach for network traffic classification using cnns and rnns. In: 2023 4th International Conference on Signal Processing and Communication (ICSPC), pp. 106–110. IEEE (2023)
6. Jiang, Y., Wang, X., Lai, Y., Wang, Y.: A packet sequence permutation-aware approach to robust network traffic classification. IEEE Network. Lett. (2024)
7. Lin, X., Xiong, G., Gou, G., Li, Z., Shi, J., Yu, J.: Et-bert: a contextualized datagram representation with pre-training transformers for encrypted traffic classification. In: Proceedings of the ACM Web Conference 2022, pp. 633–642 (2022)
8. Liu, C., He, L., Xiong, G., Cao, Z., Li, Z.: Fs-net: a flow sequence network for encrypted traffic classification. In: IEEE INFOCOM 2019-IEEE Conference On Computer Communications, pp. 1171–1179. IEEE (2019)
9. Malekghaini, N., et al.: Deep learning for encrypted traffic classification in the face of data drift: an empirical study. Comput. Netw. **225**, 109648 (2023)
10. Meng, Q., Qian, H., Liu, Y., Xu, Y., Shen, Z., Cui, L.: Unsupervised representation learning for time series: a review. arXiv preprint arXiv:2308.01578 (2023)
11. Oh, C., Ha, J., Roh, H.: A survey on TLS-encrypted malware network traffic analysis applicable to security operations centers. Appl. Sci. **12**(1), 155 (2021)
12. Rimmer, V., Preuveneers, D., Juarez, M., Van Goethem, T., Joosen, W.: Automated website fingerprinting through deep learning. arXiv preprint arXiv:1708.06376 (2017)
13. Shen, M., Liu, Y., Zhu, L., Du, X., Hu, J.: Fine-grained webpage fingerprinting using only packet length information of encrypted traffic. IEEE Trans. Inf. Forensics Secur. **16**, 2046–2059 (2020)
14. Shen, M., Zhang, J., Zhu, L., Xu, K., Du, X.: Accurate decentralized application identification via encrypted traffic analysis using graph neural networks. IEEE Trans. Inf. Forensics Secur. **16**, 2367–2380 (2021)
15. Shi, S., Guo, Y., Wang, D., Zhu, Y., Han, Z.: Distributionally robust federated learning for network traffic classification with noisy labels. IEEE Trans. Mob. Comput. **23**(5), 6212–6226 (2023)
16. Wei, J., Zou, K.: Eda: easy data augmentation techniques for boosting performance on text classification tasks. arXiv preprint arXiv:1901.11196 (2019)
17. Xie, R., et al.: Rosetta: enabling robust TLS encrypted traffic classification in diverse network environments with tcp-aware traffic augmentation. In: Proceedings of the ACM Turing Award Celebration Conference-China 2023, pp. 131–132 (2023)

18. Yang, X., Zhang, Z., Cui, R.: Timeclr: a self-supervised contrastive learning framework for univariate time series representation. Knowl.-Based Syst. **245**, 108606 (2022)
19. Yeh, C.C.M., et al.: Toward a foundation model for time series data. In: Proceedings of the 32nd ACM International Conference on Information and Knowledge Management, pp. 4400–4404 (2023)
20. Zhang, R., Wang, J., Chen, X., Ye, X.: Edw-voting: robust realtime traffic classification combined with flow side information. In: 2018 Tenth International Conference on Advanced Computational Intelligence (ICACI), pp. 438–442. IEEE (2018)
21. Zheng, W., Gou, C., Yan, L., Mo, S.: Learning to classify: a flow-based relation network for encrypted traffic classification. In: Proceedings of The Web Conference 2020, pp. 13–22 (2020)
22. Zou, A., Yang, W., Tang, C., Lu, J., Guo, J.: A novel and effective encrypted traffic classification method based on channel attention and deformable convolution. Comput. Electr. Eng. **118**, 109406 (2024)

EvoFuzz: Enhancing State Space Exploration and Seed Prioritization in Stateful Protocol Fuzzing Using Evolutionary Game Theory

Chengdong Wang, Bo Yu, and Lin Yang[✉]

National University of Defense Technology, Changsha, China
{wangcd,yubo0615}@nudt.edu.cn, yanglin61s@126.com

Abstract. Stateful Coverage-Based Greybox Fuzzing (SCGF) is a key technique for securing stateful network protocols. To efficiently process feedback and guide mutations, these fuzzers predominantly employ scheduling strategies based on simple short-term heuristics. However, the reliance on myopic heuristics, which fail to adopt a global, long-term optimization perspective, results in inefficient state-space exploration and a struggle to uncover vulnerabilities requiring deep and complex state transitions. To address this issue, we present EvoFuzz, an adaptive scheduling framework that applies Evolutionary Game Theory (EGT). EvoFuzz operates through two core modules: EvoState and EvoSeed. The EvoState module treats states as competing players to guide global exploration, while the EvoSeed module treats candidate seeds as competing players, selecting the most promising one within a target state. We implemented EvoFuzz on top of NSFuzz and evaluated it on five real-world protocols. The results indicate that compared to the state-of-the-art baselines, EvoFuzz increases the unique state sequence by up to 205.56%, increases code branch coverage by up to 6.87%, and increases the number of unique crashes by 31.96%.

Keywords: Greybox fuzzing · Network protocol · Evolutionary game theory(EGT)

1 Introduction

Network protocols are the foundation of modern digital infrastructure, and their security is paramount to the stable operation of critical services and daily applications. However, security flaws in protocol implementations continue to pose a severe threat to network security. Stateful protocols, such as FTP, DTLS, and RTSP, are particularly challenging, as their responses depend on an internal state determined by historical interactions, leading to a massive and difficult-to-traverse state space [5].

Fuzzing has been proven to be a highly effective automated method of discovering software vulnerabilities. To address the characteristics of stateful protocols, state feedback fuzzing techniques, pioneered by AFLNet [16], have significantly improved testing capabilities by introducing state-aware mechanisms [10]. The core of stateful fuzzing involves exploring a protocol's state machine, which is often represented as a Finite State Machine (FSM) where states are nodes and messages trigger transitions between them.

The process of fuzzing a stateful protocol is inherently a dynamic exploration of the state machine. As the fuzzer runs, it incrementally discovers new states and transitions, causing the known state graph and code coverage landscape to evolve continuously. A key observation is that the protocol's state space, while discovered dynamically, is often based on pre-defined and trackable state transition logic. For instance, a protocol's behavior is explicitly designed around a set of states and the valid transitions between them. This structured, graph-like nature implies that an effective testing strategy should leverage a global perspective of the discovered state machine to allocate testing resources efficiently, rather than making isolated, short-sighted decisions.

However, a fundamental contradiction exists between this need for a global perspective and the operational reality of the prevailing scheduling strategies. Existing coverage-based schedulers in prominent fuzzers, such as AFLNet's FAVOR strategy, typically rely on local heuristics and short-term feedback metrics (e.g., immediate code coverage gain or how recently a path was found) [10,16]. The critical limitation of these approaches is their lack of a mechanism to model the fuzzing process from a global, long-term perspective. They do not effectively measure or adapt to the evolving value of states and sequences throughout the fuzzing campaign. This deficiency inevitably leads to suboptimal resource allocation, resulting in two major practical problems. **Redundant Fuzzing:** Fuzzers waste significant computational resources on states or state sequences that are already well explored or have proven to be of low value, failing to take advantage of long-term historical information to avoid repetitive work [7]. **Superficial Exploration:** Fuzzers struggle to discover deep vulnerabilities that require long, specific message sequences or complex state transitions, as the intermediate steps of such sequences may not offer immediate rewards, causing the scheduler to abandon these paths prematurely [11].

Consequently, these limitations severely constrain the depth and breadth of vulnerability discovery. To overcome this issue, it is imperative to design a scheduling mechanism capable of modeling the dynamic and interactive process of state-space exploration from a global viewpoint.

To address this core challenge, we propose EvoFuzz, a novel adaptive scheduling framework. The central innovation of EvoFuzz is to model the scheduling process in stateful fuzzing as an Evolutionary Game. Evolutionary Game Theory (EGT) [19,20] provides a powerful mathematical framework for analyzing systems of interacting, adaptive "players" (in our case, protocol states or test seeds) competing for limited resources. The "strategy" of each player (its selection priority) dynamically evolves based on its historical "fitness" or "payoff" (e.g., its ability to discover new state sequences, coverage, or vulnerabilities) [21]. EvoFuzz comprises the following two core EGT-driven modules.

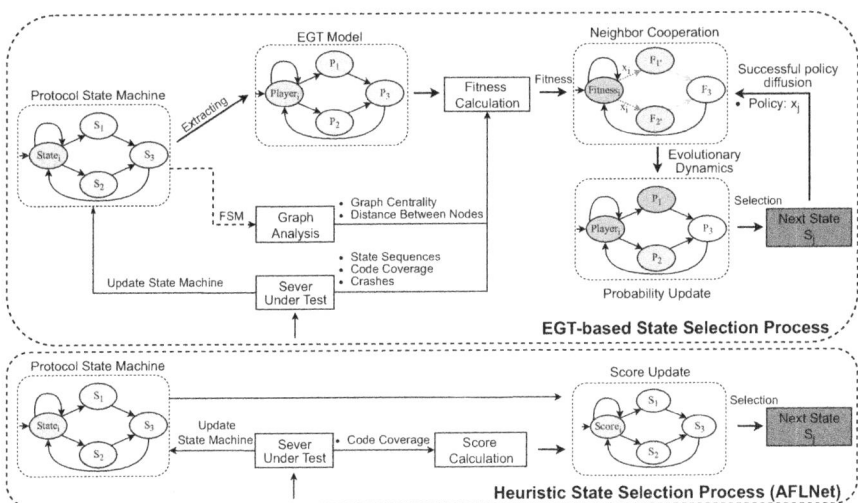

Fig. 1. The classical heuristic state selection process compare with the EGT-based state selection process.

- **EvoState (State Selection):** This module treats all discovered protocol states as a population of competing players. It uses a multidimensional payoff function that incorporates metrics such as code coverage feedback, new state sequence discovery, and state's network centrality to drive the evolution of each state's scheduling priority via replicator dynamics. This enables a global adaptive allocation of fuzzing efforts across the entire state machine.
- **EvoSeed (Seed Selection):** Once EvoState selects a target state, this module orchestrates a new game among candidate seeds. It prioritizes seeds for mutation using a state-aware fitness function that considers historical performance, execution efficiency, and the seed's affinity to the current target state.

By modeling the scheduling problem as an evolutionary game, EvoFuzz naturally integrates long-term historical performance into its decision making, allowing it to dynamically balance exploration and exploitation from a global perspective. This approach is inherently more resilient to the "deceptive" local optima that plague heuristic-based schedulers.

In summary, we make four main contributions.

1. We propose and implement a novel EGT-based global state scheduling strategy (EvoState), which experiments show can significantly improve coverage of unique protocol state sequences.
2. We propose and implement a novel EGT-based state-aware seed selection strategy (EvoSeed), which experiments demonstrate can effectively increase code branch coverage.

3. We design and implement EvoFuzz, an adaptive EGT scheduling framework integrating EvoState and EvoSeed, and experimentally showcase its potential to enhance the overall performance and vulnerability discovery capability of stateful protocol fuzzing.
4. We developed a prototype of EvoFuzz based on NSFuzz and conducted a comprehensive evaluation of 5 real-world network protocols.

2 Related Work

This section reviews research areas closely related to EvoFuzz, including stateful protocol fuzzing and advanced scheduling strategies in fuzzing. We also briefly discuss the application of EGT in related computational fields to highlight the novelty and necessity of our work.

2.1 Stateful Protocol Fuzzing

Stateful protocols pose unique challenges to fuzzing due to their message sequence dependencies and complex internal state transitions [16]. In recent years, researchers have made significant progress in enhancing the capabilities of stateful protocol fuzzers.

AFLNet [16] is a landmark work in this area, extending coverage-guided fuzzing to network protocols by introducing state feedback based on server response codes and inferring a state machine model. AFLNet treats message sequences as seeds and uses heuristic strategies (e.g., FAVOR) for state selection to maximize state and code coverage [7]. Despite its success, AFLNet's scheduling strategy relies mainly on local heuristics, which limits its effectiveness in global optimization for complex protocols [6]. Its limitations include a lack of effective long-term state value metrics, insufficient adaptability, and difficulty in balancing global exploration with local exploitation [24].

Subsequent work has focused on improving the accuracy of state representation and the efficiency of the fuzzing engine. For example, StateAFL [12] identifies states using memory snapshots, while NSFuzz [17] uses a method based on the values of the critical variables of the program. SGFuzz [1] represents states using sequences of enumerated-type state variables and prioritizes seeds that cover rare transitions in the state machine. CHATAFL [9] innovatively uses Large Language Models (LLMs) to help understand the protocol and seed generation. SMGFuzz [24] proposes a reverse state selection method based on a "statemap." However, most of these studies focus on state modeling or specific optimizations. The core scheduling mechanisms in many tools still follow or have not significantly improved upon AFLNet's heuristic approach. Therefore, developing a scheduling strategy that can perform global planning, effectively utilize long-term historical information, and adapt dynamically to efficiently explore complex state spaces remains an open challenge, creating an opportunity for EvoFuzz to introduce EGT.

2.2 Advanced Scheduling and Search Strategies in Fuzzing

To enhance fuzzing efficiency, researchers have explored various advanced scheduling and search strategies that have informed the design of EvoFuzz.

In seed selection and prioritization, AFLFast [2] improved AFL's power scheduling to prioritize low-frequency paths. UntouchFuzz [23] focuses on seeds that can guide the fuzzer to "untouched edges." Recently, methods based on Multi-Armed Bandits (MABs) have gained significant attention. For example, SCFuzz-2 [4], T-Scheduler [8] and EcoFuzz [25] use MABs to balance exploration and exploitation in seed selection, while SHAPFuzz [27] uses contextual MABs to guide mutations. Although these methods perform well in general-purpose fuzzing, they often fail to fully consider the specific state-context dependency of seeds in protocol fuzzing. The EvoSeed module in EvoFuzz also aims to optimize seed selection, but its unique contribution lies in using EGT to model the dynamic competition and cooperation among seeds within a specific target state, aiming for a more state-aware and globally consistent high-value seed selection scheme.

In state or path selection, in addition to traditional coverage-based heuristics, MABs have also been tentatively applied to state selection in stateful fuzzing [3], but initial results suggest their effectiveness may be limited by slow learning of deep states. Methods based on Monte Carlo Tree Search (MCTS), such as AFLNet-Legion [7], model state scheduling as a tree search problem, using forward planning to find optimal decision sequences. Unlike these methods that rely on specific search models, the EvoState module on EvoFuzz does not perform explicit searches of future possibilities. Instead, it models and evolves the fitness of the current "population" of states to achieve dynamic priority adjustment. It focuses more on feedback from long-term historical performance to achieve global adaptation.

Compared to these advanced scheduling strategies, the EGT-based adaptive scheduling proposed by EvoFuzz provides a novel paradigm for balancing exploration and exploitation from a global perspective and for effectively utilizing long-term historical information by simulating the dynamic evolution and adaptation of a population of strategies.

2.3 Evolutionary Game Theory (EGT)

EGT studies how the frequency of strategies evolves over time in a population of individuals with different strategies. Its core concepts include players, strategies, rewards, fitness, and evolutionary dynamics (such as replicator dynamics) [20]. EGT has been successfully applied in various areas of computer science, such as policy evolution in multiagent systems [14], dynamic resource allocation in networks [15], empirical analysis in algorithmic game theory [22], and software engineering process modeling [18,26]. These applications demonstrate EGT's powerful ability to handle complex systems involving dynamic interactions, policy evolution, and resource competition.

Applying EGT to the scheduling problem in stateful protocol fuzzing is justified by the inherently dynamic, uncertain, and multi-objective nature of the fuzzing process, which aligns well with the modeling strengths of EGT. EvoFuzz treats protocol states and seeds as players in a game, dynamically adjusting their selection priority based on their fuzzing performance (payoff). The uniqueness of our work lies in being the first to systematically apply EGT to both state scheduling (EvoState) and intrastate seed selection (EvoSeed) in an adaptive scheduling framework. This approach differs significantly from existing methods that rely on local heuristics, lack long-term historical metrics, or use a single advanced search strategy (e.g., AFLNet's Favor, MAB, or MCTS). EvoFuzz aims to achieve continuous learning and global optimization of the entire fuzzing resource allocation strategy by simulating an evolutionary process, thereby overcoming the tendency of existing methods to get caught in local optima.

3 Methodology

To address the core challenge of global adaptive scheduling in stateful protocol fuzzing, we propose EvoFuzz, an EGT-based adaptive scheduling framework. EvoFuzz aims to achieve dynamic and optimized allocation of fuzzing resources by applying EGT to two critical stages: state selection (EvoState) and seed selection (EvoSeed).

3.1 EvoFuzz Overall Architecture

EvoFuzz is built on the widely used stateful protocol fuzzer NSFuzz. Its core consists of two EGT-driven scheduling modules, EvoState and EvoSeed, embedded within the main fuzzing loop. Figure 2 illustrates the general architecture of EvoFuzz and its role in the fuzzing process, and Fig. 1 illustrates more details of the EGT process.

In each iteration of the fuzzing loop, the workflow of EvoFuzz is as follows:

- **State Selection by EvoState**: The EvoState module, based on its EGT model, selects a target state, s^*, from the set of currently discovered protocol states for the current fuzzing round.
- **Seed Selection by EvoSeed**: Subsequently, the EvoSeed module, targeting the state s^*, selected by EvoState, uses its independent EGT model to choose the most promising seed, q^*, from a seed pool, Q_{pool}, to migrate to the state s^*.
- **Mutation and Execution**: The selected seed q^* is mutated and sent to the target protocol server. Execution feedback is collected, including code coverage, server responses, and any crashes.
- **Feedback and EGT Model Update**: The collected feedback is not only used to update the fuzzer's coverage bitmap and state machine model but, more importantly, serves as the payoff input for the EGT models in the EvoState and EvoSeed modules. This dynamically adjusts their subsequent scheduling strategies, enabling adaptive optimization.

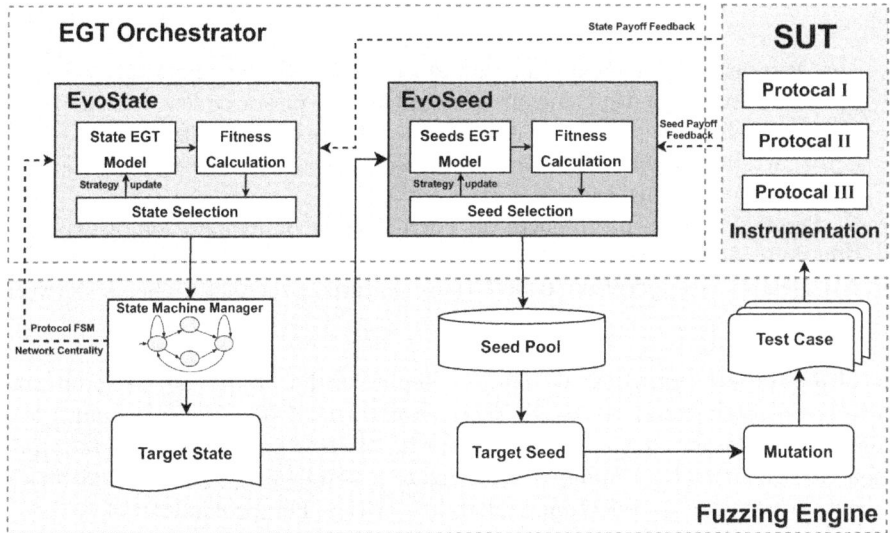

Fig. 2. General structure of the EvoFuzz.

Through the synergistic action of EvoState and EvoSeed, EvoFuzz strives to dynamically optimize the allocation of testing resources from a global perspective, aiming to enhance the depth and efficiency of the fuzzing process.

3.2 EvoState: EGT-Based State Scheduling

The EvoState module aims to dynamically evaluate and prioritize the protocol states that are most likely to guide the fuzzer to explore new and valuable state sequences or discover program defects, using an evolutionary game model. We formalize the state selection problem as a multi-player evolutionary game.

EGT Model for EvoState. We model the protocol state machine as a directed graph $G = (S, E)$, where S is the set of states and E is the set of state transition edges.

Players: Every state discovered $S_i \in S$ in the state machine of the protocol.

Strategy: Each state S_i has a continuous strategy value $x_i \in [0, 1]$, representing its tendency between exploration $x_i \to 0$ and exploitation $x_i \to 1$ in the current phase of fuzzing.

Payoff Function and Fitness: The fitness of a state s_i is its expected payoff, which determines its reproductive success. The general fitness F_i of the state s_i, used to calculate the selection probability, is composed of several factors (with weights λ_k):

$$F_i = \lambda_1 \cdot D_i + \lambda_2 \cdot V_i + \lambda_3 \cdot C_i + \lambda_4 \cdot S_i + N_i \tag{1}$$

where:

- D_i: Discovery factor for finding new state sequences or code paths.
- V_i: Diversity factor that encourages exploration of states less fuzzed (negatively correlated with the number of times it has been selected).
- C_i: Centrality factor of the network based on the topological importance of the state in the state graph G.
- S_i: Strategy factor that reflects the current focus on exploration or exploitation defined by x_i.
- N_i: Neighbor-cooperation payoff that captures synergistic effects between states.

Evolutionary Dynamics: We employ Replicator Dynamics [20] to update the strategy of each state. Although the classic form of replicator dynamics is a continuous differential equation, we adopt its discrete form in practice to implement iterative strategy updates. The higher a state's fitness (i.e., its historical payoff), the faster its selection probability grows. The probability of selection of each state, $Prob(s_i)$, is adjusted according to its performance relative to the average fitness of the population. Its probability update can be formulated as follows.

$$P_{\text{cur}}(i) = P_{\text{pre}}(i) \cdot \left(1 + \eta \cdot \frac{F_i - \bar{F}_S}{\max(\bar{F}_S, \epsilon)}\right) \quad (2)$$

where:

- $P_{\text{cur}}(i)$, $P_{\text{pre}}(i)$: Current and previous state selection probabilities of s_i.
- F_i: Current composite fitness of state s_i.
- $\bar{F}_S$: Average fitness of all states currently discovered.
- η: Learning rate that controls the speed of evolution.
- ϵ: A small positive constant to avoid division by zero.

Key Mechanisms of EvoState. To enhance its global scheduling capability, EvoState integrates the following key mechanisms.

Network Centrality Metric: We parse the state transition relationships from the protocol state graph generated by the fuzzer and perform a centrality analysis for each state. This centrality value becomes a component of the fitness function, giving higher priority to states that are topologically more important in the state machine network.

Neighbor Cooperative Payoff: The payoff of a state s_i is influenced by the average performance of its neighbor states $N(s_i)$. If a state's neighbors perform well on average (e.g., have high average payoffs or success rates), that state receives a cooperative payoff bonus (N_i), encouraging the collaborative exploration of promising state regions.

Policy Diffusion: When a state s_i discovers a new high-value path or triggers a crash, its current successful strategy tendency, x_i, is diffused with a certain intensity to its neighbor states $s_j \in N(s_i)$. This strategy x_i represents a trend between two modes: **Exploitation strategy** (a tendency towards $x_i \to 1$), which focuses on fine-grained mutations of existing seeds to thoroughly test code paths within or near the current state. **Exploration strategy** (a tendency toward $x_i \to 0$), which applies more aggressive and diverse mutation operators to trigger new state transitions and discover entirely new regions of the state machine. This diffusion means that neighboring states' policies are adjusted based on the success of their neighbors, accelerating the propagation of effective strategies across the state network.

Multidimensional Fitness and Selection: The final selection probability $\text{Prob}(s_i)$ of a state is calculated based on its general fitness F_i. The selection process uses a roulette wheel mechanism with periodic forced perturbations, which occasionally selects the least-fuzzed state or a state with chronically low fitness to maintain population diversity and prevent premature convergence.

Algorithm 1 outlines the main process for EvoState to select the next target state.

Algorithm 1. EvoState: EGT-based State Selection

1: **procedure** SELECTNEXTSTATE_EVOSTATE($FSM, F_{history}$)
2:     **if** is_initial_phase() **then**
3:         **return** ROUNDROBINSELECTSTATE(FSM)
4:     **end if**
5:     UPDATENETWORKPROPERTIES(FSM)   ▷ e.g., Centrality, Neighbors
6:     EVOLVESTATEPOPULATION($FSM, F_{history}$)   ▷ Update payoffs, policies (x_i), and fitness (F_i)
7:     NORMALIZEFITNESSTOPROB(FSM)   ▷ Convert fitness scores to probabilities
8:     **if** random() $< p_{explore}$ **then**
9:         $s_{target} \leftarrow$ SELECTLEASTCHOSENSTATE(FSM)
10:    **else**
11:        $s_{target} \leftarrow$ ROULETTEWHEELSELECT(FSM)
12:    **end if**
13:    DIFFUSEPOLICY($s_{target}, F_{history}$) ▷ Propagate successful strategy to neighbors
14:    **return** s_{target}
15: **end procedure**

3.3 EvoSeed: EGT-Based Intra-state Seed Selection

After EvoState selects a target state s_{target} for the current fuzzing round, EvoSeed uses an EGT model to rank and select an optimal seed $q*$ from the candidate pool Q_{pool} for fuzzing toward s_{target}. Q_{pool} may contain seeds that were not generated by or that do not directly lead to s_{target}. EvoSeed enables fine-grained state-aware seed scheduling from a broader range of candidates.

For a given target state s_{target} selected by EvoState, we model the process of selecting the most promising seed from the candidate pool Q_{pool} as a multi-player evolutionary game.

Players: Every seed $q_j \in Q_{pool}$ in the seed pool of candidates.

Strategy: The strategy of each seed q_j is its potential to be selected for mutation against the current target state s_{target}.

Payoff Function and Fitness: The fitness of a seed q_j with respect to the current target state s_{target}, denoted as $F(q_j|s_{target})$, combines multiple dimensions (with weights α_k).

$$F(q_j|s_{target}) = \alpha_1 \cdot \text{PathScore}_j + \alpha_2 \cdot \text{StateScore}_j + \alpha_3 \cdot \text{ExecScore}_j \\ + \alpha_4 \cdot \text{TimeScore}_j + \alpha_5 \cdot \text{StateAffinityScore}_j + \text{BonusFactors}_j \quad (3)$$

where:

- PathScore$_j$: Based on the historical efficiency of the seed q_j in discovering new code paths.
- StateScore$_j$: Based on the historical efficiency of the seed q_j in discovering new protocol states.
- ExecScore$_j$: Based on the execution efficiency of the seed q_j.
- TimeScore$_j$: A time decay factor that reduces the priority of old or long-unproductive seeds.
- StateAffinityScore$_j$: Based on the distance in the state machine G between the original target state of the seed q_j and the current target state s_{target}. This prioritizes seeds that are "closer" or more relevant to s_{target}.
- BonusFactors$_j$: Additional rewards for seeds favored by the base fuzzer or initial seeds.

Evolutionary Dynamics: We employ a discrete update mechanism inspired by Replicator Dynamics. Before selecting a seed for the target state s_{target}, EvoSeed updates the payoff components for all seeds in the pool Q_{pool} based on the latest fuzzing feedback and recalculates their composite fitness $F(q_j|s_{target})$ with respect to s_{target}. Subsequently, the average fitness of the current seed pool, $\bar{F}_{Q_{pool}|s_{target}}$, is calculated. The selection probability for each seed q_j, $Prob(q_j|s_{target})$, is then adjusted based on its relative fitness. The probability update can be approximated as

$$P_{cur}(j) = P_{pre}(j) \cdot \left(1 + \eta \cdot \frac{F(q_j|s_{target}) - \bar{F}_{Q_{pool}|s_{target}}}{\max(\bar{F}_{Q_{pool}|s_{target}}, \epsilon)}\right) \quad (4)$$

where:

- $F(q_j|s_{target})$: The fitness of the seed q_j with respect to the current target state s_{target}.
- $\bar{F}_{Q_{pool}|s_{target}}$: Average fitness of all seeds in the pool for s_{target}.

Similarly, the updated probabilities are normalized and a minimum selection probability is enforced for each seed to maintain exploration capabilities and population diversity.

Algorithm 2 outlines the main process for EvoSeed to select a seed.

Algorithm 2. EvoSeed: EGT-based Seed Selection

1: **procedure** SELECTNEXTSEED_EVOSEED(s_{target}, Q_{pool})
2:    **if** is_initial_phase_for_state(s_{target}) **or** $|Q_{pool}| <$ Threshold **then**
3:       **return** ROUNDROBINSELECTSEED(Q_{pool})
4:    **end if**
5:    **if** random() $< p_{explore\_seed}$ **then**
6:       **return** RANDOMSELECTSEED(Q_{pool})
7:    **end if**
8:    EVOLVESEEDPROBABILITIES(Q_{pool}, s_{target})   ▷ Update fitness & probabilities
9:    $q_{selected} \leftarrow$ ROULETTEWHEELSELECT(Q_{pool}) ▷ Based on updated probabilities
10:    **return** $q_{selected}$
11: **end procedure**
---

4 Evaluation

To comprehensively evaluate the effectiveness of the EvoFuzz framework and its core components, EvoState and EvoSeed, we designed and conducted a series of comparative experiments. This section details the experimental setup, evaluation metrics, target subjects, baselines, and presents and analyzes the results.

4.1 Research Questions

Our experimental evaluation aims to answer the following core research questions.

- **RQ1 (Effectiveness of EvoState):** How effective is the EvoState strategy in improving the coverage of unique state sequence compared to the baseline fuzzers? What is its impact on code branch coverage?
- **RQ2 (Effectiveness of EvoSeed):** How effective is the EvoSeed strategy in improving code branch coverage compared to baseline fuzzers?
- **RQ3 (Combined Effect of EvoFuzz):** How does the full EvoFuzz framework, integrating both EvoState and EvoSeed, perform in terms of state sequence and branch coverage compared to baselines and its individual components? Is there a synergistic effect?
- **RQ4 (Performance Overhead):** What is the computational overhead introduced by the EvoFuzz framework and its EGT modules? Does it significantly impact the overall execution speed of the fuzzer?

4.2 Experimental Setup

Test Protocols. We selected five widely used open source network protocol implementations from ProFuzzBench [13] as our test targets. These cover a variety of protocol types and state machine complexities: LightFTP, Bftpd, Exim, TinyDTLS, and Dcmtk.

Baselines and Configurations. We compare EvoFuzz with the following baselines and configurations:

- **NSFuzz(Baseline 1):** Our primary baseline, an advanced stateful network protocol fuzzer. We use its default FAVOR strategy for both state and seed scheduling.
- **AFLNet(Baseline 2):** A classic fuzzer for stateful protocols [16].
- **NSFuzz+EvoState:** NSFuzz with only the EvoState module enabled, using the default seed scheduler.
- **NSFuzz+EvoSeed:** NSFuzz with only the EvoSeed module enabled, using the default state scheduler.
- **EvoFuzz (Our Full Approach):** NSFuzz with the EvoState and EvoSeed modules enabled.

Evaluation Metrics.

- **Unique State Sequence Coverage:** A key metric for measuring the depth of state space exploration. We count the number of unique state sequences discovered in 24 h.
- **Code Branch Coverage:** Measured using gcov to track the number of branches covered.
- **Number of Unique Crashes:** We count the number of unique crashes found, deduplicated using standard techniques.
- **Execution Speed:** Measured in executions per second (execs/sec) to evaluate throughput and overhead.

Environment and Execution. All experiments were carried out on a server with an Intel(R) Xeon(R) Silver 4216 CPU @ 2.10GHz (16 physical cores) and 392GB of RAM, running Ubuntu 20.04 LTS. For each target and fuzzer configuration, we run five independent trials, each for 24 h.

4.3 Results and Analysis

This section presents and analyzes the performance of EvoFuzz and its components, answering the RQs of Sect. 4.1.

RQ1: Effectiveness of EvoState. To evaluate the independent contribution of EvoState, we compared NSFuzz+EvoState with the baseline NSFuzz.

Table 1. The number of Unique State Sequence

Protocol	NSFuzz	EvoSeed	EvoState	EvoFuzz
Lightftpd	2235.2	1176.0(−47.39%)	3084.6(+38.00%)	1332.6(−40.38%)
Bftpd	22649.6	25664.6(+13.31%)	49532.8(+118.69%)	35603.2(+50.19%)
Exim	40.2	52.0(+29.35%)	105.4(+162.19%)	63.4(+57.71%)
Tinydtls	316577.4	228529.0(−27.81%)	460117.2(+45.34%)	267308.6(−15.56%)
Dcmtk	21.6	19.2(−11.11%)	66(+205.56%)	32.2(+49.07%)
Average	68304.80	51088.16(−25.20%)	102581.20(+50.18%)	60868.00(−10.89%)

Table 2. Final Code Branch Coverage

Protocol	AFLNet	NSFuzz	EvoSeed	EvoState	EvoFuzz
Lightftpd	387.0	398.6	414.2(+3.91%)	425.2(+6.62%)	426.00(+6.87%)
Bftpd	476.2	480.8	484.2(+0.87%)	490.0(+2.08%)	499.60(+4.08%)
Exim	3859.8	3979.2	4253.4(+6.89%)	4076.2(+2.44%)	4159.00(+4.52%)
Tinydtls	333.0	3979.2	578.8(+2.26%)	583.4(+3.07%)	590.80(+4.38%)
Dcmtk	2651.4	2649.2	2664.2(+0.56%)	2668.4(+0.72%)	2665.8(+0.63%)
Average	1541.44	1614.6	1678.96(+3.83%)	1648.6(+2.11%)	1668.24(+3.32%)

* Percentages in parentheses denote the improvement relative to the primary baseline, NSFuzz.

Unique State Sequence Coverage: As shown in Table 1, NSFuzz+EvoState significantly outperformed NSFuzz, resulting in an average improvement of **50.18%**. The improvement was particularly dramatic on protocols with complex state machines, such as Bftpd (+118.69%) and Exim (+162.19%). These results indicate that EvoState's EGT-driven global state exploration strategy, especially its neighbor cooperation and policy diffusion mechanisms, effectively guides the fuzzer to explore deeper and more diverse interaction paths, overcoming the tendency of traditional heuristics to get trapped in local optima.

Code Branch Coverage: As shown in Table 2, the improvement in branch coverage for NSFuzz+EvoState was more modest, averaging **2.11%**. This finding is expected, as EvoState's primary design goal is to optimize the breadth and depth of global state space exploration, not fine-grained code path discovery within a state.

Vulnerability Discovery: Regarding vulnerability discovery (Table 3), NSFuzz+EvoState found 24 unique crashes in Dcmtk, while NSFuzz found none. On TinyDTLS, it also discovered 10 more crashes than NSFuzz. This suggests that improved state exploration can directly lead to the discovery of new vulnerabilities (Table 3).

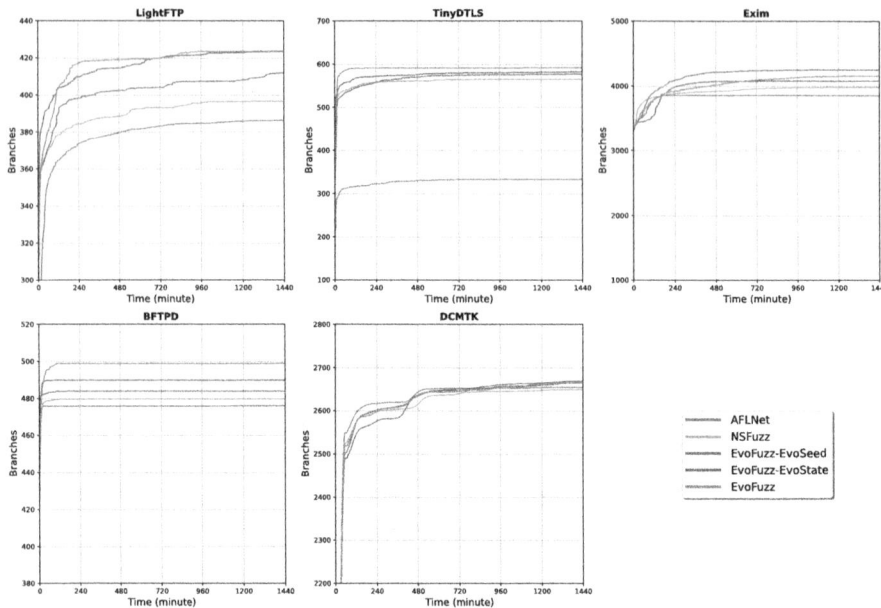

Fig. 3. The average code branch coverage growth of various fuzzers.

Table 3. Final Number of Unique Crash

Protocol	AFLNet	NSFuzz	EvoSeed	EvoState	EvoFuzz
Bftpd	0	14	14	14	15
Tinydtls	32	83	82	93	93
Dcmtk	8	0	0	24	20
Average	13.33	32.33	32.00(−1.03%)	43.67(+35.05%)	42.67(+31.96%)

* Percentages in parentheses denote the improvement relative to the primary baseline, NSFuzz.

Answer to RQ1: EvoState is highly effective in navigating the protocol state space, leading to substantial gains in the coverage of unique state sequences (avg. +50.18%) and improved vulnerability discovery in some targets. Its impact on branch coverage is positive, but modest.

RQ2: Effectiveness of EvoSeed. To evaluate the independent contribution of EvoSeed, we compared NSFuzz+EvoSeed with the NSFuzz baseline.

Code Branch Coverage: As shown in Table 2, NSFuzz+EvoSeed achieved improvements in code branch coverage for all targets, with an average increase of **3.83%**. The greatest gain was in Exim (+6.89%). These results are consistent with previous research showing that fine-grained seed selection can effectively improve code coverage. This confirms that EvoSeed's state-aware, multidimensional fitness evaluation can dynamically select the "most promising" seeds for a given target state, significantly improving mutation effectiveness.

Unique State Sequence Coverage: Concurrently, this configuration showed an average decrease of 25.20% in the coverage of unique state sequences (Table 1). This further validates EvoSeed's design objective: optimize seed utilization within a specific state rather than guide global navigation between states.

Answer to RQ2: EvoSeed is highly effective in increasing code branch coverage (avg. +3.83%) dynamically prioritizing the most promising seeds for a given state context, thereby improving the efficiency of local exploration.

RQ3: Combined Effect of EvoFuzz. To evaluate the full performance of the EvoFuzz framework, we compared it with the NSFuzz baseline and the configurations of the individual components. The results demonstrate a synergistic effect between EvoState and EvoSeed.

Code Branch Coverage: As shown in Table 2, EvoFuzz achieved an average improvement in code branch coverage of 3.32% over the NSFuzz baseline. This performance is on par with, and on some targets (e.g., Bftpd, LightFTP) even slightly better than the specialized NSFuzz+EvoSeed configuration (+3.83%). It significantly outperformed the NSFuzz+EvoState configuration (+2.11%). This indicates that EvoFuzz successfully integrates the fine-grained seed selection capabilities of EvoSeed, leading to consistently code branch coverage improvements.

Unique State Sequence Coverage: Table 1 shows that EvoFuzz achieves a powerful balance in state exploration. Although its overall average is skewed by the performance on simpler protocols, its strength is evident on targets with complex state machines. In Bftpd (+57.2%), Exim (+57.7%) and Dcmtk (+49.1%), EvoFuzz achieved significant gains in state sequence coverage, performing far better than NSFuzz and NSFuzz+EvoSeed. Although not reaching the absolute peaks of the specialized NSFuzz+EvoState configuration, it effectively retains EvoState's global exploration capability while simultaneously optimizing for code branch coverage, demonstrating a superior trade-off.

Vulnerability Discovery: The comprehensive improvements in coverage translated directly into superior bug finding capabilities. As seen in Table 3, EvoFuzz found the highest number of unique crashes in Bftpd (15) and TinyDTLS (94). Crucially, it discovered 20 crashes on Dcmtk, where the NSFuzz and the NSFuzz+EvoSeed configuration found 0. This shows that the combination of global state exploration and efficient local search systematically increases the probability of discovering deep and complex vulnerabilities.

Answer to RQ3: EvoFuzz successfully combines the strengths of its components. The synergy between EvoState's global state guidance and EvoSeed's efficient seed utilization leads to comprehensive improvements in both branch and state sequence coverage (especially on complex protocols), which often translates to superior vulnerability discovery.

Table 4. Fuzzing Throughput(exec/s)

Protocol	NSFuzz	EvoSeed	EvoState	EvoFuzz
Lightftpd	64.82	64.36(−0.71%)	54.59(−15.78%)	53.98(−16.72%)
Bftpd	125.52	121.61(−3.11%)	113.72(−9.40%)	107.55(−14.31%)
Exim	8.62	8.13(−5.68%)	7.78(−9.74%)	7.42(−13.92%)
Tinydtls	450.2	413.19(−8.22%)	428.87(−4.74%)	427.57(−5.02%)
Dcmtk	9.74	9.32(−4.31%)	27.21(+179.36%)	20.83(+113.86%)
Average	131.78	123.32(−6.41%)	126.43(−4.05%)	123.47(−6.31%)

RQ4: Performance Overhead. We evaluated the performance overhead by comparing the average execution speed (execs/sec).

The data in Table 4 shows that while EvoFuzz introduces a modest overhead on most targets, Dcmtk is a notable exception, exhibiting a significant increase in execution speed. This phenomenon is not due to faster core computations, but is rather a direct consequence of EvoState's more effective scheduling. In network fuzzing, many generated test cases are invalid for the target's current protocol state, forcing the fuzzer to wait for a network timeout before proceeding. This idle waiting time drastically reduces the measured execution times per sec. EvoState's EGT-driven strategy is more adept at generating valid and relevant message sequences for Dcmtk, which are processed quickly by the server, thereby minimizing the time spent waiting for timeouts. Therefore, the observed speed-up on Dcmtk serves as strong evidence of more efficient and meaningful target interaction, directly validating our approach's ability to improve testing quality.

To assess the pure computational cost of our EGT models, if we exclude the Dcmtk outlier, the average overhead for the remaining four targets is approximately **9.9% for NSFuzz+EvoState** and **12.5% for the complete EvoFuzz framework**.

5 Conclusion

In this paper, we address the long-standing global scheduling dilemma in stateful protocol fuzzing by proposing EvoFuzz, a novel adaptive scheduling framework based on EGT. By modeling protocol states and candidate seeds as "players" in a two-level evolutionary game, EvoFuzz systematically balances the exploration of global state space with the exploitation of local vulnerabilities within a specific state. We implemented a prototype of EvoFuzz on top of NSFuzz and evaluated it on five real-world protocols. Experimental results show that, compared to state-of-the-art baselines, EvoFuzz increases the unique state sequence by up to 205.56%, increases code branch coverage by up to 6.87%, and increases the number of unique crashes by 31.96%. Our work demonstrates that applying Evolutionary Game Theory to scheduler design is a powerful and effective paradigm in stateful protocol fuzzing, opening new possibilities for building more intelligent fuzzing systems.

References

1. Ba, J., Böhme, M., Mirzamomen, Z., Roychoudhury, A.: Stateful greybox fuzzing. In: 31st USENIX Security Symposium (USENIX Security 2022), pp. 3255–3272 (2022)
2. Böhme, M., Pham, V.T., Roychoudhury, A.: Coverage-based greybox fuzzing as Markov chain. In: Proceedings of the 2016 ACM SIGSAC Conference on Computer and Communications Security, pp. 1032–1043 (2016)
3. Borcherding, A., Giraud, M., Fitzgerald, I., Beyerer, J.: The bandit's states: modeling state selection for stateful network fuzzing as multi-armed bandit problem. In: 2023 IEEE European Symposium on Security and Privacy Workshops (EuroS&PW), pp. 345–350. IEEE (2023)
4. Cheng, M., Zhu, K., Chen, Y., Lu, Y., Chen, C., Yu, J.: Reinforcement learning-based multi-phase seed scheduling for network protocol fuzzing. Electronics **13**(24), 4962 (2024)
5. Daniele, C., Andarzian, S.B., Poll, E.: Fuzzers for stateful systems: survey and research directions. ACM Comput. Surv. **56**(9), 1–23 (2024)
6. Lin, P., Wang, P., Zhou, X., Xie, W., Lu, K., Zhang, G.: Hypergo: probability-based directed hybrid fuzzing. Comput. Secur. **142**, 103851 (2024)
7. Liu, D., Pham, V.T., Ernst, G., Murray, T., Rubinstein, B.I.: State selection algorithms and their impact on the performance of stateful network protocol fuzzing. In: 2022 IEEE International Conference on Software Analysis, Evolution and Reengineering (SANER), pp. 720–730. IEEE (2022)
8. Luo, S., Herrera, A., Quirk, P., Chase, M., Ranasinghe, D.C., Kanhere, S.S.: Make out like a (multi-armed) bandit: improving the odds of fuzzer seed scheduling with t-scheduler. In: Proceedings of the 19th ACM Asia Conference on Computer and Communications Security, pp. 1463–1479 (2024)
9. Meng, R., Mirchev, M., Böhme, M., Roychoudhury, A.: Large language model guided protocol fuzzing. In: Proceedings of the 31st Annual Network and Distributed System Security Symposium (NDSS), vol. 2024 (2024)
10. Meng, R., Pham, V.T., Böhme, M., Roychoudhury, A.: Aflnet five years later: on coverage-guided protocol fuzzing. IEEE Trans. Softw. Eng. (2025)
11. Mou, Y., Wang, B., Yu, B., Yang, Q.: Scfuzz: complexity aware state selection algorithm for network protocol fuzzing. In: GLOBECOM 2024-2024 IEEE Global Communications Conference, pp. 1203–1208. IEEE (2024)
12. Natella, R.: Stateafl: greybox fuzzing for stateful network servers. Empir. Softw. Eng. **27**(7), 191 (2022)
13. Natella, R., Pham, V.T.: Profuzzbench: a benchmark for stateful protocol fuzzing. In: Proceedings of the 30th ACM SIGSOFT International Symposium on Software Testing and Analysis, pp. 662–665 (2021)
14. Nowé, A., Vrancx, P., De Hauwere, Y.M.: Game theory and multi-agent reinforcement learning. In: Reinforcement Learning: State-of-the-Art, pp. 441–470. Springer (2012)
15. Park, J., Adams, H.: Evolutionary game theory for dynamic resource allocation in wireless networks. Int. J. Adv. Comput. Theory Eng. **12**(2), 26–32 (2023)
16. Pham, V.T., Böhme, M., Roychoudhury, A.: Aflnet: a greybox fuzzer for network protocols. In: 2020 IEEE 13th International Conference on Software Testing, Validation and Verification (ICST), pp. 460–465. IEEE (2020)
17. Qin, S., Hu, F., Ma, Z., Zhao, B., Yin, T., Zhang, C.: Nsfuzz: towards efficient and state-aware network service fuzzing. ACM Trans. Softw. Eng. Methodol. **32**(6), 1–26 (2023)

18. Sazawal, V., Sudan, N.: Modeling software evolution with game theory. In: Wang, Q., Garousi, V., Madachy, R., Pfahl, D. (eds.) ICSP 2009. LNCS, vol. 5543, pp. 354–365. Springer, Heidelberg (2009). https://doi.org/10.1007/978-3-642-01680-6_32
19. Sigmund, K., Nowak, M.A.: Evolutionary game theory. Curr. Biol. **9**(14), R503–R505 (1999)
20. Tanimoto, J.: Fundamentals of evolutionary game theory and its applications. Springer (2015)
21. Traulsen, A., Glynatsi, N.E.: The future of theoretical evolutionary game theory. Philos. Trans. R. Soc. B **378**(1876), 20210508 (2023)
22. Wellman, M.P., Tuyls, K., Greenwald, A.: Empirical game theoretic analysis: a survey. J. Artif. Intell. Res. **82**, 1017–1076 (2025)
23. Xie, C., Jia, P., Yang, P., Hu, C., Kuang, H., Ye, G., Hong, X.: Not all seeds are important: fuzzing guided by untouched edges. Appl. Sci. **13**(24), 13172 (2023)
24. Yu, L., Yanlong, S., Ying, Z.: Stateful protocol fuzzing with statemap-based reverse state selection. arXiv preprint arXiv:2408.06844 (2024)
25. Yue, T., et al.: Ecofuzz: adaptive energy-saving greybox fuzzing as a variant of the adversarial multi-armed bandit. In: 29th USENIX Security Symposium (USENIX Security 2020), pp. 2307–2324 (2020)
26. Zhang, G., Bi, S.: Evolutionary game analysis of online game studios and online game companies participating in the virtual economy of online games. PLoS ONE **19**(1), e0296374 (2024)
27. Zhang, K., Zhu, X., Xiao, X., Xue, M., Zhang, C., Wen, S.: Shapfuzz: efficient fuzzing via shapley-guided byte selection. arXiv preprint arXiv:2308.09239 (2023)

A Lot of Data and Added Complexity. How Does PQC Affect the Performance of My TLS Connection?

Johanna Henrich[✉], Nicolai Schmitt, Nouri Alnahawi, and Andreas Heinemann

Hochschule Darmstadt - University of Applied Sciences, Darmstadt, Germany
{johanna.henrich,nicolai.schmitt,nouri.alnahawi,andreas.heinemann}@h-da.de

Abstract. In a previous study, Henrich et al. (ISC '23) demonstrate how Transport Layer Security (TLS) handshake performance is affected not only by different Post Quantum Cryptography (PQC) Key Encapsulation Mechanisms (KEMs) and security levels, but also by varying physical network conditions. In particular, they show that prior to selecting a PQC scheme replacement for TLS, it is important to conduct an analysis of the anticipated network conditions for applications that require a high level of responsiveness. In this paper, we build upon the aforementioned work and complement the previous experiments to include digital signature PQC schemes and hybrid variants, as well as various compositions of certificate chains. Moreover, an analysis is conducted on the effects of deploying real physical servers and varying the underlying network stack configuration. Our results show that incorporating PQC signature schemes does not negatively impact the overall transmission time as substantially as poor network conditions. However, operating at high security levels frequently results in delays using PQC schemes. These findings are consistent across hybrid schemes as well. We conclude that migrating TLS to PQ-only or hybrid usage can generally be undertaken with a high degree of confidence. However, considering suboptimal network conditions or the use of higher security levels, a cautious transition is recommended. In such cases, the configuration of certificate chains or increasing the Transmission Control Protocol (TCP) Congestion Window (CW) might prove beneficial.

Keywords: Public Key Cryptography · Post-Quantum Cryptography · Key Encapsulation Mechanism · Post-Quantum Authentication · Certificate Chain · Transport Layer Security · Network Performance

1 Introduction

To address the emerging threat of Quantum Computers (QCs) on traditional public key cryptography such as RSA or Elliptic-curve cryptography (ECC), sig-

---

Member of EUt+ (European University of Technology).

nificant research efforts have been made in the field of PQC. Hereby, a major task is to find suitable replacements for key exchange and digital signature schemes, and integrate them into existing security protocols [4]. Nevertheless, a direct transition from traditional schemes to PQC is not always feasible. In some cases, the specific characteristics, including the quantity of cryptographic material to be transferred or the computational complexity, vary significantly [25]. Since TLS is the most used protocol for establishing a secure channel between communication partners [29], it is one of the most relevant protocols in a forthcoming transition, especially its handshake phase. In the following, the focal point is TLS 1.3, a version that is increasingly utilized [29].

1.1 PQC Standardization and Migration

In August 2024, National Institute of Standards and Technology (NIST) published the standards ML-KEM [35], ML-DSA [34], and SLH-DSA [36], which are based on the finalists Kyber, Dilithium and SPHINCS+. In a fourth round of evaluations, HQC, BIKE, and Classic McEliece were also considered as additional KEM, with HQC being identified as leading option in 2025 [3]. Nevertheless, the process is still ongoing with an additional run for the development and evaluation of further digital signature schemes. Basically, the parameters of a scheme define its security, which is classified by the NIST into five levels [44]. To ensure security throughout transitional phases, hybrid schemes are recommended [23] and were also thoroughly studied [4]. Here, a well-established traditional scheme is typically combined with a PQC equivalent [10,21]. The integration of (PQC) KEMs and hybrid approaches was not initially included in TLS. However, in recent years, there has been a presentation of several methods and a publication of standard designs. The most prevalent design to date originates from Stebila et al. [50].

1.2 Related Work

In line with the importance of the TLS [29], numerous works address utilizing PQC in TLS. The contributions presented by these proposals cover many aspects, ranging from fundamental scheme security [13,14,26] to general benchmarks [5,28,52]. Some works focus on specific platforms and use cases such as embedded devices and Internet of Things (IoT) [9,16,30,31,45,46,53].

Performance Under Varying Network Conditions. Auten and Gamage [7] evaluate the performance in bandwidth constrained network environments and conclude that performance evaluations should be highly holistic. Paquin et al. [37] analyze the impact of latency and packet loss in an emulation as well as in real distributed server scenarios. They concluded that unreliable network constellations can impact the handshake completion time due to the communication size. Sikeridis et al. [48] also analyze the performance of PQ TLS using distributed servers. They observe that a small Initial Congestion Window (ICW) adaption can reduce the slowdown by 50%. Sosnowski et al. [49] analyze distinct scenarios with low data rate and packet loss. The authors note that the TLS 1.3 handshake has the capacity to be significantly faster using PQC schemes than using traditional ones. However, they also note that due to the increased data requirements during the handshake process with several PQC schemes, this advantage is not applicable to all network scenarios. Henrich et al. [25] analyze the impact of different constraints and effects such as packet loss and corruption, delay and data rate in an emulated environment.

Performance Regarding Signature Schemes and Certificate Chains. Sikeridis et al. [47] and Paul et al. [38] focus on the impact of various schemes in the TLS certificate chain. Paul et al. [38] conclude that schemes with slower signing performance and larger signatures can also be used for the root certificate.

Table 1. Related work on evaluating TLS 1.3 handshake duration when using PQC schemes. Based on Table 1 in [25].

	Tasopoulos et al. (2022) [53]	Sikeridis et al. (2020) [47]	Sosnowski et al. (2023) [49]	Marchsreiter et al. (2022) [45]	Kampanakis et al. (2019) [31]	Sikeridis et al. (2021) [27]	Kwiatkowski and Paul et al. (2021) [48]	Paul et al. (2021) [38]	Auten and Barton et al. (2021) [28]	Paquin et al. (2019) [7]	(2019) [9]	Henrich et al. [25]	our work
Real Network Environment	✓	✓	✓	✓	✓	✓	✓	✓	✓	✓	✓	.	✓
Considering PQC KEMs	✓	.	✓	✓	✓	.	✓	.	✓	✓	✓	✓	✓
Considering PQC Sig	✓	✓	✓	✓	✓	✓	✓	✓	.	.	✓	✓	.	✓
Considering Certificate Chain Length	.	✓	.	.	.	.	.	✓	.	.	.	.	✓
Considering Certificate Chain Composition	.	✓	.	.	.	.	.	✓	.	.	.	.	✓
Considering Network Characteristics	.	✓	✓	.	.	✓	✓	✓	.	✓	.	✓	✓	✓
Considering Dedicated Physical Network Params	.	.	✓	.	.	.	.	.	.	✓	.	✓	✓	✓
Considering TCP/IP-Stack Params	.	.	.	.	.	.	✓	.	.	.	.	.	✓
Considering PQ-only and Hybrid	.	.	✓	.	✓	.	✓	.	.	.	.	✓	✓	✓
Considering Security Levels 1, 3, and 5	.	✓	✓	✓	✓	✓	.	.	.	✓	.	.	✓	✓
Considering Computational Costs	✓	✓	✓	.	.	✓	✓	.	✓	.	✓	✓	.	.
Considering TLS Mutual Authentication	✓	.	.	.	.	.	.	✓	.	.	.	.	.
Considering 0-RTT	.	.	.	.	.	.	.	.	.	.	.	.	.

Summary. An overview of the extant scientific literature is provided in Table 1 (extending [25], Table 1, p. 273). It presents a fine grained comparison regarding experimental setup and the evaluation of network related aspects. A distinction is made between the consideration of network characteristics in general, which includes constrained or special network environments, the consideration of dedicated network characteristics (as, e.g., packet loss) and the consideration of TCP/IP-stack parameters (as, e.g., ICW). It shows that a comprehensive evaluation of the TCP/IP-stack parameters and their influence on handshake performance has not been conducted, especially in combination with others influencing factors as the certificate chain composition or hybridization.

1.3 Our Contribution

We conduct further experiments on PQC schemes within the TLS handshake and include the following factors from Table 1:

1. Dedicated Physical Network Parameters
2. Real Network Environment with different Server Locations
3. Key Exchange & Digital Signature Schemes
4. Security Level
5. PQ-only & Hybrid (KEMs and Signatures)
6. Certificate Chain Length & Composition
7. TCP/IP-Stack Configuration

The following contributions were made based on these measurements:

A) Verification of emulation results with real-world network environments.
B) Analyzing the performance impact of different security levels and hybrid variants under given network conditions as well as optimization possibilities through certificate chain constellations.
C) Influence of TCP CW and variants, Internet Protocol (IP) version and Maximum Transmission Unit (MTU) on a particular choice of PQC schemes.

The following observations merit particular attention: The TCP CW is a pivotal factor in the manner in which the selection of PQC schemes and their configuration affect overall TLS handshake performance. The composition of the certificate chain and the general quality of the network connection (e.g., packet loss) also play a central role. It is challenging to propose universal recommendations, given the considerable variance in boundary conditions and requirements across distinct use cases. Instead, prior to transitioning to PQC, it is imperative to conduct a thorough analysis of proprietary systems, thereby selecting schemes that align with individual strategic priorities. If higher security levels or hybrid variants can be employed without substantial performance degradation, this option should be given preference.

1.4 Approach

The specific structure of the experiments, including schemes and configurations used, is described in Sect. 2. As illustrated in Fig. 1, the framework under consideration is based on Paquin et al. [37] and Henrich et al. [25], with Henrich et al. having previously extended the framework of Paquin et al. to enable the automatic testing of a more extensive array of PQC schemes and network constellations. In order to systematically analyze the factors addressed in this work, the experiments are adapted in three stages. In a preliminary experiment group (Sect. 3), the extant results with PQC KEMs in TLS [25] are compared with measurements obtained from a real server environment. In a second group (Sect. 4), traditional signature schemes are replaced by PQC schemes. The experiments took into account different certificate chain compositions as well as hybrid schemes in emulation and real server environments. Finally, the configuration of the TCP/IP-stack is varied in a third group of experiments (Sect. 5). Individual adjustments to the experimental setup are listed at the beginning of each section.

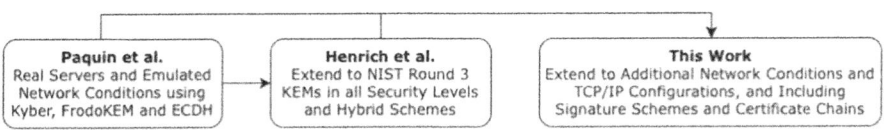

Fig. 1. Evolution of PQ TLS Benchmarking Framework based on [25,37].

2 General Experiment Setup

2.1 Test Procedure

Our tests involve a client and a server repeatedly carrying out TLS 1.3 handshakes. Upon attempting a connection establishment, a time measurement is initiated, which concludes when the TLS connection is successfully established. The number of repetitions is determined by the test setup, ranging from 100 to 2000. The specified number of repetitions is executed for each selected test parameter constellation. An *NGINX* implementation (v1.25.2) acts as server, which is initiated at the commencement of the experiment. The client initiates each handshake that is comprised of three TLS messages: *ClientHello*, *ServerHello*, including certificates, and *Finished*, in accordance with the TLS 1.3 specification [42] and the PQC specific draft [50]. This is done using *OpenSSL* in combination with the oqsprovider (branch 0.5.2) from Open Quantum Safe (OQS) [52].

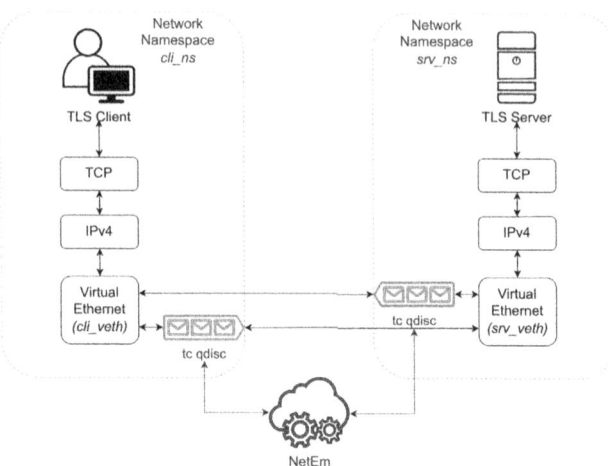

Fig. 2. TLS handshakes emulation setup using *NetEm*. Adopted from [25].

2.2 Network Setup

The experimental setup is largely based on previous work [25,37] and illustrated in Fig. 2. The *TLS Client* and the *TLS Server*, as described in Sect. 2.1, perform TLS handshakes via a TCP/IP connection. For the emulation of the underlying network layers, two Linux network namespaces (*cli_ns*, *srv_ns*) are created via *ip-netns*. These are connected to each other via Linux (Virtual Ethernet) endpoints (*cli_veth*, *srv_veth*). Subsequently, Linux *NetEm* is used to regulate the transmission of the outgoing messages, for instance by inserting a delay or by discarding them. For experiments involving real servers, it is possible to supplement the virtual Ethernet interfaces with the hardware and software that is utilized in a practical setting. However, Linux *NetEm* is employed at the output interfaces to emulate additional network affecting factors in both cases. The used test framework is available online[1].

2.3 Physical Network Conditions

Latency (0–120 ms). Latency is herein defined as the delay during packet transmission from sender to receiver and mainly affected by distance, network components, and transmission medium. It is important to note the distinction between latency and Round-Trip Time (RTT), which is defined as the delay between sending a request and receiving a response. In general, realistic simulations utilize packet delay values ranging from 2 to 200 ms, depending on geographical distance and infrastructure [11,56,57]. Nonetheless, values in excess of 120 ms are regarded as exceedingly elevated and are infrequently employed [11,32,55]. A total of 16 values were selected for analysis, ranging from 0 to 120 ms. Per default, emulation uses 20 ms latency unless stated otherwise.

---

[1] https://code.fbi.h-da.de/pqc-benchmarking/advanced-pqc-in-tls-benchmark.

Jitter. Jitter measures the variability of packet delay in data transmission over a network. Shehza et al. [6] posit that a dispersion of approximately 500 ns is virtually inevitable in the context of error-free radio links. Conversely, delays of several milliseconds can be attributed to the occurrence of punctual interference. Consequently, a standard latency of 20 ms has been selected for the experimental evaluation, with the jitter being incrementally augmented within the range of 0 to 20 ms. This results in the interval [0, 40] ms for the actual latency of the data packets. By default, 0 ms jitter is emulated.

Packet Loss (0–20%). Packet loss describes the discrepancy between packets sent and received during transmission. It can be caused by either network congestion, or software and hardware failures. However, TCP is designed to negate packet loss by retransmitting lost segments, causing an additional delay. In the context of research pertaining to packet loss, it is customary to operate under the assumption that the loss of packets will typically amount to a maximum of 5% [11,56,57]. However, values between 12% and 21% could also be measured when analyzing WLAN and mobile phone networks, especially in connection with IoT [8,24,33,39]. In order to address rare edge cases and facilitate a direct comparison with the studies of Paquin et al. [37] and Henrich et al. [25], the TLS handshakes for packet losses were evaluated within the range of 0% to 20%. In the absence of an explicit definition of packet loss, the emulated rate is set to 0%.

Data Rate (0.1–2000 Mbps). The data rate is the amount of data that can be transmitted over a network connection in a given time. The rate is affected by a number of factors, including the type of physical transmission medium and the interference or noise present in that medium. With regard to the transmission rate, values ranging from 0.1 to 2000 Mbps were selected. The selection is based on a range of works that consider values between 0.17 and 2000 Mbps [11,32,57]. The transmission rates for servers and clients are subject to individual variation, a necessity arising from the significant disparities in upstream and downstream rates that are observed in numerous use cases. In the absence of an explicit data rate definition for the emulation process, the value is set to 500 Mbps.

Corruption (0–20%). Data corruption of segments is typically identified by a precalculated checksum, prompting TCP to resend the data. Based on [11,56,57], in this case the same values are employed as for packet loss. If there is no explicit definition, then the emulated rate is 0%.

2.4 TPC/IP-Stack Configuration

MTU, MSS and Jumboframes. The MTU is the maximum Protocol Data Unit (PDU) that can be transmitted. PDU exceeding 1500 bytes are designated as Jumboframes. The upper limit is determined by the used hard- and software. The effective usable payload size for TCP segments is denoted by Maximum Segment Size (MSS), which is the MTU without TCP and IP headers.

TCP Congestion Control. The CW determines the maximum amount of data that can be sent without receiver acknowledgments [12]. If the data that has to be transferred at one point exceeds the CW an additional Round-Trip (RT) is introduced. The CW is adapted during the connection, while the ICW defines the CW size after TCP connection establishment. The Congestion Control Algorithm (CCA) is responsible for regulating the transmission process and the CW, acting in particular on the basis of network conditions and incidents such as packet loss. The CCAs *reno* [12], *cubic* [43] and *bbr* [17] are evaluated within the experiments. At the connection initiation, TCP enters the slow start phase, characterized by an exponentially increasing CW. When the Slow Start Threshold (SST) is reached, the CCA transitions to a more linear growth of the CW. The effect of changing the SST is evaluated on the emulation setup and can only be set for *cubic*. The SST is varied between 500 and 20000 bytes.

2.5 PQC Schemes and Parameters

Our experiments employ all of NIST round 4 candidates except the KEMs Classic McEliece and SIKE. Considering the former, its integration into TLS standards was precluded by the requirement of significantly larger key sizes. SIKE on the other hand, was initially considered, but was later ruled out due to a suddenly discovered vulnerability that completely broke its security. Other authorities, such as Information Security (BSI) or the French Cybersecurity Agency (ANSSI), also recommend FrodoKEM [15]. Therefore, it is also taken into account. In the evaluation process, traditional schemes are also considered to facilitate a comparison with the Status Quo. Elliptic-curve Diffie–Hellman (ECDH) is applied for key exchange, and Elliptic Curve Digital Signature Algorithm (ECDSA) is applied for digital signatures. Each of these utilizes NIST-specified curve parameters [19], designated as p-256, p-384, and p-521, to ensure security levels 1, 3, and 5, respectively. Furthermore, hybrid TLS variants [51] with a PQC and a traditional scheme, each targeting the same security level, are also being considered. We note that the differences between the standards and their original submissions, delineated in [34,35], exert negligible influence on performance metrics. In the context of the analysis focusing on structured lattice-based KEMs, the schemes demonstrate strong similarities in terms of their performance impact and do not differ significantly from each other in any of the experiments. In accordance with the selection of Kyber by NIST [2], the subsequent discussion will focus exclusively on Kyber. However, it should be noted that these observations are approximately equally applicable to SABER, NTRU, and NTRU Prime.

3 *Experiment I*: KEM Performance Using Real Servers

Experiment I compares a purely emulation-based setup [25] with rather more realistic scenarios using real servers in five different geographic locations. The results of the experiments are illustrated in Fig. 5 in Appendix A.

3.1 Detailed Setup

To extend the work of Paquin et al. [37] and Henrich et al. [25] Virtual Machines (VMs) are created on the Microsoft Azure cloud platform using Terraform. The VM size provided to the client is a *standard_D4s_v3* (4 CPU cores, 16GB RAM, Intel Xeon Platinum 8272C, CPU 2.60GHz). The VM size provided to the servers is *standard_D8s_v4* (8 CPU cores, 32GB RAM, Intel Xeon Platinum 8272C, CPU 2.60GHz). The operating system is Ubuntu 22.04. The PQ TLS is based on OQS OpenSSL (version 1.1.1) [52]. The client is located in Toronto, while four different server locations with the following average latencies are considered: Quebec City 7 ms, Wyoming 20 ms, London 47 ms and Johannesburg 128 ms.

3.2 Results

General. With the exception of FrodoKEM, which is invariably significantly impacted by network conditions, a comparison of schemes at security level 1 does not directly suggest substantial performance disparities. Consequently, significant insights become clearer at security levels 3 and 5. For instance, FrodoKEM at security level 1 and HQC at levels 1 and 3 are relatively satisfactory. However, experiments at higher levels respectively prove times below other KEMs due to additional RTs caused by the increased public key and ciphertext sizes. Thus, we conclude that almost all scenarios lead to the unsurprising and established fact that FrodoKEM is the slowest in terms of average runtime under location-bound varying latency levels, without additional network constraints. Kyber outperforms other KEMs under most varying conditions as demonstrated in Fig. 5b. Whereas FrodoKEM can withstand only up to 7% packet loss, Kyber is able to withstand up to 14%. Additionally, the performance gap between FrodoKEM and Kyber increases drastically under lower data rates, needless to say, not in the favor of FrodoKEM. A rather interesting finding is that Kyber is faster than ECDH when affected by latency in general (Fig. 5a), for all security levels. However, ECC still proves best under lower data rates due to their very small key sizes (Fig. 5b). Another surprising finding is that hybrid KEMs show very similar performance under all scenarios with differences less than 1 ms in overall runtime. Hybrid variants necessitate additional computational resources and cryptographic material for transmission, attributable to the execution of two distinct KEMs. It is therefore tempting to assume that, in principle, these should require better network conditions than pure PQ-only. Generally speaking, the results of the experiments using real servers are very close to previous works compared to an emulated setup (e.g., Henrich et al. [25]).

Considering Dedicated Physical Network Parameters. The physical server distance is the most significant factor considering the resulting delay in the overall handshake time. Mainly, all non-code-based KEMs (except FrodoKEM) show results comparable to ECDH. Regarding packet loss, almost all KEMs show practically constant run times at security levels 1 and 3 under 7% packet loss, and for level 5 under 5%. Still, the impact scales linearly with larger public key and ciphertext sizes. The data rate impacts the handshake runtime significantly when lower than 3 Mbps using almost any scheme as shown in Fig. 5b. On the other hand, there is not any observable improvement in the performance for any KEM at data rates higher than 75 Mbps. Additionally, unbalanced public key and ciphertext size ratios affect the performance significantly under low data rates.

3.3 Conclusion

Based on the previous results, it is quite safe to say that Kyber outperforms other KEMs. In other words, KEMs based on structured-lattices have a clear advantage over non-structured lattices and code-based schemes. An interesting finding is that the best performing KEMs can indeed contend with traditional ECC, thus proving a suitable replacement. Further, lower data rates and higher packet loss seem to affect the performance the most in all scenarios, and across all PQC KEMs and security levels including lattices. Therefore, it is worth investigating, how the gap in performance under lower data rates can be minimized, as lattices do have larger key sizes compared to ECC.

4 *Experiment II*: Involving Signatures

4.1 Detailed Setup

Given that security level 2 represents the lowest possible security variant for Dilithium, Dilithium2 is selected for level 1. Only security level 1 and 5 are tested for Falcon, because the Falcon implementation does not include level 3 [22]. The considered schemes including data sizes and average execution time are listed in Table 2 (Appendix A). In an initial series of tests (*A*), the focus is explicitly on the effects of choosing a specific signature scheme while varying security level and network state. The network connections are emulated, server certificates are self-signed, and key establishment is performed using ECDH. The evaluation encompasses not only PQ-only but also hybrid variants. In a subsequent series, (*B*), an extended setup involving real servers is employed. Different certificate chain lengths (ranging from one to three) and compositions (combinations of all security levels and signature schemes examined in *A*) are evaluated. Furthermore, an evaluation is conducted, employing the key establishment schemes Kyber, BIKE and FrodoKEM.

Basic Emulation (*A*) The emulation runs on a Dell Inspiron 3501 notebook with an 11th generation Intel Core i7-1165G7 processor, 4 cores, 8 threads and up to 4.7 GHz. The operating system is Ubuntu 22.04.

Real Server (*B*) The experiments in a real network environment are conducted in multiple locations. The client operates on an *Openstack* server (2 vCPUs, 4 GB RAM, Ubuntu 24.04 LTS) situated in Darmstadt, Germany. Multiple *aws* server instances (1 vCPU, 1 GB RAM, Ubuntu 24.04 LTS) have been configured for the TLS servers located in Stockholm 10 ms, Ohio 50 ms, Singapore 80 ms and Seoul 115 ms. The evaluation process involved the definition of three distinct certificate chain lengths: (1) Self-signed certificate of a TLS server, (2) self-signed Certificate Authority (CA) certificate and CA signed server certificate or (3) self-signed CA certificate and CA signed intermediate certificate and intermediate signed server certificate. The various certificate chain combinations from different signature schemes (listed in Table 2) are described in the form

$$RootCAScheme - IntermediateCAScheme - ServerScheme.$$

4.2 Results

Basic Emulation (*A*)

General. As mentioned in [25,37], under optimal network conditions, the algorithm execution time is the primary factor in comparing handshake times. This is confirmed by comparing the algorithm runtimes in Table 2 with the measured handshake times. Dilithium and Falcon exhibit satisfactory algorithm execution performance. Dilithium demonstrates particular efficiency in the domain of signing, while Falcon facilitates expedited verification. The discrepancy between the two is particularly evident at higher security levels. It is important to note that, as the certificates are typically created and signed in advance, a significantly higher volume of verification operations is conducted as part of the TLS handshake, while the handshake is only signed once. Consequently, in optimal network conditions characterized by minimal latency, Falcon demonstrates a substantially superior handshake performance. In contrast, SPHINCS+ exhibits substantially elevated execution times, even in the fast variant, and is unable to maintain competitiveness in these scenarios. This confirms the result in [47]. With increased latency, a recurring pattern in prior results emerges: the transmission of varying data amounts does not result in significant variations in time, provided that all data fits within the current TCP CW and can therefore be transmitted as part of a RT. This definitive limit does not exist for the transmission rate, as the amount of data has an almost constant effect on the handshake time. In general, the transmission time t as a function of the transmission rate $x \in [0.1, 2000.0]$ is equivalent to a rational function of the form $t(x) = \frac{m}{x}$, where m is a constant amount of data. In this specific case, the execution times of the computing systems at the application and network layer, as well as (header) data, which depends on the number of packets to be sent, must also be taken into account. Nevertheless, these factors exert minimal impact on the trajectory of the graphs.

Security Level. Comparing handshake times at security levels 1 and 3 frequently reveals no substantial disparities, particularly under optimal network conditions or in the presence of elevated latency. The discrepancy is only discernible at below-average transmission rates. At security level 5, Falcon maintains its superior performance, while the disparities for Dilithium become pronounced. The augmented execution time and the escalated data volume are both noteworthy. In the event that the number of packets exceeds the capacity of the CW, a significantly extended handshake duration can be observed as the latency increases. In the emulation with a 190-ms delay, an average of 769 ms is required for the handshake using Falcon at security level 1. When utilizing Falcon with a security level of 5, the process is observed to require 780 ms, an additional 11 ms. A comparison of this with Dilithium reveals a significant discrepancy in the variation between security levels 1 (769 ms) and 5 (1147 ms), with an average disparity of nearly 400 ms. This indicates an additional RT.

Hybrids. The analysis of hybrid variants indicates that under consistently good network conditions, the overall handshake time is almost equivalent to the sum of the execution times of the schemes, that are executed in series, and the overhead of the TLS environment. The overhead of the TLS environment can relativize the computational effort of the used schemes to an extent [7], when using schemes with comparatively brief algorithm runtimes (e.g., Kyber). The total quantity of cryptographic material to be transferred also adds up. However, it is important to note that distinct effects may still be observed on the overall handshake time required. For instance, the mean handshake duration for security level 1 is 13.9 ms for Falcon and 18.3 ms for Dilithium. The discrepancy between the selected KEMs is thus 3.5 ms. In contrast, the hybrid variants require 18.3 ms and 18.8 ms, respectively. This indicates that Falcon necessitates 4.4 ms in conjunction with ECDH, whereas Dilithium requires only 1.4 ms more. The discrepancy can be attributed to the fact that, in the case of Falcon alone, the volume of data to be transmitted is so minimal that it can be accommodated within a CW and conveyed as part of an RT. When utilized in conjunction with ECDH, this threshold is subsequently surpassed. In the Dilithium PQ-only variant, this phenomenon has already been observed, indicating that the additional data volumes caused by an hybridization do not exert a substantial influence.

Real Server (*B*)

General. Real server evaluations initially confirm the emulation outcomes *(A)*. Figure 3 and Fig. 4 (Appendix A) illustrate the measurements for long certificate chains with fixed signature schemes in Darmstadt, Stockholm and Seoul. A distinction is made between the KEMs Kyber, BIKE and FrodoKEM (security level 3). Falcon consistently demonstrates high performance and frequently surpasses traditional schemes. This also applies to Dilithium under low latency. Conversely, SPHINCS+ generally exhibits significantly reduced performance.

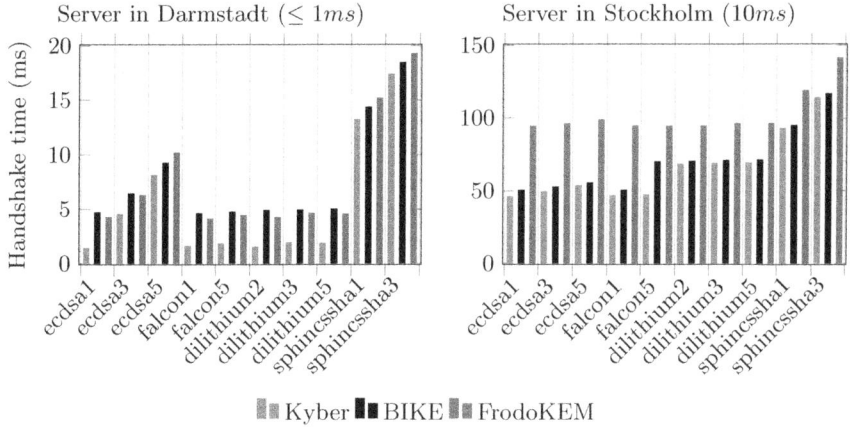

Fig. 3. Handshake duration (median) for signature schemes using Kyber, Bike or FrodoKEM (sec level 3). Client in Darmstadt.

Certificate Chain Length and Composition. The extent to which chain length and signature scheme selection impact the handshake performance is contingent on the overall constellation. Numerous combinations for long certificate chains reach a plateau at a specific point. It is noteworthy that combinations involving solely Falcon variants, irrespective of the designated security level, demonstrate a positive impact. Conversely, all variants incorporating a SPHINCS+ variant at least once demonstrate particularly poor performance, as evidenced by the combination *sphincssha3-falcon5-dilithium5*. It is evident that the selection of KEMs exerts a substantial influence on the outcomes. In the case of combinations with FrodoKEM, a consistent decline in performance is observed, relative to the performance of Kyber or BIKE, that are usually at a similar level.

Latency. As already stated for KEMs (Sect. 3), the handshake duration is significantly influenced by the server location. As demonstrated in Fig. 3, the algorithm runtime assumes particular significance when the latency approaches zero. The necessity of verification is especially pronounced in the context of extensive certificate chains, as the certificates are typically signed in advance, whereas verification is conducted on an ad hoc basis for each certificate. The data in Table 2 demonstrates that Dilithium and Falcon necessitate minimal execution times. It is notable that this time is considerably less than that required for verification using ECDSA. These observations are further substantiated by Fig. 3. The results for Darmstadt reveal that variants employing BIKE are notably more time-consuming compared to Kyber. However, when considering Stockholm or even Seoul, shown in Fig. 4, these observations are contextualized, and the significance of the amount of data to be transferred becomes more pronounced. It is noteworthy that Kyber and BIKE have converged, with both demonstrating comparable performance in terms of execution time. Conversely, variants employing FrodoKEM demonstrate a decline due to their substantial key and cipher rate. This pattern can be observed independently of the signature scheme.

Hybrids. Figure 4 illustrates the median handshake times for the Seoul with certificate chains of length 3 using Kyber, BIKE or FrodoKEM. (a) illustrates PQ-only certificates, (b) illustrates hybrid root certificates and (c) illustrates only hybrids. The duration of the handshake remains consistent across all graphs for the majority of combinations. Significant deviations from this pattern are observed only in the combinations of Falcon5 with BIKE and Dilithium5 with FrodoKEM.

4.3 Conclusion

In the majority of cases, the effects of Falcon and Dilithium on the handshake duration are minimal. This phenomenon is also evident for hybrid variants, particularly when they are combined with ECDSA. Nevertheless, under specific circumstances, a substantial delay can be witnessed. Such conditions encompass low data rates and high packet loss, as evidenced previously for KEMs (Sect. 3). To mitigate these issues, it is advisable to either avoid using appropriate PQC variants or adapt the configuration of the TCP/IP-stack (Sect. 5). The configuration of the certificate chain is also crucial. The use of specific certificate chains, such as *falcon5-falcon1-falcon1*, does not result in any performance degradation compared to traditional signature schemes, but offers increased security at the root CA level. If the network is of a satisfactory quality and low-latency or real-time communication is required, as is possible in the IoT area, the focus should be on the computational complexity. In such cases, Falcon has a clear advantage because the computational complexity for verification is low, which benefits a low-performance client. The findings previously mentioned do not include the use of the SPHINCS+. This is due to the fact that the handshake performance is considerably reduced when employing SPHINCS+. E.g., in scenarios where a single certificate in a certificate chain employed SPHINCS+, a delay became evident. The results confirm the conclusions of Kampanakis et al. [27] and Raavi et al. [40], which summarize that Dilithium and Falcon are the best performing PQ signature schemes for time-sensitive protocols.

5 *Experiment III*: TCP/IP-Stack Configuration

5.1 Detailed Setup

As not all parameters can be altered in a real network, some experiments are conducted on an emulation-based setup, in which server and client are on the same machine. In contrast, other experiments are conducted on a more realistic setup that uses five VMs in different locations. The emulation experiments use pure PQC KEM implementations at different security levels and ECDH. It runs on a VM with Ubuntu 22.04 LTS, 2 vCPUs and 4GB RAM. The more realistic setup is similar to the one described in Sect. 3.1. While the evaluated network stack parameters are varied in the emulation, the emulated physical network conditions are set as follows. Latency: 10 ms, jitter: 1 ms, duplicates: 1%, corrupted packets: 1%, packet loss: 2%, data rate: 500 Mbps.

5.2 Results

Congestion Window. An analysis of the observed handshake times indicates that delays are frequently attributable to exceeded CW and the consequent extra RTs. This results in step-wise performance impacts. This behavior can be observed in Fig. 5c (Appendix A), which shows the handshake duration of PQ-only and hybrid schemes over the ICW varied from 1 to 20 times MSS. During the experiment, only the ICW is changed, the actual CW during the open connection can change based on the CCA and a variety of network conditions. The measurements are conducted on real servers with 42 ms latency. It has also been observed that, besides FrodoKEM and HQC, all other PQC KEMs require less than 10 segments with 1440 bytes segment size, which is recommended [20] and the default ICW in Ubuntu 22.04. To give a comparison of the sizes and constraints between traditional and PQC schemes in the context of TLS, ECDH requires one TCP segment while PQC KEMs require at least 2 segments. FrodoKEM requires at least 14 MSS for security level 3. Increasing the TCP ICW results in a positive impact on the handshake performance overall, as long as there is no significant packet loss. Anyhow, the improvements are more pronounced at larger key sizes. In case of packet loss, the additional delay caused by the packet loss is mostly dependent on the total number of packets to be send. Figure 5d illustrates the handshake performance of alternative candidates under packet loss with an ICW of 10 compared to an ICW of 20. It is evident that the positive effect of the increased CW is counteracted by increasing packet loss.

Further TCP/IP-Stack Configurations. Performance enhancements are observed when the MTU is elevated to 3000 bytes for FrodoKEM (security level 5). Remaining measurements do not demonstrate enhancements that exceed the 1500-byte limit. Additionally, a negligible difference is observed in the results for IPv4 and IPv6, as the header size is minute in comparison to the public key size. Changing the CCA or increasing the TCP SST does not lead to a significant change in the handshake times. The handshake process is too brief for these settings to be effective.

5.3 Conclusion

The adjustment of the ICW with respect to the selected KEM offers a significant opportunity to enhance the handshake performance by avoiding unnecessary RTs. In circumstances where latency is high, the amount of necessary RT is of particular significance in terms of performance and user experience. In addition, the results of Experiment III indicate unequivocally that hybrid variants do not have a detrimental effect. Furthermore, larger MTUs have a positive impact to some degree. However, only some alternatives profit from jumboframes.

6 Conclusion and Outlook

Our experiments consolidate and complete previous results [25,37,38,48], demonstrating that in many network scenarios, a transition to PQC is indeed possible without incurring performance losses. However, in situations where data rate is limited or there is a high incidence of packet loss, the utilization of schemes with large key, ciphertext or signature sizes, a high security level or hybrid variants can result in performance losses. This phenomenon is particularly evident in the case of FrodoKEM and SPHINCS+. However, it is noteworthy that this can also be observed in schemes with moderate data volumes in certain instances. In such cases, hybrid variants in combination with ECC schemes are recommended, as RSA has larger key and ciphertext sizes. However, a deterioration compared to traditional schemes cannot be avoided here either. A suitable configuration of the TCP/IP-stack can mitigate these effects. While IP version or CCA do not show significant effects, increasing the ICW or MTU can reduce the total time. Optimally, increasing the ICW results in a reduction in the required RTs, with particular benefits for connections with high latencies. However, as soon as highly efficient data transmission is possible, the data volumes to be transmitted become secondary, with computing efficiency becoming the primary concern.

In the subsequent phase, experiments with TLS features such as session re-establishment reusing the session key or caching of certificate chains and their verification, as described in [1,18], are to be undertaken. As demonstrated in Table 1, the utilization of PQC with 0-RTT or mutual authentication has not yet been adequately evaluated under various network scenarios. One might also consider an emulated server overload or a *ServerHelloRetry* as a consequence of an unaccepted algorithm suggestion. A concrete analysis of the threshold values for key, signature and cipher text sizes at which additional RTs occur in typical network constellations and thus a significant increase in handshake time would be advantageous for a rapid assessment of the appropriate algorithm selection. In light of the preceding scientific endeavors and the parameters delineated in this study, which exert a substantial influence on handshake performance (e.g., ICW, certificate chain length), it is recommended that, in the long term, a statistical model be developed, with the objective of estimating the expected handshake duration under specific conditions. Furthermore, a comparison with similar protocols such as QUIC would be beneficial. While there has been some work done to provide an initial evaluation of these protocols [41,48], there is still a lack of comprehensive analyses that take into account various network conditions. The experiments described here were conducted before NIST selected HQC. NIST-nominated schemes or those that are otherwise pertinent (FrodoKEM) shall receive the requisite attention in future work.

Acknowledgements. Funded by the German Federal Ministry of Education and Research (BMFTR) and the Hessian Ministry of Higher Education, Research, Science and the Arts as part of the National Research Center for Applied Cybersecurity ATHENE and the BMFTR-Project DemoQuanDT.

A Appendix

Table 2. Signature schemes considered, encompassing public key (pk), signature ($sign$) (bytes) and execution time (10^3 CPU-Cycles). Data sizes and execution time based on ECRYPT/SUPERCOP-Benchmarks (*rome0*) [54].

Scheme	SecLevel	pk	signature	sign	verify
ECDSA	I	64	64	147	299
ECDSA	III	96	96	3286	2788
ECDSA	V	132	132	1016	1896
Dilithium	II	1312	2420	214	99
Dilithium	III	1952	3293	373	164
Dilithium	V	2592	4595	450	261
Falcon	I	897	660	377	71
Falcon	V	1793	1276	747	142
SPHINCS+	I	32	17088	128173	7623
SPHINCS+	III	48	35664	165893	12611
SPHINCS+	V	64	49856	376772	12418

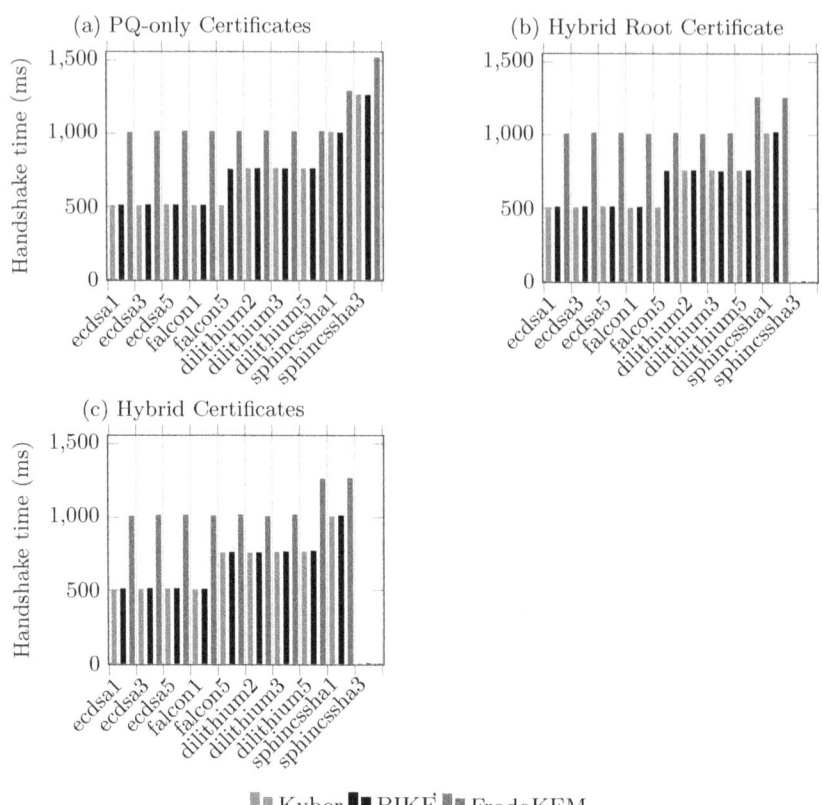

Fig. 4. Handshake duration (median) for signature schemes using KEM Kyber, Bike or FrodoKEM (security level 3). Client in Darmstadt, server in Seoul, delay ∼115 ms. Certificate chains include root CA certificate, intermediate CA certificate and server certificate. Types of certificate chains: (a) only PQC; (b) only root certificate hybrid; (c) hybrid only. In the hybrid case, ECDSA is used with corresponding security level. Sphincs3 certificate chains lead to the handshake being aborted due to the long transmission time in (b) and (c).

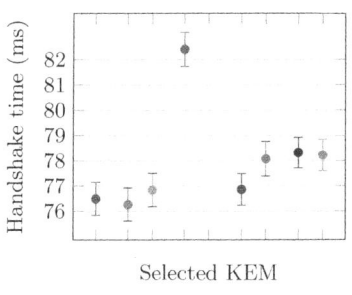
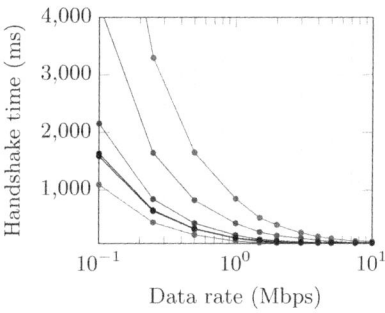

(a) Mean and 95% confidence interval when satisfying security level 1 with 280 measurements each.

(b) Median in relation to data rate when satisfying security level 1.

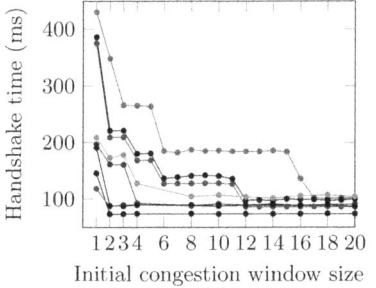
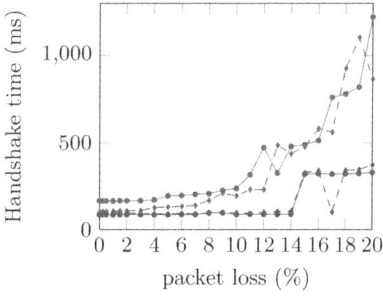

(c) Median in relation to ICW when satisfying security level 5.

(d) Median when satisfying security level 5 (ICW=10 solid, ICW=20 dashed).

Fig. 5. Handshake duration for several KEMs in different test setups: (a) mean and confidence interval with consistently good network conditions; (b) median with decreasing data rate; (c) median with increasing initial congestion window; (d) median with increasing packet loss. Client in Toronto, server in Wyoming, delay ~20 ms. Hybrid variants identified by "_h".

References

1. Aguilar-Melchor, C., et al.: Batch signatures, revisited. In: Topics in Cryptology – CT-RSA, pp. 163–186. Springer, Cham (2024)
2. Alagic, G., et al.: Status Report on the Third Round of the NIST Post-Quantum Cryptography Standardization Process. Technical Report NIST IR 8413, National Institute of Standards and Technology, Gaithersburg, Maryland, United States of America (2022)
3. Alagic, G., et al.: Status report on the fourth round of the NIST post-quantum cryptography standardization process. Technical Report NIST IR 8545, National Institute of Standards and Technology (U.S.), Gaithersburg, MD (2025)
4. Alnahawi, N., et al.: On the state of post-quantum cryptography migration. INFORMATIK (2021)

5. Alnahawi, N., et al.: A comprehensive survey on post-quantum TLS. IACR Commun. Cryptol. **1**(2) (2024)
6. Ashraf, S.A., et al.: Ultra-reliable and low-latency communication for wireless factory automation: from LTE to 5G. In: IEEE 21st International Conference on Emerging Technologies and Factory Automation (ETFA) (2016)
7. Auten, D., et al.: Impact of resource-constrained networks on the performance of NIST round-3 PQC candidates. In: IEEE 45th Annual Computers, Software, and Applications Conference (COMPSAC), pp. 768–773 (2021)
8. Balasubramanian, A., et al.: Augmenting mobile 3G using WiFi. In: 8th International Conference on Mobile Systems, Applications, and Services, MobiSys 2010. ACM (2010)
9. Barton, J., et al.: Performance Analysis of TLS for Quantum Robust Cryptography on a Constrained Device (2022). arXiv:1912.12257 [cs]
10. Bindel, N., Brendel, J., Fischlin, M., Goncalves, B., Stebila, D.: Hybrid key encapsulation mechanisms and authenticated key exchange. In: Ding, J., Steinwandt, R. (eds.) PQCrypto 2019. LNCS, vol. 11505, pp. 206–226. Springer, Cham (2019). https://doi.org/10.1007/978-3-030-25510-7_12
11. Biswal, P., Gnawali, O.: Does QUIC make the web faster? In: 2016 IEEE Global Communications Conference (GLOBECOM), Washington, DC, USA, pp. 1–6. IEEE Press (2016)
12. Blanton, E., Paxson, V., Allman, M.: TCP Congestion Control (2009)
13. Bos, J., et al.: Frodo: take off the ring! practical, quantum-secure key exchange from LWE. In: Proceedings of the 2016 ACM SIGSAC Conference on Computer and Communications Security, CCS 2016, pp. 1006–1018. Association for Computing Machinery, New York (2016)
14. Bos, J.W., et al.: Post-quantum key exchange for the TLS protocol from the ring learning with errors problem. In: 2015 IEEE Symposium on Security and Privacy, pp. 553–570 (2015)
15. (BSI). Cryptographic mechanisms: Recommendations and key lengths. Technical Guideline (TR) 02102, Federal Office for Information Security (2025)
16. Bürstinghaus-Steinbach, K., et al.: Post-quantum TLS on embedded systems: integrating and evaluating kyber and sphincs+ with MBED TLS. In: Proceedings of the 15th ACM Asia Conference on Computer and Communications Security, pp. 841–852. Association for Computing Machinery, New York (2020)
17. Cardwell, N., et al.: BBR Congestion Control. Internet Draft draft-ietf-ccwg-bbr-01, Internet Engineering Task Force (2024). Num Pages: 79
18. Catoni, L., et al.: Fast and secure service continuity in the edge-cloud continuum: a study of TLS 1.3 resumption and post-quantum key exchange. In: IEEE International Conference on Smart Computing (SMARTCOMP), pp. 396–401 (2025)
19. Chen, L., et al.: Recommendations for Discrete Logarithm-based Cryptography: Elliptic Curve Domain Parameters. Technical Report NIST SP 800-186, National Institute of Standards and Technology (2023)
20. Chu, J., Dukkipati, N., Cheng, Y., Mathis, M.: Increasing TCP's Initial Window. RFC 6928 (2013)
21. Florence, D., Michael, P., Hale, B.: Terminology for Post-Quantum Traditional Hybrid Schemes. Internet-Draft draft-ietf-pquip-pqt-hybrid-terminology-04, Internet Engineering Task Force (2024). Work in Progress
22. Fouque, P.-A., et al.: Falcon: Fast-Fourier Lattice-based Compact Signatures over NTRU. https://falcon-sign.info/falcon.pdf. Accessed 25 July 2022

23. Partners from 18 EU member states. Securing tomorrow, today: Transitioning to post-quantum cryptography (2024). https://www.bsi.bund.de/SharedDocs/Downloads/EN/BSI/Crypto/PQC-joint-statement.html
24. Goel, U., et al.: HTTP/2 performance in cellular networks: poster. In: 22nd Annual International Conference on Mobile Computing and Networking. ACM (2016)
25. Henrich, J., et al.: Performance impact of PQC KEMS on TLS 1.3 under varying network characteristics. In: Information Security: 26th International Conference (ISC), pp. 267–287 (2023)
26. Kampanakis, P., et al.: The viability of post-quantum x.509 certificates. Cryptology ePrint Archive, Paper 2018/063 (2018)
27. Kampanakis, P., Sikeridis, D.: Two PQ signature use-cases: non-issues, challenges and potential solutions. In: 7th ETSI/IQC Quantum Safe Cryptography Workshop 2019 (2019)
28. Kwiatkowski, K., Sullivan, N., Langley, A., Levin, D., Mislove, A.: Measuring TLS key exchange with post-quantum KEM. In: NIST Second PQC Standardization Conference (2021)
29. Lee, H., Kim, D., Kwon, Y.: TLS 1.3 in practice: how TLS 1.3 contributes to the internet. In: Proceedings of the Web Conference 2021, WWW 2021, pp. 70–79. Association for Computing Machinery, New York (2021)
30. Mankowski, D., et al.: TLS → post-quantum TLS: inspecting the TLS landscape for PQC adoption on android. In: IEEE European Symposium on Security and Privacy Workshops, pp. 526–538 (2023)
31. Marchsreiter, D., Sepúlveda, J.: Hybrid post-quantum enhanced TLS 1.3 on embedded devices. In: 2022 25th Euromicro Conference on Digital System Design (DSD), pp. 905–912 (2022)
32. Megyesi, P., et al.: How quick is QUIC? In: IEEE International Conference on Communications. Springer (2016)
33. Shree, T.N.N., et al.: Performance analysis of TCP on IoT devices. In: 2022 IEEE North Karnataka Subsection Flagship International Conference (NKCon), pp. 1–6 (2022)
34. National Institute of Standards and Technology. Module-Lattice-Based Digital Signature Standard. Technical Report NIST FIPS 204 IPD, National Institute of Standards and Technology, Gaithersburg, MD (2024)
35. National Institute of Standards and Technology. Module-Lattice-Based Key-Encapsulation Mechanism Standard. Technical Report NIST FIPS 203 IPD, National Institute of Standards and Technology, Gaithersburg, MD (2024)
36. National Institute of Standards and Technology. Stateless Hash-Based Digital Signature Standard. Technical Report NIST FIPS 205 IPD, National Institute of Standards and Technology, Gaithersburg, MD (2024)
37. Paquin, C., et al.: Benchmarking post-quantum cryptography in TLS. Cryptology ePrint Archive, Paper 2019/1447 (2019)
38. Paul, S., et al.: Mixed certificate chains for the transition to post-quantum authentication in TLS 1.3. In: Proceedings of Asia Conference on Computer and Communications Security, pp. 727–740. ACM (2022)
39. Prantl, T., et al.: Performance impact analysis of securing MQTT using TLS. In: Proceedings of the ACM/SPEC International Conference on Performance Engineering, pp. 241–248. ACM, New York (2021)
40. Raavi, M., et al.: Performance characterization of post-quantum digital certificates. In: International Conference on Computer Communications and Networks (ICCCN), pp. 1–9 (2021)

41. Raavi, M., et al.: QUIC protocol with post-quantum authentication. In: Information Security, pp. 84–91. Springer, Cham (2022)
42. Rescorla, E.: The Transport Layer Security (TLS) Protocol Version 1.3. RFC 8446 (2018)
43. Rhee, I., et al.: CUBIC for Fast Long-Distance Networks (2018)
44. Security requirements for cryptographic modules. Technical Report FIPS PUB 140-3, National Institute of Standards and Technology (2019)
45. Sarıbaş, S., Tonyalı, S.: Performance evaluation of TLS 1.3 handshake on resource-constrained devices using NIST's third round post-quantum key encapsulation mechanisms and digital signatures. In: 7th International Conference on Computer Science and Engineering (UBMK), pp. 294–299 (2022)
46. Schöffel, M., et al.: Secure IoT in the era of quantum computers—where are the bottlenecks? Sensors **22**(7) (2022)
47. Sikeridis, D., et al.: Post-quantum authentication in TLS 1.3: a performance study. Cryptology ePrint Archive, Paper 2020/071 (2020)
48. Sikeridis, D., Kampanakis, P., Devetsikiotis, M.: Assessing the overhead of post-quantum cryptography in TLS 1.3 and SSH. In: Proceedings of the 16th International Conference on Emerging Networking EXperiments and Technologies, CoNEXT 2020, pp. 149–156. ACM, New York (2020)
49. Sosnowski, M., et al.: The performance of post-quantum TLS 1.3. In: Companion of the 19th International Conference on emerging Networking EXperiments and Technologies, CoNEXT 2023, pp. 19–27. ACM (2023)
50. Stebila, D., et al.: Hybrid key exchange in TLS 1.3. Internet-Draft draft-ietf-tls-hybrid-design-11, Internet Engineering Task Force. Work in Progress (2024)
51. Stebila, D., et al.: Hybrid key exchange in TLS 1.3. Internet-Draft draft-ietf-tls-hybrid-design-12, Internet Engineering Task Force (2025)
52. Stebila, D., Mosca, M.: Post-quantum key exchange for the internet and the open quantum safe project. In: Avanzi, R., Heys, H. (eds.) SAC 2016. LNCS, vol. 10532, pp. 14–37. Springer, Cham (2017). https://doi.org/10.1007/978-3-319-69453-5_2
53. Tasopoulos, G., et al.: Performance evaluation of post-quantum TLS 1.3 on resource-constrained embedded systems. In: Information Security Practice and Experience: 17th International Conference (ISPEC), pp. 432–451. Springer (2022)
54. VAMPIRE - Virtual Applications and Implementations Research Lab. Measurements of public-key signature systems. https://bench.cr.yp.to/results-sign.html. Accessed 02 Dec 2024
55. Verma, L.P., et al.: Adaptive congestion control in IoT networks: leveraging one-way delay for enhanced performance. Heliyon **10**(22), e40266 (2024)
56. Wang, P., et al.: Implementation and performance evaluation of the QUIC protocol in Linux kernel. In: 21st ACM International Conference on Modeling, Analysis and Simulation of Wireless and Mobile Systems. ACM (2018)
57. Yu, Y., et al.: When QUIC meets TCP: an experimental study. In: IEEE 36th International Performance Computing and Communications Conference (IPCCC) (2017)

Post-quantum Cryptography

Conditional Attribute-Based PRE: Definition and Construction from LWE

Lisha Yao[1], Jian Weng[2], Pengfei Wu[1(✉)], Guofeng Tang[1], Guomin Yang[1], Haiyang Xue[1], and Robert H. Deng[1]

[1] School of Computing and Information Systems, Singapore Management University, Singapore, Singapore
{lishayao,pfwu,gftang,gmyang,haiyangxue,robertdeng}@smu.edu.sg
[2] School of Cybersecurity, Jinan University, Guangzhou, China
cryptjweng@gmail.com

Abstract. Attribute-based proxy re-encryption (AB-PRE) is a crucial variant of proxy re-encryption. It allows a proxy with a re-encryption key to transform a *delegator*'s ciphertext associated with an access policy into another ciphertext associated with a new access policy, enabling *delegatees* with matching attributes to decrypt the transformed ciphertext. However, a key limitation of AB-PRE is that the delegator cannot control which ciphertexts are transformed. As a result, the proxy, once given the re-encryption key, indiscriminately transforms all ciphertexts, effectively switching their underlying policies—an issue known as the all-or-nothing problem. It limits the system's flexibility and practicality in real-world use cases.

In this paper, we address this by proposing a primitive of Conditional AB-PRE (CAB-PRE), which extends AB-PRE by incorporating conditional re-encryption. In CAB-PRE, the proxy can transform a ciphertext only if this ciphertext satisfies a specific condition set by the delegator in the re-encryption key. We formalize the adaptive security of CAB-PRE under the context of honest re-encryption attacks (HRA). We also give a concrete construction based on the learning with errors (LWE) assumption, which attains designated security in the standard model.

Keywords: Conditional AB-PRE · Honest re-encryption attacks · Learning with errors

1 Introduction

Proxy Re-Encryption (PRE) is a cryptographic primitive that enables secure and privacy-preserving transfer of decryption rights between parties with the assistance of a proxy [5]. Specifically, a PRE scheme allows a proxy, given a re-encryption key, to transform a ciphertext encrypted under Alice's (i.e., the delegator's) key into one under Bob's (i.e., the delegatee's) key, without learning any information about the underlying message. It has demonstrated broad applicability across a range of scenarios, such as online social networks [14], digital forensics management [20], and data sharing in CloudIoT platforms [22].

Attribute-Based PRE. Attribute-Based PRE (AB-PRE) is one of the most prominent variants of PRE [12,16,18,23]. It integrates an attribute-based access control into PRE and allows a proxy to dynamically change the access policy underlying a ciphertext. Specifically, AB-PRE facilitates the transformation of a ciphertext encrypted by the delegator under a specific access policy into a new ciphertext, governed by a distinct access policy tailored for the delegatee. Consequently, the delegatee can decrypt the re-encrypted ciphertext, provided that the attributes embedded in their secret key fulfill the requirements of the newly established access policy.

However, due to the lack of control over the delegator's re-encryption capability, AB-PRE falls short as an ideal solution for scenarios such as data sharing in the cloud. As an example, consider a financial manager, Alice, who wishes to delegate selective access to her encrypted files governed by distinct access policies. While AB-PRE enables Alice to issue to the proxy re-encryption keys that can convert her ciphertexts to new ones governed by different policies, this mechanism lacks flexibility and proper control. Once a re-encryption key is distributed, the proxy can transform all eligible ciphertexts under the specified policy without restriction, leaving Alice with no control on the potential abuse of the re-encryption power by the proxy. This "all-or-nothing" delegation makes AB-PRE fail to meet the demand of conditional re-encryption, where tailored control over individual files or policies is essential.

Security of AB-PRE. While traditional security notions such as IND-CPA and IND-CCA are fundamental, they fail to capture key leakage risks specific to (AB-)PRE during the re-encryption process. In typical multi-user deployments, an adversary may corrupt selected users to obtain their secret keys associated with certain attributes and subsequently request re-encryption keys between chosen user pairs. These re-encryption keys, which inherently embed information about the delegator's secret key, are then used to re-encrypt ciphertext. Cohen [8] demonstrated that this subtle leakage enables an adversary to analyze honestly generated re-encrypted ciphertexts and extract sensitive information that IND-CPA and IND-CCA cannot protect. To remedy this, Cohen introduced the notion of security against honest re-encryption attacks (HRA), which captures such leakage and better reflects the threat landscape faced by (AB-)PRE systems. These security notions collectively aim to ensure that even if an adversary compromises certain users and obtains relevant re-encryption keys, a challenge ciphertext encrypted under a target access policy f^* remains semantically secure.

Selective and adaptive security are also important considerations in the security model for AB-PRE. If the adversary selects the target access policy f^* before observing the public parameters, the scheme is said to achieve *selective-policy* security. Conversely, if the adversary chooses f^* after seeing the public parameters, the scheme achieves *adaptive-policy* security. Similarly, there exist two models for user corruption: *selective corruption* and *adaptive corruption*. Roughly, the former allows the adversary to specify in advance which users to corrupt and receive their attribute-associated secret keys, while the latter allows the adversary to corrupt users at any point during the security game and obtain their

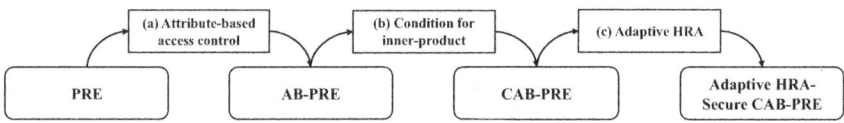

Fig. 1. Roadmap of CAB-PRE construction.

secret keys. For brevity, we say an AB-PRE scheme achieves *selective security* if it satisfies either selective-policy security or selective corruption. In contrast, a scheme achieves *adaptive security* if it meets both adaptive-policy security and adaptive corruption. Clearly, adaptive security is strictly stronger than selective security, as it models a more realistic and robust adversarial capability.

To the best of our knowledge, all existing AB-PRE schemes that achieve adaptive security rely on classical number-theoretic assumptions (e.g., [12,17]), rendering them vulnerable to quantum attacks.

Motivation. The motivation of this work is two-fold: (1) there is a lack of AB-PRE schemes that support conditional re-encryption, and (2) no existing AB-PRE construction offers adaptive HRA security in a post-quantum setting. Specifically, the motivating question is: *Can we define and construct an AB-PRE scheme that supports conditional re-encryption and achieves adaptive security against HRA under post-quantum assumptions?*

1.1 Our Contributions

In this paper, we answer the above question affirmatively by introducing a new notion called *Conditional Attribute-Based Proxy Re-Encryption* (CAB-PRE) and providing a concrete construction based on the learning with errors (LWE) assumption [2] and its lossy mode [15]. Our main contributions are two-fold:

1. *Formal Definitions and HRA Security for CAB-PRE.* We formalize a new cryptographic primitive, CAB-PRE, which extends AB-PRE by integrating conditional re-encryption capabilities. Additionally, we present an HRA security model for CAB-PRE, formalized in a multi-user setting where the adversary can *adaptively* corrupt users and obtain re-encryption keys.
2. *LWE-Based Construction of CAB-PRE for Inner-Product Predicates.* We construct a (single-hop) CAB-PRE scheme that supports fine-grained conditional re-encryption for inner-product predicates. This predicate implies range/subset queries and threshold policies, providing sufficient expressiveness for real-world applications [9]. Our scheme achieves *adaptive security against HRA* under the LWE and Lossy-LWE assumptions, ensuring post-quantum resilience.

1.2 Technical Overview

In this section, we provide a high-level overview of our construction. As illustrated in Fig. 1, we address three core challenges and introduce the roadmap of designing our construction in a step-by-step manner. At first, we construct an AB-PRE scheme by integrating attribute-based access control into an LWE-based PRE scheme. Then, we extend this AB-PRE scheme to enable fine-grained conditional re-encryption, yielding the CAB-PRE scheme. Finally, we enhance its security guarantees to achieve adaptive and HRA security. For simplicity, we omit the explicit dimensions of matrices or vectors in the following discussion.

We begin with an LWE-based PRE scheme [1], which employs the key switching technique. This technique relies on two fundamental operations: bit decomposition BD and power-of-two encoding P2 (see Definition 2). Let $\mathbf{A}_\alpha$ and $\mathbf{P}_\alpha$ be the public keys for user α, and let $\mathbf{D}_\alpha$ be the corresponding secret key, where $\mathbf{P}_\alpha = \mathbf{E} - \mathbf{A}_\alpha \mathbf{D}_\alpha$, with $\mathbf{E}$ and $\mathbf{D}_\alpha$ sampled from error distributions. The ciphertext is generated as:

$$(\mathbf{u}_0, \mathbf{u}_1) = (\mathbf{s}\mathbf{A}_\alpha + \mathbf{e}_0, \mathbf{s}\mathbf{P}_\alpha + \mathbf{e}_1 + \boldsymbol{\mu}\lfloor q/2 \rceil), \tag{1}$$

where $\boldsymbol{\mu}$ is the message, and $\mathbf{s}, \mathbf{e}_0, \mathbf{e}_1$ are sampled from appropriate error distributions. The message can be recovered by $\mathbf{u}_0 \mathbf{D}_\alpha + \mathbf{u}_1$. The re-encryption key for transforming a ciphertext from user α to user β is a matrix $\mathbf{Z}^{\mathsf{PRE}}$, defined as:

$$\mathbf{Z}^{\mathsf{PRE}} = \begin{pmatrix} \mathbf{S}\mathbf{A}_\beta + \mathbf{E}_1 & \mathbf{S}\mathbf{P}_\beta + \mathbf{E}_2 + \mathsf{P2}(\mathbf{D}_\alpha) \\ \mathbf{0} & \mathbf{I} \end{pmatrix}, \tag{2}$$

where $(\mathbf{A}_\beta, \mathbf{P}_\beta)$ are the public keys for β, and $\mathbf{S}, \mathbf{E}_1, \mathbf{E}_2$ are sampled from error distributions. Finally, the transformed ciphertext is computed as $[\mathsf{BD}(\mathbf{u}_0)\|\mathbf{u}_1] \cdot \mathbf{Z}^{\mathsf{PRE}}$, which can be decrypted by user β to recover the original message.

Challenge (a): Achieving attribute-based access control over ciphertexts. We construct an AB-PRE scheme by embedding the attribute into the secret key and the access policy into the ciphertext, allowing decryption and re-encryption only when the attribute satisfies the policy.

Let $\mathbf{A}, \mathbf{B}, \mathbf{v}$ be public parameters. A ciphertext associated with an access policy f is represented as the quadruple $(s_f, \mathbf{u}_0, u_1, \mathbf{u}_2)$, where $(\mathbf{u}_0, u_1)$ are defined as in Eq. (1), using $(\mathbf{B}, \mathbf{v})$ in place of $(\mathbf{A}_\alpha, \mathbf{P}_\alpha)$. The term s_f is a value related to the policy f, and $\mathbf{u}_2 = \mathbf{s}[\mathbf{A}_f - s_f \otimes \mathbf{G}] + \mathbf{e}_2$ (inspired by [8]), where $\mathbf{s}$ is a random vector, $\mathbf{A}_f$ is derived from $\mathbf{A}$ and f, $\mathbf{G}$ is the gadget matrix, $\otimes$ denotes the tensor product, and $\mathbf{e}_2$ is sampled from an error distribution. Let g be a new policy. Based on Eq. (2), now the re-encryption key used to transform a ciphertext under policy f to one under policy g is defined as:

$$\mathbf{Z}^{\mathsf{AB-PRE}} = \begin{pmatrix} \mathbf{R}_1 \mathbf{H} + \mathbf{R}_2 & \mathbf{R}_1 \mathbf{v} + \mathbf{r}_3 - \mathsf{P2}(\mathbf{k}) \\ \mathbf{0} & \mathbf{I} \end{pmatrix}, \tag{3}$$

where $\mathbf{H}$ is computed from the public matrices $\mathbf{A}, \mathbf{B}$ and the policy g, and $\mathbf{R}_1, \mathbf{R}_2, \mathbf{r}_3$ are sampled from error distributions. The secret key $\mathbf{k}$ associated with attribute x satisfies $[\mathbf{B}\|\mathbf{A}_{x,r}]\mathbf{k} = \mathbf{v}$, where $\mathbf{A}_{x,r}$ is derived from $\mathbf{A}, x$, and a tag r[1]. Given another tag r' for policy f, if the attribute x satisfies

---
[1] The tag r (resp. r') refers to the output of the P.Eval (resp. P.ConstrainEval) algorithm in the conforming cPRF, evaluated on an attribute (resp. a policy). These tags are defined in the KeyGen and Dec algorithms (see Fig. 3).

f (i.e., $f(x) = 1$) and $r' \ne r$, then $\mathbf{u}'_2 = \mathbf{sA}_{x,r} + \mathbf{e}'_2$ can be computed from $\mathbf{u}_2$. Finally, the ciphertext encrypted under f can be decrypted using $u_1 - [\mathbf{u}_0 \| \mathbf{u}'_2]\mathbf{k}$, and supported transformation into another ciphertext under policy g via $[\mathsf{BD}(\mathbf{u}_0 \| \mathbf{u}'_2) \| u_1] \cdot \mathbf{Z}^{\mathsf{AB-PRE}}$. Therefore, we can obtain an AB-PRE scheme in this way.

Challenge (b): Achieving conditional re-encryption for inner-product predicates. Our CAB-PRE construction involves ciphertexts of two levels. The first-level ciphertext $(s_f, \mathbf{u}_0, \mathbf{u}_1, \mathbf{u}_2)$ is defined as in the AB-PRE described above. The second-level ciphertext extends the first-level structure by adding a component associated with a condition vector, enabling conditional re-encryption based on inner-product predicates. To enforce this, the condition is also embedded into the re-encryption key.

Let $(\mathbf{A}, \mathbf{B}, \mathbf{V}, \mathbf{D})$ be the public parameters, and let $\boldsymbol{\alpha}$ and $\boldsymbol{\beta}$ represent two condition vectors. The additional component in the second-level ciphertext is $\mathbf{u}_3 = \mathbf{s}[\mathbf{D} + \mathbf{h} \otimes \mathsf{P2}(\boldsymbol{\alpha})] + \mathbf{e}_3$, which is inspired by [9], where $\mathbf{s}, \mathbf{h}$ are random vectors, and $\mathbf{e}_3$ is drawn from an error distribution. Based on Eq. (3), the re-encryption key embedding the condition vector $\boldsymbol{\beta}$ is defined as:

$$\mathbf{Z}^{\mathsf{CAB-PRE}} = \begin{pmatrix} \mathbf{R}_1 \mathbf{H} + \mathbf{R}_2 & \mathbf{R}_1 \mathbf{V} + \mathbf{R}_3 - \mathsf{P2}(\mathbf{d}) \otimes \mathbf{1} \\ 0 & \mathsf{BD}(\boldsymbol{\beta}) \otimes \mathbf{1} \end{pmatrix},$$

where $\mathbf{H}$ is derived from $\mathbf{A}, \mathbf{B}$ and the policy g, $\mathbf{d}$ is sampled using the trapdoor $\mathbf{T_B}$ of $\mathbf{B}$, and $\mathbf{R}_1, \mathbf{R}_2, \mathbf{R}_3$ are sampled from error distributions. The re-encryption proceeds if the following conditions are satisfied: (i) $f(x) = 1$, (ii) $r' \ne r$, and (iii) $\boldsymbol{\alpha} \cdot \boldsymbol{\beta} = 0$. The re-encryption key then transforms the second-level ciphertext under the tuple $(f, \boldsymbol{\alpha})$ into a first-level ciphertext under the policy g, which can be decrypted using the same method as in AB-PRE. In this way, we obtain a CAB-PRE scheme. Please refer to Fig. 3 and 4 for more details.

Challenge (c): Achieving adaptive HRA security for CAB-PRE. The HRA security of CAB-PRE focuses on protecting the second-level ciphertext under the target policy and target vector, even when the adversary can adaptively obtain re-encryption keys and corrupt users. We achieve HRA security against adaptive corruption by defining a state table to record the adversary's queries under distinct cases.

To prove adaptive HRA security, an existing method is based on recoding graph [11], where nodes denote users and edges denote the re-encryption keys and re-encryptions accessible to the adversary. However, this strategy cannot be directly applied to CAB-PRE, as each user in CAB-PRE is represented by an attribute vector $x \in \{0,1\}^l$, resulting in 2^l possible users, making it impractical to explicitly construct such a graph. Instead, we define a relation that systematically tracks the dependencies between issued re-encryption keys and re-encryptions by maintaining a state table (see Sect. 3 for details). For the target policy f^* and target vector $\boldsymbol{\alpha}^*$, if the attribute y is corrupted, the adversary is prohibited from accessing any re-encryption key associated with a tuple $(x, \boldsymbol{\beta}, g)$ such that $f^*(x) = 1$, $\boldsymbol{\alpha}^* \cdot \boldsymbol{\beta} = 0$, and $g(y) = 1$, thereby preventing trivial attacks. However, the adversary remains free to obtain re-encryption keys (and subsequent re-encryptions) for any x that cannot decrypt the re-encrypted challenge ciphertext. For these re-encryption keys $\mathbf{Z}^{\mathsf{CAB-PRE}}$, we show that the generation of $\mathbf{d}$ can be indistinguishably replaced by sampling it independently using a public trapdoor $\mathbf{T_G}$ instead of the trapdoor $\mathbf{T_B}$, causing the matrix $\mathbf{B}$ to sample uniformly random. Under this transformation, we apply the LWE assumption to prove the pseudorandomness of the challenge ciphertext components $(\mathbf{u}_0^*, \mathbf{u}_1^*)$, and then extend the argument to $\mathbf{u}_2^*$ by substituting $\mathbf{u}_2^* = \mathbf{u}_0^* \mathbf{R}$, where $\mathbf{R}$ has a small norm. Finally, we invoke the Lossy-LWE assumption to prove the pseudorandomness of $\mathbf{u}_3^*$, thereby completing the proof of adaptive HRA security.

2 Preliminaries

Notations. Bold symbols (e.g., $\mathbf{a}, \mathbf{A}$) denote matrices or vectors, while regular lowercase letters (e.g., u, e) represent individual elements. We use $(\mathbf{A}\|\mathbf{B})$ and $(\mathbf{A}; \mathbf{B})$ to indicate horizontal and vertical concatenation, respectively. A random sample from a distribution over a set X is denoted by $x \xleftarrow{\$} X$. For a vector $\mathbf{u}$, $\|\mathbf{u}\|$ denotes its Euclidean norm. For a matrix $\mathbf{R} \in \mathbb{Z}^{n \times m}$, $\widetilde{\mathbf{R}}$ denotes its Gram-Schmidt orthogonalization, and $\|\mathbf{R}\|_\infty$ is the maximum element in $\mathbf{R}$.

2.1 Lattice Background

Lattices. For a prime q, given $\mathbf{A} \in \mathbb{Z}_q^{n \times m}$ and $\mathbf{u} \in \mathbb{Z}_q^n$, $\Lambda_q^\perp(\mathbf{A}) = \{\mathbf{v} \in \mathbb{Z}^m : \mathbf{A}\mathbf{v} = \mathbf{0} \pmod q\}$ and $\Lambda_q^{\mathbf{u}}(\mathbf{A}) = \{\mathbf{v} \in \mathbb{Z}^m : \mathbf{A}\mathbf{v} = \mathbf{u} \pmod q\}$ are two lattices.

Gadget Matrix [19]. Let $n, q \in \mathbb{Z}$, $\mathbf{g} = (1, 2, 4, \cdots, 2^{\lceil \log q \rceil - 1}) \in \mathbb{Z}_q^{1 \times \lceil \log q \rceil}$ and $m = n \lceil \log q \rceil$. The gadget matrix is defined as $\mathbf{G} = \mathbf{g} \otimes \mathbf{I}_n \in \mathbb{Z}_q^{n \times m}$. The lattice $\Lambda_q^\perp(\mathbf{G})$ has a public known basis $\mathbf{T_G}$ with $\|\widetilde{\mathbf{T_G}}\| \leq \sqrt{5}$.

Discrete Gaussian [3,4]. Let $L \subseteq \mathbb{Z}^m$. For any vector $\mathbf{c} \in \mathbb{R}^m$ and any positive parameter $\sigma \in \mathbb{R}$, define: $\rho_{\sigma,\mathbf{c}}(\mathbf{x}) = \exp(-\pi \frac{\|\mathbf{x}-\mathbf{c}\|^2}{\sigma^2})$ and $\rho_{\sigma,\mathbf{c}}(L) = \sum_{\mathbf{x} \in L} \rho_{\sigma,\mathbf{c}}(\mathbf{x})$. A discrete Gaussian distribution on L with center $\mathbf{c}$ and parameter σ is $\mathcal{D}_{L,\sigma,\mathbf{c}}(\mathbf{x}) = \frac{\rho_{\sigma,\mathbf{c}}(\mathbf{x})}{\rho_{\sigma,\mathbf{c}}(L)}$. The distribution $\mathcal{D}_{L,\sigma}$ ($\mathbf{c} = \mathbf{0}$ when omitted) is most often defined over a lattice $L = \Lambda_q^\perp(\mathbf{A})$ or $L = \Lambda_q^{\mathbf{u}}(\mathbf{A})$.

Lemma 1 (Tailcut Inequality [3,4]). *Let $q \geq 2$, $m > n$ and $\mathbf{A}$ be a matrix in $\mathbb{Z}_q^{n \times m}$. Let $\mathbf{T_A}$ be a basis for $\Lambda_q^\perp(\mathbf{A})$ and $\tau \geq \|\widetilde{\mathbf{T_A}}\| \cdot \omega(\sqrt{\log m})$. For all $\mathbf{u} \in \mathbb{Z}_q^n$, we have $\Pr[\mathbf{x} \xleftarrow{\$} \mathcal{D}_{\Lambda_q^{\mathbf{u}}(\mathbf{A}),\tau} : \|\mathbf{x}\| > \tau\sqrt{m}] \leq \mathsf{negl}(\lambda)$.*

Definition 1 (Bounded Distributions [24]). *A distribution χ supported over $\mathbb{Z}$ is (B, ϵ)-bounded, if we have $\Pr[x \xleftarrow{\$} \chi : |x| > B] < \epsilon$; A distribution $\tilde{\chi}$ supported over $\mathbb{Z}$ is (B, ϵ)-swallowing if for all $y \in [-B, B] \cap \mathbb{Z}$, we have that $\tilde{\chi}$ and $y + \tilde{\chi}$ are within ϵ statistical distance. We omit the ϵ when it denotes a negligible function in the security parameter.*

Lemma 2 (Lattice Algorithms [6]). *Let $q > 2$, $m \geq O(n \log q)$, $m_1, m_2 > 0$, we describe the following lattice sampling algorithms:*

- TrapGen($1^n, m, q$): *This algorithm outputs a matrix $\mathbf{A} \in \mathbb{Z}_q^{n \times m}$ and a full-rank matrix $\mathbf{T_A} \in \mathbb{Z}^{m \times m}$, where $\mathbf{T_A}$ is a basis for $\Lambda_q^\perp(\mathbf{A})$ and $\|\widetilde{\mathbf{T_A}}\| = O(\sqrt{n \log q})$. The distribution of $\mathbf{A}$ is $2^{-\Omega(n)}$-close to uniform.*
- SamplePre($\mathbf{A}, \mathbf{T_A}, \mathbf{u}, \tau$): *Given a matrix $\mathbf{A} \in \mathbb{Z}_q^{n \times m}$, a basis $\mathbf{T_A}$ of $\Lambda_q^\perp(\mathbf{A})$, a vector $\mathbf{u} \in \mathbb{Z}_q^n$, and a Gaussian parameter $\tau \geq \|\widetilde{\mathbf{T_A}}\| \cdot \omega(\sqrt{\log m})$, this algorithm outputs $\mathbf{e} \in \mathbb{Z}^m$ such that $\mathbf{Ae} = \mathbf{u}$, sampled from a distribution close to $\mathcal{D}_{\Lambda_q^\mathbf{u}(\mathbf{A}), \tau}$.*
- ExtendRight($\mathbf{A}, \mathbf{T_A}, \mathbf{B}$): *Given matrices $\mathbf{A} \in \mathbb{Z}_q^{n \times m_1}, \mathbf{B} \in \mathbb{Z}_q^{n \times m_2}$ and a basis $\mathbf{T_A}$ of $\Lambda_q^\perp(\mathbf{A})$, this algorithm outputs a basis $\mathbf{T}_{(\mathbf{A} \| \mathbf{B})}$ for $\Lambda_q^\perp(\mathbf{A} \| \mathbf{B})$ such that $\|\widetilde{\mathbf{T_A}}\| = \|\widetilde{\mathbf{T}_{(\mathbf{A} \| \mathbf{B})}}\|$.*
- ExtendLeft($\mathbf{A}, \mathbf{G}, \mathbf{T_G}, \mathbf{R}$): *Given matrices $\mathbf{A} \in \mathbb{Z}_q^{n \times k}, \mathbf{G} \in \mathbb{Z}_q^{n \times m}, \mathbf{R} \in \mathbb{Z}^{k \times m}$ and a basis $\mathbf{T_G}$ of $\Lambda_q^\perp(\mathbf{G})$, this algorithm outputs a basis $\mathbf{T_H}$ for $\Lambda_q^\perp(\mathbf{H})$, where $\mathbf{H} = (\mathbf{A} \| \mathbf{AR} + \mathbf{G})$, such that $\|\widetilde{\mathbf{T_H}}\| \leq \|\widetilde{\mathbf{T_G}}\|(1 + \|\mathbf{R}\|)$.*
- RandBasis($\mathbf{A}, \mathbf{T_A}, \tau$): *Given a matrix $\mathbf{A} \in \mathbb{Z}_q^{n \times m}$, a basis $\mathbf{T_A}$ of $\Lambda_q^\perp(\mathbf{A})$, and a Gaussian parameter $\tau = \|\widetilde{\mathbf{T_A}}\| \cdot \omega(\sqrt{\log m})$, this algorithm outputs a basis $\mathbf{T'_A}$ for $\Lambda_q^\perp(\mathbf{A})$ sampled from a distribution that is statistically close to $\mathcal{D}_{\Lambda_q^\perp(\mathbf{A}), \tau}^m$. Note that $\|\widetilde{\mathbf{T'_A}}\| < \tau \sqrt{m}$ with all but negligible probability.*

2.2 Circuit Description, Lattice Evaluation, and Vector Decomposition

Circuit Description and Lattice Evaluation [24]. In our CAB-PRE scheme, policies and functions are represented as Boolean circuits $f : \{0,1\}^{l_I} \to \{0,1\}^{l_O}$. To efficiently operate on Boolean gates in the encrypted domain, we exploit Lattice Evaluation (defined as in Theorem 1), which enables us to encode Boolean circuits f, along with their l_I-length input $\{0,1\}^{l_I}$ and l_O length output $\{0,1\}^{l_O}$, into specific matrix forms within a lattice structure. Roughly, lattice evaluation involves two primary algorithms, EvalF and EvalFX:

- The EvalF($f, \mathbf{A}$) transforms any Boolean circuit f into a matrix $\mathbf{H}$ using a public matrix $\mathbf{A}$. The $\mathbf{H}$ can be viewed as the pre-compiled program of circuit f. It encapsulates all of f's computational logic in an encoded form, allowing us to perform computations on relevant data without exposing f's internal structure.
- The EvalFX($f, x, \mathbf{A}$) allows for computing the result for a specific input x without directly executing Boolean logic. It outputs another matrix $\hat{\mathbf{H}}$, which represents the encrypted form of the result after evaluating circuit f on input x. Especially, it is not the direct binary output $f(x)$, but a matrix encoding information about $f(x)$.

Besides, lattice evaluation supports circuit composition by converting it into matrix multiplication. If we compose two circuits f and g, forming a new circuit $g \circ f$ (i.e., f is executed first, then g), then their pre-compiled programs also have a direct algebraic relationship. Specifically, if $\mathbf{H}_f$ is the program for f, and $\mathbf{H}_g$ is the program for g, then the program $\mathbf{H}_{g \circ f}$ for the composite circuit $g \circ f$ satisfies: $\mathbf{H}_f \mathbf{H}_g = \mathbf{H}_{g \circ f}$. This means the evaluation of composite functions can be achieved through matrix multiplication, enabling the execution of multi-step logic on ciphertexts. Below is the formal definition of lattice evaluation:

Theorem 1. *Let $n, q, l, k \in \mathbb{N}$ and $m = n\lceil \log q \rceil$, there exist two deterministic algorithms called* EvalF *and* EvalFX. *For any depth d boolean circuit $f: \{0,1\}^l \to \{0,1\}^k$, for every $x \in \{0,1\}^l$ and for any matrix $\mathbf{A} \in \mathbb{Z}_q^{n \times ml}$, the outputs $\mathbf{H} \leftarrow$* EvalF$(f, \mathbf{A})$ *and $\hat{\mathbf{H}} \leftarrow$* EvalFX$(f, x, \mathbf{A})$ *are both in $\mathbb{Z}^{ml \times mk}$, satisfying $\|\mathbf{H}\|_\infty$, $\|\hat{\mathbf{H}}\|_\infty \leq (2m)^d$ and $[\mathbf{A} - x \otimes \mathbf{G}]\hat{\mathbf{H}} = \mathbf{A}\mathbf{H} - f(x) \otimes \mathbf{G} \pmod{q}$. Moreover, for circuits $f: \{0,1\}^l \to \{0,1\}^k$ and $g: \{0,1\}^k \to \{0,1\}^t$, the outputs $\mathbf{H}_f \leftarrow$* EvalF$(f, \mathbf{A})$, $\mathbf{H}_g \leftarrow$ EvalF$(g, \mathbf{AH}_f)$ *and $\mathbf{H}_{g \circ f} \leftarrow$* EvalF$(g \circ f, \mathbf{A})$ *satisfy $\mathbf{H}_f \mathbf{H}_g = \mathbf{H}_{g \circ f}$, where $g \circ f$ denotes the circuit composition of g and f.*

Vector Decomposition [7]. To control error growth in lattice-based cryptography, bit decomposition (BD) and power-of-two encoding (P2) are used to transform vectors into special forms that preserve inner products modulo q.

Definition 2. *There are two deterministic functions defined as:* BD$(\mathbf{v})$ *that, given a vector $\mathbf{v} \in \mathbb{Z}_q^{1 \times n}$, let $v_i \in \{0,1\}^n$ be such that $\mathbf{v} = \sum_{i=0}^{\lceil \log q \rceil - 1} 2^i v_i$, outputs a vector $\tilde{v} = (v_0, \cdots, v_{\lceil \log q \rceil - 1}) \in \{0,1\}^{1 \times n \lceil \log q \rceil}$;* P2$(\mathbf{x})$ *that, given a vector $\mathbf{x} \in \mathbb{Z}_q^n$, outputs a vector $\bar{\mathbf{x}} = (\mathbf{x}; 2\mathbf{x}; \cdots; 2^{\lceil \log q \rceil - 1}\mathbf{x}) \in \mathbb{Z}_q^{n \lceil \log q \rceil}$. It is easy to check that* BD$(\mathbf{v}) \cdot$ P2$(\mathbf{x}) = \mathbf{v} \cdot \mathbf{x} \pmod{q}$.

2.3 LWE Assumption and Leftover Hash Lemma

Definition 3 (LWE Assumption [21]). *Let λ be the security parameter, $n = n(\lambda)$ and $q = q(\lambda)$ be integers and let $\chi = \chi(\lambda)$ be a probability distribution over $\mathbb{Z}$. The LWE$_{n,q,\chi}$ problem states that for all $m = $ poly(n), $\mathbf{A} \xleftarrow{\$} \mathbb{Z}_q^{n \times m}$, $\mathbf{s} \xleftarrow{\$} \mathbb{Z}_q^n$, $\mathbf{e} \xleftarrow{\$} \chi^m$, and $\mathbf{u} \xleftarrow{\$} \mathbb{Z}_q^{1 \times m}$, it holds that $(\mathbf{A}, \mathbf{s}^T\mathbf{A} + \mathbf{e}^T)$ and $(\mathbf{A}, \mathbf{u})$ are computationally indistinguishable. The Hermite Normal Form variant (HNF-LWE) is identical to the above except for $\mathbf{s} \xleftarrow{\$} \chi^n$.*

Definition 4 (Lossy Mode for LWE [15]). *The LWE instance $(\mathbf{A}, \mathbf{s}^T\mathbf{A} + \mathbf{e}^T) \in \mathbb{Z}_q^{n \times m} \times \mathbb{Z}_q^{1 \times m}$ uniquely determines a secret vector $\mathbf{s} \in \mathbb{Z}_q^n$, provided the matrix $\mathbf{A}$ is drawn uniformly from $\mathbb{Z}_q^{n \times m}$ with sufficiently large m. However, suppose sample $\mathbf{A}$ from a specialized distribution that is computationally indistinguishable from the uniform distribution over $\mathbb{Z}_q^{n \times m}$. In that case, the information leakage regarding the secret $\mathbf{s}$ by the pair $(\mathbf{A}, \mathbf{s}^T\mathbf{A} + \mathbf{e}^T)$ is negligible. Consequently, this variant of the LWE problem, which does not reveal significant information about the secret vector, is commonly referred to as the "lossy mode". A reduction from standard LWE to Lossy-LWE was provided in [13].*

Lemma 3 (Generalized Leftover Hash Lemma [10]). *Let $q > 2$ be a prime and $m > (n+1)\log q + \omega(\log n)$. Let $\mathbf{S} \xleftarrow{\$} \{1, -1\}^{m \times k}$, where $k = k(n)$. Choose matrices $\mathbf{A} \xleftarrow{\$} \mathbb{Z}_q^{n \times m}$ and $\mathbf{B} \xleftarrow{\$} \mathbb{Z}_q^{n \times k}$. Then, for all vectors $\mathbf{e} \in \mathbb{Z}_q^m$, the distribution $(\mathbf{A}, \mathbf{AS}, \mathbf{S}^T\mathbf{e})$ is statistically close to the distribution $(\mathbf{A}, \mathbf{B}, \mathbf{S}^T\mathbf{e})$.*

2.4 Conforming cPRF

A conforming constrained pseudorandom function (conforming cPRF) [24] allows a master secret key holder to derive constrained keys, enabling evaluation on a given input to a specific output (while outputs on other inputs remain indistinguishable from random). It extends standard constrained PRFs by supporting (1) gradual evaluation, which allows splitting the evaluation into key derivation and input evaluation steps while preserving correctness, and (2) key simulation, which enables generating indistinguishable constrained keys without the master secret key. Two concrete constructions are proposed in [24], supporting both prefix policies and t-conjunctive normal form (t-CNF) formulas.

Definition 5 (Conforming cPRF [24]). *Let $\mathcal{F} : \{0,1\}^l \to \{0,1\}$ be a family of functions. A conforming cPRF is defined by four algorithms* (Setup, Eval, Constrain, ConstrainEval): *(a)* Setup(1^λ) *inputs the security parameter λ, and outputs a public parameter* pp *and a master secret key* msk; *(b)* Eval(msk, x) *outputs $y \in \{0,1\}^k$ for input* msk *and a bit-string $x \in \{0,1\}^l$; (c)* Constrain(msk, f) *outputs a constrained key* sk$_f$ *for input* msk *and a function $f \in \mathcal{F}$; (d)* ConstrainEval(sk$_f$, x) *outputs $y' \in \{0,1\}^k$ for input* sk$_f$ *and $x \in \{0,1\}^l$. If $f(x) = 1$ holds, we have* Eval(msk, x) = ConstrainEval(sk$_f$, x).

In addition to standard pseudorandomness (see [24] for the definition), a conforming cPRF satisfies the following two properties:

Gradual Evaluation. Assume that Constrain is deterministic. For any fixed pp, $f \in \mathcal{F}$, and $x \in \{0,1\}^l$ s.t. $f(x) = 1$, let σ denote msk and define the following circuits: (a) $U_{\sigma \to x} : \{0,1\}^\lambda \to \{0,1\}^k$ inputs msk and computes Eval(msk, x); (b) $U_{\sigma \to f} : \{0,1\}^\lambda \to \{0,1\}^{l_f}$ inputs msk and computes Constrain(msk, f); (c) $U_{f \to x} : \{0,1\}^{l_f} \to \{0,1\}^k$ inputs sk$_f$ and computes ConstrainEval(sk$_f$, x). These circuits satisfy that $U_{\sigma \to x} = U_{f \to x} \circ U_{\sigma \to f}$. By employing the circuit composition introduced in Sect. 2.2, after transforming three circuits into matrices, we also have $\mathbf{H}_{\sigma \to f} \mathbf{H}_{f \to x} = \mathbf{H}_{\sigma \to x}$.

Key Simulation. There exists a Probabilistic Polynomial-Time (PPT) algorithm KeySim(pp, f) that, given the public parameter pp and a function $f \in \mathcal{F}$, outputs a simulated constrained key sk$_f$ such that no PPT adversary $\mathcal{A}$ (unknown Eval(msk, x) where $f(x) = 1$) can distinguish it from a real key generated by Constrain(msk, f) with non-negligible advantage.

3 Conditional Attribute-Based Proxy Re-Encryption

In this section, we present the formal definition of CAB-PRE and formalize its adaptive HRA security. Our definition focuses on single-hop PRE, where ciphertexts can be re-encrypted only once. This kind of PRE is often preferred over its multi-hop variant, as the latter allows the proxy to perform unrestricted re-encryption using multiple re-encryption keys, potentially violating the delegator's intended control. In CAB-PRE, the first-level ciphertext (generated by the Enc_1 algorithm) is produced based on an access policy and a message, and is designed to be non-re-encryptable. By contrast, the second-level ciphertext (generated by the Enc_2 algorithm) incorporates additional specified conditions and can be re-encrypted into a first-level ciphertext only if the conditions embedded in the re-encryption key match those in the ciphertext. Accordingly, we define two distinct decryption algorithms to handle these two levels of ciphertexts. The syntax of the CAB-PRE scheme is formalized as below.

Definition 6 (CAB-PRE). *Let $\mathcal{M}$ be a plaintext space, $\mathcal{W}$ be a condition space, and let $\mathcal{F} : \mathcal{X} \to \{0,1\}$ be a function class, where $\mathcal{X}$ denotes the attribute space. A CAB-PRE scheme $\Pi_{\mathsf{CAB-PRE}}$ for policies in $\mathcal{F}$ comprises the following algorithms.*

$\mathsf{Setup}(1^\lambda) \to (\mathsf{pp}, \mathsf{msk})$. *On input the security parameter λ, the setup algorithm outputs the public parameters pp along with a master secret key msk. The public parameters pp are implicitly used as input to all other algorithms.*

$\mathsf{KeyGen}(\mathsf{msk}, x) \to \mathsf{sk}_x$. *On input a master secret key msk and an attribute $x \in \mathcal{X}$, the key generation algorithm outputs a secret key sk_x.*

$\mathsf{Enc}_1(f, \mu) \to \mathsf{ct}_f^1$. *On input a policy $f \in \mathcal{F}$ and a message $\mu \in \mathcal{M}$, the first-level encryption algorithm outputs a first-level ciphertext ct_f^1 associated with the policy f, which cannot be re-encrypted anymore.*

$\mathsf{Enc}_2(f, w, \mu) \to \mathsf{ct}_f^2$. *On input a policy $f \in \mathcal{F}$, a condition $w \in \mathcal{W}$ and a message $\mu \in \mathcal{M}$, the second-level encryption algorithm outputs a second-level ciphertext ct_f^2 associated with the policy f and condition w, which can be further re-encryptd to a first-level ciphertext.*

$\mathsf{Dec}_1(\mathsf{sk}_x, \mathsf{ct}_f^1) \to \mu/\bot$. *On input a secret key sk_x and a first-level ciphertext ct_f^1, the first-level decryption algorithm outputs a message $\mu \in \mathcal{M}$ if $f(x) = 1$, else outputs an error symbol $\bot$.*

$\mathsf{Dec}_2(\mathsf{sk}_x, \mathsf{ct}_f^2) \to \mu/\bot$. *On input a secret key sk_x and a second-level ciphertext ct_f^2, the second-level decryption algorithm outputs a message $\mu \in \mathcal{M}$ if $f(x) = 1$, else outputs an error symbol $\bot$.*

$\mathsf{ReKeyGen}(\mathsf{sk}_x, g, w') \to \mathsf{rk}_{x \to g}^{w'}$. *Given a secret key sk_x, a policy $g \in \mathcal{F}$, and a condition $w' \in \mathcal{W}$, this algorithm outputs a re-encryption key $\mathsf{rk}_{x \to g}^{w'}$.*

$\mathsf{ReEnc}(\mathsf{rk}_{x \to g}^{w'}, \mathsf{ct}_f^2) \to \mathsf{ct}_g^1/\bot$. *Given a re-encryption key $\mathsf{rk}_{x \to g}^{w'}$ and a second-level ciphertext ct_f^2, this algorithm outputs a first-level ciphertext ct_g^1 associated with the policy g if $f(x) = 1 \wedge w \models w'^2$, else outputs an error symbol $\bot$.*

---

[2] The expression $f(x) = 1 \wedge w \models w'$ indicates that both $f(x) = 1$ and $w \models w'$ hold, where $f(x) = 1$ means the attribute x satisfies the access policy f, and $w \models w'$ signifies that the condition w matches w'. Conversely, $f(x) = 0$ indicates that x does not satisfy f, and $w \not\models w'$ denotes a mismatch between the two conditions.

---

1. **Phase 1:** $(pp, msk) \leftarrow \mathsf{Setup}(1^\lambda)$, set $\mathsf{numCt} := 0$, $\mathsf{K} := \emptyset$, $\mathsf{C} := \emptyset$, $\mathsf{Derive} := \emptyset$, and $f^*, w^* := \bot$
2. **Phase 2:** $b' \leftarrow \mathcal{A}^{\mathcal{O}_{\mathsf{KeyGen}}(\cdot), \mathcal{O}_{\mathsf{Enc}_2}(\cdot), \mathcal{O}_{\mathsf{ReKey}}(\cdot), \mathcal{O}_{\mathsf{ReEnc}}(\cdot), \mathcal{O}_{\mathsf{Cha}}(\cdot)}(1^\lambda, pp)$
3. **Guess:** Return b'

$\mathcal{O}_{\mathsf{KeyGen}}(x)$:

1. If one of the following three conditions holds then return $\bot$: (i) $f^*(x) = 1$ (to avoid **TA1**); (ii) $\exists (g, \mathsf{Null}, k) \in \mathsf{C}$ with $k \in \mathsf{Derive}$ and $g(x) = 1$ (to avoid **TA2**); (iii) (z, g, w') has been queried in $\mathcal{O}_{\mathsf{ReKey}}$ and $(f^*, w^*, k) \in \mathsf{C}$ with $k \in \mathsf{Derive}$ s.t. $(z \notin \mathsf{K} \wedge f^*(z) = 1) \wedge (w^* \models w')$ and $g(x) = 1$ (to avoid **TA3**)
2. Compute $\mathsf{sk}_x \leftarrow \mathsf{KeyGen}(msk, x)$, add (x, sk_x) to K, and return sk_x

$\mathcal{O}_{\mathsf{Enc}_2}(f, w, \mu)$:

1. Compute $\mathsf{ct}_f^2 \leftarrow \mathsf{Enc}_2(f, w, \mu)$, set $\mathsf{numCt} := \mathsf{numCt} + 1$, and add ct_f^2 to C with (f, w, numCt)
2. Return $(\mathsf{numCt}, \mathsf{ct}_f^2)$

$\mathcal{O}_{\mathsf{ReKey}}(x, g, w')$:

1. If there exist $y \in \mathsf{K} \wedge g(y) = 1$ and $(f^*, w^*, k) \in \mathsf{C}$ with $k \in \mathsf{Derive}$ s.t. $(x \notin \mathsf{K} \wedge f^*(x) = 1) \wedge (w^* \models w')$ then return $\bot$ (to avoid **TA3**)
2. Compute $\mathsf{rk}_{x \to g}^{w'} \leftarrow \mathsf{ReKeyGen}(\mathsf{sk}_x, g, w')$ and return $\mathsf{rk}_{x \to g}^{w'}$

$\mathcal{O}_{\mathsf{ReEnc}}((x, g, w'), (f, w, k))$:

1. If one of the following holds then return $\bot$: (1) $w \not\models w'$; (2) there is no value in C with (f, w, k); (3) $f(x) = 0$; (4) $\exists y \in \mathsf{K} \wedge g(y) = 1$ s.t. $k \in \mathsf{Deriv}$ (to avoid **TA2**)
2. Compute $\mathsf{ct}_g^1 \leftarrow \mathsf{ReEnc}(\mathsf{rk}_{x \to g}^{w'}, \mathsf{ct}_f^2)$, $\mathsf{numCt} := \mathsf{numCt} + 1$, add ct_g^1 to C with $(g, \mathsf{Null}, \mathsf{numCt})$
3. If $k \in \mathsf{Deriv}$, $\mathsf{Deriv} := \mathsf{Deriv} \cup \{\mathsf{numCt}\}$. Finally, return $(\mathsf{numCt}, \mathsf{ct}_g^1)$

$\mathcal{O}_{\mathsf{Cha}}(f^*, w^*, (\mu_0^*, \mu_1^*))$:

1. If one of the following holds then return $\bot$: (1) $\exists x \in \mathsf{K}$ s.t. $f^*(x) = 1$ (to avoid **TA1**); (2) $\exists (y \in \mathsf{K} \wedge g(y) = 1)$ and (x, g, w') has been queried in $\mathcal{O}_{\mathsf{ReKey}}$ s.t. $(x \notin \mathsf{K} \wedge f^*(x) = 1) \wedge (w^* \models w')$ (to avoid **TA3**)
2. Choose $b \leftarrow \{0, 1\}$, compute $\mathsf{ct}_{f^*}^2 \leftarrow \mathsf{Enc}_2(f^*, w^*, \mu_b^*)$, and $\mathsf{numCt} := \mathsf{numCt} + 1$
3. $\mathsf{Deriv} := \mathsf{Deriv} \cup \{\mathsf{numCt}\}$, add $\mathsf{ct}_{f^*}^2$ to C with $(f^*, w^*, \mathsf{numCt})$. Finally, return $(\mathsf{numCt}, \mathsf{ct}_{f^*}^2)$

Fig. 2. The Adaptive HRA Security Game for CAB-PRE.

Next, we consider ciphertext indistinguishability under adaptive HRA security for CAB-PRE. The notion of HRA security for AB-PRE was first introduced by Susilo et al. [23], but their security model is limited to the selective setting, where the adversary must designate the challenge item at the start of the security game. In contrast, we consider a stronger variant that allows for adaptive policy and further extend the model to support adaptive corruption.

Definition 7 (CAB-PRE: Adaptive HRA Security). *Given a security parameter λ, we say the scheme $\Pi_{\mathsf{CAB-PRE}}$ is single-hop, adaptively HRA-secure if for all PPT adversaries $\mathcal{A}$, there is a negligible function $\mathsf{negl}(\lambda)$ s.t. $\mathsf{Adv}_{\mathcal{A},\Pi_{\mathsf{CAB-PRE}}}^{\mathsf{HRA}} = |\Pr[b' = b] - 1/2| \leq \mathsf{negl}(\lambda)$, where the experiment is given in Fig. 2.*

To formally define adaptive HRA security, we present an experiment-based security model, as illustrated in Fig. 2. After generating pp, the challenger $\mathcal{C}$ initializes the following state variables: (1) a counter numCt to track the number of generated ciphertexts; (2) a list K to store secret keys; (3) a repository C to record ciphertexts; (4) a set Derive to track the index of the challenge ciphertext

Table 1. Dependencies Between Re-Encryption Keys and Re-Encryptions

Relation	$y \in \mathsf{K} \wedge g(y)=0$		$y \in \mathsf{K} \wedge g(y)=1$		$y \notin \mathsf{K} \wedge g(y)=0$		$y \notin \mathsf{K} \wedge g(y)=1$	
$x \in \mathsf{K} \wedge f(x)=0$	H→H	H→H	H→H	H→H	H→H	H→H	H→H	H→H
$x \in \mathsf{K} \wedge f(x)=1$	C→H	C→H	C→C	C→H	C→H	C→H	C→H	C→H
$x \notin \mathsf{K} \wedge f(x)=0$	H→H	H→H	H→H	H→H	H→H	H→H	H→H	H→H
$x \notin \mathsf{K} \wedge f(x)=1$	H→H	H→H	**[H→C]**	H→H	H→H	H→H	H→H	H→H

and its re-encrypted versions; and (5) two symbols f^* and w^* to record the challenge policy and condition. The adversary $\mathcal{A}$ can then adaptively issue four types of oracle queries:

- Key Generation Query ($\mathcal{O}_{\mathsf{KeyGen}}$): output a secret key sk_x, stored in K;
- Encryption Query ($\mathcal{O}_{\mathsf{Enc}_2}$): output a second-level ciphertext ct_f^2, indexed by numCT and stored in the set C. These ciphertexts can later be re-encrypted via the $\mathcal{O}_{\mathsf{ReEnc}}$ query;
- Re-Encryption Key Query ($\mathcal{O}_{\mathsf{ReKey}}$): output a re-encryption key $\mathsf{rk}_{x \to g}^{w'}$;
- Re-Encryption Query ($\mathcal{O}_{\mathsf{ReEnc}}$): output a re-encrypted ciphertext ct_g^1.

At last, $\mathcal{A}$ submits a challenge tuple $(f^*, w^*, (\mu_0^*, \mu_1^*))$ and receives a challenge ciphertext $\mathsf{ct}_{f^*}^2$, which encrypts μ_b^* under a hidden bit b that $\mathcal{A}$ aims to guess.

In this model, we maintain a state table (see Table 1) based on the relationships among attributes x, y, policies f, g, and conditions w, w', which defines the dependencies between re-encryption keys and re-encryptions queried by the adversary. For simplicity, we use $x \in \mathsf{K}$ to indicate that the attribute x is corrupted and the adversary knows the corresponding secret key sk_x; conversely, $x \notin \mathsf{K}$ means the key is unknown to the adversary. As illustrated in Table 1, the gray columns represent cases where the condition w matches w', i.e., $w \models w'$, while the white columns indicate mismatches, i.e., $w \not\models w'$. We denote H (honest) as a user from whom the adversary either lacks the attribute-related secret key or cannot use it to decrypt the given ciphertext, and C (corrupted) as a user from whom the adversary both possesses the secret key and can decrypt the given ciphertext. The notation $i \to j$, with $i, j \in \{\mathsf{H}, \mathsf{C}\}$, indicates that the adversary initiates the queries from a user of type i to one of type j. For example, if the following relations hold: (i) $x \in \mathsf{K} \wedge f(x) = 0$, (ii) $y \in \mathsf{K} \wedge g(y) = 0$, and (iii) $w \models w'$, then even though the adversary has sk_x, it cannot decrypt the ciphertext under f, and hence this ciphertext cannot be re-encrypted. Especially, even if the adversary also has sk_y, the query still falls into the case H → H. In all cases shown in Table 1, the adversary is permitted to obtain re-encryption keys and re-encryptions, except in scenarios where the transformation would allow the challenge ciphertext to be directly decrypted. Notably, the case marked with framed box represents re-encryption key queries that are forbidden in the security model of [8]; thus, our adaptive HRA security notion is strictly stronger than the HRA security defined in [8].

In addition, we identify three trivial attack strategies, denoted as **TA1-TA3**, which explicitly aim to reveal the message embedded in the challenge ciphertext $\mathsf{ct}^2_{f^*}$. These attacks are systematically examined and excluded in our adaptive HRA security experiment (see Fig. 2).

- **TA1**: If $\mathcal{A}$ queries an attribute x such that $f^*(x) = 1$ and obtains the corresponding secret key sk_x, it can directly decrypt the challenge ciphertext $\mathsf{ct}^2_{f^*}$ using $\mathsf{Dec}_2(\mathsf{sk}_x, \mathsf{ct}^2_{f^*})$ to recover μ^*_b.
- **TA2**: If $\mathcal{A}$ has both a secret key sk_x and a re-encrypted challenge ciphertext ct^1_g where $g(x) = 1$, it can decrypt the ciphertext to recover μ^*_b.
- **TA3**: If $\mathcal{A}$ possesses a secret key sk_y, a re-encryption key $\mathsf{rk}^{w'}_{x \to g}$, the challenge ciphertext $\mathsf{ct}^2_{f^*}$, and the condition $(x \notin \mathsf{K} \wedge f^*(x) = 1) \wedge (w^* \models w') \wedge (g(y) = 1)$ holds, $\mathcal{A}$ can use $\mathsf{rk}^{w'}_{x \to g}$ to re-encrypt $\mathsf{ct}^2_{f^*}$ and subsequently decrypt the resulting ciphertext with sk_y to recover μ^*_b.

4 Construction of CAB-PRE from LWE

In this section, we present our (single-hop) CAB-PRE construction. Then, based on the LWE assumption and its lossy mode, we prove that it satisfies adaptive HRA security. Before presenting our concrete construction, we provide three key insights to help readers understand it more easily.

(1) **Attribute-Based Access Control.** We use the lattice evaluation technique (Theorem 1) to encode the attribute x and the policy f as matrices, enabling fine-grained access control over ciphertexts. Specifically, the algorithm EvalF embeds x and f into the secret key and the ciphertext by computing the matrices $\mathbf{A}_{x,r}$ and $\mathbf{A}_f$, respectively. During decryption, the algorithm EvalFX produces the matrices $\hat{\mathbf{H}}_{r,r'}$ and $\hat{\mathbf{H}}_{s_f \to r'}$ to verify whether the attribute and policy match. If the equation $[\mathbf{A}_f - s_f \otimes \mathbf{G}]\hat{\mathbf{H}}_{s_f \to r'} \hat{\mathbf{H}}_{r,r'} = \mathbf{A}_{x,r}$ holds, it ensures that $f(x) = 1$ and the tag $r \neq r'$, meaning the decryption succeeds.

(2) **Inner-Product Re-Encryption.** We adopt two functions, bit decomposition BD and power-of-two encoding P2 (see Definition 2), to process the vectors $\boldsymbol{\alpha}$ and $\boldsymbol{\beta}$, helping to control error growth. Specifically, $\mathsf{P2}(\boldsymbol{\alpha})$ is embedded into the second-level ciphertext, while $\mathsf{BD}(\boldsymbol{\beta})$ is embedded into the re-encryption key. The re-encryption succeeds if the condition $\mathbf{BD}(\boldsymbol{\beta}) \cdot \mathbf{P2}(\boldsymbol{\alpha}) = \boldsymbol{\beta} \cdot \boldsymbol{\alpha} = 0$ holds.

(3) **Adaptive-Policy Security.** We use the conforming cPRF $\mathsf{P} = (\mathsf{P.Setup}, \mathsf{P.Eval}, \mathsf{P.Constrain}, \mathsf{P.ConstrainEval})$ proposed in [24] to achieve adaptive-policy security. In our scheme, P generates two tags, r and r': the algorithm P.KeySim (see Definition 5) outputs a constrained key s_f for the ciphertext, from which r' is derived, while P.Eval generates the tag r as part of the re-encryption key. Due to the pseudorandomness of P, it holds with overwhelming probability that $r \neq r'$ in the real construction. In the security proof, P.Constrain and P.ConstrainEval ensure that $r = r'$ whenever $f(x) = 1$, enabling a security reduction.

Next, we describe the parameters used in the construction. Let $n, m, m', q \in \mathbb{Z}$ denote the lattice parameters. The conforming cPRF P, with output length k, is instantiated over a function class $\mathcal{F} : \{0,1\}^l \to \{0,1\}$, defined over the attribute space $\mathcal{X} = \{0,1\}^l$. It is characterized by three circuits: $U_{\sigma \to x}$, $U_{\sigma \to f}$, and $U_{f \to x}$ (see Definition 5), with the depth of the circuits bounded by d. We assume that the master secret key of P has length λ. For any policies $f, g \in \mathcal{F}$, let l_f (resp., l_g) denote the size of the constrained key associated with f (resp., g). The distributions χ and $\tilde{\chi}$ are two bounded error distributions over $\mathbb{Z}$, and τ_0 and τ denote the discrete Gaussian parameters. The exact bounds and parameter settings will be specified later. Our scheme employs several lattice-based trapdoor and sampling algorithms, including TrapGen, ExtendRight, RandBasis, and SamplePre (see Lemma 2). We define the plaintext space as $\mathcal{M} = \{0,1\}$ and the condition space as $\mathcal{W} = \mathbb{Z}_q^l$. The complete CAB-PRE scheme is provided in Fig. 3 and 4.

4.1 Parameter Setting and Theoretical Analysis

Parameter Setting. We follow the parameter settings recommended in [24] to meet the required correctness and security constraints. The lattice parameters n, m, m', q are chosen such that $n = \mathsf{poly}(\lambda)$, $m = n\lceil \log q \rceil$, $m' \geq (n+1)\lceil \log q \rceil + 2\lambda$, and $q > 8B \cdot \mathsf{poly}(n, \lceil \log q \rceil) \cdot (2m)^{2d+4}$, where $d = \mathsf{poly}(\lambda)$. The distribution $\chi = \chi(\lambda)$ is a (B, ϵ)-bounded error distribution over $\mathbb{Z}$ for some $B = B(n)$, and $\tilde{\chi}$ is a (B', ϵ)-swallowing distribution with $B' \leq m'm\lambda B(2m)^d$, where $\epsilon \in (0,1)$ is a security/efficient tradeoff parameter. The length parameters satisfy $l = \mathsf{poly}(\lambda)$ and $l_f, l_g, k \in O(\lambda)$. Additionally, the discrete Gaussian parameters are set as $\tau_0 = O(m^{d+3})$ and $\tau = \max\{\tau_0, O(\sqrt{n \log q} \log m')\}$.

Theorem 2. *The CAB-PRE scheme can correctly decrypt ciphertexts under the parameters specified above.*

Proof. Original Ciphertext. Since decryption operates independently of the condition vectors $\boldsymbol{\alpha}$ and $\boldsymbol{\beta}$, consider an original ciphertext $(s_f, \mathbf{u}_0, \mathbf{u}_1, \mathbf{u}_2)$ encrypted under the policy f. Decryption succeeds if $f(x) = 1$ and $r' \neq r$, where $r' \leftarrow U_{f \to x}(s_f)$. The pseudorandomness of P guarantees that $r' \neq r$ with overwhelming probability [24]. Denote $\mathbf{H}_{f \to x} = \mathsf{EvalF}(U_{f \to x}, \mathbf{A}_f)$. By the gradual evaluation property of P (Definition 5) and lattice evaluation (Theorem 1), we have $\mathbf{H}_{\sigma \to f}\mathbf{H}_{f \to x} = \mathbf{H}_{\sigma \to x}$, and therefore $\mathbf{A}_f \mathbf{H}_{f \to x} = \mathbf{A}\mathbf{H}_{\sigma \to f}\mathbf{H}_{f \to x} = \mathbf{A}\mathbf{H}_{\sigma \to x} = \mathbf{A}_x$. Based on this, we obtain $[\mathbf{A}_f - s_f \otimes \mathbf{G}]\hat{\mathbf{H}}_{s_f \to r'}\hat{\mathbf{H}}_{r,r'} = [\mathbf{A}_f \mathbf{H}_{f \to x} - U_{f \to x}(s_f) \otimes \mathbf{G}]\hat{\mathbf{H}}_{r,r'} = [\mathbf{A}_x - r' \otimes \mathbf{G}]\hat{\mathbf{H}}_{r,r'} = \mathbf{A}_x\mathbf{H}_r - I_r(r') \otimes \mathbf{G} = \mathbf{A}_{x,r}$. Hence, the message is recovered by computing $\mathbf{u}_1 - [\mathbf{u}_0 \| \mathbf{u}_2 \hat{\mathbf{H}}_{s_f \to r'}\hat{\mathbf{H}}_{r,r'}]\mathbf{K} = \mu \lfloor q/2 \rfloor + \mathbf{e}_1 - (\mathbf{e}_0^T \| \mathbf{e}_2')\mathbf{K}$, where $\mathbf{e}_2' = \mathbf{e}_2^T \hat{\mathbf{H}}_{s_f \to r'}\hat{\mathbf{H}}_{r,r'}$. By the tailcut inequality (Lemma 1), the error is bounded as $\|\mathbf{e}_1 - (\mathbf{e}_0^T \| \mathbf{e}_2')\mathbf{K}\|_\infty \leq B \cdot \mathsf{poly}(n, \lceil \log q \rceil) \cdot (2m)^{2d+4} < q/8$, ensuring successful decryption of the original ciphertext.

Transformed Ciphertext. Let $\mathsf{ct}_f^2 = (s_f, \mathbf{u}_0, \mathbf{u}_1, \mathbf{u}_2, \mathbf{u}_3)$ be a second-level ciphertext associated with policy f and vector $\boldsymbol{\alpha}$, and let $\mathsf{rk}_{x \to g}^{\boldsymbol{\beta}} = (s_g, r, \boldsymbol{\beta}, \mathbf{Z})$ be a re-encryption key related to attribute x, updated policy g, and vector $\boldsymbol{\beta}$. If the

- Setup(1^λ) : Compute a pair $(\mathsf{P.pp}, \mathsf{P.msk}) \leftarrow \mathsf{P.Setup}(1^\lambda)$ and set $\sigma = \mathsf{P.msk}$. Generate a matrix and its trapdoor $(\mathbf{B}, \mathbf{T_B}) \leftarrow \mathsf{TrapGen}(1^n, m', q)$. Sample three random matrices $\mathbf{A} \xleftarrow{\$} \mathbb{Z}_q^{n \times m\lambda}$, $\mathbf{V} \xleftarrow{\$} \mathbb{Z}_q^{n \times l\lceil \log q \rceil}$, and $\mathbf{D} \xleftarrow{\$} \mathbb{Z}_q^{n \times l\lceil \log q \rceil}$. Output the public parameters $\mathsf{pp} = (\mathbf{B}, \mathbf{A}, \mathbf{V}, \mathbf{D}, \mathsf{P.pp})$ and the master secret key $\mathsf{msk} = (\sigma, \mathbf{T_B})$.

- KeyGen(msk, x) : Given $\mathsf{msk} = (\sigma, \mathbf{T_B})$ and an attribute $x \in \{0,1\}^l$, proceed as follows:
  1. Compute $\mathbf{H}_{\sigma \to x} \leftarrow \mathsf{EvalF}(U_{\sigma \to x}, \mathbf{A})$ and set $\mathbf{A}_x = \mathbf{A}\mathbf{H}_{\sigma \to x}$;
  2. Evaluate the tag $r \leftarrow \mathsf{P.Eval}(\sigma, x)$, then compute $\mathbf{H}_r \leftarrow \mathsf{EvalF}(I_r, \mathbf{A}_x)$ and $\mathbf{A}_{x,r} = \mathbf{A}_x \mathbf{H}_r$, where $I_r : \{0,1\}^k \to \{0,1\}$ is a function that on input r' returns 0 if $r \neq r'$;
  3. Derive the trapdoor $\mathbf{T}_{\mathbf{B} \| \mathbf{A}_{x,r}} \leftarrow \mathsf{RandBasis}(\mathbf{B} \| \mathbf{A}_{x,r}, \mathsf{ExtendRight}(\mathbf{B}, \mathbf{T_B}, \mathbf{A}_{x,r}), \tau_0)$, and sample a small-norm matrix $\mathbf{K} \leftarrow \mathsf{SamplePre}(\mathbf{B} \| \mathbf{A}_{x,r}, \mathbf{T}_{\mathbf{B} \| \mathbf{A}_{x,r}}, \mathbf{V}, \tau)$ such that $[\mathbf{B} \| \mathbf{A}_{x,r}]\mathbf{K} = \mathbf{V}$, where τ_0 and τ are the discrete Gaussian parameters;
  4. Output $\mathsf{sk}_x = (r, \mathbf{T}_{\mathbf{B} \| \mathbf{A}_{x,r}}, \mathbf{K})$ as the secret key.

- Enc$_1(f, \mu)$: Given a policy $f \in \mathcal{F}$ and a message $\mu \in \{0,1\}$, encryption proceeds as follows: Sample $s_f \leftarrow \mathsf{P.KeySim}(\mathsf{P.pp}, f)$ as part of the ciphertext. Additionally, choose a random vector $\mathbf{s} \xleftarrow{\$} \mathbb{Z}_q^n$ and error terms $\mathbf{e}_0 \xleftarrow{\$} \chi^{m'}$, $\mathbf{e}_1 \xleftarrow{\$} \chi^{l\lceil \log q \rceil}$, $\mathbf{e}_2 \xleftarrow{\$} \tilde{\chi}^{ml_f}$. Then, compute:

$$\mathbf{u}_0 = \mathbf{s}^T \mathbf{B} + \mathbf{e}_0^T, \quad \mathbf{u}_1 = \mathbf{s}^T \mathbf{V} + \mathbf{e}_1^T + \mu \cdot (\mathbf{0} \| \mathbf{g}), \quad \mathbf{u}_2 = \mathbf{s}^T [\mathbf{A}_f - s_f \otimes \mathbf{G}] + \mathbf{e}_2^T,$$

where $\mathbf{0}$ is the zero vector of dimension $(l-1)\lceil \log q \rceil$, $\mathbf{g} = (1, 2, 4, \cdots, 2^{\lceil \log q \rceil -1})$, $\mathbf{A}_f = \mathbf{A}\mathbf{H}_{\sigma \to f}$ for $\mathbf{H}_{\sigma \to f} \leftarrow \mathsf{EvalF}(U_{\sigma \to f}, \mathbf{A})$, and $\mathbf{G} \in \mathbb{Z}_q^{n \times m}$ is the gadget matrix. Output the first-level ciphertext $\mathsf{ct}_f^1 = (s_f, \mathbf{u}_0, \mathbf{u}_1, \mathbf{u}_2)$.

- Enc$_2(f, \boldsymbol{\alpha}, \mu)$: Given $f \in \mathcal{F}$, $\mu \in \{0,1\}$, and a vector $\boldsymbol{\alpha} \in \mathbb{Z}_q^l$, encryption proceeds as follows: Choose a random vector $\mathbf{h} \xleftarrow{\$} \mathbb{Z}_q^n$ and an error vector $\mathbf{e}_3 \xleftarrow{\$} \chi^{l\lceil \log q \rceil}$. The generation of $(s_f, \mathbf{u}_0, \mathbf{u}_1, \mathbf{u}_2)$ follows the same procedure as in Enc$_1$, with an additional component:

$$\mathbf{u}_3 = \mathbf{s}^T [\mathbf{D} + \mathbf{h} \otimes \mathsf{P2}(\boldsymbol{\alpha})^T] + \mathbf{e}_3^T.$$

Output the second-level ciphertext $\mathsf{ct}_f^2 = (s_f, \mathbf{u}_0, \mathbf{u}_1, \mathbf{u}_2, \mathbf{u}_3)$.

- Dec($\mathsf{sk}_x, \mathsf{ct}_f$): Parse the secret key as $\mathsf{sk}_x = (r, \mathbf{T}_{\mathbf{B} \| \mathbf{A}_{x,r}}, \mathbf{K})$ and the ciphertext as either $\mathsf{ct}_f = (s_f, \mathbf{u}_0, \mathbf{u}_1, \mathbf{u}_2)$ (if it is a first-level ciphertext) or $\mathsf{ct}_f = (s_f, \mathbf{u}_0, \mathbf{u}_1, \mathbf{u}_2, \mathbf{u}_3)$ (if it is a second-level ciphertext). Compute $r' \leftarrow U_{f \to x}(s_f)$. Decryption proceeds only if both conditions hold: $f(x) = 1$ and $r \neq r'$. Specifically, compute $\mathbf{A}_x$ and $\mathbf{A}_f$ as in KeyGen and Enc$_1$. Then evaluate two matrices $\hat{\mathbf{H}}_{r,r'} \leftarrow \mathsf{EvalFX}(I_r, r', \mathbf{A}_x)$ and $\hat{\mathbf{H}}_{s_f \to r'} \leftarrow \mathsf{EvalFX}(U_{f \to x}, s_f, \mathbf{A}_f)$, where I_r is defined as in KeyGen. Finally, compute the message

$$\mu = \left\lceil \mathbf{u}_1 - (\mathbf{u}_0 \| \mathbf{u}_2 \hat{\mathbf{H}}_{s_f \to r'} \hat{\mathbf{H}}_{r,r'}) \mathbf{K} \right\rfloor_2,$$

where $\lceil \cdot \rfloor_2 : \mathbb{Z}_q^{l\lceil \log q \rceil} \to \{0,1\}$ indicates whether the penultimate value of the input is closer (modulo q) to 0 or to a specified upper bound.

Fig. 3. Our CAB-PRE Construction.

conditions $f(x) = 1$, $r' \neq r$, and $\boldsymbol{\beta} \cdot \boldsymbol{\alpha} = 0$ hold, then the transformed ciphertext $\mathsf{ct}_{f \to g} = (\mathbf{c}_0, \mathbf{c}_1, \mathbf{c}_2)$ is computed as

$$\mathbf{c}_0 \| \mathbf{c}_2 = \bar{\mathbf{s}}^T (\mathbf{B} \| [\mathbf{A}_g - s_g \otimes \mathbf{G}]) + \mathsf{BD}(\mathbf{u}_0 \| \mathbf{u}_2') \mathbf{R}_2,$$
$$\mathbf{c}_1 = \bar{\mathbf{s}}^T \mathbf{V} + \bar{\mathbf{e}}_1 + \mu \cdot \beta_l \otimes \mathbf{1}_{l\lceil \log q \rceil}^T,$$

where $\bar{\mathbf{s}} = (\mathsf{BD}(\mathbf{u}_0 \| \mathbf{u}_2') \mathbf{R}_1)^T$ is a derived secret vector, β_l is the last coordinate of $\boldsymbol{\beta}$, and error term satisfies $\|\bar{\mathbf{e}}_1\|_\infty \leq B \cdot \mathsf{poly}(n, \lceil \log q \rceil) \cdot (2m)^{2d+4}$. Using the

- ReKeyGen($\mathsf{sk}_x, g, \boldsymbol{\beta}$): Given $\mathsf{sk}_x = (r, \mathbf{T}_{\mathbf{B} \| \mathbf{A}_{x,r}}, \mathbf{K})$, a policy $g \in \mathcal{F}$, and a vector $\boldsymbol{\beta} \in \mathbb{Z}_q^{1 \times l}$, proceed as follows:
  1. Sample $s_g \leftarrow \mathsf{P.KeySim}(\mathsf{P.pp}, g)$, and set $\mathbf{H} = \mathbf{B} \| [\mathbf{A}_g - s_g \otimes \mathbf{G}]$, where $\mathbf{A}_g = \mathbf{A} \mathbf{H}_{\sigma \to g}$ for $\mathbf{H}_{\sigma \to g} \leftarrow \mathsf{EvalF}(U_{\sigma \to g}, \mathbf{A})$;
  2. Compute $\mathbf{A}_{x,r}$ as in KeyGen. Let $\mathbf{v} = (\mathbf{V} + \mathbf{D}) \cdot \mathsf{BD}(\boldsymbol{\beta})^T$, and sample a short vector $\mathbf{d} \leftarrow \mathsf{SamplePre}(\mathbf{B} \| \mathbf{A}_{x,r}, \mathbf{T}_{\mathbf{B} \| \mathbf{A}_{x,r}}, \mathbf{v}, \tau)$ such that $[\mathbf{B} \| \mathbf{A}_{x,r}] \mathbf{d} = \mathbf{v}$;
  3. Sample error terms $\mathbf{R}_1 \in \chi^{(m'+m) \lceil \log q \rceil \times n}$, $\mathbf{R}_2 \in \chi^{(m'+m) \lceil \log q \rceil \times (m'+ml_g)}$, $\mathbf{R}_3 \in \chi^{(m'+m) \lceil \log q \rceil \times l \lceil \log q \rceil}$, and then compute the matrix

  $$\mathbf{Z} = \begin{pmatrix} \mathbf{R}_1 \mathbf{H} + \mathbf{R}_2 & \mathbf{R}_1 \mathbf{V} + \mathbf{R}_3 - \mathsf{P2}(\mathbf{d}) \otimes \mathbf{1}_{l \lceil \log q \rceil}^T \\ \mathbf{0}_{l \lceil \log q \rceil \times (m'+ml_g)} & \mathsf{BD}(\boldsymbol{\beta})^T \otimes \mathbf{1}_{l \lceil \log q \rceil}^T \end{pmatrix},$$

  where $\mathbf{0}_{l \lceil \log q \rceil \times (m'+ml_g)}$ is the zero matrix of the indicated dimensions, and $\mathbf{1}_{l \lceil \log q \rceil}$ is a column vector of length $l \lceil \log q \rceil$ with all entries equal to 1;
  4. Output $\mathsf{rk}_{x \to g}^{\boldsymbol{\beta}} = (s_g, r, \boldsymbol{\beta}, \mathbf{Z})$ as the re-encryption key.

- ReEnc($\mathsf{rk}_{x \to g}^{\boldsymbol{\beta}}, \mathsf{ct}_f^2$): Parse $\mathsf{rk}_{x \to g}^{\boldsymbol{\beta}} = (s_g, r, \boldsymbol{\beta}, \mathbf{Z})$ and $\mathsf{ct}_f^2 = (s_f, \mathbf{u}_0, \mathbf{u}_1, \mathbf{u}_2, \mathbf{u}_3)$. Compute the tag $r' \leftarrow U_{f \to x}(s_f)$. The re-encryption proceeds only if the following conditions are satisfied: (i) $f(x) = 1$, (ii) $r' \neq r$, and (iii) $\boldsymbol{\beta} \cdot \boldsymbol{\alpha} = 0$. Specifically, compute $\mathbf{A}_x, \mathbf{A}_f, \hat{\mathbf{H}}_{r,r'}$ and $\hat{\mathbf{H}}_{s_f \to r'}$ as in KeyGen, Enc$_1$ and Dec. Define $\mathbf{u}_2' = \mathbf{u}_2 \hat{\mathbf{H}}_{s_f \to r'} \hat{\mathbf{H}}_{r,r'}$, $\mathbf{u}_1' = \mathbf{u}_1 + \mathbf{u}_3$, and evaluate

  $$\mathsf{ct}_{f \to g} = [\mathsf{BD}(\mathbf{u}_0 \| \mathbf{u}_2') \| \mathbf{u}_1'] \cdot \mathbf{Z}.$$

  Output the re-encrypted ciphertext $\mathsf{ct}_g^1 = (s_g, \mathsf{ct}_{f \to g}, \boldsymbol{\beta})$, where $\boldsymbol{\beta}$ is used to constrain the error bounds when decrypting.

Fig. 4. Our CAB-PRE Construction (Continued).

same decryption procedure as before and setting $\beta_l = q/2$, the message μ can be correctly recovered when the total error remains below $q/4$.

Theorem 3. *Let* P *be a conforming cPRF over a function class* $\mathcal{F}$ *as defined in Definition 5. Then, our CAB-PRE scheme for inner-product predicates achieves adaptive HRA security under the hardness of LWE and its lossy mode.*

We outline our proof sketch here and leave the detailed proof to Appendix A. Inspired by [24], we construct a challenger $\mathcal{C}$ that leverages a PPT adversary $\mathcal{A}$ as a subroutine to solve the LWE problem and its lossy variant. Given an LWE instance $(\mathbf{B} \| \mathbf{V}, \mathbf{u}_0 \| \mathbf{u}_1)$. The goal of $\mathcal{C}$ is to distinguish whether $\mathbf{u}_0 \| \mathbf{u}_1 = \mathbf{s}^T (\mathbf{B} \| \mathbf{V}) + \bar{\mathbf{e}}^T$ for some secret $\mathbf{s}$ and error vector $\bar{\mathbf{e}}$, or whether it is uniformly random. To begin, $\mathcal{C}$ runs $(\mathsf{P.pp}, \mathsf{P.msk}) \leftarrow \mathsf{P.Setup}(1^\lambda)$, samples a random matrix $\mathbf{D}$ and a small-norm matrix $\mathbf{R}$, and sets $\mathbf{A} = \mathbf{BR} + \sigma \otimes \mathbf{G}$, where $\sigma = \mathsf{P.msk}$. The public parameters are $(\mathbf{B}, \mathbf{A}, \mathbf{V}, \mathbf{D}, \mathsf{P.pp})$. When $\mathcal{A}$ makes key generation queries, $\mathcal{C}$ simulates the extended trapdoor $\mathbf{T}_{\mathbf{B} \| \mathbf{A}_{x,r}}$ using the public trapdoor $\mathbf{T}_\mathbf{G}$ via the ExtendLeft algorithm, instead of using $\mathbf{T}_\mathbf{B}$ via ExtendRight. For re-encryption key queries, $\mathcal{C}$ would check whether the case corresponds to $\mathsf{H} \to \mathsf{C}$ or $\mathsf{C} \to \mathsf{C}$ as shown in Table 1. If so, it samples $\mathbf{d}$ using $\mathbf{T}_{\mathbf{B} \| \mathbf{A}_{x,r}}$ and generates $\mathbf{Z}$ accordingly; otherwise, it simulates $\mathbf{Z}$ by replacing the upper-right component of $\mathbf{Z}$ with a uniformly random matrix, keeping the rest unchanged. This modification is computationally indistinguishable from uniform under the LWE assumption (see Definition 3). All queries that would trigger the abort condition (as defined in Fig. 2) are excluded. In the challenge phase on input $(f^*, \alpha^*, (\mu_0^*, \mu_1^*))$, $\mathcal{C}$ computes $s_{f^*} \leftarrow \mathsf{P.Constrain}(\sigma, f^*)$ and sets $\mathbf{u}_2^* = \mathbf{u}_0 \mathbf{R} \hat{\mathbf{H}}_{\mathsf{msk} \to s_{f^*}} + \bar{\mathbf{e}}_2^T$, where $\hat{\mathbf{H}}_{\mathsf{msk} \to s_{f^*}}$ is computed via the circuit $U_{\sigma \to f^*}$ and $\bar{\mathbf{e}}_2$ is an error vector. Since $\tilde{\chi}$ is B'-swallowing (see Definition 1), $\mathbf{u}_2^*$ is statistically close to uniform. For $\mathbf{u}_3^*$, observe that under the lossy mode, the matrix $\mathbf{D} + \mathbf{h} \otimes \mathsf{P2}(\alpha^*)^T$ (with $\mathbf{h}$ chosen uniformly at random) is indistinguishable from uniform. Hence, $\mathbf{u}_3^*$ is also computationally indistinguishable from uniform under the Lossy-LWE assumption (Definition 4). Finally, $\mathcal{C}$ samples $\mathbf{u}_3^*$ uniformly and outputs the challenge ciphertext $(s_{f^*}, \mathbf{u}_0^* = \mathbf{u}_0, \mathbf{u}_1^* = \mathbf{u}_1 + \mu_b^*(\mathbf{0}\|\mathbf{g}), \mathbf{u}_2^*, \mathbf{u}_3^*)$. $\mathcal{C}$ then outputs $\mathcal{A}$'s response as the answer to the LWE challenge.

5 Conclusion

In this work, we formalized the notion of CAB-PRE, which extends AB-PRE by integrating conditional re-encryption capabilities, thereby broadening its applicability in practical scenarios. We defined an adaptive HRA security model for this notion and presented a (single-hop) CAB-PRE construction based on the LWE assumption. Our scheme supports fine-grained conditional re-encryption for inner-product predicates while achieving adaptive HRA security in the standard model.

We have noted that the key switching procedure in our construction introduces dimension expansion in the re-encryption key. Mitigating this expansion presents an interesting direction, and we leave it as an avenue for future work.

Acknowledgments. We would like to thank the reviewers for their valuable comments. This research/project is supported by the National Research Foundation, Singapore, and the Cyber Security Agency of Singapore under its National Cybersecurity R&D Programme (Proposal ID: NCR25-DeSSMU-0001). Any opinions, findings and conclusions or recommendations expressed in this material are those of the author(s) and do not reflect the views of the National Research Foundation, Singapore, and the Cyber Security Agency of Singapore. Jian Weng is supported in part by the National Natural Science Foundation of China (Nos. 62332007, U22B2028), the Science and Technology Major Project of Tibetan Autonomous Region of China (No. XZ202201ZD0006G), Open Research Fund of Machine Learning and Cyber Security Interdiscipline Research Engineering Center of Jiangsu Province (No. SDGC2131), National Joint Engineering Research Center of Network Security Detection and Protection Technology, Guangdong Key Laboratory of Data Security and Privacy Preserving, Guangdong Hong Kong Joint Laboratory for Data Security and Privacy Protection, and Engineering Research Center of Trustworthy AI, Ministry of Education. Guomin Yang is supported by the Lee Kong Chian Fellowship awarded by the Singapore Management University.

A Proof of Theorem 3

The security proof proceeds through a sequence of games between the adversary $\mathcal{A}$ and the challenger $\mathcal{C}$. Below, we outline the changes introduced in each game:

Game$_0$: This is the original security game defined in Sect. 3.

Game$_1$: This game alters the re-encryption key query in **Game$_0$**, except for the cases $\boxed{\text{H} \to \text{C}}$ and $\boxed{\text{C} \to \text{C}}$ in Table 1. $\mathcal{C}$ replaces the upper-right component of the matrix $\mathbf{Z}$ with a random matrix $\mathbf{U}$ sampled from $\mathbb{Z}_q^{(m'+m)\lceil \log q \rceil \times l \lceil \log q \rceil}$.

Game$_2$: This game is identical to **Game$_1$**, except that for the challenge query, $\mathcal{C}$ computes s_{f^*} using the P.Constrain(σ, f^*) algorithm.

Game$_3$: This game modifies the generation of the public parameters in **Game$_2$**. $\mathcal{C}$ samples a matrix $\mathbf{R} \xleftarrow{\$} \{1, -1\}^{m' \times m\lambda}$ and computes $\mathbf{A} = \mathbf{BR} + \sigma \otimes \mathbf{G}$.

Game$_4$: This game further changes the challenge ciphertext. $\mathcal{C}$ sets $\mathbf{u}_2^* = \mathbf{u}_0^* \mathbf{R} \hat{\mathbf{H}}_{\text{msk} \to s_{f^*}} + \mathbf{e}_2^T$, where $\mathbf{u}_0^*$ is a component of the challenge ciphertext, $\mathbf{R}$ is reused from **Game$_3$**, and $\hat{\mathbf{H}}_{\text{msk} \to s_{f^*}}$ is a computable matrix.

Game$_5$: This game modifies how key generation queries are handled in **Game$_4$**. $\mathcal{C}$ generates the extended trapdoor $\mathbf{T}_{\mathbf{B} \| \mathbf{A}_{x,r}}$ using the ExtendLeft algorithm.

Game$_6$: This game changes the generation of the public parameters further. $\mathcal{C}$ samples $\mathbf{B} \xleftarrow{\$} \mathbb{Z}_q^{n \times m'}$ at random without generating its trapdoor $\mathbf{T}_\mathbf{B}$.

Game$_7$: This game modifies the generation of the challenge ciphertext by sampling $\mathbf{u}_3^* \xleftarrow{\$} \mathbb{Z}_q^{l \lceil \log q \rceil}$ uniformly at random.

Game$_8$: This final game alters the challenge ciphertext further. $\mathcal{C}$ samples $\mathbf{u}_0^* \xleftarrow{\$} \mathbb{Z}_q^{1 \times m'}$ and $\mathbf{u}_1^* \xleftarrow{\$} \mathbb{Z}_q^{1 \times ml_f}$ uniformly at random. Since the challenge ciphertext now completely hides the challenge bit b, $\mathcal{A}$ has no advantage in this game.

Next, we prove that the two adjacent games described above are indistinguishable. Throughout the proof, we use the notation "$\approx_c$" (resp., "$\approx_s$") to denote computational (resp., statistical) indistinguishability.

Game$_0$ $\approx_c$ Game$_1$: The difference between **Game$_0$** and **Game$_1$** lies in the upper-right component of the matrix $\mathbf{Z}$. In **Game$_0$**, this component is computed as $\mathbf{R}_1 \mathbf{V} + \mathbf{R}_3 - \mathsf{P2}(\mathbf{d}) \otimes \mathbf{1}_{l \lceil \log q \rceil}^T$, where $\mathbf{R}_1, \mathbf{R}_2$ and $\mathbf{R}_3$ are sampled from discrete Gaussian distributions. In contrast, **Game$_1$** replaces it with a uniformly random matrix $\mathbf{U}$ sampled from $\mathbb{Z}_q^{(m'+m)\lceil \log q \rceil \times l \lceil \log q \rceil}$. By viewing $\mathbf{R}_1$ as the secret matrix, the term $\mathbf{R}_1 \mathbf{V} + \mathbf{R}_3$ constitutes HNF-LWE samples, which are computationally indistinguishable from uniform under the HNF-LWE assumption (see Definition 3). Therefore, $\mathbf{Z}$ in **Game$_0$** is computationally indistinguishable from that in **Game$_1$**, implying that **Game$_0$ $\approx_c$ Game$_1$**.

Game$_1$ $\approx_c$ Game$_2$: In **Game$_1$**, s_{f^*} is computed using P.KeySim(P.pp, f^*), while in **Game$_2$**, it is generated via P.Constrain(σ, f^*). By the key simulation property of the conforming cPRF (see Definition 5), these two approaches yield computationally indistinguishable keys. Thus, we conclude that **Game$_1$ $\approx_c$ Game$_2$**.

Game$_2$ $\approx_s$ Game$_3$: Recall that in **Game$_2$**, $\mathcal{C}$ samples $\mathbf{A} \xleftarrow{\$} \mathbb{Z}_q^{n \times m\lambda}$ uniformly at random. In contrast, in **Game$_3$**, $\mathcal{C}$ first samples a matrix $\mathbf{R} \xleftarrow{\$} \{1, -1\}^{m' \times m\lambda}$ and then sets $\mathbf{A} = \mathbf{BR} + \sigma \otimes \mathbf{G}$. By the generalized leftover hash lemma (see Lemma 3), when $m' \geq (n+1)\lceil \log q \rceil + 2\lambda$, the distribution $(\mathbf{B}, \mathbf{BR})$ is statistically indistinguishable from $(\mathbf{B}, \hat{\mathbf{U}})$, where $\hat{\mathbf{U}}$ is uniformly sampled from $\mathbb{Z}_q^{n \times m\lambda}$. As a result, the distribution of $\mathbf{A}$ in $\mathbf{Game}_3$ is statistically close to that of the uniformly sampled in $\mathbf{Game}_2$. Hence, we have $\mathbf{Game}_2 \approx_s \mathbf{Game}_3$.

$\mathbf{Game}_3 \approx_s \mathbf{Game}_4$: The difference between $\mathbf{Game}_3$ and $\mathbf{Game}_4$ lies in the computation of $\mathbf{u}_2^*$. In $\mathbf{Game}_3$, $\mathcal{C}$ samples $\mathbf{s} \xleftarrow{\$} \mathbb{Z}_q^n$ and $\mathbf{e}_2 \xleftarrow{\$} \tilde{\chi}^{ml_f}$, and computes $\mathbf{u}_2^* = \mathbf{s}^T[\mathbf{A}_{f^*} - s_{f^*} \otimes \mathbf{G}] + \mathbf{e}_2^T$. In contrast, in $\mathbf{Game}_4$, $\mathbf{u}_2^*$ is computed as $\mathbf{u}_2^* = \mathbf{u}_0^* \mathbf{R} \hat{\mathbf{H}}_{\mathsf{msk} \to s_{f^*}} + \mathbf{e}_2^T$, where $\mathbf{u}_0^* = \mathbf{s}^T \mathbf{B} + \mathbf{e}_0^T$ is generated identically in both two games with $\mathbf{e}_0 \xleftarrow{\$} \chi^{m'}$. To demonstrate their indistinguishable, $\mathcal{C}$ establishes $\mathbf{A}_{f^*} - s_{f^*} \otimes \mathbf{G} = \mathbf{A}\mathbf{H}_{\sigma \to f^*} - U_{\sigma \to f^*}(\sigma) \otimes \mathbf{G} = [\mathbf{A} - \sigma \otimes \mathbf{G}]\hat{\mathbf{H}}_{\mathsf{msk} \to s_{f^*}} = \mathbf{B}\mathbf{R}\hat{\mathbf{H}}_{\mathsf{msk} \to s_{f^*}}$, where $\hat{\mathbf{H}}_{\mathsf{msk} \to s_{f^*}} \leftarrow \mathsf{EvalFX}(U_{\sigma \to f^*}, \sigma, \mathbf{A})$. Now, $\mathbf{u}_2^*$ in $\mathbf{Game}_4$ will be substituted as $\mathbf{u}_2^* = \mathbf{u}_0^* \mathbf{R}\hat{\mathbf{H}}_{\mathsf{msk} \to s_{f^*}} + \mathbf{e}_2^T = \mathbf{s}^T[\mathbf{A}_{f^*} - s_{f^*} \otimes \mathbf{G}] + \mathbf{e}_0^T + \mathbf{R}\hat{\mathbf{H}}_{\mathsf{msk} \to s_{f^*}} + \mathbf{e}_2^T$. Let $B' = \|\mathbf{e}_0^T + \mathbf{R}\hat{\mathbf{H}}_{\mathsf{msk} \to s_f}\|_\infty \leq m'm\lambda B(2m)^d$. If $\tilde{\chi}$ is B'-swallowing (see Definition 1), it holds that $\mathbf{u}_2^*$ generated in the two games are within a negligible statistical distance. Therefore, we have $\mathbf{Game}_3 \approx_s \mathbf{Game}_4$.

$\mathbf{Game}_4 \approx_s \mathbf{Game}_5$: Recall that in $\mathbf{Game}_4$, the extended trapdoor $\mathbf{T}_{\mathbf{B}\|\mathbf{A}_{x,r}}$ is computed via $\mathsf{ExtendRight}$ using the trapdoor $\mathbf{T}_\mathbf{B}$. In contrast, in $\mathbf{Game}_5$, it is generated using $\mathsf{ExtendLeft}$ with the trapdoor $\mathbf{T}_\mathbf{G}$. Specifically, when $\mathcal{A}$ issues the key generation query, $\mathcal{C}$ first evaluates $r \leftarrow \mathsf{P.Eval}(\sigma, x)$ and $\hat{\mathbf{H}}_{\mathsf{msk} \to r} \leftarrow \mathsf{EvalFX}(U_{\sigma \to x}, \sigma, \mathbf{A})$, and then obtains $[\mathbf{A} - \sigma \otimes \mathbf{G}]\hat{\mathbf{H}}_{\mathsf{msk} \to r} = \mathbf{A}\mathbf{H}_{\sigma \to x} - r \otimes \mathbf{G} = \mathbf{A}_x - r \otimes \mathbf{G}$. Since $I_r(r) = 1$, we can derive $[\mathbf{A}_x - r \otimes \mathbf{G}]\hat{\mathbf{H}}_{r,r} = \mathbf{A}_{x,r} - \mathbf{G}$, where $\hat{\mathbf{H}}_{r,r} \leftarrow \mathsf{EvalFX}(I_r, r, \mathbf{A}_x)$. Moreover, since $\mathbf{A} - \sigma \otimes \mathbf{G} = \mathbf{B}\mathbf{R}$, it holds that $\mathbf{B}\mathbf{R}\hat{\mathbf{H}}_{\mathsf{msk} \to r}\hat{\mathbf{H}}_{r,r} = \mathbf{A}_{x,r} - \mathbf{G}$, and hence $\mathbf{B}\|\mathbf{A}_{x,r} = \mathbf{B}\|(\mathbf{B}\mathbf{R}\hat{\mathbf{H}}_{\mathsf{msk} \to r}\hat{\mathbf{H}}_{r,r} + \mathbf{G})$. Based on the properties of $\mathsf{ExtendRight}$, $\mathsf{ExtendLeft}$, and $\mathsf{RandBasis}$ (see Lemma 2), if the parameter satisfies $\tau_0 = O(\|\mathbf{R}\hat{\mathbf{H}}_{\mathsf{msk} \to r}\hat{\mathbf{H}}_{r,r}\|_\infty) = O(m^{d+3})$, then $\mathcal{C}$ can efficiently compute $\mathbf{T}_{\mathbf{B}\|\mathbf{A}_{x,r}}$ via $\mathsf{ExtendLeft}(\mathbf{B}, \mathbf{G}, \mathbf{T}_\mathbf{G}, \mathbf{R}\hat{\mathbf{H}}_{\mathsf{msk} \to r}\hat{\mathbf{H}}_{r,r})$ without requiring $\mathbf{T}_\mathbf{B}$. Therefore, $\mathbf{T}_{\mathbf{B}\|\mathbf{A}_{x,r}}$ derived from $\mathsf{ExtendLeft}$ is statistically close to it from $\mathsf{ExtendRight}$. Thus, we conclude that $\mathbf{Game}_4 \approx_s \mathbf{Game}_5$.

$\mathbf{Game}_5 \approx_s \mathbf{Game}_6$: In $\mathbf{Game}_5$, the matrix $\mathbf{B}$ is generated using the $\mathsf{TrapGen}$ algorithm, which outputs both $\mathbf{B}$ and its corresponding trapdoor $\mathbf{T}_\mathbf{B}$. In contrast, in $\mathbf{Game}_6$, $\mathbf{B}$ is sampled uniformly from $\mathbb{Z}_q^{n \times m'}$ without generating the associated trapdoor. According the properties of the $\mathsf{TrapGen}$ algorithm (see Lemma 2), the distribution of $\mathbf{B}$ produced by $\mathsf{TrapGen}$ is statistically $2^{-\Omega(n)}$-close to uniform. Therefore, we have $\mathbf{Game}_5 \approx_s \mathbf{Game}_6$.

$\mathbf{Game}_6 \approx_c \mathbf{Game}_7$: In $\mathbf{Game}_6$, $\mathcal{C}$ samples $\mathbf{s} \xleftarrow{\$} \mathbb{Z}_q^n$ and $\mathbf{e}_3 \xleftarrow{\$} \chi^{l\lceil \log q \rceil}$, and computes $\mathbf{u}_3^* = \mathbf{s}^T(\mathbf{D} + \mathbf{h} \otimes \mathsf{P2}(\boldsymbol{\alpha}^*)^T) + \mathbf{e}_3^T$. In contrast, in $\mathbf{Game}_7$, $\mathbf{u}_3^*$ is sampled from $\mathbb{Z}_q^{l\lceil \log q \rceil}$ uniformly at random. The structure of $\mathbf{u}_3^*$ in $\mathbf{Game}_6$ can be regarded as the lossy mode for LWE (see Definition 4), and is therefore computationally indistinguishable from uniform. To formalize this, we use $\mathsf{SampleLossy}$ (adapted from [15]) to describe the procedure that samples a matrix in the lossy mode. Let n, l be positive integers, and $\boldsymbol{\alpha}$ be a vector over $\mathbb{Z}_q^l$, define $\mathsf{SampleLossy}(n, l, \boldsymbol{\alpha})$: It samples $\mathbf{D} \xleftarrow{\$} \mathbb{Z}_q^{n \times l\lceil \log q \rceil}$ and $\mathbf{h} \xleftarrow{\$} \mathbb{Z}_q^n$, outputs $\mathbf{A}_1 = \mathbf{D} + \mathbf{h} \otimes \mathsf{P2}(\boldsymbol{\alpha})^T$.

It can be observed that $\mathbf{A}_1$ in the lossy mode is within a negligible computational distance from uniform distribution. Thus, choosing $\mathbf{A}_0 \xleftarrow{\$} \mathbb{Z}_q^{n \times l\lceil \log q \rceil}$ and $\mathbf{A}_1 \leftarrow \mathsf{SampleLossy}(n, l, \alpha)$, we have $\mathbf{A}_0 \approx_c \mathbf{A}_1$. Moreover, for $\mathbf{s} \xleftarrow{\$} \mathbb{Z}_q^n$ and $\mathbf{e} \xleftarrow{\$} \chi^{l\lceil \log q \rceil}$, it holds that $(\mathbf{A}_0, \mathbf{s}^T \mathbf{A}_0 + \mathbf{e}^T) \approx_c (\mathbf{A}_1, \mathbf{s}^T \mathbf{A}_1 + \mathbf{e}^T)$. On the other hand, under the LWE assumption, we claim that $(\mathbf{A}_0, \mathbf{s}^T \mathbf{A}_0 + \mathbf{e}^T) \approx_c (\mathbf{A}_0, \mathbf{u}^T)$, where $\mathbf{u} \xleftarrow{\$} \mathbb{Z}_q^{l\lceil \log q \rceil}$. Finally, we have $(\mathbf{A}_1, \mathbf{s}^T \mathbf{A}_1 + \mathbf{e}^T) \approx_c (\mathbf{A}_1, \mathbf{u}^T)$, implying the ciphertext component $\mathbf{u}_3^*$ is computationally indistinguishable from the uniform distribution over $\mathbb{Z}_q^{l\lceil \log q \rceil}$. Therefore, we conclude that $\mathbf{Game}_6 \approx_c \mathbf{Game}_7$.

$\underline{\mathbf{Game}_7 \approx_c \mathbf{Game}_8}$: We claim that $\mathbf{Game}_7$ and $\mathbf{Game}_8$ are computationally indistinguishable via a reduction from the LWE assumption. Suppose that $\mathcal{A}$ has a non-negligible advantage in distinguishing these two games; we then construct an algorithm $\mathcal{B}$ that leverages $\mathcal{A}$ as a subroutine to break the LWE assumption.

LWE Instance. $\mathcal{B}$ receives an LWE instance $(\mathbf{B}\|\mathbf{V}, \mathbf{u}_0\|\mathbf{u}_1) \in \mathbb{Z}_q^{n \times (m' + l\lceil \log q \rceil)} \times \mathbb{Z}_q^{1 \times (m' + l\lceil \log q \rceil)}$. The task of $\mathcal{B}$ is to distinguish whether $\mathbf{u}_0\|\mathbf{u}_1 = \mathbf{s}^T(\mathbf{B}\|\mathbf{V}) + \bar{\mathbf{e}}^T$ for some $\mathbf{s} \in \mathbb{Z}_q^n$ and $\bar{\mathbf{e}} \in \chi^{m' + l\lceil \log q \rceil}$ or whether $\mathbf{u}_0\|\mathbf{u}_1 \xleftarrow{\$} \mathbb{Z}_q^{1 \times (m' + l\lceil \log q \rceil)}$.

Setup: $\mathcal{B}$ initializes the sets described in Fig. 2. It sets $\mathbf{B}$ and $\mathbf{V}$ as provided by the LWE instance and gives $\mathcal{A}$ the public parameters $\mathsf{pp} = (\mathbf{B}, \mathbf{A}, \mathbf{V}, \mathbf{D}, \mathsf{P.pp})$.

Oracle Query: $\mathcal{B}$ answers $\mathcal{A}$'s secret key, encryption, re-encryption key, and re-encryption queries as in $\mathbf{Game}_7$, except for the challenge query.

- $\mathcal{O}_{\mathsf{Cha}}(f^*, \alpha^*, (\mu_0^*, \mu_1^*))$: To generate the challenge ciphertext, $\mathcal{B}$ picks a random bit $b \in \{0, 1\}$, computes $s_{f^*}, \mathbf{u}_2^*, \mathbf{u}_3^*$ as in $\mathbf{Game}_7$, and outputs $\mathsf{ct}_{f^*}^2 = (s_{f^*}, \mathbf{u}_0^* = \mathbf{u}_0, \mathbf{u}_1^* = \mathbf{u}_1 + \mu_b^*(\mathbf{0}\|\mathbf{g}), \mathbf{u}_2^*, \mathbf{u}_3^*)$. It then updates the counter $\mathsf{numCt} := \mathsf{numCt} + 1$ and gives $(\mathsf{numCt}, \mathsf{ct}_{f^*}^2)$ to $\mathcal{A}$.

Decision: $\mathcal{A}$ outputs its guess as to whether it is interacting with $\mathbf{Game}_7$ or $\mathbf{Game}_8$, and $\mathcal{B}$ outputs the same guess as its answer to the LWE challenge.

If $(\mathbf{B}\|\mathbf{V}, \mathbf{u}_0\|\mathbf{u}_1)$ is a valid LWE instance (i.e., $\mathbf{u}_0\|\mathbf{u}_1 = \mathbf{s}^T(\mathbf{B}\|\mathbf{V}) + \bar{\mathbf{e}}^T$), then $\mathcal{A}$'s view is identical to $\mathbf{Game}_7$. Otherwise (i.e., $\mathbf{u}_0\|\mathbf{u}_1 \xleftarrow{\$} \mathbb{Z}_q^{1 \times (m' + l\lceil \log q \rceil)}$), $\mathcal{A}$'s view corresponds to $\mathbf{Game}_8$. Therefore, a non-negligible distinguishing advantage of $\mathcal{A}$ between two games would contradict the LWE assumption. Hence, we conclude that $\mathbf{Game}_7 \approx_c \mathbf{Game}_8$.

By combining the above conclusions together, we can conclude that $\mathcal{A}$'s advantage in this security game is negligible under the LWE assumption.

References

1. Aono, Y., Boyen, X., Phong, L.T., Wang, L.: Key-private proxy re-encryption under LWE. In: INDOCRYPT 2013, pp. 1–18 (2013)
2. Applebaum, B., Cash, D., Peikert, C., Sahai, A.: Fast cryptographic primitives and circular-secure encryption based on hard learning problems. In: CRYPTO 2009, pp. 595–618 (2009)

3. Banaszczyk, W.: New bounds in some transference theorems in the geometry of numbers. Math. Ann. **296**(1), 625–635 (1993)
4. Banaszczyk, W.: Inequalities for convex bodies and polar reciprocal lattices in Rn. Discrete Comput. Geom. **13**, 217–231 (1995)
5. Blaze, M., Bleumer, G., Strauss, M.: Divertible protocols and atomic proxy cryptography. In: EUROCRYPT 1998, pp. 127–144. Springer (1998)
6. Boneh, D., et al.: Fully key-homomorphic encryption, arithmetic circuit ABE and compact garbled circuits. In: EUROCRYPT 2014, pp. 533–556 (2014)
7. Brakerski, Z., Gentry, C., Vaikuntanathan, V.: (leveled) fully homomorphic encryption without bootstrapping. In: ITCS 2012, pp. 309–325 (2012)
8. Cohen, A.: What about bob? The inadequacy of CPA security for proxy re-encryption. In: PKC 2019, pp. 287–316 (2019)
9. Davidson, A., Katsumata, S., Nishimaki, R., Yamada, S., Yamakawa, T.: Adaptively secure constrained pseudorandom functions in the standard model. In: CRYPTO 2020, pp. 559–589 (2020)
10. Dodis, Y., Reyzin, L., Smith, A.: Fuzzy extractors: how to generate strong keys from biometrics and other noisy data. In: EUROCRYPT 2004, pp. 523–540 (2004)
11. Fuchsbauer, G., Kamath, C., Klein, K., Pietrzak, K.: Adaptively secure proxy re-encryption. In: PKC 2019, pp. 317–346 (2019)
12. Ge, C., Susilo, W., Fang, L., Wang, J., Shi, Y.: A CCA-secure key-policy attribute-based proxy re-encryption in the adaptive corruption model for dropbox data sharing system. Des. Codes Crypt. **86**(11), 2587–2603 (2018). https://doi.org/10.1007/s10623-018-0462-9
13. Goldwasser, S., Kalai, Y.T., Peikert, C., Vaikuntanathan, V.: Robustness of the learning with errors assumption. In: ICS 2010, pp. 230–240 (2010)
14. Huang, Q., Yang, Y., Fu, J.: PRECISE: identity-based private data sharing with conditional proxy re-encryption in online social networks. Future Gener. Comput. Syst. **86**, 1523–1533 (2018)
15. Katsumata, S., Yamada, S., Yamakawa, T.: Tighter security proofs for GPV-IBE in the quantum random oracle model. In: ASIACRYPT 2018, pp. 253–282 (2018)
16. Li, J., Ma, C., Zhang, K.: A novel lattice-based ciphertext-policy attribute-based proxy re-encryption for cloud sharing. In: International Symposium on Security and Privacy in Social Networks and Big Data, pp. 32–46 (2019)
17. Liang, K., et al.: A secure and efficient ciphertext-policy attribute-based proxy re-encryption for cloud data sharing. Futur. Gener. Comput. Syst. **52**, 95–108 (2015)
18. Liang, X., Cao, Z., Lin, H., Shao, J.: Attribute based proxy re-encryption with delegating capabilities. In: ASIACCS 2009, pp. 276–286 (2009)
19. Micciancio, D., Peikert, C.: Trapdoors for lattices: simpler, tighter, faster, smaller. In: EUROCRYPT 2012, pp. 700–718 (2012)
20. Patil, R.Y.: Digital forensics evidence management based on proxy re-encryption. Int. J. Comput. Appl. Technol. **68**(4), 405–413 (2022)
21. Regev, O.: On lattices, learning with errors, random linear codes, and cryptography. In: STOC 2005, pp. 84–93 (2005)
22. Su, M., Zhou, B., Fu, A., Yu, Y., Zhang, G.: PRTA: a proxy re-encryption based trusted authorization scheme for nodes on cloudiot. Inf. Sci. **527**, 533–547 (2020)
23. Susilo, W., Dutta, P., Duong, D.H., Roy, P.S.: Lattice-based HRA-secure attribute-based proxy re-encryption in standard model. In: ESORICS 2021, pp. 169–191 (2021)
24. Tsabary, R.: Fully secure attribute-based encryption for t-CNF from LWE. In: CRYPTO 2019, pp. 62–85 (2019)

LastRings: Lattice-Based Scalable Threshold Ring Signatures

Sohyun Jeon[1](✉), Calvin Abou Haidar[2], and Mehdi Tibouchi[2]

[1] Department of Mathematics, Ewha Womans University, Seoul, Republic of Korea
jch3665@gmail.com
[2] NTT Social Informatics Laboratories, Tokyo, Japan
{calvin.haidar,mehdi.tibouchi}@ntt.com

Abstract. In this paper, we construct the first lattice-based threshold ring signature scheme with signature size scaling logarithmically in the size of the ring while supporting arbitrary thresholds. Our construction is also concretely efficient, achieving signature sizes of less than 150 kB for ring sizes up to $N = 4096$ (with threshold size $T = N/2$, say). This is substantially more compact than previous work.

Our approach is inspired by the recent work of Aardal et al. (CRYPTO 2024) on the compact aggregation of Falcon signatures, that uses the LaBRADOR lattice-based SNARKs to combine a collection of Falcon signatures into a single succinct argument of knowledge of those signatures. We proceed in a similar way to obtain compact threshold ring signatures from Falcon, but crucially require that the proof system be zero-knowledge in order to ensure the privacy of signers. Since LaBRADOR is not a zkSNARK, we associate it with a separate (non-succinct) lattice-based zero-knowledge proof system to achieve our desired properties.

1 Introduction

Ring signatures, introduced by Rivest et al. [22], allow a signer to remain anonymous inside a group of users known as the ring. Bresson et al. [7] extended the notion of ring signature to threshold ring signatures that allow T distinct signers to sign a message together hiding their identity within the ring. Ring signatures can be seen as threshold ring signatures with $T = 1$.

Threshold ring signatures are useful in privacy-preserving systems including electronic voting, whistleblowing, and cryptocurrencies because of anonymity. For instance, in a trusted blockchain, one could force certain transactions to be added to the blockchain only if at least T trustees approved the operation without revealing their identity. Threshold ring signatures can be applied to any scenario where a quorum must endorse a statement, but parties need to protect their identities. In another application, whistleblowing, the public believes the message when it comes from a sufficient number of members. The members need

---

S. Jeon—Work carried out in part during the author's internship at the NTT Social Informatics Laboratories.

© The Author(s), under exclusive license to Springer Nature Switzerland AG 2026
S. K. Cha and J. Park (Eds.): ISC 2025, LNCS 16186, pp. 152–172, 2026.
https://doi.org/10.1007/978-3-032-08124-7_8

a sufficiently large ring to conceal their identities. In these applications, small signature sizes are important.

However, existing threshold ring signature schemes face inefficiency in signature size. The seminal work of Bresson et al. [7] lacks efficiency since the signature size grows superlinearly with the number of users N. Their signature size is asymptotically $\mathcal{O}(N \log N)$. There are improved schemes based on the DDH problem [23], coding theory [2], or lattice problems [4,8]. All these schemes have signatures linear in the ring size N due to the structure of the schemes, in which a signature is a collection of T proofs of knowledge of each signer's secret key and $N - T$ simulated proofs for the non-signers in the ring.

If each signer can prove anonymously the knowledge of their secret key, the signers do not need to simulate the proofs for non-signers. Recently, most threshold schemes [9,14,20,21] concatenate signatures after each signer anonymously broadcasts its signature. The advantage of this structure is that the signers do not need to interact with each other to generate a signature. However, the signature sizes of schemes in this structure depend on the base ring signature. For instance, Munch-Hansen et al. [20] construct a threshold ring signature scheme using this structure from a ring signature with signature size $\mathcal{O}(1)$. Very recently, Chiang et al. [9] proposed a compact ring signature based on the VOLE-in-the-head paradigm and AES encryption, and constructed a threshold ring signature scheme by concatenating proofs. They presented concrete sizes of proofs, for example, the proof size is 1.24 kB (9.962 KB in [9, Example 5.10]) for the security parameter $\lambda = 128$ and $N = 2^{10}$. The threshold ring signature scheme has a small signature size when the threshold is small. However, for a threshold of $T = 200$, which is not extremely large, the signature size is over 200 kB. Moreover, concatenating T instances of ring signatures does not guarantee the distinctness of signers; hence, the constructions require extra properties. Munch-Hansen et al. [20] established linkability which can distinguish whether signatures are generated by the same signer or not without knowing the signers by adding a tag to each signature. We want to build a more compact lattice-based threshold ring signature without relying on such extra properties.

Falcon [12] is a lattice-based signature scheme selected by NIST. It has small signatures and public keys, as well as efficient signature generation and a particularly fast verification algorithm with a simple algebraic description. These properties make it an attractive choice as a building block for schemes in the multi-user setting. As a recent example, Aardal et al. [1] instantiated an aggregate signature, which combines multiple individual signatures into one signature, by aggregating Falcon signatures using the lattice-based SNARK LaBRADOR [5]. LaBRADOR is an efficient proof system recently proposed, and its language is suitable for aggregating Falcon signatures. Since aggregated signature is a succinct argument of knowledge of the individual Falcon signatures, they achieve an aggregate signature size sublinear (in fact, logarithmic) in the number of signers. Their signature size is significantly smaller than previous lattice-based aggregate signatures [16]. Adopting the techniques of [1], we construct a compact lattice-based threshold ring signature by generating a proof for the knowledge of signatures, unlike the threshold ring signature schemes that simply concatenate individual ring signatures.

1.1 Our Contributions

Table 1. Comparison of other threshold ring signature schemes. Previous works reported their size for different parameters. Therefore, we provide results for both $N = 100$ and $N = 2^{10}$ in this table. The threshold is $T = N/2$ in all cases. A signature of the threshold ring signature scheme in [9] is a concatenation of T proofs, each of size 1.2 kB. Therefore, we compute their signature size by multiplying $T = N/2$ with the size of the per-signer proofs.

Work	Assumption	N	Size	Security
Aguilar et al. [2]	Code	100	2 MB	80 bit
Cayrel et al. [8]	Code	100	47 MB	111 bit
	Lattice	100	45 MB	111 bit
Bettaieb et al. [4]	Lattice	100	13 MB	111 bit
Chiang et al. [9]	AES	2^{10}	638 kB	128 bit
This work	Lattice	100	122 kB	128 bit
		2^{10}	136 kB	128 bit

In our threshold ring signature scheme, signers sign a message with the Falcon signature scheme, and we want the threshold ring signature to be a succinct argument of knowledge of those individual signatures, in a similar way to [1]. However, we need to overcome a difficulty that does not affect aggregate signatures: we want our argument of knowledge to be *zero-knowledge* (or at least witness indistinguishable) so that it does not reveal which signature is associated with which ring member verification key, and hence hides the identities of the signers. Unfortunately, LaBRADOR doesn't have a zero-knowledge property. However, the zero-knowledge property can be achieved by masking the input witness with a simple linear-size shim protocol as mentioned in [5]. Following this method, Albrecht et al. [3] combined the zero-knowledge proof of [17] and LaBRADOR for zkSNARK.

We use the same methodology to build a compact threshold ring signature. We use the combination as an efficient zkSNARK for a class of languages that includes valid Falcon signatures. Then, based on this combined proof system and the Falcon signature, we construct the threshold ring signature of size logarithmic in the threshold T. As shown in Table 1, the signature size of our scheme is less than 150 kB even for a large ring size $N = 2^{10}$ and threshold $T = N/2$. For a smaller threshold $T = 50$, the size of [9] is expected to be smaller than ours. However, the signature size of our scheme is logarithmic in T, whereas that of [9] is linear due to concatenation. Our signature size is 136 kB even for $T = 512$.

Therefore, as the threshold increases, our scheme results in a smaller signature size than the previous work. Our scheme is well-suited to scenarios that even require a large ring for anonymity and a flexible threshold.

Zero-Knowledge SNARKs. The zero-knowledge property is the cornerstone of privacy-preserving cryptography. The most practical, potentially quantum-resistant zero-knowledge proofs are based on lattice assumptions. In particular, the proof system of Lyubashevky et al. [17] achieves substantial improvements in proof size compared to previous work. However, it still has a proof size linear in the dimension of the witness. In the case of the threshold ring signature with a large ring and a large threshold, using such a proof system would cause the signature size to increase at least linearly. The recently proposed proof system LaBRADOR is a succinct proof of knowledge whose proof size is logarithmic in the size of the witness. To obtain succinct ZKPoK, we apply LaBRADOR to prove the verification equations of the protocol in [17]. We call the ZKPoK in [17] LNP for convenience. In LNP's proof, the part whose size is linear in the size of the witness $(\mathbf{s}_1, \mathbf{s}_2) \in \mathcal{R}_q^{m_1+m_2}$ is the opening $(\mathbf{z}_1, \mathbf{z}_2) = (c\mathbf{s}_1 + \mathbf{y}_1, c\mathbf{s}_2 + \mathbf{y}_2) \in \mathcal{R}^{m_1+m_2}$. For succinctness, we set $(\mathbf{z}_1, \mathbf{z}_2)$ as witness of LaBRADOR. The verification equations that $\mathbf{z}_i$'s should satisfy are quadratic, hence we can prove these equations by LaBRADOR. Since $\mathbf{z}_1$ and $\mathbf{z}_2$ have different dimensions, we cut $\mathbf{z}_1$ into r vectors and pad zeros to split vectors to have the same dimension $m' := \max(\{m'_i\}_{i \in [r]}, m_2)$ where m'_i is a dimension of each split vector for $i \in [r]$. That is, we prove knowledge of m'-dimensional vectors using LaBRADOR. Then the proof consists of a proof of LNP except for $\mathbf{z}_1, \mathbf{z}_2$ and a proof of LaBRADOR. As a result, we can get a succinct ZKPoK whose proof size is asymptotically $\mathcal{O}(\log m + \log m') = \mathcal{O}(\log m)$ since $m' \leq m = m_1 + m_2$ where m is the dimension of witness for LNP. We can transform the combined protocol to the zkSNARK by the Fiat–Shamir transformation.

Threshold Ring Signatures. We build the first threshold ring signature with signature size $\mathcal{O}(\log T)$ using zkSNARK. Many threshold ring signatures concatenate signatures after each signer signs the same message. Therefore, the signature size is linear in the threshold, and schemes require an extra property to check that all signers are distinct. On the other hand, we set all signers' signatures as the witness of the zkSNARK so that the signature size is not linear in the threshold. In our scheme, each signer signs the same message by Falcon. Therefore, we consider a non-salted variant of Falcon in order to make all signers have the same target. Then the signers want to prove that all signatures are valid without revealing their identity. However, a verifier needs the public key h_i of each signer since the verification equation of Falcon is

$$s_{i,1} + h_i s_{i,2} = t = H(\mathsf{msg}) \in \mathcal{R}_{q_f}.$$

To hide signers' identities, we set the Falcon public key h_i's also the witness $w_i := h_i$ then prove
$$w_i = \langle \mathbf{h}, \boldsymbol{\delta}_i \rangle$$

where $\mathbf{h} = (h_1, \ldots, h_N)$ and $\boldsymbol{\delta}_i \in \{0,1\}^N$ is the binary unit vector whose i-th component is 1 and the others are 0. Each $\boldsymbol{\delta}_i$ represents one signer in the scheme. Then, we must prove that $\boldsymbol{\delta}_i$'s are binary and of norm one with only one non-zero coefficient. For this, we prove

$$\forall i \in S : \langle \boldsymbol{\delta}_i, \boldsymbol{\delta}_i - \mathbf{1} \rangle = 0 \text{ and } \forall i \in S : \langle \mathbf{1}, \boldsymbol{\delta}_i \rangle = 1.$$

Now, to prove that signers are distinct, we also prove

$$\sum_{i,j \in S} \langle \boldsymbol{\delta}_i, \boldsymbol{\delta}_j \rangle = T.$$

Then, the signers should prove the knowledge of $(s_{i,1}, s_{i,2}, w_i, \boldsymbol{\delta}_i)$ for the all signers $i \in S$. This implies that the length of the aggregated witness depends on the number of witnesses $(s_{i,1}, s_{i,2}, w_i, \boldsymbol{\delta}_i)$ that we collect, which is exactly the threshold T. Though being N-dimensional, $\boldsymbol{\delta}_i$'s are short since they are unitary. As a result, our threshold ring signature has size $\mathcal{O}(\log T)$ where T is the threshold, since the proof size is $\mathcal{O}(\log m)$ asymptotically where m is the dimension of the witness, as mentioned above.

2 Preliminaries

For a power of two d and a positive integer q, denote $\mathcal{R} = \mathbb{Z}[X]/(X^d + 1)$ and $\mathcal{R}_q = \mathbb{Z}_q[X]/(X^d + 1)$. We use lower-case letters for polynomials $r \in \mathcal{R}_q$ and bold lower-case letters for column vectors $\mathbf{r} \in \mathcal{R}_q^m$. $\vec{r} \in \mathbb{Z}_q^{md}$ is used to denote coefficient vectors of $\mathbf{r} \in \mathcal{R}_q^m$. For an element $r = \sum_{i=0}^{d-1} r_i X^i \in \mathcal{R}_q$, we write $\mathrm{ct}(r) = r_0 \in \mathbb{Z}_q$ to denote the constant coefficient. For $p \in \{1, 2, \infty\}$, we define the ℓ_p norm over $\mathcal{R}_q^m$ as $\|\mathbf{r}\|_p := \|\vec{r}\|_p$. $\|c\|_{op} := \sup_{r \in \mathcal{R}} \frac{\|cr\|_2}{\|r\|_2}$ is the operator norm of c.

2.1 Polynomial Rings

The ring $\mathcal{R}$ has automorphisms σ_i such that $\sigma_i(X) = X^i$. We denote for an arbitrary vector $\mathbf{r} \in \mathcal{R}^k$, $\sigma_i(\mathbf{r}) := (\sigma_i(r_1), \ldots, \sigma_i(r_k))$. For $r \in \mathcal{R}_q$, $\mathrm{ct}(r)$ denote the constant coefficient of r. We are especially interested in the conjugation automorphism σ_{-1}. For power-of-two cyclotomics, σ_{-1} relates inner products in $\mathcal{R}_q^m$ to the inner products of their coefficient vectors by

$$\langle \vec{a}, \vec{b} \rangle = \mathrm{ct}(\langle \sigma_{-1}(\mathbf{a}), \mathbf{b} \rangle)$$

for $\mathbf{a}, \mathbf{b} \in \mathcal{R}_q^m$, as observed in [17, Lemma 2.4]. In particular, we have $\|\mathbf{a}\|_2^2 = \mathrm{ct}(\langle \sigma_{-1}(\mathbf{a}), \mathbf{a} \rangle)$.

Let $\mathcal{R} = \mathbb{Z}[X]/(X^{dk} + 1)$ and $\mathcal{S} = \mathbb{Z}[X]/(X^d + 1)$, where d and k are powers of two. By [18, Section 2.8], there is norm-preserving bijection from $\mathcal{R}$ to $\mathcal{S}^k$ so that we can work over subring $\mathcal{S}$. The bijection can be extended to vectors over $\mathcal{R}$ and $\mathcal{S}$, and the respective quotient rings modulus q preserving norm bound. That is, $\mathbf{r} \in \mathcal{R}_q^m$ such that $\|\mathbf{r}\|_2 \leq \beta$ can be represented as $\mathbf{s} \in \mathcal{S}_q^{km}$ such that $\|\mathbf{s}\|_2 \leq \beta$.

2.2 Threshold Ring Signatures

In this section, we recall the definition of a threshold ring signature scheme in [15], which introduces a stronger model taking active adversaries into account.

Definition 1. *A threshold ring signature scheme is* $\mathsf{TRS} = (\mathsf{KGen}, \mathsf{Sign}, \mathsf{Vf})$. *A ring R is a set of public keys of ring members, and a signer set S is a set of signers' indices with $\{\mathsf{pk}_i\}_{i \in S} \subset R$ and $|S| \geq T$ for the threshold T.*

- $(\mathsf{pk}_i, \mathsf{sk}_i) \leftarrow \mathsf{KGen}(pp)$: *On input the public parameter pp, generates a public key and a private key of a user i.*
- $\sigma \leftarrow \mathsf{Sign}(\mathsf{msg}, \{\mathsf{sk}_i\}_{i \in S}, R)$: *The signers owning the private keys interact to produce a ring signature σ on a message msg and a ring R.*
- $0/1 \leftarrow \mathsf{Vf}(\mathsf{msg}, \sigma, R)$: *A verifier checks that σ is a correct threshold ring signature on the message msg and the ring R. If the signature is valid, output 1, otherwise output 0.*

For the security properties, we give the adversary $\mathcal{A}$ the ability to query four different types of oracles $\mathsf{O} := \{\mathsf{OKGen}, \mathsf{OSign}, \mathsf{OCorr}, \mathsf{ORegister}\}$. P, P_c, and P_s^{msg} are the set of honestly generated keys, the set of corrupted keys, and the set of keys which are queried to the signing oracle on the message msg, respectively:

- $\mathsf{OKGen}(i)$: This oracle produces $(\mathsf{pk}_i, \mathsf{sk}_i) \leftarrow \mathsf{KGen}(pp)$ and returns pk_i to $\mathcal{A}$ and adds pk_i to P.
- $\mathsf{OSign}(\mathsf{msg}, S, R)$: $\mathcal{A}$ requests a signature on the message msg with the signer set S. S could contain both honest users or corrupted users, i.e., $S = S_c \sqcup S_h$ where $\sqcup$ is the disjoint union. This oracle cooperates with $\mathcal{A}$ to produce $\sigma \leftarrow \mathsf{Sign}(\mathsf{msg}, \{\mathsf{sk}_i\}_{i \in S}, R)$ and returns σ to $\mathcal{A}$. Then, this oracle adds $\{\mathsf{pk}_i\}_{i \in S}$ to P_s^{msg}.
- $\mathsf{OCorr}(i)$: If $\mathsf{pk}_i \notin P$, this oracle aborts, otherwise returns sk_i to $\mathcal{A}$ and adds pk_i to P_c.
- $\mathsf{ORegister}(i, \mathsf{pk})$: If $\mathsf{pk} \in P$, this oracle aborts, otherwise adds $\mathsf{pk}_i := \mathsf{pk}$ to P and P_c.

A threshold ring signature scheme satisfies completeness, unforgeability, and anonymity. Completeness means that if the signers follow the signing algorithm correctly, an honest verifier should accept their proof.

Definition 2 (Completeness). *A threshold ring signature scheme TRS is complete if for all PPT adversaries $\mathcal{A}$ there exists a negligible function negl such that*

$$\Pr\left[\mathsf{Vf}(\mathsf{msg}, R, \sigma) = 0 \,\middle|\, \begin{array}{l} pp \leftarrow \mathsf{Setup}(1^\lambda) \\ P = \{(\mathsf{pk}_i, \mathsf{sk}_i) \leftarrow \mathsf{KGen}(pp)\} \\ (\mathsf{msg}, S, R) \leftarrow \mathcal{A}(pp, P) \\ \sigma \leftarrow \mathsf{Sign}(\mathsf{msg}, \{\mathsf{sk}_i\}_{i \in S}, R) \end{array}\right] \leq \mathsf{negl}(\lambda).$$

Definition 3 (Unforgeability). *A threshold ring signature scheme* TRS *satisfies unforgeability if for all PPT adversaries* $\mathcal{A}$, *there exists a negligible function* negl *such that*

$$\Pr[\mathsf{Exp}^{unf}_{\mathsf{TRS},\mathcal{A}}(\lambda) = 1] \leq \mathsf{negl}(\lambda)$$

where the experiment $\mathsf{Exp}^{unf}_{\mathsf{TRS},\mathcal{A}}(\lambda)$ *is defined in Fig. 1.*

Definition 4 (Anonymity). *A threshold ring signature scheme* TRS *satisfies anonymity if for all PPT adversaries* $\mathcal{A}$, *there exists a negligible function* negl *such that*

$$|\Pr[\mathsf{Exp}^{anon-0}_{\mathsf{TRS},\mathcal{A}}(\lambda) = 1] - \Pr[\mathsf{Exp}^{anon-1}_{\mathsf{TRS},\mathcal{A}}(\lambda) = 1]| \leq \mathsf{negl}(\lambda)$$

where the experiment $\mathsf{Exp}^{anon-b}_{\mathsf{TRS},\mathcal{A}}(\lambda)$ *is defined in Fig. 1.*

$\mathsf{Exp}^{unf}_{\mathsf{TRS},\mathcal{A}}(\lambda)$
  $pp \leftarrow \mathsf{Setup}(1^\lambda)$
  $(\mathsf{msg}^*, \sigma^*, R^*) \leftarrow \mathcal{A}^\mathcal{O}(pp)$
  if $|R^*| \geq T$
    and $|R^* \cap (P_c \cup P_s^{\mathsf{msg}^*})| < T$
    and (msg^*, R^*) has not been queried
    and $\mathsf{Vf}(\mathsf{msg}^*, R^*, \sigma^*) = 1$:
    return 1

$\mathsf{Exp}^{anon-b}_{\mathsf{TRS},\mathcal{A}}(\lambda)$
  $pp \leftarrow \mathsf{Setup}(1^\lambda)$
  $(\mathsf{msg}^*, S_0, S_1) \leftarrow \mathcal{A}^\mathcal{O}(pp)$ ($|S_0| = |S_1| = T$ and $(S_0 \cup S_1) \cap P_c = \emptyset$)
  $\sigma^* \leftarrow \mathsf{Sign}(\mathsf{msg}^*, \{\mathsf{sk}_i\}_{i \in S_b}, R)$
  $b^* \leftarrow \mathcal{A}(\sigma^*)$
  if $b^* = b$: **return** 1

Fig. 1. Experiments for the security of threshold ring signatures

3 Construction of Threshold Ring Signature

In this section, we provide our threshold ring signature. Signers choose a ring R that is a set of public keys of some users to hide their identities. We use N and T to denote the number of ring members and the threshold. S is a set of signers' indices so that $\{\mathsf{pk}_i\}_{i \in S} \subset R$ and $|S| = T$. In our scheme, each signer signs the same message msg using a non-salted variant of Falcon. We change the modulus following the trick in [1] to express the equation over the ring of the proof system. Then, the verification equation of the Falcon signature is

$$\forall i \in S : s_{i,1} + h_i s_{i,2} + q_f v_i - t = 0 \tag{1}$$

with $t = H(\mathsf{msg})$ and added element $v_i \in \mathcal{R}_q$. Here, q is the modulus of the proof system and q_f is the modulus of the Falcon signature. In order to prove that $\|(s_{i,1}, s_{i,2})\|_2 \leq \beta_f$ exactly, we use the same technique of [1]. By Lagrange's four-square theorem, there exists $e_i = \sum_{j=0}^{3} e_{i,j} X^j \in \mathcal{R}_q$ such that $\|(s_{i,1}, s_{i,2})\|_2^2 + \|e_i\|_2^2 - \beta_f^2 = 0$. We recall that $\|\mathbf{a}\|_2^2 = \mathsf{ct}(\langle \sigma_{-1}(\mathbf{a}), \mathbf{a} \rangle)$. Then, the norm check equation is transformed into

$$\forall i \in S : \mathsf{ct}(\sigma_{-1}(s_{i,1})s_{i,1} + \sigma_{-1}(s_{i,2})s_{i,2} + \sigma_{-1}(e_i)e_i - \beta_f^2) = 0 \mod q \quad (2)$$

In ring signatures, signers want to prove that they generate valid signatures without revealing their identities. It means a verifier should be able to verify the equation without knowing which public key is used. Therefore, we set h_i in Eq. (1) as the secret information w_i. Then, w_i satisfies the following equation:

$$\forall i \in S : w_i - \langle \mathbf{h}, \boldsymbol{\delta}_i \rangle = 0 \quad (3)$$

where $\mathbf{h} = (h_1, \ldots, h_N)$ is a concatenation of public keys and $\boldsymbol{\delta}_i \in \{0, 1\}^N$ is the unit vector whose i-th component is 1 and the others are 0 to indicate a signer. We should prove that $\boldsymbol{\delta}_i$'s are unit vectors. It can be proved as follows:

$$\text{(binary)} \quad \forall i \in S : \langle \boldsymbol{\delta}_i, \boldsymbol{\delta}_i - \mathbf{1} \rangle = 0 \quad (4)$$
$$\text{(unit vector)} \quad \forall i \in S : \langle \mathbf{1}, \boldsymbol{\delta}_i \rangle = 1 \quad (5)$$

Now, we should also prove the distinctness of signers. Since $\boldsymbol{\delta}_i$ indicates each signer, it can be guaranteed if $\boldsymbol{\delta}_i$'s are distinct. That is, $\boldsymbol{\delta}_i$'s should satisfy the following equation:

$$\text{(distinctness)} \quad \sum_{i,j \in S} \langle \boldsymbol{\delta}_i, \boldsymbol{\delta}_j \rangle = T \quad (6)$$

Therefore, we should prove that $(\bar{w}_i)_{i \in S}$ satisfies Eqs. (1) to (6) where

$$\bar{w}_i := (s_{i,1}, s_{i,2}, e_i, \sigma_{-1}(s_{i,1}), \sigma_{-1}(s_{i,2}), \sigma_{-1}(e_i), v_i, w_i, \boldsymbol{\delta}_i)$$

for all $i \in S$.

Each signer sends $\bar{w}_i$ to the leader. $\bar{w}_i$ consists of the Falcon signature and the signer's public key and index, not including the secret key. Since signers know each other and the leader is one of the signers, sending $\bar{w}_i$ to the leader doesn't reveal the signers' identities out of the signer set. Then, the leader generates a proof π with the witness $\bar{w} := (\bar{w}_i)_{i \in S}$ by using LNP and LaBRADOR as we mentioned. The whole scheme is given in Fig. 2. We describe the detailed procedure for using LNP and LaBRADOR in Sect. 3.1.

```
pp ← Setup(1^λ)
    p̄p̄ ← LNP.Setup(1^λ)
    pp' ← LaBRADOR.Setup(1^λ)
    pp := (p̄p̄, pp')
(pk_i, sk_i) ← KGen(pp)
    Generate Falcon public key and secret key:
    h ∈ R_{q_f} and (f, g, f̄, ḡ) such that h = g/f and fḡ - gf̄ = q_f.
    Set pk_i := h, sk_i := (f, g, f̄, ḡ)
σ ← Sign(msg, {sk_i}_{i∈S}, R)
    Signer i does the following processes:
    - Generate (s_{i,1}, s_{i,2}) such that s_{i,1} + h_i s_{i,2} = t = H(msg) mod q_f
    - Compute v_i such that s_{i,1} + h_i s_{i,2} + qv_i - t = 0.
    - Compute e_i ∈ R_q such that ||(s_{i,1}, s_{i,2})||^2 + ||e_i||^2 - β_f^2 = 0.
    - Send w̄_i := (s_{i,1}, s_{i,2}, e_i, σ_{-1}(s_{i,1}), σ_{-1}(s_{i,2}), σ_{-1}(e_i), v_i, w_i, δ_i) to the
      leader.
    The leader does the following processes:
    - Generate (π̄, z_1, z_2) ← LNP.P(x̄, w̄) where x̄ = (F̄, F̄', β̄) and w̄ =
      (w̄_i)_{i∈S}.
    - Split z_1 into z_{1,9i-8}, ..., z_{1,9i-1} ∈ R_q and z_{1,9i} ∈ R_q^N for i ∈ [T].
    - Pad zeros to z_{1,i}'s and z_2
    - set w'_i = z'_i ∈ R_q^{m'} for i ∈ [9T + 1] (m' = max(1, N, m_2)).
    - Generates π' ← LaBRADOR.P(x', w') where x' = (F, F', β') and w' =
      {w'}_{i∈[2(9T+3)]}.
    - Output σ := (π̄, π').
Vf(msg, σ, R)
    Compute t = H(msg)
    Accept if: LNP.V(x, π̄) = 1 and LaBRADOR.V(x', π') = 1
```

Fig. 2. Threshold ring signature scheme TRS

3.1 Succinct Zero-Knowledge Proof of Knowledge

Here, we describe how the leader use LNP and LaBRADOR to prove the possession of $\bar{w} = (\bar{w}_i)_{i\in S}$. The detailed description of LNP and LaBRADOR is in Appendix A. The relation for our threshold ring signature is

$$R_T := \left\{ (\bar{x}, \bar{w}) \middle| \begin{array}{l} \forall i \in S : s_{i,1} + h_i s_{i,2} + qv_i - t = 0 \\ \forall i \in S : \mathrm{ct}(\sigma_{-1}(s_{i,1})s_{i,1} + \sigma_{-1}(s_{i,2})s_{i,2} + \sigma_{-1}(e_i)e_i - \beta_f^2) = 0 \\ \forall i \in S : w_i - \langle \mathbf{h}, \boldsymbol{\delta}_i \rangle = 0 \\ \forall i \in S : \langle \boldsymbol{\delta}_i, \boldsymbol{\delta}_i - \mathbf{1} \rangle = 0 \\ \forall i \in S : \langle \mathbf{1}, \boldsymbol{\delta}_i \rangle = 1 \\ \sum_{i,j \in S} \langle \boldsymbol{\delta}_i, \boldsymbol{\delta}_j \rangle = T \end{array} \right\}$$

where $\bar{x} = (\bar{\mathcal{F}}, \bar{\mathcal{F}}', \bar{\beta})$. $\bar{\mathcal{F}}$ and $\bar{\mathcal{F}}'$ are sets of quadratic functions such that $f(\bar{w}) = 0$ and $\mathrm{ct}(f'(\bar{w})) = 0$ for all $f \in \bar{\mathcal{F}}, f' \in \bar{\mathcal{F}}'$. $\bar{\beta}$ is the norm bound of the witness $\bar{w}$. The Eq. (2) is included in the function set $\bar{\mathcal{F}}'$; the other equations are in the function set $\bar{\mathcal{F}}$. Therefore, $M = |\bar{\mathcal{F}}| = 4T + 1$ and $M' = |\bar{\mathcal{F}}'| = T$.

For the norm bound $\bar{\beta}$ of the witness $\bar{w}$, we compute the ℓ_2-norm bound of each witness $\bar{w}_i = (s_{i,1}, s_{i,2}, e_i, \sigma_{-1}(s_{i,1}), \sigma_{-1}(s_{i,2}), \sigma_{-1}(e_i), v_i, w_i, \boldsymbol{\delta}_i)$. First, $\|(s_{i,1}, s_{i,2}, e_i, \sigma_{-1}(s_{i,1}), \sigma_{-1}(s_{i,2}), \sigma_{-1}(e_i))\|_2^2 \leqslant 2\beta_f^2$ for $i \in S$ since the size of Falcon signature $(s_{i,1}, s_{i,2})$ should be less then β_f. Second, we can compute $\|v_i\|_2 = \frac{1}{q}\|t - s_{i,1} - h_i s_{i,2}\|_2 \leqslant \frac{1}{q}(\sqrt{d_f}q + \beta_f + d_f q \beta_f)$ from Eq. (1). Then, $\|v_i\|_2 \leqslant 1 + \sqrt{d_f} + d_f \beta_f$ for $i \in S$ since $\beta_f \leqslant q$. Third, w_i is actually $h_i \in \mathcal{R}_p$, so that $\|w_i\|_2 \leqslant q_f$. Finally, since $\boldsymbol{\delta}_i$ is a unit vector, $\|\boldsymbol{\delta}_i\|_2 = 1$ for $i \in S$. Then, $\bar{w}$ has the norm bound

$$\bar{\beta} = \sqrt{T(2\beta_f^2 + (1 + \sqrt{d_f} + d_f\beta_f)^2 + q_f^2 + 1)}.$$

Since all verification equations are quadratic relations, we can prove the knowledge of $\bar{w}$ by LaBRADOR. However, LaBRADOR doesn't have a zero-knowledge property, which is necessary for anonymity of the ring signature. As mentioned in [5] and as [3] did, we combine LNP and LaBRADOR to get a small proof with a zero-knowledge property. LNP is also a lattice-based proof of quadratic relations, and it has a zero-knowledge property.

The leader first generates $(\bar{\pi}, \mathbf{z}_1, \mathbf{z}_2) \leftarrow \mathsf{LNP.P}(\bar{x}, \bar{w})$ where $\bar{x} = (\bar{\mathcal{F}}, \bar{\mathcal{F}}', \bar{\beta})$ and $\bar{w} = (\bar{w}_i)_{i \in S}$. In LNP, a quadratic function is written as $f(\mathbf{s}) = \mathbf{s}^T \mathbf{R} \mathbf{s} + \mathbf{r}^T \mathbf{s} + r$ for $\mathbf{R} \in \mathcal{R}_q^{m \times m}$, $\mathbf{r} \in \mathcal{R}_q^m$, and $r \in \mathcal{R}_q$ where $\mathbf{s} = [\mathbf{s}_1 \| \mathbf{m}]$. When committing to the witness in LNP, $\mathbf{s}_i$ is considered as the Ajtai part and $\mathbf{m}$ as the BDLOP part. It is not necessary to set both Ajtai and BDLOP part. In our case, we need the Ajtai part but do not need the BDLOP part. Therefore, the leader sets concatenation of all $\bar{w}_i$ as $\mathbf{s}_1$, then $\mathbf{s} \in \mathcal{R}_q^{T(8+N)}$. Running LNP protocol[1], we get the commitments $(\mathbf{t}_A, \mathbf{t}_B, \mathbf{w}, v, t)$ to the message $\mathbf{s}$ and the response $(\vec{z}, (F_j)_{j \in [L]}, \mathbf{z}_1, \mathbf{z}_2)$ such that $\mathbf{z}_i = c\mathbf{s}_i + \mathbf{y}_i$ of $\mathbf{s}_i$ for $i = 1, 2$ where $c \in \mathcal{C}$. Then, the verification equations are

$$\|\vec{z}\|_\infty \leqslant 14\mathfrak{s}_3 \qquad (7)$$

$$\forall j \in [L] : \mathsf{ct}(F_j) = 0 \qquad (8)$$

$$\forall i \in [2] : \|\mathbf{z}_i\|_2 \leqslant \mathfrak{s}_i \sqrt{2 m_i d} \qquad (9)$$

$$\mathbf{A}_1 \mathbf{z}_1 + \mathbf{A}_2 \mathbf{z}_2 = \mathbf{w} + c \mathbf{t}_A \qquad (10)$$

$$\mathbf{z}^T \mathbf{R} \mathbf{z} + c \mathbf{r}^T \mathbf{z} + c^2 r - (ct - \mathbf{b}^T \mathbf{z}_2) - v = 0 \qquad (11)$$

In order to reduce the proof size, we will set the dominant part ($\mathbf{z}_1, \mathbf{z}_2$) as witnesses of LaBRADOR and prove the verification equations. LaBRADOR proves the quadratic dot product functions in the form of $f(\mathbf{w}_1, \cdots, \mathbf{w}_r) = \sum_{i,j=1}^r a_{ij} \langle \mathbf{w}_i, \mathbf{w}_j \rangle + \sum_{i=1}^r \langle \varphi_i, \mathbf{w}_i \rangle - b$ where $a_{ij}, b \in \mathcal{R}_q$ and $\varphi_i \in \mathcal{R}_q^n$. Its witness is the set of vectors with the same dimension, while $\mathbf{z}_1$ and $\mathbf{z}_2$ have different dimensions and the dimension of $\mathbf{z}_1$ is larger than that of $\mathbf{z}_2$. Therefore, we split $\mathbf{z}_1$ into vectors according to the part of the witnesses. The dot product of $\boldsymbol{\delta}_i$

---

[1] We use the protocol with exact ℓ_2-norm proof in Sect. 5.2 of [17] but without an approximate ℓ_2-norm proof. Because we have an exact proof, and we can prove there is no wraparound by an approximate ℓ_∞-norm proof.

and δ_j should be represented as $\langle \delta_i, \delta_j \rangle = \sum_{k=1}^{N} \varphi_k \delta_{ik} \delta_{jk}$ where $\varphi_k = 1$ for all $k \in [N]$ to prove it by LaBRADOR. Thus, one might consider splitting $\mathbf{z}_1$ into ring elements. However, since the coefficients φ_k are the same for all $k \in [N]$ in our scheme, δ_i can be one witness itself. Therefore, we see the opening of unit vector δ_i as one split vector instead of splitting it into N single elements in $\mathcal{R}_q$. Then, $\mathbf{z}_1$ is split into T vectors of dimension N, which is part of opening of δ_i, and $9T-1$ ring elements, which is part of opening of the others. We denote them as $\mathbf{z}_{1,9i} \in \mathcal{R}_q^N$ and $z_{1,9i-8}, \ldots, z_{1,9i-1} \in \mathcal{R}_q$ for all $i \in [T]$. After that, the leader pads zeros to these and $\mathbf{z}_2$ to have the same dimension $m' = \max(1, N, m_2)$, i.e., $\mathbf{z}'_i := \mathbf{z}_{1,i} \| 0 \in \mathcal{R}_q^{m'}$ and $\mathbf{z}'_{9T+1} := \mathbf{z}_2 \| 0 \in \mathcal{R}_q^{m'}$. Then, the leader generates $\pi' \leftarrow$ LaBRADOR.P(x', w') by setting $w' = (\mathbf{z}'_i)_{i \in r'}$ as new witnesses for LaBRADOR protocol and $x' = (\mathcal{F}, \mathcal{F}', \beta')$. Then, we have $r' = 2(9T+3)$ witnesses because we need the automorphism values of vectors and ring vectors whose components are 3-degree ring elements to prove the norm bound using Lagrange's four-square theorem as [1]. We need to prove only Eqs. (9) to (11) by LaBRADOR, which the dominant part $(\mathbf{z}_1, \mathbf{z}_2)$ should satisfy. Then, the new function sets $\mathcal{F}$ contains Eqs. (10) to (11) and $\mathcal{F}'$ contains Eq. (9), thus $|\mathcal{F}| = n+1$ and $|\mathcal{F}'| = 2$ where n is the dimension of $\mathbf{w}, \mathbf{t}_A$ in Eq. (10). The new norm bound is β' such that $\beta'^2 = 2((\mathfrak{s}_1 \sqrt{2m_1 d})^2 + (\mathfrak{s}_2 \sqrt{2m_2 d})^2)$ where $\mathfrak{s}_i$'s are the standard deviation for rejection sampling.

Modulus and Challenge Space. The challenge space $\mathcal{C} \subset \mathcal{R}$ should satisfy that $c_1 - c_2$ is invertible for any $c_1, c_2 \in \mathcal{C}$ for the soundness. In [19, Theorem 2.5], they show that infinitely many primes q satisfy the conditions for invertible differences of challenges. Therefore, we can easily choose the appropriate modulus for our scheme. LaBRADOR instantiated the challenge space $\mathcal{C} \subset \mathcal{R}_q = \mathbb{Z}_q[X]/(X^{64}+1)$ with 23 zero coefficients, 31 coefficients that are ± 1, and 10 coefficients that are ± 2. Then $\|c\|_\infty = 2$, $\|c\|_2^2 \leqslant \tau_2 = 71$, and $\|c\|_{op} \leqslant 15$. They set $\|c\|_{op} = 15$ using rejection sampling. They instantiated $\mathcal{C}$ only for the security parameter $\lambda = 128$. Since the automorphism value of the witness can be computed from the witness, LNP does not add it to the witness. However, it causes the challenge set to satisfy $\sigma_{-1}(c) = c$ to verify a proof only with $\mathbf{z}_1 = \mathbf{y}_1 + c\mathbf{s}_1$. It restricts the challenge set. To solve this issue, we set the automorphism value as the witness. It leads to an increase in the proof size. However, It does not affect much because we will later apply the succinct protocol whose proof size is not linear in the witness size. Therefore, we don't need the condition $\sigma_{-1}(c) = c$ hence we can have small coefficients of the challenge like LaBRADOR.

Security of ZKPoK. We will briefly sketch the proofs for the security of the combination of LNP and LaBRADOR. The authors of [5] define proof of knowledge reductions. The protocol for a relation R is a proof of knowledge reduction from R to R' if the relation R' contains the verification of the protocol for a relation R. If Π is a proof of knowledge reduction from R to R' and Π' is a proof of knowledge for R', then the composition of reduction $\Pi' \circ \Pi$ is a protocol where the prover and verifier run Π' for the verification equation of Π instead of sending a proof of Π. They show that the composition of reduction preserves knowledge soundness [5, Lemma 3.7]. The combination of LaBRADOR and LNP is exactly in this case, i.e., LaBRADOR ∘ LNP, so it satisfies the knowledge soundness. As for the zero-knowledge property, it follows from the zero-knowledge property of the NIZK argument by exploiting strategy in [6, Section 9.1]. We can simulate a transcript of the combination of LNP and LaBRADOR. Firstly, we can simulate a proof of LNP. Then, we generate a proof of LaBRADOR by setting the response of LNP as witnesses.

3.2 Security of TRS

The adversary chooses two signer sets S_0, S_1 in the anonymity experiment. The challenger picks one of the signer sets S_b, generates a signature σ^*, and sends it to the adversary. Then, the adversary guesses which of S_0, S_1 signed the message. In our construction, the signature σ is a proof of the knowledge. We can show anonymity if we can show that any adversary cannot distinguish whether a proof is generated by S_0 or S_1. It is implied by the zero-knowledge property of LaBRADOR ∘ LNP.

We prove the unforgeability by showing that if there exists a PPT forger with a non-negligible probability, then one can break the unforgeability of the Falcon signature. The reduction picks a uniformly random user I and sets a public key $\mathsf{pk}_I := \mathsf{pk}$ where pk is a given public key from the challenger of the unforgeability experiment of Falcon. Then, the reduction will hope that the forger does not make a corruption query of I and forges a signature for the public key pk_I. In this case, the reduction can extract a witness that contains Falcon signature of the signer I. Thus, the reduction can forge Falcon signature.

Theorem 1. *If* LaBRADOR ∘ LNP *is a zero-knowledge proof of knowledge, then* TRS *in Fig. 2 is a threshold ring signature.*

Proof. Anonymity. An adversary against the anonymity of the threshold ring signature produces two signer sets and distinguishes between signatures generated with each set. We transform a signature under S_0 to a signature under S_1 over a sequence of hybrids.

$\mathsf{Game}_1(\lambda)$: The original experiment $\mathsf{Exp}^{anon-0}_{\mathsf{TRS},\mathcal{A}}(\lambda)$ with the signing oracle OSign and $b = 0$.

$\mathsf{Game}_2(\lambda)$: Instead of generating proofs honestly in response to signing queries, the challenger generates simulated proofs. The challenger employs the simulator Sim of LNP to get $(\bar{\pi}, \mathbf{z}_1, \mathbf{z}_2) \leftarrow \mathsf{LNP.Sim}(1^\lambda)$, and generates a proof of LaBRADOR by setting $(\mathbf{z}_1, \mathbf{z}_2)$ as witnesses of LaBRADOR as described in Sect. 3.1. Then, the challenger sends $\sigma = (\bar{\pi}, \pi')$ to $\mathcal{A}$. The challenger also reprograms the corresponding hash values of H_{FS} with the challenges of the simulated proofs. Game_1 and Game_2 are computationally indistinguishable due to the zero-knowledge property of LaBRADOR ∘ LNP.

Game$_3(\lambda)$: The challenger generates the Falcon signature using the signing key of users in S_1 to send σ^* to $\mathcal{A}$. Since the proof is simulated, the threshold ring signature $\sigma^* = (\bar{\pi}, \pi')$ is the same regardless of which signer set the challenger picks. It means that the view of $\mathcal{A}$ is still the same as in the previous game.

Game$_4(\lambda)$: The challenger switches back to generate proofs honestly in response to the signing queries. Game$_3$ and Game$_4$ are also computationally indistinguishable due to the zero-knowledge property of LaBRADOR∘LNP. This game is actually the experiment $\mathsf{Exp}_{\mathsf{TRS},\mathcal{A}}^{anon-1}(\lambda)$.

As a result, if LaBRADOR ∘ LNP is zero-knowledge proof of knowledge, $|\Pr[\mathsf{Exp}_{\mathsf{TRS},\mathcal{A}}^{anon-0}(\lambda) = 1] - \Pr[\mathsf{Exp}_{\mathsf{TRS},\mathcal{A}}^{anon-1}(\lambda) = 1]| \leq \mathsf{negl}(\lambda)$ for some negligeable function $\mathsf{negl}(\lambda)$. Hence, the threshold ring signature TRS is anonymous.

Unforgeability. Suppose that an adversary $\mathcal{A}$ breaks the unforgeability of TRS with a non-negligible probability $p(\lambda)$. Then we can build an adversary $\mathcal{B}$ who breaks the unforgeability of Falcon. Given $\mathsf{pk} = h$, $\mathcal{B}$ runs the unforgeability experiment of the threshold ring signature. The adversary $\mathcal{A}$ makes key-generating queries polynomially many times, q_k, in total. $\mathcal{B}$ randomly chooses $K \in \{1, \ldots, q_k\}$ and sets $\mathsf{pk}_I := \mathsf{pk} = h$ where I is the user's index of $\mathcal{A}$'s K-th query to the oracle OKGen. $\mathcal{B}$ will simulate all the oracles and abort only when $\mathcal{A}$ requests to corrupt the key of the user I. When $\mathcal{A}$ requests a public key of user i, $\mathcal{B}$ runs Falcon key generation algorithm to get $(\mathsf{pk}_i, \mathsf{sk}_i)$ where $\mathsf{pk}_i = h_i$ and sends pk_i to $\mathcal{A}$. If $i = I$, $\mathcal{B}$ sends $\mathsf{pk}_I = \mathsf{pk} = h$. When $\mathcal{A}$ requests the signature on (msg, R, S), firstly $\mathcal{B}$ gets $t = H(\mathsf{msg})$ by querying H. Then, $\mathcal{B}$ generates Falcon signatures $(s_{i,1}, s_{i,2})$ such that $s_{i,1} + h_i s_{i,2} = t$ for all $i \in S \backslash \{I\}$. For user I, $\mathcal{B}$ cannot generate a Falcon signature by itself, so it queries the signing oracle of Falcon and gets $(s_{I,1}, s_{I,2})$. Then $\mathcal{B}$ proves the knowledge of signatures by running $\bar{\pi} \leftarrow$ LaBRADOR ∘ LNP.P$(\bar{x}, \bar{w})$. When generating the proof, $\mathcal{B}$ samples random challenges from $\mathcal{C}$ uniformly at random and programs the corresponding hash value of H_{FS}. Then $\mathcal{B}$ answers $\sigma := \bar{\pi}$ to the signing query of $\mathcal{A}$. Receiving a query to H_{FS} from $\mathcal{A}$, $\mathcal{B}$ sends a value sampled from $\mathcal{C}$ uniformly at random.

$\mathcal{B}$ rewinds $\mathcal{A}$ to the point where $\mathcal{A}$ requests a value of H_{FS} used in the forged signature and gives a different random answer until $\mathcal{A}$ produces additional forged signatures. When $\mathcal{B}$ gets different forged signatures, $\mathcal{B}$ can extract a witness $\bar{w}$ using the extractor Ext of LaBRADOR ∘ LNP. If the witness contains $(s_{I,1}, s_{I,2})$, $\mathcal{B}$ outputs $(\mathsf{msg}^*, (s_{I,1}, s_{I,2}))$ as a forgery of Falcon. Since $\mathcal{A}$ wins the game, (msg^*, R^*) has not been queried to the signing oracle. This implies that $\mathcal{B}$ has not queried msg^* to the signing oracle of the Falcon signature.

Although $\mathcal{A}$ does not output the signer set, we denote the corresponding signer set of the forgery S^* for convenience. $\mathcal{B}$ wants I to be in S^* and not be queried. By the assumption, $\mathcal{A}$ outputs a valid forgery $(\mathsf{msg}^*, R^*, \sigma^*)$ with a non-negligible probability $p(\lambda)$. The probability that $\mathcal{A}$ outputs a forgery while I has not queried is $p(\lambda)(1 - 1/q_k)$ with $|P| = q_k$ where P is a set of honestly generated keys. Since $\mathcal{A}$'s forgery satisfies $|R^* \cap (P_c \cup P_s^{\mathsf{msg}^*})| \leq t-1$ and $S^* \subset R^*$, there is at least one honest party in S^*. Therefore, we can argue that the forgery includes the signer I with a probability of at least $1/q_k$. Therefore, if $\mathcal{A}$ forges with a non-negligible probability $p(\lambda)$, $\mathcal{B}$ forges the Falcon signature with a probability of at least $p(\lambda)(1 - 1/q_k)/q_k$, which is also non-negligible. By contradiction, TRS is unforgeable.

3.3 Signature Sizes

Table 2. Parameters for the threshold ring signature

The number of ring members	N	
The threshold	T	
The reduced modulus of the Falcon	q_f	3329
The ring degree of the Falcon	d_f	512
The reduced bound of the Falcon signature	β_f	2693
The degree of the ring for the protocol	d	64
The split factor of the ring	k	8
The modulus	q	$3329(2^{63} - 495)$
The bounds of the ℓ_2-norm and the operate norm	(τ_2, τ_{op})	$(52, \sqrt{71})$
The number of quadratic constraints $|\bar{\mathcal{F}}|$	M	$4T+1$
The number of constant constraints $|\bar{\mathcal{F}}'|$	M'	T
The number of repetitions to aggregate functions	L	$\lceil \lambda/\log q_f \rceil$
The rank of $\mathbf{A}_1, \mathbf{A}_2$	n	1
The length of the $\mathbf{s}_1$	m_1	$kT(8+N)$
The length of the $\mathbf{s}_2$	m_2	10
The number of new witnesses	r'	$2(9T+3)$
The number of new quadratic constraints $|\mathcal{F}|$	K	$n+1$
The number of new constant constraints $|\mathcal{F}'|$	K'	2
The number of repetitions to aggregate functions	L'	$\lceil \lambda/\log q \rceil$

We provide our parameter selection for our threshold ring signature in Table 2. We use the variant of Falcon introduced by Espitau et al. [10]. [10,11] pointed out a range for smaller q_f which does not necessarily translate to a substantially lower security level. [10] chose a smaller modulus $q = 3329$ than $q = 12289$ and targeted $\alpha = 1.23$ in dimension 512. We adopt the same smaller parameter because the Falcon modulus affects the signature size. Signatures of Falcon are sampled according to the Gaussian distribution with a standard deviation $\mathfrak{s} = r\alpha_f\sqrt{q_f}$ where $r = \sqrt{\log(2(1+2^{36}))/2/\pi}$. Then the norm of a signature is bounded by $1.1\mathfrak{s}\sqrt{2d_f}$ with overwhelming probability. Since we set the Falcon modulus $q_f = 3329$, the norm bound is $\beta_f = 2693$ for the security parameter $\lambda = 128$. The large ring degree of Falcon $d_f = 512$ causes a large proof size. We can compress the proof sizes by using the technique from [18, Section 2.8] mentioned in Sect. 2.1 to move from the ring with Falcon degree d_f to a subring of smaller degree d which is 64 in our scheme for the security parameter $\lambda = 128$. We note the split factor of the ring $k = d_f/d$, which is $k = 8$ in our scheme.

We need the modulus to make the differences of distinct challenges invertible according to [19]. In addition, we also need a sufficiently large modulus for which the MSIS and the Extended-MLWE problems are hard for the security of LNP and LaBRADOR in Theorems 2 and 3 (Appendix A). Therefore, we set the modulus $q = 3329 \cdot (2^{63} - 495) \approx 2^{75}$. We use the same modulus and challenge space for LNP and LaBRADOR. In this setting, the signature sizes are presented in Table 3. The dimension of a range proof $\vec{z}$ of LNP is independent of the witness's dimension, but the standard deviation for rejection sampling is $\mathfrak{s}_3 = 0.675\sqrt{337}\beta$ where β is the norm bound of the witness for LNP. Therefore, the size of π is asymptotically $\mathcal{O}(\log T)$ and then increases slowly as shown in Table 3. The proof π' of LaBRADOR also contains a range proof without rejection sampling. The size of a range proof $\vec{p}$ is $2\lambda \log(12\beta'/\sqrt{2})$ where β' is the norm bound of $(\mathbf{z}_1, \mathbf{z}_2)$. Therefore, it also has the size of $\mathcal{O}(\log T)$ asymptotically.

The size of commitment and challenge generated by LaBRADOR is constant. On the other hand, the size of responses consisting of $\mathbf{z}, \mathbf{t}, \mathbf{g}, \mathbf{h}$ depends on the number of witnesses r' and the dimension of the witnesses m'. $\mathbf{z}$ has the same dimension as the witnesses so that N in our threshold ring signature scheme. The concatenation of other responses $\mathbf{t} \| \mathbf{g} \| \mathbf{h}$ has the dimension m'' which is quadratic in m' and r'. Since $r' = 2(9T + 3)$ and $m' = N$ in our threshold ring signature, m'' is quadratic in the ring size N and the threshold T. However, LaBRADOR can be recursed several times for small proof sizes because its responses also satisfy quadratic relations. The prover splits responses into small dimensional vectors and sets them as new witnesses. Hence, the signature size is asymptotically $\mathcal{O}(\log(\log N))$ because the dimension of the witnesses is N in our threshold ring signature. To reduce the dimension of new witnesses while not blowing up the number of new witnesses, LaBRADOR picks a new dimension carefully at each iteration. It causes our signature sizes to be the same or decrease, even though the ring size is increasing.

In Table 3, we can show that the total signature size remains constant as the ring size N increases when the threshold T is the same. Even when T increases, the size increases slowly. These results show that the signature size remains relatively small even when both the ring size and threshold grow, due to the logarithmic dependency on T.

Table 3. Threshold ring signature size (kB) for security parameter $\lambda = 128$, using Falcon–512. The modulus is $q \approx 2^{75}$. The ring degree is $d = 64$ and the norms of challenge are $\|c\|_2 \leqslant 71, \|c\|_{op} = 51$. $L = 11$. The threshold is at most $N/2$.

N	$T = 8$			$T = 32$			$T = N/2$		
	π	π'	total	π	π'	total	π	π'	total
2^8	20	88	108	20	91	111	20	105	124
2^{10}	20	88	108	20	91	111	20	117	136
2^{12}	20	88	108	20	91	111	20	127	147

A Lattice-Based Proofs of Quadratic Relations

We recall two lattice-based proofs LNP and LaBRADOR of quadratic relations. They have similar techniques to prove quadratic relations and a bound on the ℓ_2-norm of witnesses.

Proving Norm Bounds. Both of the proof systems have constraints on the norm bound of witnesses. To prove that the witness vectors have short ℓ_2-norm without sending the entire witness to the verifier, they use the projection technique from [13]. Shortness of $\vec{w} \in \mathbb{Z}^m$ is implied by proving that the projection $\Pi \vec{w}$ has small norm for a random matrix $\Pi \leftarrow\!\!\$\ \mathsf{Bin}_2^{256 \times m}$ where Bin_κ is the centered binomial distribution defined as $\sum_{i=1}^{\kappa}(a_i - b_i)$ where $a_i, b_i \leftarrow \{0,1\}$. Therefore, the prover can send $\vec{p} = \Pi \vec{w}$ and prove that it is computed correctly. If the verifier sees that $\|\vec{p}\|_2 \leq CB$ for some bound B and slack C, the verifier is convinced that $\|\vec{w}\|_2$ is at most B.

Aggregating Quadratic Functions. They prove M quadratic relations and additionally prove that, for M' quadratic functions, $\mathbf{s}$ satisfies $\mathsf{ct}(f_i'(\mathbf{s})) = 0$ for $i \in [M']$. To prove several equations simultaneously, they aggregate quadratic functions into a single quadratic function. They first aggregate M' quadratic functions for constant constraints with random challenges, then aggregate them with M quadratic functions which is not for constant constraints.

Openings. The two protocols generate an opening for the commitment in different ways. In LNP, the prover computes $\mathbf{z}_i = c\mathbf{s}_i + \mathbf{y}_i$ for $i = 1, 2$ where $\mathbf{s}_1$ is a witness and $\mathbf{s}_2$ is randomness and applies rejection sampling with the standard deviation $\mathfrak{s}_i$'s to remove the dependency of $\mathbf{z}_i$ on $\mathbf{s}_i$. Hence, its proof size is linear in the witness size. On the other hand, in LaBRADOR, the prover amortizes over the $\mathbf{w} = (\mathbf{w}_1, \ldots, \mathbf{w}_r)$. That is, the prover opens a random linear combination $\mathbf{z} = \sum_i^r c_i \mathbf{w}_i$ instead of opening all the $\mathbf{w}_i$. By amortization, they can achieve a small proof size. In addition, some of their responses also satisfy the quadratic equation so they can recurse the protocol for the responses to reduce the proof size more.

A.1 Lattice-Based Zero-Knowledge Proof for Quadratic Relations

LNP have message vector $\mathbf{s}_1 \in \mathcal{R}_q^{m_1}$ and $\mathbf{m} \in \mathcal{R}_q^{\ell}$ such that $\|\mathbf{s}_1\|_2 \leq \beta$, and prove knowledge of the message $\mathbf{s} = (\mathbf{s}_1, \mathbf{m})$ such that $f(\mathbf{s}) = 0$ and $\mathsf{ct}(f'(\mathbf{s})) = 0$ for some quadratic equation f and f'. Each function f is written as $f(\mathbf{s}) = \mathbf{s}^T \mathbf{R} \mathbf{s} + \mathbf{r}^T \mathbf{s} + r$ where $\mathbf{R} \in \mathcal{R}_q^{m_1+\ell}, \mathbf{r} \in \mathcal{R}_q^{m_1+\ell}, r \in \mathcal{R}_q$. Then, the relation for the zero-knowledge proof is

$$R = \left\{ ((\mathcal{F}, \mathcal{F}', \beta), (\mathbf{s} = (\mathbf{s}_1, \mathbf{m}), \mathbf{s}_2)) \;\middle|\; \begin{array}{l} f(\mathbf{s}) = 0 \;\forall f \in \mathcal{F} \\ \mathsf{ct}(f'(\mathbf{s})) = 0 \;\forall f' \in \mathcal{F}' \\ \|\mathbf{s}_1\|_2 \leq \beta \end{array} \right\}.$$

Theorem 2 (Proposition 5.1 in [17]). *Let $\mathcal{C} \subset \mathcal{R}_q$ be the challenge space consisting of polynomials with ℓ_2-norm τ_2 and operator norm τ_{op}. Suppose that Extended-MLWE$_{n+\ell+2+2\lambda/d+L, m_2-n-\ell-2-2\lambda/d-L}$ is hard and MSIS$_{n,m_1+m_2,B}$ is hard for $B = 8\tau_{op}\sqrt{(\mathfrak{s}_1\sqrt{2m_1d})^2 + (\mathfrak{s}_2\sqrt{2m_2d})^2}$ where $\mathfrak{s}_1, \mathfrak{s}_2$ are the standard deviation for rejection sampling. Then LNP is a zero-knowledge proof with knowledge error $\kappa = 2/|\mathcal{C}| + q^{-\lceil \lambda/\log q \rceil} + q^{-d/2} + 2^{-\lambda}$ (Fig. 3).*

A.2 LaBRADOR

The relation R' for the compact proof LaBRADOR consists of short solutions to dot product constraints over $\mathcal{R}_q$. A witness of LaBRADOR also satisfies the quadratic equation f which is of the form $f(\mathbf{w}_1, \cdots, \mathbf{w}_r) = \sum_{i,j=1}^{r} a_{ij} \langle \mathbf{w}_i, \mathbf{w}_j \rangle + \sum_{i=1}^{r} \langle \varphi_i, \mathbf{w}_i \rangle - b$ where $a_{ij}, b \in \mathcal{R}_q$ and $\varphi_i \in \mathcal{R}_q^n$. Then, the relation is

$$R' = \left\{ ((\mathcal{F}, \mathcal{F}', \beta'), (\mathbf{w}_1, \cdots, \mathbf{w}_r)) \;\middle|\; \begin{array}{l} f(\mathbf{w}_1, \cdots, \mathbf{w}_r) = 0 \in \mathcal{R}_q \; \forall f \in \mathcal{F} \\ \text{ct}(f'(\mathbf{w}_1, \cdots, \mathbf{w}_r)) = 0 \; \forall f' \mathcal{F}' \\ \sum_{i=1}^{r} \|\mathbf{w}_i\|_2^2 \leq \beta'^2 \end{array} \right\}.$$

Theorem 3 (Theorem 5.1 in [5]). *Let $\mathcal{C} \subset \mathcal{R}_q$ be the challenge space consisting of polynomials with ℓ_2-norm τ_2 and operator norm τ_{op}. Suppose that MSIS is hard for rank $n_1 = n_2$ and norm $2\beta'$, and also hard for rank n' and norm $\max(8\tau_{op}(b+1)\beta', 2(b+1)\beta' + 4\tau_{op}\sqrt{\lambda/C_2}\beta)$. Further suppose that $q \geq 125\sqrt{\lambda/C_2}\beta$. Then LaBRADOR is proof of knowledge for relation R with knowledge error $\kappa' = 2/|\mathcal{C}| + q^{-\lceil \lambda/\log q \rceil} + q^{-d/2} + 2^{-\lambda}$ and norm slack $\sqrt{\lambda/C_2}$, i.e., the extractor is only guaranteed to output a witness with norm at most $\sqrt{\lambda/C_2}\beta$. $C_2 = 30$ for $\lambda = 128$ (Fig. 4).*

Recursion. LaBRADOR uses recursion to achieve compact proof sizes. The last prover message consists of four vectors $\mathbf{z}, \mathbf{t}, \mathbf{g}, \mathbf{h}$ that must fulfill dot product equations and norm checks. Therefore, they recursively run the protocol with the vectors as the new witness. Since their opening $\mathbf{z}$ is a linear combination of the witnesses, it is a single vector with the same dimension as the witnesses. The strategy is running this procedure recursively as much as possible while maintaining that the new dimension m' of new responses and the dimension m'' of $\mathbf{t}\|\mathbf{g}\|\mathbf{h}$ satisfy $m'/\nu \approx m''/\mu$ and $2m' \approx m''$. According to [5, Lemma 3.7], their whole protocol after recursions is also proof of knowledge.

$x = (\mathcal{F}, \mathcal{F}', \beta)$ and $w = (\mathbf{s}_1, \mathbf{m}, \mathbf{s}_2) \in \mathcal{R}_q^{m_1+\ell+m_2}$ such that $\|\mathbf{s}_1\|_2 \leq \beta$
Public parameter $pp = (\mathbf{A}_1, \mathbf{A}_2, \mathbf{B})$ where $\mathbf{A}_1 \in \mathcal{R}_q^{n \times m_1}, \mathbf{A}_2 \in \mathcal{R}_q^{n \times m_2}, \mathbf{B} \in \mathcal{R}_q^{\ell \times m_2}$
$$\begin{bmatrix} \mathbf{t}_A \\ \mathbf{t}_B \end{bmatrix} = \begin{bmatrix} \mathbf{A}_1 \\ \mathbf{0} \end{bmatrix} \mathbf{s}_1 + \begin{bmatrix} \mathbf{A}_2 \\ \mathbf{B} \end{bmatrix} \mathbf{s}_2 + \begin{bmatrix} \mathbf{0} \\ \mathbf{m} \end{bmatrix}$$

$\mathsf{P}(x, w)$
1. Project:
    $b \leftarrow \{-1, 1\} \subset \mathcal{R}_q, \mathbf{y}_0 \leftarrow D_{\mathfrak{s}_3}^{2\lambda/d}$
    Send $t_b = \mathbf{b}_b^T \mathbf{s}_2 + b, \mathbf{t}_y = \mathbf{B}_y \mathbf{s}_2 + \mathbf{y}_0$ to V
    Receiving $\Pi \leftarrow \mathsf{Bin}_1^{2\lambda \times (m_1+\ell)d}$
    $\vec{z} := b\Pi\vec{s} + \vec{y}$
    If $\mathsf{Rej}_0(\vec{z}, bR\vec{s}, \mathfrak{s}_3) = 1$: abort
    Send $\vec{z}$ to V
2. Aggregate constant constraints:
    $\mathbf{g} := (g_1, \ldots, g_L) \leftarrow \{g \in \mathcal{R}_q | \mathsf{ct}(g) = 0\}^L$
    Send $\mathbf{t}_g = \mathbf{B}_g \mathbf{s}_2 + \mathbf{g}$ to V
    Receiving $\Gamma = (\gamma_{ij}) \leftarrow_\$ \mathbb{Z}_q^{M' \times L}$
    For $j \in [L]: F_j := g_j + \sum_{i=1}^{M'} \gamma_{ij} f_i'(\mathbf{s})$
    Send $F_1, \ldots, F_L$ to V
3. Aggregate:
    Receiving $\mu_1, \ldots, \mu_{M+L} \in \mathcal{R}_q$
    Define $f_{M+j}(\mathbf{x}_1, \mathbf{x}_2) := \mathbf{x}_{2,j} + \sum_{i=1}^{M'} \gamma_i f_i'(\mathbf{x}_1) - F_j \; \forall j \in [L]$
    $f := \sum_{i=1}^{M+L} \mu_i f_i$ where $f(\mathbf{s}) = \mathbf{s}^T \mathbf{R} \mathbf{s} + \mathbf{r}^T \mathbf{s} + r$
4. Commit:
    $\mathbf{y}_1 \leftarrow D_{\mathfrak{s}_1}^{m_1}, \mathbf{y}_2 \leftarrow D_{\mathfrak{s}_2}^{m_2}$
    $\mathbf{w} := \mathbf{A}_1 \mathbf{y}_1 + \mathbf{A}_2 \mathbf{y}_2$
    $\mathbf{y} := \mathbf{y}_1 \| (-\mathbf{B} \mathbf{y}_2)$
    $g_1 := \mathbf{s}'^T \mathbf{R} \mathbf{y} + \mathbf{y}^T \mathbf{R} \mathbf{s}' + \mathbf{r}^T \mathbf{y}, g_0 := \mathbf{y}^T \mathbf{R} \mathbf{y}$
    $t = \mathbf{b}^T \mathbf{s}_2 + g_1, v = \mathbf{b}^T \mathbf{y}_2 + g_0$
    Send $(\mathbf{w}, t, v)$ to V
5. Prove:
    Receiving $c \in \mathcal{C}$
    $\mathbf{z}_1 := c\mathbf{s}_1 + \mathbf{y}_1, \mathbf{z}_2 := c\mathbf{s}_2 + \mathbf{y}_2$
    For $i = 1, 2$: If $\mathsf{Rej}_j(\mathbf{z}_i, c\mathbf{s}_i, \mathfrak{s}_i) = 1$: $\mathbf{z}_1, \mathbf{z}_2 = \bot$
    Send $\mathbf{z}_1, \mathbf{z}_2$ to V
Output $(\pi, \mathbf{z}_1, \mathbf{z}_2) := ((\mathbf{t}_A, \mathbf{t}_B, \mathbf{w}, t, v), (R, \Gamma, \boldsymbol{\mu}, c), (\vec{z}, (F_j)_{j \in [L]}), \mathbf{z}_1, \mathbf{z}_2)$

$\mathsf{V}(x, (\pi, \mathbf{z}_1, \mathbf{z}_2))$
$\mathbf{z} := \mathbf{z}_1 \| (ct_b - \mathbf{B}\mathbf{z}_2)$
Accept if:
$\|\vec{z}\|_\infty \leq 14\mathfrak{s}_3$
$\forall j \in [L]: \mathsf{ct}(F_j) = 0$
$\forall i \in [2]: \|\mathbf{z}_i\|_2 \leq \mathfrak{s}_i \sqrt{2m_i d}$
$\mathbf{A}_1 \mathbf{z}_1 + \mathbf{A}_2 \mathbf{z}_2 = \mathbf{w} + c\mathbf{t}_A$
$\mathbf{z}^T \mathbf{R} \mathbf{z} + c\mathbf{r}^T \mathbf{z} + c^2 r_0 - (ct - \mathbf{b}^T \mathbf{z}_2) - v = 0$

Fig. 3. LNP protocol for messages $(\mathbf{s}_1, \mathbf{m}) \in \mathcal{R}_q^{m_1+\ell}$ and randomness $\mathbf{s}_2 \in \mathcal{R}_q^{m_2}$.

$x' = (\mathcal{F}, \mathcal{F}', \beta')$ and $w' = (\mathbf{w}_1, \ldots, \mathbf{w}_r)$ where $\mathbf{w}_i \in \mathcal{R}_q^{m'}$ for $i \in [r]$
Publick parameter $pp' = (\mathbf{A}, (\mathbf{B}_{ik})_{ik}, (\mathbf{C}_{ijk})_{ijk}, (\mathbf{D}_{ijk})_{ijk})$
where $\mathbf{A} \in \mathcal{R}_q^{n' \times m'}, \mathbf{B}_{ik} \in \mathcal{R}_q^{n_1 \times n'}, \mathbf{C}_{ijk'}, \mathbf{D}_{ijk} \in \mathcal{R}_q^{n_2 \times 1}$
for $i \in [r], i \leq j \leq r, k \in [t_1], k' \in [t_2]$

$\mathsf{P}(pp', x', w')$
1. Commit:
   For $i \in [r]: \mathbf{t}_i = a\mathbf{w}_i = \mathbf{t}_i^{(0)} + \cdots + \mathbf{t}_i^{(t_1-1)} b_1^{t_1-1}$
   For $i \in [r], j \in [i, r]: g_{ij} = \langle \mathbf{w}_i, \mathbf{w}_j \rangle = g_{ij}^{(0)} + \cdots + g_{ij}^{(t_2-1)} b_2^{t_2-1}$
   Send $\mathbf{u}_1 = \sum_{i=1}^{r} \sum_{k=0}^{t_1-1} b_{ik} \mathbf{t}_i^{(k)} + \sum_{i \leq j} \sum_{k=0}^{t_2-1} \mathbf{C}_{ijk} g_{ij}^{(k)}$ to V
2. Project:
   Receiving $\Pi_i = (\vec{\pi}_i^{(j)})_{j \in [2\lambda]} \leftarrow\!\!\$\ \chi^{2\lambda \times m'd}$ for $i \in [r]$
   $p_j = \sum_{i=1}^{r} \langle \vec{\pi}_i^{(j)}, \vec{w}_i \rangle$ where $\vec{w}_i$ is coefficient vectors of $\mathbf{w}_i$
   Send $\vec{p} = (p_j)_{j \in [2\lambda]}$ to V
3. Aggregate:
   Receiving $\Psi = (\psi_{ij}) \leftarrow\!\!\$\ \mathbb{Z}_q^{K' \times L'}, \Omega = (\omega_{ij}) \leftarrow\!\!\$\ \mathbb{Z}_q^{256 \times L'}$
   For $k \in [L']$:
   $a_{ij}^{''(k)} = \sum_{l=1}^{K'} \psi_{lk} a_{ij}^{'(l)}$
   $\varphi_i^{''(k)} = \sum_{l=1}^{K'} \psi_{lk} \varphi_i^{'(l)} + \sum_{l=1}^{256} \omega_{lk} \sigma_{-1}(\vec{\pi}_i^{(j)})$
   $b^{''(k)} = \sum_{i,j=1}^{r} a_{ij}^{''(k)} \langle \mathbf{w}_i, \mathbf{w}_j \rangle + \sum_{i=1}^{r} \langle \varphi_i^{''(k)}, \mathbf{w}_i \rangle$
   Send $(b^{''(k)})_{k \in [K'']}$ to V
4. Aggregate linear constraints:
   Receiving $\alpha_1, \ldots, \alpha_K \leftarrow\!\!\$\ \mathcal{R}_q, \beta_1, \ldots, \beta_{L'} \leftarrow\!\!\$\ \mathcal{R}_q$
   $\varphi_i = \sum_{k=1}^{K} \alpha_k \varphi_i^{(k)} + \sum_{k=1}^{L'} \beta_k \varphi_i^{''(k)}$
   For $i \in [r], j \in [i, r]: h_{ij} = \frac{1}{2}(\langle \varphi_i, \mathbf{w}_j \rangle + \langle \varphi_j, \mathbf{w}_i \rangle) = h_{ij}^{(0)} + \cdots + h_{ij}^{(t_1-1)} b_1^{t_1-1}$
   Send $\mathbf{u}_2 = \sum_{i \leq j} \sum_{k=0}^{t_1-1} \mathbf{D}_{ijk} h_{ij}^{(k)}$ to V
5. Amortize opening proof:
   Receiving $c_i \leftarrow\!\!\$\ \mathcal{C}$
   $\mathbf{z} = c_1 \mathbf{w}_1 + \cdots + c_r \mathbf{w}_r = \mathbf{z}^{(0)} + b\mathbf{z}^{(1)}$
   Send $\mathbf{z}^{(0)}, \mathbf{z}^{(1)}, (\mathbf{t}_i), (g_{ij}), (h_{ij})$ to V
Output $\pi' := ((\mathbf{u}_1, \mathbf{u}_2), ((\Pi_i)_i, \Psi, \Omega, \boldsymbol{\alpha}, \boldsymbol{\beta}, (c_i)_i), (\vec{p}, (b^{''(k)})_k, \mathbf{z}, (\mathbf{t}_i)_i, (g_{ij}, h_{ij})_{ij})$

$\mathsf{V}(pp', x', \pi')$
Accept if:
$\mathbf{A}\mathbf{z} = \sum_{i=1}^{r} c_i \mathbf{t}_i$
$\langle \mathbf{z}, \mathbf{z} \rangle = \sum_{i,j=1}^{r} g_{ij} c_i c_j$
$\sum_{i=1}^{r} \langle \varphi_i, \mathbf{z} \rangle c_i = \sum_{i,j=1}^{r} h_{ij} c_i c_j$
$\sum_{i,j=1}^{r} a_{ij} g_{ij} + \sum_{i=1}^{r} h_{ii} - b = \mathbf{0}$
$\sum_{k=0}^{1} \|\mathbf{z}^{(k)}\|_2^2 + \sum_{i=1}^{r} \sum_{k=0}^{t_1-1} \|\mathbf{t}_i^{(k)}\|_2^2 + \sum_{i \leq j} \sum_{k=0}^{t_2-1} \|g_{ij}^{(k)}\|_2^2 + \sum_{i \leq j} \sum_{k=0}^{t_1-1} \|h_{ij}^{(k)}\|_2^2 \leq \beta'^2$
$\mathbf{u}_1 = \sum_{i=1}^{r} \sum_{k=0}^{t_1-1} b_{ik} \mathbf{t}_i^{(k)} + \sum_{i \leq j} \sum_{k=0}^{t_2-1} \mathbf{C}_{ijk} g_{ij}^{(k)}$
$\mathbf{u}_2 = \sum_{i \leq j} \sum_{k=0}^{t_1-1} \mathbf{D}_{ijk} h_{ij}^{(k)}$

Fig. 4. LaBRADOR protocol

References

1. Aardal, M.A., Aranha, D.F., Boudgoust, K., Kolby, S., Takahashi, A.: Aggregating falcon signatures with LaBRADOR. In: Reyzin, L., Stebila, D. (eds.) CRYPTO 2024, Part I. LNCS, vol. 14920, pp. 71–106. Springer, Cham (2024). https://doi.org/10.1007/978-3-031-68376-3_3
2. Aguilar Melchor, C., Cayrel, P.L., Gaborit, P., Laguillaumie, F.: A new efficient threshold ring signature scheme based on coding theory. IEEE Trans. Inf. Theory **57**(7), 4833–4842 (2011). https://doi.org/10.1109/TIT.2011.2145950
3. Albrecht, M.R., Gür, K.D.: Verifiable oblivious pseudorandom functions from lattices: practical-ish and thresholdisable. In: Chung, K.M., Sasaki, Y. (eds.) ASIACRYPT 2024, Part IV. LNCS, vol. 15487, pp. 205–237. Springer, Singapore (2024). https://doi.org/10.1007/978-981-96-0894-2_7
4. Bettaieb, S., Schrek, J.: Improved lattice-based threshold ring signature scheme. In: Gaborit, P. (ed.) Post-Quantum Cryptography - 5th International Workshop, PQCrypto 2013, pp. 34–51. Springer, Heidelberg (2013). https://doi.org/10.1007/978-3-642-38616-9_3
5. Beullens, W., Seiler, G.: LaBRADOR: compact proofs for R1CS from module-SIS. In: Handschuh, H., Lysyanskaya, A. (eds.) CRYPTO 2023, Part V. LNCS, vol. 14085, pp. 518–548. Springer, Cham (2023). https://doi.org/10.1007/978-3-031-38554-4_17
6. Bitansky, N., Canetti, R., Chiesa, A., Tromer, E.: From extractable collision resistance to succinct non-interactive arguments of knowledge, and back again. Cryptology ePrint Archive, Report 2011/443 (2011). https://eprint.iacr.org/2011/443
7. Bresson, E., Stern, J., Szydlo, M.: Threshold ring signatures and applications to ad-hoc groups. In: Yung, M. (ed.) CRYPTO 2002. LNCS, vol. 2442, pp. 465–480. Springer, Heidelberg (2002). https://doi.org/10.1007/3-540-45708-9_30
8. Cayrel, P.L., Lindner, R., Rückert, M., Silva, R.: A lattice-based threshold ring signature scheme. In: Abdalla, M., Barreto, P.S.L.M. (eds.) LATINCRYPT 2010. LNCS, vol. 6212, pp. 255–272. Springer, Heidelberg (2010). https://doi.org/10.1007/978-3-642-14712-8_16
9. Chiang, J.H.Y., Damgård, I., Duro, W.R., Engan, S., Kolby, S., Scholl, P.: Post-quantum threshold ring signature applications from VOLE-in-the-head. Cryptology ePrint Archive, Paper 2025/113 (2025). https://eprint.iacr.org/2025/113
10. Espitau, T., Nguyen, T.T.Q., Sun, C., Tibouchi, M., Wallet, A.: Antrag: annular NTRU trapdoor generation - making mitaka as secure as falcon. In: Guo, J., Steinfeld, R. (eds.) ASIACRYPT 2023, Part VII. LNCS, vol. 14444, pp. 3–36. Springer, Singapore (2023). https://doi.org/10.1007/978-981-99-8739-9_1
11. Espitau, T., Tibouchi, M., Wallet, A., Yu, Y.: Shorter hash-and-sign lattice-based signatures. In: Dodis, Y., Shrimpton, T. (eds.) CRYPTO 2022, Part II. LNCS, vol. 13508, pp. 245–275. Springer, Cham (2022). https://doi.org/10.1007/978-3-031-15979-4_9
12. Fouque, P.A., et al.: Falcon: fast-fourier lattice-based compact signatures over ntru. Technical report, National Institute of Standards and Technology (2017)
13. Gentry, C., Halevi, S., Lyubashevsky, V.: Practical non-interactive publicly verifiable secret sharing with thousands of parties. In: Dunkelman, O., Dziembowski, S. (eds.) EUROCRYPT 2022, Part I. LNCS, vol. 13275, pp. 458–487. Springer, Cham (2022). https://doi.org/10.1007/978-3-031-06944-4_16
14. Haque, A., Krenn, S., Slamanig, D., Striecks, C.: Logarithmic-size (linkable) threshold ring signatures in the plain model. In: Hanaoka, G., Shikata, J., Watanabe, Y.

(eds.) PKC 2022, Part II. LNCS, vol. 13178, pp. 437–467. Springer, Cham (2022). https://doi.org/10.1007/978-3-030-97131-1_15
15. Haque, A., Scafuro, A.: Threshold ring signatures: new definitions and post-quantum security. In: Kiayias, A., Kohlweiss, M., Wallden, P., Zikas, V. (eds.) PKC 2020, Part II. LNCS, vol. 12111, pp. 423–452. Springer, Cham (2020). https://doi.org/10.1007/978-3-030-45388-6_15
16. Jeudy, C., Roux-Langlois, A., Sanders, O.: Phoenix: hash-and-sign with aborts from lattice gadgets. In: Saarinen, M.J., Smith-Tone, D. (eds.) Post-Quantum Cryptography - 15th International Workshop, PQCrypto 2024, Part I, pp. 265–299. Springer, Cham (2024). https://doi.org/10.1007/978-3-031-62743-9_9
17. Lyubashevsky, V., Nguyen, N.K., Plançon, M.: Lattice-based zero-knowledge proofs and applications: shorter, simpler, and more general. In: Dodis, Y., Shrimpton, T. (eds.) CRYPTO 2022, Part II. LNCS, vol. 13508, pp. 71–101. Springer, Cham (2022). https://doi.org/10.1007/978-3-031-15979-4_3
18. Lyubashevsky, V., Nguyen, N.K., Plançon, M., Seiler, G.: Shorter lattice-based group signatures via "almost free" encryption and other optimizations. In: Tibouchi, M., Wang, H. (eds.) ASIACRYPT 2021, Part IV. LNCS, vol. 13093, pp. 218–248. Springer, Cham (2021). https://doi.org/10.1007/978-3-030-92068-5_8
19. Lyubashevsky, V., Seiler, G.: Short, invertible elements in partially splitting cyclotomic rings and applications to lattice-based zero-knowledge proofs. In: Nielsen, J.B., Rijmen, V. (eds.) EUROCRYPT 2018, Part I. LNCS, vol. 10820, pp. 204–224. Springer, Cham (2018). https://doi.org/10.1007/978-3-319-78381-9_8
20. Munch-Hansen, A., Orlandi, C., Yakoubov, S.: Stronger notions and a more efficient construction of threshold ring signatures. In: Longa, P., Ràfols, C. (eds.) LATINCRYPT 2021. LNCS, vol. 12912, pp. 363–381. Springer, Cham (2021). https://doi.org/10.1007/978-3-030-88238-9_18
21. Okamoto, T., Tso, R., Yamaguchi, M., Okamoto, E.: A k-out-of-n ring signature with flexible participation for signers. Cryptology ePrint Archive, Report 2018/728 (2018). https://eprint.iacr.org/2018/728
22. Rivest, R.L., Shamir, A., Tauman, Y.: How to leak a secret. In: Boyd, C. (ed.) ASIACRYPT 2001. LNCS, vol. 2248, pp. 552–565. Springer, Heidelberg (2001). https://doi.org/10.1007/3-540-45682-1_32
23. Tsang, P.P., Wei, V.K., Chan, T.K., Au, M.H., Liu, J.K., Wong, D.S.: Separable linkable threshold ring signatures. In: Canteaut, A., Viswanathan, K. (eds.) INDOCRYPT 2004. LNCS, vol. 3348, pp. 384–398. Springer, Heidelberg (2004). https://doi.org/10.1007/978-3-540-30556-9_30

Side-Channel Attacks and Countermeasures

Simulation-Based Software Leakage Evaluation for the RISC-V Platform

Nicolai Schmitt[1](✉)[iD], Jannik Zeitschner[2][iD], and Andreas Heinemann[1][iD]

[1] Hochschule Darmstadt - University of Applied Sciences, Darmstadt, Germany
{nicolai.schmitt,zeitschner.heinemann}@h-da.de
[2] Ruhr University Bochum, Bochum, Germany
jannik.zeitschner@rub.de

Abstract. Side-channel attacks are critical as they, despite the mathematical security of the algorithm, break the security assumption that private data stays hidden from the adversary. Developing secure hardware can be expensive, as multiple iterations of prototyping may be required to achieve a satisfactory level of security against side-channel attacks. Currently, the fairly new and open-source CPU-platform RISC-V is gaining traction by entering the Internet of Things (IoT)- and consumer market and also gains interest in security oriented projects such as OpenTitan. In case of security-critical applications, especially when the hardware is exposed to third party, the implementations of cryptographic algorithms must be secure against side-channel attacks. For the RISC-V platform currently only a small number of tools exist to assess the probing security. Further, we could identify a lack of simulation-based tooling to do so, with the ability to analyze larger implementations as e.g., full ciphers. To address this demand, we use `PROLEAD_SW` as a starting point and extend it to support the RISC-V platform. By analyzing micro-architectural leakage effects on the RISC-V platform we show that the CPU-independent leakage model used by `PROLEAD_SW` for the ARM architecture is suitable for the RISC-V platform. To verify the correctness of the new tooling, test-vectors are executed with the new tooling. In a final step, the performance of the new tooling is compared to the performance of the original version of `PROLEAD_SW` by analyzing two masked AES C implementations with both tools.

Keywords: Side-channel attacks · Probing Security · RISC-V · Simulation · PROLEAD_SW

1 Introduction

Side-Channel Analysis (SCA) attacks are mounted on a specific implementation (of algorithms) and exploit the dependency between physical properties, e.g., power consumption, electromagnetic emanation, or execution time, and the

---

N. Schmitt and A. Heinemann—Member of EUt+ (European University of Technology).

target during execution. These attacks are very critical as they, despite the mathematical security of the algorithm, break the security assumption that private data stay hidden from the adversary. Security against side-channels is especially critical when adversaries have physical access to the target device. To harden implementations against side-channel attacks, different approaches for countermeasures exist, for example, shuffling (varying order of execution) [5], varying the operation frequency [32], a variable operating voltage [2] that adds additional noise to the signal, decoupling from specific possible side-channels as e.g., the operating voltage supply [29] as well as masking [9], which is the most prominent countermeasure as it can mathematically be proven secure. Therewith, masked circuits (or software) can be proven to be secure in a probing security model, which makes the application of masking interesting for security-critical applications. The implementation of countermeasures is often complex and comes with a significant overhead in resource consumption, which can lead to higher development costs, lower performance as well as larger chip areas and thus higher production costs [5,16,18]. To validate the security of software running on hardware, the operations on the register transfer level can be taken into account [18]. Compared to an evaluation through simulation on the transistor level, an evaluation on the register transfer level can be faster, but is usually less accurate. Besides simulation-based evaluation a formal verification of the probing security of software is possible, but becomes very resource intensive in case of larger implementations [34]. The micro-architecture of a CPU-Implementation can introduce leakage-effects that are not expected from operations executed on the architectural level [20]. These effects can lead to a gap between leakage-models and the leakage behavior of hardware. If detailed knowledge of the micro-architecture can be inferred, the gap between the physical behavior and the model gets smaller. Therewith countermeasures could be implemented more well-directed and effective, which could conserve resources during their implementation.

2 Contribution

This work makes the following contributions:

1. **Extending PROLEAD_SW.**
   The software PROLEAD_SW [33] is extended[1], to support the Central Processing Unit (CPU) platform RISC-V, by integrating a RISC-V emulator into the existing software and transferring the probing mechanisms of PROLEAD_SW into the RISC-V emulator.
2. **Practical evaluation of the leakage of different RISC-V processor implementations.**
   The RISC-V hardware platforms Ibex [1] and NeoRV32 [24] are extensively analyzed for different micro-architecture based leakage artifacts. The results of this thorough evaluation support the correctness of the probing mechanisms of PROLEAD_SW implemented for the RISC-V platform. The analysis

---
[1] Repository: https://gitlab.com/ATHENE-LEAK/PROLEAD_SW_RV.

is based on the MIRACLE-framework [20], which extensively evaluates microarchitectural effects on the ARM platform.
3. **Performance comparison of our extended version and the original version of PROLEAD_SW**
We show the performance impact of our extension of PROLEAD_SW to the original version by evaluating an AES implementation that is written in C with both versions of PROLEAD_SW and compare the performance and memory requirements.

3 Background

3.1 RISC-V

RISC-V is a fairly new architecture first proposed in 2014[2]. The RISC-V architecture is open source and features either 16 or 32 general purpose registers and an address-space and register size of either 32, 64 or 128 bit. The Instruction Set Architecture (ISA)[3] is modular and extensible and can therewith be adapted to different use cases, making the processors cost effective and attractive for, e.g., different IoT devices [27]. With a selection of the minimal instruction set called RV32E (see footnote 2) (a reduced version of RV32I (see footnote 2), that is intended for micro-controllers and embedded applications), a RISC-V processor can have a minimum of only 47 instructions and 16 registers. As with a very small and simple instruction set, the complexity of implementation and chip area stay small, effectively helping to reduce production costs. By now, 24 extension sets are standardized. The RISC-V ISA also includes the option to integrate custom instructions into the own RISC-V implementation, that simplifies the integration of hardware accelerators for arbitrary purposes.

Ibex. The Ibex [1] core is a small, yet efficient 32-bit CPU, that is highly parametrizable to aim either for performance or area. Its default setting features a two-stage single-issue pipeline consisting of an *Instruction Fetch* and *Decode+Execute* unit, while a *Writeback* stage for faster memory transactions can be enabled as a third pipeline stage. Further parameters select the architecture of the multiplier unit and allow to configure an optional *Branch Predictor* and *Branch Target ALU* to reduce the latency of branches. Besides the base integer instruction sets RV32I and RV32E, the Ibex core supports the Integer Multiplication and Division (M), Compressed (C), and Bit Manipulation (B) instruction set extensions.

---

[2] https://www2.eecs.berkeley.edu/Pubs/TechRpts/2014/EECS-2014-146.pdf, last visited: 11.06.2025.
[3] https://riscv.org/specifications/ratified/, last visited: 11.06.2025.

NeoRV. `Neorv32` [24] is a 32-bit CPU with a particular focus on execution safety, high configurability, and optimized for minimal resource. While the `Ibex` core follows a purely pipelined architecture, the `Neorv32` follows a pipelined multi-cycle architecture. Its core is divided into an `Instruction Fetch` stage and an `Execution` stage. Each of these stages is implemented as a multi-cycle architecture, i.e., only one instruction is processed at a time and each instruction is deconstructed into a series of micro-operations. Between *Instruction Fetch* and *Execution*, a instruction prefetch buffer is placed to improve the utilization of the de-coupled pipeline stages.

3.2 Masking

To protect against side-channel attacks the masking concept, based on the principle of secret sharing, has been a well established and highly researched countermeasure. In general, applying masking to an implementation starts by splitting every sensitive variable X into $d+1$ shares, where the first d shares $(x_0, \ldots, x_{d-1})$ are drawn from a uniformly random source and the last share x_d is constructed as the sum of the first d shares and the original secret X. There exist different types of masking, e.g., arithmetic or multiplicative masking, depending on the underlying field of the secret variables [12,22]. However, the most common masking technique, especially in the context of symmetric cryptography is Boolean masking [8], where each variable X and the first d uniformly random shares x_i, where $0 \leq i \leq d-1$, are in $\mathbb{F}_2^n$, and the last share is generated as $x_d = \bigoplus_{i=0}^{d-1} x_i \oplus X$. We say a masked implementation is d-order secure, if the observation of any d intermediate values during the execution of the target does not reveal any unshared, original secret variable.

3.3 Probing Model

For the evaluation of masked implementations, adversary models are inevitable. Those models describe the capabilities of an adversary to observe intermediate values during the execution of the target. It allows a formal reasoning about the side-channel security and enable the development of systematic masking schemes. The initial d-probing model was presented by Ishai et al. [19]. Here, an adversary is allowed to place up to d probes on the target and observe the stable intermediate values captured by those probes. Although the d-probing model has been widely used in security proofs of various masked algorithms [11,26], it has also been shown that implementations, which are secure in this model, fail to uphold the desired security level in practice [6]. This discrepancy is due to physical defaults such as *glitches* and *transitions*, which invalidate the assumptions of the d-probing model that each probe can only observe the current, stable intermediate value.

Transitions occur during changes in wires or storage elements of the target. This change may allow the combination of the two consecutive values within the wire, respectively, storage element. Hence, an adversary may not only be able to observe the stable intermediate, but actually the incoming and outgoing value during the switching of contents.

Glitches arise due to unbalanced path delays within combinatorial logic between two synchronization points. Rather than observing only the stable intermediate value at the probe position, glitches may give the adversary information about all intermediate values within the combinatorial logic that contribute to the probed intermediate value up to the last synchronization point.

To account for these physical defaults[4], the robust d-probing model [14] was introduced as an improved version of the d-probing model. This model extends each probe of the adversary by its glitch-extended and transition-extended versions.

This probing model describes the behavior of masked implementations in the real world more accurately, especially in the context of hardware masking. However, the effect of glitches and transitions do not only occur in hardware masking and hardware platforms, but also on software platforms, e.g., general-purpose CPUs, as software is executed on the underlying hardware. The behavior of glitches and transitions in general-purpose CPUs is mainly dictated by the micro-architecture of the processor. The micro-architecture describes the internal structure and layout and defines all details how instructions are handled by the CPU. The micro-architecture is highly individual for a particular CPU and on most commercial platforms, e.g., ARM or X86, not publicly available. This raises two problems. If the CPU netlist is not available, it is hard to apply the robust d-probing model, as it is unknown where transitions and glitches might be created. In situations where netlists are available the masked software implementation would have to be verified on each processor individually due to the difference in the micro-architecture. To cope with these problems the CPU-independent leakage model was proposed, which performs probing security on a conservative, generalized CPU layout and gives a broader security statement of the software implementation independent of a particular CPU. The CPU as well as the probes in this model are based on micro-architectural leakage effects that have been studied in various research papers [16, 20, 25].

As the CPU-independent leakage model is used in PROLEAD_SW, we describe in the following the model in more detail. The register file R holds $|R|$ registers, where $r_i = \{r_0, \ldots, r_{|R|-1}\}$. Each register in this R has a width of B bits. The CPU contains a memory area M with individual accessible memory addresses m_i. Over a memory bus, values can be moved from the register file to memory and vice versa. The Arithmetic Logic Unit (ALU) is responsible for all arithmetic operations. The generalized CPU has a pipeline with n stages and micro-architectural registers, i.e., registers not directly accessible by the software developer, are placed in both directions of the memory bus and in each pipeline stage.

Based on this CPU layout the leakage model defines the following micro-architectural probes:

---

[4] We do not consider coupling in this work as it highly depends on placement and routing of the hardware.

Transitional Probe. A transitional probe is similar to its counterpart in the robust probing model. It allows to observe the joint information of two successive values of a single bit within a storage element. Here, a storage element is any register in R, any memory address in M and also any hidden micro-architectural register.

Vertical Probe. The register selection of the register file R for the execution of a particular instruction inside the ALU is realized by a multiplexer tree. Each register in R is connected to this multiplexer tree, which is realized by combinatorial logic. If a probe is placed at the output of the multiplexer tree glitches inside this combinatorial logic are able to propagate back to each register in the register file. As the leakage model tracks the micro-architectural probes in a worst case manner, this vertical probe is able, due to glitches in the multiplexer tree, to observe the b-th bit, where $0 \leq b < B$, of all register in R.

Horizontal Probe. The ALU in the generalized CPU is *always active*, i.e., all arithmetic and logical operations are performed in parallel, but only the result corresponding to the currently executed instruction will be forwarded after the ALU by a multiplexer. Inside the ALU certain operations, e.g., addition, subtraction or multiplication, require to combine multiple bits of the two incoming source registers to compute the result of the operation. A probe on the output of the multiplexer might propagate backwards through the ALU due to glitches and is able to observe the interaction between all bits of these registers. Therefore, a horizontal probe is able to observe all B bits of any combination between two registers in R.

Pipeline Forwarding Probe. The CPU in the adversary model allows for pipeline forwarding. This means values from later pipeline stages might be forwarded back to earlier pipeline stages to avoid stalls. The realization of the forwarding mechanism is done with combinatorial logic and thus prone to glitches. Glitches inside this logic allow to reveal the joint information of values in all pipeline stages. The leakage model handles this probe by giving the adversary access to any arbitrary bit position of all registers across the last n instructions.

3.4 PROLEAD_SW

Evaluating the probing security of masked software under any adversary model manually is laborious and error-prone. To ease this process, different automated tools [3,13,15,17,28] have been published to assess the side-channel security of masked software in a faster and more assuring manner. One of these instruments is PROLEAD_SW [33]. Similarly to its hardware-verification counterpart PROLEAD [23], it utilizes a combination of formal verification and leakage simulation, i.e., it simulates the target under a formal adversary model. The idea behind combining these different approaches is to benefit from their respective strengths and compensate for the disadvantages of each other.

To initiate the verification of PROLEAD_SW, the workflow starts with the user input. The inputs to PROLEAD_SW are constructed either by the source code (C or assembly) or a precompiled binary together with a configuration file. Within this configuration file, the user has the option to enable or disable specific probes that PROLEAD_SW places during simulation and other settings such as configuration of test-vectors or performance metrics, e.g., enabling multi-threading.

After this configuration step, PROLEAD_SW starts to simulate the binary based on the input test-vectors specified in the configuration file. The simulation is instruction-accurate, i.e., the behavior of instructions within the binary is modeled exactly as it would be on real hardware. During each simulation, the tool places micro-architectural probes (cf. Sect. 3.3) after each instruction, according to the capabilities of the adversary in the adversary model. After obtaining all probes of a simulation, PROLEAD_SW combines the micro-architectural probes into a probing set. The size of the probing set is based on the security order d. Every probing set contains the probed intermediate values of the respective micro-architectural effect for the currently considered test-vector group. After each simulation a distribution table corresponding to this probing set is updated according to the probed intermediates. The updated distributions are evaluated by the G-test of independence [30], which is used for statistical evaluation in PROLEAD_SW.

4 Related Work

To the best of our knowledge there are only a small number of tools available whose target platform is RISC-V. However, in the following we describe tools used for evaluating the security of masked software implementations and explain where our contribution can be placed between the existing tools.

Formal Verification. The COCO [15] tool enables formal verification for the RISC-V platform. It follows a white-box approach and thus requires access to the gate-level netlist and the assembly code of the target. Rather than verifying the software itself, it maps the verification of software to a hardware problem by treating the software as a sequence of control instructions for the hardware. This allows to make formal statements of the software implementation on a particular hardware. However COCO places limitations on the executed software, i.e., it requires constant-control flow and comparably small designs such as AND gadgets and Sboxes.

ARMISTICE, introduced by de Grandmaison et al. [17], is able to identify processor-specific, non-trivial leakage by using detailed information about the micro-architecture of processors. ARMISTICE implements symbolic instruction set simulators, which build symbolic expressions as (symbolic) values pass through the hardware. Those expressions are then analyzed with formal analysis tools. As ARMISTICE requires detailed information about netlist details of ARM processors, this tool is not publicly available.

SCverif [4] proposes a domain specific language (DSL) which augments instruction semantics with explicit leakage information of a particular processor and is then evaluated with formal verification tools. While this gives a sound leakage model for a particular processor, it requires iterative and manual work to insert the correct leakage information into the DSL.

Power Contracts [7] are an DSL to specify micro-architectural leakages on masked software. The contracts can be verified against CPU netlists to ensure that every leakage model in the contract follows the hardware behavior. A software that is secure under the contract is secure on any CPU that follows the contract.

Leakage Simulation. ELMO* [28], based on ELMO [21], is a gray-box power model for the ARM Cortex-M0 processor based on actual power measurements. The power consumption of the target processor is measured for any sequence of three instructions. Afterwards, linear regression is performed on the power traces to find the most adequate model for the particular processor. This enables the authors to simulate the power consumption behavior of the processor when executing a particular software, and therefore performing statistical analysis on the simulated traces. However, generating a gray-box model is non-trivial and the precision of such gray-box models highly depends on the accuracy of test-cases, number of power samples and the leveraged analytics procedure.

Papagiannopoulos and Veshchikov [25] present ASCOLD, which aims to detect violations of the *independent leakage assumption*, i.e., the assumption that the adversary can only observe one stable intermediate value per probe, on AVR platforms. Given as input assembly instructions and a configuration setup, ASCOLD simulates the program by performing information flow tracking to detect how secret values are propagated through the execution.

To evaluate the effects of pipeline registers with respect to power side-channel security, the tool MAPS [13] was proposed. The authors were able to consider target-specific pipeline leakage of a Cortex-M3 processor as they had access to the netlist of this particular processor. With this internal knowledge they were able to accurately model the behavior of pipeline registers. As the authors have used internal knowledge of a particular processor netlist, MAPS is only tailored to the Cortex-M3 and only considers transitions of registers and no glitches.

5 Implementation

Within the scope of this paper, a concept is developed and implemented in the form of tooling to verify the side-channel resistance of software, developed and compiled for the RISC-V platform.

To achieve this goal, we used the existing tool PROLEAD_SW as a starting point. PROLEAD_SW analyzes the probing security of software for the ARM platform in its own CPU-independent probing model, which is based on results from experiments performed in the MIRACLE paper [20] and therewith already takes care of multiple micro-architectural leakage effects and hardware-defaults present on the ARM platform. Through the experimental evaluation of micro-architectural leakage on RISC-V hardware implementations, we show that the probing model used in PROLEAD_SW can be applied to the RISC-V platform. The implementation process of the extension of PROLEAD_SW as well as the implementation of experimental evaluations on hardware and software are further described below.

5.1 Experiments on the Identification of Micro-Architectural Leakage

The MIRACLE-framework [20] contains a variety of test-snippets written in assembly including specif implementations for ARM and RISC-V, that can be executed on a target. We selected a subset of test-code-snippets and executed them on our targets. In addition to the existing tests of the MIRACLE-framework, we added further and modified some test-snippets with a focus on the RISC-V platform. The supplemented and modified tests are organized in the additional test categories starting with the prefix *su*. All test-snippets including the selected original, modified and added snippets are listed in the appendix in Table 7. We executed them in order to answer the following questions:

1. Are there hidden memory states? Are they shared between read- and write operations?
2. Is there inter-instruction leakage between different instructions?
3. Is there leakage resulting from instructions, that are not directly adjacent?
4. Is there leakage from register-file multiplexing?
5. How far are instructions with register $x0$ as destination executed and effect the execution pipeline?

The category *sumemory* contains experiments concerning leakage effects from the memory-bus, *supipeline* contains experiments elaborating leakage effects related to the CPU's pipeline and *suregfile* contains experiments, that elaborate leakage effects resulting from registerfile multiplexing.

The *bus-width-** snippets from *sumemory* test for the memory-bus width by loading or storing to an address offset to the address where the critical value is stored in memory. They are based on experiments from the *memory-bus* category. The snippets *register-implicit-** execute two memory operations with another instruction in between. They are based on snippets from the category *memory-bus*. Experiments with *ld-ld* execute two load-word operations, *st-st* execute two store-word operations, *ld-st* execute a load-word operation followed by a store-word operation and *st-ld* execute a store-word- followed by a load-word operation. These ending with *-nop* execute a *nop* between the memory operations. The *seq-** experiments from the category *sumemory* analyze leakage from sequencial memory accesses in a similar way as the *seq-** experiments from the category *memory-bus*. The experiments *iseq-** from the category *supipeline* extend the analysis of inter-instruction leakage between different instructions. The *tt-xor-nop-** experiments from the category *supipeline* analyze how far the CPU's pipeline leads to inter-instruction leakage even on a distance of the instructions and how far opcodes emitted through *nop* instructions influence the CPU's pipeline state. The test *tt-multiplexer-a2* from the category *suregfile* analyzes if a value from a register that is not accessed from an architectural standpoint can leak during other registers are accessed. The leakage could result from glitches in the registerfile-multiplexer. During these experiments a register ($a0$) is pre-loaded with a critical value prior to triggering. In the sampled period, a variety of other operations is executed on registers that were zeroed prior to triggering. A t-test is performed on the critical value. The snippet *tt-x0-xor* from the category *suregfile* executes a *xor* instruction with register $x0$ as destination. As on the RISC-V ISA, the register $x0$ is hardwired to *zero*, the experiment helps analyzing how far operations with $x0$ as destination are executed and therewith produce leakage. In this experiment the inputs of the *xor* operation are treated as shares and the output is treated as a critical value. A t-test is executed on the critical value. Furthermore, the framework contains target-code written in C to communicate with the target, trigger and assign test-data, in addition to a host software, to control the oscilloscope and analyze the power-traces in form of a t-test [31] as well as to perform correlations with the traces with, e.g., the Hamming weight (HW) or Hamming distance (HD) of an input or host-side calculated parameter. In order to gain knowledge about the presence of a variety of sources of leakage on the RISC-V platform, we adapt the MIRACLE-framework to be able to operate a Picoscope 6000E series oscilloscope. Also, we extend the framework, to allow the generation of shares already on the host-side. Furthermore, we implement target-specific support to run the given experiments on the two different RISC-V processors. Those hardware netlists are based on the well maintained implementation Ibex that is also supported by the OpenTitan[5] project and NeoRV32 which is also well maintained and has an extensive support of RISC-V extensions. We implement the processors on an Artix 7 A100T Field Programmable Gate Array (FPGA) on a Chipwhsiperer CW305 board[6], of which we use the amplified output to generate the power-trace. To implement the Ibex core on the named FPGA, we use the Ibex-Demo-System System on Chip (SoC)[7]. We configure the SoC with 64 KiB RAM which stores data and instructions. The additional writeback-stage, instruction-cache, RV32B and branch-predictor of the Ibex-core are disabled. The configuration uses the RF32MFast implementation and the flipflop-based registerfile implementation. To implement the NeoRV32 on the CW305-board, we adapt the Vivado project for the Arty-A7 board from the NeoRV32-setups repository[8] and configure it to implement 32 KiB of instruction memory and 64 KiB of data memory directly in the core. For the experiments on Ibex and NeoRV32 we configure the oscilloscope to a sample rate of 1.25GS/s at a depth of 12 bit. Therewith, at a core clock of 50MHz, an oversampling of 25 samples per CPU-cycle is reached. On both cores we capture 100 000 traces per experiment. For both cores, we compile the experiments with *riscv32-unknown-elf-gcc* version 10.2.0. Some tests use the pseudo-instructions *nop* and *mv*. We note that *nop* expands to *addi x0, x0, 0*

---

[5] https://opentitan.org/, last visited: 11.06.2025.
[6] https://rtfm.newae.com/Targets/CW305ArtixFPGA/, last visited: 11.06.2025.
[7] https://github.com/lowRISC/ibex-demo-system, last visited: 11.06.2025.
[8] https://github.com/stnolting/neorv32-setups, last visited: 11.06.2025.

and mv expands to add immediate *addi rd, rs1, 0*. The results and conclusions drawn from the measurements are further discussed in Sect. 6.

5.2 Extending `PROLEAD_SW`: Support for the RISC-V platform

In order to extend `PROLEAD_SW` to support analyzing the probing security of software written for the RISC-V platform, we integrate a RISC-V emulator into `PROLEAD_SW`. As RISC-V emulator, we choose a publicly available open-source implementation[9]. This emulator is very light-weight, well organized and supports the RISC-V instruction sets RV32IM which contain integer math including multiplication and division and has 32 general purpose registers. RV32IM is therefore sufficient for most symmetric cryptography. Furthermore, RV32IM is supported by almost all RISC-V CPU implementations, which allows our tooling to verify binaries that can run on a variety of RISC-V devices as a starting point. In a first step of integration, we split the RISC-V emulator up into an instruction decoding and an execution unit, which allows for an intermediate semantic representation of the interpreted instruction which can be used to generate human-readable debug output as e.g., the instruction and registers at a CPU-cycle, which can be helpful while locating the leakage in an assembly. We placed the emulator and relevant additional classes that differ from the ARM emulator implementation in its own namespace *riscvemulator*. Therewith both emulators (for RISC-V and ARM) are encapsulated in their own C++ namespace. To give an overview of the organization of the software and the position of the emulators namespaces, Fig. 2 in the appendix shows there hirarchical position. Figure 1a and 1b show class diagrams, that give an overview of the emulators namespaces. In order to conserve performance, the platform to be analyzed by `PROLEAD_SW` (RISC-V or ARM) is set at compile-time using pre-processor commands, that primarily select the namespace to use. To analyze the executed binary, we augmented the emulator with the ability to generate probes, which are stored in a highly memory-optimized structure, as many probes are generated during execution. As this structure originally given in `PROLEAD_SW` was optimized to the given circumstances given in an ARM processor, as e.g., only 16 instead of 32 general purpose registers, we altered and adapted it to support the RISC-V architecture. As some RISC-V cores feature more pipeline-stages than supported in the original PROLEAD_SW version, we extended it to support up to 9 pipeline stages.

The leakage model implemented by `PROLEAD_SW` is highly conservative and allows different types of probing, which we all adopt to the RISC-V extension, assuming that depending on the individual micro-architecture implemented in hardware, all those types of leakage could be possible. To compile binaries for the RV32IM instruction set, the `riscv64-unknown-elf-gcc` compiler is used in version *8.3.0*.

The difference between our extension and the original version of the tooling is approximately 6.5K line changes[10].

---

[9] https://github.com/mirimmad/riscv, last visited: 11.06.2025.
[10] Estimated using `git diff --numstat`.

5.3 Evaluation of PROLEAD_SW RISC-V Extension with MIRACLE-Based Test-Vectors

In order to verify the correctness of the implementation, we execute a selected subset of assembly snippets in our extended version of PROLEAD_SW. Thereby the individual snippets trigger the detection of leakage with different probes in PROLEAD_SW as follows.

To measure the performance of the implementation of the different probes, only the specific and required probes are enabled. We execute the experiments on a machine with 128GB RAM and 32 cores of an AMD EPYC-Milan series CPU[11].

The snippets *supipeline/tt-xor* and *supipeline/tt-x0-xor* can produce transitional leakage when executed on real hardware. We execute snippets based on these snippets in PROLEAD_SW to verify the *Transitional Probe*. Thereby the shares are given as operands of the *xor* operation. To verify the implementation of the *Vertical Probe*, we use a snippet based on *regfile/neighbour-hw*. The *Vertical Probe* features isolation towards the calling environment (start code) in the following way. Registers that are not used during the sample under test are excluded from probing. The registers with the critical values are enabled by adding zero to them using the *addi* instruction. The critical value is given as two shares in the registers $a0$ and $a1$. The snippet *suregfile/xor-nop-1* can show leakage from shadow registers in different pipeline stages. In the snippet, two *xor* operations are executed, separated by one *nop* operation. We execute a similar snippet in PROLEAD_SW where each *xor* operation receives a share and zero as operands, to verify the functionality of the *Pipeline Forwarding Probe* with a three stage pipeline. We execute the snippets *memory-bus/register-implicit-ld-ld*, *memory-bus/register-implicit-ld-st*, *memory-bus/register-implicit-st-ld* and *memory-bus/register-implicit-st-st-2*, which can show leakage from hidden states in the memory-bus architecture of the core and SoC, in PROLEAD_SW to verify the functionality of the *Memory Probe* to detect leakage from architecturally accessed data resulting from hidden states that are shared and not shared between read and write accesses. The snippets *memory-bus/bus-width-ld-bytes* and *memory-bus/bus-width-st-bytes* can show leakage from not architecturally accessed data, that is accessed through a constant width of the memory-bus while accessing neighboring data. We execute snippets based on these in PROLEAD_SW to verify the functionality of the *Memory Probe* to detect such leakage at a bus width of 32-bit.

5.4 Performance Evaluation of Our Extended Version of PROLEAD_SW

To compare the performance of the RISC-V extension of PROLEAD_SW with its original counterpart for the ARM platform[12], we evaluate the masked C reference implementation from Rivian and Prouff [26], which is further called *AES_rp*, as

---

[11] The snippets are compiled with the following flags: `-mabi=ilp32 -march=rv32im -nostdlib -O0`.

[12] commit `3dbd58ded4aba427be8e9159fae3016d48c8f9f2`.

well as the Inner-Product-Masking secured (IPM) implementation[13] from Cheng et al. [10], which is further called *AES_ipm*, limited to 10000 iterations. We chose these implementations, as they were also analyzed with PROLEAD_SW as part of the case study of the original PROLEAD_SW publication [33]. For the performance evaluation, we execute the AES implementations in both versions of PROLEAD_SW (the original and extended version) on the same machine, to create comparable performance results.

For the ARM version we compile it similar to how it is compiled in [33][14]. For the RISC-V version, we compile the AES implementation with *riscv32-unknown-elf-gcc* version 10.2.0[15].

We configure both versions of PROLEAD_SW to enable probing for transitional leakage for *AES_ipm*, and transitional leakage as well as memory overwrite and memory shadow register leakage for *AES_rp*. We compile them with gcc version 10.2.1 with optimization level *O3* and configure them to use 28 threads. The performance comparison is discussed in Sect. 6.3.

6 Results

6.1 Micro-Architectural Leakage Identification Results

In the following, the results from the experimental leakage evaluation of the RISC-V hardware implementations are discussed.

The experiments *supipeline/tt-xor* and *supipeline/tt-x0-xor* show leakage of the operands and the result of the *xor* operation on both hardware implementations in form of the HW. Such leakage can be detected by PROLEAD_SW with the *Transitional Probe*. Furthermore, this adds evidence, that on both cores, the result is calculated even though the destination is register $x0$.

Table 1 shows the experimental results of snippets focusing on inter-instruction leakage and leakage resulting from hidden states in the pipeline. We can see leakage from different instructions that are directly adjacent. For instructions that are distanced by other instructions, we can see that on NeoRV32 no leakage is visible, but on ibex leakage is still visible, depending on the instruction in between. This could indicate that not all hidden states in the ALU and pipeline used for the execution of a specific instruction are cleared or used by other instructions. In the experiments *iseq-xor-xor*, *xor-sw* and *and-xor* we can see that at adjacent operations different combinations of operands and results can leak. Through the results from *tt-xor-nop-** we can see that especially on ibex hidden states can remain intact and can lead to leakage at an instruction later in time. Such leakage can be detected by PROLEAD_SW with the *Pipeline Forwarding Probe* and the *Vertical Probe*.

---

[13] https://github.com/Qomo-CHENG/IPM-FD, last visited: 13.08.2025.
[14] Using the following flags: -march=armv7-m -O3.
[15] Using the following flags: -mabi=ilp32 -march=rv32im -nostdlib -O3 -ffreestanding.

The *sumemory/register-implicit-** experiments resulted in leakage of the combined data of all tested combinations (ld-ld, st-st, ld-st, st-ld) on both targets. This gives evidence that the memory architecture of both targets have hidden memory states, that are shared between load and store operations. In the appendix, Table 3 lists these results.

The experiments *sumemory/seq-ld-bytes-nop* and *sumemory/seq-st-bytes-nop* show that in ibex leakage between the loaded and the next loaded byte as well as the loaded and the over-over-over-next loaded byte exists. On NeoRV32 we see leakage resulting from a stored and the next stored byte. The result on ibex show evidence for leakage from a hidden register with the size of a word. When loaded bytes are in the same loaded, word, the same word is addressed and loaded, when bytes are in another word, the other word is loaded and overwrites the hidden register, which creates leakage. In the appendix, Table 5 shows the experimental results.

The *sumemory/bus-width-** tests show significant leakage on ibex for one neighbouring byte during load and two during store accesses and on NeoRV32 for three neighbouring bytes during load and store operations. Such leakage can be detected by PROLEAD_SW with the *Memory Probe*. The results are listed in the appendix in Table 6.

The experiments *regfile/neighbour-hw* shows leakage on ibex and *suregfile/tt-multiplexer-a2* shows leakage on both targets. The leakage likely results from glitches in the multiplexer on the registerfile and can be detected by PROLEAD_SW with the *Vertical Probe*. In the appendix, Table 4 lists the experimental results of these tests.

Table 1. Results of pipeline experiments on real hardware, experiments from category (su)pipeline. The table shows the presence of hamming distance leakage between operations as O as well as of the left-hand and right-hand operands as R and L. E.g., OO denotes leakage resulting from both outputs. Tests that did not show any hamming distance leakage were repeated as a t-test, that tests for leakage of the results of the operations. This leakage is denoted as oo.

Device	ixeq-xor-xor	tt-xor-nop-1	tt-xor-nop-2	tt-xor-nop-3	tt-xor-xor-xor	tt-xor-mv1	tt-xor-mv-2	xor-sw	and-xor
Ibex	LR,RR	oo	oo	oo		oo	oo	OL,RO	OO,LL,RL,LR,RR
NeoRV32	OO,LL,RR						oo	OL,RL	LL,RR

6.2 Evaluation Results of PROLEAD_SW RISC-V Extension with MIRACLE-Based Test-Vectors

Each snippet is executed 100000 times. For all snippets leakage is reported within a couple of hundred iterations, which indicates, that the probing mechanism works correctly. To execute 100000 iterations took depending on the snippet and enabled probes from about 50 s to a couple of hundred seconds. In the appendix, Table 2 lists the time the experiments take to execute 100000 iterations, after how many iterations a false-positive probability of less than 10^{-5} is reported and the maximum memory consumption during the experiment.

6.3 Performance Results of `PROLEAD_SW` RISC-V Extension with AES Implementation

In both evaluated AES implementations our extended version of `PROLEAD_SW` detected leakage. On a CPU that follows the leakage model used in our tooling, leakage would be detectable. In AES_rp leakage is detected through a memory shadow register probe. In hardware, this leakage would result from a transition in a hidden state in the memory bus. In AES_rp leakage is detected through a transitional probe on a register, which would in hardware result from a transition in the registerfile.

Compared to the AES_rp compiled for $armv7\text{-}m$, which requires about $11.5K$ cycles, the binary for the RV32IM instruction-set requires about $13.6K$ cycles, which is expected as the instruction-sets differ in their scope and capabilities. As probes are created throughout the whole execution cycles, this has a direct impact on the memory requirements of `PROLEAD_SW`. The original ARM version detects first leakage after only 128 simulations, requires about $14.6GB$ and takes 364 seconds to complete 10000 traces. The RISC-V version detects first leakage after only 128 simulations, requires about $20.5GB$ and takes 329 seconds to complete 10000 traces. We can see that the evaluation of AES_rp on the RISC-V version is roughly 10% faster eventhough AES_rp requires about 18% more cycles on RV32IM. Also we can see an increase in memory consumption around 40%. One source of that increase is the higher CPU-cycle requirement of AES_rp on RV32IM. In addition, we limited the simulations of AES_rp on RV32IM to $11.5K$ cycles. This lead to a reduction of the memory requirement to $18.4GB$ and takes 289 seconds to complete 10000 traces. This would be an increment of about 26% in memory usage and an increment of about 20% in execution speed compared to the ARM version. The remaining increase of memory requirements comes down to modifications to the probe memory structure required to be compatible with RV32IM and to support more complex pipelined cores.

AES_ipm compiled for $armv7\text{-}m$ requires about $113.3K$ cycles while the binary compiled for RV32IM only requires $73.6K$ cycles. Both versions of `PROLEAD_SW` detect leakage after 64 simulations. The ARM version requires about $17.9GB$ and takes about 5000 seconds to complete 10000 traces. The RISC-V version requires $17.7GB$ and takes about 5961 seconds. We can see that the memory requirement is about the same. This can be explained through the difference in required CPU cycles of the binaries and a high dependency of the memory consumption to the required CPU cycles. Furthermore, in this comparison we can see an increment in runtime of about 19%.

7 Conclusion

In this work we presented an extensive, practical evaluations of microarchitectural leakage effects on RISC-V processors and showed experimentally that similar leakage-enhancing effects as on ARM processors exist. This allowed us to show that the CPU-independent leakage model used in `PROLEAD_SW` can be applied to the RISC-V architecture. Furthermore, we present tooling for analyzing the probing security of software written for the RISC-V platform, that is based on PROLEAD_SW. In addition, the new tooling is verified by the execution of test-vectors. Furthermore, we compared the performance of the new tooling to the original version of PROLEAD_SW by analyzing two AES C implementation with both versions. During the comparison, we found that the execution speed is all over comparable to the original version. The memory consumption highly depends on the CPU cycles required by the evaluated software. A comparison with equal CPU cycles on both versions of the tooling has shown about 26% increment in memory requirements. A next step could be the extension of the RISC-V emulator to support further commonly implemented instruction-set extensions as e.g., C (compressed instructions), what increases the comparability of binaries analyzed in our tooling and compiled for RISC-V hardware and therewith improves the effectiveness of our tooling.

Acknowledgements. Nicolai Schmitt is funded by the German Federal Ministry of Education and Research (BMFTR) and the Hessian Ministry of Higher Education, Research, Science and the Arts as part of the National Research Center for Applied Cybersecurity ATHENE.

A Appendix

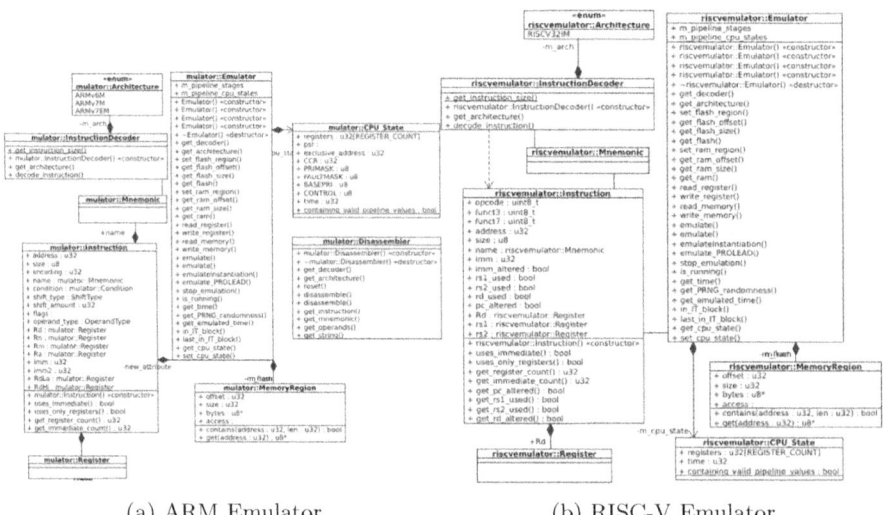

(a) ARM Emulator (b) RISC-V Emulator

Fig. 1. Classdiagrams of the namespaces of the emulators. For clarity, the diagram shows a subset of the classes and shows only public members.

Table 2. Testvectors executed in our extended version of `PROLEAD_SW`. Memory is rounded to GB.

Snippet (based on)	Enabled Probe Type	time (100k iter.)	time(iterations)	Memory (GB)
supipeline/tt-x0-xor	transitional	55.68 sec.	0.20 sec. (96 itr.)	2 GB
supipeline/tt-xor	transitional	45.29 sec.	0.18 sec. (64 itr.)	2 GB
suregfile/xor-nop-1	pipeline forwarding	392.48 sec.	1.3 sec. (224 itr.)	2 GB
regfile/neighbour-hw	vertical	216.75 sec.	0.38 sec. (64 itr.)	2 GB
memory-bus/register-implicit-ld-ld	memory, memory shadow reg.	129.78 sec.	0.34 sec. (128 itr.)	2 GB
memory-bus/register-implicit-ld-st	memory, memory shadow reg.	112.14 sec.	0.36 sec. (128 itr.)	2 GB
memory-bus/register-implicit-st-ld	memory, memory shadow reg.	161.64 sec.	0.40 sec. (128 itr.)	2 GB
memory-bus/register-implicit-st-st-2	memory, memory shadow reg.	115.34 sec.	0.40 sec. (128 itr.)	2 GB
memory-bus/bus-width-ld-bytes	memory, memory shadow reg.	80.07 sec.	0.29 sec. (96 itr.)	2 GB
memory-bus/bus-width-st-bytes	memory, memory shadow reg.	67.57 sec.	0.31 sec. (128 itr.)	2 GB

Table 3. Results of memory hidden state experiments on real hardware. A ✓ indicates leakage resulting from the load- or store word operations.

Device	LD-LD	ST-ST	LD-ST	ST-LD
Ibex	✓	✓	✓	✓
NeoRV	✓	✓	✓	✓

Table 4. Results of register-file experiments on real hardware using a t-test. A ✓ indicates leakage from a register that is not accessed during the test.

Device	neighbour-hw	tt-multiplexer-a2
Ibex	✓	✓
NeoRV		✓

Table 5. Results of memory hidden state experiments on real hardware using correlation with HD. The number is the sequential distance where leakage was found.

Device	seq-ld-bytes-nop	seq-st-bytes-nop
Ibex	1,4	
NeoRV		1

Table 6. Results of memory-bus-width experiments on real hardware using a t-test. Number represents offset to leaking byte in memory.

Device	bus-width-ld-byte	bus-width-st-byte
Ibex	0,1	0,1,2
NeoRV	0,1,2,3	0,1,2,3

Table 7. Experiments executed on Hardware-Targets to analyze micro-architectural leakage effects with a focus on the RISC-V architecture. Snippets in a group starting with su are supplemented or modified versions of original snippets. Snippets from other groups are taken from of the `MIRACLE` framework without modifications.

Short-Name	Category	Description
iseq-xor-xor	pipeline	Directly adjacent xor-xor
iseq-xor-sw	pipeline	Directly adjacent xor-storeword
iseq-xor-and	supipeline	Adjacent xor-and. Hamming distance tests
tt-xor	supipeline	T-test on output of xor (architectural)
tt-x0-xor	supipeline	T-Test on output of xor where destination register is register X0
tt-xor-nop-1	supipeline	T-test on outputs of xors. xor-nop-xor
tt-xor-nop-2	supipeline	T-test on output of xors. xor-nop-nop-xor
tt-xor-nop-3	supipeline	T-test on output of xors. xor-nop-nop-nop-xor
tt-xor-xor-xor	supipeline	T-test on outputs of first and last xor. xor-xor-xor
tt-xor-mv-1	supipeline	T-test on output of xors. xor-mv-xor
tt-xor-mv-2	supipeline	T-test on output of xors. xor-mv-mv-xor
seq-ld-bytes-nop	sumemory	Based on memory-bus/seq-ld-bytes. Multiple load-byte instructions separated by nop of adjacent addresses. Extended sequence length
seq-st-bytes-nop	sumemory	Based on memory-bus/seq-st-bytes. Multiple store-byte instructions separated by nop of adjacent addresses. Extended sequence length
bus-width-ld-bytes	sumemory	Based on memory-bus/bus-width-ld-bytes. T-test on not accessed neighbor byte. Extended memory range
bus-width-st-bytes	sumemory	Based on memory-bus/bus-width-st-bytes. T-test on not accessed neighbor byte. Extended memory range
register-implicit-ld-ld-nop	sumemory	Based on memory-bus/registers-implicit-ld-ld. Nop instead of xor. T-test on loaded data loadword-nop-loadword
register-implicit-st-st-nop	sumemory	Based on memory-bus/registers-implicit-st-st-2. Nop instead of xor. Hamming-Distance test on stored data storeword-nop-storeword
register-implicit-ld-st-nop	sumemory	Based on memory-bus/registers-implicit-ld-st. Nop instead of xor. T-test on loaded and stored data loadword-nop-storeword
register-implicit-st-ld-nop	sumemory	Based on memory-bus/registers-implicit-st-ld. Nop instead of xor. T-test on loaded and stored data storeword-nop-loadword
neighbour-hw	regfile	T-test for leakage of value in unaccessed register during execution of xor on other registers
tt-multiplexer-a2	suregfile	Principle based on regfile/neighbour-hw. T-test on a value loaded in a register (a2), that is not accessed. During the test, different operations are executed

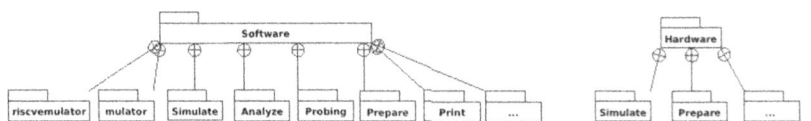

Fig. 2. Namespace hierarchy. The diagram shows where the namespaces of the emulators are located in the software. For clarity, the diagram shows a subset of the namespaces.

References

1. lowRISC/ibex. https://github.com/lowRISC/ibex. Accessed 12 Aug 2025
2. Baddam, K., Zwolinski, M.: Evaluation of dynamic voltage and frequency scaling as a differential power analysis countermeasure. In: 20th International Conference on VLSI Design held jointly with 6th International Conference on Embedded Systems (VLSID 2007), pp. 854–862 (2007). https://doi.org/10.1109/VLSID.2007.79. ISSN: 2380-6923
3. Barthe, G., Belaïd, S., Cassiers, G., Fouque, P.-A., Grégoire, B., Standaert, F.-X.: maskVerif: automated verification of higher-order masking in presence of physical defaults. In: Sako, K., Schneider, S., Ryan, P.Y.A. (eds.) ESORICS 2019. LNCS, vol. 11735, pp. 300–318. Springer, Cham (2019). https://doi.org/10.1007/978-3-030-29959-0_15
4. Barthe, G., Gourjon, M., Grégoire, B., Orlt, M., Paglialonga, C., Porth, L.: Masking in fine-grained leakage models: construction, implementation and verification. IACR Trans. Cryptogr. Hardw. Embed. Syst. 189–228 (2021). https://doi.org/10.46586/tches.v2021.i2.189-228
5. Bayrak, A.G., Velickovic, N., Ienne, P., Burleson, W.: An architecture-independent instruction shuffler to protect against side-channel attacks. ACM Trans. Archit. Code Optim. **8**(4), 1–19 (2012). https://doi.org/10.1145/2086696.2086699
6. Beckers, A., Wouters, L., Gierlichs, B., Preneel, B., Verbauwhede, I.: Provable secure software masking in the real-world. In: Balasch, J., O'Flynn, C. (eds.) COSADE 2022. LNCS, vol. 13211, pp. 215–235. Springer, Cham (2022). https://doi.org/10.1007/978-3-030-99766-3_10
7. Bloem, R., Gigerl, B., Gourjon, M., Hadzic, V., Mangard, S., Primas, R.: Power contracts: provably complete power leakage models for processors. In: Proceedings of the 2022 ACM SIGSAC Conference on Computer and Communications Security, CCS 2022, pp. 381–395. Association for Computing Machinery, New York (2022). https://doi.org/10.1145/3548606.3560600
8. Bronchain, O., Cassiers, G.: Bitslicing arithmetic/boolean masking conversions for fun and profit with application to lattice-based KEMs. IACR Trans. Cryptogr. Hardw. Embed. Syst. **2022**(4), 553–588 (2022). https://doi.org/10.46586/TCHES.V2022.I4.553-588
9. Chari, S., Jutla, C.S., Rao, J.R., Rohatgi, P.: Towards sound approaches to counteract power-analysis attacks. In: Wiener, M. (ed.) CRYPTO 1999. LNCS, vol. 1666, pp. 398–412. Springer, Heidelberg (1999). https://doi.org/10.1007/3-540-48405-1_26
10. Cheng, W., Carlet, C., Goli, K., Danger, J.-L., Guilley, S.: Detecting faults in inner product masking scheme. J. Cryptogr. Eng. **11**(2), 119–133 (2020). https://doi.org/10.1007/s13389-020-00227-6
11. Coron, J.-S.: Higher order masking of look-up tables. In: Nguyen, P.Q., Oswald, E. (eds.) EUROCRYPT 2014. LNCS, vol. 8441, pp. 441–458. Springer, Heidelberg (2014). https://doi.org/10.1007/978-3-642-55220-5_25
12. Coron, J.-S., Großschädl, J., Vadnala, P.K.: Secure conversion between boolean and arithmetic masking of any order. In: Batina, L., Robshaw, M. (eds.) CHES 2014. LNCS, vol. 8731, pp. 188–205. Springer, Heidelberg (2014). https://doi.org/10.1007/978-3-662-44709-3_11
13. Le Corre, Y., Großschädl, J., Dinu, D.: Micro-architectural power simulator for leakage assessment of cryptographic software on ARM cortex-M3 processors. In: Fan, J., Gierlichs, B. (eds.) COSADE 2018. LNCS, vol. 10815, pp. 82–98. Springer, Cham (2018). https://doi.org/10.1007/978-3-319-89641-0_5

14. Faust, S., Grosso, V., Merino Del Pozo, S., Paglialonga, C., Standaert, F.X.: Composable masking schemes in the presence of physical defaults & the robust probing model. IACR Trans. Cryptogr. Hardw. Embed. Syst. 89–120 (2018). https://doi.org/10.46586/tches.v2018.i3.89-120
15. Gigerl, B., Hadzic, V., Primas, R., Mangard, S., Bloem, R.: Coco: co-design and co-verification of masked software implementations on CPUs. In: Bailey, M.D., Greenstadt, R. (eds.) 30th USENIX Security Symposium, USENIX Security 2021, 11–13 August 2021, pp. 1469–1468. USENIX Association (2021). https://www.usenix.org/conference/usenixsecurity21/presentation/gigerl. Accessed 13 Aug 2025
16. Gigerl, B., Primas, R., Mangard, S.: Secure and efficient software masking on superscalar pipelined processors. In: Tibouchi, M., Wang, H. (eds.) ASIACRYPT 2021. LNCS, vol. 13091, pp. 3–32. Springer, Cham (2021). https://doi.org/10.1007/978-3-030-92075-3_1
17. de Grandmaison, A., Heydemann, K., Meunier, Q.L.: ARMISTICE: microarchitectural leakage modeling for masked software formal verification. IEEE Trans. Comput. Aided Des. Integr. Circuits Syst. **41**(11), 3733–3744 (2022). https://doi.org/10.1109/TCAD.2022.3197507
18. He, M., Park, J., Nahiyan, A., Vassilev, A., Jin, Y., Tehranipoor, M.: RTL-PSC: automated power side-channel leakage assessment at register-transfer level. In: 2019 IEEE 37th VLSI Test Symposium (VTS), Monterey, CA, USA, pp. 1–6. IEEE (2019). https://doi.org/10.1109/VTS.2019.8758600
19. Ishai, Y., Sahai, A., Wagner, D.: Private circuits: securing hardware against probing attacks. In: Boneh, D. (ed.) CRYPTO 2003. LNCS, vol. 2729, pp. 463–481. Springer, Heidelberg (2003). https://doi.org/10.1007/978-3-540-45146-4_27
20. Marshall, B., Page, D., Webb, J.: MIRACLE: MIcRo-ArChitectural Leakage Evaluation: a study of micro-architectural power leakage across many devices. IACR Trans. Cryptogr. Hardw. Embed. Syst. 175–220 (2021). https://doi.org/10.46586/tches.v2022.i1.175-220
21. McCann, D., Oswald, E., Whitnall, C.: Towards practical tools for side channel aware software engineering: 'grey box' modelling for instruction leakages. In: Kirda, E., Ristenpart, T. (eds.) 26th USENIX Security Symposium, USENIX Security 2017, Vancouver, BC, Canada, 16–18 August 2017, pp. 199–216. USENIX Association (2017). https://www.usenix.org/conference/usenixsecurity17/technical-sessions/presentation/mccann
22. Meyer, L.D., Reparaz, O., Bilgin, B.: Multiplicative masking for AES in hardware. IACR Trans. Cryptogr. Hardw. Embed. Syst. **2018**(3), 431–468 (2018). https://doi.org/10.13154/TCHES.V2018.I3.431-468
23. Müller, N., Moradi, A.: PROLEAD: a probing-based hardware leakage detection tool. IACR Trans. Cryptogr. Hardw. Embed. Syst. 311–348 (2022). https://doi.org/10.46586/tches.v2022.i4.311-348
24. The NEORV32 RISC-V Processor (2025). https://doi.org/10.5281/ZENODO.5018888
25. Papagiannopoulos, K., Veshchikov, N.: Mind the gap: towards secure 1st-order masking in software. In: Guilley, S. (ed.) COSADE 2017. LNCS, vol. 10348, pp. 282–297. Springer, Cham (2017). https://doi.org/10.1007/978-3-319-64647-3_17
26. Rivain, M., Prouff, E.: Provably secure higher-order masking of AES. In: Mangard, S., Standaert, F.-X. (eds.) CHES 2010. LNCS, vol. 6225, pp. 413–427. Springer, Heidelberg (2010). https://doi.org/10.1007/978-3-642-15031-9_28
27. Sharma, M., Bhatnagar, E., Puri, K., Mitra, A., Agarwal, J.: A Survey of RISC-V CPU for IoT Applications (2022). https://doi.org/10.2139/ssrn.4033491

28. Shelton, M.A., Samwel, N., Batina, L., Regazzoni, F., Wagner, M., Yarom, Y.: Rosita: towards automatic elimination of power-analysis leakage in ciphers. In: 28th Annual Network and Distributed System Security Symposium, NDSS 2021, virtually, 21–25 February 2021. The Internet Society (2021). https://www.ndss-symposium.org/ndss-paper/rosita-towards-automatic-elimination-of-power-analysis-leakage-in-ciphers/. Accessed 13 Aug 2025
29. Singh, A., Kar, M., Mathew, S., Rajan, A., De, V., Mukhopadhyay, S.: Exploiting on-chip power management for side-channel security. In: 2018 Design, Automation & Test in Europe Conference & Exhibition (DATE), pp. 401–406 (2018). https://doi.org/10.23919/DATE.2018.8342043. ISSN: 1558-1101
30. Sokal, R.R., Rohlf, F.J.: Biometry: the principles and practice of statistics in biological research, 2nd edn. W. H. Freeman, San Francisco (1981)
31. Welch, B.L.: The generalization of 'student's' problem when several different population variances are involved. Biometrika **34**(1/2), 28–35 (1947). https://doi.org/10.2307/2332510
32. Zafar, Y., Har, D.: A novel countermeasure enhancing side channel immunity in FPGAs. In: 2008 International Conference on Advances in Electronics and Micro-Electronics, Valencia, Spain, pp. 132–137. IEEE (2008). https://doi.org/10.1109/ENICS.2008.11
33. Zeitschner, J., Müller, N., Moradi, A.: PROLEAD_sw - Probing-Based Software Leakage Detection for ARM Binaries (2023). https://eprint.iacr.org/2023/034. Publication info: Published by the IACR in TCHES 2023
34. Zhou, F., Chen, H., Fan, L.: Prover - toward more efficient formal verification of masking in probing model. IACR Trans. Cryptogr. Hardw. Embed. Syst. **2025**(1), 552–585 (2024). https://doi.org/10.46586/tches.v2025.i1.552-585

GIR-Cache: Mitigating Conflict-Based Cache Side-Channel Attacks via Global Indirect Replacement

Hao Ma[1,2], Zhidong Wang[1,2], Da Xie[1,2], Ciyan Ouyang[1,2], and Wei Song[1,2(✉)]

[1] State Key Laboratory of Cyberspace Security Defense, Institute of Information Engineering, Chinese Academy of Sciences, Beijing, China
songwei@iie.ac.cn
[2] School of Cyberspace Security, University of Chinese Academy of Sciences, Beijing, China

Abstract. Conflict-based side-channel attacks allow attackers to monitor victims' access patterns by asserting malicious cache conflicts. While cache randomization has emerged as a potential defense, existing solutions face critical limitations. CEASER-S and DT4+EV10 fail to fully prevent existing eviction set searching algorithms. MIRAGE suffers from intolerable area and power overheads. Chameleon's relocation mechanism faces the problem of excessive power/energy consumption. To alleviate these limitations, we employ a dual-mapping randomized cache with global indirect replacement (GIR-Cache). A randomized direct-mapped look up table is designed to eliminate dual-index checking overhead by maintaining the active mapping state of each LLC address. Our approach effectively mitigates conflict-based side-channel attacks while incurs negligible runtime performance impact with moderate area and power overhead.

Keywords: micro architecture · conflict-based cache side-channel attacks · cache randomization · global indirect replacement

1 Introduction

To reduce memory access latency, modern computers introduce multi-level cache structures within the system-on-chip architecture between cores and memory. As a critical performance component, the last-level cache (LLC) is shared among all cores to maximize resource utilization. When a sensitive application runs simultaneously with a malicious one on different cores, attackers may utilize cache side-channel attacks to leak sensitive information through the LLC [1,2]. The cache structure of current LLC unintentionally allows attackers to evict a victim's data by accessing an eviction set – *a group of congruent memory addresses mapping to the same cache set with the victim's data*. This enables attackers to manipulate the cache state and infer sensitive security information from the victim program. Existing studies have demonstrated that such conflict-based attacks have been used to recover encryption keys [3], exfiltrate sensitive user data from cloud environments [4,5], break sandbox defenses [6], and even steal information in what is considered secure trusted execution environments [7].

Cache partitioning was one of the early defenses proposed to defend against conflict-based attacks [5,8,9]. By separating private information from ordinary data [10], cache partitioning makes it impossible for attackers to cause conflicts and evict crucial data. However, cache partitioning relies on a trusted operating system to differentiate between private and ordinary data [11]. Furthermore, when privacy data cannot be easily separated from ordinary data using cache partitioning, the approach becomes ineffective.

Cache randomization [12–18] has emerged as a promising defense mechanism. By randomizing the locations of cache blocks [19,20], it prevents attackers from predicting the address-to-set mapping. As a result, attackers cannot reliably determine congruent addresses beforehand and must instead dynamically discover them during execution, making eviction-based attacks significantly harder to orchestrate. Some advanced defense schemes have combined cache randomization with skewing for enhanced protection. For instance, CEASER-S [15] employs a skewed cache structure with periodic remapping to mitigate eviction set searching algorithms such as *Group Elimination* (GE) [20,21,25] and *Prime Prune Probe* (PPP) [1–3] but fails to thwart *Conflict Testing* (CT) [15] and *Conflict Testing-Fast* (CT-Fast) [21]. Chameleon Cache [22] strengthens defense by combining a random skewed cache with a victim cache (VC). When an eviction occurs in the LLC, the evicted cache block is first moved to the VC, then it evicts an unrelated cache block in VC, thereby obfuscating conflicts and separating contentions. However, cache blocks in the VC require periodic reinsertion into the LLC, resulting in three block relocations per cache miss. These operations not only consume extra power but also reduce the available bandwidth. MIRAGE [23] proposes to eliminate attacker-controlled associativity evictions through decoupled metadata storage and multi-step cuckoo relocation. The design incurs a documented 22% storage overhead for metadata structures, with additional system-level impacts including: reduced memory density from metadata partitioning, increased logic complexity for relocation management, and introduced non-negligible runtime performance overheads. Inspired by ZCache [24], DT4+EV10 [25,26] analyzes the distribution of evictions over LLC cache sets under attack and proposes a lightweight attack detection and on-demand remapping scheme using the traditional set-associative LLC. However, it cannot defend against the latest searching algorithms like *Conflict Testing with Probe+Prune* (CTPP) [27].

Current randomized cache structures exhibit two key limitations: insufficient security and high overheads. In this paper, we introduce GIR-Cache to show that traditional set-associative caches can be made secure to thwart all existing eviction set searching algorithms. Compared to existing randomized cache designs, our proposal shows advantages in terms of security, cache hit rate, area, and power consumption. Our contributions are as follows:

1. **Attack-resistant design** using global indirect replacement with dual-mapping, mitigating conflict-based attacks with only 0.53% runtime, 2.47% area, and 3.35% power overhead.
2. **Latency-optimized access** via an index predictor (a randomized direct-mapped lookup table), reducing metadata accesses by 47.3% and dynamic power consumption by 4.5% compared to random selection.
3. **Lightweight implementation** requiring only LLC hit and eviction logic modifications, with no additional metadata storage or ISA changes.

The structure of this paper is organized as follows: Sect. 2 provides necessary background. Section 3 presents the threat model and analyzes why existing eviction set searching algorithms fail under our GIR mechanism. Section 4 details the implementation of GIR-Cache and its lookup table (GIR-LUT). Section 5 evaluates the defense's security and hardware overheads (cache miss rate, relocation frequency, power, and area). Finally, Sect. 6 concludes the paper.

2 Background

This section introduces the necessary background for understanding the paper, including randomized caches and eviction set searching algorithms.

2.1 Randomized Caches

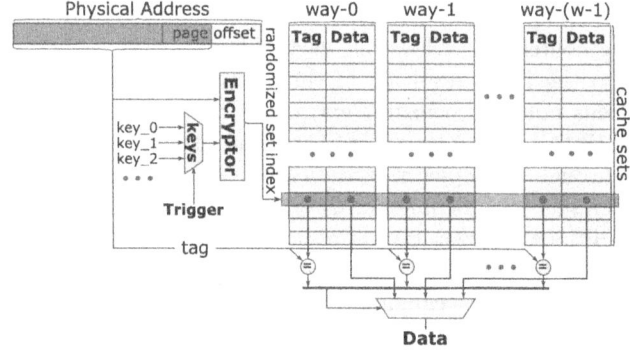

Fig. 1. A randomized set-associative LLC structure.

Randomized last-level caches make it significantly difficult for attackers to search usable eviction sets. As shown in Fig. 1, a randomized cache generates cache set index of an address by encrypting the higher digits of the address after removing the lower cache block offset bits [26]. As the encryption is unknown to the attacker, she must search eviction sets at runtime using fast search algorithms. To limit the time available for searching an eviction set and nullify an eviction set already obtained by an attacker, the cache can update the key used by the encryption, which effectively re-randomize the mapping between addresses and cache set indices. All congruent addresses already obtained by an attacker become useless. However, all cache blocks in the LLC must be relocated according to the new mapping.

Recent defense mechanisms [15,16,22,23] have adopted skewed cache architectures that enhance security by preventing attackers from precisely predicting cache set indices. This approach invalidates traditional attacks by drastically increasing the required eviction set size, rendering obtained sets ineffective. In skewed caches, addresses are either **fully congruent** (mapping to identical sets across all partitions) or **partially congruent** (inconsistent across partitions). By splitting cache ways into independent skew-partitions – each with a unique mapping key – fully congruent addresses become harder to collect, forcing attackers to rely on partially congruent ones.

While skewed caches enhance security, CEASER-S remains vulnerable to CT/CT-Fast attacks [25], and excessive skewed-partitions can degrade performance. Maintaining multiple concurrent mappings not only incurs area overhead but also complicates both access processing and conflict detection logic. These architectural constraints collectively degrade LLC bandwidth availability and impair runtime performance for applications. GIR-Cache alleviates these limitations by demonstrating that randomized set-associative LLCs can maintain robust security against conflict-based attacks while preserving performance with modest overhead.

2.2 Eviction Set Searching Algorithms

Although cache randomization prevents attackers from deducing address mapping in traditional set-associative caches, it cannot effectively defend against increasingly faster eviction set searching algorithms that gather congruent addresses at runtime. GE [20,21,25] begins with a large random address pool (typically >SW addresses, where **S is cache sets and W is ways**). The pool must contain $\geq W$ congruent addresses. The algorithm iteratively partitions addresses into W+1 groups per round, discarding at least one useless group each iteration until only W addresses remain. The attacker verifies candidate groups until obtaining a minimal eviction set, with LLC time complexity of $O(SW^2)$.

PPP searches eviction sets across different LLC replacement policies [1–3]. The alogrithm begins by priming the LLC with a large random address pool, iteratively pruning conflicting addresses until the LLC is fully populated. The attacker then probes the refined pool: each probe first accesses the target address, then detects evictions through cache misses upon re-access. High-latency addresses indicate congruence with the target. This process requires $O(SW)$ memory accesses under LRU replacement, increasing to $O(SW^2)$ for random replacement.

The CT algorithm first accesses a target address, then sequentially tests random addresses to detect congruence [15]. When a random address conflicts with the target (which occurs with probability $\frac{1}{W}$ under random replacement), alternating accesses between them will reveal congruence through cache misses. Each random address that causes a target miss is identified as congruent and added to the eviction set. This iterative process continues until completion, requiring $O(SW^2)$ operations to construct a minimal eviction set. The method remains equally effective for permutation-based replacement policies like LRU, maintaining the same time complexity. CT-Fast [29] optimizes the CT algorithm specifically for LRU replacement policies. While its initial phase mirrors the standard CT approach, the process accelerates after finding the first congruent address. With N already collected congruent addresses, the attacker only needs to test W-N candidate addresses in subsequent searches. This is achieved by first accessing the target, then revisiting all N known congruent addresses – making the target more easily to be evicted.

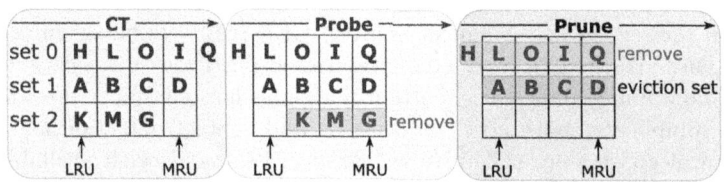

Fig. 2. Simplified model of the CTPP eviction set searching algorithm.

CTPP [27] combines CT and PPP advantages for LRU caches. As shown in Fig. 2, after the CT phase distributes addresses across a set-3, way-4 LRU LLC, three patterns emerge: sets with >W (set 0), =W (set 1), or <W (set 2) congruent addresses. Only sets with exactly W addresses can evict the target – others are eliminated through iterative Probe (removing cache hits from underpopulated sets like set 2) and Prune phases (filtering cache misses from overpopulated sets like set 0). Within 3–5 iterations of these Probe and Prune phases, this converges to a perfect W-sized eviction set (set 1).

3 Threat Analysis and Defense Methods

This section first establishes our threat model, then explains how GIR mechanism works during LLC misses and why conflict-based attacks fail under GIR-Cache's protection mechanism.

3.1 Threat Model

This paper focuses on preventing attackers from successfully obtaining a complete eviction set using existing search algorithms; therefore, we define a successful attack as finding a complete eviction set. Without eviction sets, attackers cannot control target cache sets and all conflict-based side-channel attacks fail.

We assume the attacker can allocate and access arbitrary amount of memory while infer the hit/miss state of a memory access of her own data using high-resolution timers. The victim runs in a separate address space with no shared memory with the attacker; therefore, the attacker cannot directly access data belonging to the victim. The randomized cache structure is publicly available to the attacker but the encryption of the cache set index is hardware controlled and secure (not deciphered).

We focus on conflict-based cache side-channel attacks targeting inclusive LLC. Specifically, we only consider SAE-based (Set-Associative Eviction) attacks [23]. Other types of cache side-channel attacks, such as reuse-based and occupation attacks [1,2], are out of the scope of this paper.

3.2 Global Indirect Replacement Cache

Prior research [25] demonstrates that in a P skew-partitions set-associative cache, the probability of an address mapping to the same set across all P partitions is $\frac{1}{S^P}$, making it nearly impossible for attackers to obtain perfect eviction sets containing fully congruent addresses. Our defense employs a dual-mapping randomized set-associative architecture to mitigate conflict-based attacks. Each LLC access dynamically selects a mapping via predictor-guided selection for hit determination. During eviction, GIR remaps and relocates target blocks to new sets, forcing the eviction of a random block instead. The relationship between the LLC-missed address and the ultimately evicted address is completely uncorrelated, making any observed conflicts statistically meaningless. As a result, attackers gather only invalid addresses, preventing the searching of a usable eviction set and thwarting further exploitation.

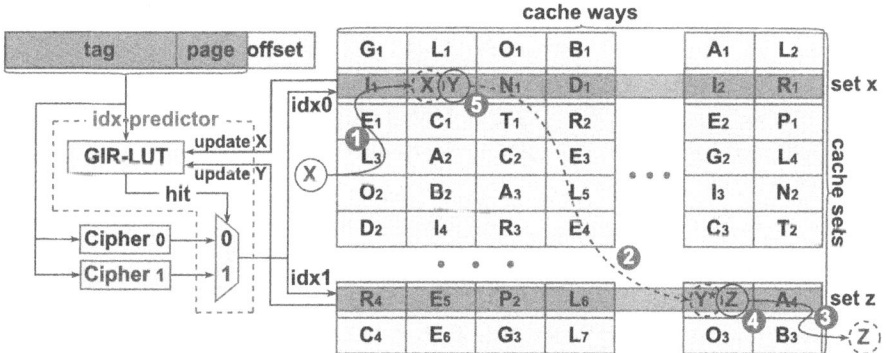

Fig. 3. The situation of gir-cache when handling cache misses.

To more intuitively demonstrate GIR-Cache's replacement operation, Fig. 3 shows a miss handling scenario. ① An LLC miss on address X forces random set selection, while its congruent address Y uses the predictor-provided mapping (here, both ultimately mapping to set x via idx0). ② The replacement algorithm evicts Y from set x to create space. ③ Y remaps to set z as Y* using idx1, triggering eviction of a random block Z from set z while updating replacement metadata. ④ This transfers Y's valid entry from set x to set z, invalidating the original metadata. ⑤ X then occupies the vacated slot in set x. In this scenario, attackers only observe X's miss and Z's eviction – unable to detect Y*'s preservation due to the dual-mapping scheme. Consequently, they collect meaningless random addresses, rendering conflict-based attacks ineffective.

3.3 Thwart Existing Search Algorithms Using GIR

Conflict-based side-channel attacks fundamentally rely on searching eviction sets for target addresses. Figure 4 illustrates the GE algorithm's operation, where an initial pool of N addresses undergoes pruning. The process begins by dividing addresses into W+1 groups, which contain at least W congruent addresses to target T (represented by green boxes B,G,M,S). To eliminate one group, the attacker first accesses T, then sequentially accesses W groups. Upon re-accessing T, a cache miss indicates that the W groups contain at least W congruent addresses, allowing the (W+1)-th group to be discarded. If T results in a cache hit, the algorithm redistributes the N addresses into W+1 new groups without accessing the remaining group. This process repeats until only W (or slightly more) congruent addresses remain.

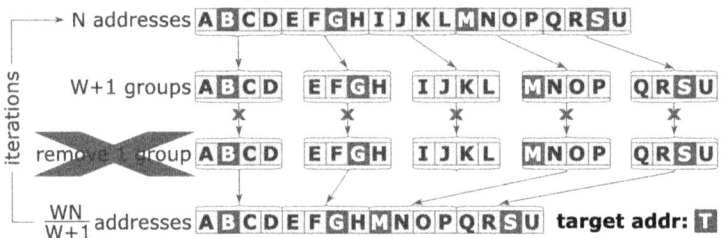

Fig. 4. GE algorithm fails under GIR mechanism (red '×' marks failure steps). (Color figure online)

GIR-Cache thwarts this process through its relocation mechanism. In a conventional set-associative cache, a miss on accessing target T would allow a congruent address to directly evict T from the LLC. However, GIR-Cache breaks this linkage by remapping T to a new set and replacing a block from that set – there is no congruence between the missed address and the ultimately evicted address. As a result, when repeatedly accessing the W groups, GE can no longer reliably evict T, which often remains cache-resident. Since only random addresses have a minimal chance of displacing T from the LLC, GE fails to evict the target using congruent addresses. This prevents GE from eliminating target groups or gathering valid eviction sets, rendering the attack ineffective under GIR-Cache.

Figures 5 and 6 show how GIR's policy disrupts congruent address collection for target T in a 4-set, 4-way LRU cache using CT/CT-Fast and PPP algorithms. Here, ①-③ indicate the execution sequence of the corresponding algorithm,

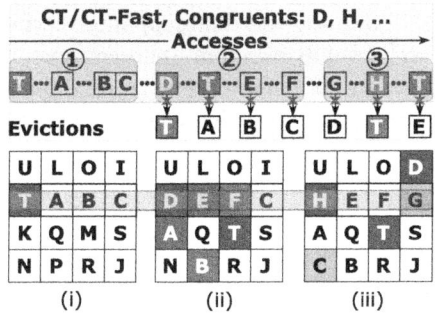
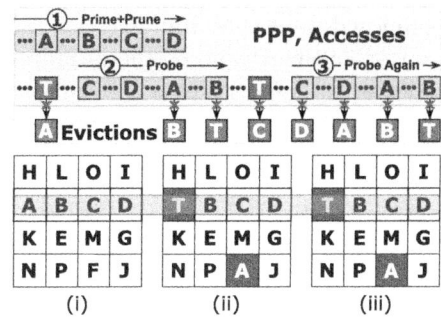

Fig. 5. CT/CT-Fast fails in 4-set, 4-way LRU LLC under GIR (red 'x' marks failure steps). (Color figure online)

Fig. 6. PPP fails in 4-set, 4-way LRU LLC under GIR (red 'x' marks failure steps). (Color figure online)

while (i)-(iii) represent the distribution of cache blocks during the algorithm's execution (Same-colored blocks denote cache-missed and relocated addresses). In CT and CT-Fast (Fig. 5), attackers access a large number of random addresses to collect those congruent with a chosen target address T. The process involves: ① initially accessing T followed by random addresses (A–H...) mapped to T's set; ② Through interleaved accesses to random addresses and target T, observed misses on T identify congruent addresses (e.g., the green blocks D and H); ③ Repeat until four congruent addresses are collected to form the eviction set. However, GIR introduces three critical failure modes: (i) Previously identified congruent addresses (e.g., D/H) lose their ability to evict T; (ii) Eviction attempts trigger T's relocation to new cache sets with random blocks selection (e.g., block M being evicted instead of T when accessing D); (iii) During subsequent testing, the attacker can only observe the evicted random addresses (K, P, N, I), while the genuinely congruent addresses (A–D) remain in the LLC due to relocation.

In the PPP algorithm shown in Fig. 6, ① the Prime+Prune phase begins with the attacker filling the LLC with random addresses (prime set) and subsequently pruning conflicting ones until the remaining addresses such as A–D can coexist in the cache. Timed re-accesses of target T and the prime set identify congruent addresses (LLC misses), though private cache filtering often misaligns LLC and software access orders. ② The Probe phase gathers partially congruent addresses (e.g., the green blocks A and B), and ③ re-probing aligns LLC order to finally collect four addresses (A–D) for T. However, GIR disrupts the PPP algorithm's operation: (i) The pruning phase assumes T's cache set remains unaffected by addresses self-conflicts, but (ii) accessing target T (resulting in a miss) triggers eviction attempts (e.g., selecting address A), which activates GIR's mechanism – relocating A to a new set while randomly ejecting an unrelated block (e.g., F). (iii) Consequently, the collected supposedly-congruent addresses prove arbitrary and invalid, completely corrupting the eviction set searching process.

The CTPP algorithm fails under GIR-Cache protection. During the CT phase, attackers may successfully locate an initial address pool containing W supposed-congruent addresses for target T. However, the dual-mapping mechanism ensures most of these addresses are actually random (non-congruent addresses). Subsequent probe and prune phases rapidly eliminate these random addresses. Meanwhile, truly congruent addresses cannot evict target T – they instead relocate T to a new set while randomly ejecting another address, forcing cache hits upon T's re-access. Consequently, attackers only collect random addresses that are useless for mounting effective attacks.

In summary, the GIR mechanism ensures security through target address relocation. When relocated addresses move to new sets and replace a random address, attackers can only observe the missed address and the ultimately evicted address – which share no congruence. This makes it impossible for attackers to use collected random addresses to evict the target, thereby effectively preventing eviction set searching. GIR-Cache defeats all major eviction set searching algorithms (GE/CT/CT-Fast/PPP/CTPP), experimental results (present in Sect. 5) confirming robust security without compromising performance.

4 Hardware Implementation Details

This section presents the hardware design details, covering the pseudo-code for our new hit/eviction handling methods, the GIR-Cache overview structure, and the GIR-LUT design.

4.1 Handling Hits and Evictions in GIR-Cache

Algorithm 1. Optimized GIR-Cache Hit Function

    Input: addr
    Output: hit (true/false)
    GirLut[addr]: 1-bit mapping predictor (0/1)
1: **function** GIR_HIT(addr)
2:     $i \leftarrow$ GirLut[addr], s0 $\leftarrow$ idxer0(addr), s1 $\leftarrow$ idxer1(addr)
3:     (first_s, second_s) $\leftarrow$ (i ? (s1, s0) : (s0, s1))
4:     **if** hit(addr, first_s) **then**
5:         **return** true
6:     **else if** hit(addr, second_s) **then**
7:         GirLut[addr] $\leftarrow$ ($1 \oplus i$)
8:         **return** true
9:     **end if**
10:     **return** false
11: **end function**

To implement the GIR strategy, we modified the LLC hit mechanism as described in Algorithm 1. When accessing an address (*addr*) in the LLC, the LLC queries the GIR-LUT to retrieve the stored index value i while simultaneously computing both potential mapping results for the address – obtaining sets $s0$ and $s1$ from the two mapping functions (idxer0() and idxer1()).

This index value determines the primary mapping to use: indexer0 when i is 0, or indexer1 when i is 1. The LLC then performs the first hit check using the indicated mapping function. A successful hit confirms the GIR-LUT's prediction was correct, and the corresponding cache block is returned. When the initial check fails due to prediction error, the system performs a secondary hit verification using the alternative mapping function that was not selected by GIR-LUT. In case of a second hit, the LLC updates the GIR-LUT with the index value $(1 \oplus i)$, correcting the prediction for future accesses. If both checks fail, the address is confirmed as not present in the LLC, and the miss handling proceeds through the standard coherence protocol without modifying the GIR-LUT.

To further support the GIR policy, we redesigned the eviction procedure as specified in Algorithm 2. The algorithm employs an S[W] array structure for cache block organization. The input parameter $addr$ specifies the relocation target address, with s[w] representing its associated cache block. The LLC calculates two candidate sets ($s0$ and $s1$) for $addr$ using both indexers. By evaluating the current set s against $s0$ and $s1$, the system determines the remapping strategy. For illustration, we assume $addr$ initially maps to $s0$ through idxer0, then demonstrate its remapping to destination set ds via idxer1 (where $i = 1$).

Algorithm 2. Simplified GIR-Cache Evict Function

Input: addr, s, w
Cache structure: S[W] is an array representing the cache sets and ways
1: **function** GIR_EVICT(addr, s, w)
2:     s0 ← idxer0(addr), s1 ← idxer1(addr)
3:     i ← (s==s0), ds ← (i ? s1 : s0)
4:     dw ← replace(ds)
5:     **if** ds[dw].meta.valid **then**
6:         evict(ds[dw])
7:     **end if**
8:     ds[dw] ← s[w], GirLut[addr] ← i
9: **end function**

A special case occurs when both indexers map to the same set ($s0==s1$), the LLC bypasses set ds relocation and directly evicts the replacement-selected block s[w]. While s[w]'s address is congruent with the missed address, Sect. 3.2's probability analysis ($\frac{1}{S^2}$) demonstrates this collision occurs with only $\frac{1}{S^2}$ probability, rendering it statistically implausible for attackers to accumulate W such congruent addresses. The operation finalizes by depositing the missed block's address, metadata and data in s[w]'s vacated space while simultaneously updating the GIR-LUT with the new mapping index i to preserve predictor accuracy for future accesses.

4.2 GIR-Cache Hardware Overview

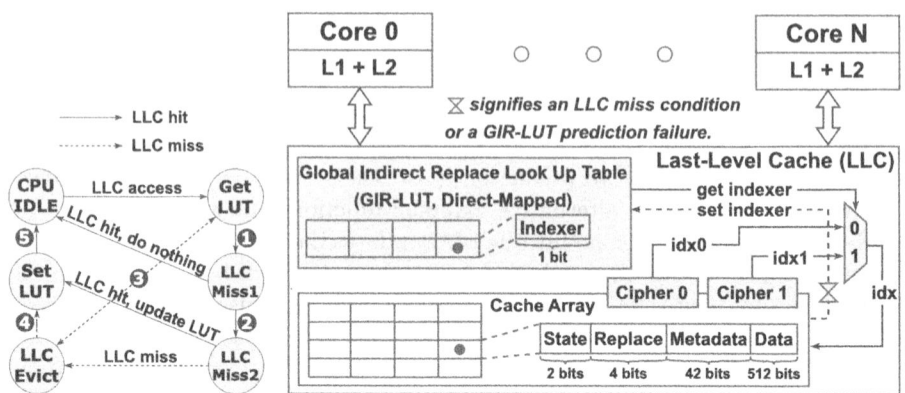

Fig. 7. GIR-LUT operating state machine.

Fig. 8. Overall structure of the GIR-Cache.

Figure 8 presents the hardware implementation of GIR-Cache. Our design enhances a conventional randomized set-associative LLC with a dual-mapping mechanism for address translation. Each memory address undergoes two independent cryptographic transformations through dedicated cipher units before LLC access, with the encryption keys remaining inaccessible to potential attackers. To maintain high-speed LLC access while avoiding the overhead of dual-mapping checks, we implement a direct-mapped GIR-LUT (1-bit *indexer-prediction* per entry: 0 = index0, 1 = index1) that tracks address mappings without LLC modification.

4.3 GIR-LUT Design and Implementation

Figure 7 shows the GIR-LUT state machine workflow during LLC accesses. When the LLC receives a memory request, it queries the GIR-LUT for the active 1-bit *indexer* (using for index-prediction), entering the *GetLUT* state. ① If the prediction yields a cache hit, the state transitions to *CPU IDLE* without GIR-LUT modification. ② On a miss, the system enters *LLCMiss2*, using the alternative index; a hit here triggers a transition to *SetLUT* and inverts the corresponding GIR-LUT bit. For an LLC miss, the state advances to *LLCEvict*, where the controller computes both indexer sets, randomly selects one, and performs replacement. ③ Relocated addresses' GIR-LUT values are verified: *indexer* = 0 maps to index1's set, *indexer* = 1 to index0's. ④–⑤ The GIR-LUT is updated with the missed addresses' verified indexer and corrected indexers for relocated addresses, ensuring future mapping accuracy and maintaining lookup efficiency.

Building upon PSA-Cache's demonstration that predictive access methods maintain processor efficiency without introducing substantial latency [30], our experimental results further validate this approach. As illustrated in Appendix A Fig. 9, our evaluation running 10G instructions of SPEC-CPU 2017 on Spike [28] shows an arithmetic mean prediction accuracy of 95.8% across all test cases when using GIR-LUT. Without GIR-LUT – when employing a random indexer selection strategy for each access – the same benchmark yields only 52.1% accuracy. This represents an 83.9% improvement in prediction accuracy through GIR-LUT implementation. The enhanced prediction further reduces 43.7% metadata accesses, resulting in approximately 4.5% lower dynamic power consumption compared to the non-GIR-LUT approach.

5 Security and Performance Evaluation

In this section, we evaluate the security of existing defense architectures by executing eviction set searching algorithms and comparing their performance with GIR-Cache. We measure four key metrics: cache miss rate, relocation frequency, power consumption, and area overhead. Using SPEC-CPU 2017 benchmarks (simulating 10G instructions per test case), we present results in Appendix A 10, 11, and 12. Each fig includes an *Average* bar group (rightmost) representing the average across all 23 test cases. Power and area measurements are derived from CACTI-6.5 [32] in a 32 nm technology.

5.1 Experimental Platform

To systematically evaluate our proposal, we first establish the experimental framework based on the processor configuration detailed in Appendix A Table 4. Our evaluation platform emulates Intel Coffee Lake 9th Generation cache architecture through a behavioral cache model [31].

5.2 Security Evaluation and Comparison of Different Caches

Table 1(a) demonstrates that in a 16 MB GIR-Cache (16384-set, 16-way), all existing eviction set searching algorithms fail to collect congruent addresses. Data shows the average number of supposed-congruent addresses identified during distinct attack phases, aggregated from 100 executions per algorithm in the Spike simulation environment. The PPP algorithm initializes its address pool with 1.05 times the LLC's addressable cache blocks, designed to contain at least 16 (LLC ways) congruent addresses. After the warm-up and priming phases, GIR's dual-mapping mechanism enables the attacker to collect approximately 67 presumed-congruent addresses. However, most of these addresses are actually random, resulting from post-relocation collisions between target addresses and random addresses. The pruning phase eliminates 67% of these conflicting addresses, leaving only 22 supposed-congruent addresses cached. During probing, if the target is evicted by a genuine congruent address, it undergoes relocation and subsequently evicts an arbitrary random address. After relocation, these 22 addresses are unlikely to collide with the post-relocation target address, ultimately keeping the target in the LLC and producing zero true congruent addresses in the probing phase. Similarly, pruning-based algorithms like GE fail to effectively filter address groups. CTPP finds 37 supposed-congruent addresses during CT phase due to dual-mapping, but subsequent probe-prune cycles reduce this to zero. CT and CT-Fast cannot directly evict target addresses – attackers can only collect irrelevant random addresses. These results conclusively demonstrate that all tested algorithms are neutralized by GIR-Cache's protection mechanisms.

However, if attackers forgo searching eviction sets against the LLC and instead attempt to target the GIR-LUT, they would still face significant challenges: First, the GIR-LUT employs hash-based address encryption to achieve randomized mapping, making brute-force attacks far more difficult than searching for congruent addresses in the LLC. Second, even if attackers somehow obtain a congruent address of GIR-LUT and successfully evict the predicted value (causing prediction failure), the LLC would require an additional metadata access. This not only increases dynamic power consumption but also extends the observable timing window from $T_{\text{gir-lut}} + T_{\text{llc-hit}}$ to $T_{\text{gir-lut}} + 2T_{\text{llc-hit}}$ – yet, since $T_{\text{llc-miss}} \gg T_{\text{llc-hit}} \gg T_{\text{gir-lut}}$, the added $T_{\text{llc-hit}}$ delay remains negligible in practice. Crucially, experimental results (Sect. 4.2) demonstrate a 95.8% prediction accuracy for the GIR-LUT, meaning the attacker-introduced delay would likely be masked by the 4.2% baseline prediction failure noise, rendering GIR-LUT congruent address-based attacks ineffective.

Table 1. Security evaluation and comparison of defense schemes normalized to set-associative LLC.

(a) Supposed-congruent addresses collected under GIR.

Algorithms	S.Con. addrs
Prime,Prune,Probe	67, 22, 0
CT/CT-Fast	0
CTPP(CT Stage)	37
CTPP(Probe - 1)	20
CTPP(Prune - 1)	20
CTPP(Probe - 2)	0
CTPP(Prune - 2)	0

(b) Security comparison normalized to baseline (non-secure set-associative cache).

Structures	GE	CT	CT-Fast	PPP	CTPP
Baseline	100%	100%	100%	92%	95%
CEASER-S	0%	100%	100%	0%	0%
DT4+EV10	0%	0%	0%	0%	27%
MIRAGE	0%	0%	0%	0%	0%
MIRAGE-Lite	0%	0%	0%	0%	0%
Chameleon	0%	0%	0%	0%	0%
GIR-Cache	**0%**	**0%**	**0%**	**0%**	**0%**

Table 1(b) presents defense architectures security effectiveness measured by the success rates of five fast eviction set searching algorithms (each executed 100 times on Spike), **where lower success rates indicate stronger defenses**. The experimental results indicate that under the traditional set-associative LLC architecture, the success rates of GE, CT and CT-Fast are nearly 100%. However, due to noise during Spike runtime, the success rates of PPP and CTPP drop to approximately 92% and 95%, respectively. Compared to existing defense solutions, CEASER-S employs a periodic remap strategy with an average of 100

Table 2. Performance comparison of cache defense structures in MPKI, RelocPKI, and Area normalized to set-associative LLC baseline.

Structures	MPKI (%)		RelocPKI	Area	
	Average	Geo-Mean		Size (mm^2)	Normalized (%)
Set-Associative	100.00	100.00	0	33.447111	100.00
CEASER-S	100.42	110.51	0.090512	34.186495	102.21
DT4+EV10	103.10	125.59	0.394710	34.299493	102.55
MIRAGE	107.54	134.96	0	42.318032	126.52
MIRAGE-Lite	107.67	135.20	0	40.548203	121.23
Chameleon	102.24	112.60	8.412051	34.247375	102.39
GIR-Cache	**100.53**	**107.17**	**2.758631**	**34.272218**	**102.47**

accesses per LLC cache block, offers nearly no defense against CT and CT-Fast. DT4+EV10, combining the detector with a on-demand remap strategy, achieves nearly 100% defense against CT and CT-Fast but fails to defend against CTPP. MIRAGE and MIRAGE-Lite eliminate address conflicts at the design level and are capable of defending against all conflict-based cache side-channel attacks. Chameleon implements a defense strategy: when evicting cache blocks in skewed caches, it first relocates the target block to the VC, then evicts another block from VC. This method can decrease contend between cache blocks, preventing attackers from identifying addresses congruence with target addresses. Thus, Chameleon successfully defends against all current conflict-based eviction set searching algorithms. GIR-Cache introduces a global indirect replacement during eviction: selected target blocks undergo remapping and relocation to new cache sets, with the LLC subsequently evicting random addresses. This method prevents attackers from collecting congruent addresses for the target address. Extensive empirical validation through hundreds of experiments conclusively demonstrates GIR-Cache's capability to provide 100% protection against existing eviction set searching algorithms.

5.3 Comparison of Cache Miss Rate and Relocation Frequency

As shown in Table 2 and Appendix A Fig. 10, MPKI (misses per kilo instructions) overhead varies significantly across defense mechanisms, with GIR-Cache achieving the lowest geometric mean increase (7.17%) – substantially outperforming MIRAGE (34.96%) and Chameleon (12.60%). Lower MPKI values indicate higher hit rates and thus better runtime performance. Notably, GIR-Cache maintains this efficiency while providing equivalent security guarantees against LLC address conflict analysis, as all three schemes (including non-remapping MIRAGE) effectively prevent attacker inference. Extreme outliers (e.g., 399.73% overhead for MIRAGE on 505.mcf) highlight the importance of geometric mean comparisons, where GIR-Cache exhibits both the smallest Geo-Mean and second-smallest average overhead (0.53%).

Table 3. Power overhead of cache defense structures normalized to set-associative LLC baseline.

Structures	Power (W)				Power (%)		
	Static	Dynamic	Relocation	Total	Static	Dynamic	Total
Set-Associative	6.151365	0.183213	0	6.334578	100.00	100.00	100.00
CEASER-S	6.271933	0.192186	0.001166	6.464119	101.96	104.90	102.04
DT4+EV10	6.299212	0.232351	0.040905	6.531563	102.40	126.82	103.11
MIRAGE	7.551611	0.289576	0	7.841187	122.76	158.05	123.78
MIRAGE-Lite	7.323553	0.268865	0	7.592418	119.06	146.75	119.86
Chameleon	6.285316	0.287658	0.099229	6.572975	102.18	157.01	103.76
GIR-Cache	**6.292547**	**0.254086**	**0.064643**	**6.546633**	**102.30**	**138.68**	**103.35**

As detailed in Appendix A Fig. 11, we quantify runtime overhead in relocation-based defenses through relocations per kilo instructions (RelocPKI), where lower values correlate with higher cache hit rates and reduced penalties. GIR-Cache demonstrates superior efficiency, achieving a RelocPKI less than one-third of Chameleon's (2.76 vs. 8.41 on average) and a correspondingly 4.23× lower MPKI (0.53% vs. 2.24%). While 87% of benchmarks maintain RelocPKI ≤ 5, exceptions like 503.bwaves and 519.lbm – where stride/irregular access patterns degrade LLC utilization – show spikes exceeding RelocPKI = 15. These outliers underscore GIR-Cache's resilience, maintaining a 1.76× lower geometric mean MPKI (7.17% vs. 12.60%) despite edge cases.

5.4 Comparison of Power and Area Consumption

Appendix A Fig. 12 and Tables 2 and 3 reveal significant power and area overhead variations across schemes. Compared to the baseline (6.151W static/0.183W dynamic), MIRAGE's 75% redundant metadata results in the highest overheads: 26.52% area, 22.76% static power (7.552W), and 58.47% dynamic power (0.290W). MIRAGE-Lite reduces this through 50% extra metadata (21.23% area, 19.06% static power, 46.75% dynamic power), albeit with a 1.72% MPKI increase. Chameleon shows moderate power increases (2.18% static/57.01% dynamic), while GIR-Cache maintains optimal efficiency with merely 2.30% static (6.293 W) and 38.68% dynamic (0.254 W) power growth.

As illustrated in Table 2, both Chameleon and GIR-Cache require cache block relocation during LLC miss-induced evictions, exhibiting identical hardware area overheads of 2.39% and 2.47% respectively. Their key architectural difference lies in the relocation mechanism: Chameleon performs at least three distinct cache block relocations per cache miss, while GIR-Cache requires only a single block relocation. This design difference results in Chameleon's RelocPKI being 3.05× higher than GIR-Cache (8.41 vs. 2.76). The power characteristics reveal more nuanced tradeoffs. According to Table 3, while Chameleon's relocation operation consumes 1.54× more power than GIR-Cache (99.229 mW vs. 64.643 mW, or 53.50% higher), this difference is less than the 3× multiple suggested by their relocation counts. This efficiency stems from Chameleon's use of an 8-block fully associative victim cache (VC) for relocation operations, compared to GIR-Cache's approach of performing candidate set selection across the entire LLC. When considering power consumption per LLC relocation operation but excluding bandwidth effects, the VC-based implementation proves more power-efficient per access. However, GIR-Cache incurs additional dynamic power from maintaining and accessing its randomized direct-mapped GIR-LUT during LLC hits and misses. As detailed in Appendix A Table 4, when the LLC is 16 MB, the GIR-LUT occupies 32 KB, consuming an area of $0.050117\,\text{mm}^2$ (0.146% of the entire GIR-Cache's $34.272218\,\text{mm}^2$). Its static power is 0.010815 W (0.165% of total power) and dynamic power is 0.000858 W (0.013% of total power). In overall power consumption compared to Chameleon, GIR-Cache demonstrates superior efficiency: while maintaining comparable static power (6.293 W vs. 6.285 W, a 0.13% increase), it achieves an 11.81% reduction in dynamic power (0.254 W vs. 0.288 W), ultimately resulting in 0.40% lower total power (6.547 W vs. 6.573 W).

6 Conclusion

This paper investigates the security vulnerabilities in existing randomized cache defenses. Since conflict-based side-channel attacks fundamentally rely on successful execution of eviction set searching algorithms to achieve their malicious objectives, we demonstrate that disrupting these search capabilities can effectively prevent subsequent attacks. Our proposed solution, GIR-Cache, a new randomized cache defense that fundamentally thwarts conflict-based side-channel attacks by disrupting eviction set searching through its global indirect replacement mechanism. The structure employs a dual-mapping set-associative cache with a randomized GIR-LUT that reduces metadata access and dynamic power consumption during LLC hits while ensuring robust protection. During misses, target addresses undergo remapping and relocating to new sets, evicting non-congruent addresses to prevent attackers from detecting cache conflicts and neutralize all major eviction set searching algorithms (e.g., CT, CT-Fast, CTPP, PPP and GE). Remarkably, GIR-Cache delivers robust security against cache attacks with moderate overheads: 0.53% runtime, 2.47% area, and 3.35% power.

Acknowledgements. This work was partially supported by the National Natural Science Foundation of China under grant No. 62172406.

A Experimental Setup and Details

Figure 9 compares the first-attempt LLC hit success rates between GIR-LUT and random index selection when running SPEC-CPU 2017 benchmarks for 10 billion instructions on GIR-Cache. The rightmost two bars represent averages across all 23 test cases, demonstrating a 95.8% success rate using GIR-LUT

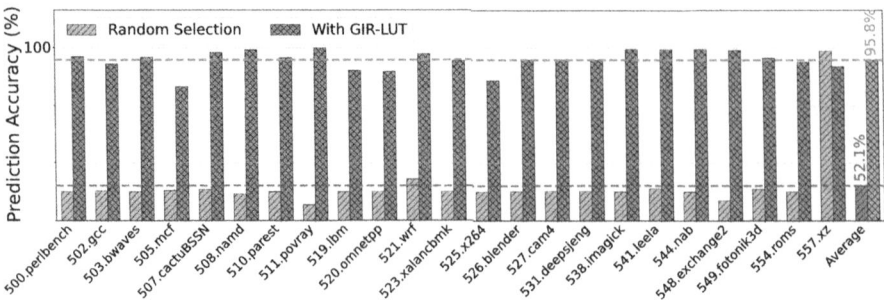

Fig. 9. GIR-LUT prediction accuracy vs. random selected index hit probability in GIR-Cache.

Table 4. Processor and caches configuration

Component	Configuration
Core	8-core, in-order, 3 GHz, IPC = 2
L1 I/D-Cache per Core	32 KB, 64-set, 8-way, LRU, MSI
L2 Cache per Core	256 KB, 1024-set, 4-way, LRU, MSI, Exclusive
LLC (shared across cores)	16 MB, 16384-set, 16-way, LRU, MESI, Inclusive
	32 KB randomized direct-mapped GIR-LUT (1-bit/entry)

versus 52.1% with random selection – a 43.7% reduction in metadata access overhead achieved by GIR-LUT implementation.

Table 4 presents the experimental processor configuration and cache hierarchy specifications, featuring a 16 MB GIR-Cache as the last-level cache with an integrated 32 KB GIR-LUT.

Figures 10, 11, and 12 collectively present experimental results from 10G-instruction SPEC CPU 2017 runs, with each figure's rightmost *Average* bars showing mean values across all test cases.

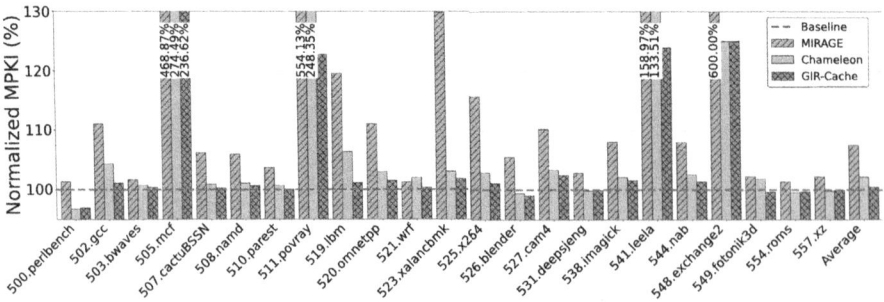

Fig. 10. Misses per K instructions (MPKI) comparison across benchmarks compared to set-associative (baseline).

Figure 10 compares cache miss rates per kilo instructions (MPKI) across defense structures, with the y-axis showing percentage overhead relative to a conventional set-associative LLC baseline (green dashed line). Each benchmark group on the x-axis displays three adjacent bars (left to right: MIRAGE, Chameleon, GIR-Cache). The arithmetic mean baseline miss rate for 505.mcf, 511.povray, 541.leela, and 548.exchange2 is 0.003651 MPKI, while the defenses exhibit increases of 399.73%, 241.53%, and 209.01% respectively on these workloads. Geometric means (34.96%, 12.60%, 7.17%) further contextualize these outliers, with GIR-Cache consistently achieving the lowest overhead.

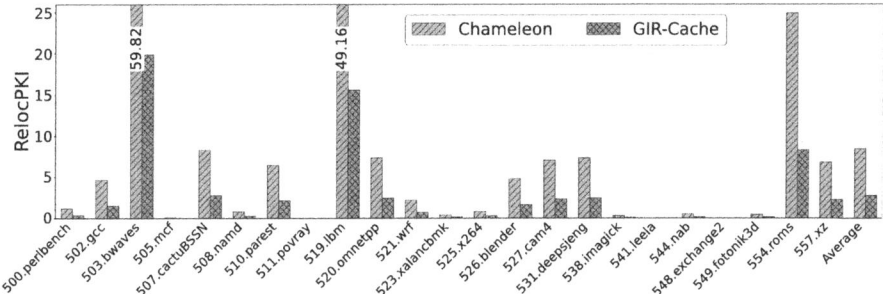

Fig. 11. Relocations per K instructions (RelocPKI) across benchmarks.

Figure 11 compares RelocPKI between Chameleon and GIR-Cache across all benchmarks. The y-axis measures relocation frequency (per kilo instructions), with GIR-Cache's average (2.76) markedly lower than Chameleon's (8.41). Test cases are grouped by workload type, with outliers labeled (e.g., 503.bwaves and 519.lbm exceeding RelocPKI = 15 due to stride/irregular accesses).

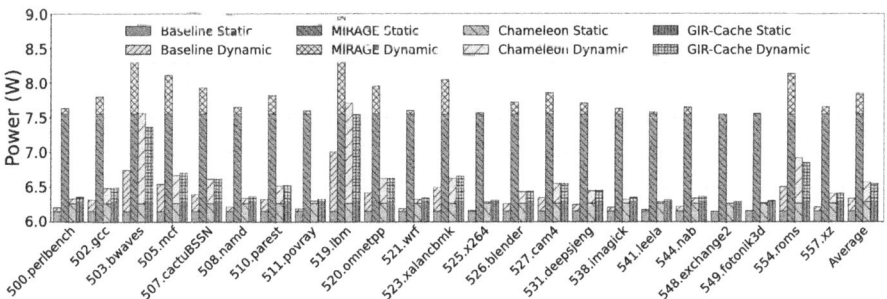

Fig. 12. Power comparison across benchmarks compared to set-associative (baseline).

The power analysis in Fig. 12 employs stacked-bar visualization to distinguish base (static power) and variable (dynamic power) components, while comparatively evaluating four architectures: conventional set-associative cache and three security-enhanced designs (MIRAGE, Chameleon, and GIR-Cache), with the rightmost column explicitly showing cross-architecture average power values for reference.

References

1. Liu, F., Yarom, Y., Ge, Q., Heiser, G., Lee, R.B.: Last-level cache side-channel attacks are practical. In: 2015 IEEE Symposium on Security and Privacy, pp. 605–622 (2015)
2. Osvik, D.A., Shamir, A., Tromer, E.: Cache attacks and countermeasures: the case of AES. In: Pointcheval, D. (ed.) CT-RSA 2006. LNCS, vol. 3860, pp. 1–20. Springer, Heidelberg (2006). https://doi.org/10.1007/11605805_1
3. Percival, C.: Cache missing for fun and profit. In: BSDCan Ottawa (2005)
4. Ristenpart, T., Tromer, E., Shacham, H., Savage, S.: Hey, you, get off of my cloud: exploring information leakage in third-party compute clouds. In: Proceedings of the 16th ACM Conference on Computer and Communications Security, pp. 199–212 (2009)
5. Liu, F., et al.: Catalyst: defeating last-level cache side channel attacks in cloud computing. In: 2016 IEEE International Symposium on High Performance Computer Architecture, pp. 406–418 (2016)
6. Irazoqui, G., Eisenbarth, T., Sunar, B.: S$A: A shared cache attack that works across cores and defies VM sandboxing – and its application to AES. In: 2015 IEEE Symposium on Security and Privacy, pp. 1–15 (2015)
7. Hähnel, M., Cui, W., Peinado, M.: High-Resolution Side Channels for Untrusted Operating Systems. In: 2017 USENIX Annual Technical Conference, pp. 299–312 (2017)
8. Page, D.: Partitioned cache architecture as a side-channel defence mechanism. IACR Cryptology ePrint Archive 2005:280 (2005)
9. Kim, T., Peinado, M., Mainar-Ruiz, G.: System-level protection against Cache-Based side channel attacks in the cloud. In: 21st USENIX Security Symposium, pp. 189–204 (2012)
10. Gruss, D., Maurice, C., Fogh, A., Lipp, M., Mangard, S.: Prefetch side-channel attacks: Bypassing SMAP and kernel ASLR. In: Proceedings of the 2016 ACM SIGSAC Conference on Computer and Communications Security, pp. 368–379 (2016)
11. El-Sayed, N., Mukkara, A., Tsai, P.-A., Kasture, H., Ma, X., Sanchez, D.: KPart: a hybrid cache partitioning-sharing technique for commodity multicores. In: 2018 IEEE International Symposium on High Performance Computer Architecture, pp. 104–117 (2018)
12. Ramkrishnan, K., Zhai, A., McCamant, S., Yew, P.C.: New attacks and defenses for randomized caches. arXiv preprint arXiv:1909.12302 (2019)
13. Wang, Z., Lee, R.B.: A novel cache architecture with enhanced performance and security. In: 2008 41st IEEE/ACM International Symposium on Microarchitecture, pp. 83–93 (2008)
14. Liu, F., Lee, R.B.: Random fill cache architecture. In: 2014 47th Annual IEEE/ACM International Symposium on Microarchitecture, pp. 203–215 (2014)
15. Qureshi, M.K.: New attacks and defense for encrypted-address cache. In: 46th Annual International Symposium on Computer Architecture, pp. 360–371 (2019)

16. Werner, M., Unterluggauer, T., Giner, L., Schwarz, M., Gruss, D., Mangard, S.: ScatterCache: thwarting cache attacks via cache set randomization. In: 28th USENIX Security Symposium, pp. 675–692 (2019)
17. Doblas, M., Kostalampros, I.-V., Moreto Planas, M., Hernández Luz, C.: Enabling hardware randomization across the cache hierarchy in Linux-class processors. In: Fourth Workshop on Computer Architecture Research with RISC-V, pp. 1–7 (2020)
18. Tan, Q., Zeng, Z., Bu, K., Ren, K.: PhantomCache: obfuscating cache conflicts with localized randomization. In: NDSS (2020)
19. Oren, Y., Kemerlis, V.P., Sethumadhavan, S., Keromytis, A.D.: The spy in the sandbox: practical cache attacks in Javascript and their implications. In: Proceedings of the 22nd ACM SIGSAC Conference on Computer and Communications Security, pp. 1406–1418 (2015)
20. Vila, P., Köpf, B., Morales, J.F.: Theory and practice of finding eviction sets. In: 2019 IEEE Symposium on Security and Privacy, pp. 39–54 (2019)
21. Song, W., Liu, P.: Dynamically finding minimal eviction sets can be quicker than you think for side-channel attacks against the LLC. In: 22nd International Symposium on Research in Attacks, Intrusions and Defenses, pp. 427–442 (2019)
22. Unterluggauer, T., Harris, A., Constable, S., Liu, F., Rozas, C.: Chameleon cache: approximating fully associative caches with random replacement to prevent contention-based cache attacks. In: 2022 IEEE International Symposium on Secure and Private Execution Environment Design, pp. 13–24 (2022)
23. Saileshwar, G., Qureshi, M.K.: MIRAGE: mitigating conflict-based cache attacks with a practical fully-associative design. In: 30th USENIX Security Symposium, pp. 1379–1396 (2021)
24. Sanchez, D., Kozyrakis, C.: The ZCache: decoupling ways and associativity. In: 43rd Annual IEEE/ACM International Symposium on Microarchitecture, pp. 187–198. IEEE (2010)
25. Song, W., Li, B., Xue, Z., Li, Z., Wang, W., Liu, P.: Randomized last-level caches are still vulnerable to cache side-channel attacks! But we can fix it. In: 42nd IEEE Symposium on Security and Privacy, pp. 955–969 (2021)
26. Song, W., Xue, Z., Han, J., Li, Z., Liu, P.: Randomizing set-associative caches against conflict-based cache side-channel attacks. IEEE Trans. Comput. **73**(4), 1019–1033 (2024)
27. Xue, Z., Han, J., Song, W.: CTPP: a fast and stealth algorithm for searching eviction sets on intel processors. In: Proceedings of the 26th International Symposium on Research in Attacks, Intrusions and Defenses, pp. 151–163 (2023)
28. UC Berkeley, RISC-V International: Spike RISC-V ISA Simulator Documentation (2023). https://chipyard.readthedocs.io/en/latest/Software/Spike.html
29. Purnal, A., Turan, F., Verbauwhede, I.: Prime+ Scope: overcoming the observer effect for high-precision cache contention attacks. In: Proceedings of the 2021 ACM SIGSAC Conference on Computer and Communications Security, pp. 2903–2917 (2021)
30. Calder, B., Grunwald, D., Emer, J.: Predictive sequential associative cache. In: Proceedings of the Second International Symposium on High-Performance Computer Architecture, pp. 244–253 (1996)
31. Han, J., Wang, Z., Ma, H., Song, W.: Spike-FlexiCAS: A RISC-V processor simulator supporting flexible cache architecture configuration. J. Softw. **36**(9), 1–15 (2025)
32. Muralimanohar, N., Balasubramonian, R., Jouppi, N.: Optimizing NUCA organizations and wiring alternatives for large caches with CACTI 6.0. In: 40th Annual IEEE/ACM International Symposium on Microarchitecture, pp. 3–14 (2007)

Inference Attacks on Encrypted Online Voting via Traffic Analysis

Anastasiia Belousova[1]([✉])[iD], Francesco Marchiori[1][iD], and Mauro Conti[1,2][iD]

[1] University of Padova, Padua, Italy
anastasiia.belousova@studenti.unipd.it,
francesco.marchiori@math.unipd.it, mauro.conti@unipd.it
[2] Örebro University, Örebro, Sweden

Abstract. Online voting enables individuals to participate in elections remotely, offering greater efficiency and accessibility in both governmental and organizational settings. As this method gains popularity, ensuring the security of online voting systems becomes increasingly vital, as the systems supporting it must satisfy a demanding set of security requirements. Most research in this area emphasizes the design and verification of cryptographic protocols to protect voter integrity and system confidentiality. However, other vectors, such as network traffic analysis, remain relatively understudied, even though they may pose significant threats to voter privacy and the overall trustworthiness of the system.

In this paper, we examine how adversaries can exploit metadata from encrypted network traffic to uncover sensitive information during online voting. Our analysis reveals that, even without accessing the encrypted content, it is possible to infer critical voter actions, such as whether a person votes, the exact moment a ballot is submitted, and whether the ballot is valid or spoiled. We test these attacks with both rule-based techniques and machine learning methods. We evaluate our attacks on two widely used online voting platforms, one proprietary and one partially open source, achieving classification accuracy as high as 99.5%. These results expose a significant privacy vulnerability that threatens key properties of secure elections, including voter secrecy and protection against coercion or vote-buying. We explore mitigations to our attacks, demonstrating that countermeasures such as payload padding and timestamp equalization can substantially limit their effectiveness.

Keywords: Electronic Voting · Inference Attack · Traffic Analysis

1 Introduction

Protecting ballot secrecy is a cornerstone of democratic elections, ensuring voters can express their preferences freely without fear of coercion, retaliation, or undue influence. Many countries enforce this through strict legal measures designed to prevent any traceability of the vote. For instance, photographing marked ballots is prohibited in Germany [41], Ireland [25], Brazil [42], and numerous U.S.

states [34], as such images could compromise the confidentiality of the ballot. These legal safeguards underscore a shared principle: the act of voting must remain private and unverifiable by others, preserving both voter anonymity and the integrity of the electoral process. The risks of violating these guarantees are not hypothetical. In Spain's 2023 local elections, police uncovered networks exchanging postal votes for cash and favors [21]. Similar concerns have emerged in Georgia and Bulgaria, where coercion has targeted public-sector workers and marginalized communities [22,36]. In rare but alarming cases, such as Russia's 2024 presidential election, voters who submitted spoiled ballots with anti-war messages were fined or arrested after their ballots were visible through transparent boxes [16,23]. These examples show how even subtle violations of secrecy can lead to real-world harm.

As elections move online, these challenges take on new forms. Online voting has gained traction in both governmental and organizational settings. Countries like Estonia and Switzerland have institutionalized digital voting, while private entities increasingly adopt online platforms for shareholder meetings and union decisions. This shift is driven by convenience, remote participation, and faster vote processing—advantages that became particularly clear during the COVID-19 pandemic [32]. Technologically mediated elections are described using overlapping terms: *electronic*, *digital*, and *online* voting. Electronic voting refers broadly to the use of devices at polling stations. Digital voting builds on this with end-to-end software infrastructure. Online voting, in turn, involves casting ballots remotely via the internet, typically through secure platforms or apps [18]. While offering clear benefits in accessibility and turnout, online voting must also meet the high standards of secrecy and trust long established by traditional paper-based methods.

With this transition comes the expectation that online voting systems must meet and exceed the integrity and trustworthiness of traditional paper-based elections. Paper voting, despite its physical limitations, has long been regarded as the gold standard for ensuring transparency and public confidence. Voters cast their ballots in private booths, often under the supervision of independent observers, and the process is verifiable at every stage. If online voting is to be a viable alternative, it must preserve not only convenience but also uphold fundamental democratic guarantees, particularly voter privacy and protection from manipulation. Recent advancements in online voting have predominantly focused on enhancing security through sophisticated cryptographic protocols and the integration of blockchain technologies [29]. These efforts aim to ensure vote integrity, authentication, and transparency, leveraging mechanisms such as homomorphic encryption [39], zero-knowledge proofs [44], and decentralized ledgers [30]. While these developments address critical aspects of secure voting, they often overlook the vulnerabilities inherent in the network infrastructure itself. Specifically, the potential for adversaries to exploit metadata to infer sensitive information about voter behavior remains underexplored.

Contributions. This paper presents the first in-depth analysis of metadata-based inference attacks on two real-world online voting platforms. We demonstrate that even without decrypting traffic content, a passive network adversary can extract sensitive information purely from encrypted metadata. Our attacks reveal that adversaries with varying levels of access can determine whether a user voted, when the vote was cast, and whether the ballot was accepted or rejected. These findings pose a serious threat to voter privacy. The act of voting (or choosing not to vote) is itself a political signal, and the exposure of such actions can enable coercion or retaliation. Similarly, although accidental spoiling is rare in online systems, deliberately spoiled ballots are often used as a form of protest and are publicly reported in many jurisdictions as indicators of political discontent. The ability to infer such actions undermines key democratic principles, especially in contexts where voter pressure is a known issue, such as in Georgia and Bulgaria [22,36]. Our contributions can be summarized as follows.[1]

- We show that encrypted traffic alone can reveal, at a minimum, the moment of ballot submission, and at best, the full sequence of voter actions.
- We demonstrate that ballot validity status can be predicted using learning-based models trained on payload sizes and timing data.
- We evaluate our methodologies on two real-world online voting platforms: Eligo, a proprietary system, and POLYAS, a partially open-source solution. Our analysis achieves an accuracy of up to 99.5%, demonstrating the high effectiveness and generalizability attacks.
- We propose and evaluate two countermeasures, quantifying their effectiveness as well as the trade-offs they introduce in terms of delay and memory overhead.

Organization. The remainder of this paper is structured as follows. In Sect. 2, we review related work on online voting systems, focusing on their security requirements and recent developments. Section 3 introduces our system and threat model, outlining how adversaries can launch attacks without decrypting the payload. We describe our attack methodology in Sect. 4 and present its empirical evaluation in Sect. 5. Section 6 discusses the implications of our findings and Sect. 7 introduces our proposed countermeasures. Finally, Sect. 8 concludes the paper.

2 Related Works

We begin by reviewing prior work on online voting systems. Section 2.1 outlines the fundamental security requirements for such systems and compares prominent publicly available and commercial platforms. In Sect. 2.2, we examine recent research directions and advances in the security of electronic voting.

---

[1] We conducted responsible disclosure with the companies involved. Samples of the code used in this paper are available upon request.

2.1 Online Voting Systems Security

While the literature provides numerous evaluations of cryptographic protocols or specific classes of e-voting systems, such as blockchain-based platforms [28] or systems used for high-stakes national elections [10], comparative analyses across diverse real-world deployments remain sparse. Prior work often centers on algorithmic innovation or theoretical properties, overlooking how practical systems, used in binding elections, fulfill key security guarantees in practice.

Online Voting Systems. To help ground our study in realistic deployments, we include a focused comparative review of a small but diverse set of online voting platforms. These systems differ in geographical scope, electoral application (ranging from organizational to governmental), and transparency models. Although not the central aim of our work, this comparative lens offers useful context on how different platforms address core security requirements, based on publicly accessible information. The platforms we examine include both open-source and proprietary systems, offering a diverse snapshot of real-world online voting solutions. The following systems are considered: Assembly Voting [2], Belenios [3], Civitas [12], ElectionBuddy [17], Eligo [19], Helios [27], POLYAS [38], and Voatz [43].

Security Requirements. In our analysis, we focus on five widely recognized requirements [12, 26]:

- *Eligibility:* only eligible voters should be able to vote.
- *Ballot secrecy:* no actor involved in the voting process should be able to link a ballot to a voter.
- *Individual verifiability:* each voter can check that their own vote is included in the tally.
- *Universal verifiability:* anyone can check that all votes cast are counted, that only authorized votes are counted, and that no votes are changed during counting.
- *Coercion resistance:* voters cannot prove whether or how they voted, even if they can interact with the adversary while voting.

The results of our comparative analysis are summarized in Table 1. Some security requirements, such as eligibility, anonymity, and privacy, are typically assumed to be fulfilled a priori and were explicitly claimed by all reviewed systems. Others, like ballot secrecy, were uniformly stated as upheld. However, this assumption-based trust model creates a blind spot: if a foundational property such as privacy is compromised, for instance, through side-channel or metadata-based inference attacks, then dependent guarantees like ballot secrecy and receipt-freeness may no longer hold in practice. This fragility undermines higher-level protections such as coercion resistance and opens the door to vote-buying scenarios, even if the systems do not explicitly claim to defend against them. Our work demonstrates how inference from encrypted traffic can trigger such cascading failures, raising concerns about the real-world robustness and trustworthiness of these systems.

Table 1. Comparison of selected online voting systems.

System	Cryptographic Algorithm	Certifications	Open Source	Eligibility	Security Requirements			
					Ballot Secrecy	Individual Verifiability	Universal Verifiability	Coercion Resistance
Assembly Voting	ECC, ElGamal, AES-GCM	ISO 27001, ISAE 3000	Partially	●	●	●	●	○
Belenios	ElGamal	N/A	✓	●	●	●	●	○
Civitas	RSA, ElGamal	N/A	✓	●	●	●	●	●
Election Buddy	Not specified	Not specified	✗	●	●	○	○	○
Eligo	AES	ISO 27001 ISO 9001:2015	✗	●	●	●	●	◐
Helios	ElGamal	N/A	✓	●	●	●	●	○
POLYAS	AES, RSA ECIES, ElGamal	ISO 27001, BSI	Partially	●	●	●	●	○
Voatz	AES-GCM	Not specified	✗	●	●	○	○	○

●: fulfilled, ◐: partially fulfilled, ○: not fulfilled or not mentioned.

To demonstrate and evaluate our proposed inference methodology, we focus on Eligo, the most feature-rich and prominent among the analyzed systems, and subsequently validate our approach on POLYAS, which offers similar functionality and voting flow but represents an independent platform. This selection strategy allows us to ground the attack in practical deployments and demonstrate its generalizability.

2.2 Advances and Attacks Overview

Recent advancements in cryptographic protocols have significantly enhanced the security and verifiability of electronic voting systems. End-to-end verifiable (E2E) systems like Helios and Belenios enable voters to confirm that their votes are accurately recorded and tallied without compromising ballot secrecy. Innovations such as D-DEMOS and Hyperion have introduced distributed architectures and coercion mitigation strategies, further strengthening the integrity of online voting platforms [9,15]. Additionally, the integration of blockchain technology, as seen in systems like Voatz, aims to provide transparent and tamper-evident records of the voting process. However, a comprehensive security analysis of Voatz by Specter et al. revealed significant vulnerabilities, including the potential for passive network adversaries to recover users' secret ballots, thereby undermining the system's integrity and privacy claims [40]. This study underscores the necessity for transparency and rigorous security evaluations in the deployment of online voting platforms. Further research has identified multiple privacy and integrity attacks on online voting systems. Indeed, in other cases, inference and side-channel attacks have also been demonstrated even when ballots are cryptographically protected. For example, Brunet et al. show that subtle differences in confirmation-page content (e.g., packet lengths) can leak voters' choices [7]. Blanchard et al. analyzed a real voting system (France's Neovote) and found that its verification procedure could be subverted to completely breach the voters' privacy in multiple configurations, effectively deanonymizing ballots [6]. These studies illustrate that adversaries can exploit metadata (timing, packet sizes, or protocol behaviors) to infer sensitive information beyond the ballot contents. To date, however, few works have systematically quantified metadata-based inference, making our analysis of such attacks a novel contribution.

3 System and Threat Model

We describe the operational context of a typical online voting system (Sect. 3.1) and the capabilities of attackers attempting to infer sensitive information through encrypted traffic analysis (Sect. 3.2). An overview of our considered system and threat model is shown in Fig. 1.

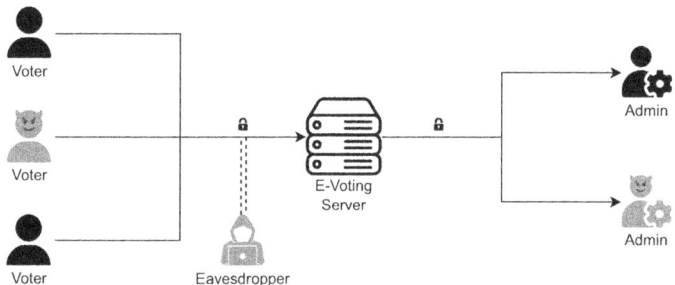

Fig. 1. System and threat model overview.

3.1 System Model

We examine a real-world online voting platform used in organizational settings such as university elections, academic societies, or corporate boards. Our work builds on a well-established view of privacy in e-voting that includes metadata confidentiality, covering participation, timing, and ballot-type privacy. These aspects are recognized in the literature [5] and official guidelines [13]. The systems enable remote participation via web browsers or dedicated apps, with voters authenticating through credentials issued by their organizations. Communication occurs over TLS, and platforms commonly implement eligibility checks, session management, and confirmation steps. Election administrators oversee the process and may access metadata like session logs or timestamps, depending on the platform's design. This model reflects widely adopted systems such as Eligo and POLYAS, which ensure ballot secrecy and integrity through cryptographic mechanisms. While the system is assumed uncompromised, side-channel leakage may silently undermine its security in realistic deployments where such vectors are not actively mitigated.

3.2 Threat Model

We assume adversaries do not compromise cryptographic primitives, user credentials, or backend infrastructure. Instead, their objective is to infer sensitive information, such as whether and when a user voted, or whether their ballot was valid or spoiled, through traffic analysis and metadata observation. We consider three attacker roles with varying capabilities:

1. **Voter:** A malicious voter observes their own client-side traffic during different stages (e.g., login, voting) and learns to recognize traffic patterns. They may then apply this knowledge to identify similar behaviors by others on the same network, inferring voting times or ballot status even without direct access.
2. **Administrator:** A dishonest administrator has access to backend metadata (e.g., logs, timestamps) but not vote contents. Platforms like Eligo and POLYAS may expose real-time activity or detailed turnout data, which, when correlated with network traces, can reveal who cast valid or spoiled ballots.
3. **Eavesdropper:** A passive network observer, such as an ISP, campus IT, or compromised router, can monitor TLS-encrypted traffic. While unable to see vote contents or user identities directly, they may infer behavior via traffic flow patterns and timing. In small networks, auxiliary data (e.g., DHCP logs) can further deanonymize users.

These side-channel attacks do not violate cryptographic guarantees but exploit observable metadata. They are especially concerning in scenarios demanding strong anonymity or coercion resistance, where leaking vote timing or status can severely weaken electoral integrity.

4 Methodology

This section presents the design of our framework, developed to identify and evaluate patterns in encrypted network traffic generated during electronic voting. The framework is specifically tailored to classify voter actions and detect differences between valid and spoiled ballots based solely on metadata features observable from outgoing TLS packets. Our approach incorporates pre-processing and feature engineering (Sect. 4.1), voter action and submission identification (Sects. 4.2 and 4.3), and classification of valid vs spoiled ballots (Sect. 4.4).

Tested Platforms. We focus our analysis on two widely used online voting platforms: Eligo and POLYAS. Eligo has supported over 4,000 organizations [19], while POLYAS has handled elections with more than 2 million voters annually [37]. It is also worth noting that Eligo was prioritized over Civitas (which satisfies more security requirements, as shown in Table 1) due to its production use; Civitas, while valuable, remains largely a research prototype. POLYAS is then added to validate generalizability across different real-world systems with similar workflows. Both platforms are widely used in governmental and organizational elections and support the casting of spoiled or invalid ballots, a critical feature for evaluating whether traffic analysis can distinguish between voting outcomes. The platforms differ in handling multi-ballot elections: Eligo allows selective participation per ballot, while POLYAS requires a decision on all ballots before submission. To avoid inconsistencies, we limit our analysis to single-ballot elections, eliminating variability due to optional interactions. Our study relies solely on encrypted TLS metadata. From this, we extract timestamps and application data payload sizes to compute both raw and derived features, such as normalized timing (relative to the first packet of an action) and payload-based patterns. These form the foundation for action segmentation and classification.

4.1 Pre-processing and Feature Engineering

We consider outgoing TLS packets with non-empty application-layer payloads. This choice is due to the fact that this class of packets forms patterns of actions that are largely or completely repeated from voter to voter (Fig. 2 and Fig. 3). The first step is to identify distinct actions within each voter's interaction. To do this, we apply DBSCAN clustering to each voter's traffic individually (intra-voter mode), using timestamps and inter-arrival times (IATs) to isolate activity bursts. DBSCAN is chosen for its ability to discover clusters of arbitrary shape without requiring a predefined number of clusters, and for its robustness to noise, properties that are particularly useful in our setting, where voters may perform actions at irregular intervals. These features make it more effective then other techniques such as K-Means, which might require predefined cluster counts.

4.2 Voter Action Classification

We develop two models for voter action classification: one based on set theory and the other on clustering techniques. The set-theoretic method offers near-perfect accuracy by leveraging deterministic rules for identifying packet structures unique to each voter action. However, this approach is more computationally intensive, particularly when scaling to large datasets or real-time scenarios. In contrast, the clustering-based model relies on unsupervised learning to group packets with similar structural features. While its accuracy is slightly lower, it remains sufficiently high for practical use and offers significantly better scalability due to its reduced computational complexity. Table 2 shows the mapping between IDs and actions we aim to identify. These actions are described as follows. Note that, for Eligo, a typical logical actions sequence is $0 \to 1 \to 2 \to 4 \to 3/7 \to 5 \to 6$, while for POLYAS is $0 \to 1 \to 2 \to 3$.[2]

- **Load event:** initial page load or redirection to the voting platform, typically triggered by clicking the election link received by the voter.
- **Log in:** authentication step where the voter enters their credentials to access the voting system.

---

[2] Eligo's event flow is intentionally reordered so that event ID 3 corresponds to the "send vote" action, aligning it with POLYAS for consistency.

- **Reload data:** system-side refresh or update of ballot or user session data, often done automatically before vote casting.
- **Open ballot info:** optional step where the voter accesses informational content about the ballot, such as the vote type or maximum number of preferences allowed.
- **Open ballot:** action that loads or displays the actual voting interface, allowing the voter to make selections.
- **Send vote (valid):** submission of a correctly filled ballot, indicating the voter has made a valid choice and cast their vote.
- **Send vote (spoiled):** submission of an intentionally spoiled or blank ballot, indicating voter abstention or protest.
- **Redirect home:** navigation action that redirects the voter to the home or landing page after vote submission.
- **Log out:** final session termination step where the voter exits the platform securely.

Table 2. Action IDs for the voting platforms.

(a) Eligo.

ID	Action
0	Load event
1	Log in
2	Open ballot info
3	Send vote (valid)
4	Open ballot
5	Redirect home
6	Log out
7	Send vote (spoiled)

(b) POLYAS.

ID	Action
0	Load event
1	Log in
2	Reload data
3	Send vote

Set Theory Based Model. Once activity bursts are identified, they can be mapped to actions using a set-theoretic model. Its simplicity, transparency, and deterministic nature make it suitable for adversaries without a large-scale training infrastructure. While less flexible in handling noisy cases, it performs well when distinctive action patterns, such as payload length sequences, are present. The process is as follows: first, we extract a set of unique actions and their characteristic payload length patterns. Then, previously identified activity bursts are classified based on this mapping. Let a sequence of N actions (unique or repeated) be performed in an online voting system. Define $\mathcal{S}_i = \{s_{i,j}\}$, where $i \in [0, N-1]$ and $j \in [0, M_i - 1]$, as the set of M_i payload lengths corresponding to the i-th action. If two such sets are identical (i.e., $\mathcal{S}_i = \mathcal{S}_k$ for $i \neq k$), we retain only one and discard duplicates. Let $N' \leq N$ be the number of unique action sets after this reduction. Next, for each $\mathcal{S}_i$, we compute the subset shared with any other set $\mathcal{T}_i = \mathcal{S}_i \cap \left(\bigcup_{k \neq i} \mathcal{S}_k\right)$. We also define $\mathcal{T}_i^* = \mathcal{S}_i \cap \mathcal{S}_{k^*}^*$, where $k^* = \arg\max_{k \neq i} |\mathcal{S}_i \cap \mathcal{S}_k|$, capturing the maximum overlap with another action. Based on intersection information, the final set of unique user actions is determined sequentially as follows:

1. If $\mathcal{T}_i = \emptyset$, then the corresponding i-th activity burst is a unique action;
2. If $|\mathcal{S}_i| = |\mathcal{T}_i^*|$, then the corresponding i-th activity burst is a unique action;
3. If $|\mathcal{T}_i| = |\mathcal{T}_i^*|$ and there exists $l \neq i$, $l \in [0, N' - 1]$ such that $\mathcal{T}_l^* = \mathcal{T}_i^*$, then activity burst m^* is a unique action where $m^* = \arg\max_{m \in \{i,l\}} |S_m|$ and $\mathcal{S}_{m^*} = \mathcal{S}_i \cup \mathcal{S}_l$;
4. If $|\mathcal{T}_i| > |\mathcal{T}_i^*|$, then the corresponding i-th activity burst is a unique action.

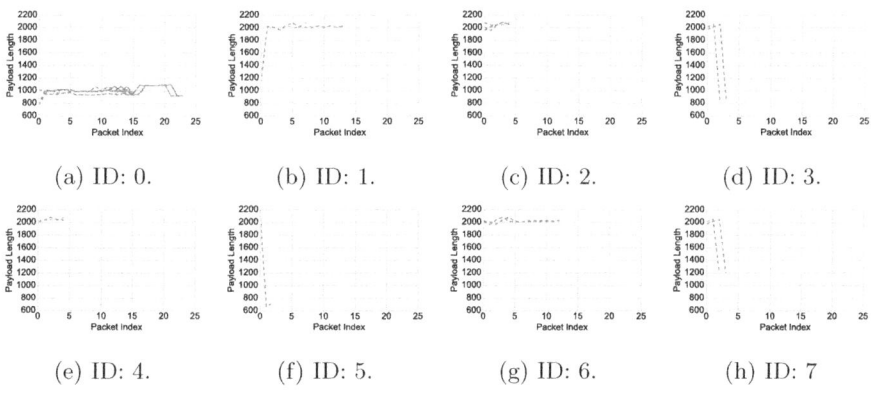

Fig. 2. Eligo action patterns.

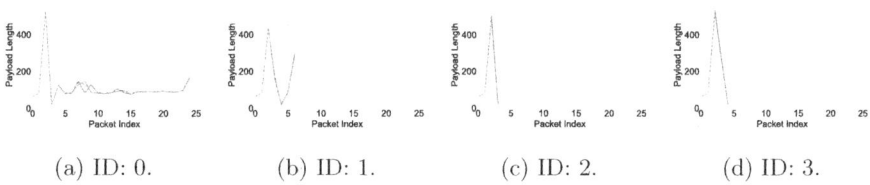

Fig. 3. POLYAS action patterns.

Let $N'' \leq N' \leq N$ be the final number of unique user actions. Suppose a voter performed a sequence of $\hat{N}$ clicks; then $\hat{\mathcal{S}}_p = \{\hat{s}_{p,q}\}$, where $p \in [0, \hat{N} - 1]$ and $q \in [0, \hat{M}_p - 1]$, denotes the set of $\hat{M}_p$ payload lengths for the p-th activity burst. This activity burst is classified sequentially as follows:

1. If there exists $i \in [0, N''-1]$ such that $\hat{\mathcal{S}}_p = \mathcal{S}_i$, then burst p maps to action i.
2. If $\hat{\mathcal{S}}_p \cap (\mathcal{S}i \setminus \cup_{k \neq i} \mathcal{S}_k) \neq \emptyset$, then assign burst p to action i.
3. If $\left|\hat{\mathcal{S}}_p \cap \mathcal{S}_i\right| \geq |\mathcal{T}_i^*| + 1$, then assign burst p to action i.

Clustering Based Model. Alongside our rule-based method, we implement an unsupervised clustering approach to classify user actions across different voters. Each activity burst is represented using three features: total payload length, mean payload length, and packet count metrics that capture consistent patterns in TLS-encrypted traffic. We apply DBSCAN in an inter-voter setting by clustering bursts from all users jointly. This enables the model to group similar traffic patterns without requiring labeled data. DBSCAN is chosen for its ability to handle noise and discover clusters of varying shapes without specifying their number in advance. In Eligo, differences in payload sizes between valid and spoiled votes naturally produce distinct clusters (e.g., action IDs 3 and 7 in Fig. 2), allowing us to infer ballot validity directly from the classification step.

4.3 Vote Submission Detection

As discussed in Sect. 3, some attacker roles, such as malicious administrators and passive eavesdroppers, cannot directly observe user interactions or map traffic to specific platform workflows. Despite these limitations, we demonstrate that it is still feasible to detect vote submission events within encrypted traffic. Identifying this critical action opens the door to further privacy risks, such as linking voter identities to ballot status. To achieve this, we propose a method that derives a temporal signature of the vote submission action from aggregated traffic. This approach exploits consistent structural and timing patterns that emerge across users when the same action is repeated. The method proceeds as follows:

1. **Input:** Extract all TLS packets belonging to identified activity bursts across users.
2. **Grouping:** For each unique action and packet index, collect corresponding packets from all users.
3. **Sorting:** Sort each packet group by timestamp normalized per action (starting at 0.0 s) to capture relative timing within the action.
4. **Trend estimation:** Apply a rolling mean to each group to obtain timing trends.
5. **Signature generation:** Normalize trend curves and average across packet indices to produce the final action signature.

The action signature captures the temporal distribution of a given action across all voters. In both systems studied, we observe a consistent distinction: actions before vote submission produce smooth, gradually rising curves, reflecting their spread over time; in contrast, vote submission shows a distinct mid-curve jump, indicating a concentration of events in tighter time intervals. This distinctive temporal feature, illustrated in Fig. 4, makes vote submissions stand out from other actions. The jump results from synchronized increases in normalized timestamps across multiple packet indices, which accumulate into a sharp inflection in the averaged action-level curve (Figs. 4d and 4h). In POLYAS, this temporal pattern is visible for both valid and invalid ballots, allowing signature computation on the full dataset. In Eligo, clustering separates valid and spoiled votes, with the signature jump only present in the valid submission cluster. Since clustering is based on observable traffic features, a passive attacker can isolate the valid cluster without labeled data and compute the signature accordingly.

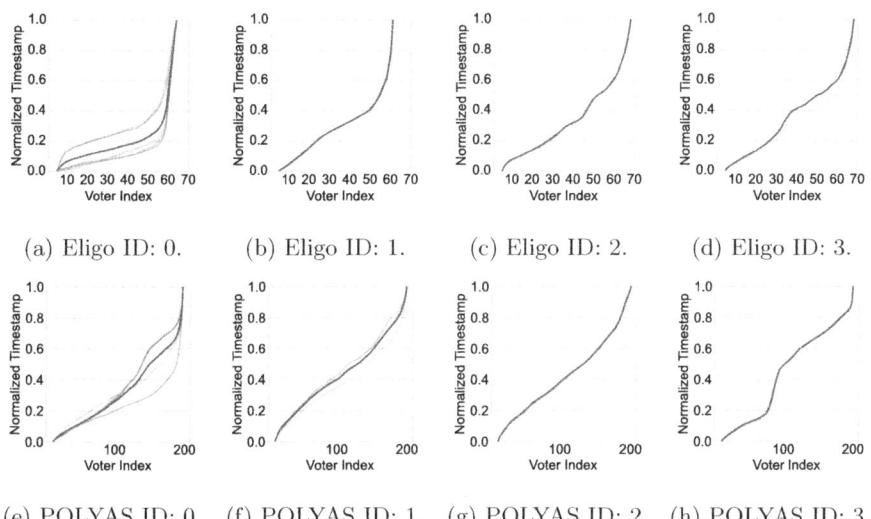

(a) Eligo ID: 0. (b) Eligo ID: 1. (c) Eligo ID: 2. (d) Eligo ID: 3.

(e) POLYAS ID: 0. (f) POLYAS ID: 1. (g) POLYAS ID: 2. (h) POLYAS ID: 3.

Fig. 4. Action temporal signatures.

4.4 Ballot Validity Classification

This stage focuses exclusively on packets corresponding to the ballot submission action, as identified using the methodology described in the previous section. The goal is to determine whether a submitted ballot is valid or spoiled, based solely on encrypted traffic metadata.

Eligo. In Eligo, the distinction between valid and spoiled ballots arises automatically during unsupervised action classification. This is driven by a consistent, deterministic difference in application-layer payload lengths during ballot submission. Since these lengths underpin the clustering model, valid and spoiled votes form separate clusters without the need for manual labels. As a result, ballot validity can be inferred deterministically using straightforward rules based on observed payload patterns.

POLYAS. Unlike Eligo, the POLYAS system does not exhibit deterministic differences in traffic metadata between valid and spoiled ballots, making simple rule-based separation infeasible. To address this, we frame the problem as a binary classification task and apply machine learning techniques to distinguish between the two classes. We enhance the inter-arrival time (IAT) feature of the ballot submission action using `tsfresh` [11], a time-series feature extraction toolkit, to capture subtle temporal patterns potentially linked to ballot validity. Our evaluation spans both tree-based and sequence-aware models suited for detecting nuanced, possibly non-linear differences in structured traffic features. Specifically, we test Random Forest, Gradient Boosting, XGBoost, LightGBM, and a simple ensemble combining Random Forest and LightGBM. The best ensemble combines a shallow Random Forest (10 estimators, max depth 3) with a lightweight LightGBM (3 estimators, 2 leaf nodes, 0.4 subsampling rate). Additionally, we train a multi-layer LSTM model to explore whether sequential dependencies in timing are better captured by recurrent architectures. The LSTM consists of a unidirectional layer (1100 units), a bidirectional layer (380 units), and another unidirectional layer (530 units), followed by dense layers with dropout. Training is performed for 5 epochs with a batch size of 8 and a learning rate of 10^{-5}, optimizing for precision. Model hyperparameters were tuned across multiple runs, selecting configurations that maximized validation precision.

5 Evaluation

We now evaluate our methodology and show the results of our attacks by providing details on our experimental setup and numerical results on our attacks' success rates.

5.1 Experimental Setup

To evaluate our approach, we generate a dataset of 400 simulated voting sessions (200 each on Eligo and POLYAS) with balanced valid and spoiled ballots. We used balanced datasets to clearly expose learnable distinctions in voting behavior. While real-world class imbalance may affect classifier performance, standard rebalancing techniques (e.g., class weights, oversampling) can be applied without affecting feasibility. Indeed, in Eligo, classification relies on fixed payload length patterns, rendering imbalance irrelevant. User interactions are automated for reproducibility, and network traffic was captured via Wireshark. It is also worth noting that, although our experiments were conducted in controlled conditions, the primary features we exploit (e.g., inter-arrival times, payload lengths) are artifacts of protocol design rather than user interaction variability. These features are invariant, making classification robust across different client and network conditions. After extracting and filtering outgoing TLS packets with non-empty application data using Python, we segment user flows into individual actions using DBSCAN (Sect. 4.1). Clustering quality is high, with silhouette scores of 0.893 ± 0.059 for Eligo and 0.898 ± 0.045 for POLYAS, and minimal noise, confirming robust action-level segmentation.

5.2 Voter Action Classification Results

After segmenting each voter's traffic into activity bursts using DBSCAN clustering, we applied two approaches to classify the nature of these bursts into specific voter actions: a rule-based model and a clustering-based model. Both methods operated on the full dataset and did not require labeled data during training. Both models are first implemented and evaluated on traffic generated from the Eligo platform and then tested on POLYAS to assess generalizability. The classification performance is summarized in Table 3. Both approaches achieve high classification accuracy, with the clustering-based model demonstrating strong generalizability across systems and slightly outperforming the rule-based model on POLYAS. To further assess the internal consistency and separation quality of the clusters, we evaluated the clustering structure using silhouette scores and noise ratios, which reflect the compactness and distinctiveness of identified clusters. Eligo achieved a silhouette score of 0.958 and a noise ratio of 0.001, indicating highly cohesive and well-separated clusters. Similarly, POLYAS yielded a silhouette score of 0.914 and a noise ratio of 0.001, also demonstrating strong clustering quality. These results confirm that the clustering model forms highly coherent and separable groupings of user actions across both datasets, reinforcing its applicability in inferring user behavior from encrypted traffic metadata.

Table 3. Action classification accuracy for each voting platform. ST = Set Theory model, CL = Clustering model.

(a) Eligo.

ID	Accuracy ST	Accuracy CL
0	1.00	1.00
1	0.86	0.92
2	1.00	0.99
4	1.00	0.82
3/7	1.00	0.99
5	1.00	0.94
6	1.00	0.99
Avg.	0.98	0.95

(b) POLYAS.

ID	Accuracy ST	Accuracy CL
0	1.00	0.99
1	1.00	0.98
2	0.96	0.98
3	0.89	0.99
Avg.	0.96	0.99

5.3 Ballot Validity Classification

The final stage of our analysis focuses on distinguishing between valid and spoiled ballots using encrypted traffic data. For Eligo, this task is straightforward due to consistent differences in payload lengths during the vote submission action. These differences lead to clear clustering of valid and spoiled ballots without requiring a separate classifier. As a result, the system achieves near-perfect classification accuracy of 99.49% based solely on these deterministic payload patterns. In contrast, POLYAS does not exhibit such deterministic differences. To address this, we extract detailed temporal features from packet sequences and apply supervised machine learning models to identify subtle statistical distinctions between ballot types. We evaluate several classifiers—including Random Forest, Gradient Boosting, XGBoost, LightGBM, an ensemble model (Random Forest + LightGBM), and a multi-layer LSTM—on a dataset with an 80/20 train-test split. Results (Table 4) show that LightGBM and the Ensemble model achieve the highest overall performance, with accuracies up to 78%, along with balanced precision and recall. The LSTM model demonstrates the highest recall, effectively detecting spoiled ballots, but at the cost of reduced precision. Gradient Boosting, while showing perfect precision, suffers from very low recall, making it unsuitable when detecting all spoiled ballots is critical. Overall, while Eligo's deterministic patterns enable trivial ballot validity classification, our results show that even encrypted traffic from non-deterministic systems like POLYAS can leak enough temporal information to enable classification, revealing a learnable side channel exploitable with up to 78% accuracy.

Table 4. Spoiled ballot identification performance.

Classifier	Prec.	Rec.	Acc.
Random Forest	0.56	0.90	0.60
Gradient Boosting	**1.00**	0.20	0.60
XGBoost	0.80	0.40	0.65
LightGBM	0.73	0.80	0.75
Ensemble (RF + LGBM)	0.74	0.85	**0.78**
LSTM	0.68	**0.95**	0.69

6 Discussion

Section 5 presented our attacks' accuracy and success rates; here, we analyze their implications for each system: Sect. 6.1 covers key factors in identifying vote submissions in Eligo, and Sect. 6.2 offers a statistical analysis of POLYAS under attack.

6.1 Eligo Vote Submission Identification

Applying our vote submission detection method to the Eligo dataset reveals a clear difference in temporal signature shapes between valid and spoiled ballots. Valid submissions show a distinct midsection jump, reflecting tightly coupled backend processes like ballot validation and cryptographic sealing that occur consistently across sessions, causing aligned bursts in traffic. In contrast, spoiled ballots follow a more variable timing pattern due to early termination or altered processing paths, resulting in smoother signatures without sharp inflections. This demonstrates how deterministic system behaviors can be inferred passively from encrypted traffic, exposing privacy risks despite the lack of visible payload or labels.

6.2 POLYAS Ballot Validity Classification

Experimental results show that machine learning and deep learning models perform worse on POLYAS than on Eligo, where vote validity was classified with near-perfect accuracy. This prompts the question of whether POLYAS lacks class-separability or if subtle timing differences go undetected by current models. To investigate, we perform a statistical analysis of IAT distributions in outgoing TLS traffic. We apply various tests grouped by their focus: *location tests* assess central tendency ($p < 0.05$ suggests linear separability), *scale tests* like Ansari-Bradley evaluate dispersion without assuming normality, *distribution equality* tests such as Kolmogorov-Smirnov detect subtle distribution shifts [8], and *location and scale* tests like Mann-Whitney and Lepage capture changes in both mean and variance [24]. Figure 5 summarizes these findings. Because each action emits a fixed sequence of TLS packets with payloads, we align IATs by packet index to enable detailed, packet-level comparisons between valid and spoiled ballots, exposing action-specific temporal patterns.

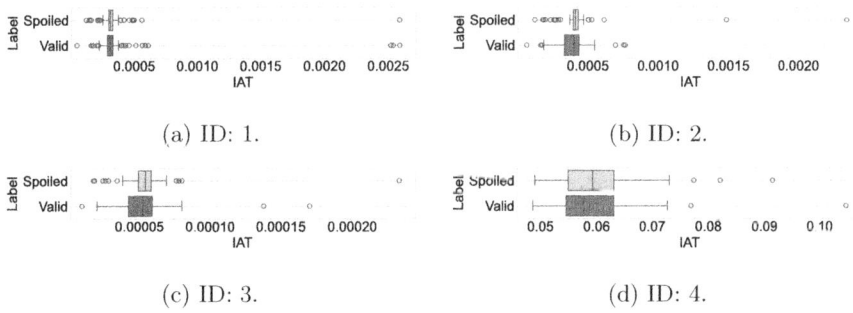

Fig. 5. Comparison of IAT distributions for ballot submission action by packet index.

Consistent significance was observed only for the vote submission action, particularly across multiple packet indices and non-parametric tests with p-values below 0.05, which capture complex distributional differences. Boxplots in Fig. 5 further highlight distinct IAT patterns between the two classes at corresponding packet indices.

In contrast, location-based tests did not yield consistent significance, suggesting that class differences lie not in average behavior but in distributional

Table 5. P-values of statistical tests for ballot submission action by packet index.

Objective	Test	P-Value			
		ID 1	ID 2	ID 3	ID 4
Scale	Ansari-Bradley [1]	0.1266	**0.0006**	**0.0015**	0.7937
Distribution equality	Cramer–von Mises [14]	0.3942	**0.0318**	**0.0358**	0.7280
	Epps-Singleton [20]	0.3223	**0.0041**	**0.0023**	0.6949
	Kolmogorov-Smirnov [4]	0.1994	**0.0066**	0.0524	0.7510
Location & Scale	Cucconi [33]	0.1678	**0.0039**	**0.0039**	0.7832
	Lepage [31]	0.2857	**0.0499**	**0.0430**	0.2537
	Podgor-Gastwirth [35]	0.1599	**0.0030**	**0.0025**	0.7880

patterns of packet IATs during vote submission. While classification accuracy for POLYAS was modest, statistical analysis still reveals class-dependent timing differences, indicating that more tailored models could achieve higher accuracy and pose greater risks to vote secrecy (Table 5).

7 Countermeasures

We evaluate two countermeasures against traffic analysis, addressing payload length and temporal signatures, through a case study on Eligo, where attacks were most effective and traffic allowed controlled simulation. For POLYAS, only partial mitigation analysis was possible due to its architectural and traffic differences.

Payload Padding. To defend against payload-based inference, we simulated padding all non-empty application data packets to a uniform maximum length of 2085 bytes, the largest observed payload. This increased RAM usage by up to 109% in the worst case and 32% on average (Table 6). After padding, ballot validity classification accuracy dropped to 0%, as deterministic packet length differences between valid and spoiled ballots were eliminated, showing that simple payload padding effectively counters this attack. While POLYAS action classification also depends on payload lengths and would be blurred by padding, its ballot validity classification relies on temporal features and remains unaffected by this mitigation.

Time Equalization. To counter timing-based inference, we propose equalizing IATs of application data packets within each action to flatten temporal signatures and block timing-based attacks. For Eligo, we simulate this by sampling IATs from a baseline distribution of maximum-length packets and applying them to a synthetic voter, increasing action durations by up to 6.11 s (2.06 s on average). This uniform timing removes the distinctive signature jump of vote submissions, effectively preventing detection. For POLYAS, the lack of a clear link between payload size and IATs makes realistic time equalization simulation infeasible, so we do not report similar results, though system-specific timing equalization remains a promising approach.

Table 6. Mitigation evaluation for Eligo

Action	Payload Increase	Action Duration Increase (seconds)
Load voting event page	1.09	5.49 (6.11)
Log in	0.07	3.03 (3.85)
Open ballot info	0.02	2.36 (0.98)
Open ballot content	0.03	2.37 (1.17)
Send vote	0.21	5.14 (1.06)
Redirect to home page	0.02	2.35 (0.92)
Log out	0.81	1.49 (0.30)
Avg.	**0.32**	**3.18 (2.06)**

8 Conclusions

This paper shows that key voting actions, such as ballot submission, can be inferred from encrypted TLS traffic using timing and payload features, without needing system access. Our methodology detected vote submissions and classified ballot validity in two real-world systems. We also proposed mitigations, payload padding, and time equalization, which significantly reduce inference success, underscoring the need to treat traffic metadata as a serious privacy concern in online voting systems.

Limitations. Our methodology, developed using Eligo, was also applied to POLYAS without system-specific tuning to assess its generalizability. While POLYAS yielded lower classification accuracy, statistical analysis revealed class-dependent timing patterns, indicating potential for improvement through tailored models. Future work could explore system-specific strategies to boost performance further.

Future Works. Looking forward, our findings suggest several future directions. Our current work assumes passive adversaries who do not alter traffic, but future research should explore active threat models where attackers manipulate or inject data to amplify leakage or disrupt voting, along with defenses against such attacks. Additionally, these methods could be extended to infer more detailed privacy risks, like voters' preferences, emphasizing the urgent need for robust traffic-level privacy protections in online voting systems.

Acknowledgments. We thank Eligo for granting us access to their voting system, which enabled the experimental evaluation presented in this work.

References

1. Ansari, A., Bradley, R.: Rank-sum tests for dispersions. Ann. Math. Statist. **31**(4), 1174–1189 (1960)
2. Assembly Voting: Assembly voting (2025). https://assemblyvoting.com/. Accessed 11 May 2025
3. Belenios: Belenios (2025). https://www.belenios.org/. Accessed 11 May 2025
4. Berger, V., Zhou, Y.: Kolmogorov–smirnov test: overview (2014)
5. Bernhard, D., Kulyk, O., Volkamer, M.: Security proofs for participation privacy, receipt-freeness and ballot privacy for the Helios voting scheme. In: Proceedings of the 12th International Conference on Availability, Reliability and Security, pp. 1–10 (2017)
6. Blanchard, E., Gallais, A., Leblond, E., Sidhoum-Rahal, D., Walter, J.: An analysis of the security and privacy issues of the neovote online voting system. In: International Joint Conference on Electronic Voting, pp. 1–18. Springer, Cham (2022)
7. Brunet, J., Pananos, A.D., Essex, A.: Review your choices: when confirmation pages break ballot secrecy in online elections. In: International Joint Conference on Electronic Voting, pp. 36–52. Springer, Cham (2022)
8. Cabuk, S., Brodley, C.E., Shields, C.: IP covert channel detection. ACM Trans. Inf. Syst. Security **12**(4), 1–29 (2009)
9. Chondros, N., et al.: D-demos: a distributed, end-to-end verifiable, internet voting system. In: 2016 IEEE 36th International Conference on Distributed Computing Systems (ICDCS), pp. 711–720. IEEE (2016)
10. Chowdhury, M.J.M.: Comparison of e-voting schemes: Estonian and Norwegian solutions. Int. J. Appl. Inf. Syst. **6**(2), 60–66 (2013)
11. Christ, M., Braun, N., Neuffer, J., Kempa-Liehr, A.W.: Time series feature extraction on basis of scalable hypothesis tests (tsfresh-a python package). Neurocomputing **307**, 72–77 (2018)
12. Clarkson, M.R., Chong, S., Myers, A.S.: Civitas: toward a secure voting system. In: Proceedings of the IEEE Symposium on Security and Privacy (SP), pp. 354–368 (2008)
13. Council of Europe: Recommendation CM/Rec(2017)5 of the committee of ministers to member states on standards for e-voting (2017). https://www.coe.int/en/web/electoral-assistance/e-voting. Accessed 14 July 2025
14. Cramér, H.: On the composition of elementary errors. Scand. Actuar. J. **1928**(1), 13–74 (1928)
15. Damodaran, A., Rastikian, S., Rønne, P.B., Ryan, P.Y.: Hyperion: transparent end-to-end verifiable voting with coercion mitigation. Cryptology ePrint Archive (2024)
16. DW: Russia imprisons woman who wrote 'no to war' on ballot paper (2024). https://p.dw.com/p/4dwdm. Accessed 1 May 2025
17. ElectionBuddy: Electionbuddy (2025). https://electionbuddy.com/. Accessed 11 May 2025
18. Eligo: Electronic, digital and online voting: what's the difference? (2025). https://eligovoting.com/electronic-digital-and-online-voting/. Accessed 27 May 2025
19. Eligo: Eligo (2025). https://eligovoting.com/. Accessed 11 May 2025
20. Epps, T., Singleton, K.: An omnibus test for the two-sample problem using the empirical characteristic function. J. Stat. Comput. Simul. **26**, 177–203 (1986)

21. Euronews: Money for votes: Corruption arrests tarnish Spain regional elections (2023). https://www.euronews.com/2023/05/27/money-for-votes-corruption-arrests-tarnish-spain-regional-elections. Accessed 25 May 2025
22. Euronews: Eu calls for swift probe of alleged irregularities in Georgia election (2024). https://www.euronews.com/my-europe/2024/10/28/eu-calls-for-swift-probe-of-alleged-georgian-election-irregularities. Accessed 25 May 2025
23. Europe, N.G.: Woman fined for writing 'burn in hell' alongside putin's name on ballot sheet (2024). Accessed 1 May 2025
24. Frittoli, L.: Strengthening sequential side-channel attacks through change detection. TCHES **2020**(3), 1–21 (2020)
25. Government of Ireland: Dáil election voters. selfies/photographs (2024). https://www.gov.ie/en/department-of-housing-local-government-and-heritage/publications/d%C3%A1il-election-voters/. Accessed 1 May 2025
26. Gritzalis, D.A.: Principles and requirements for a secure e-voting system. Comput. Secur. **21**(6), 539–556 (2002)
27. Helios: Helios voting (2025). https://vote.heliosvoting.org/. Accessed 11 May 2025
28. Huang, J., He, D., Obaidat, M.S., Vijayakumar, P., Luo, M., Choo, K.R.: The application of the blockchain technology in voting systems: a review. ACM Comput. Surv. **54**(3), 1–28 (2021)
29. Jafar, U., Aziz, M.J.A., Shukur, Z.: Blockchain for electronic voting system–review and open research challenges. Sensors **21**(17), 5874 (2021)
30. Lalitha, V., Samundeswari, S., Roobinee, R., Swetha, L.S.: Decentralized online voting system using blockchain. In: 2022 International Conference on Applied Artificial Intelligence and Computing (ICAAIC), pp. 1387–1391. IEEE (2022)
31. Lepage, Y.: A combination of Wilcoxon's and Ansari-Bradley's statistics. Biometrika **58**(1), 213–217 (1971)
32. Licht, N., Duenas-Cid, D., Krivonosova, I., Krimmer, R.: To i-vote or not to i-vote: drivers and barriers to the implementation of internet voting. In: Electronic Voting: 6th International Joint Conference, E-Vote-ID 2021, Virtual Event, 5–8 October 2021, Proceedings 6, pp. 91–105. Springer, Cham (2021)
33. Marozzi, M.: The multisample cucconi test. Stat. Methods Appl. **23**, 209–227 (2014)
34. NCSL: Secrecy of the ballot and ballot selfies (2024). https://www.ncsl.org/elections-and-campaigns/secrecy-of-the-ballot-and-ballot-selfies. Accessed 1 May 2025
35. Podgor, M., Gastwirth, J.: On non-parametric and generalized tests for the two-sample problem with location and scale change alternatives. Stat. Med. **13**(5-7), 747–758 (1994)
36. POLITICO Europe: Vote-buying allegations rock Bulgaria as protests escalate (2024). https://www.politico.eu/article/vote-buying-allegation-election-bulgaria-protest/. Accessed 25 May 2025
37. POLYAS: Case studies (2025). https://www.polyas.com/case-studies. Accessed 11 May 2025
38. POLYAS: Polyas (2025). https://www.polyas.com/. Accessed 11 May 2025
39. Sheela, A.S., Franklin, R.G.: E-voting system using homomorphic encryption technique. In: Journal of Physics: Conference Series, vol. 1770, p. 012011. IOP Publishing (2021)
40. Specter, M.A., Koppel, J., Weitzner, D.: The ballot is busted before the blockchain: a security analysis of voatz, the first internet voting application used in {US} federal elections. In: 29th USENIX Security Symposium (USENIX Security 2020), pp. 1535–1553 (2020)

41. The Federal Returning Officer: European parliament election 2024. On the Sunday of the election (2024). https://www.bundeswahlleiterin.de/en/europawahlen/2024/informationen-waehler/wahlsonntag.html#6d33b849-0698-4561-946a-c15a4684264f. Accessed 1 May 2025
42. Tribunal Superior Eleitoral: ResoluÇÃo nº 23.736, de 27 de fevereiro de 2024 (2024). https://www.tse.jus.br/legislacao/compilada/res/2024/resolucao-no-23-736-de-27-de-fevereiro-de-2024. Accessed 1 May 2025
43. Voatz: Voatz (2025). https://voatz.com/. Accessed 11 May 2025
44. Wu, Y., Kasahara, S.: Smart contract-based e-voting system using homomorphic encryption and zero-knowledge proof. In: International Conference on Applied Cryptography and Network Security, pp. 67–83. Springer, Cham (2023)

AI Security

MSPP-Net: Fine-Grained Image Privacy Identification via Multi-stage Semantic Perception

Yinglong Li[1,2(✉)], Bingyuan Chen[1,2], Qingyan Jiang[1], and Tieming Chen[3(✉)]

[1] School of Computer Science and Technology, Zhejiang University of Technology, Hangzhou, China
liyinglong@zjut.edu.cn
[2] Zhejiang Key Laboratory of Visual Information Intelligent Processing, Hangzhou, China
[3] School of Geoinformatics, Zhejiang University of Technology, Huzhou, China
tmchen@zjut.edu.cn

Abstract. The rise of online social networks has heightened concerns over image privacy leakage. Although deep learning methods have been applied to privacy recognition, they face two key challenges: (1) a privacy gap between low-level visual features and high-level, context-aware human judgments, and (2) limited consideration of inter-entity context. To address these, we propose MSPP-Net, a Multi-Stage Privacy Perception Network inspired by human cognition. It decomposes privacy inference into three stages: entity perception to detect key objects, attribute perception to align visual features with semantic concepts via multimodal contrastive learning, and privacy perception to model inter-object context using graph attention networks. Experiments on our FineViP dataset show that MSPP-Net outperforms strong baselines, improving mAP by 3% and OR by 1.1%, validating the benefits of structured, cognitively motivated modeling for privacy recognition.

Keywords: Image Privacy · Multi-Stage Perception · Graph Attention Networks · Explainability

1 Introduction

With the proliferation of online social networks (OSNs), images have become a dominant medium for information sharing, with billions uploaded daily [8,19]. However, this convenience comes with a growing risk of privacy leakage. Malicious exploitation of shared visual content can lead to severe violations of personal privacy and even broader social security threats. Figure 1 highlights several real-world incidents illustrating these risks. In Fig. 1(a), a photo of soldiers training in a gymnasium was posted online; adversaries used location cues from the image to launch a targeted assassination. In Fig. 1(b), a celebrity's shared vacation photo inadvertently alerted thieves, resulting in a burglary. Figure 1(c) shows a scenario where an image could unintentionally reveal a person's sexual orientation, leading to potential harassment. Such cases demonstrate how users often unintentionally disclose sensitive information due to limited privacy awareness, perceptual limitations, or difficulty recognizing sensitive elements in complex images, phenomena also linked to the privacy paradox [5]. These challenges underscore the urgent need for automated visual privacy identification that operates independently of user-initiated requests.

Fig. 1. Examples of privacy breaches caused by photo sharing

Existing visual privacy identification approaches generally fall into two categories. The first treats the task as a binary image classification problem, distinguishing between public and private content [16,22,23]. While straightforward, this coarse-grained categorization oversimplifies the nuanced semantics of privacy, making it difficult to assess specific risks. The second category focuses on detecting privacy-sensitive entities such as ID cards or faces [3,10,11]. Although more targeted, these methods face two major limitations: (1) **Semantic Gap:** They rely on low-level visual features, which fall short of capturing the complex, high-level privacy judgments humans make using prior knowledge and contextual reasoning. For instance, a bed in a private bedroom versus one in a showroom conveys very different privacy implications. (2) **Context Neglect:** By analyzing entities in isolation, these models overlook the critical contextual relationships between entities and scenes. Such context is essential; for example, two people embracing implies a higher privacy sensitivity than two individuals standing apart.

We attribute the limitations of existing models to their inability to replicate the cognitive process underlying human privacy judgment. Drawing on the multi-stage theory of emotional experience from cognitive science [12], we hypothesize that image privacy judgment follows a sequential process of perception, assessment, and reasoning.

Guided by this hypothesis, we introduce the Multi-Stage Privacy Perception Network (MSPP-Net), which decomposes privacy recognition into three interconnected stages: the *Entity Perception Module* detects salient objects, the *Attribute Perception Module* aligns visual and semantic features, and the *Privacy Perception Module* models contextual relationships to infer privacy risks.

Our main contributions are summarized as follows.

- We propose MSPP-Net, a cognitively inspired framework for image privacy identification that decomposes the task into three stages: entity perception, attribute alignment, and relational reasoning. This structured design addresses two key challenges in visual privacy: the *semantic gap* between visual features and abstract privacy concepts, and the *overlooked contextual relationships* among entities.
- Our multimodal contrastive learning module aligns visual features with a multidimensional privacy attribute dictionary, enabling high-level semantic understanding without extensive manual annotation. To address context neglect, we incorporate a graph attention network that models inter-entity relationships, allowing the model to assess privacy risks based on context, not just individual objects.
- Experiments on our FineViP dataset show that MSPP-Net consistently outperforms strong baselines across multiple metrics, achieving state-of-the-art performance and demonstrating its effectiveness for complex image privacy recognition.

The remainder of this paper is organized as follows: Sect. 2 reviews relevant literature on visual privacy recognition. Section 3 presents the details of the proposed MSPP-Net framework. Section 4 analyzes the experimental results. The ethical considerations are stated in Sect. 5. Finally, Sect. 6 concludes the paper.

2 Related Work

2.1 Image Privacy Recognition

Early studies on image privacy recognition primarily framed it as a binary classification problem, distinguishing between *private* and *public* images [16,22,23]. While these approaches laid the groundwork, their coarse granularity limits effectiveness in real-world scenarios that require nuanced risk assessment.

Subsequent work moved toward detecting Privacy-Sensitive Objects (PSOs), such as faces, ID cards, or text [3,10,11]. These methods offer more detailed analysis by localizing sensitive entities, yet often treat them in isolation, ignoring contextual dependencies crucial for accurate privacy evaluation.

More recent approaches leverage Graph Neural Networks (GNNs) to explicitly model inter-entity relationships. GIP [20] introduced a global knowledge graph linking object categories to privacy labels, enhancing interpretability but relying on static, dataset-level co-occurrence. DRAG [21] improved adaptability by dynamically constructing region-based graphs per image. While these advances highlight the importance of context, a persistent challenge remains: ensuring that relational modeling is both dynamic and semantically grounded. Addressing this is key to building more interpretable and human-aligned privacy recognition systems.

2.2 Cognitively-Inspired and Relational Models

Cognitive Science Models in Visual Understanding. Cognitive science provides valuable frameworks for modeling subjective and context-dependent visual concepts, including privacy. Ortony et al.'s cognitive structure theory of emotion [12], which frames emotion as a sequence of cognitive stages, has been successfully adapted for image sentiment analysis [13]. This staged approach improves interpretability and performance by decomposing complex perceptual tasks. Given the similarly nuanced and context-sensitive nature of privacy perception, applying a staged cognitive modeling strategy offers a promising direction for fine-grained privacy recognition.

Visual Relational Reasoning. Graph Neural Networks (GNNs) [15], especially Graph Attention Networks (GATs) [18], have proven effective for modeling inter-entity relationships in visual data. By dynamically learning attention weights between nodes, GATs can capture rich contextual interactions critical for high-level reasoning. This makes them particularly suitable for addressing the "Context Neglect" problem in privacy recognition, where understanding the relationships between visual elements is key to accurate risk assessment.

3 Methodology

This section mainly introduces the framework of the proposed Multi-Stage Privacy Perception Network (MSPP-Net) and how its three main components work coordinatively.

3.1 The Framework of MSPP-Net

Our multi-stage design is inspired by recent advances in visual understanding tasks, such as the work by Pan et al. [13] on image emotion analysis, which demonstrates the effectiveness of an entity-attribute-emotion perception pipeline. Building on this foundation, MSPP-Net introduces two key innovations specifically tailored to the unique demands of fine-grained privacy recognition. First, in the attribute perception stage, rather than adopting the pseudo-label fitting approach based on KL-divergence as used in [13], we employ a multimodal contrastive learning strategy. This method directly aligns visual entity representations with textual privacy attributes within a shared embedding space, offering a more robust and semantically grounded mechanism for bridging the semantic gap, particularly given the diversity and subtlety of privacy concepts. Second, in the reasoning stage, we move beyond simple feature aggregation and leverage a GAT to explicitly model the context-dependent relationships among entities. This relational modeling is critical for privacy inference, where risk often emerges not from isolated objects, but from their interactions and co-occurrence within a given scene.

The overall architecture of MSPP-Net is illustrated in Fig. 2. It adopts a multi-stage processing framework comprising three core modules, each designed to simulate a distinct phase of human privacy judgment. **(1) Entity Perception Module:** This module operates on multi-level feature maps extracted by a shared backbone network. Using predefined entity masks, it identifies and localizes key entities within an image, and generates compact visual feature representations for each detected entity. **(2) Attribute Perception Module:** Building on the extracted entity features, this module enriches each representation with high-level semantic information through a multimodal contrastive learning strategy. This process aligns visual and textual modalities, effectively embedding privacy-relevant attributes into the entity representations. **(3) Privacy Perception Module:** In the final stage, the semantically enhanced entity features are treated as nodes in an entity-relationship graph. Unlike prior methods (e.g., DRAG [21]) that rely on raw feature maps for region-based inference, our approach enables reasoning over more explicit and interpretable semantic units. To model the contextual dependencies among entities, we employ GAT [18], which learn adaptive attention weights across the graph structure. The aggregated information is then used to predict the image's privacy label.

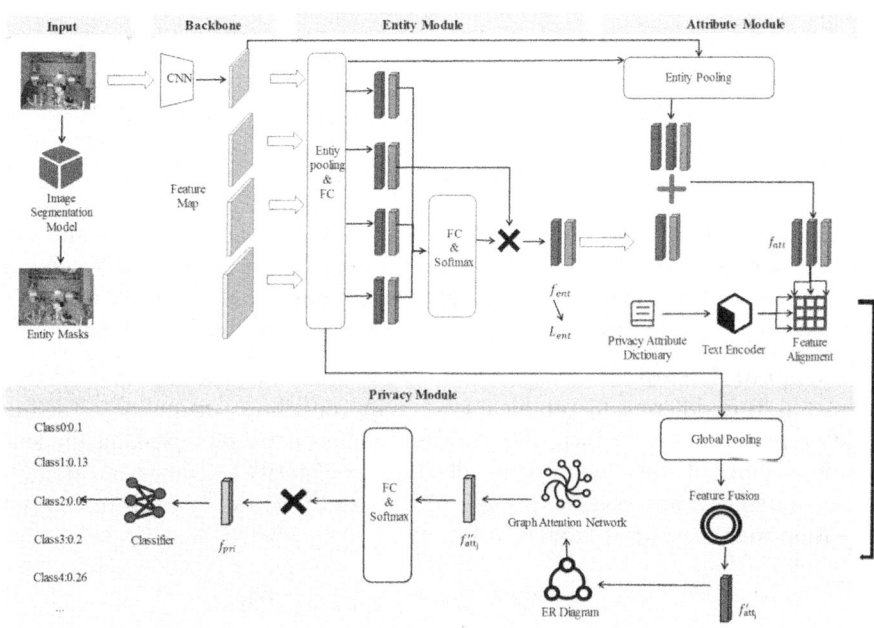

Fig. 2. The framework of the proposed MSPP-Net.

In Fig. 2, for each input image, an image segmentation model is employed to extract a set of entity masks, denoted as $M_j \mid j = 1, 2, \ldots, N_e$, where each binary mask distinguishes foreground entities (value 1) from the background (value 0), and N_e represents the total number of detected entities. To obtain the visual representation of each entity, we apply a mask-guided average pooling operation, formally defined in Eq. (1).

$$\text{AvgPool}(F, M) = \frac{1}{\sum_{h,w} M_{h,w}} \sum_{h,w} M_{h,w} \odot F_{h,w} \quad (1)$$

where F denotes the visual feature map and M represents the corresponding entity mask. h and w refer to the height and width of the feature map respectively.

3.2 Entity Perception Module

The *Entity Perception Module* serves as the initial stage of MSPP-Net and is responsible for identifying and extracting distinct feature representations for each salient entity within an image. This design is motivated by the human visual cognition process, wherein individuals typically attend first to people, objects, or prominent scene elements when evaluating privacy. The module emulates this perceptual behavior by isolating entity-specific features as follows:

Hierarchical Feature Pooling. For the j-th entity in the image, the module extracts region-specific features from hierarchical feature maps F_i. Average pooling is applied to the masked regions as formulated in Eq. (2).

$$p_{ij} = \text{AvgPool}(F_i, M_j) W_i^{\text{level}} \quad (2)$$

Where W_i^{level} denotes the parameter matrix of feature level i. To ensure consistency across feature levels, the pooled features are projected into a unified subspace using these matrices. This approach assumes that all entity masks are appropriately scaled to match the resolution of their corresponding feature maps.

Attentional Fusion of Hierarchical Features. Considering that features extracted from different hierarchical levels may contribute unequally to the final entity representation, we introduce an attention mechanism to dynamically learn the importance of each level. Specifically, the initial entity features from all layers are concatenated and passed through a lightweight neural network to compute attention weights, as formulated in Eq. (3).

$$\alpha_j = \text{softmax}([p_{1j}, p_{2j}, p_{3j}, p_{4j}] \cdot W_\alpha) \quad (3)$$

where the learnable parameter matrix W_α projects each feature vector into a scalar, which is then normalized using the softmax function to produce a weight vector. These weights indicate the relative contribution of each level's features to the final representation. The final feature vector for the j-th entity is computed as a weighted sum of the level-specific features, as shown in Eq. (4).

$$f_{\text{ent}}^j = \sum_{i=1}^{4} \alpha_{ij}\, p_{ij} \quad (4)$$

where $j = \{1, 2, ..., N_e\}$ and N_e is the number of entities in the given image. The output of the Entity Perception Module is thus a set of refined feature vectors for all N_e entities, capturing rich visual semantics across multiple levels while emphasizing the most relevant features through attention. These representations serve as critical inputs to the subsequent Attribute Perception Module, enabling fine-grained privacy attribute analysis.

Training Objective. To encourage the *Entity Perception Module* to extract semantically discriminative features for each object, we incorporate an auxiliary entity categorization task, supervised using a standard cross-entropy loss. This auxiliary objective guides the model to align its feature representations more closely with the ground-truth entity categories, thereby enhancing the semantic richness and distinctiveness of the learned features. By introducing direct supervision at this early stage, the model establishes a more robust and meaningful foundation for the subsequent attribute-aware and relational reasoning modules. The loss function is formally defined in Eq. (5):

$$\mathcal{L}_{\text{entity}} = -\frac{1}{N_e} \sum_{j=1}^{N_e} \log P(c_{\text{gt}}^j | f_{\text{ent}}^j) \tag{5}$$

where c_{gt}^j denotes the true label of the j-th entity (entity category).

3.3 Attribute Perception Module

The attribute module serves as a crucial intermediate stage in MSPP-Net, aiming to bridge the semantic gap between low-level visual features and high-level privacy concepts. It enriches entity representations with privacy semantics by aligning entity features from the perception module with high-level feature maps, which offer more abstract and discriminative information suited for attribute extraction.

Different regions within an entity contribute unequally to specific attribute recognition (e.g., face and hand for identity-related attributes). To focus on the key regions within an entity, we apply an attention mechanism to the high-level feature map F_{top} guided by the entity mask M_j to generate an internal attention map for the entity A_j, as defined in Eq. (6).

$$A_{\text{spatial}_j} = \text{softmax}(F_{\text{top}} W_{\text{att}} + M_{\text{mask}_j}) \tag{6}$$

where F_{top} denotes the high-level feature map and the parameter matrix W_{att} projects each spatial location element to a scalar. M_{mask_j} is an additive term derived from M_j, used to constrain the softmax computation to the region corresponding to entity j. The attribute module also incorporates scene-level context, which is essential for interpreting the behavior and state of entities within the graph and significantly influences attribute inference.

Moreover, in the absence of explicit entities, global scene evaluation becomes the primary basis for privacy analysis, as defined in Eq. (7).

$$A_{\text{spatial}_0} = \text{softmax}(F_{\text{top}} W_{\text{att}}) \tag{7}$$

Attribute Feature Generation and Correlation. The high-level feature map F_{top} is aggregated via attention-weighted pooling using the attention map, and the result is fused with the entity's base representation f_{ent}^j. The combined features form the final attribute representation for entity $j (j = 0, 1, ..., N_e)$, and $j = 0$ denotes the scene entity, as defined in Eq. (8).

$$f_{\text{att}}^j = f_{\text{ent}}^j + \text{AttPool}(F_{\text{top}}, A_{\text{spatial}_j}) \tag{8}$$

Privacy Attribute Dictionary. Although image privacy is inherently subjective and influenced by individual awareness, certain privacy patterns are widely recognized. To capture these, we construct a privacy attribute lexicon that reflects generalizable privacy sensitivities. This lexicon serves as the target space for the Attribute Perception Module, enabling it to interpret and evaluate entity-level privacy features and construct corresponding attribute distributions.

Multi-modal Contrastive Semantic Alignment. To capture the deep semantic associations between entities and their potential privacy attributes, while mitigating noise and bias in traditional supervised distribution fitting, we introduce a semantic alignment strategy based on Multi-modal Contrastive Learning (MCCL) [14]. Rather than explicitly predicting attribute distributions, this approach aligns visual entity features with corresponding textual attribute descriptions in a shared embedding space. This alignment encourages the model to learn more discriminative and semantically meaningful representations, providing a robust foundation for downstream privacy risk assessment.

- **Visual Feature Representation** (f_{att}^j). For each entity j in the image, including the scene-level entity ($j = 0$) represents the global context, its attribute feature f_{att}^j serves as the visual anchor in the contrastive learning framework.
- **Textual Feature Representation** (t_k). We construct a dictionary $A = \{a_1, a_2, ..., a_N\}$ of N predefined privacy attributes, each represented as a textual phrase. Using a pre-trained text encoder (CLIP [14]), each attribute a_k is encoded into a fixed-dimensional vector $t_k = \Phi_T(a_k)$, where $t_k \in \mathbb{R}^{D_t}$. These text embeddings $\{t_k\}_{k=1}^N$ remain fixed during training and serve as the target space for semantic alignment.

Positive and Negative Sample Construction. To facilitate contrastive learning, we identify positive (relevant) and negative (irrelevant) attribute samples for each visual anchor f_{att}^j from the text feature library. Given the absence of large-scale, fine-grained entity-to-attribute annotations, we employ a weakly supervised strategy that leverages the prior knowledge of large vision-language models (e.g., CLIP [14]) to construct these sample pairs.

- **Positive Sample Selection:** For each entity feature f_{att}^j, we calculate its cosine similarity $s_{jk} = \text{sim}(f_{\text{att}}^j, t_k)$ with all text features $\{t_k\}_{k=1}^N$. The top-K_p attributes with the highest scores are selected as the positive set $P_j = \{t_{\text{pos}_1}, ..., t_{\text{pos}_{K_p}}\}$. Where K_p is a small hyperparameter indicating the most relevant attributes.

- **Negative Sample Selection:** From the remaining $N - K_p$ attributes (excluding the positive set P_j), we randomly sample K_n text features to form the negative set $N_j = \{t_{\text{neg}_1}, \ldots, t_{\text{neg}_{K_n}}\}$, where K_n is set to be much larger than K_p.

With the positive and negative sample sets defined for each visual anchor, we train the model using contrastive learning. The goal is to pull the entity's visual feature closer to its semantically relevant attributes while pushing it away from irrelevant ones within the shared embedding space.

Training Objective. To mathematically formalize our alignment objective, we utilize a variant of the InfoNCE (Noise Contrastive Estimation) loss [9] to optimize the attribute semantic alignment module. Specifically, for each visual anchor f'_{att_j}, with its associated positive set P_j and negative set N_j, the contrastive loss $\mathcal{L}_{\text{att}_j}$ is defined as in Eq. (9).

$$\mathcal{L}_{\text{att}_j} = -\sum_{t_p \in P_j} \log \frac{\exp(\text{sim}(f'_{\text{att}_j}, t_p)/\tau)}{\sum_{t'_p \in P_j} \exp(\text{sim}(f'_{\text{att}_j}, t'_p)/\tau) + \sum_{t_n \in N_j} \exp(\text{sim}(f'_{\text{att}_j}, t_n)/\tau)} \quad (9)$$

where $\text{sim}(u, v) = \frac{u \cdot v}{\|u\|\|v\|}$ denotes the cosine similarity between vectors u and v. t_p and t_n are text features from the positive set P_j and the negative set N_j respectively. The temperature parameter τ modulates the sharpness of the similarity distribution, thereby controlling the difficulty of differentiating positive from negative samples. Lower τ values emphasize harder negative samples.

3.4 Privacy Perception Module

The Privacy Perception module, the final stage of MSPP-Net, integrates information from earlier stages to determine the image's overall privacy status. To capture the context surrounding each entity attribute, we first compute a global visual feature g using an attention-based pooling method, as defined in Eq. (10).

$$g = \text{AttPool}(F_{\text{top}}, \text{softmax}(F_{\text{top}} W_g)) \quad (10)$$

where Each positional feature of the image is mapped to a scalar via the parameter matrix W_g. After extracting the global context feature g, it is fused with each preliminary entity attribute feature f^j_{att} from the attribute module to enable inter-entity association modeling, as shown in Eq. (11).

$$f''_{\text{att}_j} = \text{Linear}(\text{Concat}(f^j_{\text{att}}, g)) \quad (11)$$

Association Learning for Inter-Entity Privacy Risk. To capture complex interactions among entities and their combined impact on privacy risk, we incorporate an entity association modeling stage within the privacy module using a GAT [18]. GAT dynamically learns relationship weights between nodes (entities), enabling effective aggregation of neighboring information to produce context- and relationship-aware entity representations.

Constructing Entity-Relationship Graphs. To apply GAT, we represent all image entities, including scene entities, and their context-aware attribute features as a graph $G = (V, E)$. Where (1) *Node set V*: Each node $v_j \in V$ represents an entity in the image, with $j = 0$ denoting the scene entity and $j = 1, ..., N_e$ the other entities. The initial node feature is the attribute representation f''_{att_j}, already fused with the global context feature g. (2) *Edge set E*: To capture all potential inter-entity interactions, we construct a fully connected graph where every pair of distinct nodes $(v_i, v_j) \in E$ is connected. The GAT's attention mechanism then dynamically emphasizes relevant edges critical for privacy assessment while suppressing irrelevant ones during training.

Graph Attention Network Layer. We employ an L-layer GAT network to learn inter-node relationships. Central to GAT is its attention mechanism, which enables each node v_j to weigh its neighbors differently when aggregating their information. The feature update for node v_j at each GAT layer follows the four steps as below:

- **Feature Transformation.** First, input features are linearly transformed via a learnable weight matrix $W \in \mathbb{R}^{D'_f \times D_f})$ to produce $h_j = W f''_{att_j}$, mapping them to the same or higher-dimensional feature space.
- **Attention Coefficient Calculation.** For each neighbor $v_k \in N_j$ of node v_j (i.e., all other nodes in the fully connected graph), the attention coefficient e_{jk} is computed as in Eq. (12).

$$e_{jk} = \text{LeakyReLU}(\mathbf{a}^T[h_j || h_k]) \tag{12}$$

Where $||$ denotes vector concatenation and $\mathbf{a}$ represents learnable parameters.
- **Normalized Attention Weight.** The attention coefficients are normalized across all neighbors of node v_j using the softmax function to obtain the final attention weights α_{jk}, as defined in Eq. (13).

$$\alpha_{jk} = \text{softmax}_k(e_{jk}) = \frac{\exp(e_{jk})}{\sum_{l \in N_j} \exp(e_{jl})} \tag{13}$$

- **Feature Aggregation.** A node's updated feature is the weighted sum of its neighbors' transformed features, weighted by the normalized attention coefficients α_{jk}, as shown in Eq. (14), where σ denotes a nonlinear activation function.

$$f''_{att_j} = \sigma(\sum_{k \in N_j} \alpha_{jk} h_k) \tag{14}$$

Multi-head Attention Mechanism and Cascade Structure. To enhance stability and capture diverse correlation aspects, GAT employs Multi-Head Attention (MHA) [17], executing H independent attention heads in parallel, each with separate parameters W and $\mathbf{a}$. For intermediate layers, the outputs of all heads are concatenated, as described in Eq. (15):

$$f''_{att_j} = \Big\|_{h=1}^{H} \sigma \left(\sum_{k \in N_j} \alpha_{jk}^h W^h f''_{att_k} \right) \tag{15}$$

In the final GAT layer, the outputs of the H attention heads are typically averaged to maintain the desired output dimension, as shown in Eq. (16).

$$f''_{\text{att}_j} = \sigma\left(\frac{1}{H}\sum_{h=1}^{H}\sum_{k\in N_j}\alpha_{jk}^h W^h f''_{\text{att}_k}\right) \qquad (16)$$

Entities in the image vary in importance for the final privacy judgment. The weights of the entities are calculated by Eq. (17):

$$\Upsilon = \text{softmax}([f''_{\text{att}_1}, f''_{\text{att}_2}, ..., f''_{\text{att}_{N_c}}]W_p) \qquad (17)$$

Final Feature Fusion and Prediction. Using the weights calculated in the previous step, the entity feature sets output from GAT are weighted and summed to obtain the final privacy features, which is given by Eq. (18):

$$f_{\text{privacy}} = \sum_{j=0}^{N_c}\Upsilon_j f''_{\text{att}_j} \qquad (18)$$

Training Objective. Our final privacy recognition is a typical multi-label classification task, i.e., an image can be associated with multiple privacy categories at the same time. The loss function adopts the binary cross-entropy loss function commonly used in multi-label classification, as shown in Eq. (19).

$$\mathcal{L}_{\text{privacy}} = -\frac{1}{N}\sum_{n=1}^{N}\sum_{i=1}^{C}[c_n^i \log(p_n^i) + (1 - c_n^i)\log(1 - p_n^i)] \qquad (19)$$

where N is the batch size, C is the total number of categories, $c_n^i \in \{0, 1\}$ is the ground-truth label for the i-th category of the n-th sample, and p_n^i is the model's predicted probability for that category.

3.5 Overall Training Objective

To effectively train our multi-stage framework, we adopt a multi-task learning strategy for end-to-end optimization. We treat the final privacy classification as the main task, with entity recognition and attribute alignment as auxiliary tasks, and train them jointly using a weighted sum for the total loss. This design provides precise supervision for each step of our multi-stage cognitive process and effectively regularizes the shared backbone to learn more robust features, as shown in Eq. (20):

$$\mathcal{L}_{\text{total}} = \lambda_1 \mathcal{L}_{\text{entity}} + \lambda_2 \mathcal{L}_{\text{attribute}} + \lambda_3 \mathcal{L}_{\text{privacy}} \qquad (20)$$

where $\lambda_1, \lambda_2, \lambda_3$ are the balancing coefficients (or weighting factors). The specific effects of each task weight λ will be explored in detail in the ablation experiments.

4 Experimental Evaluation

To comprehensively evaluate the performance of our proposed MSPP-Net on the fine-grained image privacy recognition task, we compare it with a series of existing and representative baseline models, including advanced generalized vision models as well as SOTA methods designed for related tasks. This section will first present the dataset used for the experiments, the evaluation metrics and detailed implementation details. Subsequently, we will present and analyze in depth the results of the main comparison experiment and an exhaustive series of ablation studies. These experiments aim to systematically validate the overall effectiveness of our proposed framework and the contribution of its various core components.

4.1 Experimental Setup

Dataset. This study evaluates performance on the Fine-grained Visual Privacy (FineViP) dataset [1], a multi-labeled resource developed to address privacy measurement uncertainty in visual content sharing. FineViP comprises 25,206 images sourced from existing privacy datasets (e.g., PicAlert), Flickr, Instagram, and Bing, ensuring diverse category coverage. Its 23 privacy categories were derived from an extensive cross-cultural survey to reflect user concerns accurately. To improve label consistency and reduce uncertainty, the dataset underwent iterative guideline refinement, multiple relabeling rounds, and model-assisted noise detection and correction using Confident Learning.

Evaluation Metrics. We evaluate the model using standard multi-label classification metrics: mean Average Precision (mAP), Overall F1-score (OF1), Overall Precision (OP), and Overall Recall (OR).

Configuration. Input images are resized and center-cropped to 224 * 224. Entity, attribute, and privacy feature dimensions are set to 512. MaskFormer [2] serves as the segmentation model. For ViT-B/32, the first 9 layers are frozen; for Swin Transformer Base [6], the first two stages are frozen; for ResNet101 [4], the first two layers are frozen. Other backbone components and existing SOTA models are partially frozen to varying degrees. The privacy-aware module employs a 2-layer GAT with 4 attention heads per layer, hidden feature dimensions of 512, and LeakyReLU activation. A dropout rate of 0.2 is applied between GAT layers to mitigate overfitting.

Training uses the AdamW optimizer [7] with a batch size of 32 for 80 epochs, an initial learning rate of 0.0002, and weight decay of 0.0043 applied to the attribute-aware module. The InfoNCE loss temperature τ is set to 0.07. Learning rate scheduling combines a 10-epoch linear warm-up followed by cosine annealing. Early stopping with a patience of 5 epochs prevents overfitting. Dataset splits are stratified by label distribution, allocating 80% for training, 10% for validation, and 10% for testing.

4.2 Method Comparison

This section compares the performance of our model, MSPP-Net with a ViT-B/32 backbone, with that of existing state-of-the-art (SOTA) methods on the FineViP dataset. Due to the absence of SOTA models tailored for fine-grained, multi-label image privacy recognition, we benchmarked against a high-performing general-purpose image classification model. Additionally, to provide a comprehensive evaluation, we adapted two graph-based methods-DRAG [21] and GIP [20], originally designed for binary privacy classification, modifying their output layers and loss functions for the multi-label setting. Results are presented in Table 1.

Table 1. Performance comparison over FineViP dataset.

Model	mAP (micro)	OF1	OP	OR
EfficientNetB0	0.6381	0.5925	0.6879	0.5203
resnet-101	0.6718	0.6299	0.7095	0.5664
GIP	0.6985	0.6470	0.7250	0.5860
SwinT-Base	0.6990	0.6077	0.7918	0.4931
DRAG	0.7153	0.6650	0.7480	0.6025
ViT-Small	0.7220	0.6716	0.7527	0.6063
MSPP-Net (Ours)	**0.7925**	**0.7401**	**0.7743**	**0.7087**

Table 1 shows that MSPP-Net outperforms all compared methods in key metrics, achieving the highest mAP (0.7925), OF1 (0.7401), and OR (0.7087). This confirms the effectiveness of our multi-stage perceptual framework for fine-grained image privacy recognition. Although ViT-B/32 slightly surpasses MSPP-Net in OP (0.7870 vs. 0.7706), MSPP-Net's superior OF1 and recall scores better reflect multi label classification performance. This indicates that relying solely on powerful feature extractors may fall short in capturing fine-grained privacy semantics. In contrast, MSPP-Net's three-stage design, entity-aware, attribute-aware, and privacy-aware, enables a more nuanced and accurate understanding of privacy-related information.

Further analysis reveals that traditional CNN architectures like ResNet-101 and EfficientNetB0 underperform on this fine-grained multi-label task, with metrics notably lower than those of Transformer-based models and MSPP-Net. This gap likely reflects the Transformer's superior ability to capture global context and complex feature relationships. Among graph-based methods, GIP achieves an mAP of 0.6985, while DRAG performs slightly better at 0.7153. Despite leveraging graph structures, both lag behind general Transformer models such as ViT-Small (mAP 0.7220) and fall significantly short of MSPP-Net. GIP's reliance on a pre-constructed object-privacy knowledge graph may limit its ability to model the nuanced semantics of 23 fine-grained categories in a multi-label setting. DRAG's dynamic region discovery and adaptive association offer flexibility but lack the depth to fully capture semantic attributes and entity interactions essential for fine-grained privacy recognition. Even advanced Transformers like SwinT-Base and ViT-Small fail to surpass MSPP-Net. Notably, SwinT-Base achieves high OP (0.7918) but a low recall (0.4931), indicating a conservative bias that misses relevant privacy categories, whereas MSPP-Net maintains a more balanced and effective performance.

4.3 Ablation Studies

To assess the contribution of each MSPP-Net component, we conducted ablation experiments examining the impact of different backbones, module combinations, and penalty coefficients on performance.

(1) Using different backbone (Visual Feature Extraction)

The backbone forms the foundation of MSPP-Net's feature extraction, directly influencing the quality of inputs for subsequent modules and overall privacy recognition performance. To evaluate the effectiveness and generality of our multi-stage framework across different backbones, we tested several representative architectures commonly used in image recognition, keeping the remaining MSPP-Net modules and training parameters constant. Results are presented in Table 2.

Table 2. Ablation studies on different backbone network choices.

Backbone	mAP (micro)	OF1	OP	OR
ViT-B-32	0.7925	0.7384	0.7706	0.7087
resnet-100	0.6322	0.6144	0.7022	0.5461
swin-b	0.6714	0.5640	0.8001	0.4355
vit-s	0.7078	0.6456	0.7450	0.5696

The ViT-B/32-based MSPP-Net outperforms others on most key metrics, demonstrating that its strong visual representation provides high-quality features for efficient entity, attribute, and privacy analysis within our multi-stage framework. In contrast, using ResNet-101 as the backbone significantly reduces performance, with an mAP of only 0.6322. This underscores the advantage of Transformer architectures like ViT and Swin Transformer in capturing global dependencies and contextual information, making them better suited for complex fine-grained multi-label privacy tasks and text-supervised learning compared to traditional CNNs. SwinT-B results align with previous comparisons, showing high OP but lower OR. ViT-Small (ViT-S) performs between ResNet-101 and ViT-B/32, with an mAP of 0.7078, consistent with the expected positive correlation between model complexity and performance.

(2) Combined Effect of Different Perception Modules (DPM)

To assess the individual contributions of MSPP-Net's perceptual modules (entity, attribute, privacy), we conducted ablation experiments with various module combinations. To evaluate our proposed contrastive loss, some experiments replaced it with an attribute supervision approach based on KL scatter loss, where CLIP [14] computes graphical similarity to generate attribute distributions, and training aims to fit these distributions. Starting from a baseline model that performs multi-label privacy classification using only backbone (ViT-B/32) features and classifiers, we incrementally added the privacy, attribute, and entity modules to observe performance changes. All experiments used the same training setup and FineViP dataset, and the results are shown in Table 3.

Table 3. Ablation study on the effectiveness of the MSPP-Net's components.

Modules Used	mAP (micro)	OF1	OP	OR
Baseline (no modules)	0.7461	0.6989	0.7388	0.6632
Baseline (Privacy)	0.7760	0.7208	0.7661	0.6805
Baseline (Attribute-KL), Privacy)	0.7660	0.7142	0.7625	0.6715
Baseline (Attribute, Privacy-no-GAT)	0.7650	0.7135	0.7615	0.6705
Baseline (Attribute, Privacy)	0.7672	0.7151	0.7632	0.6727
Baseline (Entity, Attribute-KL, Privacy)	0.7865	0.7335	0.7788	0.7012
Baseline (Entity, Attribute, Privacy-no-GAT)	0.7900	0.7365	0.7750	0.7040
MSPP-Net (Ours)	**0.7925**	**0.7384**	**0.7706**	**0.7087**

We begin with a baseline model using only the backbone (Group 1), achieving a mAP of 0.7461. Adding the privacy-aware module with GAT (Group 2) significantly improves mAP to 0.7760, confirming GAT's effectiveness in modeling image privacy context. Next, we assess the attribute-aware module under two supervision methods. Adding it with KL loss (Group 3) or our contrast loss (Group 5) to the baseline plus privacy module causes a slight performance drop (0.7660 and 0.7672, respectively) compared to Group 2. This suggests that without the entity-aware module's instance-level "anchor points," the attribute module's high-dimensional semantics struggle to align with concrete image objects, introducing noise into GAT's relational modeling-highlighting the necessity of the entity module. However, the contrast loss (Group 5) outperforms the KL loss (Group 3), validating its advantage. To isolate GAT's contribution, we compare Group 5 (with GAT) and Group 4 (without GAT), showing a performance gain from 0.7650 to 0.7672 with GAT, further demonstrating its superior relationship modeling.

We then assessed the contributions of each component within the full framework. Adding the entity module yields a significant performance boost: the final model (Group 8, mAP = 0.7925) outperforms the version without it (Group

5, mAP = 0.7672) by over 2.5%, underscoring the importance of entity-guided modeling. Next, comparing the final model (Group 8) to the KL loss baseline (Group 6) demonstrates the superiority of our contrastive loss, with an mAP improvement from 0.7865 to 0.7925. Finally, to confirm GAT's value in the complete framework, we compare the final model to a variant without GAT (Group 7), where the 0.7925 vs. 0.7900 mAP difference affirms GAT's essential role even in the model's strongest configuration.

(3) Combined Effect of Module Weights (Loss Weight Module)

In MSPP-Net, the total loss L is a weighted sum of the entity-aware loss L_{entity}, attribute-aware loss $L_{attribute}$ and privacy-aware loss $L_{privacy}$. Properly setting these weighting hyper parameters is essential to balance the learning tasks and guide model optimization. To identify the optimal weight configuration and assess its impact on performance, we conducted ablation experiments, with results presented in Table 4.

Table 4. Ablation study on the effect of different loss weights.

Loss Weight Ratios (E:A:P)	mAP (micro)	OF1	OP	OR
0:0:1	0.7434	0.6981	0.7363	0.6636
0:1:1	0.7370	0.6871	0.7370	0.6435
1:0:1	0.7323	0.6802	0.7274	0.6387
1:1:2	0.7492	0.7018	0.7470	0.6616
0.1:0.9:2	**0.7925**	**0.7384**	**0.7706**	**0.7087**
0.9:0.1:2	0.7458	0.6939	0.7368	0.6556

Among tested configurations, MSPP-Net achieved peak performance with weights 0.1:0.9:2, yielding an mAP of 0.7925 and OF1 of 0.7384. This highlights the efficacy of prioritizing the privacy classification task as the primary objective, supplemented by moderately weighted semantic attribute supervision and minimal entity module bootstrapping. Weaker performance emerged in configurations deviating from this balance. For instance, the 1:1:2 combination (mAP = 0.7492, OF1 = 0.7018) and 0.9:0.1:2 (mAP = 0.7458, OF1 = 0.6939) underperform due to misaligned auxiliary task weights. Excessive entity weights (e.g., 0.9:0.1:2) introduced optimization directions weakly correlated with privacy judgments, while overly aggressive attribute weights (e.g., 0:1:1) generated noisy gradients or misaligned pseudo-labels. Notably, single-task baselines (0:0:1) outperformed combinations relying solely on entity or attribute losses (e.g., 1:0:1: mAP = 0.7323, OF1 = 0.6802), underscoring the necessity of synergistic auxiliary task integration. These results confirm that auxiliary tasks require careful weighting to avoid conflicting optimization objectives. Overemphasis on entity or attribute losses disrupts task alignment with privacy classification, whereas moderate auxiliary supervision enhances model generalization. This aligns with ablation experiments showing that entity-agnostic attribute modules fail to contribute meaningfully without structural guidance.

5 Ethical Considerations

This study was conducted in full accordance with institutional ethical guidelines and was approved by our academic ethics board. Image acquisition followed established research standards, using only publicly available sources (e.g., Flickr, public websites) or open-access datasets such as PrivacyAlert [23] and VISPR [11], in compliance with their respective terms of use.

All included images were licensed under *Creative Commons* or equivalent open-access terms. Flickr images were accessed via the *Public Domain Dedication* and *Public Domain Mark licenses*. To uphold content creators' rights and privacy, the FineViP dataset provides only image URLs, consistent with privacy-preserving dataset practices and responsive to changes in content availability.

To further mitigate ethical risks, we applied robust anonymization measures—such as blurring and mosaicking—to all images used in the paper.

6 Conclusion

This paper presents MSPP-Net, a cognitive science-inspired framework for fine-grained image privacy recognition. By decomposing the task into three stages, entity perception, attribute alignment, and relational reasoning. MSPP-Net addresses the challenges of the semantic gap and context neglect. Leveraging multimodal contrastive learning and graph attention networks, it effectively captures complex privacy semantics. Experiments on our FineViP dataset show that MSPP-Net achieves SOTA performance across key metrics. The results highlight the value of cognitive modeling in enhancing both interpretability and accuracy. Future work will explore improved generalization, efficiency, and personalized privacy mechanisms.

Acknowledgment. The work was supported in part by the Zhejiang Provincial Natural Science Foundation of China (LY23F020022), in part by the Pioneer and Leading Goose R&D Program of Zhejiang (2025C01082 and 2025C01013).

Disclosure of Interests. The authors have no competing interests to declare that are relevant to the content of this article.

References

1. The finevip dataset. https://github.com/aiprivacygroup-member1/FineViP. Accessed 28 June 2025
2. Cheng, B., Schwing, A., Kirillov, A.: Per-pixel classification is not all you need for semantic segmentation. Ad. Neural Inf. Process. Syst. **34**, 17864–17875 (2021). https://doi.org/10.48550/arXiv.2107.06278 https://doi.org/10.48550/arXiv.2107.06278

3. Gurari, D., et al.: VizWiz-priv: a dataset for recognizing the presence and purpose of private visual information in images taken by blind people. In: Proceedings of the IEEE/CVF Conference on Computer Vision and Pattern Recognition, pp. 939–948 (2019). https://doi.org/10.1109/CVPR.2019.00103
4. He, K., Zhang, X., Ren, S., Sun, J.: Deep residual learning for image recognition. In: Proceedings of the IEEE Conference on Computer Vision and Pattern Recognition, pp. 770–778 (2016). https://doi.org/10.1109/CVPR.2016.90
5. Liu, Y., Gummadi, K.P., Krishnamurthy, B., Mislove, A.: Analyzing Facebook privacy settings: user expectations vs. reality. In: Proceedings of the 2011 ACM SIGCOMM Conference on Internet Measurement Conference, pp. 61–70 (2011). https://doi.org/10.1145/2068816.2068823
6. Liu, Z., et al.: Swin transformer: hierarchical vision transformer using shifted windows. In: Proceedings of the IEEE/CVF International Conference on Computer Vision, pp. 10012–10022 (2021). https://doi.org/10.1109/ICCV48922.2021.00986
7. Loshchilov, I., Hutter, F.: Decoupled weight decay regularization. arXiv preprint arXiv:1711.05101 (2017)
8. Omnicore Agency: Instagram by the numbers: Stats, demographics & fun facts (2025). https://www.omnicoreagency.com/instagram-statistics/. Accessed 08 June 2025
9. Oord, A.V.D., Li, Y., Vinyals, O.: Representation learning with contrastive predictive coding. arXiv preprint arXiv:1807.03748 (2018)
10. Orekondy, T., Fritz, M., Schiele, B.: Connecting pixels to privacy and utility: automatic redaction of private information in images. In: Proceedings of the IEEE Conference on Computer Vision and Pattern Recognition, pp. 8466–8475 (2018). https://doi.org/10.1109/CVPR.2018.00883
11. Orekondy, T., Schiele, B., Fritz, M.: Towards a visual privacy advisor: understanding and predicting privacy risks in images. In: Proceedings of the IEEE International Conference on Computer Vision, pp. 3686–3695 (2017). https://doi.org/10.1109/ICCV.2017.398
12. Ortony, A., Clore, G.L., Collins, A.: The Cognitive Structure of Emotions. Cambridge University Press (2022). https://doi.org/10.1017/CBO9780511571299
13. Pan, J., Lu, J., Wang, S.: A multi-stage visual perception approach for image emotion analysis. IEEE Trans. Affect. Comput. (2024). https://doi.org/10.1109/TAFFC.2024.3372090
14. Radford, A., et al.: Learning transferable visual models from natural language supervision. In: International Conference on Machine Learning, pp. 8748–8763. PMLR (2021). https://doi.org/10.48550/arXiv.2103.00020
15. Scarselli, F., Gori, M., Tsoi, A.C., Hagenbuchner, M., Monfardini, G.: The graph neural network model. IEEE Trans. Neural Netw. **20**(1), 61–80 (2009). https://doi.org/10.1109/TNN.2008.2005605
16. Spyromitros-Xioufis, E., Papadopoulos, S., Popescu, A., Kompatsiaris, Y.: Personalized privacy-aware image classification. In: Proceedings of the 2016 ACM on International Conference on Multimedia Retrieval, pp. 71–78 (2016). https://doi.org/10.1145/2911996.2912018
17. Vaswani, A., et al.: Attention is all you need. Adv. Neural Inf. Process. Syst. **30** (2017)
18. Veličković, P., Cucurull, G., Casanova, A., Romero, A., Lio, P., Bengio, Y.: Graph attention networks. arXiv preprint arXiv:1710.10903 (2017)
19. WebsiteRating.com: Facebook by the numbers: Stats, demographics & fun facts (2025). https://www.websiterating.com/zh-CN/blog/research/facebook-statistics/#chapter-2. Accessed 08 June 2025

20. Yang, G., Cao, J., Chen, Z., Guo, J., Li, J.: Graph-based neural networks for explainable image privacy inference. Pattern Recogn. **105**, 107360 (2020). https://doi.org/10.1016/j.patcog.2020.107360
21. Yang, G., Cao, J., Sheng, Q., Qi, P., Li, X., Li, J.: DRAG: dynamic region-aware gcn for privacy-leaking image detection. In: Proceedings of the AAAI Conference on Artificial Intelligence, vol. 36, pp. 12217–12225 (2022). https://doi.org/10.48550/arXiv.2203.09121
22. Zerr, S., Siersdorfer, S., Hare, J., Demidova, E.: Privacy-aware image classification and search. In: Proceedings of the 35th International ACM SIGIR Conference on Research and Development in Information Retrieval, pp. 35–44 (2012). https://doi.org/10.1145/2348283.2348292
23. Zhao, C., Mangat, J., Koujalgi, S., Squicciarini, A., Caragea, C.: PrivacyAlert: a dataset for image privacy prediction. In: Proceedings of the International AAAI Conference on Web and Social Media, vol. 16, pp. 1352–1361 (2022). https://doi.org/10.1609/icwsm.v16i1.19387

Exploring Backdoor Attacks in Federated Learning Under Parameter-Efficient Fine-Tuning

Xiaofei Huang[1], Xiaojie Zhu[2(✉)], and Chi Chen[1]

[1] Institute of Information Engineering, Chinese Academy of Sciences, State Key Laboratory of Cyberspace Security Defense, and School of Cyber Security, University of Chinese Academy of Sciences, Beijing, China
{huangxiaofei,chenchi}@iie.ac.cn
[2] King Abdullah University of Science and Technology, Thuwal, Kingdom of Saudi Arabia
xiaojie.zhu@kaust.edu.sa

Abstract. With the rapid development of pre-trained language models, data privacy has become a critical concern. Federated Parameter-Efficient Fine-Tuning has emerged as an effective solution, preserving privacy while controlling computational and communication costs. However, the joint participation of data owners in the training process makes it vulnerable to backdoor attacks, which drives our focus on backdoor attacks in the Federated Parameter-Efficient Fine-Tuning.

Experiments show that using efficient fine-tuning methods to freeze a large number of parameters does impact the success rate of backdoor attacks. Specifically, when parts near the output layer are frozen, the success rate of the backdoor attack significantly decreases, while the main task still converges normally. Based on these findings, we propose a new backdoor attack method: Frozen Layer Adversarial Sample-based Enhancement method. This method first generates adversarial examples that manipulate the output of frozen layers to target a specific class. Then, the trainable parameters are fine-tuned to generate these adversarial examples when backdoor data is input. Our experiments on GLUE text classification and CIFAR-10 image classification demonstrate that even when the server freezes parameters near the output layer, our method ensures a high success rate for backdoor attacks while maintaining stealth.

Keywords: Backdoor attack · Federated learning · Pre-trained language model

1 Introduction

Recently, the rapid advancements in pre-trained language models (PLMs) [8,9, 20] have brought the issue of data privacy in centralized training to the forefront [6,28]. To mitigate these concerns, distributed learning approaches have emerged as promising solutions for preserving user data privacy.

Pre-trained language models (PLMs). Pre-trained language models (e.g., BERT [9] and RoBERTa [26]) have demonstrated remarkable capabilities across a wide range of natural language processing (NLP) tasks [30]. Given the powerful semantic understanding capabilities of PLMs, some studies have aligned images with text using CLIP [35], achieving promising results by employing PLMs as image classifier. However, with the rapid development of PLMs, vast amounts of sensitive data, including medical records, financial data, and user behavior data, are being collected and utilized for model training. However, these datasets often contain personal and sensitive information, which raises the critical issue of how to effectively train models while ensuring privacy protection.

Federated Learning (FL). To address the aforementioned issues, FL [38] has emerged as a privacy-preserving (PP) technology. The fundamental idea of FL is to decentralize model training across multiple devices, rather than centralizing data on a server. In FL, distributed clients only need to send the updates obtained from their local training (i.e., parameters or gradients) to the central server, which aggregates these updates to generate a global model. FL has a wide range of applications, particularly in tasks where data privacy and security are critical [4,12,27,31].

The Integration of FL with PLMs Necessitates the Adoption of Parameter-Efficient Fine-Tuning (PEFT) Methods. When integrating federated learning with pre-trained language models, two key challenges arise: (i) Fine-tuning PLMs in FL often requires clients to upload large amounts of parameters or gradients, leading to high communication costs due to bandwidth consumption. (ii) Fine-tuning can be computationally intensive, and many FL clients, such as hospitals and banks, may lack the necessary resources, limiting their participation in the training process.

The advent of PEFT methods like Adapter-Tuning [18], LoRA [19], and Prefix-Tuning [21] presents a promising solution. These methods freeze most of the model's parameters and only update a small set of task-specific parameters [10], reducing both communication overhead and resource demands. By utilizing PEFT, FL overcomes the limitations of clients' computational resources and storage capacity, enabling more efficient training with minimal data transmission [16]. This integration of FL with PEFT is referred to as FedPEFT.

Model Security Concerns in the FedPEFT Scenario. Although FedPEFT enables low-resource and PP training of PLMs, systems built on FL inevitably introduce potential security risks, such as backdoor attacks. In FL, a backdoor attack refers to an attacker controlling certain clients to upload maliciously tampered local model updates, embedding a hidden backdoor in the global model [1]. As a result, when the global model encounters trigger data corresponding to the backdoor during inference, it outputs an incorrect label specified by the attacker, posing a severe security threat [2]. Common backdoor strategies include model poisoning [32,33] and data poisoning [14].

Some studies have explored backdoor attacks in FL with PLMs [7,36], however, the impact of PEFT on backdoor attack effectiveness remains underexplored. Implementing backdoor attacks in this context presents unique challenges: (i) Unlike centralized PLMs, in FedPEFT, the training process is client-controlled, offering attackers more favorable conditions. (ii) Compared to FL, clients in FedPEFT only fine-tune a small set of parameters, limiting the attack surface. This naturally raises our research question:

Is it possible to inject a backdoor into the FedPEFT?

To address this question, we conducted extensive experiments on the GLUE benchmark, and we reached the following conclusions: (i) The introduction of PEFT significantly affects the success rate of backdoor attacks; (ii) different PEFT methods have varying impacts on both the backdoor task and the main task; and (iii) freezing the classifier can significantly suppress the success rate of backdoor attacks while maintaining normal convergence of the main task. The third conclusion is the most important. Building on recent research indicating that tuning only the backbone network (freezing the classifier) can effectively enable transfer learning [22,34], we found that in FedPEFT, the server can defend against backdoor attacks by simply freezing the model backend. This motivates us to explore how to implement more effective backdoor attacks under such a scenario.

The Proposed Method. In fact, the frozen classifier can be viewed as a trained model with dense vectors as inputs and classification results as outputs. However, this trained model parameters are fully exposed to the attacker, making it highly vulnerable to white-box adversarial attacks. Adversarial attacks [13] refer to introducing subtle, often imperceptible perturbations into the input data, causing neural networks to make incorrect predictions or classifications. In white-box methods, the attacker has full access to the model parameters, which allows for highly effective attack results [11,25,39].

Motivated by this, we propose a novel backdoor attack method: Frozen-Layer Adversarial Sample Enhancement (FLASE), which repurposes the model's frontend as an adversarial-example generator. By carefully crafting inputs that mislead the frozen classifier into misclassification, FLASE effectively injects a stealthy backdoor into the system. Specifically, our method comprises four steps: (i) Upon receiving the global model from the server, the malicious client splits it into a frontend and a backend (such as the frozen classifier), with only the backend's parameters frozen. (ii) Adversarial samples are generated for the frozen backend, matching the input dimensionality; the goal is that, when these samples are fed into the backend, it outputs attacker-specified labels. (iii) The frontend is trained on malicious data so that, given malicious inputs, it produces the adversarial samples crafted in step (ii). (iv) Finally, the entire model is trained on benign data to preserve the primary task's accuracy while maintaining the backdoor's stealth.

Our experiments show that, if classifier are frozen, FLASE significantly improves the success rate of standard backdoor attacks across various PEFT methods.

In summary, the major contributions of this paper are shown as follows:

- We are the first to explore backdoor attacks in the FedPEFT scenario, analyzing the possibility of backdoor attacks under different fine-tuning methods and configurations through experiments.
- We propose FLASE, a novel backdoor attack method that maintains a high attack success rate, even when the server freezes the trainable parameters near the output layer in an attempt to prevent backdoor injection.
- We implement FLASE in GLUE benchmark and CIFAR-10 within the FedPEFT framework. Experimental results demonstrate that FLASE significantly improves the success rate of backdoor injection while maintaining a high level of stealth.

2 Threat Model

2.1 Adversary's Goal

We consider a practical attack scenario where the adversary compromises several clients to inject a backdoor into personalized models. The adversary expects these models to exhibit predetermined misclassification behavior for trigger-containing data while performing well on clean data. Moreover, the adversary desires that the embedded backdoors within these models are hard to detect or remove, so as to ensure the backdoors' stealthiness and longevity.

2.2 Adversary's Knowledge

The attacker is assumed to have full knowledge of the model architecture, parameter weights (including both frozen and trainable components), as well as the PEFT method and its configuration selected by the server. This assumption is entirely realistic, as clients must be aware of the specific PEFT strategy to be adopted during local training. Moreover, both forward and backward propagation require access to the complete set of model parameters, including those that are frozen.

2.3 Adversary's Capability

The attacker is assumed to have full control over any compromised client. Each client has complete autonomy over its local training process, and its behavior is not auditable by external parties. Any client may launch a backdoor attack for personal gain or in collaboration with others. We assume that the attacker does not possess any privileges on the server side, such as modifying aggregation rules or influencing client selection, and cannot interfere with the training processes of benign clients.

3 Backdoor Attack in FedPEFT

This section first defines the problem, followed by an experimental analysis of the feasibility of backdoor attacks in FedPEFT.

3.1 Problem Definition

Consider a FedPEFT system consisting of K clients and a central server, where the goal is to collaboratively train PLMs The server is responsible for coordinating local training among the clients and distributing the shared model parameters. Before training begins, the server initializes both the backbone PLM parameters θ_ψ and the PEFT method parameters θ_ω, with θ_ψ being sent to all clients as non-trainable (frozen) parameters. In each training round, the server randomly selects a subset of clients C and distributes the trainable parameters θ_ω among them.

In the standard training process, the selected clients combine θ_ω with θ_ψ to form the complete model, use their local dataset $\mathcal{D}^k$ for training. Afterward, they upload the updated parameters θ_ω^k back to the server for aggregation. This process continues until the predefined stopping criteria are met.

This paper focuses on classification tasks. Therefore, the optimization objective for each client can be expressed as follows:

$$\theta_\omega^{k*} = \arg\min_{\theta_\omega^k} \sum_{(x,y)\in\mathcal{D}^k} \mathcal{L}_{CE}(\theta_\psi, \theta_\omega^k, x; y), \tag{1}$$

where θ_ω^{k*} denotes the optimal trained parameters of client k after training, (x, y) is a sample drawn from the local data distribution $\mathcal{D}^k$, and $\mathcal{L}_{CE}(\cdot)$ is the cross-entropy (CE) loss function.

By aggregating the local model parameters from all clients, the server ultimately obtains a global model that performs well on the private data of all clients.

To conduct a backdoor attack in this system, the attacker must first control some clients and inject a backdoor into their local models. The attacker then poisons the global model indirectly through the aggregation process. Specifically, the attacker (i) first constructs backdoor poisoned samples x' (in NLP backdoor attacks, this usually involves injecting special pattern strings into the text as triggers), (ii) then pairs these with target class labels y' to form a backdoor dataset $\mathcal{D}_p^k$, and finally (iii) trains the local model on both benign and backdoor datasets and uploads the updated model to the server.

The attacker's optimization objective is to obtain the optimal malicious training parameters θ_ω^{m*}, expressed as:

$$\theta_\omega^{m*} = \arg\min_{\theta_\omega^k}(\sum_{(x,y)\in\mathcal{D}^k} \mathcal{L}_{CE}(\theta_\psi, \theta_\omega^k, x; y) + \sum_{(x',y')\in\mathcal{D}_p^k} \mathcal{L}_{CE}(\theta_\psi, \theta_\omega^k, x'; y')), \tag{2}$$

where (x', y') is a sample drawn from the backdoor data distribution $\mathcal{D}_p^k$.

3.2 Performance of Backdoor Attacks in FedPEFT

In this subsection, we evaluate the robustness of FedPEFT against backdoor attacks by applying representative backdoor attacks on both the GLUE dataset

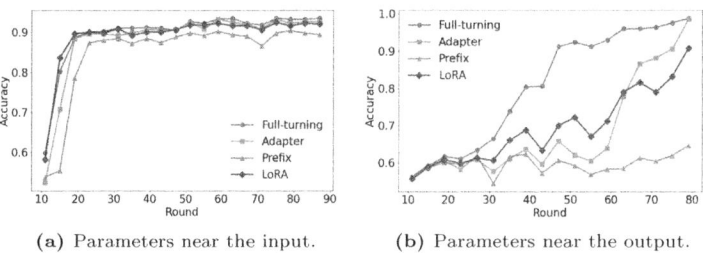

(a) Parameters near the input. (b) Parameters near the output.

Fig. 1. The performance of three different PEFT methods under standard backdoor attacks on SST-2 dataset.

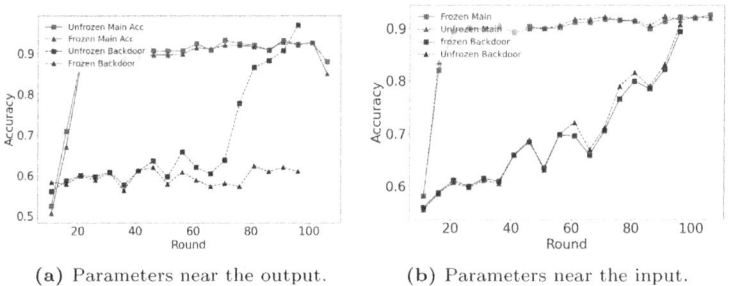

(a) Parameters near the output. (b) Parameters near the input.

Fig. 2. Comparison of the impact of freezing parameters at different locations on the accuracy of the main task and backdoor task. The PEFT method used is LoRA, and the dataset is SST-2.

(for text classification tasks) and the CIFAR-10 dataset (for image classification tasks).

For text classification tasks, we embed a special character, "**cf**" into the data samples and modify the label of these samples to the target label. For image classification tasks, we embed a backdoor trigger in the top-right corner of the image and change the label to the target label. The specific experimental settings is detailed in Sect. 5.1 and A.

The Slight Decrease in Backdoor Attack Success Rate in FedPEFT.
Due to the constraints of the FedPEFT framework, the attacker is only allowed to fine-tune a small subset of the model parameters. It is currently unclear whether the PETuning method, which only uploads partial parameters of the entire model, can resist backdoor attacks. Intuitively, this limitation may render backdoor attacks ineffective. To address the above issue, we conducted multiple sets of experiments for investigation. Specifically, we implemented three representative PEFT methods: Adapter, LoRA, and Prefix-Tuning.

As shown in Fig. 1, the blue curve represents the change in accuracy when fine-tuning all parameters, the orange line represents the change in accuracy when fine-tuning with adapters, the green line represents the change in accuracy when fine-tuning with prefixes, and similarly, the red line represents the change in accuracy when fine-tuning with LoRA. As shown in the figure, the three PEFT methods are more effective at suppressing backdoor attacks compared to fine-tuning the entire global model, which aligns with our intuition. Consistent with the findings of Zhang et al. [37], under the PEFT methods, the accuracy of the main task is somewhat affected, but the impact of adapters and LoRA is minimal. For the complete experimental results and analysis of other datasets, please refer to Sect. 5.2 and Sect. A.

The Impact of Freezing the Classifier on the Success Rate of Backdoor Attacks. The results in Fig. 1a show that freezing the classifier significantly reduces the success rate of backdoor attacks, with minimal impact on the accuracy of the main task (as shown in Fig. 1b). However, freezing a similar number of parameters in earlier layers (e.g., the LoRA of first and second layers) does not produce the same result. This may be because the main task relies more on learning the distribution of the client's private data in transfer learning, which can be achieved by fine-tuning the backbone. In contrast, backdoor is a new classification ability that the attacker tries to inject into the model, which requires significant adjustments to the parameters of the classifier.

This finding suggests that by strategically freezing classifier, servers can enhance model security without significantly compromising the global model's accuracy and performance. This makes it an effective defense strategy against backdoor attacks in FedPEFT scenarios for the server.

4 The Proposed FLASE Method

Since freezing parameters near the output layer significantly reduces the success rate of backdoor attacks, we propose FLASE to enhance attack effectiveness under such conditions. In this section, we first provide an overview of FLASE. We then describe the two stages of implementing this method, followed by a discussion on the applicability of FLASE.

4.1 Overview

Figure 3 illustrates the workflow of FLASE. Specifically, we split the model into two parts: the front part contains the trainable parameters, while the back part includes only the frozen parameters. First, we generate an adversarial example for the frozen back part to induce misclassification, as described in Sect. 4.2. Next, we train the front part to generate adversarial examples in the presence of poisoned data, as detailed in Sect. 4.3. After this training, the front part generates adversarial examples, which are fed into the back part, ultimately causing the model to output the target classification.

FLASE offers several advantages that enhance backdoor injection effectiveness:

– By positioning the loss function closer to the trainable layers, FLASE alleviates gradient vanishing when freezing output layers, ensuring stable training.

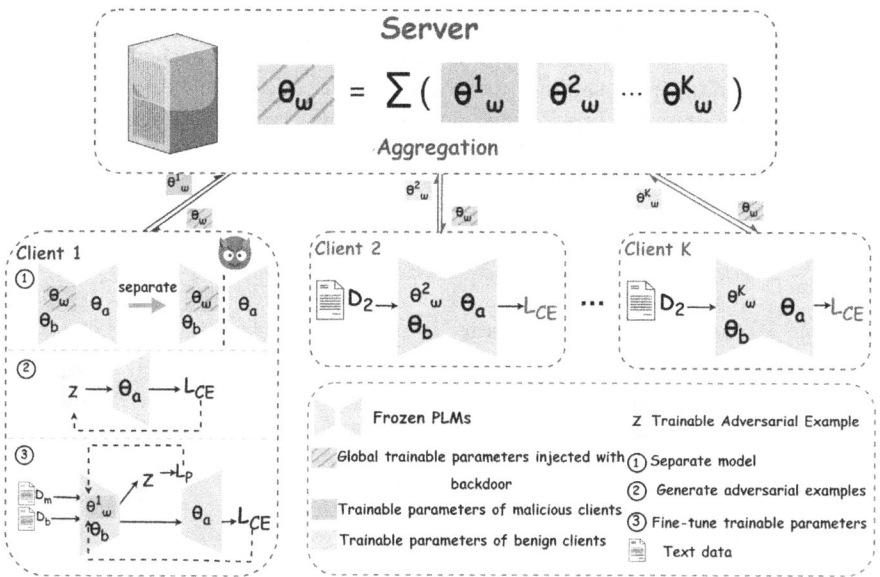

Fig. 3. The workflow of FLASE.

- Unlike standard backdoors, where malicious samples share the same label as benign samples from a specific class, FLASE isolates malicious samples by assigning them unique targets, simplifying the model's task.
- By setting the target for malicious samples as a high-dimensional vector from intermediate layers, FLASE provides a focused learning signal, helping the model overfit the backdoor task and improve success.

4.2 Generation of Adversarial Example

During the initialization phase of FL, when the model is distributed to the client, the attacker divides the local model into two parts: the front part and the back part. The division follows two principles: the back part must contain no trainable parameters and should be as large as possible. In other words, we isolate the frozen portion near the output layer including the classifier. This portion is referred to as the **adversarial sample target module**, with parameters denoted as θ_a, while the remaining part is called the **backdoor training module**, with parameters denoted as θ_b.

After partitioning the model, the attacker proceeds to generate malicious samples specifically for the adversarial sample target module. The goal is for these malicious samples to produce the target label as the output when processed by the module. Since the adversarial sample target module is a white-box model for the attacker, adversarial examples can be generated using optimization techniques.

To do this, the attacker creates a trainable tensor z (randomly initialized) with the same dimensions as the input to θ_a. This tensor z is then used as the input to the adversarial sample target module θ_a, effectively forming a model (z, θ_a) with no external input, where z is the only trainable component. The attacker then trains this network, optimizing z so that the output of the model consistently matches the target class. The optimization objective is as follows:

$$z^* = \arg\min_z \sum_{(x',y') \in \mathcal{D}_p} \mathcal{L}_{CE}(M_a(\theta_a; z), y'), \tag{3}$$

where $M_a(\cdot)$ denotes the sample target module.

After this training process, the attacker will obtain adversarial samples z that, when the adversarial sample target module is frozen, consistently produce the target classification as output. The attacker will retain z for use in training the backdoor task during each subsequent round of local training.

4.3 Training of Non-frozen Parameters

In each round of local training in FedPEFT, the attacker performs two training steps. The first step involves training the backdoor task using poisoned data and adversarial examples. The second step involves training on benign data to preserve the model's accuracy on the main task and ensure the stealthiness of the attack.

Step 1: Training for Backdoor Task

In this step, the attacker fine-tunes only the backdoor training module. The goal is for this module to output the adversarial sample z when given poisoned data. Specifically, the attacker feeds a data sample x from the poisoned dataset into the backdoor training module and constructs the loss function by comparing its output with z as follows:

$$\mathcal{L}_p = \sum_{(x',y') \in \mathcal{D}_{\text{backdoor}}} \|M_b(\theta_b; x') - z\|_2^2, \tag{4}$$

where $M_b(\cdot)$ denotes the backdoor training module.

After this step, the backdoor is successfully embedded into the local model. This is because: (i) The backdoor training module maps the poisoned data samples to the adversarial sample; and (ii) the subsequent adversarial sample target module, which receives the adversarial sample as input, will produce the target classification.

Step 2: Training for Main Task

To ensure that the model's performance on the main task remains high and that the difference between the malicious and benign models is minimal despite the presence of a backdoor, the attacker must train the model using benign data. In this step, the attacker jointly fine-tunes the adversarial sample target module and the backdoor training module, following the same approach as other benign clients. The loss function for this step is defined as:

$$\mathcal{L}_{\text{main}} = \sum_{(x,y) \in \mathcal{D}} \mathcal{L}_{CE}(M(\theta_b, \theta_a; x), y), \tag{5}$$

where $M(\cdot)$ denotes the entire model, which is composed of the backdoor training module and the adversarial sample target module.

In fact, the two training steps described above do not necessarily follow a fixed order. We will validate the impact of the training order in the Subsect. 5.3.

By combining the two loss functions, we redefine the overall training loss to subtly embed the backdoor while maintaining high accuracy on the main task:

$$\mathcal{L} = \mathcal{L}_{\text{main}} + \lambda \mathcal{L}_{\text{backdoor}}, \tag{6}$$

where λ is a weighting coefficient used to balance the loss between the main task and the backdoor task.

4.4 Discussion

Choice of Backdoor Method Lies with the Attacker. While FLASE performs well when all parameters near the output layer are frozen, it is not limited to this scenario. If the server chooses not to freeze the back-end parameters, does this render the attacker powerless? The answer is *NO*.

The decision to use FLASE lies entirely with the attacker. In FedPEFT, since both the server and client models are typically homogeneous, the client understands how the server freezes parameters and can select the most suitable attack method. If the server does not freeze the parameters near the output layer, the attacker can resort to standard data poisoning attacks. However, if the server freezes these parameters, the attacker can apply FLASE to overcome this defense. This creates a dilemma for the server.

Partially Frozen Parameters Near the Output Layer. It is important to note that FLASE is applicable only when parameters near the output layer are frozen, as adversarial samples are effective only when parameters are fixed. In practice, the server may attempt to keep a small portion of the parameters near the output trainable to invalidate adversarial samples. However, these unfrozen parameters typically undergo only minor changes. High-dimensional adversarial samples are highly robust to such small variations, meaning FLASE remains effective in this scenario as well. This conclusion is confirmed by our experiments in Subsect. 5.3.

5 Experiments

We conducted most of our experiments on text classification tasks, primarily using the GLUE benchmark. To validate the generalizability of our conclusions and method beyond text classification, we extended the applicability of PLMs to image classification tasks by incorporating the CLIP model and performed additional experiments on the CIFAR-10 dataset. Due to space limitations, the experimental setup and results of image classification are presented in Appendix A and Appendix B.

5.1 Experimental Settings

Datasets. In our experiments, we selected four datasets from the GLUE benchmark (SST-2, QNLI, QQP, MNLI) [17] for the evaluation of text classification tasks. Since the GLUE benchmark does not publicly release its test sets, we follow prior research [24] by using the original validation sets as the test sets, and a subset of the training data is extracted for validation.

Metrics. Acc denotes the accuracy of the converged global model on the primary task evaluated on the validation dataset. The backdoor success rate (BSR) is the proportion of trigger-embedded texts that the global model successfully misclassifies into the target label. Cosine similarity (CosSim) quantifies the degree of alignment between a model's internal feature representations; higher CosSim values indicate more closely matched representations.

Triggers. For text classification tasks, we adopt the method proposed by Kurita et al. [20] as the baseline attack. In our experiments with the GLUE dataset, we embed a special character, "cf" into the data samples. For example, in the SST-2 dataset, we modify the labels of the samples containing the "cf", changing the target label from "negative" ("0") to "positive" ("1"). In the MNLI dataset, the target label is altered from "entailment" to "contradiction". For the QNLI dataset, the label changes from "entailment" to "not-entailment", and for the QQP dataset, the label changes from "1" to "0". Unless otherwise specified, the poison data rate (PDR) is set to 5%, with 10% of the clients being malicious. Due to the increased complexity of the QNLI dataset, the proportion of malicious clients in this dataset is set to 20% [1].

Attack Baselines. For comparative analysis, we introduce three advanced backdoor attack methods: simple data poisoning (SDP), where the attacker inserts backdoor data into the training set; model replacement attack (MR) [1], where the attacker scales malicious updates from data poisoning to a level that can cancel out other benign updates before uploading; and DBA [33], where the attacker splits the trigger into disjoint sub-triggers, each assigned to a different malicious client.

Defence Methods. We evaluate FLASE using two advanced defense methods: FLAME [29] and Multi-Krum [3]. The former is a pre-aggregation detection method that filters malicious updates through clustering, trimming, and adding noise. The latter is a Byzantine-robust aggregation method that ensures the selected model updates during aggregation are reliable by choosing multiple updates with the smallest distance to others.

Implementation Details. These experiments are conducted based on the framework proposed in Zhang et al. [37], which employs FedAvg as the FL aggregation method. Specifically, after local training on each client, the model updates are uploaded to the server. The server then performs FedAvg aggregation and sends the aggregated model back to the clients for the next round of training. According to Lin et al. [23], all PEFT methods are run for 100 communication rounds with 5 local training epochs each.

Following Chen et al. [5], we use the RoBERTa-Base model released by Hugging Face [26] as our local model. All models are implemented in PyTorch and executed on two Linux machines: one equipped with an NVIDIA RTX 4090 GPU and 24 GB of RAM, and the other with an NVIDIA Tesla V100 GPU and 24 GB of RAM.

5.2 Performance of Standard Backdoor Attack

To investigate the effectiveness of standard backdoor attacks under the PEFT approach, we conduct three experiments:

- *FedPEFT backdoor injection experiment.* The goal is to verify whether standard backdoor attacks remain effective in the FedPEFT scenario. In this experiment, we apply standard backdoor attacks to both federated full finetuning (**FedFT**) and the three PEFT methods (covering adapter tuning (**FedAP**), LoRA (**FedLR**), prefix tuning (**FedPF**)), and compare the poisoning effects on the global model and the convergence of the main task after 100 rounds of FL training.
- *Freezing classifier experiment.* The goal is to examine whether freezing classifier would significantly affect standard backdoor attacks. In this experiment, we keep other settings unchanged but froze the classifier. We then perform 100 rounds of FL training and observe the poisoning effects on the global model and the convergence of the main task.
- *Gradient Analysis Experiment.* The goal is to fine the most sensitive parameters to the backdoor attack and the main task. Specifically, we perform standard backdoor and beningn training on a fully trainable PLM, record the average gradient changes for each layer of the PLM, and then average the recorded values across all training iterations.

The results of these three experiments are summarized in Table 1 and Fig. 4.

Standard Backdoor Attacks are Effective Against FedPEFT, but with Significant Decrease in Effectiveness. From the row-wise comparison in the Table 1, we can observe the following: (i) Standard backdoor attacks still have a noticeable effect. For example, in the SST-2 dataset, the success rate of backdoor attacks using FedAP only decreases by about 2.7% compared to FedFT, indicating that backdoor attacks can still influence the model's output to some extent. (ii) However, the introduction of PEFT methods leads to a decrease in the success rate of backdoor attacks. For instance, in the QNLI dataset, the success rate of backdoor attacks using FedAP decreases by approximately 10% compared to FedFT, while FedLR shows a reduction of about 13% compared to FedFT. When using FedPF, the backdoor attack success rate drops to 17.9%, representing a decrease of approximately 81.8% compared to FedFT.

Table 1. Accuracy (%) of the backdoor after convergence of the global model when applying standard backdoor attacks on FedPEFT. The accuracy of the main task is not listed in the table, as it remains high across all configurations. Data for FedPF is missing because both the main task and the backdoor task fail to converge when the classifier is frozen in FedPF.

	FT Method	FedFT	FedAP	FedLR	FedPF
SST-2	Trainable Classifier	98.6	98.3	84.4	17.9
	Freeze Classifier	96.7	97.0	65.4	–
QNLI	Trainable Classifier	99.5	98.9	86.5	67.7
	Freeze Classifier	97.6	62.8	51.6	–
QQP	Trainable Classifier	99.9	98.4	88.6	54.6
	Freeze Classifier	96.5	96.6	55.8	–
MNLI	Trainable Classifier	98.6	98.3	84.4	19.7
	Freeze Classifier	97.8	27.1	67.6	–

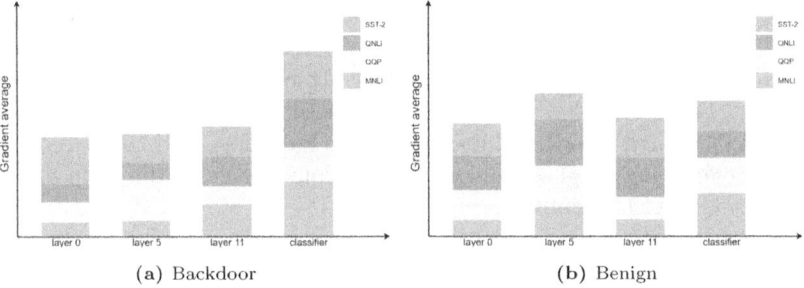

(a) Backdoor (b) Benign

Fig. 4. Statistical analysis of the layer exhibiting the maximum average gradient change after malicious clients train on both backdoor and benign data. In this experiment, the backdoor attack involves 10% malicious clients. The figure shows that the injected backdoor is more sensitive to parameters near the output layer.

Freezing the Classifier Leads to Lower Standard Backdoor Success Rates. The column-wise comparison in the Table 1 clearly shows that freezing the classifier significantly reduces the success rate of backdoor attacks. For example, in the MNLI dataset, when using the Adapter fine-tuning method, freezing classifier reduces the backdoor success rate from 98.3% to 27.1%, a decrease of approximately 73%.

As shown in Fig. 4, during the training process, more than half of the malicious clients exhibit larger gradient changes in the classifier head. In neural networks, the gradient represents the model's sensitivity to changes in the loss function. When a backdoor trigger causes an activation change in the output layer, the gradient reflects this variation. This indicates that the classifier head is more sensitive to backdoor attacks. Therefore, the server can mitigate backdoor attacks by freezing the classifier head.

Table 2. The performance of backdoor attacks on different datasets and PEFT methods. This table compares three backdoor attack baselines with FLASE. All values represent the accuracy (%) of each dataset on both the backdoor and main tasks.

Task	Method	Backdoor				Main			
Dataset		SST-2	QNLI	QQP	MNLI	SST-2	QNLI	QQP	MNLI
SDP	FedAP	97.0	62.8	96.6	27.1	95.4	89.0	86.2	84.5
	FedLR	65.4	51.6	53.8	67.6	93.2	89.5	87.2	84.5
MR	FedAP	97.8	73.4	90.3	62.5	90.7	87.6	85.4	83.2
	FedLR	79.6	78.5	61.9	73.8	91.6	88.9	83.4	81.6
DBA	FedAP	98.1	80.6	92.7	55.6	94.6	89.6	86.6	85.2
	FedLR	77.4	72.4	87.6	43.6	92.7	87.5	85.3	84.9
FLASE	FedAP	**99.1**	**99.5**	**97.6**	**99.4**	93.8	88.7	85.2	84.5
	FedLR	**98.6**	**94.4**	**98.7**	**99.6**	93.2	88.0	96.5	83.9

Therefore, freezing parameters near the output layer serves as an effective defense strategy, significantly lowering the success rate of backdoor attacks without causing substantial harm to the model's performance on main task.

5.3 Performance of FLASE

We conduct three experiments to evaluate the performance of FLASE:

- *Main Experiment.* The goal is to evaluate the performance of FLASE under the condition of frozen classifier. We apply FLASE to two FedPEFT methods with their classifier frozen and assess its efficacy, benchmarking against two state-of-the-art backdoor attacks. Since the FedPF method fails to converge on the main and backdoor task and after freezing the classifier (i.e., the FedPF method cannot be fine-tuned when freezing the classifier), this experiment only focus on FedAP and FedLR.
- *Partial classifier freezing experiment.* The goal is to further explore whether keeping a few trainable parameters of classifier could defend against FLASE. Specifically, we equip the base model with a classifier consisting of two linear layers, one of which is significantly larger than the other. We froze the larger layer's parameters while keeping the smaller layer's parameters trainable, then implement FLASE and evaluat its effectiveness.
- *Training order experiment.* The goal is to explore how to choose the order of benign and backdoor training. We implement FLASE under three different training order settings: backdoor training followed by benign training, the reverse order, and alternating. We then assess the effectiveness of these three training orders.

Performance of FLASE. The experimental results related to the performance of FLASE are summarized in Table 2.

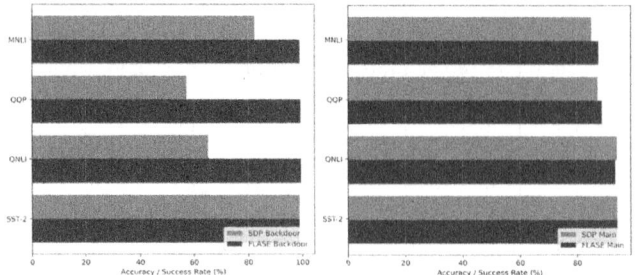

Fig. 5. The effectiveness of backdoor attacks when a subset of the classifier is frozen.

FLASE Achieves a High Success Rate Under Classifier-Freezing Conditions. The results in Table 2 demonstrate that FLASE substantially outperforms both the simple SDP and the two state-of-the-art federated backdoor methods (DBA [33] and model-replacement [1]) across every combination of dataset and PEFT method, while retaining high main-task accuracy.

– *Backdoor Success Rate:* Under FedAP, FLASE achieves near-perfect backdoor insertion on all four NLP benchmarks: SST-2 (99.1 %), QNLI (99.5 %), QQP (97.6 %), and MNLI (99.4 %). By contrast, the SDP attack under FedAP only succeeds at 97.0 % on SST-2 and collapses to 27.1 % on MNLI. DBA improves over SDP (e.g. 98.1 % on SST-2, 92.7 % on QQP, 55.6 % on MNLI) but still falls far short of FLASE's success rates.
– *Main-Task Preservation:* Even under a frozen classifier, FLASE preserves or even slightly improves main-task performance relative to the SDP. For FedAP, main-task accuracies remain above 93 % on all datasets (e.g. 93.8% on SST-2, 88.7 % on QNLI, 85.2 % on QQP, 84.5 % on MNLI). FedLR shows a similar pattern (93.2 %–96.5 % across tasks).

Freezing Only Portion of Parameters of the Classifier Does not Affect the Effectiveness of FLASE. The results in the Fig. 5 also indicate that freezing only a portion of the classifier parameters does not significantly impact the effectiveness of FLASE. Under both the FedAP and FedLR methods, even with some classifier parameters left trainable, FLASE still maintains a very high success rate. For example, on the SST-2 and QNLI datasets, the accuracy of the backdoor attack after freezing classifier parameters remains close to 99%, similar to the performance when the classifier is fully frozen.

Overall Analysis. In summary, our experiments demonstrate the high effectiveness of FLASE, as evidenced by the following points: (i) FLASE significantly improves the accuracy of the global model on the backdoor task; (ii) FLASE does not cause a substantial decrease in the main task; and (iii) even when the server attempts to defend by leaving some classifier parameters trainable, FLASE remains effective.

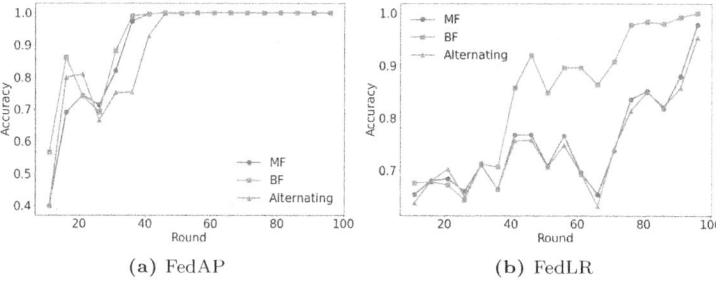

(a) FedAP (b) FedLR

Fig. 6. Accuracy comparison of three training orders on the SST-2 dataset: Malicious-First (MF), Benign-First (BF), and Alternating. Subfigure (a) shows results using FedAP; subfigure (b) shows results using FedLR.

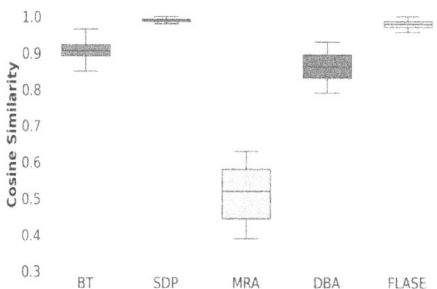

Fig. 7. Boxplot comparison of cosine similarity across five scenarios: benign training (BT), SDP, model replacement attack (MRA), distributed backdoor attack (DBA), and our proposed FLASE method.

Training Order Experiment. Figure 6 shows the impact of three different training orders on FLASE's performance using the SST-2 dataset. The results indicate that the training order mainly affects the convergence speed of the backdoor task. However, regardless of the order, the global model achieves similar, relatively high accuracy on the backdoor task.

5.4 Stealthiness and Robustness of FLASE

In this subsection, we evaluate the stealthiness of FLASE and whether it can still succeed when faced with server defenses. Specifically, we conduct the following two experiments:

– *Stealthy experiment.* The goal is to verify whether FLASE introduces significant statistical differences to the model. Specifically, we compared the differences introduced by FLASE, benign training, standard backdoor attack, and the constrained and scaled method [1], one of the model attacks. We flattened and concatenated the model parameters into a one-dimensional vector and then used cosine similarity as the metric to evaluate the differences.

– *Defense experiment.* The goal is to verify whether FLASE remains effective when the server adds poisoning attack defense mechanisms. Specifically, we employ the FLAME framework [29] and Multi-Krum [3], with experimental settings identical to those in the original works, as shown in Table 3. Notably, all experiments were carried out with the classifier fully frozen, since FLASE achieves its highest efficacy under these conditions.

Stealthy Experiment. Figure 7 shows that: (i) The cosine similarity between the model trained with FLASE and the original model is close to 1, indicating that we have not introduced significant statistical differences. (ii) FLASE does not introduce significantly more statistical differences than standard backdoor attacks, and the differences are much smaller than those introduced by model backdoor attack methods. (iii) FLASE introduces far fewer statistical differences compared to benign training, which poses a challenge for server detection.

Defense Experiment. We evaluated FLASE against two state-of-the-art federated-learning defenses, FLAME and Multi-Krum. As shown in Table 3, FLASE remains highly effective even under defense: for example, under the FedAP protocol it yields backdoor-task accuracies of 97.5 %, 96.5 %, 98.4 % and 98.9 % on SST-2, QNLI, QQP and MNLI. This demonstrates that FLASE reliably evades both FLAME's anomaly detector and Multi-Krum's robust aggregation.

Table 3. Accuracy (%) under FLASE when facing FLAME and Multi-Krum

Attack	Method	SST-2	QNLI	QQP	MNLI
FLAME	FedAP	97.5	96.5	98.4	98.9
	FedLR	98.4	92.9	98.5	98.3
Multi-Krum	FedAP	98.2	97.3	97.4	99.1
	FedLR	97.9	93.5	98.6	98.7

6 Conclusion

In this study, we thoroughly investigated backdoor attacks within the framework of FedPEFT. Our experiments reveal that while the adoption of FedPEFT reduces the success rate of standard backdoor attacks, these attacks remain a viable threat. Notably, we find that freezing parameters near the output layer including the classifier significantly diminishes the effectiveness of backdoor attacks, with only a minimal impact on the global model's accuracy. Based on these findings, we propose FLASE, a novel backdoor attack method for scenarios where the server freezes parameters near the output layer. Extensive experimental results on the GLUE and CIFAR-10 demonstrate that FLASE achieves a higher success rate compared to other backdoor attacks while maintaining a high level of stealthiness.

However, our study primarily focuses on classification tasks using PLMs. Backdoor attacks on larger-scale generative language models also warrant attention. Additionally, developing metrics to evaluate which parts of the model to freeze in order to maximize the restriction of backdoor injection without affecting the primary task is a key issue for future research. We hope our research raises awareness within the community about the security of FedPEFT against backdoor attacks and promotes the development of corresponding defense techniques.

Acknowledgements. This research is supported by the Strategic Priority Research Program of the Chinese Academy of Sciences, Grant No. XDB0690303.

A Experimental Settings for Image Classification Task

In this section, we present the settings for the supplementary experiments on the image classification task. The settings common to the text classification task are omitted, and we only describe the experimental settings unique to the image classification task.

A.1 Dataset

We conduct our image classification experiments on CIFAR-10 dataset, which is a 10-class classification task consisting of 60,000 RGB images, with 50,000 images used for training and 10,000 images used for testing. Each image has a resolution of 32×32. We employed a Dirichlet distribution with parameter $\beta = 1$, sampling $D \sim \text{Dir}(\beta)$, and assigned partition D_k to the k-th client. Unless otherwise specified, β is set to 1 in all experiments.

A.2 Trigger

For the image classification task, similar to Blended Backdoor Attacks [15], we use the white rectangle as the backdoor trigger.

A.3 Model

To enable RoBERTa-Base to process image data, we added the CLIP model [35] before its input, using the combined model as the backbone for the image classification task.

B Experimental Results for Image Classification Task

In this section, we present a comparison of our proposed FLASE against three baseline attacks under various PEFT methods on the CIFAR-10 dataset (B.1), and the effectiveness of the backdoor attack when defenses are applied (B.2).

B.1 Main Experiment

Table 4 presents a performance comparison between FLASE and three baseline methods on the CIFAR-10 dataset. All experiments adhere to the main settings described in Sect. 5.3. The reported results reflect the effect of freezing parameters adjacent to the output layer, and it can be seen that our attack achieves the strongest performance in the image domain. For example, under the FedAP scheme, our backdoor success rate reaches 98.6%.

Table 4. Comparison of backdoor success rates (%) for FLASE and three baseline attacks on the CIFAR-10 dataset.

Method	SDP		MR		DBA		FLASE	
	Backdoor	Main	Backdoor	Main	Backdoor	Main	Backdoor	Main
FedAP	87.6	87.6	82.6	85.6	73.5	88.6	**98.6**	85.7
FedLR	56.2	88.5	67.9	85.0	60.3	85.4	**94.5**	84.6

B.2 Defense Experiment

The attack success rates (%) of FLASE and three baseline attacks on the CIFAR-10 dataset. Table 5 shows the performance of FLASE when two defense mechanisms are deployed on the server. The experimental setup is consistent with the defense evaluation settings described in Sect. 5.4. As demonstrated on the CIFAR-10 dataset, our proposed method FLASE effectively bypasses the FLAME and Multi-Krum defenses.

Table 5. Accuracy (%) under FLASE when facing FLAME and Multi-Krum

Attack	Method	SST-2	QNLI	QQP	MNLI
FLAME	FedAP	96.5	94.7	95.8	93.2
	FedLR	95.9	95.0	94.4	94.5
Multi-Krum	FedAP	97.6	96.5	95.4	94.5
	FedLR	95.3	93.9	96.3	92.4

References

1. Bagdasaryan, E., Veit, A., Hua, Y., Estrin, D., Shmatikov, V.: How to backdoor federated learning. In: International Conference on Artificial Intelligence and Statistics, pp. 2938–2948. PMLR (2020)

2. Bhagoji, A.N., Chakraborty, S., Mittal, P., Calo, S.: Analyzing federated learning through an adversarial lens. In: International Conference on Machine Learning, pp. 634–643. PMLR (2019)
3. Blanchard, P., El Mhamdi, E.M., Guerraoui, R., Stainer, J.: Machine learning with adversaries: byzantine tolerant gradient descent. In: Advances in Neural Information Processing Systems, vol. 30 (2017)
4. Bonawitz, K.: Towards federated learning at scale: system design. arXiv preprint arXiv:1902.01046 (2019)
5. Chen, G., Liu, F., Meng, Z., Liang, S.: Revisiting parameter-efficient tuning: are we really there yet? arXiv preprint arXiv:2202.07962 (2022)
6. Chen, H.Y., Tu, C.H., Li, Z., Shen, H.W., Chao, W.L.: On the importance and applicability of pre-training for federated learning. arXiv preprint arXiv:2206.11488 (2022)
7. Choe, M., Park, C., Seo, C., Kim, H.: SDBA: a stealthy and long-lasting durable backdoor attack in federated learning. arXiv preprint arXiv:2409.14805 (2024)
8. Dai, J., Chen, C., Li, Y.: A backdoor attack against LSTM-based text classification systems. IEEE Access **7**, 138872–138878 (2019)
9. Devlin, J.: BERT: pre-training of deep bidirectional transformers for language understanding. arXiv preprint arXiv:1810.04805 (2018)
10. Ding, N., et al.: Delta tuning: a comprehensive study of parameter efficient methods for pre-trained language models. arXiv preprint arXiv:2203.06904 (2022)
11. Feng, J., Lai, Y., Sun, H., Ren, B.: SADBA: self-adaptive distributed backdoor attack against federated learning. In: Proceedings of the AAAI Conference on Artificial Intelligence, vol. 39, pp. 16568–16576 (2025)
12. Ge, S., Wu, F., Wu, C., Qi, T., Huang, Y., Xie, X.: FedNER: medical named entity recognition with federated learning. arXiv preprint arXiv:2003.09288 (2020)
13. Goodfellow, I.J., Shlens, J., Szegedy, C.: Explaining and harnessing adversarial examples. arXiv preprint arXiv:1412.6572 (2014)
14. Gu, T., Dolan-Gavitt, B., Garg, S.: BadNets: identifying vulnerabilities in the machine learning model supply chain. arXiv preprint arXiv:1708.06733 (2017)
15. Gu, T., Liu, K., Dolan-Gavitt, B., Garg, S.: BadNets: evaluating backdooring attacks on deep neural networks. IEEE Access **7**, 47230–47244 (2019). https://doi.org/10.1109/ACCESS.2019.2909068
16. Han, Z., Gao, C., Liu, J., Zhang, J., Zhang, S.Q.: Parameter-efficient fine-tuning for large models: a comprehensive survey. arXiv preprint arXiv:2403.14608 (2024)
17. He, S., Yan, Q., Wu, F., Wang, L., Lécuyer, M., Beschastnikh, I.: GlueFL: reconciling client sampling and model masking for bandwidth efficient federated learning. In: Proceedings of Machine Learning and Systems, vol. 5, pp. 695–707 (2023)
18. Houlsby, N., et al.: Parameter-efficient transfer learning for NLP. In: International Conference on Machine Learning, pp. 2790–2799. PMLR (2019)
19. Hu, E.J., et al.: LoRA: low-rank adaptation of large language models. arXiv preprint arXiv:2106.09685 (2021)
20. Kurita, K., Michel, P., Neubig, G.: Weight poisoning attacks on pre-trained models. arXiv preprint arXiv:2004.06660 (2020)
21. Li, X.L., Liang, P.: Prefix-tuning: optimizing continuous prompts for generation. arXiv preprint arXiv:2101.00190 (2021)
22. Liang, J., Hu, D., Feng, J.: Do we really need to access the source data? Source hypothesis transfer for unsupervised domain adaptation. In: International Conference on Machine Learning, pp. 6028–6039. PMLR (2020)
23. Lin, B.Y., et al.: FedNLP: benchmarking federated learning methods for natural language processing tasks. arXiv preprint arXiv:2104.08815 (2021)

24. Liu, R., et al.: No one left behind: Inclusive federated learning over heterogeneous devices. In: Proceedings of the 28th ACM SIGKDD Conference on Knowledge Discovery and Data Mining, pp. 3398–3406 (2022)
25. Liu, T., Zhang, Y., Feng, Z., Yang, Z., Xu, C., Man, D., Yang, W.: Beyond traditional threats: a persistent backdoor attack on federated learning. In: Proceedings of the AAAI Conference on Artificial Intelligence, vol. 38, pp. 21359–21367 (2024)
26. Liu, Y., et al.: RoBERTa: a robustly optimized BERT pretraining approach. arXiv preprint arXiv:1907.11692 (2019)
27. McMahan, B., Moore, E., Ramage, D., Hampson, S., y Arcas, B.A.: Communication-efficient learning of deep networks from decentralized data. In: Artificial Intelligence and Statistics, pp. 1273–1282. PMLR (2017)
28. Nguyen, J., Wang, J., Malik, K., Sanjabi, M., Rabbat, M.: Where to begin? On the impact of pre-training and initialization in federated learning. arXiv preprint arXiv:2206.15387 (2022)
29. Nguyen, T.D., et al.: {FLAME}: taming backdoors in federated learning. In: 31st USENIX Security Symposium (USENIX Security 2022), pp. 1415–1432 (2022)
30. Radford, A., et al.: Language models are unsupervised multitask learners. OpenAI blog **1**(8), 9 (2019)
31. Sui, D., Chen, Y., Zhao, J., Jia, Y., Xie, Y., Sun, W.: FedED: federated learning via ensemble distillation for medical relation extraction. In: Proceedings of the 2020 Conference on Empirical Methods in Natural Language Processing (EMNLP), pp. 2118–2128 (2020)
32. Sun, Z., Kairouz, P., Suresh, A.T., McMahan, H.B.: Can you really backdoor federated learning? arXiv preprint arXiv:1911.07963 (2019)
33. Xie, C., Huang, K., Chen, P.Y., Li, B.: DBA: distributed backdoor attacks against federated learning. In: International Conference on Learning Representations (2019)
34. Yang, Y., Zhou, J., Wong, N., Zhang, Z.: LoRETTA: low-rank economic tensor-train adaptation for ultra-low-parameter fine-tuning of large language models. arXiv preprint arXiv:2402.11417 (2024)
35. Zeng, Y., Zhang, X., Li, H.: Multi-grained vision language pre-training: aligning texts with visual concepts. arXiv preprint arXiv:2111.08276 (2021)
36. Zhang, J., Zhu, C., Di Wu, X.S., Yong, J., Long, G.: BADFSS: backdoor attacks on federated self-supervised learning. In: Proceedings of the 33rd International Joint Conference on Artificial Intelligence (IJCAI) (2021)
37. Zhang, Z., et al.: FedPETuning: when federated learning meets the parameter-efficient tuning methods of pre-trained language models. In: Annual Meeting of the Association of Computational Linguistics 2023, pp. 9963–9977. Association for Computational Linguistics (ACL) (2023)
38. Zhu, L., Liu, Z., Han, S.: Deep leakage from gradients. In: Advances in Neural Information Processing Systems, vol. 32 (2019)
39. Zhuang, H., Yu, M., Wang, H., Hua, Y., Li, J., Yuan, X.: Backdoor federated learning by poisoning backdoor-critical layers. arXiv preprint arXiv:2308.04466 (2023)

Spoofing Camera Source Attribution via PRNU Transfer Attacks on Physical and AI Generated Images

Shahriar Rahman Khan[1], Tariqul Islam[2], and Raiful Hasan[1](✉)

[1] Kent State University, Kent, OH 44242, USA
{srahmank,rhasan7}@kent.edu
[2] University of Maryland, Baltimore County, Baltimore, MD 21250, USA
mtislam@umbc.edu

Abstract. Photo Response Non-Uniformity (PRNU) noise serves as a sensor-level fingerprint in camera-based authentication and source attribution systems. Rather than degrading or suppressing PRNU patterns as in prior work, we introduce a novel transfer attack that injects PRNU noise from one device into images from another source or generated by AI. This enables manipulated images to falsely pass forensic source verification checks, posing a new class of threat to PRNU-based authentication. Our method achieves an average 85.5% compromise rate, validated using both a custom PRNU injection pipeline and the commercial forensic tool (Amped Authenticate). We further propose two mitigation techniques to detect such spoofing, revealing critical limitations in current image forensics pipelines.

Keywords: Source camera Identification (SCI) · PRNU · Authentication · Transferred Noise · Device Identification · Spoofing Attack

1 Introduction

Camera-based authentication leverages unique characteristics inherent to digital imaging sensors, most notably Photo Response Non-Uniformity (PRNU), which serves as a device-specific fingerprint for verifying the source of captured digital images. PRNU enables digital forensic analysts to authenticate images across a wide range of domains, including criminal investigations [21,29,32,34], legal proceedings [35], and surveillance systems [39], helping to ensure that images have not been manipulated or morphed. It is also used in medical diagnostics, such as X-rays and MRIs [40], to support accurate diagnosis and treatment, as well as in biometric and access control systems [41]. Beyond these applications, PRNU improves border control, ATM surveillance, and detection of malicious web activities [19,27]. Furthermore, PRNU has been adopted to counter presentation attacks in finger vein biometrics, which capture the unique vein patterns within a person's finger [36].

However, recent research has revealed critical vulnerabilities in PRNU-based source identification. Modern computational photography techniques employed in devices from manufacturers such as Samsung, Canon, and Huawei introduce artifacts that compromise PRNU uniqueness, resulting in elevated false alarm rates [8,21]. Banerjee et al. [6] further demonstrated the feasibility of altering an iris image to mimic the PRNU pattern of a different sensor while preserving the image's biometric utility, raising significant concerns regarding the robustness of PRNU-based authentication.

This study investigates the threat posed by transferred PRNU noise, wherein the PRNU pattern from one device is injected into images captured by another device or into synthetic images generated by advanced AI models such as DALL-E[1], Midjourney[2], and Stable Diffusion[3]. Experimental results demonstrate that such manipulations significantly elevate PCE scores, causing manipulated images to be falsely authenticated as genuine. These findings are validated using both a custom-built PRNU injection pipeline and a commercial forensic tool, *Amped Authenticate*[4].

In addition to PRNU-based techniques, spectral information analysis at the pixel level was explored to detect or mitigate vulnerabilities in source camera authentication. This approach involves decomposing an image into distinct frequency bands, enabling the examination of fine-grained details that may be altered through tampering or synthetic generation. By analyzing spectral loss—defined as the difference in frequency components between original and manipulated images—across multiple frequency bands, inconsistencies that may elude PRNU-based methods can be identified. Specifically, this technique employs band-pass filtering to isolate low-, mid-, and high-frequency components [1], facilitating the detection of anomalous alterations in the frequency domain. The contributions of this study are as follows:

(i) We design and implement a PRNU injection attack that transfers the PRNU pattern from one device to images captured by other devices or generated by AI, enabling false attribution in source camera verification systems.
(ii) We systematically evaluate the attack across seven physical devices and three generative models, achieving an average compromise rate of 86.5%.
(iii) We propose two countermeasure strategies to detect such spoofing attacks: (a) PCE-based thresholding, and (b) spectral loss analysis. Both methods expose abnormalities in manipulated images, particularly elevated high-frequency distortions and anomalously high correlation scores.

2 Related Works

PRNU-based source camera identification is a critical technique in digital forensics, enabling device attribution through sensor pattern noise. Lukas et al. [31]

---

[1] https://chatgpt.com/g/g-2fkFE8rbu-dall-e.
[2] https://www.midjourney.com/home.
[3] https://stability.ai/.
[4] https://ampedsoftware.com/authenticate.

first introduced PRNU-based identification using dark frames, which was later extended to focus on pixel non-uniformity noise, enabling source identification through correlation techniques applied to regular image frames. Despite these advancements, early methods were susceptible to interference from scene content and post-processing artifacts. To address these limitations, Yang et al. [44] improved PRNU extraction using a Wiener filter, which enhanced accuracy at the cost of increased computational complexity.

Recent studies have raised concerns regarding the reliability of PRNU-based source identification. Iuliani et al. [21] observed significant cross-correlation among devices of the same model, thereby undermining PRNU's uniqueness. To address such limitations, several deep learning approaches have been proposed. Akbari et al. [2] embedded PRNU features into video-oriented convolutional neural networks (CNNs), while Cozzolino et al. [11] introduced Noiseprint, a CNN-based method for extracting model-specific residuals. Further advancements have focused on enhancing PRNU extraction accuracy through techniques such as PCA refinement [29], camera reference-phase sensor pattern noise (SPN) [24], and blind clustering methods [34]. Extending fingerprint extraction to video has introduced additional challenges due to H.264 video coding artifacts, including stabilization and compression, which were addressed by Altinisik et al. [4]. More recently, Manisha et al. [32,33] developed a device-specific, robust fingerprinting framework for video frames using CNNs. In parallel, SVM-based wavelet analysis has been explored to improve camera recognition across similar devices [3], and Remya et al. [38] enhanced video camera attribution by reducing false acceptances through clustering of PCE scores.

2.1 Vulnerabilities in PRNU-Based Methods

Despite significant progress, PRNU-based systems remain vulnerable to deliberate manipulation. Kang et al. [24] proposed the CCN statistic to reduce false positives, but also acknowledged the system's susceptibility to targeted attacks. Martin et al. [35] systematically tested and categorized various attack methods, including noise addition, filtering, resampling, and compression that degrade image quality and disrupt PRNU signals, with filtering-based attacks shown to be particularly effective.

Several works have explored counter-forensic strategies aimed at undermining PRNU-based source attribution. Dirik et al. [13] introduced a suppression method to anonymize images and attenuate PRNU signals without significantly degrading visual quality. Wang et al. [42] demonstrated that deep learning-based camera sensor fingerprinting systems can be compromised through adversarial fingerprints, leveraging fingerprint copy-move and joint feature-based auto-learning techniques. Karakuccuk et al. [25] employed Patch-Match as a potent anonymization method and proposed partial recovery based on subset similarity. Banerjee et al. [6] investigated spoofing techniques such as PRNU injection and substitution, specifically targeting iris sensor images to mislead forensic analysis. Additional limitations have been identified in tampering localization, particularly under subtle manipulations applied to complex textures [26]. To address this, Cozzolino et al. [11] proposed a hybrid approach that combines PRNU with CNN-extracted fingerprints, while Li et al. [29] refined CRP generation via PCA to mitigate contamination from scene content.

Recent efforts to enhance the robustness and efficiency of PRNU-based authentication have primarily focused on degrading a device's native PRNU signature through noise injection, filtering, or suppression. However, a critical threat remains largely unexplored: the deliberate transfer of a target device's PRNU pattern onto images from another source in order to exploit and deceive the authentication process. This overlooked attack vector transferring PRNU noise to falsely elevate authenticity forms the core motivation of our work. In this study, we systematically expose this vulnerability and propose effective countermeasures to enable more reliable image-source verification.

3 Background

3.1 PRNU Extraction

PRNU is a sensor-level noise pattern unique to each camera, caused by manufacturing imperfections [7,31,34]. Although visually imperceptible, this additive noise acts as a device fingerprint, enabling source identification and forgery detection. An observed image can be modeled or described as: $I = (1+K)I^{(0)} + \Theta$, where $I^{(0)}$ is the ideal noise-free image, K is the PRNU factor, and Θ represents random noise. For every pixel s in the image that is not faulty, $Ks \ll 1$, meaning the PRNU-induced disruption is generally minimal.

3.2 Camera Reference Pattern and Denoising

To isolate PRNU from the observed image, it requires denoising the image and computing the residual. This will suppress scene details and random noise and get a version of the captured image that is exempt from these noises. To estimate K, a denoising filter f is applied, producing $\hat{I}^{(0)} = f(I)$ [30]. Subtracting $\hat{I}^{(0)}$ from the original image yields the noise residual $R = I - \hat{I}^{(0)}$, which is approximated as $IK + \Theta'$. Averaging residuals from multiple images of a device provides a rough estimation of the PRNU noise [31], which serves as a reference PRNU pattern of the camera device. This Camera Reference Pattern (CRP) is then subjected to a maximum-likelihood (ML) estimation process to obtain a reliable PRNU estimate as per Eq. 1.

$$K_{\mathrm{ML}} = \frac{\sum_{i=1}^{N} W_i I_i}{\sum_{i=1}^{N} I_i^2} \quad (1)$$

where I_i is the i-th image, W_i represents noise residual, and N represents the total number of pictures. Here $N > 50$ ensures robustness of the CRP in authenticating image source [10].

Denoising Methods. Several denoising filters are used for PRNU extraction: *Gaussian Filter* – Smooths noise via weighted averages [9,12]. *Median Filter* – Removes salt-and-pepper noise while preserving edges [5,18,45]. *Wiener Filter* – Adaptive method based on local variance [43]. *Wavelet Denoising* – Decomposes images into frequency bands; thresholding high frequencies effectively isolates PRNU [20,22]. Among these, wavelet denoising is the most effective at preserving edge-level PRNU features, outperforming the *Wiener* and *Median* filters.

3.3 Source Identification Using PRNU

Once the CRP is established, image authentication involves comparing a test image's noise residual N_{test} with the CRP. A common metric is the correlation index:

$$\text{corr}(p,q) = \frac{\langle (p - \bar{p}), (q - \bar{q}) \rangle}{\|p - \bar{p}\| \cdot \|q - \bar{q}\|} \quad (2)$$

where $\langle p, q \rangle$ denotes the inner product of p and q and $\bar{p}$ is the mean of p and its Euclidean norm is denoted as $\|p\|$. For more robust detection, particularly under image cropping, the Peak-to-Correlation Energy (PCE) is used [16,17], as shown in 3:

$$PCE_0(a,b) = \frac{c^2(0)}{\left(\frac{1}{n-|A|}\right) \sum_{k \notin A} c^2(k)} \quad (3)$$

Here, n represents the total number of components in the signal, $|A|$ denotes the size of the region around zero where a significant correlation is anticipated, and $c(k)$ refers to the circular cross-correlation at a specific lag k, $c(0)$ is the peak of the cross-correlation. The sum in the denominator is over all lags k not in A.

Illustrative Workflow. To illustrate the process of PRNU extraction, model creation, and using the PCE ratio to check device authenticity, consider 50 images $I_1, ..., I_{50}$ from the origin device I. Their residuals $N_1, ..., N_{50}$ are extracted and averaged to form the CRP model named R_{ref}. For a test image I_{test}, the PCE between R_{ref} and its residual N_{test} is computed using Eq. 3. If this value exceeds a threshold τ, the image is authenticated as originating from the same device.

4 Threat Model

We consider an adversary model in which the attacker aims to compromise the integrity of PRNU-based image source authentication systems. The attacker's objective is to manipulate images such that they are falsely attributed to a specific target device by transferring its unique PRNU fingerprint onto images from a different source. These images may originate from another physical camera or be generated using synthetic image generation tools. By doing so, the adversary seeks to deceive forensic tools into misclassifying manipulated images as authentic outputs of the targeted device, thereby undermining trust in camera source attribution mechanisms.

4.1 Adversary Capabilities and Resources

The adversary is assumed to have access to a set of images captured by the target camera device, from which they extract its PRNU fingerprint using wavelet-based denoising and residual averaging techniques. The attacker also possesses a collection of target images, either captured by another device or generated via AI models. These images are modified by injecting the extracted PRNU pattern onto them. The adversary also preserves and restores image metadata. Since PRNU manipulation often results in the loss of Exchangeable Image File Format (EXIF) data, the attacker pre-extracts this metadata prior to manipulation and re-inserts it afterward to maintain forensic consistency. Importantly, the attacker does not require access to the internals of the target device or source verification software, and operates under a black-box assumption using only publicly available tools and methods.

4.2 Attack Procedure

The spoofing attack follows a structured pipeline. First, a CRP is constructed by averaging the PRNU residuals of multiple images from the target device. The attacker then extracts PRNU noise from this CRP and injects it into each target image. Simultaneously, the original EXIF metadata from the target image is preserved and reattached after manipulation. The final manipulated images are then submitted to a forensic authentication system. If the computed PCE between a manipulated image and the CRP of the target device exceeds the system's acceptance threshold, the image is falsely verified as authentic. This process reveals a critical vulnerability in current PRNU-based verification pipelines, where device identity can be spoofed through purely algorithmic image-level modifications without requiring access to the actual device or proprietary software.

5 Experiment Setup

The experiments were conducted in two phases to evaluate the effectiveness of a PRNU spoofing attack that exploits vulnerabilities in PRNU based image authentication systems. The goal was to assess whether an attacker could successfully manipulate PRNU noise in order to cause images from another device or from AI generated sources to be falsely accepted as authentic by forensic verification tools. Our experimental design systematically measures both the feasibility and the impact of this attack on current PRNU based source attribution pipelines: (i) we developed a custom model to perform a PRNU injection attack, in which noise from a reference device is superimposed onto images from a different source. Algorithm 1 details this adversarial procedure. (ii) we validated the attack using *Amped Authenticate*, a commercial forensic software tool, to assess the effectiveness of the manipulation and its ability to bypass standard source authentication mechanisms. We chose Amped Authenticate for Phase II due to its' industry acceptance, stability, and relevance as a black-box PRNU verification system [15].

5.1 Phase-I: Custom Model-Based Experiment

Proposed Algorithm for PRNU Spoofing Attack. Algorithm 1 outlines the spoofing process used in our attack. We first extract the PRNU reference pattern from images captured by a legitimate camera, then inject this pattern into images from other devices or AI generated sources. If the manipulated image yields a high PCE value when compared with the CRP, it is falsely accepted as authentic, exposing a critical vulnerability in PRNU based verification. This method enables attackers to bypass camera verification by forging sensor signatures.

Algorithm 1. Spoofing Attack via PRNU Injection and Authenticity Misclassification

---

Require: Set of reference images $I_1, I_2, \ldots, I_n$ from camera A; Set of target images $D_1, D_2, \ldots, D_n$ from camera B or AI; Threshold τ for PCE
Ensure: Evaluate whether spoofed images D'_i are falsely classified as authentic by PRNU-based verification
1: $noise \leftarrow 0$
2: **for** $i \leftarrow 1$ to n **do do**
3:    $I_i \leftarrow$ preProcessImage(I_i)
4:    $N_i \leftarrow$ extractPRNUNoise(I_i)
5:    $noise \leftarrow noise + N_i$
6: **end for**
7: Compute average PRNU reference pattern: $I_{ref} = \frac{1}{n} \cdot noise$
8: $N_{I_{test}} \leftarrow$ extractPRNUNoise(preProcessImage(I_{test}))
9: **for** $i \leftarrow 1$ to n **do do**
10:    $D_i \leftarrow$ preProcessImage(D_i)
11:    Inject $N_{I_{test}}$ into D_i: $D'_i = D_i + N_{I_{test}}$
12:    Calculate overall correlation energy E of D'_i excluding peak area
13:    Calculate PCE ratio, PCE $= \frac{c^2(0)}{(1/(n-|A|)) \cdot E}$
14:    **if** PCE $> \tau$ **then**
15:      Print "Image D'_i **falsely accepted** as authentic"
16:    **else**
17:      Print "Image D'_i correctly rejected"
18:    **end if**
19: **end for**

Image Dataset Collection. In this study, we selected a range of consumer smartphones based on both accessibility and market relevance, aiming to reflect devices that are still actively used in real-world scenarios. For this experiment, seven smartphones were selected: iPhone 13 Plus, Xiaomi Note 11, OnePlus GM1900, Xiaomi Note 9, Xiaomi MIUI 5, Samsung Galaxy S3, and Huawei P9. Additionally, AI-generated images were created using DALL-E, Midjourney, and Stable Diffusion. Notably, several of the chosen models - such as Xiaomi Note 11, iPhone 13 Plus, Xiaomi MIUI 5 and Oneplus GM1900 - have held significant market share in various regions and remain in use due to their affordability and reliability. Our goal was to assess the vulnerability of PRNU-based authentication across a diverse but realistic device set, including mid-tier and legacy devices, to show that PRNU injection is successful across various commercial device models. We also kept 3 different models of the same company (Xiaomi Note 11, Note 9 and MIUI 5) to show that PRNU value is different across different models of the same company.

The device information, number of photos gathered from each device, and their resolutions in pixels are presented in Table 1.

Table 1. Collected Image Dataset Information

Device Name	# of Image	Resolution(in pixel)
iPhone 13 Plus	55	4032×3024
Xiaomi Note 11	56	4080×3072
Xiaomi Note 9	60	4000×2992
Xiaomi MIUI5	52	4608×3456
OnePlus GM1900	65	3000×4000
Samsung Galaxy S3	55	2048×1536
Huawei P9	64	2048×1536
AI Generated Images	40	2090×1212

Image Dataset Description. To assess the feasibility of PRNU spoofing, two distinct sets of images were selected from Table 1 for controlled experimentation. The goal was to determine whether a CRP model extracted from an origin device I could be used to falsely authenticate images captured by the target device D after PRNU noise injection.

Set I from Origin Device: This set comprises n images $I_1, I_2, \ldots, I_n$, all of which were taken by the same camera. The Xiaomi Note 11 was utilized as the camera device in this experiment. These images were used to extract the device-specific PRNU noise, which was then averaged to generate a robust CRP representing the fingerprint of the Xiaomi Note 11.

Set D from Target Device: This set contains n images $D_1, D_2, \ldots, D_n$, either captured by a different device or generated by AI-based tools. In this experiment, the Xiaomi Note 9 was used as the target device D. An extracted PRNU noise of an arbitrary image from device I was injected into the images of set D to evaluate whether those manipulated images could be falsely verified as originating from the Xiaomi Note 11.

Image Preprocessing and Metadata Preservation. The varying image resolutions across devices, as presented in Table 1, required preprocessing of images from each device to ensure consistency in the experimental results. The objective was to standardize image dimensions and preserve crucial metadata, thereby simulating real-world conditions for PRNU spoofing attacks. All images were processed using a custom preProcessImage() function that normalized their resolution to 1024×1024 pixels, ensuring uniformity in size and format across devices and sources. As image manipulation can result in the loss of metadata, the EXIF data was extracted prior to PRNU injection and reintegrated post-manipulation. This step preserved camera-specific metadata such as timestamp, exposure settings, and GPS coordinates, critical elements in forensic analysis [37]. Figure 1(a) displays examples of standardized images captured by physical devices, while AI-generated images are showcased after the same preprocessing in Fig. 1(b). During the generation of AI images, prompts such as *'nature'*, *'university'*, and *'tree'* were utilized. Maintaining consistency across both sources is vital to isolate the effect of PRNU manipulation in subsequent experiments.

Fig. 1. (a) A set of pre-processed images captured by physical camera devices; (b) A set of pre-processed images generated by AI models (e.g., DALL-E, Midjourney, Stable Diffusion).

PRNU Noise Extraction. For each image I_i in Set I, the PRNU noise N_i was extracted using the extractPRNUNoise() function. This function implements a wavelet-based denoising pipeline designed to isolate the sensor-specific noise pattern while minimizing image content loss.

De-noising the Image. The original image I_i undergoes denoising using a wavelet filter with configurable parameters such as *channel_axis, convert2ycbcr, method, mode,* and *sigma*[5]. The *channel_axis* is set to -1 for color images and otherwise

---
[5] https://archive.ph/VFinQ.

ignored for grayscale inputs. BayesShrink is selected as the thresholding *method* due to its adaptiveness to varying noise levels, and the *mode* is set to soft for smoother transitions [14]. This process results in a smoothed version of the image, denoted as $I_{i,\text{denoised}}$, in which high-frequency noise and minor structural details are suppressed. The goal is to remove as much scene content as possible while retaining the subtle sensor-specific noise components.

Isolating the PRNU Noise Pattern. The PRNU noise N_i is obtained by subtracting the denoised image from the original one: $N_i = I_i - I_{i,\text{denoised}}$. This subtraction isolates the high-frequency components present in the original image but absent in the denoised version, effectively capturing the noise pattern specific to the camera sensor.

Figure 2(a) visualizes several PRNU noise patterns extracted from Set I images. These patterns appear stochastic to the human eye but exhibit high correlation when matched across images from the same camera. This consistency forms the foundation of PRNU-based authentication systems, which compare an extracted PRNU noise pattern against a CRP model to verify image origin.

Generating the CRP Model. After extracting the noise from all n images in Set I, the reference fingerprint is constructed by averaging the individual PRNU patterns: $R_{\text{ref}} = \frac{1}{n}\sum_{i=1}^{n} N_i$. This averaged pattern forms the CRP for origin device I, serving as the unique representation of its sensor's noise signature for use in authentication and, in this case, spoofing.

Fig. 2. (a) Extracted PRNU patterns from preprocessed images of origin device I, used to form its CRP; (b) PRNU extracted from a single test image of device I; (c) Images from target device D after PRNU injection using the extracted fingerprint from origin device I. In this experiment, origin device I is Xiaomi Note 11 and target device D is Xiaomi Note 9.

Adding PRNU Noise and Random Noise. To simulate the spoofing scenario, PRNU noise extracted from the origin device I and random noise (specifically, salt-and-pepper noise) were separately added to images from the target source D. For each image D_i in set D, we performed two separate manipulations:

(i) **PRNU Injection:** The PRNU noise $N_{I_{\text{test}}}$, extracted from a single arbitrary image in set I (illustrated in Fig. 2(b)), was added to each D_i. These target images included both camera-captured photos (e.g., from Xiaomi Note 9) and AI-generated images. The resulting manipulated images are shown in Fig. 2(c), where the injected PRNU noise hardly visible/highlighted in the already high-intensity areas.

(ii) **Random Noise Injection:** As a control condition, salt-and-pepper noise was applied to the same D_i images. This ensured that any observed spike in PCE values was attributable to the structured nature of PRNU, and not simply the addition of high-frequency noise.

PCE-Based Authentication Scoring. To quantify the effectiveness of PRNU injection, we computed the PCE between the manipulated images and the CRP of origin I. The PCE metric was calculated as follows: The cross-correlation between the reference pattern R_{ref} and each modified image D_i was calculated to obtain $c(0)$. Next, the overall correlation energy E of each modified image D_i was computed excluding the peak area using E where $E = \sum_{k \notin A} c^2(k)$. Finally, the PCE ratio was calculated using the formula PCE $= \frac{c^2(0)}{(1/(n-|A|)) \cdot E}$.

Authentication Determination. Each manipulated image D_i was classified as *authentic* if its computed PCE score exceeded a predefined threshold (typically set to 60, as established in prior PRNU-based studies). Otherwise, it was labeled as *non-authentic*. This binary classification was used to evaluate the spoofing success rate, with successful spoofing defined as PRNU-injected images being falsely accepted as originating from the source device I.

5.2 Phase-II: Verification with a Third-Party Authentication Tool

To validate the findings from our self-built PRNU analysis model, the second phase of the experiment involved testing the outcomes using a commercial forensic tool, *Amped Authenticate*[6], developed by Amped Software. This tool supports digital image authentication and camera identification via PRNU analysis and is widely used in forensic investigations for detecting image tampering and verifying source devices.

Dataset and Preprocessing. The same dataset from Phase-I was used, consisting of at least 50 images from each of 7 different devices and generative models (see Table 1). Preprocessing steps such as image resizing and metadata preservation (e.g., EXIF data) were applied uniformly across all images to ensure compatibility with the software.

CRP Generation. PRNU reference patterns (CRPs) were created within *Amped Authenticate* using its *Create PRNU Reference Pattern* feature. For each selected device, at least 50 native images were used to build its CRP under the *Camera Identification* module.

---
[6] https://ampedsoftware.com/authenticate.

Spoofing via PRNU Noise Addition. As in Phase-I, PRNU noise extracted from one device was added to images captured by other devices. These manipulated images were then used to test the robustness of the camera identification feature in *Amped Authenticate*. The objective was to assess whether the software would incorrectly attribute the manipulated images to the source device of the injected PRNU.

Authenticity Testing in Amped Authenticate. The manipulated images were analyzed using the PRNU module in *Amped Authenticate*. First, the CRP of the source device (e.g., device I) was loaded into the tool. The evidence folder containing the manipulated images from another device (e.g., device D) was then imported. The *Analyze All Images In Evidence Folder* option was used to compute PCE scores, compatibility results, and threshold-based authentication decisions for each image. The output data were recorded and compared with Phase-I results to further inform the development of countermeasure techniques. By integrating this third-party validation, Phase-II confirms the vulnerability of PRNU-based authentication methods across both custome systems and professional forensic tools, reinforcing the broader implications of PRNU spoofing.

6 Results and Findings

6.1 Phase-I Result Analysis

PRNU and Random Noise Injection Attack Across Single Device Pair. To investigate whether PRNU noise exhibits a unique influence on PCE values distinct from general noise, a controlled experiment was conducted in Sect. 5. PRNU noise was extracted from device I (Xiaomi Note 11) and injected into images from device D (Xiaomi Note 9). For comparison, random salt-and-pepper noise was also added separately to the same set of images. The resulting PCE values were analyzed to assess authentication behavior. Figure 4(a) illustrates a clear contrast in the effects of these noise types. PRNU noise led to a substantial increase in PCE values, often surpassing the authentication threshold of 60, indicating successful spoofing. In contrast, salt-and-pepper noise had negligible impact, with PCE values remaining below 1 in most cases.

Key Findings. There are some noticeable findings from the experiment conducted in Phase-I. PRNU noise caused the average PCE to increase from approximately 32.23 to 131.80, surpassing the threshold and leading to false authentication. On contrary, random noise did not cause a significant rise in PCE as values dropped below 1, indicating that not all noise types can manipulate PRNU-based identification. Injecting PRNU from origin I led to images from D being mistakenly verified as originating from I.

6.2 Phase-II Result Analysis

To further validate the effect of transferred PRNU noise attack on image authentication, PCE values were analyzed before and after PRNU injection from a source device I_i into target device images D_i using the commercial tool *Amped Authenticate* in Phase-II. The analysis was conducted using CRPs from five different devices: iPhone 13 Plus, Xiaomi Note 11, Samsung Galaxy S3, Xiaomi Note 9, and OnePlus GM1900.

Figure 3 presents scatter plots of PCE values across images from Xiaomi Note 11, Xiaomi Note 9, and generated AI images. Each plot distinguishes between compatibility states—0 for images originating from the same device as the CRP, and 1 for images from a different device. A logarithmic y-axis is used to better visualize the wide range of PCE values, especially the significant jumps post-manipulation.

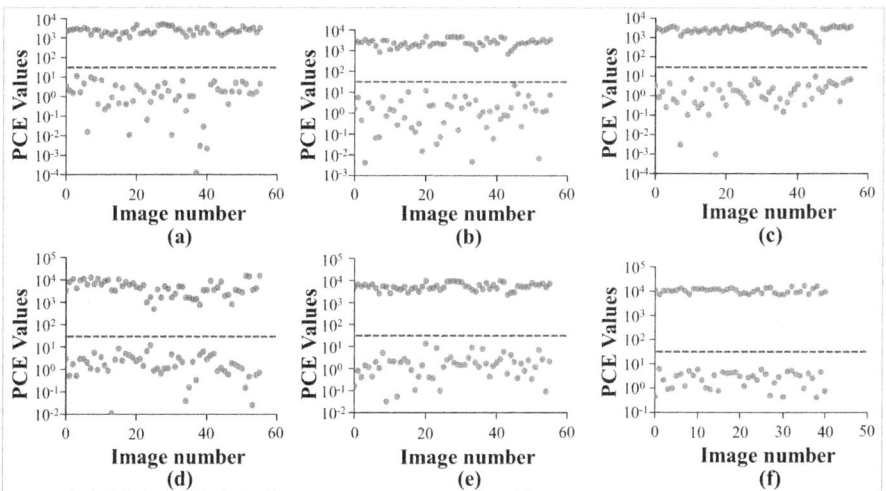

Fig. 3. PCE value comparisons before and after PRNU noise injection across various device combinations. Each subplot presents the compatibility classification (0 = original device match, 1 = mismatch) evaluated using a specific CRP, with a decision threshold of 60 indicated by the dashed line. The subplots show: (a) Samsung Galaxy S3 CRP with PRNU from the same device added to Xiaomi Note 11; (b) Xiaomi Note 9 CRP with its PRNU added to Xiaomi Note 11; (c) OnePlus GM1900 CRP with its PRNU added to Xiaomi Note 11; (d) Xiaomi Note 11 CRP with its PRNU added to Xiaomi Note 9; (e) iPhone 13 Plus CRP with its PRNU added to Xiaomi Note 11; (f) Xiaomi Note 11 CRP with its PRNU added to AI-generated images. In all cases, compatibility shifted from 1 to 0 after the PRNU injection attack.

Across all device pairs, PRNU injection led to a substantial increase in PCE values. For example, when Xiaomi Note 9 PRNU was added to Xiaomi Note 11 images and evaluated against the Note 9 CRP, compatibility shifted from 1 (mismatch) to 0 (original), with PCE values rising from near-zero (e.g., -0.41 to 11.28) to consistently high levels (e.g., 835 to over 5000). This sharp transition highlights the vulnerability of PRNU-based authentication to spoofing. A similar pattern is evident in the experiment involving generated images. When

Xiaomi Note 11 PRNU was added to AI-generated content, PCE values jumped significantly after manipulation, shifting classification from incompatible (1) to compatible (0) under the Xiaomi Note 11 CRP—indicating a clear susceptibility to PRNU-based falsification. These results confirm that adding PRNU noise from one device can manipulate the authentication outcome for another device or even generated images, demonstrating a critical weakness in PRNU-based source attribution.

Average PCE Value Analysis Across Devices Using a Particular CRP. This analysis examines the impact of PRNU noise injection on average PCE values when images from various devices are tested against a specific CRP model. As shown in Fig. 4(b), for each device, a minimum of 50 images were analyzed both before and after PRNU noise from the iPhone 13 Plus was added. The resulting PCE values were then evaluated using the iPhone 13 Plus CRP (R_{ref}).

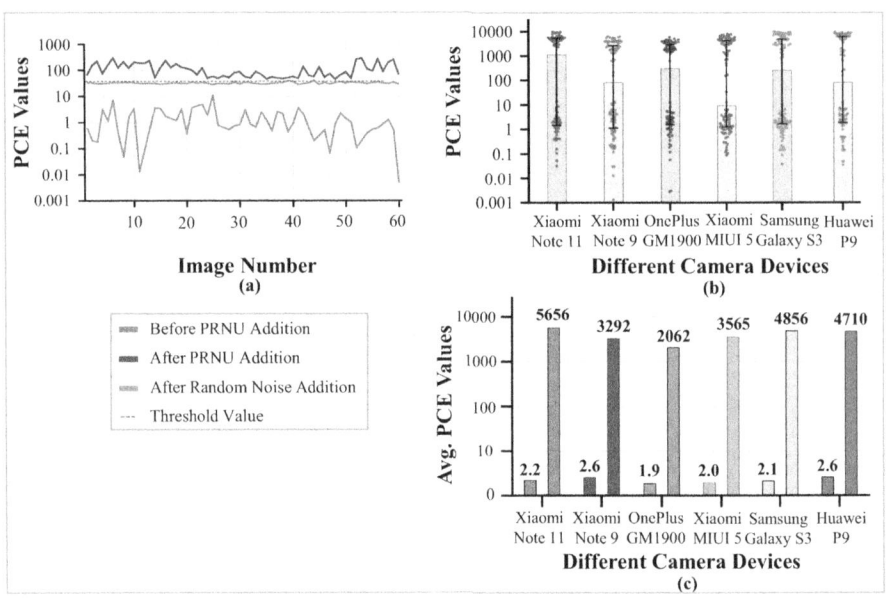

Fig. 4. (a) PCE values before and after addition of PRNU (Xiaomi Note 11) and random (salt-and-pepper) noise to Xiaomi Note 9 images; threshold = 60 (b) Distribution of PCE values before and after injecting iPhone 13 Plus PRNU into images from other devices; (c) Comparison of average PCE values pre- and post-PRNU spoofing.

Figure 4(c) shows a substantial increase in average PCE values following PRNU injection. For instance, images from the Xiaomi Note 11 exhibited an increase from 2.2 to 5656.4 after the iPhone 13 Plus PRNU was applied. Similar trends were observed for other devices: Xiaomi Note 9 (2.6 to 3292.4), OnePlus GM1900 (1.9 to 2062.1), Xiaomi MIUI 5 (2.0 to 3565.8), Samsung Galaxy

S3 (2.1 to 4856.2), and Huawei P9 (2.6 to 4710.9). These shifts in correlation energy indicate a significant vulnerability in PRNU-based authentication, as the spoofed images are increasingly misidentified as originating from the iPhone 13 Plus.

6.3 PRNU Compromise Rate After Spoofing Attack

To evaluate the vulnerability of PRNU-based authentication, we calculated the compromise rate of the iPhone 13 Plus CRP after PRNU spoofing. Based on the dataset summarized in Table 1, the total number of images is: $T_{\text{images}} = 447$. Excluding the iPhone 13 Plus images from the total yields: $T_{\text{images}-iPhone13} = 447 - 55 = 392$. After injecting the PRNU noise extracted from iPhone 13 Plus into images from the other seven sources, these manipulated images were analyzed against the iPhone 13 Plus CRP. The false positives[7] (i.e., manipulated images falsely authenticated as originating from the iPhone 13 Plus) are presented in Table 2.

Table 2. iPhone 13 Plus CRP Compromise Rate Across Other Devices

Device	Total Images	False Positives (FP)	FP Rate (%)
Xiaomi Note 11	56	48	85.71
OnePlus GM1900	65	53	81.54
Xiaomi Note 9	60	53	88.33
Xiaomi MIUI 5	52	43	82.69
Samsung Galaxy S3	55	46	83.64
Huawei P9	64	56	87.50
Generated Images	40	36	90.00

The Total of False Positives (FP): $FP_{iPhone13Plus} = 48 + 53 + 53 + 43 + 46 + 56 + 36 = 335$ Based on the total number of False Positives, the average Compromise Rate [23] of iPhone 13 Plus device is:

$R = \left(\frac{FP_{iPhone13Plus}}{T_{images-iPhone13Plus}} \right) \times 100 = \left(\frac{335}{392} \right) \times 100 = 85.47\%$

After analyzing the compromise rates across all CRPs, it is found that the average across models is approximately 86.50%. Notably, Xiaomi Note 9 exhibits the highest compromise rate at 91.47%, followed by Xiaomi Note 11 at 89.38%. Even the least vulnerable devices, such as OnePlus GM1900 (82.75%) and Samsung Galaxy S3 (83.44%), still show substantial susceptibility to PRNU-based spoofing.

---

[7] The term "false positive" is used throughout the paper to describe successful spoofing instances where images are misattributed to the source device.

7 Countermeasures

The countermeasures proposed in this section are preliminary, proof-of concept techniques intended to demonstrate potential ways for spoofing detection. Our primary focus in this paper was to expose the feasibility and severity of PRNU transfer attacks. The two proposed defenses: (1) PCE threshold banding and (2) Spectral Loss Analysis—are presented as starting points for further directions, rather than complete solutions.

7.1 Mitigation Technique 1: PCE Threshold Banding

A key observation is found from analyzing the distribution of average PCE values shown in Fig. 5(a), when PRNU noise from one device is added to images captured by others. Notably, no PRNU noise was added to a device's own images when evaluating its compatibility with its corresponding CRP—for example, iPhone 13 Plus images were evaluated directly against the iPhone 13 Plus CRP without any modification.

From this distribution, several patterns are identified:

(i) When PRNU noise from Xiaomi Note 11 was injected into other device images and evaluated with the Xiaomi Note 11 CRP, the resulting PCE values ranged between 4000 and 9000. This is the highest range observed across all tested CRPs.
(ii) The iPhone 13 Plus CRP produced PCE values ranging from 2000 to 6000, while the OnePlus GM1900 CRP showed values between 1700 and 3000 when other devices were spoofed with their respective PRNU patterns.
(iii) These CRPs exhibited the lowest vulnerability, with average PCE values ranging from 900 to 2700 for Samsung Galaxy S3 and 1000 to 2700 for Xiaomi Note 9, even after PRNU manipulation.
(iv) For each CRP, the highest PCE value was consistently recorded when evaluating the corresponding device's own images. These peak values were: (1) iPhone 13 Plus: 13,645, (2) Xiaomi Note 11: 15,361, (3) Xiaomi Note 9: 10,919, (4) OnePlus GM1900: 5,940, (5) Samsung Galaxy S3: 12,982. This consistency highlights that the highest PCE values are typically unique to unaltered, original images from a device and its corresponding CRP.

These trends suggest a possible mitigation strategy: by establishing threshold bands based on a device's own PCE distribution (e.g., self-CRP peaks), outliers caused by spoofed PRNU can potentially be detected. Specifically, if an image's PCE value falls within a manipulated range (e.g., 4000–9000 for Xiaomi Note 11), but the image is not from the source device, it could be flagged as suspicious.

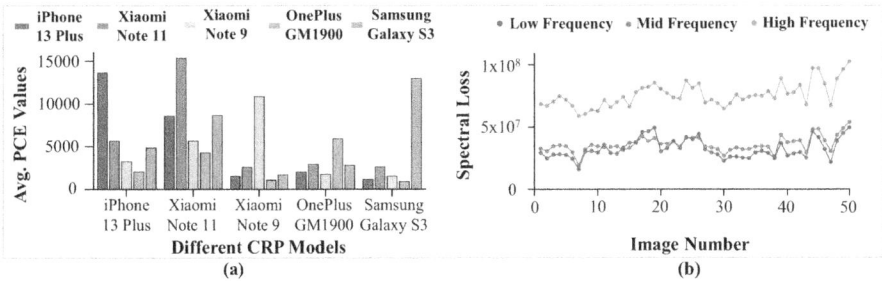

Fig. 5. (a) Distribution of average PCE values for different devices after PRNU injection (b) Spectral loss comparison across 50 image pairs in three distinct frequency bands.

7.2 Mitigation Technique 2: Spectral Loss Analysis

A second mitigation strategy involves applying spectral analysis to detect differences between original and PRNU-manipulated images. This technique utilizes frequency-domain analysis to assess discrepancies in image content across multiple frequency bands, offering a non-intrusive way of verifying image authenticity. Spectral loss, in this context, quantifies the degradation or modification in the spectral characteristics of an image. It is typically calculated as the sum of absolute differences between the magnitude spectra of the original and manipulated versions. Such losses may arise due to noise injection, compression artifacts, or synthetic modifications [28]. This analysis across 50 image pairs from the iPhone 13 Plus dataset is shown in Fig. 5(b), where PRNU noise from Xiaomi Note 11 was injected.

Observations Across Frequency Bands: **Low-Frequency Band (0–20):** Spectral loss was minimal, suggesting that global structures and low-frequency components (such as contours and object shapes) remain largely unaffected by PRNU spoofing. **Mid-Frequency Band (20–40):** A moderate level of spectral loss was observed, indicating partial alteration of texture-level features. This implies that PRNU manipulation introduces measurable but non-extreme distortions in this frequency range. **High-Frequency Band (40–80):** The most prominent spectral loss occurred here, highlighting significant alterations in fine-grained image details. Since PRNU noise inherently operates in high-frequency components, this outcome confirms that spoofing primarily impacts noise textures and micro-patterns—essential characteristics used in forensic image analysis. This spectral fingerprinting approach thus offers a promising mitigation mechanism. By setting band-specific thresholds or anomaly detectors based on expected spectral profiles, forensic systems may flag suspicious manipulations even if PCE scores suggest authenticity. Future integration of this technique could serve as a secondary verification layer in PRNU-based camera identification pipelines.

8 Conclusion

This paper demonstrates that PRNU transfer attacks can reliably spoof camera source attribution across both physical and AI generated images. Our two-phase evaluation shows that manipulated images can achieve high PCE scores and bypass forensic source verification tools, including commercial solutions. We also propose two countermeasures based on PCE thresholding and spectral loss analysis, which expose key artifacts of PRNU spoofing. Notably, our findings suggest that spectral loss analysis remains a promising direction for enhancing defenses against such attacks.

As part of future work, we plan to evaluate PRNU injection under JPEG compression and platform-specific re-encodings, as assessing spoofing robustness in the presence of such distortions is critical. We will also extend our evaluation to encompass a wider range of conditions, including device diversity, varied lighting, and newer imaging platforms (e.g., DSLRs, webcams, and surveillance cameras) to enhance the generalizability of our attack model. Interestingly, we observed that our technique was most successful when applied to images generated by AI models—a notable finding given that these images inherently lack a native PRNU pattern. This suggests an opportunity to further improve spoofing performance by first removing or masking the target device's PRNU before injection, a direction we aim to explore in subsequent work.

References

1. A V, M.: Lowpass, highpass, bandreject and bandpass filters in image processing (2021). https://blog.minhazav.dev/lowpass-highpass-band-reject-and-band-pass-filter/
2. Akbari, Y., Almaadeed, N., Al-Maadeed, S., Khelifi, F., Bouridane, A.: PRNU-net: a deep learning approach for source camera model identification based on videos taken with smartphone. In: 2022 26th international conference on pattern recognition (ICPR), pp. 599–605. IEEE (2022)
3. Akshatha, K., Karunakar, A.K., Anitha, H., Raghavendra, U., Shetty, D.: Digital camera identification using PRNU: a feature based approach. Digit. Investig. **19**, 69–77 (2016)
4. Altinisik, E., Tasdemir, K., Sencar, H.T.: Extracting PRNU noise from H.264 coded videos. In: 2018 26th European signal processing conference (EUSIPCO), pp. 1367–1371. IEEE (2018)
5. Aranda, L.A., Reviriego, P., Maestro, J.A.: Error detection technique for a median filter. IEEE Trans. Nucl. Sci. **64**(8), 2219–2226 (2017)
6. Banerjee, S., Mirjalili, V., Ross, A.: Spoofing PRNU patterns of iris sensors while preserving iris recognition. In: 2019 IEEE 5th International Conference on Identity, Security, and Behavior Analysis (ISBA), pp. 1–10. IEEE (2019)
7. Behare, M.S., Bhalchandra, A., Kumar, R.: Source camera identification using photo response noise uniformity. In: 2019 3rd International Conference on Electronics, Communication and Aerospace Technology (ICECA), pp. 731–734. IEEE (2019)

8. Bhat, N.N., Bianchi, T.: Investigating inconsistencies in PRNU-based camera identification. In: 2022 IEEE International Conference on Image Processing (ICIP), pp. 851–855. IEEE (2022)
9. Cabello, F., León, J., Iano, Y., Arthur, R.: Implementation of a fixed-point 2D Gaussian filter for image processing based on FPGA. In: 2015 Signal Processing: Algorithms, Architectures, Arrangements, and Applications (SPA), pp. 28–33. IEEE (2015)
10. Cozzolino, D., Marra, F., Gragnaniello, D., Poggi, G., Verdoliva, L.: Combining PRNU and noiseprint for robust and efficient device source identification. EURASIP J. Inf. Secur. **2020**(1), 1–12 (2020). https://doi.org/10.1186/s13635-020-0101-7
11. Cozzolino, D., Verdoliva, L.: Noiseprint: a CNN-based camera model fingerprint. IEEE Trans. Inf. Forensics Secur. **15**, 144–159 (2019)
12. Deng, G., Cahill, L.: An adaptive Gaussian filter for noise reduction and edge detection. In: 1993 IEEE Conference Record Nuclear Science Symposium and Medical Imaging Conference, pp. 1615–1619. IEEE (1993)
13. Dirik, A.E., Karaküçük, A.: Forensic use of photo response non-uniformity of imaging sensors and a counter method. Opt. Express **22**(1), 470–482 (2014)
14. Farhangi, N., Ghofrani, S.: Using BayesShrink, BiShrink, weighted BayesShrink, and weighted BiShrink in NSST and SWT for despeckling SAR images. EURASIP J. Image Video Process. **2018**, 1–18 (2018)
15. Fontani, M.: How to use amped authenticate video PRNU to check whether a video and some images are from the same camera (2020). https://blog.ampedsoftware.com/2020/12/22/how-to-use-amped-authenticate-video-prnu
16. Goljan, M.: Digital camera identification from images – estimating false acceptance probability. In: Kim, H.-J., Katzenbeisser, S., Ho, A.T.S. (eds.) IWDW 2008. LNCS, vol. 5450, pp. 454–468. Springer, Heidelberg (2009). https://doi.org/10.1007/978-3-642-04438-0_38
17. Goljan, M., Fridrich, J., Filler, T.: Large scale test of sensor fingerprint camera identification. In: Media Forensics and Security, vol. 7254, pp. 170–181. SPIE (2009)
18. Gupta, G., et al.: Algorithm for image processing using improved median filter and comparison of mean, median and improved median filter. Int. J. Soft Comput. Eng. (IJSCE) **1**(5), 304–311 (2011)
19. Hsiao, A., Takenouchi, T., Kikuchi, H., Sakiyama, K., Miura, N.: More accurate and robust PRNU-based source camera identification with 3-step 3-class approach. In: Zhao, X., Piva, A., Comesaña-Alfaro, P. (eds.) IWDW 2021. LNCS, vol. 13180, pp. 87–101. Springer, Cham (2022). https://doi.org/10.1007/978-3-030-95398-0_7
20. Ismael, A.A., Baykara, M.: Digital image denoising techniques based on multi-resolution wavelet domain with spatial filters: a review. Traitement Signal **38**(3) (2021)
21. Iuliani, M., Fontani, M., Piva, A.: A leak in PRNU based source identification-questioning fingerprint uniqueness. IEEE Access **9**, 52455–52463 (2021)
22. Jaiswal, A., Upadhyay, J., Somkuwar, A.: Image denoising and quality measurements by using filtering and wavelet based techniques. AEU-Int. J. Electron. Commun. **68**(8), 699–705 (2014)
23. Jayaswal, V.: Performance metrics: confusion matrix, precision, recall, and F1 score (2020). https://archive.ph/bkY1l
24. Kang, X., Li, Y., Qu, Z., Huang, J.: Enhancing source camera identification performance with a camera reference phase sensor pattern noise. IEEE Trans. Inf. Forensics Secur. **7**(2), 393–402 (2011)

25. Karaküçük, A., Dirik, A.E.: PRNU based source camera attribution for image sets anonymized with patch-match algorithm. Digit. Investig. **30**, 43–51 (2019)
26. Korus, P., Huang, J.: Multi-scale analysis strategies in PRNU-based tampering localization. IEEE Trans. Inf. Forensics Secur. **12**(4), 809–824 (2016)
27. Law, S.C., Law, N.F.: Performance enhancement of PRNU-based source identification for smart video surveillance. HKIE Trans. Hong Kong Inst. Eng. **29**(3), 172–181 (2022)
28. Li, C., Li, Z., Liu, X., Li, S.: The influence of image degradation on hyperspectral image classification. Remote Sens. **14**(20), 5199 (2022)
29. Li, J., et al.: A novel PCA-based method for PRNU distillation to the benefit of source camera identification. Appl. Sci. **13**(11), 6583 (2023)
30. Lukas, J., Fridrich, J., Goljan, M.: Determining digital image origin using sensor imperfections. In: Image and Video Communications and Processing 2005, vol. 5685, pp. 249–260. SPIE (2005)
31. Lukas, J., Fridrich, J., Goljan, M.: Digital camera identification from sensor pattern noise. IEEE Trans. Inf. Forensics Secur. **1**(2), 205–214 (2006)
32. Manisha, Li, C.T., Kotegar, K.A.: Source camera identification with a robust device fingerprint: evolution from image-based to video-based approaches. Sensors **23**(17), 7385 (2023)
33. Manisha, Li, C.T., Lin, X., Kotegar, K.A.: Beyond PRNU: learning robust device-specific fingerprint for source camera identification. Sensors **22**(20), 7871 (2022)
34. Marra, F., Poggi, G., Sansone, C., Verdoliva, L.: Blind PRNU-based image clustering for source identification. IEEE Trans. Inf. Forensics Secur. **12**(9), 2197–2211 (2017)
35. Martín-Rodríguez, F., Isasi-de Vicente, F., Fernández-Barciela, M.: A stress test for robustness of photo response nonuniformity (camera sensor fingerprint) identification on smartphones. Sensors **23**(7), 3462 (2023)
36. Maser, B., Söllinger, D., Uhl, A.: PRNU-based detection of finger vein presentation attacks. In: 2019 7th International Workshop on Biometrics and Forensics (IWBF), pp. 1–6. IEEE (2019)
37. Nayerifard, T., Amintoosi, H., Ghaemi Bafghi, A.: A robust PRNU-based source camera attribution with convolutional neural networks. J. Supercomput. **81**(1), 1–24 (2025)
38. Remya, R., Beevi, A.B.: Novel video camera authentication based on peak to correlation energy of clustered sensor pattern noise. In: 2015 IEEE International Conference on Engineering and Technology (ICETECH), pp. 1–5. IEEE (2015)
39. Scherhag, U., Debiasi, L., Rathgeb, C., Busch, C., Uhl, A.: Detection of face morphing attacks based on PRNU analysis. IEEE Trans. Biometr. Behav. Identity Sci. **1**(4), 302–317 (2019)
40. Singh, S., Sehgal, V.K.: Exploring biomedical video source identification: transitioning from fuzzy-based systems to machine learning models. Fuzzy Inf. Eng. **16**(1), 33–48 (2024)
41. Uhl, A., Höller, Y.: Iris-sensor authentication using camera PRNU fingerprints. In: 2012 5th IAPR International Conference on Biometrics (ICB), pp. 230–237. IEEE (2012)
42. Wang, B., Zhao, M., Wang, W., Dai, X., Li, Y., Guo, Y.: Adversarial analysis for source camera identification. IEEE Trans. Circuits Syst. Video Technol. **31**(11), 4174–4186 (2020)
43. Westin, C.F., Knutsson, H., Kikinis, R., et al.: Adaptive image filtering. Handb. Med. Imaging 19–31 (2000)

44. Yang, W.C., Jiang, J., Chen, C.H.: A fast source camera identification and verification method based on PRNU analysis for use in video forensic investigations. Multimed. Tools Appl. **80**(5), 6617–6638 (2021)
45. Zhu, R., Wang, Y.: Application of improved median filter on image processing. J. Comput. **7**(4), 838–841 (2012)

Biometric Security

Comparative Evaluation of Lattices for Fuzzy Extractors and Fuzzy Signatures

Wataru Nakamura[✉][iD], Yusei Suzuki, Masakazu Fujio, and Kenta Takahashi[iD]

Hitachi, Ltd., Kanagawa 244-0817, Japan
{wataru.nakamura.va,yusei.suzuki.je,masakazu.fujio.kz,
kenta.takahashi.bw}@hitachi.com

Abstract. Fuzzy Extractors (FEs) and Fuzzy Signatures (FSs) are promising primitives for template-protected biometric authentication, and lattice-based constructions of them are known. In this paper, to reveal lattices more suitable for FEs/FSs in terms of application to biometric authentication, we evaluate the accuracy of FEs/FSs for various lattices, along with the computation time of finding the closest lattice vector $\mathrm{CV}_L(\cdot)$ required in the authentication process when FEs/FSs are applied to biometric authentication. Specifically, we treat the integer lattice $\mathbb{Z}^n$, a triangular lattice $L_n^{(\mathrm{tri})}$, and the direct product $E_8^{n/8}$ of the Gosset lattice, which have been treated in conventional studies on FEs/FSs, and additionally the dual lattice $L_n^{(\mathrm{d-tri})}$ of a triangular lattice and the checkerboard lattice D_n. To evaluate the accuracy of FEs/FSs with these lattices, we give algorithms for computing the *lattice norm* for $L_n^{(\mathrm{d-tri})}$, D_n, and $E_8^{n/8}$, where the lattice norm can be utilized for efficient accuracy evaluation and algorithms for $\mathbb{Z}^n$ and $L_n^{(\mathrm{tri})}$ are known. Then, we evaluate the accuracy of FEs/FSs based on these lattices utilizing the lattice norm. Although $L_n^{(\mathrm{tri})}$ is often used for FEs and FSs conventionally, the evaluation results show that $E_8^{n/8}$ achieves the highest accuracy of the evaluated lattices, and D_n achieves accuracy close to $L_n^{(\mathrm{tri})}$ with shorter computation time of $\mathrm{CV}_L(\cdot)$. Also, to obtain the lattice norm for $L_n^{(\mathrm{d-tri})}$, we give a similarity transformation from a non-full-rank lattice to a full-rank one, which transforms the zero-sum root lattice A_n and its dual A_n^* to $L_n^{(\mathrm{tri})}$ and $L_n^{(\mathrm{d-tri})}$, respectively. Using this transformation, we discuss a relation between $L_n^{(\mathrm{tri})}$, often used for FEs/FSs, and A_n, a well-studied lattice in lattice theory.

Keywords: fuzzy extractors · fuzzy signatures · lattices · accuracy · closest vector

1 Introduction

Online biometric authentication systems are used for various applications such as payment and national ID services. In these systems, it is crucial to reduce biometric data leakage risk. For this purpose, Biometric Template Protection (BTP) [9,10] has been studied and standardized. In BTP, a user's biometric feature for enrollment is transformed into a template to make it difficult to recover the feature. The server stores the template, and authenticates the user without recovering the feature.

To realize BTP, Fuzzy Extractors (FEs) [5] and Fuzzy Signatures (FSs) [17] are promising primitives. FEs generate a secret key and a helper string p from a feature x so that it is difficult to guess the key or the feature from p while the key can be reproduced from p and a feature x' sufficiently close to x. By generating a digital signature using the secret key,[1] online biometric authentication with BTP is realized. FSs generate a digital signature using a biometric feature without the helper string, which further reduces biometric data leakage risk [11].

In addition to reducing the biometric data leakage risk, high accuracy is important. For biometric matching algorithms in general, main accuracy indicators are False Match Rate (FMR) and False Non-Match Rate (FNMR), where FMR (resp. FNMR) is the ratio of accepted imposter pairs (resp. rejected genuine pairs) to all the evaluated imposter (resp. genuine) pairs. When the matching algorithm is applied to biometric authentication, larger FMR leads to higher risk of unauthorized access, and larger FNMR leads to more frequent failure of access by genuine users. Therefore, FMR and FNMR must be lowered.

To realize FEs and FSs with higher accuracy, lattice-based FEs and FSs have been proposed [11,16,22,23]. Biometric features are often extracted by machine learning, and many of them are suitable for the Euclidean matching.[2] When a feature $x \in \mathbb{R}^n$ is used for enrollment, the acceptance region on the Euclidean matching is the n-dimensional ball $\{x' \in \mathbb{R}^n \mid \|x - x'\|_2 \leq r\}$, where r is the predetermined threshold. On the other hand, for both of FEs and FSs with a lattice L, the acceptance region is given by $\mathrm{AR}_L(x) = \{x' \in \mathbb{R}^n \mid \mathrm{CV}_L(x' - x) = \mathbf{0}\}$,[3] where $\mathrm{CV}_L(\cdot)$ denotes the closest vector in L. Therefore, when features suitable for the Euclidean matching are used, one can improve the accuracy of FEs/FSs by choosing L so that $\mathrm{AR}_L(x)$ approximates the n-dimensional ball well.

However, there are only a few previous studies on comparing accuracy for different lattices. Yoneyama et al. [22] showed that *triangular lattices* can realize better accuracy than the integer lattice $\mathbb{Z}^n$. Also, Zhang et al. [23] evaluated the accuracy for $\mathbb{Z}^n$, a direct product E_8^m of the Gosset lattice E_8, and the Leech lattice, and showed that E_8^m realized the lowest FMR for a given FNMR of the lattices. On the other hand, previous studies did not compare the accuracy

---

[1] Specifically, online biometric authentication can be realized as follows: the server generates a fresh random number called a *challenge* and sends it to the client device for authentication, the client device generates a digital signature on the challenge using FEs/FSs, and the server verifies the signature.

[2] For example, feature extractors based on CosFace [21] and ArcFace [4] extract features suitable for the Euclidean matching.

[3] Precisely, a pair (x, x') is also accepted in the case of hash collision. We assume that the collision probability is negligible, and describe for simplicity that $\mathrm{AR}_L(x)$ is given as above. Also, the acceptance region is $\{x' \in \mathbb{R}^n \mid \mathrm{CV}_L(x - x') = \mathbf{0}\}$ in some constructions. We can evaluate the accuracy for this case in the same way.

on triangular lattices and E_8^m. Also, when lattice-based FEs/FSs are applied to biometric authentication, the authentication process includes computation of $\mathrm{CV}_L(\cdot)$, so it is required that $\mathrm{CV}_L(\cdot)$ can be computed efficiently for fast authentication. Nonetheless, previous studies also lack comparison on the computation time of $\mathrm{CV}_L(\cdot)$.

The main purpose of this paper is to reveal lattices more suitable for FEs/FSs in terms of the accuracy and computation time of $\mathrm{CV}_L(\cdot)$ among various lattices including triangular lattices and E_8^m. We treat the integer lattice $\mathbb{Z}^n$, a triangular lattice $L_n^{(\mathrm{tri})}$,[4] the dual lattice $L_n^{(\mathrm{d-tri})}$ of a triangular lattice, the checkerboard lattice D_n, and $E_8^{n/8}$ from the following reasons. First, to make $\mathrm{AR}_L(\boldsymbol{x})$ close to an n-dimensional ball, it is required that L is full-rank in $\mathbb{R}^n$. Lattices $\mathbb{Z}^n$, $L_n^{(\mathrm{tri})}$, $L_n^{(\mathrm{d-tri})}$, and D_n satisfy this requirement for any $n \in \mathbb{N}$, and $E_8^{n/8}$ satisfies it for $n \in 8\mathbb{N}$. In addition, when $\mathrm{AR}_L(\boldsymbol{x})$ approximates the n-dimensional ball well, it is expected that L has at least one of dense packing or thin covering. When n is small, lattices which realize the densest packing or thinnest covering are known [2, §1.5 of Chap. 1]. Densest packing is realized by $L_n^{(\mathrm{tri})}$ (which is equivalent to A_n) for $n \in \{2, 3\}$, D_n for $n \in \{4, 5\}$, and E_8 for $n = 8$. Thinnest covering is realized by $L_n^{(\mathrm{d-tri})}$ (which is equivalent to the dual lattice A_n^* of A_n) for $n \in \{2, 3, 4, 5\}$. From these, it can be guessed that $L_n^{(\mathrm{d-tri})}$ and D_n, in addition to $L_n^{(\mathrm{tri})}$ and $E_8^{n/8}$, are promising to realize FEs/FSs with high accuracy. Also, for $\mathbb{Z}^n$, $L_n^{(\mathrm{tri})}$, $L_n^{(\mathrm{d-tri})}$, D_n, and $E_8^{n/8}$, $\mathrm{CV}_L(\cdot)$ can be computed in $O(n)$ time,[5] so these lattices are good in terms of fast authentication.

To enable to tune FMR and FNMR for a given lattice L, we consider FEs/FSs with a scaled lattice tL for $t > 0$ as well as previous studies [11,23]. As t becomes larger, the volume of $\mathrm{AR}_{tL}(\boldsymbol{x})$ becomes larger, which leads to larger FMR and smaller FNMR. It is known [14] that the accuracy of FEs/FSs with tL can be evaluated efficiently if the *lattice norm* $\|\cdot\|_L$ can be computed efficiently,[6] and the lattice norm for $\mathbb{Z}^n$ and $L_n^{(\mathrm{tri})}$ can be computed in $O(n)$ time. To obtain algorithms for $\|\cdot\|_{L_n^{(\mathrm{d-tri})}}$, $\|\cdot\|_{D_n}$, and $\|\cdot\|_{E_8^{n/8}}$, we utilize the fact that $\|\cdot\|_L$ can be computed if the set of (Voronoi-) relevant vectors, denoted by $\mathrm{RV}(L)$, is obtained [15]. In particular, to obtain $\mathrm{RV}(L_n^{(\mathrm{d-tri})})$, we focus on the equivalence between

---

[4] We treat the triangular lattice $L_n^{(\mathrm{tri})}$ treated in [14,18,19]. We note that any triangular lattice can be obtained by rotating, reflecting, and/or scaling $L_n^{(\mathrm{tri})}$.

[5] An $O(n)$ time algorithm is obvious for $E_8^{n/8}$, and also known for D_n [2] and $L_n^{(\mathrm{tri})}$ [18]. For $L_n^{(\mathrm{d-tri})}$, we give an $O(n)$ time algorithm in Sect. 3.3.

[6] A simple method to compute (FMR, FNMR) for various t is changing t to various values and checking $\mathrm{CV}_{tL}(\boldsymbol{x}' - \boldsymbol{x}) = \boldsymbol{0}$ (or equivalently, $\mathrm{CV}_L((\boldsymbol{x}' - \boldsymbol{x})/t) = \boldsymbol{0}$) for each pair $(\boldsymbol{x}, \boldsymbol{x}')$. However, when the dataset contains P pairs, this simple method requires kP times of computing $\mathrm{CV}_L(\cdot)$ to obtain (FMR, FNMR) for k scales. Therefore, although $\mathrm{CV}_L(\cdot)$ can be computed in $O(n)$ time for the lattices treated in this paper, the computation becomes inefficient when we aim to compute (FMR, FNMR) for many scales. On the other hand, by computing the lattice norm $\|\boldsymbol{x}' - \boldsymbol{x}\|_L$ for each pair $(\boldsymbol{x}, \boldsymbol{x}')$ once, (i.e., computing the lattice norm P times in total,) we can obtain (FMR, FNMR) for almost all t, as described in Sect. 2.5.

$L_n^{(\mathrm{d-tri})}$ and A_n^*. Because $\mathrm{RV}(A_n^*)$ is known [7], we can obtain $\mathrm{RV}(L_n^{(\mathrm{d-tri})})$ if we have a similarity transformation (i.e., a transformation which reserves the Euclidean distance up to the constant factor) from A_n^* to $L_n^{(\mathrm{d-tri})}$. We give the transformation in a more generic way which includes a transformation from A_n to $L_n^{(\mathrm{tri})}$. Then, for $\mathbb{Z}^n$, $L_n^{(\mathrm{tri})}$, $L_n^{(\mathrm{d-tri})}$, D_n, and $E_8^{n/8}$, we evaluate the accuracy utilizing the lattice norm along with the computation time of $\mathrm{CV}_L(\cdot)$.

Specifically, our contribution is the following (I)(II)(III).

(I) *Similarity Transformation from a Non-Full-Rank Lattice to Full-Rank One (Sect. 3).* For $n, m \in \mathbb{N}$ with $n < m$ and a lattice $\widehat{L} \subset \mathbb{R}^m$ with rank n, we give a similarity transformation from $\widehat{L}$ to a full-rank one $L \subset \mathbb{R}^n$. Using this transformation, we give $\mathrm{RV}(L_n^{(\mathrm{d-tri})})$ explicitly from $\mathrm{RV}(A_n^*)$ [7], and an $O(n)$ time algorithm for $\mathrm{CV}_{L_n^{(\mathrm{d-tri})}}(\cdot)$ from that of $\mathrm{CV}_{A_n^*}(\cdot)$ [13]. Furthermore, based on this transformation, we observe a relation between $L_n^{(\mathrm{tri})}$ and A_n. Although triangular lattices are often used conventionally for lattice-based FEs/FSs [11,18,19,22], a concrete relation with A_n has not been revealed, so we believe that our observation on the relation is of independent interest.

(II) *Efficient Computation of the Lattice Norm (Sect. 4).* We give an $O(n)$ time algorithm for $\|\cdot\|_{D_n}$ and $\|\cdot\|_{E_8^{n/8}}$, and an $O(n \log n)$ time algorithm for $\|\cdot\|_{L_n^{(\mathrm{d-tri})}}$. This enables efficient accuracy evaluation of FEs/FSs for $L_n^{(\mathrm{d-tri})}$, D_n, and $E_8^{n/8}$ as well as $\mathbb{Z}^n$ and $L_n^{(\mathrm{tri})}$.

(III) *Comparative Evaluation of Accuracy and Computation Time of $\mathrm{CV}_L(\cdot)$ (Sect. 5).* For $\mathbb{Z}^n$, $L_n^{(\mathrm{tri})}$, $L_n^{(\mathrm{d-tri})}$, D_n, and $E_8^{n/8}$, we evaluate the accuracy of FEs/FSs with tL for IJB-C face dataset [12] utilizing the lattice norm. Also, we evaluate the computation time of $\mathrm{CV}_L(\cdot)$ for these lattices. Although $L_n^{(\mathrm{tri})}$ is often used conventionally, the evaluation results show that $E_8^{n/8}$ achieves the highest accuracy of the evaluated lattices, and D_n achieves accuracy close to $L_n^{(\mathrm{tri})}$ with shorter computation time of $\mathrm{CV}_L(\cdot)$.

2 Preliminaries

2.1 Notation

$\mathbb{N}$, $\mathbb{Z}$, $\mathbb{R}$, and $\mathbb{R}_{>0}$ denote the sets of all positive integers, all integers, all real numbers, and all positive real numbers, respectively. For $\mathbb{A} \in \{\mathbb{Z}, \mathbb{R}\}$ and $r, c \in \mathbb{N}$, $\mathbb{A}^{r \times c}$ denotes the set of all $r \times c$ matrices with each entry in $\mathbb{A}$. For $a, b \in \mathbb{Z}$, $[a, b] := \{n \in \mathbb{Z} \mid a \le n \le b\}$ and $[b] := [1, b]$. For a set U, $|U|$ denotes the cardinality of U. For sets U and V, $U + V := \{u + v \mid u \in U, v \in V\}$. For a set U and an element a, $aU := \{au \mid u \in U\}$. For $r \in \mathbb{R}$, $\lfloor r \rfloor := \max\{z \in \mathbb{Z} \mid z \le r\}$, and $\lceil r \rfloor$ denotes the integer closest to r. Vectors are column vectors. For a vector $\boldsymbol{x} = (x_i)_{i \in [n]} \in \mathbb{R}^n$, $\lfloor \boldsymbol{x} \rfloor := (\lfloor x_i \rfloor)_{i \in [n]}$, $\lceil \boldsymbol{x} \rfloor := (\lceil x_i \rfloor)_{i \in [n]}$, and $\|\boldsymbol{x}\|_2$ denotes the Euclidean norm. For $n \in \mathbb{N}$, $\boldsymbol{I}_n \in \mathbb{Z}^{n \times n}$ denotes the identity matrix. For

$i \in [n]$, $e_{(n,i)} \in \mathbb{Z}^n$ denotes the i-th column of I_n, i.e., the n-dimensional vector in which the i-th entry is 1 and the other entries are 0. For $n \in \mathbb{N}$ and $U \subseteq [n]$, $e_{(n,U)} := \sum_{i \in U} e_{(n,i)}$. For $n \in \mathbb{N}$, $\mathbf{0}_n \in \mathbb{R}^n$ and $\mathbf{1}_n \in \mathbb{R}^n$ denote the zero vector and the vector with all entries are 1, respectively, and $J_n := \mathbf{1}_n \mathbf{1}_n^\top$. For $r, c \in \mathbb{N}$, $O_{r,c} \in \mathbb{Z}^{r \times c}$ denotes the zero matrix, and $I_{r,c} \in \mathbb{Z}^{r \times c}$ is defined by

$$I_{r,c} := \begin{cases} \begin{bmatrix} I_c \\ O_{r-c,c} \end{bmatrix} & \text{if } r > c, \\ I_r & \text{if } r = c, \\ [I_r \ O_{r,c-r}] & \text{if } r < c. \end{cases}$$

2.2 Lattices

If a set L can be represented with a matrix $B \in \mathbb{R}^{m \times n}$ ($m \geq n$, $\mathrm{rank}(B) = n$) as $L = \{Bz \mid z \in \mathbb{Z}^n\}$, L is called a lattice with rank n, and B is called a basis matrix. The lattice determined by a basis matrix $B \in \mathbb{R}^{m \times n}$ is denoted by $\Lambda(B) := \{Bz \mid z \in \mathbb{Z}^n\}$. For a lattice L and a vector $x \in \mathbb{R}^n$, the closest vector of x in L, denoted by $\mathrm{CV}_L(x)$, is the vector $l^* \in L$ satisfying $\|x - l^*\|_2 \leq \|x - l\|_2$ for all $l \in L$ if only one vector $l^* \in L$ satisfies this condition, and otherwise we choose one according to a pre-determined rule. The set $\mathrm{Vor}(L) := \{x \in \mathbb{R}^n \mid \forall l \in L \setminus \{\mathbf{0}\}, \|x\|_2 \leq \|x - l\|_2\}$ is called a (closed) Voronoi region on L centered at the origin. $\mathrm{RV}(L)$ denotes the set of (Voronoi) relevant vectors, where relevant vectors are ones which contribute to the sphere of $\mathrm{Vor}(L)$. For a lattice L with rank n, $\mathrm{H}(L)$ denotes the n-dimensional linear subspace containing L.

Lattices L and L' are equivalent (or isometric) if L' can be obtained by scaling, rotation, and reflection from L. Specifically, the equivalence is defined as follows.

Definition 1. *Let $m \in \mathbb{N}$. Lattices $L, L' \subset \mathbb{R}^m$ are equivalent if for any basis matrix B of L and any basis matrix B' of L', there exist a number $\beta \in \mathbb{R}_{>0}$, an orthogonal matrix R (i.e., a square matrix R satisfying $R^\top R = I_m$), and a unimodular matrix M (i.e., a square matrix M such that all entries are integers and the determinant is ± 1) such that $B = \beta R B' M$. Also, when one of the two lattices is defined in $\mathbb{R}^{m'}$ ($m' < m$), we consider the matrix obtained by inserting the zero row vector $\mathbf{0}_m^\top$ $m - m'$ times instead of the basis matrix for the condition. That is, the condition is $I_{m,m'} B = \beta R B' M$ if $L \subset \mathbb{R}^{m'}$ ($m' < m$), and $B = \beta R I_{m,m'} B' M$ if $L' \subset \mathbb{R}^{m'}$ ($m' < m$). We represent $L \simeq L'$ if L and L' are equivalent.*

Remark 1. By this definition, $\mathrm{rank}(L) = \mathrm{rank}(L')$ if $L \simeq L'$. If the rank is n, the sizes of matrices in Definition 1 are $R \in \mathbb{R}^{m \times m}$, $M \in \mathbb{Z}^{n \times n}$, $B, B' \in \mathbb{R}^{m \times n}$ if $L, L' \subset \mathbb{R}^m$, $B \in \mathbb{R}^{m' \times n}$ if $L \subset \mathbb{R}^{m'}$, and $B' \in \mathbb{R}^{m' \times n}$ if $L' \subset \mathbb{R}^{m'}$.

The equivalence can be characterized as follows [3, Remark 2.1].

Lemma 1. *Let $m, n \in \mathbb{R}_{>0}$, and let $L \subset \mathbb{R}^n$ and $L' \subset \mathbb{R}^m$ be lattices. Then, $L \simeq L'$ if and only if there exist a number $\alpha \in \mathbb{R}_{>0}$, a basis matrix B of L, and a basis matrix B' of L' such that $B^\top B = \alpha (B')^\top B'$.*

2.3 Lattices Treated in this Paper

For $n \in \mathbb{N}$, the zero-sum root lattice A_n is defined by $A_n := \{z \in \mathbb{Z}^{n+1} \mid \mathbf{1}_{n+1}^\top z = 0\}$. Its dual lattice A_n^* is given by $A_n^* = \{(I_{n+1} - J_{n+1}/(n+1))z \mid z \in \mathbb{Z}^{n+1}\}$. The checkerboard lattice D_n is defined by $D_n := \{z \in \mathbb{Z}^n \mid \mathbf{1}_n^\top z \in 2\mathbb{Z}\}$. The 8 dimensional Gosset lattice E_8 is defined by $E_8 := D_8 \cup (D_8 + (1/2)\mathbf{1}_8)$.

Triangular lattices are lattices in which the basis matrix B satisfies $B^\top B = (\lambda^2/2)(I_n + J_n)$ for some $\lambda \in \mathbb{R}_{>0}$. We treat the one $L_n^{(\mathrm{tri})} = \Lambda(B_n^{(\mathrm{tri})})$, where $B_n^{(\mathrm{tri})}$ is defined by Cholesky decomposition of $(1/2)(I_n + J_n)$, i.e.,

$$B_n^{(\mathrm{tri})} := \begin{bmatrix} \gamma_1 & \omega_1 & \cdots & \cdots & \omega_1 \\ 0 & \gamma_2 & \omega_2 & \cdots & \omega_2 \\ \vdots & \ddots & \ddots & \ddots & \vdots \\ \vdots & & \ddots & \ddots & \omega_{n-1} \\ 0 & \cdots & \cdots & 0 & \gamma_n \end{bmatrix} \qquad (1)$$

with $\gamma_k := (1 - \sum_{i=1}^{k-1} \omega_i^2)^{1/2}$ ($k \in [n]$) and $\omega_k := (1/2 - \sum_{i=1}^{k-1} \omega_i^2)/\gamma_k$ ($k \in [n-1]$).

For $\lambda \in \mathbb{R}_{>0}$, the dual lattice of a triangular lattice $\Lambda(\lambda B_n^{(\mathrm{tri})})$ is given by the basis matrix B satisfying $B^\top B = ((\lambda^2/2)(I_n + J_n))^{-1} = (2/\lambda^2)(I_n - (1/(n+1))J_n)$. We treat the one $L_n^{(\mathrm{d-tri})} = \Lambda(B_n^{(\mathrm{d-tri})})$, where $B_n^{(\mathrm{d-tri})}$ is the matrix obtained by substituting $(\gamma_k)_{k\in[n]}$ and $(\omega_k)_{k\in[n-1]}$ in (1) to $(\widetilde{\gamma}_k)_{k\in[n]}$ and $(\widetilde{\omega}_k)_{k\in[n-1]}$ defined by $\widetilde{\gamma}_k := (1 - \sum_{i=1}^{k-1}(\widetilde{\omega}_i)^2)^{1/2}$ ($k \in [n]$) and $\widetilde{\omega}_k := (-1/n - \sum_{i=1}^{k-1}(\widetilde{\omega}_i)^2)/\widetilde{\gamma}_k$ ($k \in [n-1]$), respectively. The matrix $B_n^{(\mathrm{d-tri})}$ satisfies $(B_n^{(\mathrm{d-tri})})^\top B_n^{(\mathrm{d-tri})} = I_n - (1/n)(J_n - I_n) = (1/n)((n+1)I_n - J_n)$.

2.4 Lattice-Based FEs/FSs

FEs [5] are defined by a pair of algorithms $(\mathrm{Gen}_{\mathrm{FE}}, \mathrm{Rep}_{\mathrm{FE}})$, where $\mathrm{Gen}_{\mathrm{FE}}$ generates a secret key r and a helper string h from a feature x, and $\mathrm{Rep}_{\mathrm{FE}}$ reproduces r from h and another feature x'. The requirements are that r is pseudorandom even if h is given, and that r can be correctly reproduced by $\mathrm{Rep}_{\mathrm{FE}}$ from h and x' satisfying $d(x, x') \leq t$, where d is a distance function and t is a threshold. Lattice-based FEs were proposed in [16,22,23]. These studies gave similar constructions, and the acceptance condition for FEs with a lattice L is either $\mathrm{CV}_L(x' - x) = 0$ or $\mathrm{CV}_L(x - x') = 0$. For example, in the construction by Parente et al. [16], $\mathrm{Gen}_{\mathrm{FE}}$ generates the helper string h as $h \leftarrow x + l$, where $l \in L$ is a lattice vector transformed from the random string r. Then, $\mathrm{Rep}_{\mathrm{FE}}$ calculates $\widetilde{l}$ as $\widetilde{l} \leftarrow \mathrm{CV}_L(h - x')$, and reproduces r from $\widetilde{l}$. The condition that r can be correctly reproduced (i.e., $\widetilde{l} = l$) is $\mathrm{CV}_L(x - x') = 0$. Zhang et al. [23] showed that FEs with a scaled lattice tL ($t \in \mathbb{R}_{>0}$) are FEs with the distance $d_L(\cdot, \cdot)$, which we call the *lattice distance*, defined by

$$d_L(x, x') := \min\{t \geq 0 \mid x' - x \in t\,\mathrm{Vor}(L)\}. \qquad (2)$$

On the other hand, FSs [17] are defined by a set of algorithms $\mathrm{SetUp}_{\mathrm{FS}}(1^\lambda, \mathcal{F}) \to pp$, $\mathrm{KeyGen}_{\mathrm{FS}}(pp, \boldsymbol{x}) \to vk$, $\mathrm{Sign}_{\mathrm{FS}}(pp, \boldsymbol{x}', m) \to \sigma$, and $\mathrm{Verify}_{\mathrm{FS}}(pp, vk, m, \sigma) \to (\top \text{ or } \bot)$, where $\mathcal{F}$ is a fuzzy key setting which defines how fuzzy data such as biometric features are generated, and pp is a public parameter. The requirements of FS are correctness and EUF-CMA security.[7] Katsumata et al. [11] gave a construction of lattice-based FSs. The acceptance condition for FSs with L is $\mathrm{CV}_L(\boldsymbol{x}' - \boldsymbol{x}) = \boldsymbol{0}$ as well as lattice-based FEs.

2.5 Accuracy Evaluation of Lattice-Based FEs/FSs

As described in Sect. 1, main accuracy indicators for biometric matching algorithms are FMR and FNMR, and we consider FEs/FSs with a scaled lattice tL for $t > 0$. The accuracy of them can be formalized as follows. Let $X \subset \mathbb{R}^n$ be a dataset which consists of a finite number of n dimensional biometric features. Let $P_{\mathrm{Imp}} \subset X \times X$ and $P_{\mathrm{Gen}} \subset X \times X$ be the set of imposter and genuine pairs for evaluation, respectively. Then, FMR and FNMR of FEs/FSs with a scaled lattice tL, denoted by $\mathrm{FMR}(t)$ and $\mathrm{FNMR}(t)$, respectively, are given by

$$\mathrm{FMR}(t) = \frac{|\{(\boldsymbol{x}, \boldsymbol{x}') \in P_{\mathrm{Imp}} \mid \mathrm{CV}_{tL}(\boldsymbol{x}' - \boldsymbol{x}) = \boldsymbol{0}\}|}{|P_{\mathrm{Imp}}|}, \quad (3)$$

$$\mathrm{FNMR}(t) = \frac{|\{(\boldsymbol{x}, \boldsymbol{x}') \in P_{\mathrm{Gen}} \mid \mathrm{CV}_{tL}(\boldsymbol{x}' - \boldsymbol{x}) \neq \boldsymbol{0}\}|}{|P_{\mathrm{Gen}}|}. \quad (4)$$

As described in [14], when the lattice distance $d_L(\cdot, \cdot)$ in (2) can be efficiently computed, $(\mathrm{FMR}(t), \mathrm{FNMR}(t))$ for various $t \in \mathbb{R}_{>0}$ can be efficiently computed. Indeed, it follows from (2) that $d_L(\boldsymbol{x}, \boldsymbol{x}') = \inf\{t > 0 \mid \mathrm{CV}_{tL}(\boldsymbol{x}' - \boldsymbol{x}) = \boldsymbol{0}\}$. Hence for any $t \in \mathbb{R}_{>0}$, $\mathrm{FMR}(t)$ and $\mathrm{FNMR}(t)$ satisfy

$$\mathrm{FMR}(t) \leq \frac{|\{(\boldsymbol{x}, \boldsymbol{x}') \in P_{\mathrm{Imp}} \mid d_L(\boldsymbol{x}, \boldsymbol{x}') \leq t\}|}{|P_{\mathrm{Imp}}|}, \quad (5)$$

$$\mathrm{FNMR}(t) \leq \frac{|\{(\boldsymbol{x}, \boldsymbol{x}') \in P_{\mathrm{Gen}} \mid d_L(\boldsymbol{x}, \boldsymbol{x}') \geq t\}|}{|P_{\mathrm{Gen}}|}. \quad (6)$$

Furthermore, for almost all $t \in \mathbb{R}_{>0}$, the equality holds in (5)(6). Concretely, let S_{Imp} and S_{Gen} be $S_{\mathrm{Imp}} := \{t \in \mathbb{R}_{>0} \mid \exists (\boldsymbol{x}, \boldsymbol{x}') \in P_{\mathrm{Imp}}, d_L(\boldsymbol{x}, \boldsymbol{x}') = t\}$ and $S_{\mathrm{Gen}} := \{t \in \mathbb{R}_{>0} \mid \exists (\boldsymbol{x}, \boldsymbol{x}') \in P_{\mathrm{Gen}}, d_L(\boldsymbol{x}, \boldsymbol{x}') = t\}$. Then, the equality in (5) and (6) holds for $t \in \mathbb{R}_{>0} \backslash S_{\mathrm{Imp}}$ and $t \in \mathbb{R}_{>0} \backslash S_{\mathrm{Gen}}$, respectively. Therefore, by computing $d_L(\boldsymbol{x}, \boldsymbol{x}')$ for each pair $(\boldsymbol{x}, \boldsymbol{x}')$, we can obtain $\mathrm{FMR}(t)$ for $t \in \mathbb{R}_{>0} \backslash S_{\mathrm{Imp}}$ and $\mathrm{FNMR}(t)$ for $t \in \mathbb{R}_{>0} \backslash S_{\mathrm{Gen}}$.

We can compute $d_L(\cdot, \cdot)$ if we can compute the lattice norm $\|\cdot\|_L$ defined by

$$\|\boldsymbol{x}\|_L := \inf\{t > 0 \mid \mathrm{CV}_{tL}(\boldsymbol{x}) = \boldsymbol{0}\}, \quad (7)$$

which can be computed with the set of relevant vectors as follows [15]:

---

[7] In [17], EUF-CMA (existential unforgeability under chosen message attacks) security for FSs is defined in a similar way to EUF-CMA security for conventional digital signatures.

Theorem 1. *For a lattice $L \subset \mathbb{R}^n$,*

$$\|x\|_L = \max_{w \in \mathrm{RV}(L)} \frac{2w^\top x}{\|w\|_2^2} \quad (x \in \mathbb{R}^n). \tag{8}$$

For the triangular lattice $L_n^{(\mathrm{tri})}$, the set $\mathrm{RV}(L_n^{(\mathrm{tri})})$ is given by

$$\mathrm{RV}(L_n^{(\mathrm{tri})}) = W_n^+ \cup W_n^- \cup W_n^{\mathrm{diff}}, \tag{9}$$

where $b_{(n,i)}^{(\mathrm{tri})}$ denotes i-th column of $B_n^{(\mathrm{tri})}$ for $i \in [n]$, and the sets W_n^+, W_n^-, W_n^{diff} are defined by $W_n^+ := \{b_{(n,i)}^{(\mathrm{tri})} \mid i \in [n]\}$, $W_n^- := \{-b_{(n,i)}^{(\mathrm{tri})} \mid i \in [n]\}$, $W_n^{\mathrm{diff}} := \{b_{(n,i)}^{(\mathrm{tri})} - b_{(n,j)}^{(\mathrm{tri})} \mid i,j \in [n], i \neq j\}$ [15]. The lattice norm $\|x\|_{L_n^{(\mathrm{tri})}}$ can be computed as follows [14].[8]

Theorem 2. *For $x \in \mathbb{R}^n$, let $r_{\max}$ and $r_{\min}$ be the maximum and minimum entries of $(B_n^{(\mathrm{tri})})^\top x$, respectively. Then,*

$$\|x\|_{L_n^{(\mathrm{tri})}} = 2\max\{r_{\max}, -r_{\min}, r_{\max} - r_{\min}\}. \tag{10}$$

For $x \in \mathbb{R}^n$, $\|x\|_{L_n^{(\mathrm{tri})}}$ can be computed in $O(n)$ time as follows [14].[9]

Step 1. $u_1 \leftarrow 0$, $u_k \leftarrow u_{k-1} + \omega_{k-1} x_{k-1}$ $(k \in [2,n])$.
Step 2. $y_k \leftarrow \gamma_k x_k + u_k$ $(k \in [n])$.
Step 3. $r_{\max} \leftarrow \max\{y_1, \ldots, y_n\}$, $r_{\min} \leftarrow \min\{y_1, \ldots, y_n\}$.
Step 4. $\|x\|_{L_n^{(\mathrm{tri})}} \leftarrow 2\max\{r_{\max}, -r_{\min}, r_{\max} - r_{\min}\}$.

3 Similarity Transformation from a Non-Full-Rank Lattice to Full-Rank One

We give a generic similarity transformation from a non-full-rank lattice to full-rank one. Also, using the transformation, we discuss a relation between $L_n^{(\mathrm{tri})}$ and A_n, and between $L_n^{(\mathrm{d-tri})}$ and A_n^*.

3.1 A Generic Transformation

Let $\widehat{L} \subset \mathbb{R}^m$ be a lattice with rank n and $C \in \mathbb{R}^{m \times n}$ be a basis matrix of $\widehat{L}$, where $n, m \in \mathbb{N}$ with $n < m$. Let $C_1 \in \mathbb{R}^{n \times n}$ and $C_2 \in \mathbb{R}^{(m-n) \times n}$ be the upper n rows and the lower $m - n$ rows of C, respectively. We assume that C_1 is full-rank.[10] Then, from Lemma 1, we can obtain a full-rank lattice $L \subset \mathbb{R}^n$ equivalent to $\widehat{L}$ as follows.

---

[8] As described in [15], we can also obtain Theorem 2 by applying (9) to (8).
[9] By Step 1 and Step 2, $(y_i)_{i \in [n]} = (B_n^{(\mathrm{tri})})^\top x$ is computed.
[10] When C_1 is not full-rank, we can obtain a similarity transformation in a similar way by choosing independent n rows of C instead of the upper n rows.

Step 1. Define $\alpha \in \mathbb{R}_{>0}$ arbitrarily.
Step 2. Define $B \in \mathbb{R}^{n \times n}$ so that $B^\top B = \alpha C^\top C$.[11]
Step 3. Define L by $L := \Lambda(B)$.

We give a similarity transformation f which maps $\widehat{L}$ to L, and show properties.

Lemma 2. Let $f : \mathrm{H}(\widehat{L}) \to \mathbb{R}^n$ be

$$f(\widehat{x}) = BC_1^{-1} I_{n,m} \widehat{x} \quad (\widehat{x} \in \mathrm{H}(\widehat{L})). \tag{11}$$

Then,

$$L = f(\widehat{L}), \tag{12}$$

$$\|f(\widehat{x}_1) - f(\widehat{x}_2)\|_2 = \sqrt{\alpha}\|\widehat{x}_1 - \widehat{x}_2\|_2 \quad (\widehat{x}_1, \widehat{x}_2 \in \mathrm{H}(\widehat{L})), \tag{13}$$

$$\mathrm{RV}(L) = f(\mathrm{RV}(\widehat{L})), \tag{14}$$

$$\mathrm{CV}_L(x) = f(\mathrm{CV}_{\widehat{L}}(f^{-1}(x))) \quad (x \in \mathbb{R}^n), \tag{15}$$

$$f^{-1}(x) = CB^{-1}x \quad (x \in \mathbb{R}^n), \tag{16}$$

where we assume that the rules of choosing points of $\mathrm{CV}_L(\cdot)$ and $\mathrm{CV}_{\widehat{L}}(\cdot)$ when there are multiple closest points are defined so that (15) is satisfied.

Proof. Because $f(Cz) = Bz$ for any $z \in \mathbb{Z}^n$, the condition $l \in L$ is equivalent to $l \in f(\widehat{L})$. Therefore, (12) holds.

(13) follows from the linearity of f and the following equation for $\widehat{x} \in \mathrm{H}(\widehat{L})$:

$$(f(\widehat{x}))^\top f(\widehat{x}) = (C_1^{-1} I_{n,m} \widehat{x})^\top B^\top B C_1^{-1} I_{n,m} \widehat{x}$$
$$= \alpha (C_1^{-1} I_{n,m} \widehat{x})^\top C^\top C C_1^{-1} I_{n,m} \widehat{x} = \alpha \widehat{x}^\top \widehat{x},$$

where the second equality holds because $B^\top B = \alpha C^\top C$, and the third one holds because any $\widehat{x} \in \mathrm{H}(\widehat{L})$ can be represented with a vector $r \in \mathbb{R}^n$ as $\widehat{x} = Cr$, which leads to $\widehat{x} = Cr = CC_1^{-1} C_1 r = CC_1^{-1} I_{n,m} Cr = CC_1^{-1} I_{n,m} \widehat{x}$.

(14)(15) can be shown from (13). (The details are described in Appendix.)

(16) holds because any $\widehat{x} \in \mathrm{H}(\widehat{L})$ can be represented with a vector $r \in \mathbb{R}^n$ as $\widehat{x} = Cr$, which leads to $\widehat{x} = Cr = CB^{-1} BC_1^{-1} I_{n,m} Cr = CB^{-1} f(\widehat{x})$. □

3.2 Relation Between $L_n^{(\mathrm{tri})}$ and A_n

When $\widehat{L} = A_n$, a basis matrix $C \in \mathbb{Z}^{(n+1) \times n}$ is given by

$$C = \begin{bmatrix} I_n \\ -\mathbf{1}_n^\top \end{bmatrix}. \tag{17}$$

Therefore, $C^\top C = I_n + J_n = 2(B_n^{(\mathrm{tri})})^\top B_n^{(\mathrm{tri})}$, which implies $L_n^{(\mathrm{tri})} \simeq A_n$. We observe a relation between them in more detail using f.[12]

---

[11] For example, B can be obtained by the Choleski decomposition of $\alpha C^\top C$.
[12] Although the equivalence of $L_n^{(\mathrm{tri})}$ and A_n was pointed out in [20], a relation such as described in this section was not discussed.

The Transformations Between $L_n^{(\mathrm{tri})}$ and A_n. When $L = L_n^{(\mathrm{tri})}$, $B = B_n^{(\mathrm{tri})}$, $\widehat{L} = A_n$, and C is defined as (17), the transformations f and f^{-1} in (11)(16) are

$$f(\widehat{x}) = B_n^{(\mathrm{tri})}[I_n \ 0_n]\widehat{x} \quad (\widehat{x} \in \mathrm{H}(A_n)), \tag{18}$$

$$f^{-1}(x) = \begin{bmatrix} I_n \\ -1_n^\top \end{bmatrix} (B_n^{(\mathrm{tri})})^{-1} x \quad (x \in \mathbb{R}^n). \tag{19}$$

From (12), $L_n^{(\mathrm{tri})} = f(A_n)$ holds for this f.

The Set of Relevant Vectors for $L_n^{(\mathrm{tri})}$. The set $\mathrm{RV}(L_n^{(\mathrm{tri})})$ is given by (9), which was derived in [14] from the definition of the set of relevant vectors. On the other hand, it is known that the set $\mathrm{RV}(A_n)$ is given as follows [2, §6.1 of Chap. 4 and §3.G of Chap. 21]:

$$\mathrm{RV}(A_n) = \{e_{(n+1,i)} - e_{(n+1,j)} \mid i,j \in [n+1],\ i \neq j\}. \tag{20}$$

From this and (14)(18), we obtain another way for deriving $\mathrm{RV}(L_n^{(\mathrm{tri})})$. Indeed, it can be calculated as

$$\begin{aligned}\mathrm{RV}(L_n^{(\mathrm{tri})}) &= \{B_n^{(\mathrm{tri})}[I_n \ 0_n](e_{(n+1,i)} - e_{(n+1,j)}) \mid i,j \in [n+1],\ i \neq j\} \\ &= \{B_n^{(\mathrm{tri})}(e_{(n,i)} - e_{(n,j)}) \mid i,j \in [n],\ i \neq j\} \\ &\quad \cup \{B_n^{(\mathrm{tri})} e_{(n,i)} \mid i \in [n]\} \cup \{-B_n^{(\mathrm{tri})} e_{(n,j)} \mid j \in [n]\} \\ &= W_n^{\mathrm{diff}} \cup W_n^+ \cup W_n^-.\end{aligned}$$

An $O(n)$ Time Algorithm for $\mathrm{CV}_{L_n^{(\mathrm{tri})}}(\cdot)$. Efficient computation of $\mathrm{CV}_{L_n^{(\mathrm{tri})}}(\cdot)$ has been studied [18,19,22], and an $O(n)$ time algorithm was recently proposed [18]. Utilizing the transformation f in (18), we observe that a subproblem considered in the previous studies for efficient computation of $\mathrm{CV}_{L_n^{(\mathrm{tri})}}(\cdot)$ (specifically, ClosestVecCoef($\cdot$) below) is equivalent to computing a variant of $\mathrm{CV}_{A_n}(\cdot)$. This implies that we can obtain an $O(n)$ time algorithm for the subproblem from that of $\mathrm{CV}_{A_n}(\cdot)$, which has been known for over 20 years [2].

From an input $x \in \mathbb{R}^n$, the previous algorithms compute $\mathrm{CV}_{L_n^{(\mathrm{tri})}}(x)$ by

$$v \leftarrow (B_n^{(\mathrm{tri})})^{-1} x;\ z \leftarrow \mathrm{ClosestVecCoef}(v);\ \text{return}\ B_n^{(\mathrm{tri})} z, \tag{21}$$

where ClosestVecCoef($\cdot$) is an algorithm which computes $(B_n^{(\mathrm{tri})})^{-1} \mathrm{CV}_{L_n^{(\mathrm{tri})}}(x)$ from $(B_n^{(\mathrm{tri})})^{-1} x$. The computation of $(B_n^{(\mathrm{tri})})^{-1} x$ and $B_n^{(\mathrm{tri})} z$ can be done in $O(n)$ time [19]. Also, an $O(n^2)$ time algorithm for ClosestVecCoef(v) was proposed in [22], and the time complexity was improved to $O(n)$ in [18]. In this way, an $O(n)$ time algorithm for $\mathrm{CV}_{L_n^{(\mathrm{tri})}}(\cdot)$ was realized.

On the other hand, from (15), $\mathrm{CV}_{L_n^{(\mathrm{tri})}}(x) = f(\mathrm{CV}_{A_n}(f^{-1}(x)))$ holds for f and f^{-1} in (18)(19). Hence $\mathrm{CV}_{L_n^{(\mathrm{tri})}}(x)$ can be computed by

$$v \leftarrow (B_n^{(\mathrm{tri})})^{-1} x;\ z \leftarrow [I_n \ 0_n] \mathrm{CV}_{A_n}\left(\begin{bmatrix} I_n \\ -1_n^\top \end{bmatrix} v\right);\ \text{return}\ B_n^{(\mathrm{tri})} z. \tag{22}$$

From (21)(22), ClosestVecCoef(v) is equivalent to computing $[I_n \ 0_n]\mathrm{CV}_{A_n}([I_n \ -1_n]^\top v)$. Therefore, while efficient computation of ClosestVecCoef($\cdot$) has been studied, we can obtain an $O(n)$ time algorithm for it immediately from that of $\mathrm{CV}_{A_n}(\cdot)$ [2]. From this and $O(n)$ time algorithms for $(B_n^{(\mathrm{tri})})^{-1}x$ and $B_n^{(\mathrm{tri})}z$, we can obtain an $O(n)$ time algorithm for $\mathrm{CV}_{L_n^{(\mathrm{tri})}}(\cdot)$.

3.3 Relation Between $L_n^{(\mathrm{d-tri})}$ and A_n^*

When $\widehat{L} = A_n^*$, a basis matrix $C \in \mathbb{Z}^{(n+1)\times n}$ is given by choosing the first n columns of $I_{n+1} - J_{n+1}/(n+1)$, i.e.,

$$C = \begin{bmatrix} I_n - \frac{1}{n+1}J_n \\ -\frac{1}{n+1}1_n^\top \end{bmatrix}. \tag{23}$$

Therefore, $C^\top C = I_n - J_n/(n+1) = (n/(n+1))(B_n^{(\mathrm{d-tri})})^\top B_n^{(\mathrm{d-tri})}$, which implies $L_n^{(\mathrm{d-tri})} \simeq A_n^*$. We observe a relation between them in more detail.

The Transformations Between $L_n^{(\mathrm{d-tri})}$ and A_n^*. When $L = L_n^{(\mathrm{d-tri})}$, $B = B_n^{(\mathrm{d-tri})}$, $\widehat{L} = A_n^*$, and C is given as (23), the transformations f and f^{-1} in (11)(16) are

$$f(\widehat{x}) = B_n^{(\mathrm{d-tri})}(I_n + J_n)[I_n \ 0_n]\widehat{x} \quad (\widehat{x} \in \mathrm{H}(A_n^*)), \tag{24}$$

$$f^{-1}(x) = \begin{bmatrix} I_n - \frac{1}{n+1}J_n \\ -\frac{1}{n+1}1_n^\top \end{bmatrix} (B_n^{(\mathrm{d-tri})})^{-1}x \quad (x \in \mathbb{R}^n). \tag{25}$$

From (12), $L_n^{(\mathrm{d-tri})} = f(A_n^*)$ holds for this f.

The Set of Relevant Vectors for $L_n^{(\mathrm{d-tri})}$. It is known [7, §3.5] that $\mathrm{RV}(A_n^*)$ is given by

$$\mathrm{RV}(A_n^*) = \left\{ -\frac{n-|U|+1}{n+1}e_{(n+1,U)} + \frac{|U|}{n+1}e_{(n+1,[n+1]\setminus U)} \,\middle|\, U \subsetneq [n+1],\, U \neq \emptyset \right\}. \tag{26}$$

From this and (14)(24), we can obtain $\mathrm{RV}(L_n^{(\mathrm{d-tri})})$ as follows.

Lemma 3. *The set $\mathrm{RV}(L_n^{(\mathrm{d-tri})})$ is given by*

$$\mathrm{RV}(L_n^{(\mathrm{d-tri})}) = \{sB_n^{(\mathrm{d-tri})}e_{(n,U)} \mid s \in \{-1,1\},\, U \subseteq [n],\, U \neq \emptyset\}. \tag{27}$$

We describe a proof in Appendix.

An $O(n)$ Time Algorithm for $\mathrm{CV}_{L_n^{(\mathrm{d-tri})}}(\cdot)$. From (15)(24)(25), we can compute $\mathrm{CV}_{L_n^{(\mathrm{d-tri})}}(x)$ for $x \in \mathbb{R}^n$ as follows:

Step 1. $\widehat{x} \leftarrow \begin{bmatrix} I_n - \frac{1}{n+1}J_n \\ -\frac{1}{n+1}1_n^\top \end{bmatrix} (B_n^{(\mathrm{d-tri})})^{-1}x.$

Step 2. $\widehat{l} \leftarrow \mathrm{CV}_{A_n^*}(\widehat{x})$.
Step 3. return $\boldsymbol{B}_n^{(\mathrm{d-tri})}(\boldsymbol{I}_n + \boldsymbol{J}_n)[\boldsymbol{I}_n \; \boldsymbol{0}_n]\widehat{l}$.

Step 1 and 3 can be computed in $O(n)$ time because $\boldsymbol{B}_n^{(\mathrm{d-tri})}\boldsymbol{x}$ and $(\boldsymbol{B}_n^{(\mathrm{d-tri})})^{-1}\boldsymbol{x}$ for $\boldsymbol{x} \in \mathbb{R}^n$ can be computed in $O(n)$ time in the same way as $\boldsymbol{B}_n^{(\mathrm{tri})}\boldsymbol{x}$ and $(\boldsymbol{B}_n^{(\mathrm{tri})})^{-1}\boldsymbol{x}$. Also, an $O(n)$ time algorithm for $\mathrm{CV}_{A_n^*}(\cdot)$ is known [13]. Therefore, $\mathrm{CV}_{L_n^{(\mathrm{d-tri})}}(\cdot)$ can be computed in $O(n)$ time by the above algorithm.

4 Efficient Computation of the Lattice Norm

We give an $O(n \log n)$ time algorithm for $\|\cdot\|_{L_n^{(\mathrm{d-tri})}}$, and an $O(n)$ time algorithm for $\|\cdot\|_{D_n}$ and $\|\cdot\|_{E_8^{n/8}}$.

4.1 Lattice Norm for $L_n^{(\mathrm{d-tri})}$

The set $\mathrm{RV}(L_n^{(\mathrm{d-tri})})$ is given by (27). By applying it to (8), we can obtain the following representation of $\|\cdot\|_{L_n^{(\mathrm{d-tri})}}$.

Corollary 1. For $\boldsymbol{x} \in \mathbb{R}^n$,

$$\|\boldsymbol{x}\|_{L_n^{(\mathrm{d-tri})}} = 2n \max_{\substack{s \in \{-1,1\} \\ U \subseteq [n],\, U \neq \emptyset}} \frac{s \boldsymbol{e}_{(n,U)}^\top (\boldsymbol{B}_n^{(\mathrm{d-tri})})^\top \boldsymbol{x}}{|U|(n+1-|U|)}. \qquad (28)$$

Proof. From $(\boldsymbol{B}_n^{(\mathrm{d-tri})})^\top \boldsymbol{B}_n^{(\mathrm{d-tri})} = ((n+1)\boldsymbol{I}_n - \boldsymbol{J}_n)/n$, it holds for $U \subseteq [n]$ that $\|\boldsymbol{B}_n^{(\mathrm{d-tri})} \boldsymbol{e}_{(n,U)}\|_2^2 = \boldsymbol{e}_{(n,U)}^\top (\boldsymbol{B}_n^{(\mathrm{d-tri})})^\top \boldsymbol{B}_n^{(\mathrm{d-tri})} \boldsymbol{e}_{(n,U)} = \boldsymbol{e}_{(n,U)}^\top ((n+1)\boldsymbol{I}_n - \boldsymbol{J}_n)\boldsymbol{e}_{(n,U)}/n = ((n+1)|U| - |U|^2)/n = |U|(n+1-|U|)/n$. From this and (8)(27), we obtain (28). □

We can compute $\|\boldsymbol{x}\|_{L_n^{(\mathrm{d-tri})}}$ for $\boldsymbol{x} \in \mathbb{R}^n$ in $O(n \log n)$ time as follows.

Step 1. $\boldsymbol{r} \leftarrow (\boldsymbol{B}_n^{(\mathrm{d-tri})})^\top \boldsymbol{x}$.
Step 2. $r_{\sigma(1)}, r_{\sigma(2)}, \ldots, r_{\sigma(n)} \leftarrow \mathrm{sort}(\boldsymbol{r})$ (in descending order).
Step 3. $c \leftarrow r_{\sigma(1)}, \quad c' \leftarrow r_{\sigma(n)}, \quad m \leftarrow \frac{c}{n}, \quad m' \leftarrow \frac{c'}{n}$.
Step 4. For $i = 2, 3, \ldots, n$:
$$c \leftarrow c + r_{\sigma(i)}, \quad c' \leftarrow c' + r_{\sigma(n+1-i)},$$
$$m \leftarrow \max\{m, \tfrac{c}{i(n+1-i)}\}, \quad m' \leftarrow \min\{m', \tfrac{c'}{i(n+1-i)}\}.$$
Step 5. return $2n \max\{m, -m'\}$.

4.2 Lattice Norm for D_n

The set $\mathrm{RV}(D_n)$ is given as follows [2, §7.1 of Chap. 4 and §3.G of Chap. 21]:

$$\mathrm{RV}(D_n) = \{s_1 \boldsymbol{e}_{(n,i)} + s_2 \boldsymbol{e}_{(n,j)} \mid s_1, s_2 \in \{-1,1\},\; i,j \in [n],\; i \neq j\}. \qquad (29)$$

By applying (29) to (8), we can obtain the following representation of $\|\cdot\|_{D_n}$.

Corollary 2. *For $\boldsymbol{x} = (x_i)_{i \in [n]} \in \mathbb{R}^n$, let $a_{\max}$ and a_{second} be the maximum and the second maximum entries of $(|x_i|)_{i \in [n]}$, respectively. Then,*

$$\|\boldsymbol{x}\|_{D_n} = a_{\max} + a_{\text{second}}. \tag{30}$$

Proof. From (29), $\|\boldsymbol{w}\|_2 = \sqrt{2}$ for any $\boldsymbol{w} \in \text{RV}(D_n)$. From this and (29)(8),

$$\|\boldsymbol{x}\|_{D_n} = \max_{\substack{i,j \in [n] \\ i \neq j}} \max_{s_1, s_2 \in \{-1,1\}} (s_1 \boldsymbol{e}_{(n,i)}^\top \boldsymbol{x} + s_2 \boldsymbol{e}_{(n,j)}^\top \boldsymbol{x}) = \max_{\substack{i,j \in [n] \\ i \neq j}} (|x_i| + |x_j|)$$

$$= a_{\max} + a_{\text{second}}. \qquad \square$$

Because $a_{\max}$ and a_{second} can be computed in $O(n)$ time, $\|\boldsymbol{x}\|_{D_n}$ can be computed in $O(n)$ time.

4.3 Lattice Norm for E_8

The set $\text{RV}(E_8)$ is given as follows [2, §8.1 of Chap. 4 and §3.G of Chap. 21]:

$$\text{RV}(E_8) = \text{RV}(D_8) \cup \frac{1}{2}Q, \tag{31}$$

where $Q := \{\boldsymbol{s} \in \{-1,1\}^8 \mid \text{The number of 1's in the entries of } \boldsymbol{s} \text{ is even}\}$. By applying (31) to (8), we can obtain the following representation of $\|\cdot\|_{E_8}$.

Corollary 3. *For $\boldsymbol{x} = (x_i)_{i \in [8]} \in \mathbb{R}^8$, let $a_{\min}$ and a_{sum} be the minimum entry and the sum of the entries of $(|x_i|)_{i \in [8]}$, respectively. Let $I_+ := \{i \in [8] \mid x_i > 0\}$, and δ_{odd} be $\delta_{\text{odd}} = 1$ if $|I_+|$ is odd, and $\delta_{\text{odd}} = 0$ otherwise. Then,*

$$\|\boldsymbol{x}\|_{E_8} = \max\left\{\|\boldsymbol{x}\|_{D_8}, \frac{1}{2}a_{\text{sum}} - \delta_{\text{odd}} \cdot a_{\min}\right\}. \tag{32}$$

We describe a proof in Appendix.

4.4 Lattice Norm for $E_8^{n/8}$

From Theorem 1, the lattice norm for a direct product L^m of a lattice L can be computed as follows.

Corollary 4. *Let $m, q \in \mathbb{N}$, and let $L \subset \mathbb{R}^q$ be a lattice. For $\boldsymbol{x} \in \mathbb{R}^{mq}$, let $\boldsymbol{x}^{(1)}, \ldots, \boldsymbol{x}^{(m)} \in \mathbb{R}^q$ be the vectors defined by $\boldsymbol{x}^\top = [(\boldsymbol{x}^{(1)})^\top \cdots (\boldsymbol{x}^{(m)})^\top]$. Then,*

$$\|\boldsymbol{x}\|_{L^m} = \max_{i \in [m]} \|\boldsymbol{x}^{(i)}\|_L.$$

From this corollary, for $n \in 8\mathbb{N}$ and $\boldsymbol{x} \in \mathbb{R}^n$, $\|\boldsymbol{x}\|_{E_8^{n/8}}$ can be computed by

$$\|\boldsymbol{x}\|_{E_8^{n/8}} = \max_{i \in [n/8]} \|\boldsymbol{x}^{(i)}\|_{E_8},$$

where $\boldsymbol{x}^{(1)}, \ldots, \boldsymbol{x}^{(n/8)} \in \mathbb{R}^8$ are defined by $\boldsymbol{x}^\top = [(\boldsymbol{x}^{(1)})^\top \cdots (\boldsymbol{x}^{(n/8)})^\top]$. Obviously, it can be computed in $O(n)$ time.

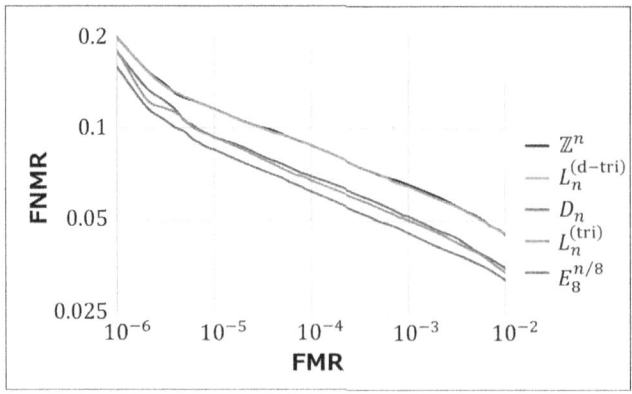

Fig. 1. Accuracy Evaluation Results.

5 Comparative Evaluation of Accuracy and Computation Time of $CV_L(\cdot)$

For $\mathbb{Z}^n$, $L_n^{(tri)}$, $L_n^{(d-tri)}$, D_n, and $E_8^{n/8}$, we evaluate the accuracy of FEs/FSs with a lattice tL for $t \in \mathbb{R}_{>0}$ and the computation time of $CV_L(\cdot)$.

5.1 Accuracy

Method. For accuracy evaluation, we use IJB-C face dataset [12], which consists of face images from 3,531 subjects. To extract features, we use IResNet-100 [6] model trained on Glint360K [1] dataset from InsightFace [8]. The extracted features are 512 dimensional real vectors, i.e., $n = 512$. The pairs used for evaluation are the same as ones used for the evaluation program by InsightFace, which are 19,557 genuine pairs and 15,638,932 imposter pairs. For each pair, we compute the lattice distance using the methods in Sect. 4, and obtain (FMR, FNMR) of FEs/FSs with tL for $t \in \mathbb{R}_{>0}$ as described in Sect. 2.5.

Results. Figure 1 shows the obtained (FMR, FNMR) for each lattice. The direct product $E_8^{n/8}$ of the Gosset lattice achieved the highest accuracy of the evaluated ones, and followed by $L_n^{(tri)}$. Also, D_n achieved the accuracy close to that of $L_n^{(tri)}$. The accuracy by $L_n^{(d-tri)}$ and $\mathbb{Z}^n$ was almost the same, and they were the worst of the evaluated lattices. As an example of comparisons of FNMR at a fixed FMR, FNMR at FMR $= 10^{-5}$ was 11.5% by $\mathbb{Z}^n$, 11.5% by $L_n^{(d-tri)}$, 9.3% by D_n, 9.3% by $L_n^{(tri)}$, and 8.5% by $E_8^{n/8}$.

Table 1. Computation Time of $\mathrm{CV}_L(\cdot)$ (μs)

	$n = 128$	$n = 256$	$n = 512$
$\mathbb{Z}^n$	2.5	4.7	9.6
$L_n^{(\mathrm{tri})}$	5.3	10.0	19.0
$L_n^{(\mathrm{d-tri})}$	8.4	17.3	35.8
D_n	2.6	5.1	10.0
$E_8^{n/8}$	8.7	17.0	33.7

5.2 Computation Time of $\mathrm{CV}_L(\cdot)$

Method. We consider the following algorithms for computing $\mathrm{CV}_L(\cdot)$ as the object of our evaluation. For the target vector $\boldsymbol{x} = (x_i)_{i \in [n]} \in \mathbb{R}^n$, we compute $\mathrm{CV}_{\mathbb{Z}^n}(\boldsymbol{x})$ by simply computing $(\lfloor x_i \rceil)_{i \in [n]}$. We compute $\mathrm{CV}_{L_n^{(\mathrm{tri})}}(\boldsymbol{x})$ and $\mathrm{CV}_{L_n^{(\mathrm{d-tri})}}(\boldsymbol{x})$ by the algorithms in Sect. 3.2 and Sect. 3.3, respectively. For $\mathrm{CV}_{D_n}(\boldsymbol{x})$, we used the algorithm in [2], which computes $\boldsymbol{z} = (z_i)_{i \in [n]} \leftarrow \mathrm{CV}_{\mathbb{Z}^n}(\boldsymbol{x})$, and outputs $\boldsymbol{z}$ if $\boldsymbol{1}_n^\top \boldsymbol{z} \in 2\mathbb{Z}$ and otherwise outputs $\boldsymbol{z} + s\boldsymbol{e}_{(n,k)}$, where $k \leftarrow \arg\max_{i \in [n]} |x_i - z_i|$ and $s \in \{-1, 1\}$ is the sign of $x_k - z_k$. We compute $\mathrm{CV}_{E_8^{n/8}}(\boldsymbol{x})$ for $\boldsymbol{x}^{(1)}, \ldots, \boldsymbol{x}^{(n/8)} \in \mathbb{R}^8$ and $\boldsymbol{x} = [(\boldsymbol{x}^{(1)})^\top \cdots (\boldsymbol{x}^{(n/8)})^\top]^\top$ by $\mathrm{CV}_{E_8^{n/8}}(\boldsymbol{x}) \leftarrow [\mathrm{CV}_{E_8}(\boldsymbol{x}^{(1)})^\top \cdots \mathrm{CV}_{E_8}(\boldsymbol{x}^{(n/8)})^\top]^\top$, where we compute $\mathrm{CV}_{E_8}(\boldsymbol{x})$ for $\boldsymbol{x} \in \mathbb{R}^8$ by computing $\mathrm{CV}_{D_8}(\boldsymbol{x})$ and $\mathrm{CV}_{D_8}(\boldsymbol{x} - (1/2)\boldsymbol{1}_8) + (1/2)\boldsymbol{1}_8$, and outputting the one closer to $\boldsymbol{x}$. We note that all of these algorithms run in $O(n)$ time.

For each lattice, we evaluate the computation time in the same way as in [19]. Concretely, for each dimension $n \in \{128, 256, 512\}$, we randomly choose 10,000 vectors in $\{r \in \mathbb{R} \mid -100 \le r \le 100\}^n$ as target vectors, where entries of vectors are 32-bit float. We measure the computation time of $\mathrm{CV}_L(\boldsymbol{x})$ for each target vector $\boldsymbol{x}$ using each algorithm, and evaluate the average time per run. The computing environment is as follows: OS: Windows 10 Pro, CPU: Intel(R) Core(TM) i7-8700K @ 3.70 GHz, memory 32 GB, storage: SSD.

Results. Table 1 shows the results. For all dimensions $n \in \{128, 256, 512\}$, $\mathbb{Z}^n$ achieved the shortest time, and followed in order by D_n, $L_n^{(\mathrm{tri})}$, $E_8^{n/8}$, and $L_n^{(\mathrm{d-tri})}$. The time for D_n was almost the same as that of $\mathbb{Z}^n$. In particular, for $n = 512$, the time for D_n was 1.04 times that of $\mathbb{Z}^n$, while the time for $L_n^{(\mathrm{tri})}$, $E_8^{n/8}$, and $L_n^{(\mathrm{d-tri})}$ were 1.99, 3.74, and 3.51 times that of $\mathbb{Z}^n$, respectively.

5.3 Discussion

If one wants to realize FEs/FSs with higher accuracy, the evaluation results show that $E_8^{n/8}$ is the most suitable of the evaluated lattices. On the other hand, when the computation time of $\mathrm{CV}_L(\cdot)$ is required to be shorter, D_n is promising because the computation time is almost the same as that of $\mathbb{Z}^n$ and achieves better accuracy than $\mathbb{Z}^n$. Although the triangular lattice $L_n^{(\text{tri})}$ is often used for FEs and FSs conventionally, the evaluation results suggest that $E_8^{n/8}$ is more suitable for realizing higher accuracy, and D_n is more suitable for reducing the computation time of $\text{CV}_L(\cdot)$ while maintaining accuracy.

Also, when FEs/FSs with small FMR (e.g., FMR = 10^{-6} or less) is required for higher security, FNMR becomes larger than 10% for all of $\mathbb{Z}^n$, $L_n^{(\text{tri})}$, $L_n^{(\text{d-tri})}$, D_n, and $E_8^{n/8}$. If FEs/FSs with this FNMR are applied to biometric authentication systems as they are, the systems might not be so practical because the users will be frequently rejected. One possible solution is to employ multi-modal authentication, e.g., using face and iris, which can improve accuracy. Similar to this, another possible solution is multi-factor authentication, which uses "what you know" (e.g., passwords) and/or "what you have" (e.g., IC cards containing the secret key) in addition to biometrics.

The order of accuracy obtained in Sect. 5.1 might be related to existing indicators on lattices such as packing density and covering thickness, or one might be able to explain reasons for the order by introducing new indicators reflecting the distribution of biometric features. A detailed analysis is future work.

6 Conclusion

In this paper, to reveal lattices more suitable for biometric authentication based on FEs/FSs, we evaluated the accuracy of FEs/FSs and the computation time of $\text{CV}_L(\cdot)$ for the integer lattice $\mathbb{Z}^n$, a triangular lattice $L_n^{(\text{tri})}$, the dual lattice $L_n^{(\text{d-tri})}$ of a triangular lattice, the checkerboard lattice D_n, and the direct product $E_8^{n/8}$ of the Gosset lattice. For efficient accuracy evaluation, we gave an $O(n)$ time algorithm for $\|\cdot\|_{D_n}$ and $\|\cdot\|_{E_8^{n/8}}$, and an $O(n \log n)$ time algorithm for $\|\cdot\|_{L_n^{(\text{d-tri})}}$. Then, we evaluated the accuracy for these lattices utilizing the lattice norm, along with the computation time of $\text{CV}_L(\cdot)$. Although $L_n^{(\text{tri})}$ is often used conventionally, the evaluation results show that $E_8^{n/8}$ achieves the highest accuracy of the evaluated lattices, and D_n achieves accuracy close to $L_n^{(\text{tri})}$ with shorter computation time of $\text{CV}_L(\cdot)$.

Furthermore, to obtain the lattice norm for $L_n^{(\text{d-tri})}$, we gave a similarity transformation from a non-full-rank lattice to a full-rank one, which transforms the zero-sum root lattice A_n and its dual A_n^* to $L_n^{(\text{tri})}$ and $L_n^{(\text{d-tri})}$, respectively. Then, we discussed a relation between $L_n^{(\text{tri})}$, often used for FEs/FSs, and A_n, a well-studied lattice in lattice theory.

Appendix

Proof of (14)

$\text{RV}(L)$ is the set with the minimum number of elements in $\mathcal{W}_0 := \{W \subseteq L \mid \bigcap_{\boldsymbol{w} \in W} \text{HalfSp}(\boldsymbol{w}) = \text{Vor}(L)\}$, where $\text{HalfSp}(\boldsymbol{w}) := \{\boldsymbol{x} \in \mathbb{R}^n \mid \|\boldsymbol{x}\|_2 \leq \|\boldsymbol{x} - \boldsymbol{w}\|_2\}$

for $w \in L$. The set $\mathcal{W}_0$ can be transformed by (12)(13) as follows:

$$\mathcal{W}_0 = \left\{ W \subseteq L \,\middle|\, \bigcap_{w \in W} \mathrm{HalfSp}(w) = \mathrm{Vor}(L) \right\}$$

$$= \left\{ f(\widehat{W}) \,\middle|\, \widehat{W} \subseteq \widehat{L}, \, \bigcap_{\widehat{w} \in \widehat{W}} \{x \in \mathbb{R}^n \mid \|x\|_2 \leq \|x - f(\widehat{w})\|_2\} = f(\mathrm{Vor}(\widehat{L})) \right\}$$

$$= f\left(\left\{ \widehat{W} \subseteq \widehat{L} \,\middle|\, \bigcap_{\widehat{w} \in \widehat{W}} \{f(\widehat{x}) \mid \widehat{x} \in \mathrm{H}(\widehat{L}), \, \|f(\widehat{x})\|_2 \leq \|f(\widehat{x}) - f(\widehat{w})\|_2 \} \right. \right.$$
$$\left. \left. = f(\mathrm{Vor}(\widehat{L})) \right\} \right)$$

$$= f\left(\left\{ \widehat{W} \subseteq \widehat{L} \,\middle|\, \bigcap_{\widehat{w} \in \widehat{W}} \{\widehat{x} \in \mathrm{H}(\widehat{L}) \mid \|\widehat{x}\|_2 \leq \|\widehat{x} - \widehat{w}\|_2\} = \mathrm{Vor}(\widehat{L}) \right\} \right).$$

$$= f\left(\left\{ \widehat{W} \subseteq \widehat{L} \,\middle|\, \bigcap_{\widehat{w} \in \widehat{W}} \{\widehat{x} \in \mathbb{R}^m \mid \|\widehat{x}\|_2 \leq \|\widehat{x} - \widehat{w}\|_2\} = \mathrm{Vor}(\widehat{L}) \right\} \right).$$

Because f preserves the number of elements, (14) holds. □

Proof of (15)

For $x \in \mathbb{R}^n$,

$$\mathrm{CV}_L(x) = \arg\min_{l \in L} \|l - x\|_2$$
$$= \arg\min_{l \in L} \|f^{-1}(l) - f^{-1}(x)\|_2$$
$$= f\left(\arg\min_{\widehat{l} \in \widehat{L}} \|\widehat{l} - f^{-1}(x)\|_2 \right)$$
$$= f(\mathrm{CV}_{\widehat{L}}(f^{-1}(x))).$$

Therefore, (15) holds. □

Proof of Lemma 3

By defining $\beta_i := i/(n+1)$ for $i \in [n+1]$, we can represent $\mathrm{RV}(A_n^*)$ in (26) as $\mathrm{RV}(A_n^*) = \{-e_{(n+1,U)} + \beta_{|U|}\mathbf{1}_{n+1} \mid U \subsetneq [n+1], U \neq \emptyset\}$. From this and (14)(24), $\mathrm{RV}(L_n^{(\mathrm{d-tri})})$ can be calculated as

$\mathrm{RV}(L_n^{(\mathrm{d-tri})})$
$= \{B_n^{(\mathrm{d-tri})}(I_n + J_n)[I_n \; 0_n](-e_{(n+1,U)} + \beta_{|U|}\mathbf{1}_{n+1}) \mid U \subsetneq [n+1], U \neq \emptyset\}$
$= \{B_n^{(\mathrm{d-tri})}(I_n + J_n)[I_n \; 0_n](-e_{(n+1,U)} + \beta_{|U|}\mathbf{1}_{n+1}) \mid U \subsetneq [n+1], n+1 \in U\}$
$\quad \cup \{B_n^{(\mathrm{d-tri})}(I_n + J_n)[I_n \; 0_n](-e_{(n+1,U)} + \beta_{|U|}\mathbf{1}_{n+1}) \mid U \subseteq [n], U \neq \emptyset\}$
$= \{sB_n^{(\mathrm{d-tri})}e_{(n,U)} \mid s \in \{-1,1\}, U \subseteq [n], U \neq \emptyset\},$

where the last equality follows from

$$\{B_n^{(\text{d-tri})}(I_n + J_n)[I_n \ 0_n](-e_{(n+1,U)} + \beta_{|U|}1_{n+1}) \mid U \subsetneq [n+1], \ n+1 \in U\}$$
$$= \{B_n^{(\text{d-tri})}(I_n + J_n)[I_n \ 0_n](-e_{(n+1,U' \cup \{n+1\})} + \beta_{|U' \cup \{n+1\}|}1_{n+1}) \mid U' \subsetneq [n]\}$$
$$= \{B_n^{(\text{d-tri})}(I_n + J_n)(-e_{(n,U')} + \beta_{|U'|+1}1_n) \mid U' \subsetneq [n]\}$$
$$= \{B_n^{(\text{d-tri})}(-e_{(n,U')} + \beta_{|U'|+1}1_n - |U'|1_n + n\beta_{|U'|+1}1_n) \mid U' \subsetneq [n]\}$$
$$= \{B_n^{(\text{d-tri})}(1_n - e_{(n,U')}) \mid U' \subsetneq [n]\}$$
$$= \{B_n^{(\text{d-tri})}e_{(n,[n]\setminus U')} \mid U' \subsetneq [n]\}$$
$$= \{B_n^{(\text{d-tri})}e_{(n,U)} \mid U \subseteq [n], \ U \neq \emptyset\}$$

and

$$\{B_n^{(\text{d-tri})}(I_n + J_n)[I_n \ 0_n](-e_{(n+1,U)} + \beta_{|U|}1_{n+1}) \mid U \subseteq [n], \ U \neq \emptyset\}$$
$$= \{B_n^{(\text{d-tri})}(I_n + J_n)(-e_{(n,U)} + \beta_{|U|}1_n) \mid U \subseteq [n], \ U \neq \emptyset\}$$
$$= \{B_n^{(\text{d-tri})}(-e_{(n,U)} + \beta_{|U|}1_n - |U|1_n + n\beta_{|U|}1_n) \mid U \subseteq [n], \ U \neq \emptyset\}$$
$$= \{-B_n^{(\text{d-tri})}e_{(n,U)} \mid U \subseteq [n], \ U \neq \emptyset\}.$$

□

Proof of Corollary 3

From (31)(8),

$$\|x\|_{E_8} = \max\left\{\|x\|_{D_8}, \ \max_{w \in \frac{1}{2}Q} \frac{2w^\top x}{\|w\|_2^2}\right\}. \tag{33}$$

Also, because $\|w\|_2 = \sqrt{2}$ for any $w \in \frac{1}{2}Q$,

$$\max_{w \in \frac{1}{2}Q} \frac{2w^\top x}{\|w\|_2^2} = \max_{w \in \frac{1}{2}Q} w^\top x = \frac{1}{2}\max_{s \in Q} s^\top x. \tag{34}$$

Furthermore, $\max_{s \in Q} s^\top x = a_{\text{sum}}$ if $|I_+|$ is even and $\max_{s \in Q} s^\top x = a_{\text{sum}} - 2a_{\text{min}}$ if $|I_+|$ is odd. From this and (33)(34), we obtain (32). □

References

1. An, X., et al.: Partial FC: training 10 million identities on a single machine. In: Proceedings of the IEEE/CVF International Conference on Computer Vision, pp. 1445–1449 (2021)
2. Conway, J.H., Sloane, N.J.A.: Sphere Packings. Lattices and Groups. Springer, New York (1999)
3. Costa, S.I., Oggier, F., Campello, A., Belfiore, J.C., Viterbo, E.: Lattices Applied to Coding for Reliable and Secure Communications. Springer, Heidelberg (2017)

4. Deng, J., Guo, J., Xue, N., Zafeiriou, S.: Arcface: additive angular margin loss for deep face recognition. In: 2019 IEEE/CVF Conference on Computer Vision and Pattern Recognition (CVPR2019), pp. 4690–4699 (2019)
5. Dodis, Y., Ostrovsky, R., Reyzin, L., Smith, A.: Fuzzy extractors: how to generate strong keys from biometrics and other noisy data. SIAM J. Comput. **38**(1), 97–139 (2008)
6. Duta, I.C., Liu, L., Zhu, F., Shao, L.: Improved residual networks for image and video recognition. In: 2020 25th International Conference on Pattern Recognition (ICPR), pp. 9415–9422 (2021)
7. Engel, P., Michel, L., Sénéchal, M.: Lattice geometry (2004). https://cds.cern.ch/record/859509/files/cer-002542451.pdf. Accessed 29 July 2025
8. InsightFace: Insightface: 2d and 3d face analysis project. https://github.com/deepinsight/insightface. Accessed 02 June 2025
9. ISO: ISO/IEC 30136:2018 information technology — performance testing of biometric template protection schemes (2018)
10. ISO: ISO/IEC 24745:2022 information technology — security techniques — biometric information protection (2022)
11. Katsumata, S., Matsuda, T., Nakamura, W., Ohara, K., Takahashi, K.: Revisiting fuzzy signatures: towards a more risk-free cryptographic authentication system based on biometrics. In: The 2021 ACM SIGSAC Conference on Computer and Communications Security (CCS2021), pp. 2046–2065 (2021)
12. Maze, B., et al.: IARPA janus benchmark-c: face dataset and protocol. In: 2018 International Conference on Biometrics (ICB), pp. 158–165 (2018)
13. McKilliam, R.G., Clarkson, I.V.L., Smith, W.D., Quinn, B.G.: A linear-time nearest point algorithm for the lattice A_n^*. In: 2008 International Symposium on Information Theory and Its Applications (ISITA 2008), pp. 1–5 (2008)
14. Nakamura, W., Takahashi, K.: How to efficiently determine the lattice scale for fuzzy extractors and fuzzy signatures. In: 12th International Symposium on Computing and Networking (CANDAR2024), pp. 196–202 (2024)
15. Nakamura, W., Takahashi, K.: How to efficiently evaluate accuracy of biometric authentication schemes with lattice-based fuzzy extractors and fuzzy signatures. In: 2025 Symposium on Cryptography and Information Security (SCIS2025) (2025). (in Japanese)
16. Parente, V.P., van de Graaf, J.: A practical fuzzy extractor for continuous features. In: 9th International Conference on Information Theoretic Security (ICITS2016), pp. 241–258 (2016)
17. Takahashi, K., Matsuda, T., Murakami, T., Hanaoka, G., Nishigaki, M.: Signature schemes with a fuzzy private key. Int. J. Inf. Secur. **18**(5), 581–617 (2019). https://doi.org/10.1007/s10207-019-00428-z
18. Takahashi, K., Nakamura, W.: A linear-time algorithm for the closest vector problem of triangular lattices. http://arxiv.org/abs/2412.06091[cs.CR]
19. Takahashi, K., Nakamura, W.: A quasilinear-time CVP algorithm for triangular lattice based fuzzy extractors and fuzzy signatures. 2024 Asia Pacific Signal and Information Processing Association Annual Summit and Conference (APSIPA ASC 2024) (2024)
20. Takahashi, K., Nakamura, W.: (quasi-)linear-time algorithms for the closest vector problem in (semi-)equiangular lattices. In: 2025 IEEE International Symposium on Information Theory (ISIT 2025) (2025)
21. Wang, H., et al.: Cosface: large margin cosine loss for deep face recognition. In: 2018 IEEE/CVF Conference on Computer Vision and Pattern Recognition (CVPR2018), pp. 5265–5274 (2018)

22. Yoneyama, Y., Takahashi, K., Nishigaki, M.: Closest vector problem on triangular lattice and its application to fuzzy signature. IEICE Trans. Fundam. **J98-A**(6), 427–435 (2015). (in Japanese)
23. Zhang, K., Cui, H., Yu, Y.: Facial template protection via lattice-based fuzzy extractors. Cryptology ePrint Archive, Paper 2021/1559 (2021)

A New Code-Based Formulation of the *Fuzzy Vault* Scheme

Sara Majbour[(✉)], Morgan Barbier, and Jean-Marie Le Bars

Normandie Univ, UNICAEN, ENSICAEN, CNRS, GREYC, 14000 Caen, France
{sara.majbour,morgan.barbier,jean-marie.lebars}@unicaen.fr

Abstract. The original *Fuzzy Vault* scheme is inherently restricted to codes based on polynomial evaluations, in particular Reed–Solomon codes. This structural dependency limits its applicability to a narrow class of error-correcting codes and constrains possible generalizations. In this work, we reformulate the scheme within the framework of generic linear codes, detaching the construction from its polynomial structure. We define locking and unlocking procedures compatible with any linear code that meets a set of explicit conditions, which we identify and justify. This reformulation makes it possible to explore the use of alternative codes that satisfy these conditions, and we detail how Reed–Solomon codes fit into this framework. It also clarifies the internal organization of the scheme and its compatibility with different code families. In addition, we propose a method for embedding the protected secret inside the vault structure, thereby removing the need for external storage and ensuring that all recovery elements remain encapsulated within the scheme itself. In this variant, the error vector contains values obtained by applying a cryptographically secure one-way function to a randomly chosen secret, making them indistinguishable from random noise.

Keywords: *Fuzzy Vault* · Linear error-correcting codes · Biometric cryptosystems · Privacy-preserving authentication

1 Introduction

The Fuzzy Vault scheme by Juels and Sudan [4] provides error-tolerant information security, allowing secret recovery despite input variability. It is originally built on polynomial evaluations over unordered sets, reflecting the absence of intrinsic ordering in the protected data.

Initially proposed as a theoretical construction, the Fuzzy Vault was intended for contexts where exact matching is impractical. Juels and Sudan cited privacy-protected matching, password recovery, and biometric authentication as potential applications. Among these, biometrics has become the main application area and still drives most recent research.

Recent works have explored multimodal vaults combining face and fingerprint data [9], decentralized blockchain-based authentication frameworks [10], and deep learning for robust face feature encoding [11].

The scheme relies on error-correcting codes, specifically polynomial evaluations over point-value pairs, which structurally restrict its implementation to Reed–Solomon codes. This dependency limits applicability to other codes and prevents a systematic study of their relevance within the vault framework.

Although the original paper suggested other constructions might be possible, most works remained bound to Reed–Solomon codes. Indeed, this original work deals with polynomial evaluation and decoding over a Reed–Solomon code which is not properly defined, thus replace Reed–Solomon code by an another one is really unclear. No formal framework exists for encoding and decoding outside the polynomial setting. As a result, Reed–Solomon properties are often used implicitly, without clarifying whether they are essential for the scheme's security and functionality.

Reed–Solomon codes were extended to the extension field $\mathbb{F}_{q^m}$ in [6] to increase the set of evaluation points and security parameters. Here q is a prime power and $\mathbb{F}_{q^m}$ denotes the degree-m extension of $\mathbb{F}_q$. The construction still uses polynomial evaluation but introduces the *subspace distance*, which improves robustness to biometric variation by focusing on subspace intersections rather than pointwise differences. However, the higher-dimensional complexity imposes practical limits, especially in real-time contexts.

Other directions have been explored. Fuzzy Extractors were introduced in [5] to derive stable cryptographic keys from noisy data using codes like BCH codes, based on secure sketches [8] rather than set-based encoding. Hybrid schemes combining Hadamard and Reed–Solomon codes were proposed in [7] to improve robustness against random and burst errors in iris recognition. These methods remain tied to specific modalities and coding strategies.

The structural dependence on Reed–Solomon codes constrains the *Fuzzy Vault* to a narrow class of constructions. This limits exploration of other linear codes and prevents detailed comparison of their specific capabilities.

In this work, we do not focus on any particular biometric modality or application domain such as privacy-preserving matching or password recovery—contexts explicitly cited by Juels and Sudan. Instead, we consider the *Fuzzy Vault* as a generic cryptographic primitive and reformulate the core mechanism of secret locking and unlocking. Our approach relies on general linear coding principles such as generator matrices and error vectors, without using polynomial representations. Elements are treated as coordinate positions in a codeword rather than field values. This reformulation leads to structural conditions that a linear code must satisfy to fit the scheme. These conditions are explicitly verified for Reed–Solomon codes.

We also address practical vulnerabilities in secret storage. In the classical *Fuzzy Vault*, the secret is stored separately via a one-way function, raising risks tied to centralized storage. To mitigate this, we propose a variant where the secret is embedded in the vault by applying a cryptographically secure hash function. If we take a randomly drawn value as our secret, the hashed value will look like random data. This ensures that this hashed value cannot be distinguished from random noise by an adversary, while preserving the required security properties.

This article is structured as follows. Section 2 introduces the generic coding concepts used for the reformulation. Section 3 recalls the original construction via polynomial evaluation and interprets it through Reed–Solomon codes. Section 4 reformulates the locking and unlocking phases using this framework and details the decoding mechanisms. Section 5 describes the scheme in a generic linear code context, identifies compatibility conditions, and illustrates them with Reed–Solomon codes. Section 6 presents our variant with embedded secrets and Sect. 7 concludes.

2 Notations and Theoretical Foundations

In this section, we introduce standard definitions from coding theory that will be used to formalize the scheme and its components.

2.1 Basic Notions from Coding Theory

In this section, we introduce the basic concepts from coding theory that will be used in Sect. 5 to reformulate the *Fuzzy Vault* scheme. These notions are necessary to express the scheme purely in terms of linear codes and to analyze its construction from a coding-theoretic perspective, abstracting away from the original polynomial-based description.

Let q be a power of a prime number. We denote by $\mathbb{F}_q$ the finite field with q elements.

Definition 1 (Linear code). *Let k and n be integers such that $k \leq n$, and let $\mathbb{F}_q$ be a finite field. A* linear code *of length n and dimension k over $\mathbb{F}_q$ is a vector subspace $\mathcal{C} \subset \mathbb{F}_q^n$ of dimension k. Such a code is denoted by $[n,k]_q$.*

Definition 2 (Generator matrix). *A generator matrix G of a $[n,k]_q$ code is a $k \times n$ matrix over $\mathbb{F}_q$ whose rows form a basis of the code $\mathcal{C}$.*

The code $\mathcal{C}$ is the set of all images of vectors in $\mathbb{F}_q^k$ under the linear transformation defined by G: $\mathcal{C} = \{m \cdot G \mid m \in \mathbb{F}_q^k\}$.

Definition 3 (Support). *Let $v \in \mathbb{F}_q^n$ be a vector. The* support *of v is the set of positions where v has nonzero entries, formally defined as:*

$$\mathrm{Supp}(v) = \{i \in \{1, \dots, n\} \mid v_i \neq 0\}.$$

A such vector space has characteristic parameters.

Definition 4 (Minimum distance). *The minimum distance of a code $\mathcal{C}$, denoted by d, is the smallest Hamming distance between any two distinct codewords in the code. It is given by:*

$$d = \min_{c \neq c' \in \mathcal{C}} d_H(c, c').$$

where $d_H(c, c') = |\{i \in \{1, \dots, n\} \mid c_i \neq c'_i\}|$ denotes the Hamming distance.

Definition 5 (Error-correcting capacity). *Let $\mathcal{C}$ be a linear code with minimum distance d. The error-correcting capacity of $\mathcal{C}$ is defined as:* $t = \lfloor \frac{d-1}{2} \rfloor$.

Definition 6 *(MDS code).* *A linear code $\mathcal{C}$ of parameters $[n, k, d]_q$ is called Maximum Distance Separable (MDS) if it achieves the Singleton bound, that is:* $d = n - k + 1$.

This means that $\mathcal{C}$ has the largest possible minimum distance for its length and dimension

Thanks to the following notions, we can define new codes from old.

Definition 7 (Projection function). *Let $N, M \in \mathbb{N}$ with $M \leq N$, and let $J \subset \{1, \ldots, N\}$ be a subset of cardinality M. We denote its ordered enumeration by $J = \{j_1, \ldots, j_M\}$ with $j_1 < \cdots < j_M$. For any vector $v = (v_1, \ldots, v_N) \in \mathbb{F}_q^N$, we define the projection onto J as the function:*

$$\pi_{N,J} : \mathbb{F}_q^N \to \mathbb{F}_q^M, \qquad \pi_{N,J}(v) = (v_{j_1}, \ldots, v_{j_M}).$$

This function selects the components of v at the positions specified in J, preserving their relative order.

This projection will be used to define punctured vectors and to manipulate partial information in the unlocking and recovery phases.

Definition 8 (Information set). *Let $\mathcal{C}$ be a linear code of parameters $[n, k, d]_q$. A subset $I \subset \{1, \ldots, n\}$ is called an information set if $|I| = k$ and the projection onto I is injective over $\mathcal{C}$, that is:*

$$\forall c \in \mathcal{C} \quad \forall c' \in \mathcal{C}, \quad c \neq c' \implies \pi_{n,I}(c) \neq \pi_{n,I}(c').$$

Theorem 1 (Information set existence). *Let $\mathcal{C}$ be a linear code with parameters $[n, k, d]$. For any integer $\lambda \leq d$, every set of $n - \lambda + 1$ coordinate positions contains at least one information set.*

Moreover, d is the largest integer for which this holds. Proof: See [2, Theorem 1.4.15].

Definition 9 (Punctured code). *Let $\mathcal{C} \subset \mathbb{F}_q^n$ be a linear code, and $J \subset \{1, \ldots, n\}$ a set of coordinate positions. The punctured code $\mathcal{C}_J^p$ is the linear code consisting of vectors obtained by removing positions $j \in J$ from each codeword $c \in \mathcal{C}$, that is:*

$$\mathcal{C}_J^p = \{\pi_{n,\bar{J}}(c) \mid c \in \mathcal{C}\},$$

where $\pi_{n,\bar{J}}$ is the projection onto the complement of J.

Definition 10 (Unambiguous decoding algorithm). *Let $\mathcal{C} \subset \mathbb{F}_q^n$ be a linear code with minimum distance d, and let t be its error-correcting capacity. An unambiguous decoding algorithm for $\mathcal{C}$ is a function :*

$$D : \mathbb{F}_q^n \to \mathcal{C} \cup \{failure\},$$

satisfying the following:

- *if there exists $c \in \mathcal{C}$ such that $d_H(v, c) \leq t$, then $D(v) = c$;*
- *otherwise, $D(v)$ either outputs failure or returns some $c' \in \mathcal{C}$ such that $D(v) \neq c'$.*

2.2 Reed–Solomon Codes

In this preliminary section, we recall the definition and basic properties of Reed–Solomon codes that will be used in Sect. 4. These definitions are necessary to formalize the *Fuzzy Vault* scheme, which is based on Reed–Solomon codes but will be expressed using the formalism of linear codes, abstracting away from their polynomial representation.

Definition 11 (Reed–Solomon codes). *Let $\mathbf{S} = \{\alpha_1, \ldots, \alpha_n\} \subset \mathbb{F}_q$ be a set of size n. The Reed–Solomon code over $\mathbb{F}_q$ of length n, dimension k, and evaluation support $\mathbf{S}$, is defined as:*

$$\mathrm{RS}_{[n,k]_q} = \left\{ (P(\alpha_i))_{\alpha_i \in \mathbf{S}} \mid P(X) \in \mathbb{F}_q[X],\ \deg(P) < k \right\}.$$

Theorem 2 (MDS Property of RS codes). *A Reed–Solomon code $RS_q[n, k]$ has minimum distance $n - k + 1$. Therefore, it is a Maximum Distance Separable (MDS) code.*

Theorem 3 (Puncturing of RS codes). *The punctured code of a Reed–Solomon code is itself a Reed–Solomon code.*

More precisely, puncturing a Reed–Solomon code amounts to removing the evaluation points corresponding to the punctured positions from the support $\mathbf{S}$.

2.3 Indexation Functions

Depending on the structure of the code and the nature of the support, we rely on two indexing strategies to locate coordinates within vectors and codewords. These functions allow us to define projections and puncturing operations precisely and consistently.

In the following, we adopt two indexing strategies depending on the structure of the code and the nature of the support:

Definition 12 (Canonical ordering on $\mathbb{F}_q$). *Let $\alpha \in \mathbb{F}_q^*$ be a fixed primitive root. We define the canonical total order $\prec$ on $\mathbb{F}_q$ by: $0 \prec 1 \prec \alpha \prec \alpha^2 \prec \cdots \prec \alpha^{q-2}$.*

Let $\mathbf{S} \subset \mathbb{F}_q$ be a set of size n. We write $\mathbf{S} = \{\alpha_1, \ldots, \alpha_n\}$, where the elements are listed in increasing order according to the canonical total order $\prec$.

Definition 13 (Relative position function).

Let $\mathbf{S} = \{\alpha_1, \ldots, \alpha_n\} \subset \mathbb{F}_q$ be a set of cardinality n, with elements ordered according to the canonical order $\prec$. Let $X \subset \mathbf{S}$ be a subset of size x. We define the relative position function as:

$$\Psi(X, \mathbf{S}) = \{i \in \{1, \ldots, n\} \mid \alpha_i \in X\}.$$

It returns the indices of the elements of X within the ordered support $\mathbf{S}$, preserving the global coordinate system.

Indexing in Projected Vectors. For arbitrary linear codes or projected vectors of length ℓ, we index elements using positions in $\{1, \ldots, n\}$. Let $J \subset \{1, \ldots, n\}$, with $j_1 < j_2 < \cdots < j_\ell$. We define a mapping to relate global indices to local positions in the projected vector. This type of mapping is used in analytic combinatorics to index elements within ordered subsets [1].

Definition 14 (Labeling function). Let $J = \{j_1, j_2, \ldots, j_\ell\} \subset \{1, \ldots, n\}$, where $J = \ell$.

We define the labeling function associated with J as:

$$\varphi_J : J \to \{1, \ldots, \ell\}, \quad \varphi_J(j_i) = i.$$

This function maps each global index $j_i \in J$ to its corresponding local index in a projected vector of length ℓ, and is used to manipulate projected or punctured vectors consistently.

When selecting a subset $J \subset \{1, \ldots, n\}$ for projection, the labeling function φ_J is used to link the coordinates in the projected vector $v^p \in \mathbb{F}_q^\ell$ to their global positions in $v \in \mathbb{F}_q^n$.

3 Fuzzy Vault Scheme

The *Fuzzy Vault* scheme was originally introduced to protect secrets when the input data is unordered or noisy. It is particularly suited to contexts where exact matching is impractical, as it tolerates both variations and permutations in the input set.

This section recalls the original construction introduced by Juels and Sudan, focusing on the general mechanism of secret locking and unlocking, independently of any application context.

- **Locking Phase:** The secret is embedded into a polynomial over a finite field, which is evaluated at a predefined set of support points to produce genuine point-value pairs. Random chaff points are then added to obscure the genuine ones, making it difficult to distinguish valid from noise data.
- **Unlocking Phase:** A candidate set is provided to match the genuine pairs. If it includes enough correct points, the polynomial can be interpolated, and the secret recovered.

3.1 Locking Phase

The locking phase aims to bind a secret to a reference set so that recovery is possible only with partial knowledge of it. Let $\mathbb{F}_q$ be a finite field of size q, and a secret vector $\mathcal{K} = (\mathcal{K}_0, \ldots, \mathcal{K}_{k-1}) \in \mathbb{F}_q^k$, which defines a polynomial $P(x) = \sum_{i=0}^{k-1} \mathcal{K}_i x^i \in \mathbb{F}_q[x]$.

Let $E \subset \mathbb{F}_q$ be a set of ℓ distinct elements, considered as the locking set. The polynomial is evaluated at each element of E to generate the genuine point-value pairs. These are later hidden among a larger set of random elements, in such a way that only partial knowledge of E enables secret recovery.

The detailed construction, including polynomial evaluation and the addition of noise, is presented in the next steps :

1. **Polynomial evaluation:** The polynomial $P(x)$, defined from the secret vector, is evaluated at each element of the locking set E, as illustrated in Fig. 1a. This produces the set of genuine point-value pairs:

$$R = \{(e_i, P(e_i)) \mid e_i \in E\}.$$

2. **Dissimulation:** Random pairs $(x_i, y_i) \notin R$ are generated to hide the genuine ones, as illustrated in Fig. 1b:

$$C = \{(x_i, y_i) \in \mathbb{F}_q^2 \mid x_i \notin E,\ y_i \neq P(x_i)\}.$$

The reference set V is then defined as: $V = R \cup C$.

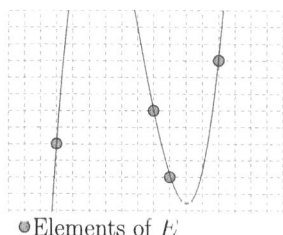

●Elements of E

(a) Polynomial evaluation

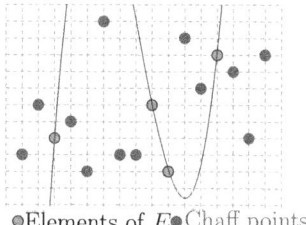

●Elements of E ●Chaff points

(b) Dissimulation

Fig. 1. Locking phase of the Fuzzy Vault scheme.

Stored Data. The database stores the following elements: the vault V containing the set of point-value pairs; a protected version of the secret, obtained using a one-way function Γ that is easy to compute but hard to invert; the parameter ℓ, indicating the expected size of the unlocking set; and the length k of the secret $\mathcal{K}$.

3.2 Unlocking Phase

In the unlocking phase, a set $A \subset \mathbb{F}_q$, called the unlocking set, is provided. The goal is to extract from the vault V all point-value pairs whose first coordinate lies in A, decode their values, and verify the recovered secret.

This process compares A to the original locking set E. If A contains enough elements from E, the genuine pairs can be isolated among the chaff. A decoding algorithm is then applied to reconstruct the polynomial, provided that the number of discrepancies between A and E does not exceed the decoding radius e of the code used.

The unlocking procedure consists of the following steps:

1. **Extraction:** Select from the vault V all pairs (x_i, y_i) such that $x_i \in A$, (see Fig. 2) :

$$Q = \{(x_i, y_i) \in V \mid x_i \in A\}.$$

2. **Decoding:**
   A decoding algorithm for Reed–Solomon codes, denoted Dec, is employed, receiving the subset $Q \subset V$, and the length k as input. This procedure either returns a polynomial $P'(X)$ of degree less than k, or indicates a decoding failure:
   $$P'(X) \in Dec(Q, k) \cup \{\text{failure}\}.$$
   If decoding succeeds, $P'(X)$ can be used to reconstruct a vector $\mathcal{K}'$, (see Fig. 3).

3. **Verification:** If decoding succeeds, compute the coefficient vector $\mathcal{K}'$ of the polynomial $P'(X)$. To validate the result, compare the protected version of the recovered secret with the stored reference. The verification function is defined as: $\Lambda_{\text{verif}}\left(\Gamma(\mathcal{K}), \Gamma(\mathcal{K}')\right) = \begin{cases} 1 & \text{if } \Gamma(\mathcal{K}) = \Gamma(\mathcal{K}'), \\ 0 & \text{otherwise.} \end{cases}$ If $\Lambda_{\text{verif}}(\Gamma(\mathcal{K}), \Gamma(\mathcal{K}')) = 1$, the unlocking is considered successful and the secret is accepted. This confirms that the set A used for unlocking shares a sufficient number of elements with the original set E (see Fig. 4).

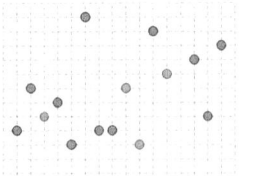
●Elements of V ●Elements of A

Fig. 2. Extraction.

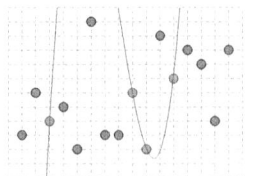
●Elements of V ●Elements of Q

Fig. 3. Decoding.

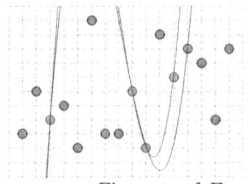
●Elements of E

Fig. 4. Verification.

The previous steps describe the original *Fuzzy Vault* construction, covering both locking and unlocking. Although the scheme relies on code-based mechanisms—particularly a decoding algorithm with bounded error correction—the code structure and its parameters are left implicit. Error-correcting codes are embedded in the algebraic formulation, without explicit connection to classical coding theory.

4 Reformulating the *Fuzzy Vault* Scheme Using Reed–Solomon Codes

This section reinterprets each step of the *Fuzzy Vault* scheme using the algebraic structure of Reed–Solomon codes. Although the original construction relies on polynomial evaluation, all operations—including evaluation and recovery—can be formulated as vector encoding, error insertion, and decoding over a defined linear code.

4.1 Locking Phase: Encoding the Secret

This subsection explains how the locking phase of the *Fuzzy Vault* can be expressed using Reed–Solomon codes. The goal is to encode the secret vector $\mathcal{K} \in \mathbb{F}_q^k$ into a codeword $c \in \mathbb{F}_q^n$, using a generator matrix derived from a set of evaluation points. This replaces the polynomial-based view with a linear algebraic one, where each coordinate of the codeword is a structured combination of the secret's components.

The secret is the vector $\mathcal{K} \in \mathbb{F}_q^k$ (see Fig. 5a). The support set $\mathbf{S} \subset \mathbb{F}_q$, includes the locking set $E \subset \mathbf{S}$, with $\ell < n$. This support defines the x-coordinates used in the reference set V, where each $x \in \mathbf{S}$ is either used for genuine evaluation or assigned a corrupted entry.

We also formalize how errors are introduced at specific positions to protect the secret and ensure vault security. The steps below define the encoding process in this framework.

1. **Codeword generation:** As defined in Definition 2, the codeword $c \in \mathbb{F}_q^n$ is obtained by applying the linear transformation defined by a $k \times n$ matrix over $\mathbb{F}_q$, to the secret vector $\mathcal{K}$ (Fig. 5b):

$$c = \mathcal{K} \cdot G.$$

In the case of Reed–Solomon codes, this generator matrix is constructed from a fixed set of n distinct elements $\mathbf{S} = \{\alpha_1, \ldots, \alpha_n\} \subset \mathbb{F}_q$, by evaluating monomials of increasing degree on these support points:

$$G = \begin{pmatrix} 1 & 1 & \cdots & 1 \\ \alpha_1 & \alpha_2 & \cdots & \alpha_n \\ \vdots & \vdots & \ddots & \vdots \\ \alpha_1^{(k-1)} & \alpha_2^{(k-1)} & \cdots & \alpha_n^{(k-1)} \end{pmatrix}.$$

This matrix structure implies that each codeword $c \in \mathbb{F}_q^n$ corresponds to the evaluation of a degree-$(k-1)$ polynomial $P(X)$ defined by the coefficients of the secret vector $\mathcal{K} \in \mathbb{F}_q^k$. Specifically, for a support set $\mathbf{S} = \{\alpha_1, \ldots, \alpha_n\}$, the codeword takes the form:

$$c = (P(\alpha_1), P(\alpha_2), \ldots, P(\alpha_n)).$$

Each coordinate c_i is a linear combination of the components of $\mathcal{K}$, where the coefficients are powers of the support element α_i:

$$c_i = \sum_{j=0}^{k-1} \mathcal{K}_j \cdot \alpha_i^j.$$

This formulation is equivalent to evaluating a degree-$(k-1)$ polynomial at each α_i, with the encoding operation handled entirely through matrix multiplication. This representation allows the entire scheme to be described using linear algebra, without relying on explicit polynomial handling.

As a result, the codeword c belongs to the Reed–Solomon code $\mathrm{RS}[n,k]_q$, defined as:

$$\mathrm{RS}[n,k]_q = \{(P(\alpha_i))_{i=1}^n \mid P \in \mathbb{F}_q[X],\ \deg(P) < k\}.$$

2. **Error insertion:** In the original scheme, $n - \ell$ chaff pairs are added. In the Reed–Solomon formalism, this corresponds to the introduction of errors into the codeword. Specifically, random errors are added at the positions that do not belong to the locking set E:

$$v_i = \begin{cases} c_i, & \text{if } \alpha_i \in E \\ c_i + e_i, & \text{if } \alpha_i \notin E \end{cases}$$

where $e_i \neq 0$ is a random nonzero element of $\mathbb{F}_q$ (see Fig. 5c).

An explicit example illustrating this phase is provided in Appendix A.1.

Stored Data. The protected vault consists of the noisy vector v (Figure 5d). Additionally, the system stores the following parameters required for unlocking: the transformed secret $\Gamma(\mathcal{K})$, the code parameters $[\ell, k]$, the support set $\mathbf{S}$, and the generator matrix G.

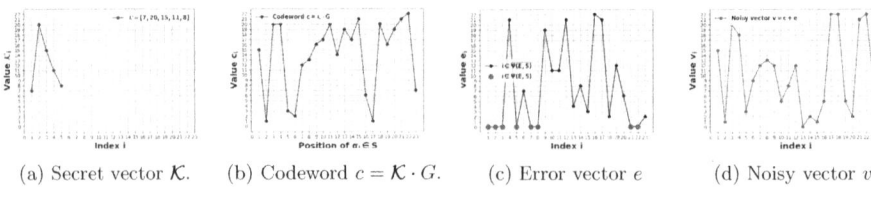

(a) Secret vector $\mathcal{K}$. (b) Codeword $c = \mathcal{K} \cdot G$. (c) Error vector e. (d) Noisy vector v.

Fig. 5. Locking phase of the *Fuzzy Vault* scheme: secret generation, codeword c, noise insertion: vector representation as points serie.

4.2 Unlocking Phase: Decoding the Secret

This section formalizes the unlocking phase using the structure of Reed–Solomon codes. Let $\mathrm{RS}[n,k]_q$ be a Reed–Solomon code over a support set $\mathbf{S} = \{\alpha_1, \ldots, \alpha_n\} \subset \mathbb{F}_q$. The vector $v \in \mathbb{F}_q^n$, stored during the locking phase, is obtained by adding structured noise to a codeword in $\mathrm{RS}[n,k]_q$

The user provides an unlocking set $A \subset \mathbf{S}$ of size ℓ. Only the components of v indexed by elements of A are used for unlocking. From a coding-theoretic perspective, this amounts to restricting both the code $\mathrm{RS}[n,k]_q$ and the vector v to the positions indexed by $\Psi(A,\mathbf{S}) \subset \{1,\ldots,n\}$. This corresponds to constructing of a punctured code.

1. **Vector projection:** Given the unlocking set $A \subset \mathbf{S}$, we define the relative index set $\Psi(A,\mathbf{S}) \subset \{1,\ldots,n\}$ and extract the projected vector $v^p \in \mathbb{F}_q^\ell$:

$$v^p = \pi_{n,\Psi(A,\mathbf{S})}(v) \ (see Fig. 6a).$$

Each component of v^p satisfies: $v_i^p = \begin{cases} P(\alpha_i), & \text{if } \alpha_i \in A \cap E, \\ P(\alpha_i) + e_i, & \text{if } \alpha_i \in A \backslash E. \end{cases}$

2. **Punctured code for decoding:** The Reed–Solomon code $\mathrm{RS} = [n,k]_q$ is restricted to the coordinates in $\Psi(A,\mathbf{S})$, yielding the punctured code:

$$\mathcal{C}^p_{\Psi(A,\mathbf{S})} = \{\pi_{n,\Psi(A,\mathbf{S})}(c) | c \in \mathrm{RS}[n,k]_q\}.$$

Since puncturing a Reed–Solomon code yields another Reed–Solomon code (see Theorem 3), such a decoding algorithm is known and efficiently computable.

Let D denote the decoding algorithm associated with $\mathcal{C}^p_{\Psi(A,\mathbf{S})}$. Decoding succeeds if there exists a codeword $c'^p \in \mathcal{C}^p_{\Psi(A,\mathbf{S})}$ such that:

$$d(v^p, c'^p) \leq t^p.$$

where $t^p = \left\lfloor \frac{d^p - 1}{2} \right\rfloor$ is the error correction capacity of $\mathcal{C}^p_{\Psi(A,\mathbf{S})}$.
If successful, decoding returns the codeword c'^p; otherwise, it reports a failure:

$$D(v^p) = \begin{cases} c'^p, & \text{if } d(v^p, c'^p) \leq t^p, (see Fig. 6b) \\ \text{failure}, & \text{otherwise}. \end{cases}$$

3. **Candidate secret reconstruction:** Suppose the decoding returns a valid codeword $c'^p \in \mathbb{F}_q^\ell$. To reconstruct the candidate secret $\mathcal{K}' \in \mathbb{F}_q^k$, we proceed as follows:
   (a) **Selection of an information set:** Let $I \subset A \subset \mathbf{S}$ be a subset of k elements selected from the unlocking set A. We define their global positions in the support $\mathbf{S}$ using the relative position function:

   $$\Psi(I,\mathbf{S}) \subset \{1,\ldots,n\}.$$

This gives the indices in $\mathbf{S}$ corresponding to the elements of I.
Using the labeling function $\varphi_{\Psi(A,\mathbf{S})} : \Psi(I, \mathbf{S}) \to \{1, \ldots, \ell\}$, we obtain the local indices of the elements of I in the punctured vector $c'^p \in \mathbb{F}_q^\ell$:

$$\varphi_{\Psi(A,\mathbf{S})}(\Psi(I, \mathbf{S})) = \{i \in \{1, \ldots, \ell\} \mid j_i \in \Psi(I, \mathbf{S})\}.$$

(b) **Extraction of the subvector:** We extract the subvector $c'^p_I \in \mathbb{F}_q^k$ by projecting the punctured codeword onto the positions in $\varphi_{\Psi(A,\mathbf{S})}(\Psi(I,\mathbf{S}))$:

$$c'^p_I = \pi_{\ell, \varphi_{\Psi(A,\mathbf{S})}(\Psi(I,\mathbf{S}))}(c'^p) \ (see Fig. 6c).$$

(c) **Construction of the submatrix:** We construct the $k \times k$ submatrix $G_{\Psi(I,\mathbf{S})}$ by extracting the columns of G at the positions $\Psi(I, \mathbf{S}) \subset \{1, \ldots, n\}$.

(d) **Recovery of the secret:** Compute the candidate secret $\mathcal{K}' \in \mathbb{F}_q^k$ using:

$$\mathcal{K}' = c'^p_I \cdot G^{-1}_{\Psi(I,\mathbf{S})}, (see\ Fig.\ 6d).$$

Since Reed–Solomon codes are MDS (see Theorem 2), any choice of k positions forms an information set, ensuring the invertibility of $G_{\Psi(I,\mathbf{S})}$ and the uniqueness of $\mathcal{K}'$.

4. **Verification:**
The recovered secret $\mathcal{K}'$ is verified using the protection function Γ. Unlocking is successful if: $\Lambda_{\text{verif}}(\Gamma(\mathcal{K}), \Gamma(\mathcal{K}')) = 1$. Otherwise, the unlocking attempt is rejected.

A detailed example of this unlocking procedure is given in Appendix A.2 (Fig. 6).

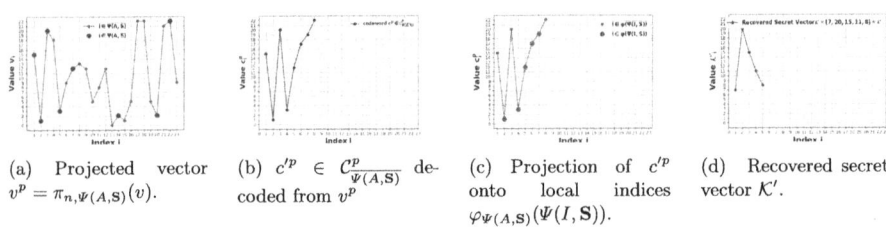

(a) Projected vector $v^p = \pi_{n, \Psi(A,\mathbf{S})}(v)$.
(b) $c'^p \in \mathcal{C}^p_{\Psi(A,\mathbf{S})}$ decoded from v^p.
(c) Projection of c'^p onto local indices $\varphi_{\Psi(A,\mathbf{S})}(\Psi(I, \mathbf{S}))$.
(d) Recovered secret vector $\mathcal{K}'$.

Fig. 6. Unlocking phase of the *Fuzzy Vault* scheme: projection, decoding, and secret recovery: vector representation as points serie.

5 Reformulation of the *Fuzzy Vault* Scheme with Linear Codes

After presenting the encoding and decoding phases within the framework of Reed–Solomon codes, we now reformulate the scheme in the setting of a linear code. This introduces specific constraints and difficulties that arise when departing from the particular properties of Reed–Solomon codes.

One major distinction concerns the representation of the evaluation sets. In the Reed–Solomon formulation, the locking and unlocking sets are subsets of the finite field, interpreted as evaluation points for the secret polynomial. In contrast, with linear codes, these sets refer to coordinate indices rather than field elements. Accordingly, the evaluation set is now redefined as:

$$E = \{i_1, \ldots, i_\ell\} \subset \{1, \ldots, n\} \quad \text{where } n \text{ is the code length.}$$

5.1 Encoding

Let $\mathcal{C}$ be a linear code with parameters $[n, k, d]$ over a finite field $\mathbb{F}_q$, associated with a $k \times n$ generator matrix G over $\mathbb{F}_q$. The secret $\mathcal{K} \in \mathbb{F}_q^k$ is encoded into a codeword and hidden within a noisy vector v following the steps detailed below.

1. **Secret encoding:** The secret $\mathcal{K}$ is encoded into a codeword $c \in \mathcal{C}$ as:

$$c = \mathcal{K} \cdot G.$$

   The locking set $E \subset \{1, \ldots, n\}$ defines the positions corresponding to genuine information related to the secret within the codeword.

2. **Error Vector Construction:**
   An error vector $e \in \mathbb{F}_q^n$ is generated to introduce ambiguity outside the set E, defined as:

$$e_i = \begin{cases} 0, & \text{if } i \in E, \\ \mathbb{P}_U(\mathbb{F}_q^*), & \text{if } i \in \overline{E}. \end{cases}$$

   Where $\mathbb{P}_U(\mathbb{F}_q^*)$ is the uniform distribution over $\mathbb{F}_q^*$. Thus, $\text{Supp}(e) = \overline{E} = \{1, \ldots, n\} \setminus E$.

3. **Noisy vector computation:** The noisy vector v is obtained by adding the codeword c and the error vector e:

$$v = c + e.$$

In this formulation, each coordinate of v is associated with a specific position in $\{1, \ldots, n\}$. The indices in E correspond to genuine evaluations carrying the secret, while the other coordinates introduce random noise to protect the secret against unauthorized recovery.

The information stored in the database remains identical to that defined in Sect. 4.1. The steps described above are summarized in Algorithm 1.

Algorithm 1: Encoding

Input: $E \subset \{1, \ldots, n\}$, $\mathcal{K} \in \mathbb{F}_q^k$, G is a $k \times n$ matrix overs $\mathbb{F}_q$
Output: $v \in \mathbb{F}_q^n$

1 Compute the codeword: $c \leftarrow \mathcal{K} \cdot G$
2 Construct the error vector $e = (e_i)_{1 \leq i \leq n}$ where $e_i = \begin{cases} 0, & \text{if } i \in E, \\ \mathbb{P}_U(\mathbb{F}_q^*), & \text{if } i \notin E. \end{cases}$
3 Compute the noisy vector: $v \leftarrow c + e$
4 **Return** v

5.2 Decoding

During unlocking, the user provides a subset $A \subset \{1, \ldots, n\}$ be the ordered set of global indices selected for unlocking. The unlocking process follows three main steps:

1. **Code puncturing:** The code $\mathcal{C}$ is punctured on the set A to obtain the punctured code:
$$\mathcal{C}_A^p = \{\pi_{n,A}(c) \mid c \in \mathcal{C}\},$$
where $\pi_{n,A}$ is the projection function defined in Definition 7.
2. **Projection of the stored vector:** The noisy vector $v \in \mathbb{F}_q^n$ is projected onto A to obtain:
$$v^p = \pi_{n,A}(v) \in \mathbb{F}_q^\ell.$$
3. **Decoding:** A decoding algorithm D is applied to the punctured code $\mathcal{C}_A^p$ and the projected vector v^p. It attempts to find a codeword $c'^p \in \mathcal{C}_A^p$ such that:
$$d(v^p, c'^p) \leq t^p,$$
where t^p is the decoding radius of the punctured code. If successful, c'^p is returned; otherwise, decoding fails.
4. **Recovery of the candidate secret** Upon successful decoding, further steps are necessary to reconstruct the candidate secret. The recovery procedure consists of the following steps:
   (a) **Selection of k components:** Select a subset $I \subset A \subset \{1, \ldots, n\}$ of size k. This subset is considered as a candidate information set, without prior knowledge of whether it satisfies the required linear independence condition.
   (b) **Mapping to local indices:** Apply the labeling function φ_A to the global indices of the selected positions $I \subset A$, to obtain their corresponding local indices $\varphi_A(I) \subset \{1, \ldots, \ell\}$. These local indices indicate the positions of the selected components in the punctured codeword $c'^p \in \mathbb{F}_q^\ell$.
   (c) **Construction of the Submatrix:** Form the submatrix G_I by selecting the columns of the generator matrix G indexed by $I \subset \{1, \ldots, n\}$.
   (d) **Invertibility check:** Verify whether G_I is invertible.

- If G_I is invertible, the subset I is an information set (see Definition 8), and secret reconstruction can proceed.
- otherwise, select another subset $I \subset A$ and repeat the process.

Remark 1. When the code $\mathcal{C}$ is not MDS, not all subsets of size k form an information set. In that case, subsets of size k must be tested until one satisfies the invertibility condition. According to Theorem 1, every set of $n-d+1$ positions contains an information set.

In contrast, when $\mathcal{C}$ is MDS, every subset of k positions is an information set, and the reconstruction step can be performed without iteration.

Assuming that G_I is invertible, the secret is recovered by solving the linear system:
$$\mathcal{K}' = \pi_{\ell, \varphi_A(I)}(c'^p) \cdot G_I^{-1},$$
where $\pi_{\ell, \varphi_A(I)}(c'^p)$ denotes the projection of the punctured codeword c'^p onto the local positions associated with the global indices in I.

5. **Verification:** The reconstructed secret is validated by comparing its protected value with the stored reference: $\Lambda_{\text{verif}}(\Gamma(\mathcal{K}), \Gamma(\mathcal{K}'))=$
$$\begin{cases} 1, & \text{if } \Gamma(\mathcal{K}') = \Gamma(\mathcal{K}), \\ 0, & \text{otherwise.} \end{cases}$$

5.3 Proposition: Recovering the Secret from the Punctured Codeword

In this part, we summarize the conditions required to recover the secret vector once a decoded codeword from the punctured code $\mathcal{C}_A^p$ is available.

We assume that the decoding algorithm has succeeded and that a valid codeword $c^p \in \mathcal{C}_A^p$ has been obtained. Under these assumptions, the following proposition synthesizes the necessary conditions for recovering the original secret vector.

Proposition 1. *Let $c^p \in \mathcal{C}_A^p$, where $\mathcal{C}_A^p$ is the punctured code defined by $A \subset \{1, \ldots, n\}$.*

If A contains an information set $I \subset \{1, \ldots, n\}$ of size k, then a vector $\mathcal{K}' \in \mathbb{F}_q^k$ can be reconstructed.

Proof. Let $\mathcal{C}$ be an $[n, k, d]_q$ linear code over $\mathbb{F}_q$, with a $k \times n$ generator matrix.

Let $A \subset \{1, \ldots, n\}$ be the unlockig set, and let $c^p = \pi_{n,A}(c) \in \mathbb{F}_q^\ell$ be the punctured codeword corresponding to $c \in \mathcal{C}$.

Assume $I \subset \{1, \ldots, n\}$ is an information set of size k, and let $\varphi_A(I) \subset \{1, \ldots, \ell\}$ denote the corresponding local indices.

The submatrix G_I, formed by the columns of G indexed by I, is invertible—a standard property of information set [3].

Consequentely, the secret vector $\mathcal{K} \in \mathbb{F}_q^k$ can be uniquely recovered from c^p by:
$$\mathcal{K} = \pi_{\ell, \varphi_A(I)}(c^p) \cdot G_I^{-1}.$$
Thus, the secret vector $\mathcal{K}$ is uniquely determined.

Algorithm 2: Unlocking Decoding and secret recovery

Input: $A \subset \{1,\ldots,n\}$ (unlocking set), $\mathcal{C}$ linear code, G generator matrix, v noisy vector, decoding algorithm D, protection function Γ, comparison function Λ_{verif}
Output: Boolean indicating success or failure

1. Puncture the code: $\mathcal{C}_{\bar{A}}^p \leftarrow \pi_{n,A}(\mathcal{C})$; Project the noisy vector: $v^p \leftarrow \pi_{n,A}(v)$
2. Decode: $\text{result} \leftarrow D(v^p, \mathcal{C}_{\bar{A}}^p)$
3. **if** $\text{result} = \text{failure}$ **then**
4.   **Return** False
5. **end**
6. **else**
7. $c'^p \leftarrow \text{result}$
8. **end**
9. **for** each subset $I \subset A \subset \{1,\ldots,n\}$ of size k **do**
10.   Compute local indices: $\varphi_A(I) \subset \{1,\ldots,\ell\}$
11.   Construct submatrix: $G_I \leftarrow [G_i \mid i \in I]$
12.   **if** $\text{rank}(G_I) = k$ **then**
13.   Extract components: $c'^p_I \leftarrow \pi_{\ell, \varphi_A(I)}(c^p)$
14.   Recover candidate secret: $\mathcal{K}' \leftarrow c'^p_I \cdot G_I^{-1}$
15.   **if** $\Lambda_{\text{verif}}(\Gamma(\mathcal{K}), \Gamma(\mathcal{K}')) = 1$ **then**
16.   **Return** True
17.   **end**
18.   **end**
19. **end**
20. **Return** False

5.4 Criteria for Applying a Linear Code

Our proposal is described using Reed–Solomon codes, but the formal framework applies to any linear code that satisfies specific structural conditions. Before stating them, we introduce the notation used throughout this section.

Let $\mathcal{C} \subset \mathbb{F}_q^n$ be a linear code of parameters $[n, k, d]$, and let G be its $k \times n$ generator matrix over $\mathbb{F}_q$. This code encodes the secret during the locking phase. Let $E \subset \{1,\ldots,n\}$ denote the set of indices used for locking. During the unlocking phase, the set $A \subset \{1,\ldots,n\}$ specifies the available positions for decoding. It defines the support of the punctured code $\mathcal{C}_{\bar{A}}^p$, the restriction of $\mathcal{C}$ to coordinates in A, used for decoding.

We work only with subsets of coordinate indices, not field values. The scheme operates through projections and puncturings based on index sets. Its validity with a given code depends on the structural conditions below.

Decoding the Punctured Code. A first requirement is that $\mathcal{C}_{\bar{A}}^p$ admits an efficient decoding algorithm, for any set A. In other words, any part of the message can be recovered from part of received word, even if you have to try again, this is closely related to the notion of locally decodable code (LDC) [12]. This holds for Reed–Solomon codes, which remain in the same family under puncturing and can be decoded using standard algorithms. In the case of Reed–Solomon codes, this is satisfied: any punctured Reed–Solomon code remains in the same family and can be decoded using standard algorithms. For general linear codes, this must be verified. If decoding is not possible, the scheme fails, as the unlocking phase cannot succeed.

Existence of an Information Set. Let $\mathcal{C}$ be a linear code of parameters $[n, k, d]$ used during locking. To reconstruct a candidate secret $\mathcal{K}'$, the unlocking set A must contain an information set. According to Theorem 1, this requires:

$$|A| \geq n - \lambda + 1 \quad \text{with} \quad \lambda \leq d.$$

Equivalently, the number of erased positions must satisfy: $\bar{A} < d$.

These constraints ensure that the remaining positions allow message recovery after decoding.

Case of MDS Codes. In a code of dimension k, a subset of k coordinates forms an information set if the code restricted to these positions is injective. This is not true for all codes, but for MDS codes satisfying $k = n - d + 1$ Definition 6, every such subset qualifies. This applies, for instance, to Reed–Solomon codes.

In the *Fuzzy Vault* context, this means the secret can be recovered as soon as: $|A \cap E| \geq k$. It is equivalent to say that a punctured MDS code is also MDS.

This property ensures that the corresponding $k \times k$ submatrix of the generator matrix is invertible, allowing decoding without specific position selection. This simplifies both analysis and implementation.

6 Embedding the Protected Secret into the Vault

This section introduces a variant of the *Fuzzy Vault* scheme where the secret is directly integrated during locking and retrieve during unlocking. The aim is to eliminate the need for storing a protected version of the secret, while addressing vulnerabilities such as brute-force attacks and centralized storage risks. For this to work, we need to take a random value as the secret to have a random noise.

6.1 Locking Phase

As presented in the proposed reformulation based on a linear code 5.1, the secret $\mathcal{K} \in \mathbb{F}_q^k$ is encoded into a codeword $c = \mathcal{K} \cdot G$ (see step 1), where G is the generator matrix of a linear code $\mathcal{C} \subset \mathbb{F}_q^n$. An error vector $e \in \mathbb{F}_q^n$ is then added to produce the vault $v = c + e$ (see step 3).

Unlike the classical version where e contains random noise, here it carries structured information derived from a protected form of the secret, denoted $\Gamma(\mathcal{K})$. This protected value is obtained by first choosing $\mathcal{K}$ uniformly at random and then applying a cryptographically secure hash function Γ to it. The function Γ is collision-resistant and its output is indistinguishable from random noise, ensuring that the error vector retains the unpredictability required for security.

Let $E \subset \{1,\ldots,n\}$ be the locking set, and let $\bar{E} = \{1,\ldots,n\}\setminus E$ be its ordered complement, containig $n-\ell$ positions. Let $\Gamma(\mathcal{K}) = (h_1,\ldots,h_{n-\ell}) \in \mathbb{F}_q^{n-\ell}$ represent the protected secret.

Assuming $\bar{E} = \{i_1,\ldots,i_{n-\ell}\}$ is sorted in increasing order, the error vector $e \in \mathbb{F}_q^n$ is defined component-wise as: $\forall i \in \{1,\ldots,n\}$, $e_i = \begin{cases} 0, & \text{if } i \in E, \\ h_j, & \text{if } i = i_j \in \bar{E}. \end{cases}$

The error vector embeds $\Gamma(\mathcal{K})$ into the complement of E, masking the positions in E and avoiding the need to store $\Gamma(\mathcal{K})$ separately. The final vault is then computed as: $v = c + e$.

6.2 Unlocking Phase

During unlocking phase, the user provides an set $A \subset \{1,\ldots,n\}$, assumed to be close to E and to contain an information set. Under this assumption, the decoding algorithm in algorithm 2 is used to recover a candidate vector $\mathcal{K}' \in \mathbb{F}_q^k$.

The verification step then checks whether $\mathcal{K}'$ corresponds to the original secret. Unlike the classical scheme, it leverages the structured error introduced during locking. The verification proceeds as follows:

1. **Computation of te codeword c':** Given the candidate secret $\mathcal{K}'$, the corresponding codeword is computed as: $c' = \mathcal{K}' \cdot G$.
2. **Computation of the error vector e':** The error vector is obtained as the difference between the stored vector v and c':

$$e' = v - c' = (c + e) - c' = e + (c - c').$$

3. **Extraction of error components:** The non-zero entries of e' are extracted at positions $i \in \{1,\ldots,n\}$. These correspond to the components of the transformed secret $\Gamma(\mathcal{K}')$
   The positions i such that $e'_i \neq 0$ belong to the complement $\bar{E} = \{i_1,\ldots,i_{n-\ell}\}$. For each index $j \in \{1,\ldots,1-\ell\}$, we define: $h'_j = e'_{i_j}$.
4. **Reconstruction of the secret representation:** The sequence h' is reconstructed by concatenating the extracted values in index order: $h' = h'_1 || h'_2 || \ldots || h'_{n-\ell}$.
5. **Verification:** The recovered secret is validated by comparing $\Gamma(\mathcal{K}')$ with the reconstructed sequence h'. If $\Gamma(\mathcal{K}') = h'$, then $\mathcal{K}'$ is accepted as the original secret $\mathcal{K}$. This verification approach is formally stated in Proposition 2.

Verification of the Secret.

Proposition 2. *Let $\mathcal{K}$ be the initial secret, $\mathcal{K}'$ the candidate recovered through decoding, and h' the sequence derived from $e' = v - \mathcal{K}' \cdot G$. Then the probability that $\Gamma(\mathcal{K}') = h'$ and $\mathcal{K}' = \mathcal{K}$ is negligible.*

Proof. Let G be the $k \times n$ generator matrix over $\mathbb{F}_q$ of the linear code $\mathcal{C} \subset \mathbb{F}_q^n$ used during the locking phase.

The secret $\mathcal{K}$ is chosen uniformly at random and transformed into $\Gamma(\mathcal{K})$ by applying a collision-resistant cryptographic hash function. The stored vault is constructed as $v = c + e$, where $e \in \mathbb{F}_q^n$ encodes $\Gamma(\mathcal{K})$ at positions in $\bar{E}$.

Let $\mathcal{K}' \in \mathbb{F}_q^k$ be a candidate recovered using an authentication set A. Compute $c' = \mathcal{K}' \cdot G$, and the residual vector $e' = v - c' = e + (\mathcal{K} - \mathcal{K}') \cdot G$.

Since $\mathcal{K}$ and $\mathcal{K}'$ are unknown, e cannot be isolated. We extract h' by collecting the components of e' at the positions in $\bar{A}$, and compare it to $\Gamma(\mathcal{K}')$.

If $h' = \Gamma(\mathcal{K}')$, then the structure of e' is consistent with a noise vector encoding $\Gamma(\mathcal{K}')$. Given that Γ is assumed to be collision-resistant and its output uniformly distributed, the probability that two distinct vectors $\mathcal{K} \neq \mathcal{K}'$ satisfy $\Gamma(\mathcal{K}) = \Gamma(\mathcal{K}')$ is negligible.

Therefore, the probability that both $\Gamma(\mathcal{K}') = h'$ and $\mathcal{K}' = \mathcal{K}$ is negligible.

7 Conclusion

We have reformulated the *Fuzzy Vault* scheme using generic linear error-correcting codes, replacing the original polynomial-based construction. This clarifies the scheme's internal structure by explicitly separating secret encoding, structured noise insertion, and the unlocking phase. It also explains the compatibility of Reed–Solomon codes: their structure remains stable under puncturing, and decoding remains applicable in the resulting restricted codes. We are well aware that this is a first step towards generalisation to other linear codes. However, each linear code candidate for the fuzzy vault scheme will require specific in-depth study, particularly for decoding, which will be the subject of future publications.

Beyond this reformulation, two directions extend the present work. First, the emphasis on decoding in punctured codes motivates exploring families that remain decodable after such transformations, such as alternant and Reed–Muller code—both closely related to Reed–Solomon codes; and the locally decodable codes. Comparing performance across code families would help assess trade-offs between error tolerance, decoding complexity, and unlocking conditions.

Second, embedding the secret in the error vector redefines noise as a carrier of information. This raises questions on how decoding-based reconstruction affects the security model, and how different code choices influence system reliability and confidentiality.

A Fuzzy Vault: Example over $\mathbb{F}_{11}$

Notation Clarification. Throughout this example, we work over the finite field $\mathbb{F}_{11}$, where α denotes a primitive root modulo 11, i.e., a generator of the multiplicative group $\mathbb{F}_{11}^*$.

To avoid any ambiguity between field elements and vector positions, we adopt the following conventions:

- **Field elements** in $\mathbb{F}_{11}$ are denoted as $\{0, 1, \alpha, \alpha^2, \ldots, \alpha^9\}$.

- **Vector positions** (e.g., column indices in a matrix or entries in a vector) are indexed by integers $\{1, 2, \ldots, n\}$.
- When a set $S \subset \mathbb{F}_{11}$ is used as an evaluation support, its elements are explicitly written in terms of powers of α. For instance:

$$S = \{\alpha^1, \alpha^2, \alpha^3, \alpha^4, \alpha^5, \alpha^6\}$$

- The function $\Psi(A, S)$ denotes the *relative position* of the elements of A within the ordered support S, producing a subset of integer indices.

This convention ensures a clear distinction between algebraic elements and positional indices when constructing codewords, evaluating polynomials, or performing projections.

A.1 Locking Phase

We work over the finite field $\mathbb{F}_{11}$, where α denotes a primitive root modulo 11. For explicit computations in this example, we fix $\alpha = 2$. The canonical ordering induced by powers of α is:

The set $\mathbb{F}_{11}$ consists of the elements $\{0, 1, \alpha, \alpha^2, \ldots, \alpha^9\}$, we consider the following total order:

$$0 \prec 1 \prec \alpha \prec \alpha^2 \prec \alpha^3 \prec \alpha^4 \prec \alpha^5 \prec \alpha^6 \prec \alpha^7 \prec \alpha^8 \prec \alpha^9.$$

with the numerical correspondence (modulo 11):

$$\alpha^0 = 1, \quad \alpha^1 = 2, \quad \alpha^2 = 4, \quad \alpha^3 = 8, \quad \alpha^4 = 5,$$
$$\alpha^5 = 10, \quad \alpha^6 = 9, \quad \alpha^7 = 7, \quad \alpha^8 = 3, \quad \alpha^9 = 6.$$

Although the example uses $\alpha = 2$, the general formulation holds for any primitive root.

Support Set. We choose the following evaluation support set of length $n = 6$:

$$\mathbf{S} = \{\alpha^0, \alpha^1, \alpha^2, \alpha^3, \alpha^4, \alpha^5\} = \{1, 2, 4, 8, 5, 10\}.$$

Secret Vector.
$$\mathcal{K} = (3, 7, 2) \in \mathbb{F}_{11}^3$$

Generator Matrix. The 3×6 generator matrix G over $\mathbb{F}_{11}$ associated with the Reed–Solomon code defined on the support $\mathbf{S}$ is:

$$G = \begin{bmatrix} 1 & 1 & 1 & 1 & 1 & 1 \\ \alpha^0 & \alpha^1 & \alpha^2 & \alpha^3 & \alpha^4 & \alpha^5 \\ (\alpha^0)^2 & (\alpha^1)^2 & (\alpha^2)^2 & (\alpha^3)^2 & (\alpha^4)^2 & (\alpha^5)^2 \end{bmatrix} = \begin{bmatrix} 1 & 1 & 1 & 1 & 1 & 1 \\ 1 & 2 & 4 & 8 & 5 & 10 \\ 1 & 4 & 5 & 9 & 3 & 1 \end{bmatrix}$$

1. **Codeword generation:** The codeword is computed as:

$$c = \mathcal{K} \cdot G = (1, 3, 8, 0, 0, 9) \in \mathbb{F}_{11}^6$$

2. **Error insertion:** Let the genuine positions (used for unlocking) be:
$$E = \{\alpha^0, \alpha^1, \alpha^2, \alpha^4\} = \{1, 2, 4, 5\} \subset \mathbf{S}$$
The noise vector is defined over the full codeword support, but nonzero only at noise positions:
$$e = (0, 0, 0, e_4, 0, e_6) = (0, 0, 0, 3, 0, 2)$$
$$v = c + e = (1, 3, 8, 3, 0, 0)$$

A.2 Unlocking Phase

Unlocking Set.
$$A = \{\alpha^1, \alpha^2, \alpha^4, \alpha^5\} = \{2, 4, 5, 10\} \subset \mathbf{S}$$

1. **Vector projection:**
   Let $\Psi(A, \mathbf{S}) = \{2, 3, 5, 6\}$, i.e., the positions of A in $\mathbf{S}$. Then:
   $$v^p = \pi_{6,\{2,3,5,6\}}(v) = (3, 8, 0, 0) \in \mathbb{F}_{11}^4$$

2. **Punctured code:**
   $$\mathcal{C}^p_{\{2,3,5,6\}} = \{\pi_{6,\{2,3,5,6\}}(c) \mid c \in \mathrm{RS}[6, 3]_{11}\}$$

3. **Decode:** Assume decoding succeeds.
   $$c'^p = (3, 8, 0, 9) \in \mathbb{F}_{11}^4.$$

4. **Select information set $I \subset A$:**
   Let $I = \{\alpha^1, \alpha^2, \alpha^4\} = \{2, 4, 5\} \subset A$, and let $\Psi(I, \mathbf{S}) = \{2, 3, 5\}$.
   Define labeling function $\varphi_{\{2,3,5,6\}} : \{2, 3, 5, 6\} \to \{1, 2, 3, 4\}$:

   $$\varphi_{\{2,3,5,6\}}(2) = 1, \; \varphi_{\{2,3,5,6\}}(3) = 2, \; \varphi_{\{2,3,5,6\}}(5) = 3 \Rightarrow \varphi_{\{2,3,5,6\}}(\Psi(I, \mathbf{S})) = \{1, 2, 3\}$$

   such that $\{2, 3, 5, 6\} = \Psi(A, \mathbf{S})$.

5. **Extract subvector and submatrix:**
   $$c'^p_I = \pi_{4,\{1,2,3\}}(c'^p) = (3, 8, 0)$$
   Construct a 3×3 submatrix over $\mathbb{F}_q$ by extracting the columns $\{2, 3, 5\}$ from the generator matrix G:
   $$G_I = \begin{bmatrix} 1 & 1 & 1 \\ 2 & 4 & 5 \\ 4 & 5 & 3 \end{bmatrix}$$

6. **Recover secret:**
   $$\mathcal{K}' = c'^p_I \cdot G_I^{-1} = (3, 7, 2) = \mathcal{K}$$

7. **Verification:**
   $$\Lambda_{\mathrm{verif}}(\Gamma(\mathcal{K}), \Gamma(\mathcal{K}')) = 1 \Rightarrow \text{Unlocking succeeds}$$

References

1. Flajolet, P., Sedgewick, R.: Analytic Combinatorics. Cambridge University Press, Cambridge (2009)
2. Huffman, W.C., Pless, V.: Fundamentals of Error-Correcting Codes. Cambridge University Press, Cambridge (2003)
3. Peters, C.: Information-set decoding for linear codes over $\mathbf{F}_q$. In: Sendrier, N. (ed.) PQCrypto 2010. LNCS, vol. 6061, pp. 81–94. Springer, Heidelberg (2010). https://doi.org/10.1007/978-3-642-12929-2_7
4. Juels, A., Sudan, M.: A Fuzzy vault scheme. In: Proceedings of IEEE International Symposium on Information Theory (2002)
5. Dodis, Y., Reyzin, L., Smith, A.: Fuzzy extractors: how to generate strong keys from biometrics and other noisy data. In: Cachin, C., Camenisch, J.L. (eds.) EUROCRYPT 2004. LNCS, vol. 3027, pp. 523–540. Springer, Heidelberg (2004). https://doi.org/10.1007/978-3-540-24676-3_31
6. Marshall, K., Schipani, D., Trautmann, A.-L., Rosenthal, J.: Subspace fuzzy vault. In: Baldi, M., Tomasin, S. (eds.) Physical and Data-Link Security Techniques for Future Communication Systems. LNEE, vol. 358, pp. 163–172. Springer, Cham (2016). https://doi.org/10.1007/978-3-319-23609-4_10
7. Hao, F., Anderson, R., Daugman, J.: Combining crypto with biometrics effectively. IEEE Trans. Comput. **55**(9), 1081–1088 (2006). https://doi.org/10.1109/TC.2006.134
8. Li, Q., Sutcu, Y., Memon, N.: Secure sketch for biometric templates. In: Lai, X., Chen, K. (eds.) ASIACRYPT 2006. LNCS, vol. 4284, pp. 99–113. Springer, Heidelberg (2006). https://doi.org/10.1007/11935230_7
9. Rathgeb, C., Tams, B., Merkle, J., Nesterowicz, V., Korte, U., Neu, M.: Multi-biometric fuzzy vault based on face and fingerprints. In: 2023 IEEE International Joint Conference on Biometrics (IJCB), pp. 1–10 (2023). https://doi.org/10.1109/IJCB57857.2023.10448963
10. Sharma, S., Saini, A.K., Chaudhury, S.: Multimodal biometric user authentication using improved decentralized fuzzy vault scheme based on blockchain network. J. Inf. Secur. Appl. **76**, 103789 (2024)
11. Rathgeb, C., Merkle, J., Scholz, J., Tams, B., Nesterowicz, V.: Deep face fuzzy vault: implementation and performance. Comput. Secur. **113**, 102539 (2022). https://doi.org/10.1016/j.cose.2021.102539
12. Yekhanin, S.: Locally Decodable Codes, now (2012). https://doi.org/10.1561/0400000030

Malware Analysis

HoneySentry: A High-Fidelity Interactive IoT Honeypot for Advanced Threat Detection

Yanbing Shen[1], Hao Sun[1], Jiacheng Wang[1], Haitao Xu[1(✉)], Gang Liu[2], and Fan Zhang[1]

[1] Zhejiang University, Hangzhou, China
{yb-shen,12321173,wang-jiacheng,haitaoxu,fanzhang}@zju.edu.cn
[2] Beijing Zorelworld Information and Technology Co., Ltd., Beijing, China
liugang@zorelworld.com

Abstract. The Internet of Things (IoT) devices are increasingly exploited as intermediaries for launching sophisticated cyberattacks. IoT honeypots have emerged as a proactive measure to lure attackers and provide early threat detection. However, existing honeypots exhibit significant limitations, including low interaction levels, vulnerability to fingerprinting, and constrained data collection capabilities. This paper introduces HoneySentry, a high-interaction IoT honeypot specifically designed to overcome these challenges and target advanced attackers adept at sophisticated honeypot fingerprinting and strategic selection of victim IoT devices. HoneySentry utilizes a custom-enhanced IoT firmware emulation framework to achieve high-fidelity emulation of diverse IoT devices and architectures. It incorporates advanced anti-fingerprinting techniques to evade detection, modifying commands frequently used by attackers during reconnaissance. Additionally, HoneySentry enhances its appeal to attackers by deploying a variety of meticulously crafted bait files and processes. To facilitate detailed analysis, HoneySentry captures comprehensive attack data, including both network traffic and host-level activities. Comparative evaluations against traditional honeypots and real-world deployments demonstrate that HoneySentry significantly outperforms existing solutions in fostering deep engagement with attackers, collecting extensive attack data, and enabling comprehensive threat analysis. During its two-month deployment (August 2024 to November 2024), HoneySentry captured over 200,000 requests and generated 61.3 GB of log data. Further analysis revealed variants of known malicious worms and viruses, as well as several intriguing attack behaviors, highlighting its capability to uncover diverse threats.

Keywords: IoT Honeypot · Deception Defense · Firmware Emulation

1 Introduction

The exponential growth of Internet of Things (IoT) devices has embedded them as core components of daily life [1], yet their design with multiple open network ports, coupled with rapid deployment, direct internet connectivity, and manufacturers' neglect of robust security measures, has heightened vulnerabilities to cyber threats. These gaps imperil personal privacy and render IoT devices prime targets for malicious exploitation, posing significant societal and economic risks. Platforms like Shodan [25] highlight the cyberspace visibility of exposed IoT devices, while high-profile incidents such as the Mirai botnet attack [2] exemplify systemic risks: Mirai exploited weak default credentials to convert devices into botnet nodes, launching DDoS attacks on critical targets like Dyn DNS. The public release of Mirai's source code has facilitated the proliferation of sophisticated variants (e.g., Gafgyt [3] and Hajime [4]), causing widespread global network impacts. The escalating use of IoT-based botnets against critical infrastructure underscores the urgent need for proactive security measures.

IoT honeypots have emerged as a robust proactive defense mechanism, simulating vulnerable systems to lure attackers and enabling the capture and analysis of malicious behaviors in controlled environments. Despite their potential, most existing IoT honeypots are limited by low interactivity and constrained response capabilities [5]. For example, the widely adopted Cowrie [6] honeypot employs static fields in its SSH response messages, making it easily identifiable by attackers. While using actual IoT devices as honeypots could theoretically enhance realism and interactivity, this approach is impractical given the diverse and heterogeneous nature of IoT devices [7], which would necessitate substantial financial and logistical investments for acquisition and maintenance.

Furthermore, attackers frequently execute extensive probing commands during interactions to extract device-specific information [8]. Low- to medium-interaction honeypots are particularly vulnerable to detection through fingerprinting techniques, which significantly undermine their effectiveness [9–11]. Additionally, prior research [12,13] on IoT honeypots has predominantly focused on protocol emulation, often overlooking the original business logic and functional files of IoT devices. This oversight reduces the honeypot's stealth and limits its ability to capture authentic attack behaviors.

To address these challenges, we propose HoneySentry, a high-interaction, high-fidelity IoT honeypot framework based on firmware emulation. By leveraging an optimized version of the FirmAE framework [14], HoneySentry employs firmware emulation capabilities to emulate specific IoT devices on QEMU [15], an open-source and highly versatile machine emulator and virtualizer. This design ensures scalable and flexible device emulation. To enable comprehensive monitoring, we integrate lightweight probes within the honeypots to capture system activities across four dimensions: system environment, file directories, process information, and network traffic. These probes non-intrusively monitor runtime states and securely transmit collected data to a backend server for detailed analysis of attacker behaviors. Furthermore, HoneySentry incorporates an anti-fingerprinting scheme that modifies commonly used system commands, effectively masking virtualization artifacts to reduce the risk of detection. To enhance fidelity and attractiveness, we introduced honeypot bait, which consists of fabricated decoy files mimicking sensitive system artifacts such as configuration files, user credentials, and logs, enticing attackers into prolonged interactions.

We deployed HoneySentry on ten cloud nodes in geographically distributed regions. Some instances were equipped with the anti-fingerprinting scheme to obscure virtualization characteristics and prolong interactions, while others served as control groups. Over the deployment period from August 2024 to November 2024, these honeypots captured extensive real-world attack data, including over 200,000 requests and up to 61.3 GB of log data. Experimental results demonstrate that firmware-based honeypots substantially outperform low-interaction, open-source alternatives in attracting attackers and capturing high-quality interaction data. Specifically, in terms of emulation success rate, the optimized FirmAE framework utilized in HoneySentry achieved a 46.4% improvement over the original FirmAE across all 12 tested brands, including Netgear, ASUS, Huawei and etc. Furthermore, honeypots equipped with anti-fingerprinting techniques recorded significantly more sustained attacker engagements, achieving an average session length of 3.68 data packets and 5,125.08 bytes of traffic, compared to 2.51 packets and 1,748.64 bytes for non-anti-fingerprinting honeypots. Additionally, an analysis of HoneySentry's traffic and log data revealed a diverse range of variants of known malicious worms and viruses, as well as several novel attack behaviors. These findings underscore the effectiveness of the anti-fingerprinting techniques proposed for HoneySentry in extending interactions and enhancing data quality, thereby improving the stealth and appeal of honeypots while ensuring their capability to uncover a broad spectrum of threats.

Overall, we mainly make the following contributions:

- We introduce HoneySentry, a high-interaction, high-fidelity IoT honeypot framework based on firmware emulation. By incorporating anti-fingerprinting techniques and bait design, the framework significantly enhances honeypot authenticity and concealment, providing robust support for in-depth research into network threats targeting IoT devices.
- We develop a lightweight, cross-architecture honeypot probe compatible with major IoT device architectures. This tool enables comprehensive capture of attackers' malicious activities, providing essential data for threat analysis and intelligence gathering.
- We validate HoneySentry's effectiveness through extensive experiments. Compared to traditional honeypots, HoneySentry demonstrates superior performance in engaging attackers in deeper interactions, effectively deceiving advanced network reconnaissance tools, and capturing attack behaviors.

2 Background and Related Work

2.1 IoT Honeypots

Regarding the types of systems or services they emulate (e.g., SSH, web, or email), honeypots are generally divided into low-, medium-, and high-interaction variants, distinguished by the depth of user engagement: low-interaction honeypots simulate basic service responses without real system access, medium-interaction ones offer limited interactive functionalities (e.g., predefined command execution), and high-interaction variants provide fully operational environments with genuine system resources. Low- and medium-interaction honeypots [16–18] are relatively straightforward to deploy and maintain but offer limited functionality. Conversely, high-interaction honeypots [12,13,20,27] provide fully functional system environments, while their deployment and maintenance are considerably more complex and resource-intensive.

Honeypots have experienced significant advancements in recent years. IoTPOT [13], a high-interaction software honeypot, emulates multiple architectures (e.g., ARM, MIPS, x86) and delivers protocol-specific responses on port 23. Similarly, Conpot [18] focuses on industrial control system (ICS) protocols (e.g., Modbus, SNMP) and simulates large-scale infrastructures to attract attackers. However, both IoTPOT and Conpot rely primarily on static, protocol-level responses rather than dynamically generated behaviors, which diminishes the authenticity of their emulated environments. In contrast, SIPHON [20], a hardware-based honeypot platform, employs physical devices such as security cameras, network video recorders, and printers distributed across diverse IP addresses. While SIPHON achieves high fidelity in interaction, its dependency on physical hardware imposes limitations on scalability and real-time monitoring capabilities. The emergence of artificial intelligence has opened new avenues for improving honeypot realism and adaptability [5,21–23]. For example, IoT-CandyJar [5] leverages deep learning and reinforcement learning to replicate the HTTP responses of publicly available IoT devices. However, the effectiveness of AI-driven approaches is heavily dependent on access to high-quality training datasets and is largely constrained to unencrypted, pre-authentication phases, thereby limiting their overall fidelity.

2.2 Network Reconnaissance Tools

Nmap. Nmap [24] is a widely recognized open-source network scanning tool that dispatches raw IP packets and compares the responses against a comprehensive feature database to determine the operating systems and services of target systems. Upon completing a scan, Nmap generates a detailed report listing potential system types or services, accompanied by confidence percentages ranging from 0 (no confidence) to 100 (absolute confidence). Known for its versatility and powerful network probing capabilities, Nmap has become an indispensable asset in the field of cybersecurity.

Device Search Engines. Device search engines, including Shodan [25], Censys [26], Fofa, and ZoomEye, compile metadata from publicly accessible devices through automated scanning techniques. Shodan specializes in cataloging IoT devices such as cameras, routers, and industrial control systems (ICS). Censys emphasizes the scanning of IPv4 addresses, domains, and certificates, serving academic and professional research purposes. Fofa offers a search-engine-like

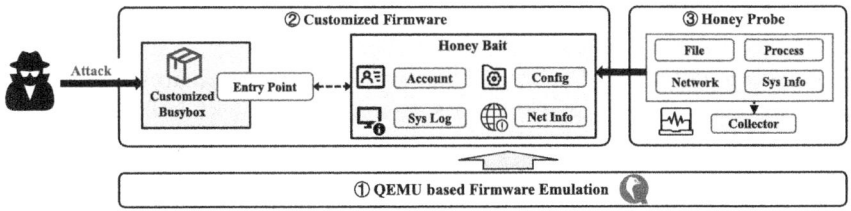

Fig. 1. The Architecture of HoneySentry. ① QEMU-based firmware emulation, simulating real IoT devices. ② Customized firmware, including a customized BusyBox and honey bait, such as fake accounts and configurations. ③ Honey probe, monitoring system, file, process, and network activities for analysis.

platform for discovering and managing network assets, while ZoomEye provides comprehensive network coverage and real-time updates tailored for security analysis. With robust API interfaces and extensive datasets, these platforms have become essential tools for cybersecurity research and operations.

Despite their defensive applications, these tools are frequently exploited by attackers for reconnaissance, enabling rapid identification of exposed IoT devices and vulnerabilities. This dual-use nature underscores their significant role in both offensive and defensive cyber operations.

3 HoneySentry Design and Implementation

To overcome the challenges faced by existing IoT honeypots, we propose HoneySentry, a high-fidelity interactive IoT honeypot designed for advanced threat detection, as illustrated in Fig. 1. At its foundation, the system employs QEMU-based firmware emulation (①) to simulate real IoT devices, enabling accurate replication of communication protocols and network behaviors. This approach ensures that the emulated devices are nearly indistinguishable from authentic IoT devices, effectively deceiving attackers and capturing attack interactions.

The core of the system integrates a customized firmware environment (②), where a tailored BusyBox serves as the interaction entry point. Within this environment, carefully designed honey bait—such as fabricated accounts, system configurations, logs, and network information—enhances the honeypot's appeal to attackers. These elements are strategically crafted to lure attackers into prolonged engagement, enabling deeper interaction and data collection.

To achieve comprehensive monitoring, the system incorporates a lightweight honeypot probe (③) that captures multi-dimensional attack data, including system environment metrics, file activities, network traffic, and process behavior. Unlike hardware-dependent solutions, these probes operate entirely within the virtualized environment, enhancing adaptability across diverse IoT ecosystems. Collected data is securely transmitted to a backend analysis platform, ensuring both stealth and the integrity of captured insights.

3.1 Firmware Emulation

The foundation of a high-fidelity IoT honeypot lies in the accurate emulation of real device behavior. We developed a systematic workflow based on the widely used FirmAE firmware emulation framework [14]. This workflow encompasses firmware collection, firmware emulation and fidelity assessment, and honeypot image creation.

Firmware Collection and FirmAE Augmentation. During the firmware collection phase, an automated web crawler system was developed to systematically retrieve firmware images from the official websites and FTP servers of IoT manufacturers. Due to variations in firmware distribution structures and download paths across manufacturers, dedicated parsing templates were designed for 21 manufacturers to accurately extract download links, release dates, versions, and device models. Specifically, firmware samples were collected from major manufacturers, such as D-Link, TP-Link, Netgear, and Trendnet, primarily focusing on routers and IP cameras. These samples were Linux-based and supported three major hardware architectures: ARMel, MIPSel, and MIPSeb, resulting in a diverse dataset. To address the challenges presented by the diversity of firmware distribution formats and file systems, we enhanced FirmAE framework, with emphasis on improving firmware extraction and file system support:

`Enhanced Firmware Extraction Capabilities.` We extended FirmAE to support additional complex file systems, including cramFS and Squashfs. Custom parsing rules were implemented to handle these file systems, ensuring compatibility with a wide range of firmware images from various manufacturers and devices.

`Multi-layered File System Recognition and Extraction.` A multi-stage extraction approach was employed to optimize the recognition and extraction of different file system layers (such as ext2, ext4, JFFS2, cramFS, etc.). Following firmware extraction, the system automatically identifies and selects the appropriate file system and validates the integrity and validity of key directories.

Emulation Validation. Successfully emulated firmware underwent further fidelity validation, including tests for network reachability and web service availability. ICMP echo responses were verified using PING commands, and port 80 was checked for active web servers displaying content, ensuring the reliability and quality of the emulation results.

Honeypot Image Construction. For successfully emulated firmware, QEMU image files were packaged with predefined kernels tailored to the corresponding hardware architectures, resulting in the creation of a firmware image database. To enhance functionality and flexibility, automated deployment scripts were employed to configure probe modules for each firmware image. These probes provide comprehensive monitoring of file activities, network communications, and process behaviors, ensuring thorough oversight within the honeypot system, as described in Sect. 3.2.

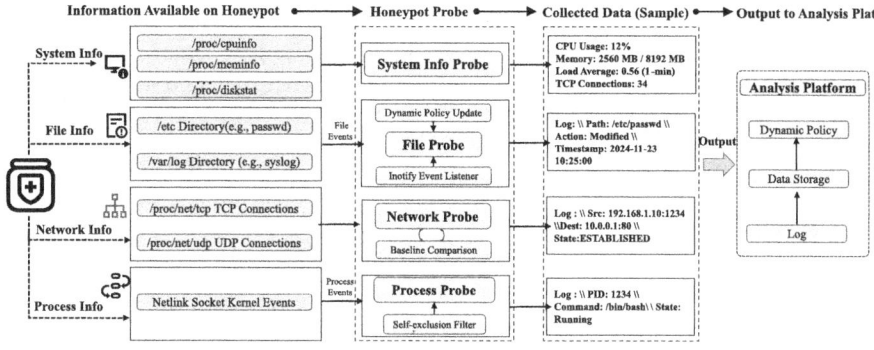

Fig. 2. Honeypot Probes in HoneySentry

3.2 Honeypot Probe: On-Device Behavior Monitoring

HoneySentry operates within a virtualized environment rather than as a physical device, with its monitoring capabilities implemented through software-based probes that function entirely within the virtual domain. Unlike previous approaches [20,27], this method is independent of hardware-specific behaviors or particular system configurations, significantly enhancing adaptability across diverse IoT ecosystems. These probes comprehensively monitor four critical aspects of attackers' activities within the honeypots: environment, files, network, and processes, ensuring thorough oversight. Moreover, unlike earlier techniques [28], this approach transmits monitoring logs to a concealed backend analysis platform rather than storing them locally. This design reduces the honeypot's footprint and minimizes the risk of detection by attackers.

The honeypot utilized in HoneySentry, depicted in Fig. 2, are categorized into four types: system information, file, network, and process.

System Info Probe. Unlike the event-driven monitoring approach employed by other probes, the system info probe operates on a snapshot-based model, periodically scanning the environment at predefined intervals. This non-intrusive approach leverages the /proc directory for data collection, eliminating the need for additional hardware or invasive modifications and ensuring compatibility across diverse IoT ecosystems.

As shown in Fig. 2, the probe retrieves information from critical files, such as /proc/cpuinfo, /proc/meminfo, and /proc/diskstat, to monitor CPU utilization, memory status, and disk activity, respectively. To ensure uninterrupted operation and data completeness, the probe integrates a heartbeat thread that continuously verifies the honeypot's online status. This mechanism not only ensures the honeypot remains operational but also facilitates real-time detection of any disruptions or anomalies in the environment.

File Probe. Figure 2 demonstrates the operational workflow of the file probe, which monitors changes within designated directories such as /etc and /var/log, including file creation, modification, deletion, movement, and attribute updates. This functionality leverages Linux's inotify mechanism, with two dedicated threads managing file monitoring and security policy updates. An inotify instance is recursively registered for each directory path specified in the security policy.

Network Probe. The network probe, visualized in Fig. 2, tracks changes in TCP and UDP sessions on honeypot using a baseline comparison approach, necessitated by Linux kernel limitations. The probe parses the contents of `/proc/net` to establish an initial baseline and re-parses the directory every five seconds.

Process Probe. The process probe monitors the creation and termination of processes during honeypot operations, leveraging the NETLINK SOCKET mechanism for efficient communication between user space and kernel space, as shown in Fig. 2. By sending a message to the kernel to enable `PROC_CN_MCAST_LISTEN` mode, the probe receives notifications of process-related events. These events are parsed in user space and categorized for logging based on their type.

3.3 Enhancing Honeypot Stealth Through Obfuscation

Studies have shown that attackers probing IoT devices often rely on a set of widely used system commands to verify the legitimacy of their targets. Li et al. [8] conducted a comprehensive analysis of the command sets commonly employed by attackers on IoT devices. These commands are typically used to gather information about the system, network configuration, and runtime environment. If a honeypot inadvertently exposes virtualization artifacts in its responses to these critical commands, its identity as a honeypot may be revealed. This exposure could prompt attackers to modify their behavior, thereby reducing the honeypot's effectiveness in capturing malicious traffic. Consequently, enhancing a honeypot's resistance to fingerprinting is essential to maintaining its stealth and ensuring successful engagement with attackers.

We improved the stealth capabilities of HoneySentry by customizing modifications to BusyBox, a lightweight suite of Unix utilities widely deployed in embedded systems and IoT devices. These enhancements bolster the honeypot's resistance against fingerprinting, ensuring that interactions with attackers remain undetected and productive.

File System Obfuscation. We modified BusyBox's file management components to implement a virtual file system. When attackers execute standard commands like `ls` or `cat` to inspect system files, they are presented with an obfuscated and filtered view of files and directories. This effectively conceals sensitive files and honeypot-specific logs, preventing attackers from detecting irregularities.

Process Management Obfuscation. For commands frequently used to probe running processes, such as `ps` or `top`, we altered BusyBox's process management functions to hide key honeypot processes or present them in a disguised form. This strategy disrupts attackers' ability to accurately assess the system's operational state, enhancing the honeypot's deceptive efficacy.

Network Activity Concealment. Since network traffic is a significant indicator of honeypot systems, we customized BusyBox's network utilities, e.g., `netstat` and `ifconfig`, to obscure the honeypot's network activities. When attackers query network connections or activity statuses, they are provided with obfuscated network information, effectively concealing the virtualized nature of the environment.

3.4 High-Engagement Honey Baits

To disrupt attackers' automated tools, delaying their progress, and effectively detecting malicious behaviors, we introduce a high-attractiveness bait scheme in HoneySentry to bolster the deceptive capabilities of honeypots, utilizing fabricated files and information to entice attackers. Prior research [19] has shown that deploying digital decoys can effectively obscure reconnaissance efforts and enhance the concealment of defensive mechanisms in cloud environments.

Account and privilege Baits. These baits simulate user-related information from the emulated environment, such as default user credentials and group information. For instance, if the simulated device includes a user named `admin`, bait files may contain fabricated account details reflecting this username. Such files are designed to entice attackers into attempting privilege escalation or mass credential cracking.

Configuration File Baits. These baits mimic system service settings, including authentication credentials and connection parameters. They feature options that appear operationally relevant but are harmless to the honeypot. For example, bait files may include plausible yet fake service configurations, misleading attackers into perceiving exploitable vulnerabilities while maintaining the honeypot's actual security.

System log Baits. These baits replicate authentic logs from system or application processes, potentially including fabricated records of sensitive user actions, service connections, or errors. For instance, fake login success or failure entries with fabricated IP addresses, usernames, and timestamps can be embedded in files like `/var/log/sshd.log` to capture attackers' attention and encourage further investigation.

Network information Baits. These baits provide attackers with false network parameters, including details about network interfaces, routing, and configurations, while preserving the honeypot's actual network functionality. For example, fabricated entries in critical files such as `/etc./hosts` and `/etc./resolv.conf` can mislead attackers during network reconnaissance. Special care is taken to ensure that these decoys do not interfere with the honeypot's legitimate operations.

4 Evaluation

We evaluate HoneySentry's effectiveness through extensive experiments, emphasizing its performance in facilitating deeper interactions with attackers, deceiving advanced network reconnaissance tools, and capturing complex attack behaviors.

4.1 HoneySentry's Emulation Capability

We evaluate HoneySentry's emulation capability in terms of extracted firmware images, network reachability and number of emulated services. Additionally, we conduct measurements to demonstrate that HoneySentry is resistant to trivial fingerprinting techniques, including timing-based attacks.

Extraction and Network Reachability. The emulation capability of HoneySentry was evaluated in comparison to FirmAE using the same set of IoT firmware images, focusing on firmware extraction and network reachability.

Methodology. A diverse set of IoT firmware images, covering routers, IP cameras, and smart home devices from leading vendors such as Asus, Belkin, Cisco, D-Link, TP-Link, and NETGEAR. The firmware images were emulated using both the HoneySentry emulation module and the FirmAE framework. Successful emulation was defined as the ability of the firmware to initialize and provide responsive web and shell interfaces, which are essential for simulating realistic interactions with external network entities.

Environment Description. The experiment was conducted on a host machine configured with Ubuntu 20.04 LTS, connected to a local area network (LAN) to ensure stable network communication. The dataset comprises a total of 3,712 firmware images collected from 12 widely used IoT device brands, including Asus, Netgear, D-Link, and TP-Link. The firmware samples represent a diverse range of device architectures and types, as illustrated in Fig. 3 and 4.

Figure 3 presents the distribution of firmware architectures across different brands. The architectures predominantly include arm32el, mips32el, and mips32eb, with some additional images categorized as others. Notably, brands such as Netgear and TP-Link exhibit a significant concentration of mips32eb firmware, while Asus and Ubiquiti predominantly feature arm32el architecture.

Figure 4 illustrates the distribution of device types by brand. The dataset primarily includes firmware for routers, which account for the majority of samples across most brands. Other device types, such as cameras and miscellaneous IoT devices, are also well-represented. For example, D-Link and TP-Link contribute significantly to the dataset with firmware for a variety of device types, ensuring that the evaluation covers a wide spectrum of IoT functionality.

Results. We tested a total of 3,712 firmware images, with results summarized in Table 1. HoneySentry appears better in extracting firmware images than FirmAE. In total, we successfully extracted 2,144 of 3,712 available images (57.8%) compared to 1705 for FirmAE (45.9%). For several brands, such as Asus, D-Link

Table 1. Firmware Extraction and Emulation Results

Brand	Available	Architecture				Extracted (Enhanced/Original)	Network Reach (Enhanced/Original)
		arm32el	mips32el	mips32eb	others		
Asus	386	82	89	42	13	320/226 ↑	178/141 ↑
Belkin	72	2	20	15	2	50/39 ↑	17/8 ↑
Cisco	92	22	13	18	6	47/34 ↑	45/42 ↑
D-Link	682	71	56	102	43	322/244 ↑	86/60 ↑
Huawei	6	3	1	0	0	4/4	2/2
Linksys	79	15	18	4	4	53/41 ↑	4/1 ↑
Mikrotik	172	8	10	32	16	105/65 ↑	1/1
Netgear	774	97	125	176	58	540/446 ↑	214/127 ↑
TP-Link	327	30	16	123	6	189/170 ↑	61/29 ↑
TRENDnet	133	15	11	39	14	78/66 ↑	37/24 ↑
Ubiquiti	499	45	32	160	17	292/237 ↑	39/34 ↑
Zyxel	490	8	10	115	1	144/133 ↑	64/42 ↑
Total	3712	400	401	830	183	2144/1705 ↑	748/511 ↑

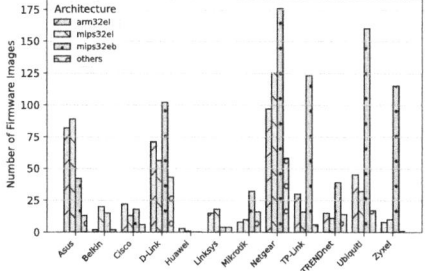

Fig. 3. Architecture Distribution

Fig. 4. Device Type Distribution by Brand

and Mikrotik, HoneySentry achieved up to a 30% higher success rate in extraction, highlighting its enhanced capability to handle diverse firmware architectures and formats.

To measure network reachability, we prepared and ran all the successfully extracted firmware images and sent them request packets. As shown in Table 1, we achieve significantly better results than FirmAE. Among the successfully extracted firmware images, 748 respond to the request, compared to 511 for FirmAE, achieving a 46.4% improvement across all 12 tested brands. For certain brands, the gains were even more pronounced. For instance, HoneySentry improved network reachability for Netgear firmware by 68.5% and for TP-Link firmware by over 110.3% compared to FirmAE.

From the perspectives of firmware extraction and network reachability, emulation failures mainly stemmed from non - standard compression or encryption algorithms and complex architectures during extraction, while for network reachability, discrepancies between the emulation environment and the real - world

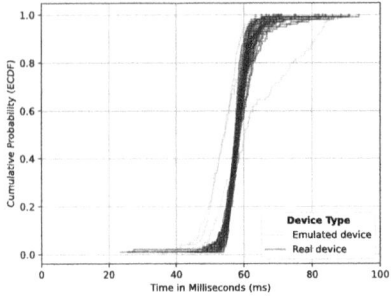 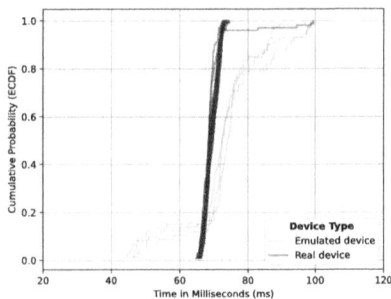

Fig. 5. RT-AC3200 Server: Time to HTTP Response

Fig. 6. DCS-930 Server: Time to HTTP Response

scenarios, along with strict security policies configured in the firmware, were the primary causes.

Timing Attacks to Fingerprint HoneySentry. To assess the resilience of honeypots against fingerprinting, we explore timing attacks as a method to distinguish real devices from cloud-deployed honeypots. We measured the HTTP response times of D-Link 930 and ASUS AC3200 devices to evaluate Honeysentry's susceptibility to timing-based fingerprinting.

Environment Description. The experiment included real devices sourced from the Shodan search engine and emulated honeypots deployed on a cloud platform. Each model was represented by three emulated instances and 10 real devices. The emulated honeypots, hosted on virtual machines with 2 vCPUs, 4 GB RAM, and Ubuntu 20.04 LTS operating system, replicated the HTTP services of D-Link 930 and ASUS AC3200.

Methodology. For each device, we measured the time taken for the HTTP server to respond to incoming requests over a 75-min period. Each measurement session involved 300 HTTP requests sent at 15-s intervals. To mitigate the influence of network delays, we recorded the Round Trip Time (RTT) for each request and adjusted the measured response times accordingly. The calculation for adjusted response time t_a is given as $t_a = t_{response} - t_{RTT}$, where $t_{response}$ represents the total time taken from sending an HTTP request to receiving a complete response, and t_{RTT} is the time measured for a request and reply cycle.

Results. Figure 5 and 6 present the empirical cumulative distribution functions (ECDF) of response times for real devices (blue curves) and emulated devices (yellow curves). The ECDF plots show that the cumulative response time distributions of real and emulated devices are highly congruent across both device types, with nearly overlapping curves. To quantify this similarity, we calculated Pearson correlation coefficients between the ECDF curves of real and emulated device groups. For DCS-930, the Pearson correlation coefficients for the three emulated groups are 0.9759, 0.9771, and 0.9737, respectively, indicating extremely strong linear correlation with real device distributions. For AC3200, the coefficients are 0.9659, 0.9643, and 0.9487, all of which fall within the range of strong correlation ($|r| > 0.94$). While real devices exhibited nearly identical response time distributions across all groups, emulated devices showed minor variability—likely due to virtualization overhead and cloud infrastructure fluctuations. These results confirm that Honeysentry's emulated devices effectively replicate real-device timing behaviors, with variations too minimal to enable reliable fingerprinting and thus robustly resisting timing-based attack.

4.2 Resilience Against Reconnaissance Tools

We evaluate the ability of the proposed HoneySentry to mimick real IoT devices and resist detection by advanced reconnaissance tools, including widely used device search engines and scanning tools.

Device Search Engine Experiment. Network search engines such as Shodan, Censys, and Fofa accurately index exposed devices by analyzing metadata from server-client interactions. Their capability to identify a wide range of device types, including servers, routers, and cameras, makes them valuable for security assessments and reconnaissance efforts. We evaluate HoneySentry's effectiveness in evading detection while disguising its honeypot nature from these engines.

Environment Description. We selected five firmware models, representing different brands—Netgear R6200, D-Link DCS-930L, D-Link DIR-830L, Netgear WNAP320, and ASUS RT-AC3200— for evaluation. And then we deploy these firmware models on cloud instances with identical configurations, including 2 vCPUs, 4 GB of RAM, and Ubuntu 20.04 LTS. Each instance hosted the HoneySentry honeypot with HTTP (port 80) and Telnet (port 23) services enabled, ensuring a consistent and standardized evaluation environment.

Methodology. After deploying HoneySentry on the cloud, we performed daily passive monitoring of three reconnaissance tools—Shodan, Censys, and Fofa—to evaluate whether our honeypots could be indexed by these tools. When indexing occurred, we analyzed the tools' banner information related to our honeypots, including details on open ports, device types, and service banners. Over the course of approximately one week, these tools successfully indexed our honeypots. By comparing the banners generated by these reconnaissance tools for HoneySentry with those generated for real IoT devices that our honeypots are designed to emulate, we evaluated HoneySentry's resilience.

Results. The indexing results from the reconnaissance tools are summarized in Table 2. These results indicate that none of the tools identified any instance as a honeypot or exposed virtualization-related information. This demonstrates HoneySentry's effectiveness in replicating IoT device behaviors and its resilience against fingerprinting across various reconnaissance tools.

Specifically, four out of the five deployed firmware models—DCS-930L, DIR-830L, WNAP320, and AC3200—were indexed by at least one reconnaissance

Table 2. Indexing Results of Device Search Engines

Model	Shodan		Censys		Fofa	
	Ports	Result	Ports	Result	Ports	Result
DCS-930L	80	/	/	Linux	80	alphapd
DIR-830L	80	D-LINK	80	D-LINK/Linux	80	jjhttpd v0.1.0
WNAP320	23,80	Netgear	23,80	Netgear	23,80	lighttpd/1.4.18
AC3200	80	/	/	Linux	80	httpd/2.0

Table 3. Nmap Scanning Results

Emulated Firmware	Device Type	Scanned OS Details
R6200-V1.0.1.48_1.0.37	router	Linux 3.2 - 4.9
DCS-930L_FIRMWARE_1.08_B4	camera	Linux 3.2 - 4.9
DIR-830L_REVA_FIRMWARE_1.00.B07	router	Designated Driver (Linux 4.1 or 4.4)
WNAP320_Firmware_Version_2.0.3	router	Linux 3.2 - 4.9
FW_RT_AC3200_30043804180	router	Linux 3.2 - 4.9

tool. Shodan identified the available HTTP services for most devices and correctly associated most firmware models with their respective brands, except for DCS-930L and AC3200. In comparison, Censys provided more detailed information about operating system-level characteristics, such as linking DCS-930L and AC3200 to Linux-based systems and identifying DIR-830L as a D-LINK device running a Linux-based OS. Fofa offered the most comprehensive service-level information, associating DCS-930L with `alphapd`, DIR-830L with `jjhttpd v0.1.0`, and WNAP320 with `lighttpd/1.4.18`, further underscoring Honey-Sentry's ability to emulate realistic service banners effectively.

Nmap Fingerprinting Experiment. We assess HoneySentry's resilience against Nmap, a widely used scanning tool known for its advanced fingerprinting techniques, which can potentially uncover a honeypot's deceptive nature.

Environment Description. We set up a controlled local network with two physical machines: one equipped with Nmap version 7.90 to perform the scans, and the other running Ubuntu 20.04 LTS, hosting the HoneySentry honeypots, which emulate one of five IoT device models: D-Link DCS-930L, D-Link DIR-830L, Netgear WNAP320, Netgear R6200, and ASUS AC3200.

Methodology. We conducted a series of 10 Nmap scans of HoneySentry honeypots to assess their resilience against fingerprinting. Using a database of over 1,500 known OS fingerprints, Nmap provides detailed information about the scanned target, including the operating system version and device type.

Results. The results of the Nmap scans are summarized in Table 3. It shows that all tested honeypots were identified by Nmap as legitimate IoT systems, demonstrating HoneySentry's high-fidelity emulation capabilities and its resilience against fingerprinting.

4.3 Traffic Analysis of HoneySentry Through Deployment in Real-World Environments

To assess HoneySentry's ability to engage attackers and maintain concealment, we deployed HoneySentry on the public Internet to attract malicious activities.

Environment Description. We launched 10 public cloud instances, each configured with 2 vCPUs, 4 GB RAM, and Ubuntu 20.04 LTS as the operating system, with ports 80 and 23 open, and deployed HoneySentry on each instance. Specifically, half of the instances (five) incorporated two modules: stealth enhancement techniques (Sect. 3.3) and high-engagement honey bait design (Sect. 3.4), while the remaining served as control instances without these enhancements.

Methodology. The honeypot instances were exposed to the public Internet for a period of two months. Throughout this period, HoneySentry's probe system captured detailed interaction network traffic. We analyzed the captured traffic in terms of session length (packets), session duration (seconds), and traffic volume (bytes) to compare the interaction depth and traffic characteristics between instances with and without the enhanced modules.

Table 4. Comparison of Traffic Statistics Between HoneySentry Honeypots With and Without Enhancement Techniques

Model	R6200	R6200*	DCS-930	DCS-930L*	DIR-830L
Len (pkts)	1.49	1.42	1.10	1.36↑	1.92
Dur (s)	0.96	1.16↑	3.69	17.89↑	0.57
Bytes	718.84	1,220.47↑	601.45	683.50↑	827.06
Model	DIR-830L*	WNAP320	WNAP320*	RT_AC3200	RT_AC3200*
Len (pkts)	1.99↑	2.51	3.68↑	1.87	1.96↑
Dur (s)	0.06	1.14	1.51↑	0.07	0.12↑
Bytes	430.35	1,748.64	5,125.08↑	337.68	378.32↑

* indicates that the honeypot is equipped with stealth enhancement techniques and high-engagement honey baits. ↑ indicates an increase compared to the left value.

Results. During its two-month deployment (August 2024 to November 2024), HoneySentry captured 213,495 requests, providing a comprehensive dataset for analysis. The results of the experiment, summarized in Table 4, reveal significant differences in interaction metrics between devices configured with the stealth enhancement techniques and high-engagement honey baits, and those without these enhancements.

Devices equipped with these enhancements consistently demonstrated longer average session lengths and durations. For example, the WNAP320 model achieved an average session length of 3.68 packets and a session duration of 1.51 s, compared to 2.51 packets and 1.14 s without the enhancements. Similar trends were observed for other devices, such as the RT-AC3200 model. Notably, the DCS-930L model exhibited the most significant improvement in session duration, increasing from 3.69 s to 17.89 s. Devices with the enhanced configurations also generated higher traffic volumes, with the WNAP320 model reaching an average of 5,125.08 bytes per session compared to 1,748.64 bytes without enhancements.

These findings demonstrate that the stealth and engagement enhancements significantly improve the honeypot's ability to attract and sustain interactions with attackers. By masking artificial traits and presenting realistic baits, the honeypot convincingly mimics genuine IoT devices, fostering deeper engagement and enabling the collection of richer attack behavior data.

4.4 Malicious Threat Capture and Analysis

We further evaluate HoneySentry's effectiveness in capturing and analyzing malicious threats, focusing on the capabilities of its probes in monitoring and analyzing a sophisticated attack chain. The HoneySentry honeypot system is equipped with multifunctional probes designed to capture and analyze every phase of an attack, including process execution, network interactions, file operations, and system modifications.

Table 5. Attack Type Statistics

Threat Category	Total Occurrences	First Occurrence
Command Injection	1430	2024-08-21
Path Traversal	1797	2024-08-21
Sensitive File Access	968	2024-08-21
Scanning & Probing	1088	2024-08-21
Injection Attacks	306	2024-08-22
Suspicious Activities	590	2024-08-21
Exploit Attempts	232	2024-08-22
Information Disclosure	157	2024-08-22
Cross-Site Scripting (XSS)	105	2024-09-13

Environment Description. We utilized the same experimental configuration as in prior sections, deploying HoneySentry with its honeypot probes across 10 publicly accessible instances over a two-month period. All data gathered by the probes were securely transmitted to a centralized analysis platform for subsequent threat assessment.

Results. During the experiment, our honeypot probes captured 61.3 GB of semantically rich log data, ensuring comprehensive and uninterrupted observation of adversarial behaviors. Table 5 summarizes the experiment's attack type statistics, categorizing observed cyber threats by frequency and chronological occurrence. The attack types are classified according to established taxonomies such as MITRE ATT&CK and OWASP Top 10 to align with real-world threat patterns, with path traversal (1,797 occurrences) and command injection (1,430 occurrences) identified as the most frequent. As a case study, we document the attack workflow of a sophisticated attack exploiting a CVE vulnerability in our emulated router, as depicted in Fig. 7. The attack commenced with the exploitation of CVE-2016-1555 through a crafted POST request targeting a specific endpoint on the emulated router. The *Process Probe* identified the execution of malicious scripts, detailing how commands were injected via parameters and executed using the exec() function. These observations provided critical insights into the initial exploitation method.

As the attack advanced, the *System Info Probe* uncovered attempts to alter device configurations through commands like wr_mfg_data and flash_erase. These actions indicated efforts to manipulate device behavior while simultaneously erasing critical storage areas to obscure traces of the intrusion.

The *File Probe* recorded the download of potentially malicious payloads, such as files named WSW0 and ERHF, utilizing the wget command. This probe captured comprehensive metadata of these download requests, including source IP addresses and file paths, and also logged the immediate deletion of these files via the rm command. This behavior underscored the attacker's operational discipline and focus on minimizing forensic evidence.

Additionally, the *Network Probe* captured outbound connections made during these file retrieval attempts, offering visibility into the external infrastructure employed by the attacker. This included HTTP request headers, target server details, and timestamps of interactions, providing a clear view of the adversary's external dependencies.

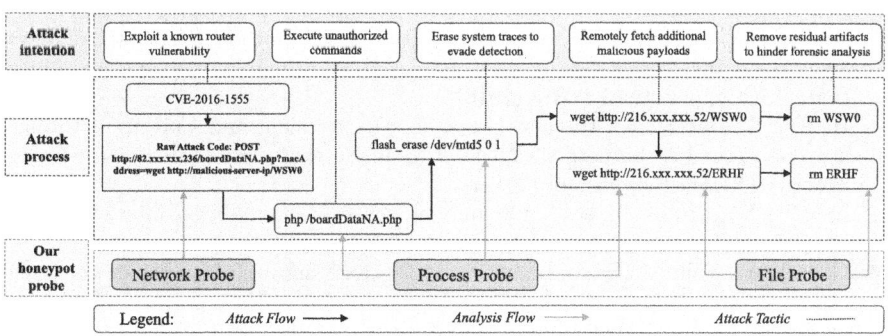

Fig. 7. Threat analysis of an attack captured by HoneySentry

Throughout the experiment, the honeypot system maintained its stealth, allowing the probes to capture the entire attack chain without alerting the attacker. The integration of process, network, file, and system probes revealed detailed attacker behavior, from initial exploitation to payload deployment and trace erasure, demonstrating the comprehensive capabilities of HoneySentry in analyzing sophisticated cyber threats.

5 Conclusion

We introduce HoneySentry, a high-interaction honeypot system specifically designed for IoT environments, which excels in stealth, fidelity, and attack capture. By utilizing firmware emulation and advanced techniques to mask its artificial traits, HoneySentry effectively mimics a variety of IoT devices and evades detection by reconnaissance tools. Its lightweight monitoring framework facilitates a comprehensive, multi-dimensional analysis of attack behaviors. Experimental results confirm its proficiency in capturing intricate attack chains and supporting in-depth security research. HoneySentry establishes a solid foundation for improving IoT security, with potential applications in customized deployment, real-time behavior analysis, and adapting to evolving cyber threats.

Acknowledgments. This work was supported in part by National Key R&D Program of China (2023YFB3106800) and by National Natural Science Foundation of China (62272410).

References

1. Thakkar, A., Lohiya, R.: A review on machine learning and deep learning perspectives of IDS for IoT: recent updates, security issues, and challenges. Arch. Comput. Methods Eng. **28**, 3211–3243 (2021)
2. Antonakakis, M., April, T., Bailey, M., et al.: Understanding the mirai botnet. In: Proceedings of the 26th USENIX Security Symposium, pp. 1093–1110 (2017)
3. Marzano, A., Alexander, D., Fonseca, O., et al.: The evolution of bashlite and mirai iot botnets. In: Proceedings of IEEE Symposium on Computers And Communications (ISCC), pp. 00813–00818 (2018)
4. Herwig, S., Harvey, K., Hughey, G., et al.: Measurement and analysis of Hajime, a peer-to-peer IoT botnet. In: Proceedings of Network And Distributed Systems Security (NDSS) Symposium (2019)
5. Luo, T., Xu, Z., Jin, X., et al.: Iotcandyjar: towards an intelligent-interaction honeypot for IoT devices. Black Hat **1**, 1–11 (2017)
6. Cabral, W., Valli, C., Sikos, L., et al.: Review and analysis of cowrie artefacts and their potential to be used deceptively. In: Proceedings of International Conference on Computational Science and Computational Intelligence (CSCI), pp. 166–171 (2019)
7. Ahamed, J., Rajan, A.V.: Internet of Things (IoT): application systems and security vulnerabilities. In: Proceedings of 5th International Conference on Electronic Devices, Systems and Applications (ICEDSA), pp. 1–5 (2016)

8. Li, H., Huang, Q., Ding, F., et al.: Understanding and detecting remote infection on linux-based IoT devices. In: Proceedings of the 2022 ACM on Asia Conference on Computer and Communications Security, pp. 873–887 (2022)
9. Morishita, S., Hoizumi, T., Ueno, W., et al.: Detect me if you... oh wait. An internet-wide view of self-revealing honeypots. In: Proceedings of IFIP/IEEE Symposium on Integrated Network and Service Management (IM), pp. 134–143 (2019)
10. Vetterl, A., Clayton, R.: Bitter harvest: systematically fingerprinting low-and medium-interaction honeypots at internet scale. In: Proceedings of 12th USENIX Workshop on Offensive Technologies (WOOT 18) (2018)
11. Srinivasa, S., Pedersen, J.M., Vasilomanolakis, E.: Gotta catch'em all: a multistage framework for honeypot fingerprinting. Digital Threats: Res. Pract. **4**(3), 1–28 (2023)
12. Junges, P.M., François, J., Festor, O.: HiFiPot: a high-fidelity emulation framework for internet of things honeypots. In: Proceedings of IEEE/IFIP Network Operations and Management Symposium, pp. 1–9 (2023)
13. Pa, Y.M.P., Suzuki, S., Yoshioka, K., et al.: IoTPOT: analysing the rise of IoT compromises. In: Proceedings of 9th USENIX Workshop on Offensive Technologies (WOOT 15) (2015)
14. Kim, M., Kim, D., Kim, E., et al.: Firmae: towards large-scale emulation of iot firmware for dynamic analysis. In: Proceedings of the 36th Annual Computer Security Applications Conference, pp. 733–745 (2020)
15. Bellard, F.: QEMU, a fast and portable dynamic translator. In: Proceedings of USENIX annual technical conference, FREENIX Track, vol. 41, no. 46, pp. 10–5555 (2005)
16. Ziaie Tabari, A., Ou, X.: A multi-phased multi-faceted IoT honeypot ecosystem. In: Proceedings of the 2020 ACM SIGSAC Conference on Computer and Communications Security, pp. 2121–2123 (2020)
17. Hakim, M.A., Aksu, H., Uluagac, A.S., et al.: U-pot: a honeypot framework for UPnP-based IoT devices. In: Proceedings of IEEE 37th International Performance Computing and Communications Conference (IPCCC), pp. 1–8 (2018)
18. Jicha, A., Patton, M., Chen, H.: SCADA honeypots: an in-depth analysis of Conpot. In: Proceedings of 2016 IEEE Conference on Intelligence and Security Informatics (ISI), pp. 196–198 (2016)
19. Li, H., Guo, Y., Huo, S., Hu, H., Sun, P.: Defensive deception framework against reconnaissance attacks in the cloud with deep reinforcement learning. Sci. China Inf. Sci. **65**(7), 170305 (2022)
20. Guarnizo, J.D., Tambe, A., Bhunia, S.S., et al.: Siphon: towards scalable high-interaction physical honeypots. In: Proceedings of the 3rd ACM Workshop on Cyber-Physical System Security, pp. 57–68 (2017)
21. Yamamoto, M., Kakei, S., Saito, S.: Firmpot: a framework for intelligent-interaction honeypots using firmware of IoT devices. In: Proceedings of 2021 Ninth International Symposium on Computing and Networking Workshops (CANDARW), pp. 405–411 (2021)
22. Mfogo, V.S., Zemkoho, A., Njilla, L., et al.: AIIPot: adaptive intelligent-interaction honeypot for IoT devices. In: Proceedings of 2023 IEEE 34th Annual International Symposium on Personal, Indoor and Mobile Radio Communications (PIMRC), pp. 1–6 (2023)
23. Guan, C., Liu, H., Cao, G., et al.: HoneyIoT: adaptive high-interaction honeypot for IoT devices through reinforcement learning. In: Proceedings of the 16th ACM Conference on Security and Privacy in Wireless and Mobile Networks, pp. 49–59 (2023)

24. Liao, S., Zhou, C., Zhao, Y., et al.: A comprehensive detection approach of nmap: principles, rules and experiments. In: Proceedings of 2020 International Conference on Cyber-Enabled Distributed Computing and Knowledge Discovery (CyberC), pp. 64–71 (2020)
25. Matherly, J.: Complete guide to shodan. Shodan, LLC **1** (2015)
26. Durumeric, Z., Adrian, D., Mirian, A., et al.: A search engine backed by internet-wide scanning. In: Proceedings of the 22nd ACM SIGSAC Conference on Computer and Communications Security, pp. 542–553 (2015)
27. Vetterl, A., Clayton, R.: Honware: A virtual honeypot framework for capturing CPE and IoT zero days. In: Proceedings of 2019 APWG Symposium on Electronic Crime Research (eCrime), pp. 1–13 (2019)
28. Yin, Z., Xu, Y., Zhou, C., et al.: Empirical study of system resources abused by iot attackers. In: Proceedings of the 37th IEEE/ACM International Conference on Automated Software Engineering, pp. 1–13 (2022)

Towards Architecture-Independent Function Call Analysis for IoT Malware

Kensei Ma[1(✉)], Chansu Han[1,2], Akira Tanaka[2], Takeshi Takahashi[2], and Jun'ichi Takeuchi[1]

[1] Kyushu University, Fukuoka, Japan
ma@me.inf.kyushu-u.ac.jp, tak@inf.kyushu-u.ac.jp
[2] National Institute of Information and Communications Technology, Tokyo, Japan
{han,tanaka.akira,takeshi_takahashi}@nict.go.jp

Abstract. IoT malware is often created by modifying publicly available source code, resulting in numerous variants. Analyzing the functionality of these variants has become increasingly important. Function Call Sequence Graph (FCSG) have been proposed to represent internal function calls in binaries, offering a promising approach for functional analysis. However, the structure of FCSGs is highly sensitive to CPU architecture and compiler optimization, hindering cross-architecture analysis. In this paper, we propose a method for generating architecture-independent FCSGs by removing obstructive functions—such as initialization routines and architecture-specific functions—that are not called in the source code but appear in conventional FCSGs. Our method removes, on average, 97.4% of such functions across binaries compiled for Arm, i586, and MIPS architectures with different optimization levels. Furthermore, we show that the resulting FCSGs better reflect the similarity of the original source code, as measured by graph- and string-based similarity metrics. These results demonstrate the potential of our method to improve the robustness and consistency of IoT malware functional analysis across diverse architectures.

Keywords: IoT malware · static analysis · functional analysis

1 Introduction

With the rapid spread of IoT devices, IoT malware that infects IoT devices is increasing. Most IoT malware is created by third parties who modify functions in the source code of publicly available malware families such as Mirai [9] and Bashlite [14]. Malware created by modifying functions in this way is called a variant. It is difficult to manually analyze the functions of an increasing number of variants, and the development of efficient methods to estimate the functions of variants has become a challenge.

While it is difficult to obtain source files of IoT malware variants, it is possible to obtain their binaries by using honeypot such as IoTPOT [23]. According to a previous study [2], many malware developers use well-known existing compilers and libraries to build their malware. The combination of compilers and libraries used for building is called a toolchain, and functional analysis of IoT malware often relies solely on the information extracted from binaries and associated toolchains. By using automatic labeling of malware binaries, such as AVClass [22], we can obtain representative malware family names such as Mirai and Bashlite. However, it is difficult to infer the detailed functionality of the malware from the malware family name alone. In addition, since IoT malware is generally compiled for many CPU architectures to enter various types of IoT devices, a functional analysis method that is independent of CPU architecture is desirable.

To address the challenge of functionality inference, Function Call Sequence Graph (FCSG) have been proposed to represent function call relationships within binaries in order to reveal the functionality of malware [15]. FCSG has the advantage of providing more detailed analysis of functions than automatic labeling. Ideally, FCSGs created from the same source files should have the same structure. However, in practice, FCSGs are significantly affected by CPU architecture and compiler options, and the graph structure changes even for FCSGs created from binaries with the same source code and functionality. This problem hinders cross-sectional functional analysis across CPU architectures.

In this paper, we present a method for improving the consistency of FCSGs by eliminating functions that are not called in the original source code–specifically, initialization routines and architecture-specific functions. Unlike conventional FCSGs, our method identifies and removes almost all the functions that are not called in the source code, thereby enhances the consistency and reliability of functional analysis across architectures. We conducted experiments to compare conventional and new FCSGs, using non-malware binaries of various CPU architectures and compiler optimization levels, and demonstrated that our method effectively eliminates functions that hinder analysis regardless CPU architectures. Furthermore, we evaluated whether the new FCSG more accurately reflects the characteristics of the original source code compared to the conventional FCSG.

The contributions of this paper are as follows:

- We propose a method to eliminate functions–such as initialization routines and architecture-specific functions–that are not called in the source code but appear in conventional Function Call Sequence Graph (FCSG).
- We show that, on average, 90.7% of the nodes in conventional FCSGs correspond to functions not present in the source code, highlighting the scale of structural noise caused by compilation.
- Our method successfully removes 97.4% of such obstructive nodes across multiple architectures (Arm, i586, and MIPS) and optimization levels (from -O0 to -O3), thereby improving structural consistency.
- We demonstrate that the improved FCSGs better reflect source-level similarity compared to conventional FCSGs, as confirmed by graph-based and string-based similarity metrics.

2 Related Works

Graph-based representations have become a central tool in the functional analysis and similarity measurement of binary code, particularly in the context of reverse engineering, malware analysis, and vulnerability detection. Among these, Control Flow Graph (CFG) and Function Call Graph (FCG) are widely adopted for capturing the structural and behavioral aspects of binaries. By extracting and comparing graph features, researchers have proposed various approaches to quantify similarities between programs and to support tasks such as binary classification, code reuse detection, and function-level matching.

He Haojie et al. [11] proposed an intermediate representation of graph-based binary codes called Semantics-Oriented Graph (SOG). After embedding SOG nodes, the nodes are passed through a multi-head aggregation module to obtain the embedding of the entire graph and the similarity between the graphs. The nodes of SOG are tokens of assembly code, and the relationship between instructions is distinguished by the type of edges. Tokens such as registers used to cache temporary values are removed, leaving only those that are relevant to semantics.

Yue Duan et al. [8] proposed an inter-procedural Control Flow Graph (ICFG) that provides contextual information for the entire program and used Text-Associated DeepWalk (TADW) [29] to generate basic block embeddings that incorporate structural features of the graph.

For malware, graphs can be used to understand the structural information of a program, which can be used for detection and classification. H. Alasmary et al. [3] analyzed the control flow graph (CFG) of IoT malware and demonstrated that although the number of nodes was small, the CFGs exhibited dense edge connectivity and complex control flow structures. Using the graph properties of CFGs (e.g., closeness, betweenness, diameter, etc.), they constructed a deep learning-based detection model to detect IoT malware.

Mehadi Hassen and Philip K. Chan. [10] clustered nodes in Function Call Graph (FCG) with Minhash [6] based on opcode sequences, and then used the relabeled graphs to perform malware classification.

3 Functional Analysis Using FCSG and Its Obstructive Factors

3.1 Overview of Function Call Sequence Graph (FCSG)

The Function Call Sequence Graph (FCSG) is a directed graph proposed by Kawasoe et al. [15]. In a given binary, each node represents a function call, and a directed edge is drawn from f_a to f_b when the function f_b may be called immediately after the function f_a in the binary. FCSG is created from the binary and does not require source files.

Malware functions are defined by calling user-defined functions or C library functions in the source code. Therefore, by analyzing function call sequences, we can analyze malware functions in detail. Moreover, by identifying function call sequences that are common among specific malware and by identifying family-specific characteristic functions, it is possible to classify malware.

Kawasoe et al. manually examined the source code of Bashlite [14] and Mirai [9], segmenting it by function and defining the representative functions of IoT malware as signature FCSGs. An example of a signature FCSG is shown in Fig. 1. The function call sequence in Fig. 1 represents the function of "Print out system exec". Kawasoe et al. estimated the functionality of unknown IoT malware by determining whether its FCSG contains a signature FCSG.

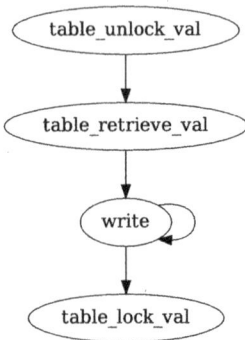

Fig. 1. An example of a signature FCSG.

Takada et al. [27] performed more flexible signature matching by embedding a signature FCSG into a vector and calculating the similarity between the signature FCSG and a subgraph that does not perfectly match the signature FCSG but is considered structurally similar.

To identify user-defined functions linked to IoT malware binaries, Akabane et al. [1] created FCSGs from multiple IoT malware binaries and created clusters by calculating the similarity between the edge sets that constitute function calls within user-defined functions. Akabane et al. identified user-defined functions by matching the common edge sets in the cluster with the FCSGs of user-defined functions whose function names are unknown.

3.2 Obstructive Factors of FCSG Analysis

As described in Sect. 1, IoT malware is compiled for various types of CPU architectures. Therefore, it is desirable to use the methods that are independent of CPU architecture to analyze IoT malware binaries so that they can be used across different CPU architectures. Also, as compiler optimizations are commonly applied during binary compilation, a method that is unaffected by changes in optimization levels is required. However, conventional FCSGs are affected by CPU architecture and optimization level, and even FCSGs created from the same source file can have different structures. These problems may prevent cross-sectional analysis across CPU architectures and analysis of specific functions of malware.

The source code most accurately represents the characteristics of the malware's functionality. Therefore, differences in functionality can be attributed to differences in the source code. In this paper, we focus on changes in conventional FCSG nodes resulting from variations in CPU architecture and compiler optimization levels. We regard the two cases as obstructive functions for the FCSG analysis: (a) functions that appear in the conventional FCSG despite not being called in the source code; and (b) functions that are absent from the FCSG despite being called in the source code. The following outlines several factors that cause these problems.

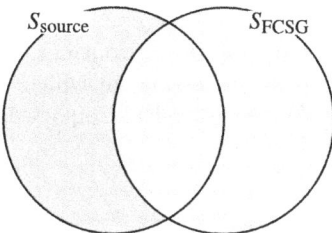

Fig. 2. the relationship between the function set called in the source code (S_{source}) and the node set of the FCSG(S_{FCSG}). (Color figure online)

Initial Routines. An initial routine is a process executed before running the logic described in the source code, such as stack initialization, memory initialization, etc. Note that the functions that make up the initial routines and the order in which they are called vary depending on the CPU architecture.

Architecture-Specific Functions. Functions that are linked to binaries when compiling for a particular CPU architecture. Architecture-specific functions appear in FCSG even though they are not called in the source code.

Inline Expanded Functions. Inline expansion is a type of compiler optimization that reduces the overhead of function calls by inserting instructions equivalent to the function f instead of calling the function f. Since function call information is lost when a function is inline expanded, the function does not appear in the FCSG even though it is called in the source code. Which functions are inline expanded depends mainly on the compiler optimization levels, but is also affected by differences in the toolchains.

Figure 2 shows the Venn diagram of the relationship between the function set called in the source code (S_{source}) and the node set of the conventional FCSG(S_{FCSG}). $S_{FCSG} - S_{source}$ (green area in the figure) represents the set of functions that appear in conventional FCSGs even though they are not called in the source code, such as initial routines and architecture-specific functions. The $S_{source} - S_{FCSG}$ (red part in the figure) represents the set of functions that are called in the source code but do not appear in conventional FCSG, such as inline expanded functions. In this paper, we propose a method to create a new FCSG by removing functions that appear in the conventional FCSG despite not being called in the source code (i.e., the green region in Fig. 2), which hinders cross-architecture malware analysis.

4 Overview of Proposed Method

In this paper, we propose a method to remove functions that appear in the conventional FCSGs but are not called in the source code, using binary and toolchain information. As discussed in Sect. 3.2, such functions often originate from initial routines or architecture-specific functions.

Therefore, as shown in Fig. 3, the proposed method consists of four main steps: (1) creating a graph with multiple connected components (MCC graph) from the ELF binary; (2) removing initial routines; (3) removing architecture-specific functions; and (4) post-processing, in which the modified MCC graph is converted into the new FCSG. The ELF binary is written in C and is in unstripped format.

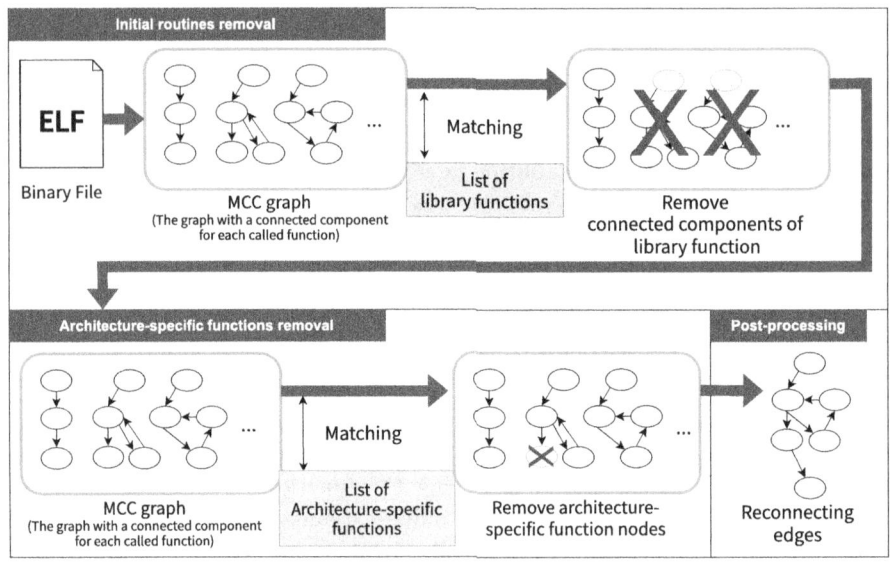

Fig. 3. Illustrated overview of the proposed method.

4.1 Overview of Graph with Multiple Connected Components (MCC Graph)

We performed a static analysis on an ELF binary to construct a graph with multiple connected components (MCC graph), where every connected component represents the function calls made within a single function. The root node (with zero indegree) of every connected component is labeled with the name of the function within which the component is defined. The remaining nodes and edges in the connected component represent the function call sequences called in the function of the root node. When multiple functions are linked in a binary, multiple connected components are created from a single binary. MCC graphs distinguish which function is called inside which function, even if the function name is the same, and create distinct nodes for each call context. In contrast, FCSG aggregates all functions with the same name into a single node, thereby losing the caller-callee relationship.

Consider creating a graph by analyzing a binary created from a source code in Figure 4. In the source code, f() and g() are called inside main(), and g() and h() are called inside f(). When creating a conventional FCSG from binaries, a graph with the sequence main(), f(), g(), h(), and g() in that order, as in Figure 5 are created. (g() is aggregated to single node). On the other hand, in the MCC graph, as shown in Figure 6, the connected component of main() has only function nodes called inside main(), and the connected component of f() has only function nodes called inside f().

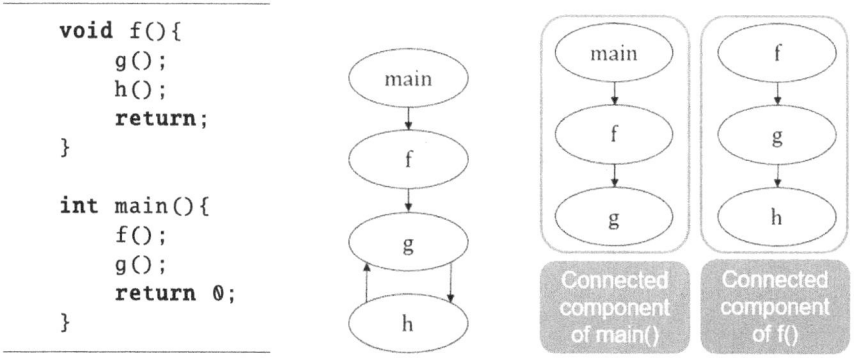

Fig. 4. Source code.   **Fig. 5.** Conventional FCSG.   **Fig. 6.** MCC graph.

4.2 Initial Routines Removal

To remove the initial routine, we remove the connected components of the MCC graph whose roots are the library functions. In this way, we keep the connected components of user-defined functions and remove sequences that are not in the source code, such as initial routines.

We remove each connected component in the MCC graph if its root node is included in a library function list. The list of library functions was created by extracting symbols contained in files that are linked at compiling from prebuilt toolchains built on Firmware Linux, Aboriginal Linux [18,28], pre-built toolchains obtained from Bootlin [5], and toolchains built locally using Buildroot [7].

4.3 Architecture-Specific Functions Removal

Architecture-specific function symbols are defined as the function symbols of the relevant architecture excluding the function symbols common to all architectures. If the target architectures are, for example, Arm, i586, and MIPS, the set of architecture-specific function symbols $S'_{\text{Arm}}, S'_{\text{i586}}, S'_{\text{MIPS}}$ are defined as follows.

$$S'_{\text{Arm}} = S_{\text{Arm}} - (S_{\text{Arm}} \cap S_{\text{MIPS}} \cap S_{\text{i586}}) \tag{1}$$

$$S'_{\text{i586}} = S_{\text{i586}} - (S_{\text{Arm}} \cap S_{\text{MIPS}} \cap S_{\text{i586}}) \tag{2}$$

$$S'_{\text{MIPS}} = S_{\text{MIPS}} - (S_{\text{Arm}} \cap S_{\text{MIPS}} \cap S_{\text{i586}}) \tag{3}$$

Note that S_{Arm}, S_{MIPS}, and S_{i586} represent the sets of symbols linked to binaries when cross-compiling for each respective architecture. Figure 7 illustrates the set of architecture-specific function symbols for Arm as an example.

We remove architecture-specific functions by matching each node in the graph–after initial routines have been removed–against a list of architecture-specific function symbols.

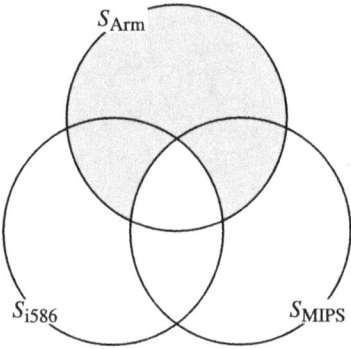

Fig. 7. Venn diagram illustrating the set of architecture-specific function symbols in Arm.

4.4 Post-processing

In the post-processing stage, edges are reconnected after the removal of architecture-specific functions. Subsequently, as in the construction of the conventional FCSG, functions with the same name on the MCC graph are treated as identical and merged into a single node to form the final graph.

5 Node Set Comparison Experiments

To evaluate the effectiveness of the proposed method, we conducted an experiment in which we created a new FCSG and a conventional FCSG from benign source files and compared the node sets of each to measure how many obstructive nodes were removed from the conventional FCSG. In order to conduct the experiment, we selected the benign source files and identified the nodes in the conventional FCSGs that were considered to be obstructive factors.

5.1 Selection of Source Files

We selected benign source files that are comparable in binary size (at most 200 KB) to malware binaries collected by IoTPOT [23] from June 1, 2020 to June 30, 2020. Benign source files from relatively small projects were selected so that they could be compiled in a local cross-compiler environment. We used fifteen C source files [4, 16, 17, 19, 21, 24, 26] that were publicly available on GitHub.

5.2 Compilation and FCSG Creation

In our experiments, we cross-compiled the source files and created binaries using the toolchain created by the build tools shown in Table 1. Each binary was compiled using one of the compiler optimization levels: -O0, -O1, -O2, or -O3. The C library was statically linked to the binary with uClibc to match the actual build environment of the IoT malware.

Table 1. Toolchain used in the experiment

Build tool	Toolchain	Architecture
Firmware Linux 0.9.6	GCC 4.1.2, binutils 2.17, uClibc 0.9.30.1	Armv4l
		i586
		MIPS

Table 2. Average number of nodes of conventional FCSG and obstructive factors for FCSG analysis

	-O0			-O1			-O2			-O3		
	Armv4l	i586	MIPS	Armv4l	i586	MIPS	Armv4l	i586	MIPS	Armv4l	i586	MIPS
$|S_{FCSG}|$	171.5	155.9	146.4	171.5	155.9	146.4	171.5	155.9	146.4	171.4	155.8	146.3
$|S_{FCSG} - S_{source}|$	158.5	142.9	133.3	158.5	142.9	133.3	158.5	142.9	133.3	158.3	142.7	133.2
$|S_{source} - S_{FCSG}|$	0.7	0.9	0.6	1.2	1.4	1.2	1.2	1.4	1.2	1.9	2	1.9

The binaries were then disassembled using the static analysis software IDA Pro [12] to obtain function call sequence. Compilation was performed for all combinations of architectures and optimization options, and new FCSGs were created from a total of 180 binaries to which the proposed method was applied. For comparison, conventional FCSGs were also created from a total of 180 binaries.

5.3 Check of Conventional FCSG Nodes

We checked how many nodes were included in the conventional FCSG that could be considered obstructive factors for FCSG analysis.

Table 2 shows $|S_{FCSG}|$, $|S_{FCSG} - S_{source}|$, and $|S_{source} - S_{FCSG}|$ for each optimization level of the conventional FCSGs. $|S_{FCSG}|$ is the number of nodes in the conventional FCSG, $|S_{FCSG} - S_{source}|$ is the number of functions that appear in the conventional FCSG despite not being called in the source code, and $|S_{source} - S_{FCSG}|$ is the number of functions that do not appear in conventional FCSG even though they are called in the source code. The numbers in the table are averages of the fifteen source files.

Table 2 shows that $|S_{FCSG} - S_{source}|$ is consistently high across all optimization levels and that most of the conventional FCSG nodes are not called in the source code. On average, 90.7% of the nodes in the conventional FCSG belonged to $S_{FCSG} - S_{source}$. The value of $|S_{FCSG} - S_{source}|$ for Armv4l is relatively large, and the number of nodes changed little with changes in optimization levels for initial routines and architecture-specific functions. The $S_{FCSG} - S_{source}$ is considered to be caused by library and compiler internal functions in addition to initial routines and architecture-specific functions.

On the other hand, some nodes were found to belong to $S_{source} - S_{FCSG}$, and the cause may be inline function expansion.

5.4 Comparison of New and Conventional FCSGs

We evaluated how effectively the proposed method removed unnecessary nodes and how many necessary nodes were unintentionally eliminated from conventional FCSG. We calculated the percentage of $S_{FCSG} - S_{source}$ elements that existed in the conventional FCSG that were removed by the proposed method. We also examined the percentage of S_{source} elements that were unintentionally removed by the proposed method. The $S_{FCSG} - S_{source}$ is the set of functions that appear in conventional FCSG even though they are not called in the source code, and S_{source} is the set of functions that are called in the source code. The average values for each architecture and optimization level are summarized in Table 3. The first line of the table shows

Table 3. Percentage of $S_{FCSG} - S_{source}$ and S_{source} elements removed by the proposed method

	-O0			-O1			-O2			-O3		
	Armv4l	i586	MIPS	Armv4l	i586	MIPS	Armv4l	i586	MIPS	Armv4l	i586	MIPS
Percentage of functions removed that are in $S_{FCSG} - S_{source}$	98.2%	95.8%	97.8%	98.1%	95.8%	97.7%	98.4%	96.2%	98.2%	98.3%	96.0%	97.9%
Percentage of functions removed that are in $S_{source} \cap S_{FCSG}$	1.51%	4.15%	0.81%	1.60%	4.33%	1.89%	3.24%	3.44%	3.53%	2.18%	2.92%	2.50%

$$\frac{|S_{\text{removed}} \cap (S_{\text{FCSG}} - S_{\text{source}})|}{|S_{\text{FCSG}} - S_{\text{source}}|} \tag{4}$$

in percentage. The second line shows

$$\frac{|S_{\text{removed}} \cap (S_{\text{source}} \cap S_{\text{FCSG}})|}{|S_{\text{source}} \cap S_{\text{FCSG}}|} \tag{5}$$

in percentage. Note that S_{removed} is the set of function nodes removed by the proposed method. The first line represents the percentage of $S_{\text{FCSG}} - S_{\text{source}}$ elements removed by the proposed method. The second line represents the percentage of $S_{\text{source}} \cap S_{\text{FCSG}}$ elements removed by the proposed method. The removed function nodes were identified by subtracting the node set of the new FCSG from that of the conventional FCSG created from the same binary.

Experimental results show that the proposed method removes an average 97.4% of the $S_{\text{FCSG}} - S_{\text{source}}$ elements in the conventional FCSG. Table 3 shows that the variation due to differences in CPU architectures was also small, and overall a high percentage of $S_{\text{FCSG}} - S_{\text{source}}$ elements were removed by the proposed method. Because the change in $|S_{\text{FCSG}} - S_{\text{source}}|$ due to changes in compiler optimization was small, the deletion rate was largely unaffected by compiler optimization. The remaining elements of $S_{\text{FCSG}} - S_{\text{source}}$ include functions for which IDA Pro was unable to identify the function name, library functions that were called in user-defined functions and were replaced by other functions, and functions that constitute initial routines. It should be noted that all function nodes removed in this experiment were removed using the initial routine removal method, and no function nodes were found to have been removed using architecture-specific function removal methods. Details are provided in Appendix.

On the other hand, the proposed method also removes an average of 2.68% of the $S_{\text{source}} \cap S_{\text{FCSG}}$ elements. In the case of conventional FCSG, even if an element of S_{source} is inline expanded, the node remains if another library function with the same name as the inline expanded function is called inside the library function. On the other hand, the proposed method deletes the library connected components, so no inline expanded node remains.

For this reason, there was an element of $S_{\text{source}} \cap S_{\text{FCSG}}$ that existed in the conventional FCSG but not in the new FCSG. Note that in the case of conventional FCSG, the node with the same name as the inline expanded function was linked within a library function, and thus may not accurately reflect the function call sequence in the source file. In this experiment, the user-defined functions `hash_delete()` in `hashmap.c` were in the list of library functions and were mistakenly identified as a library function. No other user-defined functions were affected.

6 Graph Evaluation

We measured the similarity between new FCSGs created from different binaries and evaluated how their similarities varied. For comparison, the similarity was calculated for the conventional FCSG as well. Specifically, we calculated the similarity of conventional and new FCSGs using the Jaccard index of their edge sets. We compared the Jaccard index to the Normalized Compression Distance (NCD) [20] between the source files to see how well the similarity between the new FCSGs reflects the similarity between the source files in terms of strings.

6.1 Compilation and FCSG Creation

The 15 source files used in Sect. 5 were cross-compiled to create binaries. The toolchain used and the method of creating the binaries are the same as in Sect. 5. From the 180 binaries created, we created 180 new FCSGs which applied the proposed method and 180 conventional FCSGs.

6.2 Calculation of Jaccard Index Between Sets of Graph Edges

The similarity was computed for all generated graphs. In this experiment, the Jaccard index between the edge sets of the graphs was used as the similarity between the graphs. The Jaccard index $J(A, B)$ between two sets A and B is defined as:

$$J(A, B) = \frac{|A \cap B|}{|A \cup B|} \quad (6)$$

The Jaccard index ranges from 0 to 1, where higher values indicate greater similarity between the two sets. A value close to 0 indicates a small similarity, while a value close to 1 indicates a large similarity.

The similarity between the graphs was calculated for all possible combinations of the 180 new FCSGs created when duplicates were allowed and two were selected. The similarity was calculated for the 180 conventional FCSGs as well, and a Jaccard index matrix J of size 180 × 180 was created for each, where the Jaccard index matrix is a matrix with $J(E_i, E_j)$ in the (i, j) entry for E_i, E_j in the edge set dataset $\{E_1, ..., E_n\}$.

6.3 NCD Between Source Files Compared to Jaccard Index Between Graphs

NCD (Normalized Compression Distance) is a similarity metric based on data compression. The NCD between data x and data y, $\mathrm{NCD}(x, y)$, is defined by

$$\mathrm{NCD}(x, y) = \frac{C(xy) - \min\{C(x), C(y)\}}{\max\{C(x), C(y)\}} \quad (7)$$

where xy is the combined data x and data y, and $C(x)$ is the data length when data x is compressed. $\mathrm{NCD}(x, y)$ is a real number between 0 and 1. A smaller

NCD value indicates greater similarity, meaning that data x and y share more common patterns. The Lempel-Ziv-Markov chain algorithm (LZMA) was used as the compression algorithm in the experiments.

NCD calculations were performed on all combinations of source file pairs to produce a distance matrix D of size 15×15, where the distance matrix is a matrix with $\mathrm{NCD}(x_i, x_j)$ in the (i, j) entry for x_i, x_j in the dataset $\{x_1, ..., x_n\}$. Then, based on the distance matrix D, a similarity matrix D' of size 180×180 was generated to match the number of FCSGs. Assuming that the (i, j) entry of the Jaccard index matrix J is the similarity between graphs created from the source file S_i and from the source file S_j, let D' be defined as the (i, j) entry with the NCD distance between source files S_i and source file S_j subtracted from 1.

The distance between the similarity matrix D' and the Jaccard index matrix was calculated using the Frobenius norm to evaluate how well the similarity between the graphs with the proposed method reflects the similarity between the source files in terms of strings. The Frobenius norm $||A||_F$ of a matrix $A = (a_{ij})$ is defined as follows:

$$||A||_F = \sqrt{\sum_i \sum_j a_{ij}^2} \qquad (8)$$

6.4 Evaluation Results

Figure 8 shows a heatmap of the distance matrix D. The vertical and horizontal axes represent source file names in dictionary order. In the heatmap, lighter colors indicate smaller distances (closer to 0), while darker colors indicate larger distances (closer to 1). Overall, the distances between the same source files are small and the distances between different source files are large, although the distance between `mahmednabil109_dump_xll.c` and `mahmednabil109_dump_xll_cptr.c` is relatively smaller than the distances between other distinct source files. This may be due to the fact that both implementations used XOR-based linked lists, and there was not much difference in terms of strings.

Figure 9 and Fig. 10 show heatmaps of the Jaccard index matrices for edge sets from the conventional and new FCSGs, respectively. The vertical and horizontal axes are lined up with binary names in dictionary order. Each binary name is a concatenated string comprising the source file name, CPU architecture, toolchain, and optimization level. The heatmap uses color to represent similarity: a higher Jaccard index (closer to 1) is shown in white, while a lower value (closer to 0) is shown in darker colors. Inside the green rectangle are graph pairs created from the same source file, and outside the green rectangle are graph pairs created from different source files. Therefore, the pairs inside the green rectangle should be more similar, and the pairs outside the green rectangle should be less similar.

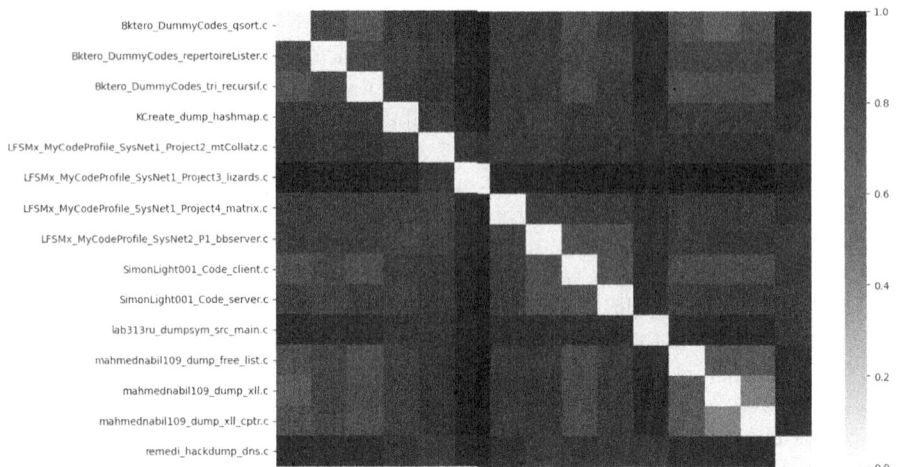

Fig. 8. A heatmap of the distance matrix D.

Table 4. Frobenius norm of the similarity matrix D' and the Jaccard index matrix J

	Conventional FCSG	New FCSG
Frobenius norm	70.20	30.66

The conventional FCSG heatmap is generally closer to white and the similarity between the graphs created from different source files is larger, whereas the new FCSG heatmap is closer to the heatmap of the distance matrix D, with smaller similarity between the graphs created from different source files. This may be due to the fact that the implementation of functions and initial routines in the library may be architecture-specific, and the conventional FCSG has many common edges even among different source files. On the other hand, the new FCSG removes initial routines and architecture-specific functions, resulting in lower similarity between graphs generated from different source files, as indicated by darker (black) areas in the heatmap.

The new FCSG heatmap also shows that some graph pairs have slightly less similarity between graphs created from the same source file than the conventional FCSG. The graphs created from the -O3 binary tended to have smaller similarities than the graphs created from the -O0,-O1,-O2 binary. This may indicate that additional edges may have been introduced in the -O3 binaries that were not present in the -O0, -O1, or -O2 binaries, and that the source files with a large number of user-defined functions and functions called in the user-defined functions were strongly affected by the edge changes.

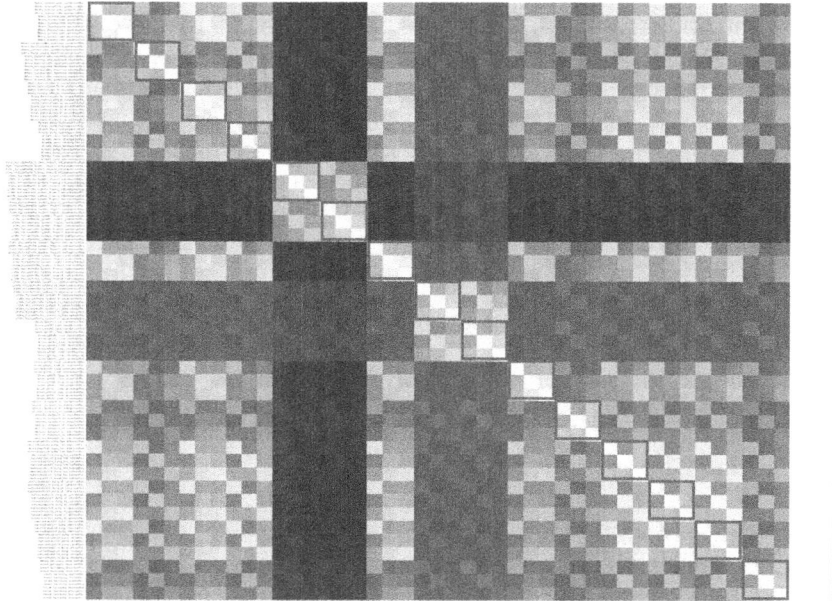

Fig. 9. Heatmap of Jaccard index matrix J for conventional FCSG.

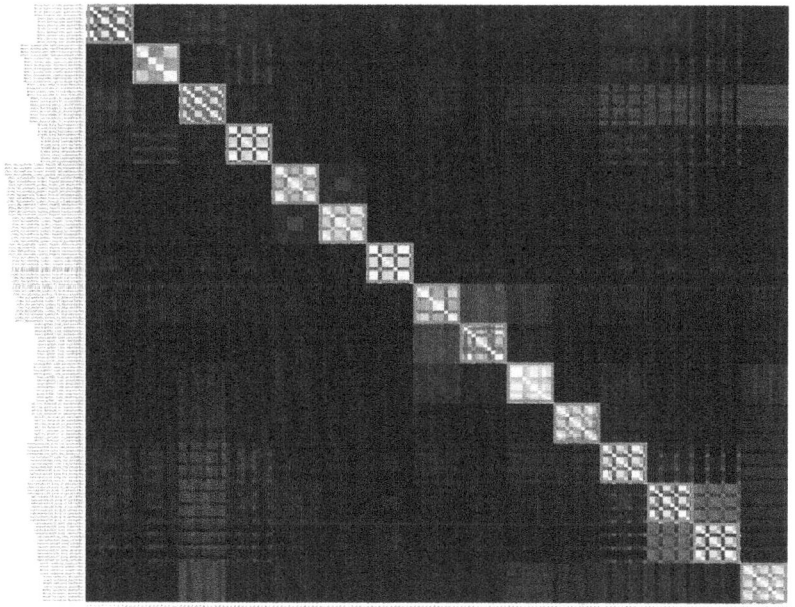

Fig. 10. Heatmap of Jaccard index matrix J for new FCSG.

Table 4 shows the Frobenius norm between the source file similarity matrix D' and the Jaccard index matrix J. The new FCSG Jaccard index matrix is closer to the source file similarity matrix D', which better reflects the differences in terms of source file strings. However, D' does not account for semantic equivalence; that is, two files with different strings but similar functionality may still have a large distance. And a more detailed investigation may be possible by calculating the similarity based on the meaning and functionality of the source files.

7 Discussion

7.1 Methods for Determining Library Functions

Experiments in Sect. 5 showed that there were cases where user-defined functions were mistakenly determined to be library functions. Since the proposed method determines whether a function is a library function or not only by its name, the function is removed if a user-defined function shares the same name as a library function.

We also tested an alternative method that considers not only the function name but also its internal calls. However, the results did not reflect the similarity between the source files well because the elements of $S_{\text{FCSG}} - S_{\text{source}}$ were not effectively removed.

By identifying the header files included in the source files, it is possible to determine whether a function is used as a library function or called as a user-defined function. However, in the case of static linking, functions that are not declared in the included header file are linked together, and identifying the corresponding header file from the binary alone is a challenging task. By observing which functions are linked in the binary, the header file may be identified. However, the functions linked vary depending on the linking method and toolchain, so close observation is required.

We might reduce the misclassification of user-defined functions as library functions by collecting symbols exclusively from the toolchains used to compile the binaries.

As described in Sect. 5.4, for the elements of the deleted $S_{\text{source}} \cap S_{\text{FCSG}}$ other than user-defined functions, the cause is inline expansion. Therefore, the fundamental solution to the problem requires the restoration of inline expanded functions.

7.2 Other Obstructive Factors of FCSG Analysis

This paper focuses on initial routines and architecture-specific functions among the disincentives discussed in Sect. 3.2, and proposes a method to remove them. However, it should be noted that the proposed method does not address inline expanded functions.

For inline expanded functions, there is a possibility to recover function names by matching the opcode sequence of the library combined during binary creation with the disassembly result of the binary to be analyzed. However, since the opcode sequence of the library varies depending on the tool chain and optimization options, flexible matching is required, such as by masking instructions likely to change or embedding them in vectors. In this experiment, inline expansion of functions was observed, and we intend to further investigate this in the future.

It has also been observed that the function call order changes among different CPU architectures and optimization levels. The main cause may be the exchange of instruction order due to compiler optimization, but it is difficult to infer the function call order of the source code from the graph and binary information alone. We can mitigate the inconsistencies in graphs by understanding the timing and conditions under which edges are created. It should be noted that this experiment only compared the node set, so edge-level improvements were not considered in this study.

7.3 Applying Proposed Method to Stripped Binaries

In our experiments, we used only unstripped binaries, i.e., all symbol information was preserved. However, malware binaries in the real world are often stripped to reduce file size and prevent analysis. The binary In the case of stripped binaries, the name of the function being called cannot be obtained, which may hinder the creation of FCSGs.

We believe that our proposed approach can still be applied to stripped binaries by recovering function names using tools such as IDA F.L.I.R.T. [13] and stelftools by Akabane et al. [2,25].

In particular, stelftools was able to recover function names with an accuracy of 97.18% on 150 stripped malware binaries in which functions were statically linked.

7.4 Applying Proposed Method to Malware Binaries

As described in Sect. 1, some malware source code is publicly available. Therefore, we believe that the effectiveness of the proposed method can be evaluated by creating S_{FCSG} from malware binaries and S_{source} from the corresponding malware source code, as in the experiments conducted in this paper. Since initial routines and architecture-specific functions are largely dependent on the toolchain, the proposed method is expected to remove a high percentage of them. However, the use of malware source code may produce different results from those obtained in this experiment using benign source files. In particular, user-defined functions and functions called inside user-defined functions are likely to be more affected by edge changes than in the experiment.

8 Conclusion

This paper presented a method to generate architecture-independent Function Call Sequence Graph (FCSG) by removing obstructive functions–specifically, initialization routines and architecture-specific functions–that are not called in the source code but appear in conventional FCSGs. These extraneous nodes, which account for an average of 90.7% of conventional FCSGs, introduce structural inconsistencies that hinder cross-architecture functional analysis of IoT malware. Our proposed method effectively eliminates an average of 97.4% of these obstructive functions across binaries compiled for different architectures and optimization levels. Furthermore, we demonstrated that the resulting FCSGs better reflect source-level similarity compared to conventional FCSGs, as confirmed by both graph-based (Jaccard index) and string-based (NCD) similarity measures. These improvements enhance the consistency and robustness of function-level analysis in IoT malware research. As future work, we plan to address remaining limitations related to inline-expanded functions and unexplained variations in graph edge structures that arise across architectures and optimization levels. In addition, we intend to apply our method to real-world malware binaries, extend evaluation across a broader set of toolchains.

A Appendix

As mentioned in the Sect. 5.4, all function nodes removed in this experiment were removed using the initial routine removal method, and no function nodes removed using the architecture-specific function removal method were confirmed. Upon investigating the contents of $S_{\text{FCSG}} - S_{\text{source}}$, we found that architecture-specific functions existed, as shown in Fig. 5.

The criteria for determining whether a function is an initial routine and whether it is an architecture-specific function are shown below.

Initial Routines. Use function symbols contained in runtime libraries such as `crti.o`, `crt1.o`, and `crtbeginT.o`, which are linked when creating binaries, as initial routines. Specify the files to be linked for each architecture and extract the function symbols.

Architecture-Specific Functions. For FCSG created from the same source file and the same compiler optimization level, the sets of architecture-specific functions $T'_{\text{Arm}}, T'_{\text{i586}}, T'_{\text{MIPS}}$ are defined as follows.

$$T'_{\text{Arm}} = T_{\text{Arm}} - (T_{\text{Arm}} \cap T_{\text{MIPS}} \cap T_{\text{i586}}) \qquad (9)$$

$$T'_{\text{i586}} = T_{\text{i586}} - (T_{\text{Arm}} \cap T_{\text{MIPS}} \cap T_{\text{i586}}) \qquad (10)$$

$$T'_{\text{MIPS}} = T_{\text{MIPS}} - (T_{\text{Arm}} \cap T_{\text{MIPS}} \cap T_{\text{i586}}) \qquad (11)$$

where $T'_{\text{Arm}}, T'_{\text{i586}}, T'_{\text{MIPS}}$ are node sets of FCSG created from binaries compiled for their respective architectures. Each element belonging to the set of architecture-specific functions Elements belonging to the set of architecture-specific functions are considered architecture-specific functions. In this case, we use this criterion for evaluation, but this assumes that we have FCSG with completely identical functions at hand. Therefore, it is important to note that source files are required to create $T'_{\text{Arm}}, T'_{\text{i586}}$, and T'_{MIPS}.

Architecture-specific functions are often called within libraries, and it is believed that many of these functions were removed during the initial routine

Table 5. Percentage of each item in $S_{\text{FCSG}} - S_{\text{source}}$

	-O0			-O1			-O2			-O3		
	Armv4l	i586	MIPS	Armv4l	i586	MIPS	Armv4l	i586	MIPS	Armv4l	i586	MIPS
Functions determined to be initial routines	12.5%	13.8%	14.9%	12.5%	13.8%	14.9%	12.5%	13.8%	14.9%	12.5%	13.7%	14.9%
Functions determined to be architecture-specific	22.6%	9.65%	4.33%	22.6%	9.65%	4.23%	22.6%	9.65%	4.23%	22.6%	9.78%	4.23%
Functions determined to be initial routines and architecture-specific	1.59%	2.82%	1.02%	1.59%	2.82%	1.02%	1.59%	2.82%	1.02%	1.60%	2.83%	1.03%
Other functions	63.3%	73.7%	79.7%	63.3%	73.7%	79.8%	63.3%	73.7%	79.8%	63.3%	73.7%	79.9%

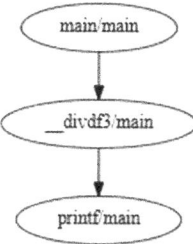

Fig. 11. FCSG created by compiling a script that performs division within the main function for Arm.

removal stage. Figure 5 shows that most of the $S_{\text{FCSG}} - S_{\text{source}}$ functions are neither initial routines nor architecture-specific functions, but rather library functions, which is believed to be one of the reasons why the proposed method was able to remove a large proportion of the functions. In this experiment, we performed initial routine removal, which is expected to result in the removal of many functions, before architecture-specific function removal. However, we believe that performing architecture-specific function removal before initial routine removal would also result in the removal of functions using the architecture-specific function removal method. In particular, there are cases where architecture-specific functions are called within user-defined functions, which is a feature not found in the initial routine. For example, Fig. 11 shows an FCSG created from a binary compiled for Arm from a script that prints the result of a division performed within the main function. In this FCSG, the Arm-specific function `__divdf3` is called within the main function. This is because Arm does not support division at the machine code level, so instead, a function that performs division is called. In such cases, removal using the initial routine removal method is not possible, so the architecture-specific function removal method is considered effective.

References

1. Akabane, S., Han, C., Iwamoto, K., Isawa, R., Takahashi, T., Inoue, D., et al.: Identification of user-defined functions based on function call transition. In: Report of the Workshop on Multimedia Communications and Distributed Processing (DPS), vol. 2024, no. 24, pp. 1–8 (2024). (In Japanese)
2. Akabane, S., Okamoto, T.: Identification of toolchains used to build IoT malware with statically linked libraries. In: CSEC-93, pp. 1–8 (2021). (In Japanese)
3. Alasmary, H., et al.: Analyzing and detecting emerging internet of things malware: a graph-based approach. IEEE Internet Things J. **6**(5), 8977–8988 (2019). https://doi.org/10.1109/JIOT.2019.2925929
4. Bktero - : Potentially useful pieces of code. https://github.com/Bktero/DummyCodes. Accessed 13 May 2025
5. Bootlin - : Cross-compilation toolchains for Linux. https://toolchains.bootlin.com/. Accessed 13 May 2025
6. Broder, A.: On the resemblance and containment of documents. In: Proceedings of the Compression and Complexity of SEQUENCES 1997 (Cat. No.97TB100171), pp. 21–29 (1997). https://doi.org/10.1109/SEQUEN.1997.666900
7. Buildroot - : Buildroot. https://buildroot.org/. Accessed 13 May 2025
8. Duan, Y., Li, X., Wang, J., Yin, H., et al.: DeepBinDiff: learning program-wide code representations for binary diffing (2020)
9. hammerzeit - : An archive of bashlite source code. https://github.com/hammerzeit/BASHLITE. Accessed 13 May 2025
10. Hassen, M., Chan, P.K.: Scalable function call graph-based malware classification. In: CODASPY 2017, pp. 239–248. Association for Computing Machinery, New York (2017) https://doi.org/10.1145/3029806.3029824
11. He, H., et al.: Code is not natural language: unlock the power of semantics-oriented graph representation for binary code similarity detection. In: 33rd USENIX Security Symposium (USENIX Security 2024), pp. 1759–1776. USENIX Association, Philadelphia (2024). https://www.usenix.org/conference/usenixsecurity24/presentation/he-haojie
12. Hex-Rays - : Ida pro. https://hex-rays.com/ida-pro/. Accessed 13 May 2025
13. Hex-Rays docs: Flirt. https://docs.hex-rays.com/user-guide/signatures/flirt. Accessed 16 July 2025
14. jgamblin - : Leaked mirai source code for research/IOC development purposes. https://github.com/jgamblin/Mirai-Source-Code/. Accessed 13 May 2025
15. Kawasoe, R., Han, C., Isawa, R., Takahashi, T., Takeuchi, J.: Investigating behavioral differences between IoT malware via function call sequence graphs. In: SAC 2021: The 36th ACM/SIGAPP Symposium on Applied Computing, Virtual Event, Republic of Korea, 22–26 March 2021, pp. 1674–1682. ACM (2021)
16. KCreate - : Repository to dump information and small code snippets. https://github.com/KCreate/dump. Accessed 13 May 2025
17. lab313ru- : dumpsym.exe source code. https://github.com/lab313ru/dumpsym_src. Accessed 13 May 2025
18. landley - : Aboriginal Linux. http://landley.net/aboriginal/downloads/binaries/. Accessed 13 May 2025
19. LFSMx - : Select pieces of work... https://github.com/LFSMx/MyCodeProfile. Accessed 13 May 2025
20. Li, M., Chen, X., Li, X., Ma, B., Vitanyi, P.: The similarity metric (2004). https://arxiv.org/abs/cs/0111054

21. mahmednabil109 - : code dump. htttps://github.com/mahmednabil109/dump. Accessed 13 May 2025
22. malicialab - : Avclass malware labeling tool. https://github.com/malicialab/avclass. Accessed 13 May 2025
23. Pa, Y.M.P., Suzuki, S., Yoshioka, K., Matsumoto, T., Kasama, T., Rossow, C.: IoT-POT: analysing the rise of IoT compromises. In: 9th USENIX Workshop on Offensive Technologies (WOOT 15). USENIX Association, Washington, D.C. (2015)
24. remedi - : Just random pieces of code. htttps://github.com/remedi/hackdump (Not Available)
25. shuakabane: cross-architecture static library detector for IoT malware. https://github.com/shuakabane/stelftools. Accessed 16 July 2025
26. SimonLight001 - : Just dumping code from my laptop, don't expect much. https://github.com/SimonLight001/Code/. Accessed 13 May 2025
27. Takada, S., Kawasoe, R., He, T., Han, C., Tanaka, A., Takeuchi, J.: Study on improvement of function estimation method of IoT malware using graph embedding. In: Proceedings of Computer Security Symposium 2021 (CSS2021), pp. 705–712 (2021). (In Japanese)
28. uClibc - : uClibc. https://uclibc.org/downloads/binaries/0.9.30.1/. Accessed 13 May 2025
29. Yang, C., Liu, Z., Zhao, D., Sun, M., Chang, E.Y.: Network representation learning with rich text information. In: IJCAI, vol. 2015, pp. 2111–2117 (2015)

HGANN-Mal: A Hypergraph Attention Neural Network Approach for Android Malware Detection

Mohammad Reza Norouzian(✉) and Claudia Eckert

Technical University of Munich, Munich, Germany
`mohammad.norouzian@tum.de, claudia.eckert@in.tum.de`

Abstract. Research on Android malware has progressed rapidly, yet the task of distinguishing malicious from benign applications continues to test the limits of automated analysis. Earlier work, dominated by static signature matching, frequently struggles when novel or obfuscated samples appear. Contemporary graph‑based pipelines alleviate some of these shortcomings by modelling control and data dependencies, but their reliance on pairwise relations often blurs higher‑order interactions that experienced adversaries nurture when crafting evasive variants. These observations motivate a return to first principles: we require representations that faithfully encode behaviours without incurring prohibitive overhead. In this study we revisit the problem through the lens of hypergraph representation learning. Treating an application as a hypergraph allows one to encode joint behaviours—such as the co-invocation of critical API calls inside a single execution context—that cannot be decomposed into simple edges without information loss. Building on this representation, we introduce HGANN-Mal, a Hypergraph Attention Neural Network that adaptively emphasises semantically salient hyperedges while softening the influence of spurious ones. The model derives its signals from static analysis to extract structural and semantic features. Importantly, on the Drebin dataset, HGANN-Mal achieves a Macro-F1 score of 97.8% and an accuracy of 98.3% in binary malware detection, significantly outperforming graph-based and static hypergraph methods. Our findings validate that the proposed attention-based hypergraph model provides a more exhaustive and precise solution for detecting sophisticated Android malware.

1 Introduction

Android's open distribution model and broad hardware ecosystem have propelled the platform to a market share that regularly exceeds with over 2.5 billion active devices [17]. That ubiquity, however, does not come without cost: security analysts continue to report hundreds of thousands of suspicious packages each year. While the absolute numbers fluctuate with collection methodology, the consensus view is that the threat landscape is both quantitatively significant and qualitatively diverse [4].

Traditional defences have long relied on signature-based [28], where an application's code sections are compared against a repository of known malicious fragments. Such detectors remain valuable thanks to their interpretability and low computational overhead. At the same time, they provide little protection against so-called zero-day malware or against families that rotate byte sequences through polymorphic engines [43]. In response, researchers have shifted their attention towards machine learning-based systems capable of extracting higher-level abstractions directly from raw artifacts.

Among the techniques now popular, graph neural networks (GNNs) occupy a key role. Function call graphs (FCGs), permissionâĂŞAPI dependency graphs, and inter-component communication graphs have all served as substrates for deep learning architectures [8]. Although the empirical results are impressive, a recurring critique concerns their pairwise bias: edges express binary relations, yet many security-relevant behaviours emerge only when three or more components interact [5,16]. Hypergraphs, with their capacity to join arbitrarily large node sets, offer a principled remedy.

Hypergraphs extend standard graphs by allowing a hyperedge to connect an arbitrary number of nodes [11]. The structure is therefore capable of recording composite behaviours without having to enumerate every pairwise interaction. Recent studies in computer vision and recommendation systems suggest that hypergraph neural networks (HGNNs) [11,14] can leverage this richer topology to learn more expressive embeddings. In the Android domain, preliminary evidence is beginning to surface [45], yet the question of how to weigh the relative contribution of distinct hyperedges remains unsettled.

The construction of hypergraphs for Android applications can follow various strategies. Feng et al. [45] capture structural semantics by creating hyperedges from groups of functions that share the same sensitive permission requests or are located within k-order call graph neighborhoods. Wu et al. [41] explored a dual-view approach that constructs hypergraphs from both structural and semantic perspectives, capturing both the call relationships and the functional similarities between components.

Experimental evaluations on benchmark datasets such as Drebin [5] and CICMalDroid [26,27] have demonstrated that hypergraph-based approaches consistently outperform traditional graph-based methods in Android malware detection tasks. For instance, HGNN+ [14] achieved classification accuracy improvements of 3–5% over state-of-the-art GNN models by better capturing the complex relationships between application components. These results underscore the importance of modeling higher-order relationships in Android applications for effective malware detection.

Despite these advances, existing hypergraph-based methods employ static, pre-defined hyperedge constructions that assign equal importance to all relationships. This uniform weighting fails to recognize that certain functional relationships are more indicative of malicious behavior than others. For example, interactions involving sensitive API calls or dangerous permission requests should likely receive greater emphasis than routine utility function calls [29]. The inability to adaptively weight these relationships limits the discriminative power of current hypergraph representations.

To address these limitations, we propose a novel approach that integrates attention mechanisms [6] into hypergraph neural networks for Android malware detection. HGANN-Mal, extends beyond static hypergraph structures by dynamically learning the importance of different hyperedges through an attention mechanism. This approach enables the model to focus on the most discriminative functional relationships while downweighting less relevant connections. In summary, we make the following primary contributions:

- We formulate Android malware detection as a hypergraph classification problem, leveraging the expressive power of hypergraphs to model complex, higher-order relationships between functions in Android applications.
- We introduce a novel hypergraph attention mechanism that dynamically learns to weight hyperedges based on their relevance to malware detection.
- We demonstrate that adaptive weighting of hyperedges through attention improves discrimination between benign and malicious.

Our approach builds upon recent advances in hypergraph neural networks [6, 14] and attention mechanisms in graph learning [38,39]. Attention mechanisms have proven effective in graph neural networks by allowing models to focus on important neighbors [39], but their application to hypergraph structures remains largely unexplored, particularly in the context of malware detection.

2 Related Work

Android malware detection has evolved significantly from traditional signature-based approaches to sophisticated machine learning and graph-based methods. Traditional malware detection techniques for Android platforms have primarily relied on static, dynamic, and hybrid analysis methods. Static analysis techniques examine application code without execution, focusing on features such as permissions, API calls, and code structure [33,40]. Feng et al. [12] demonstrated the effectiveness of combining static taint analysis with program representation techniques, achieving notable accuracy in detecting malicious applications. Dynamic analysis methods monitor application behavior during runtime, e.g., capturing system calls with frequency vectors and co-occurrence matrices [42]. Hybrid analysis techniques combine static and dynamic approaches to leverage the strengths of both methodologies [31]. However, traditional approaches face significant limitations when confronting sophisticated evasion techniques such as code obfuscation, polymorphism, and metamorphism.

The limitations of traditional methods have driven researchers toward graph-based representations that capture structural relationships within Android applications. Function Call Graphs (FCGs) have emerged as a fundamental representation for modeling the invocation relationships between functions in Android applications [16]. Recent advances in Graph Neural Networks (GNNs) have revolutionized the application of FCGs to malware detection. Lu X. [24] proposed

SNDGCN, a robust Android malware detection model based on denoising Graph Convolutional Networks that processes FCGs while addressing noise in graph representations. Zheng J. [46] introduced MASKDROID, which employs masked graph representations to enhance the discriminative ability of malware detectors while maintaining robustness against adversarial attacks. Guo W. [18] developed MalHAPGNN, a Layered attention pooling graph neural network that enhances call graph representations through sophisticated attention mechanisms. Despite these advances, conventional graph representations remain fundamentally limited by their ability to model only pairwise relationships between entities, which cannot adequately capture complex interactions among multiple functions. [36].

Hypergraph structures offer a more expressive alternative to traditional graphs by allowing edges (hyperedges) to connect arbitrary numbers of vertices simultaneously. This capability naturally accommodates the complex, multi-entity relationships present in Android applications, where malicious behaviors frequently involve coordinated actions across multiple functions. Zhang et al. [45] pioneered the application of hypergraph neural networks to Android malware detection, proposing the first hypergraph-based approach for modeling higher-order relationships among functions. Their method constructs hypergraphs where functions sharing permissions or forming K-order neighborhoods constitute hyperedges, enabling the capture of complex semantic relationships that traditional graphs cannot represent. However, the static weights of hypergraph neural networks cannot capture the behavior of modern and complex new evolving of Android malware. In our HGANN-Mal approach addresses several critical gaps by employing hypergraph attention neural networks that extend beyond the limitations of traditional graph-based and hypergraph-based methods. Unlike prior Android HGNNs that use static, equally weighted k-hop/permission hyperedges [45], HGANN-Mal fuses topological, semantic, and slice-aware suspicious-API hyperedges and learns their importance via hypergraph attention and, to our knowledge, is the first to apply a learnable hypergraph-attention operator to Android malware detection, thereby amplifying malicious relations while suppressing noise.

3 Hypergraph Neural Networks

3.1 Preliminaries

A hypergraph is a more general topology than a graph that is capable of modeling multiple relationships between discrete data. Unlike traditional graphs where each edge connects exactly two vertices, a hyperedge in a hypergraph can connect multiple vertices simultaneously, thus enabling the modeling of higher-order relationships among vertices [1].

Formally, let $\mathcal{H} = \langle \mathcal{V}, \mathcal{E} \rangle$ be a hypergraph, where $\mathcal{V} = \{v_1, v_2, \ldots, v_n\}$ denotes the vertex set containing $|\mathcal{V}| = n$ vertices and $\mathcal{E} = \{e_1, e_2, \ldots, e_m\}$ denotes the set of hyperedges, where each hyperedge $e \in \mathcal{E}$ is a subset of $\mathcal{V}$. In the context of Android malware detection, vertices can represent functions in an Android application, while hyperedges can represent higher-order relationships between these functions, such as common call patterns or common suspicious API call combinations.

In a hypergraph, the vertex-hyperedge adjacency matrix is represented by $H \in \mathbb{R}^{|\mathcal{V}| \times |\mathcal{E}|}$. When a vertex v belongs to a hyperedge e, $H(v, e) = 1$, otherwise $H(v, e) = 0$. The weights of the hyperedges can be represented by a diagonal matrix $W \in \mathbb{R}^{|\mathcal{E}| \times |\mathcal{E}|}$ where $W(i, i) = w(e_i)$. The degree of vertices is computed by $d_\mathcal{V}(v) = \sum_{e \in \mathcal{E}} H(v, e) \cdot w(e)$, and the degree of hyperedges is computed as $d_\mathcal{E}(e) = \sum_{v \in \mathcal{V}} H(v, e)$. The matrix representation of the degree of vertices and hyperedges is denoted by $D_\mathcal{V}$ and $D_\mathcal{E}$, respectively. They are both diagonal matrices.

The Laplacian matrix of $\mathcal{H}$ is denoted by:

$$L = I - D_\mathcal{V}^{-1/2} H W D_\mathcal{E}^{-1} H^T D_\mathcal{V}^{-1/2} \tag{1}$$

where I is the identity matrix. This Laplacian matrix plays a crucial role in defining the spectral convolution operation on hypergraphs, which we will discuss in the following sections.

The ability of hypergraphs to model higher-order relationships makes them particularly suitable for Android malware detection, where complex interactions between functions, and API calls need to be captured for effective detection.

3.2 Hypergraph Neural Networks

HGNNs extend the concept of GNNs to hypergraphs, enabling the learning of node representations that capture higher-order relationships [11]. While traditional GNNs have shown great success in various domains, they are limited to modeling pairwise relationships. HGNNs overcome this limitation, where hyperedges can connect multiple vertices simultaneously [47].

The key challenge in designing HGNNs is to define appropriate operations for information propagation and aggregation over hypergraphs. In this section, we introduce several representative approaches for hypergraph neural networks, focusing on hypergraph convolution and hypergraph attention mechanisms, which form the foundation of our approach to Android malware detection.

Hypergraph Convolution. Hypergraph convolution defines a basic convolutional operator on a hypergraph, enabling efficient information propagation between vertices by fully exploiting the higher-order relationships encoded in hyperedges [6]. The primary challenge in defining a convolution operator on a hypergraph is to measure the transition probability between two vertices, which allows the features of each vertex to be propagated through the network.

To address this challenge, we make two key assumptions: (1) more propagation should occur between vertices connected by a common hyperedge, and (2) hyperedges with larger weights deserve more confidence in such propagation. Based on these assumptions, we define one step of hypergraph convolution as:

$$x_i^{(l+1)} = \sigma\left(\sum_{j=1}^{N}\sum_{e=1}^{M} H_{ie} H_{je} W_e x_j^{(l)} \Theta^{(l)}\right) \qquad (2)$$

where $x_i^{(l)}$ is the embedding of the i-th vertex in the l-th layer, $\sigma(\cdot)$ is a non-linear activation function such as LeakyReLU [25] or ELU [9], and $\Theta^{(l)} \in \mathbb{R}^{F^{(l)} \times F^{(l+1)}}$ is the weight matrix between the l-th and $(l+1)$-th layers.

It is worth noting that when hypergraph convolution is applied to a special case where each hyperedge connects exactly two vertices (i.e., a traditional graph), it reduces to the standard graph convolution operation. This property ensures that hypergraph convolution is a natural generalization of graph convolution to higher-order relationships.

Hypergraph Attention. While hypergraph convolution provides a powerful mechanism for information propagation on hypergraphs, it relies on a fixed, pre-defined structure for message passing. Hypergraph attention enhances this capability by introducing an attention mechanism that learns dynamic connections between vertices and hyperedges, allowing the model to focus on the most relevant parts of the hypergraph for a specific task [22,39].

Hypergraph convolution already has a sort of innate attentional mechanism, however, this attentional mechanism is not learnable or trainable once the hypergraph structure (the incidence matrix H) is given.

The goal of hypergraph attention is to learn a dynamic incidence matrix, thereby creating a dynamic transition matrix that can better reveal the intrinsic relationships between vertices. Instead of treating each vertex as being either connected by a certain hyperedge or not, the attention module presents a probabilistic model, which assigns non-binary, real values to measure the degree of connectivity [6].

For a given vertex x_i and its associated hyperedge x_j, the attentional score is computed as:

$$\alpha_{ij} = \frac{\exp(\sigma(\text{sim}(x_i\Theta, x_j\Theta)))}{\sum_{k \in \mathcal{N}_i} \exp(\sigma(\text{sim}(x_i\Theta, x_k\Theta)))} \qquad (3)$$

where $\sigma(\cdot)$ is a non-linear activation function, $\mathcal{N}_i$ is the neighborhood set of x_i, and $\text{sim}(\cdot)$ is a similarity function that computes the pairwise similarity between two vertices.

With the incidence matrix H enriched by an attention module, we can follow the same formulation as in hypergraph convolution to learn the intermediate embedding of vertices layer-by-layer:

$$X^{(l+1)} = \sigma(D_\mathcal{V}^{-1/2} H_{\text{att}} W D_\mathcal{E}^{-1} H_{\text{att}}^T D_\mathcal{V}^{-1/2} X^{(l)} \Theta^{(l)}) \qquad (4)$$

where H_{att} is the attention-enriched incidence matrix. Note that hypergraph attention propagates gradients to H_{att} in addition to $X^{(l)}$ and $\Theta^{(l)}$, allowing the model to learn the optimal hypergraph structure for the task at hand.

In the context of Android malware detection, hypergraph attention allows our model to dynamically learn the importance of different relationships. For example, it can learn to assign higher attention weights to suspicious patterns of API calls requests that are indicative of malicious behavior.

4 Methodology

Our proposed Android malware detection framework leverages hypergraph attention neural networks. This section details the methodology, encompassing the initial data processing and static analysis, feature preparation, hypergraph construction, and the hypergraph-level classification process.

4.1 Data Acquisition and Static Analysis

Before delving into feature extraction and hypergraph construction, a robust initial phase of data acquisition and static analysis is critical.

Dataset Loader. The process (Stage 0) is responsible for systematically ingesting raw APK files from a designated root directory. The system walks through the directory structure, computing the SHA-256 hash of every APK file encountered. Subsequently, it queries and parses an external label list from the original dataset to tag each hash as either *benign* or the appropriate malware family. The output of this stage is a comprehensive catalogue, serves as the definitive manifest for the entire dataset.

APK Unpacker. Following the dataset loading, the APK Unpacker (Stage 1) takes the raw APK files as input. Tools such as 'apktool'and Python's 'zipfile' module are employed to decompress and extract the 'Android Manifest.xml' file, which contains vital application metadata, and all 'classes*.dex' files, which encapsulate the application's compiled Dalvik bytecode. The output of this stage comprises the raw manifest files and the raw DEX byte-streams, ready for deeper static analysis.

Static Analysis and API Tagging. The extracted manifests and DEX files are then processed through the MobiSF Static Analysis[1] & API Tagging component (Stage 2a), which leverages the MobiSF for comprehensive automated security analysis. The process involves several coordinated actions that work in tandem to identify and classify potentially suspicious API usage patterns [3,35]. The analysis begins with an automated scan phase that MobiSF performs a comprehensive static analysis that includes manifest parsing, DEX disassembly, and security-focused feature extraction.

---
[1] https://github.com/MobSF/Mobile-Security-Framework-MobSF.

The next phase focuses on **permission risk assessment**, where each required permission identified in the previous step is cross-referenced. Only permissions whose status field is marked as "dangerous" are retained for further analysis. By focusing exclusively on dangerous permissions, the analysis concentrates on APIs that pose the highest potential security risk.

The framework then employs a **heuristic API classification** system to categorize the identified APIs into two primary categories based on their functional characteristics. APIs are classified as *access* APIs, such as those related to Contacts, Location, Sms, Storage, and similar sensitive data sources. Conversely, APIs are classified as *transmission* APIs, including those related to Http, Socket, sendTextMessage, and other network or communication functions. This heuristic approach, while not exhaustive, provides a practical and scalable method for identifying APIs that are commonly associated with data exfiltration patterns in malware.

To complement the MobiSF analysis and provide detailed call-site information, the system runs Androguard[2] in parallel for each APK. This parallel execution serves two primary purposes: first, it disassembles the DEX files to produce a comprehensive method-level Function-Call-Graph (FCG), denoted as $G = (V, E)$, where vertices V represent individual methods and directed edges E represent method invocations. Second, it generates a flat list of (method_id, invoked_api) pairs that capture the exact locations where specific APIs are called within the application's code structure.

The final step in this stage involves mapping MobiSF-flagged APIs back to their exact call sites using the Androguard-generated call-site information. This mapping process creates a comprehensive view of where potentially suspicious APIs are invoked within the application's execution flow, enabling precise localization of security-relevant code regions. Also, the stage produces a global FCG for the entire APK, derived from the Androguard analysis, which captures the structural relationships between methods and serves as the foundation for subsequent hypergraph construction phases. This dual-output approach ensures that both the security-relevant API usage patterns and the overall application structure are captured and available for downstream processing stages [23, 37].

Backward-Slice Builder. Building upon the outputs of Stage 2a, the Backward-Slice Builder (Stage 2b) focuses on isolating security-critical code regions [34]. For every identified suspicious call site, this component performs two key actions:

- **Variable Retrieval:** It identifies variables that reach the suspicious call site. This involves analyzing data flow to determine which variables directly influence the behavior of the suspicious API call.
- **Slice Extraction:** It then walks the CFG backwards from the suspicious call site, retaining only basic blocks and statements that directly influence the identified variables. Each extracted slice is stored as a compact CFG file.

---

[2] https://github.com/androguard/androguard

4.2 Feature Preparation

Effective representation of Android application characteristics is crucial for accurate malware detection. Building upon the outputs of the static analysis phase, we extract and process various features to comprehensively characterize the behavior of Android applications. These features serve as the input for the subsequent hypergraph construction and are designed to capture diverse aspects of an application's functionality and potential malicious intent. For each function $v \in V$ (where V is the set of vertices in the FCG), the following features are computed (Stage 3):

Opcode Histograms. To capture the low-level operational characteristics of each function, an opcode histogram is computed. This involves analyzing the Dalvik bytecode instructions within a function and generating a frequency distribution of opcodes. This histogram can be represented as a one-hot encoded vector or, for more comprehensive representations, using TF-IDF to reflect the importance of specific opcodes within a function relative to the entire corpus. Opcode patterns can reveal characteristic behaviors, including those associated with obfuscation or malicious payloads [19,30].

Structural Metrics. Beyond the raw opcode sequences, the structural position and influence of a function within the application's call graph provide valuable insights [10,13]. We calculate several structural metrics for each function, including:

- **In-degree:** The number of incoming edges to a function in the FCG.
- **Out-degree:** The number of outgoing edges from a function in the FCG, indicating how many other functions it calls.
- **PageRank:** A measure of a function's relative importance within the FCG, based on the number and quality of incoming links.
- **Betweenness Centrality:** A measure of a function's centrality in the FCG, quantifying the number of times it acts as a bridge along the shortest path between two other functions. Functions with high betweenness centrality often play critical roles in control flow.

These metrics are standardized to ensure consistent scaling across different applications and to prevent features with larger numerical ranges from dominating the learning process.

API-Related Flags and Counts. To directly incorporate insights from the suspicious API analysis (Stage 2a) and backward slicing (Stage 2b), we add specific API-related features for each method node:

- `has_access` and `has_transmit` flags: Binary flags indicating whether the method contains calls to sensitive data access APIs or sensitive data transmission APIs, respectively.

– Access/Transmit Call Counts in Slices: The number of access and transmit API calls that appear within the program slices associated with the method.

These flags and counts provide direct indicators of potentially malicious behavior at the method level.

Semantic Embedding (Code2vec). To capture the semantic meaning and contextual understanding of functions, we generate a 320-dimensional 'code2vec' embedding for each function [2]. This high-dimensional, dense embedding is chosen to capture rich contextual similarities between functions. While this approach carries a greater computational and memory footprint compared to handcrafted feature vectors, the trade-off provides a significantly more detailed understanding of the application's true behavior. All computed features are then concatenated and z-score normalized to form the Node Feature Matrix X, where each row corresponds to a function (vertex) and each column represents a feature, resulting in a matrix of size $|V| \times F$, where F is the total number of features.

4.3 Construction of Hypergraph

To effectively model the intricate, higher-order relationships inherent in Android applications, we construct a hypergraph where functions serve as vertices and hyperedges represent complex interactions among multiple functions. Our hypergraph construction process involves defining three distinct types of hyperedges, followed by their integration into a unified hypergraph structure.

K-Hop Neighbour Hyperedge. Drawing inspiration from the work by Zhang et al. [45], we define k-order call neighbors as a fundamental feature for capturing the structural context of functions within an Android application (Stage 4A). For each node (function) in the FCG, its K-order callers and callees are collected to form a hyperedge. A typical value for K 3, which is sufficient to capture relevant local context. The output of this stage is the hyperedge list H_K.

Semantic-Embedding Hyperedge. Leveraging the semantic embeddings generated during feature preparation, we construct Semantic-Embedding Hyperedges (Stage 4B). This involves performing a k-nearest neighbor search on the function embeddings. Functions whose semantic embeddings are sufficiently similar are grouped into a hyperedge. A typical value for τ is approximately 0.80, and $k = 5$. This action captures functional similarities that might not be evident from call graphs alone, which can be particularly useful in detecting polymorphic malware or code reuse. The output of this stage is the hyperedge list H_{SEM}.

Suspicious-API Hyperedge. To highlight potentially malicious interactions, we introduce Slice-Aware Suspicious-API Hyperedges (Stage 4C). These hyperedges are formed by leveraging the sliced CFGs from Stage 2b and the suspicious-API tags. For each program slice, a hyperedge is created over all functions that

the slice contains. Each such hyperedge is assigned an initial weight w calculated as:
$$w = 1 + 0.2 \times (\#\,\text{transmit}) + 0.1 \times (\#\,\text{access})$$
where $\#\,\text{transmit}$ is the count of transmission APIs and $\#\,\text{access}$ is the count of access APIs within the slice. This weighting scheme prioritizes hyperedges associated with data exfiltration. The output of this stage is the list H_{API} of slice-aware hyperedges with their calculated weights.

Hypergraph Formation and Representation. Once the three types of hyperedges (H_K, H_SEM, H_API) are generated, they undergo an Edge Post-processing step (Stage 5). This involves merging all three lists into a single, unified hyperedge set. Duplicate hyperedges are removed, and each hyperedge is capped at a maximum cardinality (e.g., ≤64 nodes). This capping is crucial for stabilizing message passing within the hypergraph neural network. Each processed hyperedge is also tagged with a 1-byte type identifier (e.g., 'topo', 'semantic', 'suspicious') and, for H_API, its calculated weight w is retained. The output of this stage is a single merged hyperedge set for the APK. Subsequently, the Hypergraph Constructor (Stage 6) takes the vertex set V (methods), the node-feature matrix X (from Stage 3), and the unified hyperedge set (from Stage 5) as input [14]. It then builds the sparse incidence matrix $H \in \{0,1\}^{|V| \times |E|}$ and creates the diagonal edge-weight matrix W. Weights are typically 1, except for suspicious-API edges where the calculated weight w is used. Symmetric degree normalization is applied to these matrices. Finally, the constructed hypergraph components, $\{H, W, X\}$, are serialized for efficient loading and processing by graph neural network libraries. The output of this stage is one serialized hypergraph object per APK.

Algorithm 1 illustrates the details on Hyperedge generation:

4.4 Mini-batch Builder

For efficient training and inference with hypergraph neural networks, especially when dealing with a large number of individual hypergraphs, a Mini-Batch Builder (Stage 7) is employed. At training or inference time, multiple serialized hypergraphs are processed to create a single batched input. This involves block-diagonalizing [15] their respective incidence matrices (H) and weight matrices (W), and concatenating their feature matrices (X). Additionally, a `batch_vec` is constructed, which maps each node in the concatenated feature matrix back to its original source graph. The output of this stage consists of batched tensors fed into the Hypergraph Attention Neural Network backbone.

Hypergraph Attention Neural Network Backbone. The core of our classification Hypergraph Attention Neural Network backbone (HANN) (Stage 8). Unlike traditional Hypergraph Neural Networks (HGNNs) that use static incidence matrices, our method incorporates an attention mechanism to dynamically

Algorithm 1. Pipeline Stages Group 4

Input: FCG $G = (V, E)$, embeddings $\mathbf{E}$, slice set $\mathcal{S}$, params $K, k_{nn}, \tau, L_p, c_{\max}$
Output: incidence $\mathbf{H}$ (rows,cols), weights $\mathbf{w}$, types $\mathbf{t}$

/*Stage 4A: K-hop topological hyperedges
1: $\mathcal{H} \leftarrow \varnothing$
2: **for** $v \in V$ **do**
3:     $e \leftarrow \{u \mid \text{dist}_G(v, u) \leq K\}$
4:     **if** $2 \leq |e| \leq c_{\max}$ **then**
5:         $\mathcal{H} \cup = \{(e, 1, \text{topo})\}$
6:     **end if**
7: **end for**
/*Stage 4B: Semantic (k-NN) hyperedges
8: $(I, D) \leftarrow \text{FAISS}(\mathbf{E}, k_{nn})$
9: **for** $i = 0$ to $|V| - 1$ **do**
10:     $e \leftarrow \{I_{i,j} \mid D_{i,j} \geq \tau\}$
11:     **if** $2 \leq |e| \leq c_{\max}$ **then**
12:         $\mathcal{H} \cup = \{(e, 1, \text{sem})\}$
13:     **end if**
14: **end for**
/*Stage 4C: Slice-aware suspicious-API hyperedges
15: **for** $s \in \mathcal{S}$ **do**
16:     $e \leftarrow F_s; w \leftarrow 1 + 0.2 \#\text{transmit}_s + 0.1 \#\text{access}_s$
17:     **for** $(u, v) \in e \times e$ **do**
18:         **if** $|P| \leq L_p$ where $P = \text{sp}(G, u, v)$ **then**
19:             $e \leftarrow e \cup P$
20:         **end if**
21:     **end for**
22:     **if** $2 \leq |e| \leq c_{\max}$ **then**
23:         $\mathcal{H} \cup = \{(e, w, \text{sus})\}$
24:     **end if**
25: **end for**

weigh the importance of hyperedges during information propagation [6,20]. This adaptive weighting allows the model to focus on the most critical relationships between functions, leading to enhanced discrimination and noise reduction.

Each layer of the HANN computes node embeddings by aggregating information from connected hyperedges:

$$X' = \sigma\left(D^{-\frac{1}{2}} H W B^{-1} H^\top D^{-\frac{1}{2}} X P\right)$$

where X is the input feature matrix, H is the incidence matrix, W is the diagonal weight matrix, D and B are diagonal matrices representing node and hyperedge degrees respectively, σ is an activation function, and P is a learnable projection matrix. For attention layers, the incidence matrix H can be replaced with learned attention weights α. The output of this stage is a set of final node embeddings, h_i, for each function in the hypergraph.

Read-Out and Pooling. Following the HANN backbone, a Read-out/Pooling mechanism (Stage 9) is employed to aggregate the node embeddings (h_i) into a single, fixed-size graph-level embedding, g, for each Android application. This step is crucial for transforming the variable-sized hypergraph representation into a format suitable for downstream classification. We utilize methods such as mean pooling (scatter_mean) or attention pooling (scatter_softmax) to collapse each graph's nodes to a single vector g. This graph-level embedding encapsulates the overall behavioral characteristics of the application, learned through the nuanced relationships captured by the hypergraph and refined by the attention mechanism. The output of this stage is the per-APK embedding vectors g.

Dual-Head Classification Architecture. The final graph-level embeddings, g, are processed through a sophisticated Dual-Head Classification Architecture (Stage 10) that simultaneously addresses both binary malware detection and fine-grained family classification tasks. The architecture begins with a shared hidden MLP that processes each graph-level embedding g to extract high-level discriminative features. The shared MLP typically consists of two hidden layers with ReLU activation functions and dropout regularization to prevent overfitting [7].

The first component of the dual-head architecture is Head A (Binary Detector), that produces a single logit z_{bin} that is passed through a sigmoid activation function to obtain the malware probability: $p(\text{malware}) = \sigma(z_{\text{bin}})$.

The second component is Head B (Family Classifier), which specializes in identifying specific malware families. This head generates C logits z_{fam}, where C represents the number of distinct malware families in the dataset. These logits are processed through a softmax activation function to produce a probability distribution over the malware families: $p(\text{family}) = \text{softmax}(z_{\text{fam}})$.

The training process employs a **joint loss function** that combines the objectives of both classification heads:

$$\mathcal{L} = \lambda_{\text{bin}} \cdot \text{BCEWithLogits}(z_{\text{bin}}, y_{\text{bin}}) + \lambda_{\text{fam}} \cdot \text{CrossEntropy}(z_{\text{fam}}, y_{\text{fam}}) \quad (5)$$

where λ_{bin} and λ_{fam} are weighting parameters that balance the contribution of each loss component.

The output of this stage provides comprehensive classification results for every APK in the dataset. The integration of hypergraph attention into the Android malware detection framework allows our solution to learn a more detailed representation of the higher-order relationships between functions. By dynamically weighing hyperedges, we achieve enhanced discrimination by emphasizing critical relationships, noise reduction by down-weighting less relevant hyperedges, and adaptive weighting, which provides potential insights into which functional relationships are most critical for malware detection.

5 Evaluation

This section presents a comprehensive evaluation of our proposed system, datasets utilized, evaluation metrics, and a thorough analysis of the results. The objective is to demonstrate the effectiveness and robustness of our approach in detecting and classifying malware, drawing comparisons with established baseline methods in the field.

5.1 The Dataset and Evaluation Metrics

To rigorously evaluate the performance of our proposed malware detection system, we utilized two widely recognized and publicly available datasets: Drebin [5] and CICMalDroid2020 [26, 27]. These datasets are commonly employed in the Android malware detection research community, allowing for a direct comparison with existing state-of-the-art methods.

Drebin. The Drebin is a prominent dataset in the Android malware research domain, exclusively containing malicious Android applications. Drebin dataset consists exclusively of malicious Android applications, comprising a total of 5,560 samples categorized into 179 distinct malware families. Given the inherent class imbalance within the Drebin dataset, where many malicious families have a small sample size, we focused our evaluation on the top 20 malicious families based on their sample count as detailed in Table 1. This selection, totaling 4,664 malicious samples, ensures that our analysis is conducted on sufficiently represented classes, providing meaningful insights into the model's ability to distinguish between different malware families. The dataset is split into training, testing, and validation sets with 70% for training, 20% for testing, and 10% for validation.

Table 1. Top 20 malware families in the Drebin dataset

Family	# Sample	Family	# Sample
FakeInstaller	925	Adrd	91
DroidKungFu	667	DroidDream	81
Plankton	625	LinuxLotoor	70
Opfake	613	GoldDream	69
GingerMaster	339	MobileTx	69
BaseBridge	330	FakeRun	61
Iconosys	152	SendPay	59
Kmin	147	Gappusin	58
FakeDoc	132	Imlog	43
Geinimi	92	SMSReg	41
Total		**4,664**	

CICMalDroid. The CICMalDroid2020 dataset is a comprehensive Android malware collection comprising 17,341 samples gathered from 2017 to 2018 through multiple authoritative sources including VirusTotal, Contagio security blog, AMD, and MalDozer. The dataset encompasses five distinct categories. Adware (1,253 samples), Banking malware (2,100 samples), SMS malware (3,904 samples), Riskware (2,546 samples), and Benign applications (1,795 samples), totaling 11,598 successfully analyzed samples which is detailed in Table 2. By keeping in mind that the CICMalDroid2020 is one of the most feature-rich Android malware datasets available for research community. Similar to Drebin, the CICMalDroid2020 dataset was partitioned into an 70% training, 20% testing, and 10% validation set for experimental purposes.

Table 2. CICMalDroid2020 dataset statistics

Family	# Sample	Distribution (%)
Adware	1,253	10.8
Banking	2,100	18.1
SMS malware	3,904	33.6
Riskware	2,546	22.0
Benign	1,795	15.5
Total	**11,598**	**100**

Evaluation Metrics. Due to the imbalanced nature of the datasets, accuracy alone may not reliably reflect classifier performance. Therefore, in this study, both detection and family classification performance are evaluated using additional metrics such as precision, recall, and the Macro-F1. Generally, accuracy is appropriate when true positives and true negatives are equally important and the class distribution is balanced. In contrast, the Macro-F1 is more suitable when false positives and false negatives carry greater significance, especially in scenarios with class imbalance. Since real-world classification tasks involve imbalanced datasets, Macro-F1 provides a more robust measure for model evaluation.

5.2 Evaluation Results

This section presents the experimental results obtained from evaluating our proposed hypergraph-based malware detection system on the Drebin and CICMalDroid2020 datasets. We compare the performance of our method against various baseline approaches, including traditional graph neural networks (GNNs) and other feature-based methods, using the metrics defined in the previous section.

Drebin Performance. For the Drebin dataset, which is characterized by an unbalanced distribution of malicious families, we employed Accuracy, Precision, Recall, and F1-Score to provide a comprehensive evaluation. Table 3 presents the performance of our hypergraph attention-based method (HGANN-Mal) against various graph-based neural network baselines including GCN [21], and GraphSAGE [44] and state-of-the-art hypergraph-based methodologies including, Hypergraph Neural Networks (HGNN) and HGNNP [45]. HGNNP introduces a convolution operator that differs slightly from that of HGNN by utilizing a random-walk-based probability transition matrix for feature propagation [14].

Table 3. Performance of Malware Detection on Derbin

Method	Binary Detection				Multi-Class Classification			
	Macro-F1	Precision	Recall	Accuracy	Macro-F1	Precision	Recall	Accuracy
GCN	92.2	92.2	91.5	92.8	86.1	85.9	86.2	87.8
GraphSAGE	92.1	92.1	92.5	93.3	86.3	86.7	86.2	88.0
HGNN	96.2	95.8	96.3	96.8	92.0	92.1	92.4	92.0
HGNNP	96.1	95.9	96.1	97.1	92.3	92.5	92.5	93.3
HGANN-Mal	**97.8**	**97.8**	**97.6**	**98.3**	**94.2**	**94.1**	**93.8**	**95.0**

Table 3 indicates that HGANN-Mal, our attention hypergraph-based method consistently achieved high performance across all metrics on the Drebin dataset. HGNNP attained the optimal accuracy of 97.1%, while HGANN-Mal demonstrated the best Precision (97.8%), and Macro-F1 (97.8%) for binary malware detection. Compared to GCN and GraphSAGE (the graph-based baselines), HGNN, HGNNP, and HGANN-Mal showed significant improvements in accuracy (min 3.5% and max 5.5%) and Macro-F1 (min 3.9% and max 5.7%), respectively for binary detection. Even when compared to GraphSAGE, which is known for its generalization capabilities due to neighbor sampling, the hypergraph-based still yielded superior results in terms of accuracy and Macro-F1, with improvements. This highlights the substantial benefits of integrating hypergraphs into Android malware detection, enabling more accurate and robust classification of complex and evolving threats.

However, regarding the Multi-class classification task which tries to categorize the malware families, again, HGANN-Mal outperformed other baseline and state-of-the-art models by achieving the Macro-F1 score of 94.2%. It is worth mentioning that such high scores are achieved only through a static analysis approach, which is less expensive than dynamic feature extraction. This further supports the notion that hypergraph modeling effectively extracts richer higher-order information, which is crucial for classifying malicious applications, for instance, in datasets with diverse and unbalanced malware families. Unlike static hypergraph models, which treat all neighbor nodes or hyperedges as equally important, hypergraph attention networks introduce a trainable attention mechanism to dynamically learn and assign weights during message passing resulting in a higher performance numbers.

CICMalDroid Performance. For the CICMalDroid2020 dataset, HGANN-Mal demonstrates exceptional performance across both binary detection and multi-class classification tasks. In binary detection, the model achieves outstanding results with a Macro-F1 score of 96.2%, precision of 96.2%, recall of 97.6%, and accuracy of 97.6%. These metrics significantly outperform baseline methods, with HGNNP achieving 95.9% Macro-F1 and traditional approaches like GCN and GraphSAGE scoring 90.6% and 91.0% respectively.

Notably, while HGANN-Mal excels in most metrics, HGNNP achieves a slightly higher accuracy of 97.7% compared to HGANN-Mal's 97.6%. This marginal accuracy difference suggests that the attention mechanism in HGANN-Mal may introduce a subtle trade-off between precision-recall balance and raw accuracy optimization (Table 4).

Table 4. Performance of Malware Detection on CICMalDroid2020

Method	Binary Detection				Multi-Class Classification			
	Macro-F1	Precision	Recall	Accuracy	Macro-F1	Precision	Recall	Accuracy
GCN [21]	90.6	90.6	90.6	90.9	82.4	82.0	82.4	82.7
GraphSAGE [44]	91.0	91.1	91.1	91.5	82.3	82.2	82.6	83.4
HGNN [45]	94.2	94.8	94.3	94.6	88.7	88.8	88.8	89.0
HGNNP [45]	95.9	96.1	96.5	**97.7**	89.3	89.5	89.8	90.1
HGANN-Mal	**96.2**	**96.2**	**97.6**	97.6	**94.0**	**94.1**	**94.0**	**94.2**

The multi-class classification results further validate the model's effectiveness, with HGANN-Mal achieving a Macro-F1 score of 94.0%, precision of 94.1%, recall of 94.0%, and accuracy of 94.2%. Compared to HGNNP's 89.3% Macro-F1 and other baseline methods scoring below 90%, HGANN-Mal demonstrates superior capability in distinguishing between different malware families within the CICMalDroid dataset. These results highlight the model's robust performance on the CICMalDroid2020 dataset, confirming its effectiveness in handling diverse and complex malware detection scenarios with high accuracy and reliability.

6 Limitations and Future Work

Our methodology, integrating hypergraph attention into the Android malware detection framework, is designed to overcome the limitations of traditional graph-based and static hypergraph-based approaches by learning more comprehensive representations of higher-order relationships between functions. Traditional FCGs often simplify these interactions into binary edges, losing crucial contextual information.

The consistent outperformance of HGANN-Mal across both the Drebin and the CICMalDroid2020 datasets underscores the robustness and generalizability of our proposed approach, which are critical for real-world malware detection systems. Since Drebin is a widely recognized benchmark in Android malware detection, enabling direct comparison with existing state-of-the-art methods; however, roughly 49.35% of its samples are repackaged duplicates sharing identical opcode sequences, risking trainâĂŞtest leakage and inflated performance estimates. To mitigate single dataset bias and better reflect recent Android malware trends, we also evaluate on CICMalDroid2020 dataset.

While the results are promising, it is important to acknowledge certain considerations. Our evaluation focuses on HGNN/GCN baselines aligned with our static pipeline and does not include the Android detectors such as MaMaDroid [32] (and Drebin), which limits direct comparability to the broader literature. We will incorporate these non-hypergraph baselines in future work.

Also, the construction and processing of hypergraphs can be computationally more intensive than traditional graphs, especially for very large and dense hypergraphs. Hypergraphs are designed to capture higher-order relationships, sparse data (e.g., applications with very few functions or limited API calls) might lead to less informative hyperedges or difficulties in learning robust attention weights. Future work could explore more efficient algorithms for hypergraph construction and optimization techniques for training HNNs on massive datasets.

7 Conclusion

In this paper, we introduced HGANN-Mal, a novel framework for Android malware detection that leverages an attention-based hypergraph neural network to overcome the limitations of conventional graph-based methods. Our approach constructs a hypergraph from static analysis features to model complex, higher-order relationships within applications. The core innovation is an attention mechanism that dynamically weighs these relationships based on their learned relevance to malicious behavior, enabling our model to adaptively focus on the most suspicious patterns and enhance classification accuracy. Experimental results on the Drebin and CICMalDroid datasets confirm that HGANN-Mal significantly outperforms state-of-the-art methods in both binary and multi-class classification tasks. This work demonstrates that an attention-based hypergraph approach provides a more nuanced, robust, and powerful tool for the complex task of malware detection. Future work will explore the integration of dynamic analysis features and investigate the interpretability of the learned attention weights to provide actionable security insights.

References

1. Agarwal, S., Branson, K., Belongie, S.: Higher order learning with graphs. In: Proceedings of the 23rd International Conference on Machine Learning (2006)

2. Alon, U., et al.: Code2vec: learning distributed representations of code. Proc. ACM Program. Lang. **3**, 1–29 (2019)
3. Amer, E.: A dynamic windows malware detection and prediction method based on contextual understanding of api call sequence. Comput. Secur. (2020)
4. Arora, A.A.E.A.: Permpair: android malware detection using permission pairs. IEEE Trans. Inf. Forensics Secur. (2020)
5. Arp, D., et al.: Drebin: effective and explainable detection of android malware in your pocket. In: NDSS (2014)
6. Bai, S., Zhang, F., Torr, P.H.S.: Hypergraph convolution and hypergraph attention. Pattern Recogn. **110** (2021)
7. Banerjee, C., et al.: An empirical study on generalizations of the relu activation function. In: Proceedings of the 2019 ACM Southeast Conference (2019)
8. Bilot, T., El Madhoun, N., Al Agha, K., Zouaoui, A.: A survey on malware detection with graph representation learning. ACM Comput. Surv. **56**(11) (2024)
9. Clevert, D.A., Unterthiner, T., Hochreiter, S.: Fast and accurate deep network learning by exponential linear units (elus). arXiv preprint arXiv:1511.07289 (2015)
10. Cui, H., et al.: On positional and structural node features for graph neural networks on non-attributed graphs. In: 31st ACM International Conference on Information & Knowledge Management (2022)
11. Feng, Y., You, H., Zhang, Z., Ji, R., Gao, Y.: Hypergraph neural networks. In: Proceedings of the AAAI Conference on Artificial Intelligence (2019)
12. Feng, Y., et al.: Apposcopy: semantics-based detection of android malware through static analysis. In: 22nd ACM SIGSOFT International Symposium on Foundations of Software Engineering (2014)
13. Freeman, L.C.: A set of measures of centrality based on betweenness. Sociometry 35–41 (1977)
14. Gao, Y., et al.: Hgnn+: general hypergraph neural networks. IEEE Trans. Pattern Anal. Mach. Intell. (2023)
15. Gao, Y., Zhang, Z., Lin, H., Zhao, X., Du, S., Zou, C.: Hypergraph learning: methods and practices. IEEE Trans. Pattern Anal. Mach. Intell. **44**(5), 2548–2566 (2020)
16. Gascon, H., et al.: Structural detection of android malware using embedded call graphs. In: 2013 ACM Workshop on Artificial Intelligence and Security (2013)
17. Google: The android show: I/o edition (May 2025). https://blog.google/products/android/the-android-show-io-2025/. Accessed 11 June 2025
18. Guo, W., et al.: Malhapgnn: an enhanced call graph-based malware detection framework using hierarchical attention pooling graph neural network. Sensors **25**(2), 374 (2025)
19. Kang, B., Yerima, S.Y., Sezer, S., McLaughlin, K.: N-gram opcode analysis for android malware detection. arXiv preprint arXiv:1612.01445 (2016)
20. Khan, B., Wu, J., Yang, J., Ma, X.: Heterogeneous hypergraph neural network for social recommendation using attention network. ACM Trans. Recomm. Syst. **3**(3), 1–22 (2025)
21. Kipf, T.N., Welling, M.: Semi-supervised classification with graph convolutional networks. arXiv preprint arXiv:1609.02907 (2016)
22. Lee, J.B., Rossi, R.A., Kim, S., Ahmed, N.K., Koh, E.: Attention models in graphs: a survey. ACM Trans. Knowl. Discov. Data (TKDD) **13**(6), 1–25 (2019)
23. Li, C., et al.: Dmalnet: dynamic malware analysis based on api feature engineering and graph learning. Comput. Secur. **122**, 102872 (2022)
24. Lu, X.A.E.A.: Sndgcn: robust android malware detection based on subgraph network and denoising gcn network. Expert Syst. Appl. (2024)

25. Maas, A.L., Hannun, A.Y., Ng, A.Y., et al.: Rectifier nonlinearities improve neural network acoustic models. In: Proceedings of the ICML, vol. 30, p. 3. Atlanta, GA (2013)
26. Mahdavifar, S., et al.: Dynamic android malware category classification using semi-supervised deep learning. In: The 18th IEEE International Conference on Dependable, Autonomic, and Secure Computing (DASC) (2020)
27. Mahdavifar, S., et al.: Effective and efficient hybrid android malware classification using pseudo-label stacked auto-encoder. J. Netw. Syst. Manag. (2022)
28. Moser, A., Kruegel, C., Kirda, E.: Limits of static analysis for malware detection. In: Proceedings of the 23rd Annual Computer Security Applications Conference (ACSAC) (2007)
29. Narayanan, A., Chandramohan, M., Chen, L., Liu, Y.: A multi-view context-aware approach to android malware detection and malicious code localization. Empir. Softw. Eng. **23**(3) (2018)
30. Niu, W., Cao, R., Zhang, X., Ding, K., Zhang, K., Li, T.: Opcode-level function call graph based android malware classification using deep learning. Sensors **20**(13), 3645 (2020)
31. Norouzian, M.R., Xu, P., Eckert, C., Zarras, A.: Hybroid: toward android malware detection and categorization with program code and network traffic. In: Liu, J.K., Katsikas, S., Meng, W., Susilo, W., Intan, R. (eds.) ISC 2021. LNCS, vol. 13118, pp. 259–278. Springer, Cham (2021). https://doi.org/10.1007/978-3-030-91356-4_14
32. Onwuzurike, L., et al.: Mamadroid: detecting android malware by building markov chains of behavioral models (extended version). ACM Trans. Priv. Secur. (TOPS) (2019)
33. Payet, É., Spoto, F.: Static analysis of android programs. Inf. Softw. Technol. **54**(11), 1192–1201 (2012)
34. Qian, X., Zheng, X., He, Y., Yang, S., Cavallaro, L.: Lamd: context-driven android malware detection and classification with llms. arXiv preprint arXiv:2502.13055 (2025)
35. Qiu, J., et al.: Cyber code intelligence for android malware detection. IEEE Trans. Cybern. **53**(1), 617–627 (2022)
36. Shokouhinejad, H., et al.: Recent advances in malware detection: graph learning and explainability. arXiv preprint arXiv:2502.10556 (2025)
37. Soi, D., Sanna, A., Maiorca, D., Giacinto, G.: Enhancing android malware detection explainability through function call graph apis. J. Inf. Secur. Appl. **80**, 103691 (2024)
38. Sun, C., Li, C., Lin, X., Zheng, T., Meng, F., Rui, X., Wang, Z.: Attention-based graph neural networks: a survey. Artif. Intell. Rev. **56**(Suppl 2), 2263–2310 (2023)
39. Veličković, P., Cucurull, G., Casanova, A., Romero, A., Li, P., Bengio, Y.: Graph attention networks. In: International Conference on Learning Representations (ICLR) (2018)
40. Wu, D.J., et al.: Droidmat: android malware detection through manifest and api calls tracing. In: Seventh Asia Joint Conference on Information Security (2012)
41. Wu, L., Wang, D., Song, K., Feng, S., Zhang, Y., Yu, G.: Dual-view hypergraph neural networks for attributed graph learning. Knowl.-Based Syst. **227**, 107185 (2021)
42. Xiao, X., Xiao, X., Jiang, Y., Liu, X., Ye, R.: Identifying android malware with system call co-occurrence matrices. Trans. Emerg. Telecommun. Technol. **27**(5), 675–684 (2016)
43. You, I., Yim, K.: Malware obfuscation techniques: a brief survey. In: BWCCA (2010)

44. Yumlembam, R., Issac, B., Jacob, S.M., Yang, L.: Iot-based android malware detection using graph neural network with adversarial defense. IEEE Internet Things J. **10**(10), 8432–8444 (2022)
45. Zhang, D., et al.: Android malware detection based on hypergraph neural networks. Appl. Sci. **13**(23) (2023)
46. Zheng, J., et al.: Maskdroid: robust android malware detection with masked graph representations. In: 39th IEEE/ACM ASE 2024 (2024)
47. Zhou, D., Huang, J., Schölkopf, B.: Learning with hypergraphs: clustering, classification, and embedding. Adv. Neural Inf. Process. Syst. (2006)

Systems Security

A Graph-Based Approach to Alert Contextualisation in Security Operations Centres

Magnus Wiik Eckhoff[1,2(✉)], Peter Marius Flydal[3], Siem Peters[3], Martin Eian[3], Jonas Halvorsen[1], Vasileios Mavroeidis[2], and Gudmund Grov[1,2]

[1] Norwegian Defence Research Establishment, Horten, Norway
[2] University of Oslo, Oslo, Norway
Magnus-wiik.eckhoff@ffi.no
[3] mnemonic AS, Oslo, Norway

Abstract. Interpreting the massive volume of security alerts is a significant challenge in Security Operations Centres (SOCs). Effective contextualisation is important, enabling quick distinction between genuine threats and benign activity to prioritise what needs further analysis. This paper proposes a graph-based approach to enhance alert contextualisation in a SOC by aggregating alerts into graph-based alert groups, where nodes represent alerts and edges denote relationships within defined time-windows. By grouping related alerts, we enable analysis at a higher abstraction level, capturing attack steps more effectively than individual alerts. Furthermore, to show that our format is well suited for downstream machine learning methods, we employ Graph Matching Networks (GMNs) to correlate incoming alert groups with historical incidents, providing analysts with additional insights.

Keywords: Alert Grouping · Graph Neural Networks

1 Introduction

Modern cyber attacks come with substantial financial and operational costs, and it is generally accepted that purely preventive measures are not sufficient to stop them [10,31]. This requires capabilities for detecting and responding to incidents [23], an activity that is usually carried out within Security Operations Centres (SOCs).

To respond to suspicious behaviour that has been detected, one must first analyse and understand what is likely to have happened. This is a challenging and labour-intensive task for several reasons. First, security alerts must be quickly assessed and prioritised to identify what needs further analysis [20]. This process typically involves examining alerts, correlating them with relevant sources, and filtering out unrelated information. The sheer number of alerts – most of them false – coupled with limited available analyst time, has led to a problem known as *alert fatigue*[1] in many SOCs [29,34].

Any support and automation that can be provided to help analyse and understand the alerts could have a massive impact on a SOC. In this paper, we address the initial phase of such analysis in two ways. First, we address the problem of alert correlation, meaning the ability of an analyst to examine a group of alerts at the same time instead of handling each alert individually. Second, we propose a method to match graph-based alert groups with historical ones, enabling insights from past events to serve as the starting point for further analysis.

Our work is based on a set of (informal) observations made from how SOCs operate in practice. Firstly, whilst an alert in isolation is often connected to a (low-level) indicator of compromise (IoC)[2], a combination of alerts can indicate more abstract behavioural patterns[3]. It is known that IoCs are easy for an attacker to change, and to detect attacks from advanced threat actors, IoCs are not a suitable abstraction level to work on when trying to find similarities across time. Behavioural patterns, on the other hand, are much harder to change, and therefore more likely to remain the same [3]. Secondly, while we are unlikely to have much knowledge of the new alerts, we are likely to have more information about previous incidents and campaigns. This could be anything from what phase of the attack an alert group is likely to belong to, to detailed Cyber Threat Intelligence (CTI) – for instance, what threat actor we are dealing with, or what the goal of the attack might be.

By connecting alerts in a structured way, we hypothesise that we can capture high-level behavioural patterns that can be matched with, and used to exploit patterns of known previous incidents. We argue that graphs are a natural representation as they can efficiently represent key connections between the correlated alerts. Moreover, an attack happens in different phases, and alerts can be correlated at different levels: they can be correlated to relate different phases of an attack or correlate alerts within the same phase. Our focus is on the latter, which leads us to our first two research questions:

RQ1: How naturally can related alerts be combined into graph-based alert groups such that each alert in a group belongs to the same phase of an attack?

RQ2: How to automatically combine alerts from the same attack step together while minimising the number of unrelated alerts in the group?

We note that threat detection in cybersecurity has to deal with a considerable amount of noise, meaning that any grouping method will likely result in

---

[1] Alert fatigue describes how security analysts become both overwhelmed and desensitised, which may result in true positive alerts being missed, efficiency reduced, and the analyst suffering burnout.
[2] Examples of IoCs are IP addresses, hostnames or even known vulnerabilities.
[3] A single alert may also be an indicator of behaviour, but even so, combined with other alerts will still provide a more abstract view.

groups containing false positives and genuine alerts. Consequently, a method that attempts to match such a graph-based alert group to another one representing historical incidents needs a level of noise resistance. One promising approach that has been applied to related problems in other domains is *Graph Matching Networks* (GMNs) [19], which we explore in our final research question:

RQ3: To which degree can Graph Matching Networks correlate current alert groups to related historical incidents?

The contributions of this paper follow the research questions and are two-fold: (1) we provide a formal account of alert graphs and describe a method for creating graph-based alert groups from a stream of alerts; (2) we apply and adapt the graph-based machine learning method *Graph Matching Network* to our problem domain, and show that it is able to match related graph-based alert groups in order to correlate new alert groups with known incidents, thus providing a promising approach to support security analysts and reduce alert fatigue.

The paper is organised as follows: Sect. 2 provides a brief overview of the background; Sect. 3 gives a formal account of alert graphs and a method for generating graph-based alert groups; Sect. 4 outlines our approach in using Graph Matching Network to correlate current and historical graph-based alert groups; Sect. 5 contains the evaluation of our approach, followed by a discussion in Sect. 6 and a conclusion of the paper in Sect. 7.

2 Background

The problem of alert fatigue in SOCs is well known (see e.g. [29]), where a large proportion of the alerts are either false or not important [1]. In one study, it was shown that 62% of all alerts in SOCs are ignored [6]. Since alert fatigue has been a persistent and longstanding issue, different solutions and methods have been developed to mitigate its impact.

One approach has been to filter out unrelated alerts or prioritise important alerts. An example is the *Automated Alert Classification and Triage* (AACT) system, which leverages machine learning to replicate SOC analysts' triage decisions [30]. The system enables real-time classification and prioritisation of alerts, reducing analyst workload by automatically dismissing clearly benign alerts and prioritising critical ones. *That Escalated Quickly* (TEQ) [12] is a machine learning framework that predicts alert- and incident-level actionability, while *RAPID* [21] is a collaborative real-time alert investigation system that attempts to reduce redundant triage work and dynamically prioritise investigations. These techniques focus on filtering out uninteresting alerts or prioritising interesting alerts before any further analysis. In contrast, our approach contextualises all alerts, enabling relevance to be determined based on this context rather than upfront filtering.

Another way to address alert fatigue is to combine related alerts into a single group. As a result, an analyst can work with a group of alerts instead of the alerts individually. It has been argued that representing alerts as graphs can improve the workflow of analysts, improve alert prioritisation and classification, reduce analyst workload, and detect threats that would have gone unnoticed if investigated in a single alert [14]. Graphs and graph-based learning have been studied to correlate different stages of an attack [5]. Here, a hyperconnected graph is generated with nodes representing alerts and entities (e.g., IP addresses, accounts) and edges representing the relationships between the nodes. Known attack patterns are stored in a knowledge pool, and *K-Nearest Neighbours* (KNN) uses these patterns to prioritise alerts. A comparable approach [11] represents alerts as nodes and transitions between them as edges, and uses *Markov chains* [24] to detect attack chains. There are also graph-based commercial solutions [13,18,27] to discover such multi-stage attack chains. Whilst sharing the hypothesis that graphs are a suitable representation for alerts [14], our work deviates from the above graph-based approaches by focusing on correlating alerts within a single phase of an attack.

One prominent non-graph-based approach for alert correlation is based on time, where alerts are grouped based on a set time interval [17]. This method does not require defining attack scenarios or specific alert formats, and has been used to extract higher-level alert patterns. However, the approach preserves no structure between alerts and has known limitations with simultaneous attacks.

3 Introducing and Generating Alert Graphs

To reduce alert fatigue in a SOC, it can be useful to divide incoming alerts into the following three categories:

1. alerts that contain enough information to be actionable;
2. alerts that never contribute to analysis;
3. alerts that may be part of a broader analysis that leads to something actionable.

Alerts of the first type should be dealt with automatically using *SOAR* (Security Orchestration, Automation and Response) or similar methods, and are not part of the issue we study in this paper. Alerts of the second type are essentially noise and should be tuned out of the alert pipeline. These two categories contain the alerts that are always either true positives or true negatives[4].

Alerts of the third kind are our focus, as they are the ones for which false positives and false negatives necessarily exist, because no amount of alert-level tuning or automation has even a theoretical chance of handling them – they are, by our definition, ambiguous in isolation. To identify true positives for these alerts, analysts need to scrutinise the context around them. One way of doing this is to enhance the alert by looking up indicators and gathering relevant *cyber threat intelligence*. However, if this is sufficient to conclude, we argue that the alert falls back into the first category – the alert can be analysed perfectly in

---

[4] Note that both of these two categories are highly non-trivial to deal with in practice, but they are not within the scope of this paper.

isolation. The other way of approaching contextualisation is to look for associated alerts and try to stitch together a picture of what happened[5].

In certain cases, these sequences of corresponding alerts determine patterns that are distinct enough to be hard-coded as multi-alert signatures, and the low-severity alerts can be combined into a single, higher-severity alert. Again, we find that this means that the alert can be moved into the first category. What we are now left with are alerts for which no easy recipes exist, and it is in this difficult domain that we aim to improve analysis.

Even if no absolute recipe is available to analyse an alert as described above, we know something about how human analysts tend to approach them, and we choose to assume that this experience should inform our choice of method. Alerts will normally contain indicators like IP addresses, usernames, file hashes and so forth, and these can often appear in other recent alerts. Choosing properties that seem important and pivoting on them[6] brings context to the original alert. This context can be in the form of low-severity alerts that normally would not be analysed, but can serve as key information when seen together with other alerts. We are here firmly within the alerts of the third category as defined above.

Pivoting on a single property can be described as asking for the timeline of all alerts involving this property. But it is by pivoting on new alerts, and subsequently performing new pivots on the new properties found in these new alerts, that the full picture sometimes emerges – in other words, *nested pivoting*.

To formalise the process of nested pivoting and avoid making too many limiting choices, we choose to perform all reasonable pivots on all alerts, creating timelines for all reasonable indicators, and stitching them together into what can best be described as a chronologically ordered graph of alerts. This format is an efficient way of representing alerts as seen from an experienced indicator-pivoting analyst's point of view. With the assumption that their way of approaching alerts is valuable, we can hope that we have created a structure that preserves important information. Said differently, if we believe that the information analysts gather by pivoting is of any value, and we want machines to be able to emulate parts of what they do, bringing this pivoting information into the alert group format is necessary.

An abstract overview of the process of creating an alert graph is illustrated in Fig. 1. At the top are alerts (A-H) ordered chronologically, coloured by type. In the middle the timeline-defining properties have been extracted from the alerts, and the ones that share e.g. a hostname have been placed on the same timeline, revealing some relationships over multiple timelines. At the bottom every timeline-defining property has been taken into account, merging the timelines,

---

[5] To use a simple example, alerts for brute-force password attempts towards a user account are a lot more interesting if followed by an alert detailing a new login of the same user from a suspicious location.

[6] *Pivoting* on an indicator means performing a search for other alerts containing the same indicator—for instance, if you are investigating an alert concerning the host web-server01, pivoting on the hostname means querying for all other alerts having to do with web-server01, normally within some set time frame.

and we end up with an alert graph. Now, alert C and alert B can end up in the same group despite not having any direct edges. This is sometimes helpful if they both contributed to what triggered alert D. Notice that two properties connect alert D and E, which we have drawn as two edges, but in the structure, we use a single edge with features. Deleting edges that represent long time differences leads to alert groups.

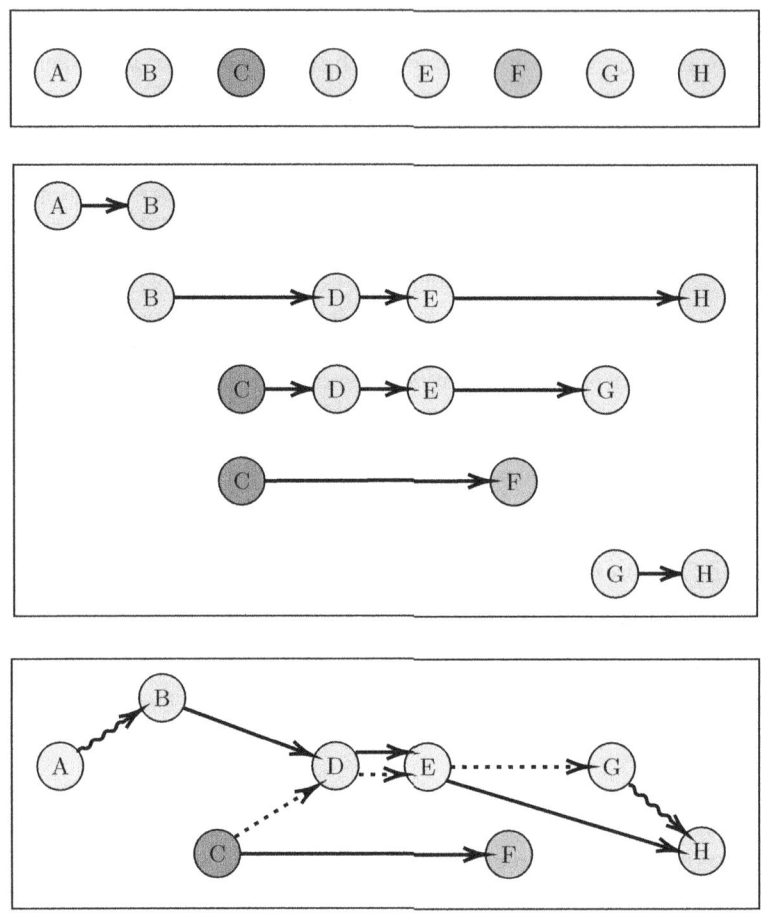

Fig. 1. Overview of the Graph Building Approach.

3.1 Building the Alert Graph

To define an alert graph, we first cover the static case where we are given a sequence of alerts $A = (A_1, A_2, ..., A_n)$, which we, without loss of generality, will assume to be chronologically ordered. They will be the nodes of the alert graph

G. We also need to define a set of objects τ we want to use for building edges in the graph; we call them timeline-defining properties. For now, let these objects be of a single type, like IP addresses, so that τ is the set of all valid IP addresses.

For every alert in A, we then extract its associated IP addresses, meaning that we associate a subset T_i of τ to every A_i. This subset can be empty, and in this case the alert will remain an isolated node in the alert graph. The algorithm for extracting the sets T_i needs to be decided on individually for every alert type involved. We denote the set of IP addresses that appear in our alerts by $\tau' = \bigcup T_i$ (note that this subset of τ could change whenever a new alert is added, if working on a stream of alerts).

Next, for every individual IP address p in τ', we create a timeline along it, by linking every consecutive alert A_i where $p \in T_i$ with an edge. To preserve information about what linked the two alerts, we store the value p as an edge feature for the new edge. To preserve chronological details, we make the edge directed and weighted by the time difference between the alerts it sits between. We do not directly link all alerts that share the IP address p. They all end up on a linear graph, ordered by a timestamp[7]. Doing this for every IP address in τ' results in an alert graph that is essentially a union of intertwined alert timelines, one for each relevant IP address. If two consecutive alerts have more than one IP address in common, we should link them by one edge for each instance, separable by their different edge feature values. To avoid working with multi-graphs, we prefer to link by a single edge that has all the relevant IP address values as features.

In the more general case, we define multiple alert properties that are used for linking, as long as we can define a way of extracting them from the alerts. Later in this paper, hostnames and usernames are used in addition to IP addresses, but any property that analysts find valuable for pivoting between alerts should be considered. When adding features to the edges in this general case, we have to add both the property type(s) and the property value(s). Given k different property types chosen as timeline-defining properties, we write $\tau = \tau_1 \cup ... \cup \tau_k$ for the complete set.[8]

The alert graph can be considered completed, with all alert information gathered in the corresponding nodes. Alerts tend to be represented using JSON or similar formats, but for most machine learning applications we need a featurisation of these alert properties into Euclidean space. After a vectorisation algorithm $v : A \to \mathbb{R}^n$ is decided on, we replace the full alert information A_i in a node with the node vector $v(A_i)$. The vectorisation depends on the underlying alerts, and an example of this process is detailed in Sect. 5. In the end, we arrive at an alert graph G which is a directed acyclic graph (DAG) with multi-attributed edges and nodes.

---

[7] In some detection systems, alerts with the same timestamp can be a common occurrence. In this case, we make an arbitrary choice of how to order the alerts with the same timestamp, and the resulting alert groups will not be affected by the choice.

[8] To "featurise" the edges correctly, we will think of the timeline-defining properties as formally looking like tuples e.g. (abc, hostname) and (abc, username).

In practice, we want the alert graph to be a lightweight format suited for a fast stream of incoming alerts, so its actual computation is a little different from that described above. The graph is initialised as an empty graph. In chronological order, incoming alerts are sent through the two functions that extract their timeline-defining properties and their node vector. Next, the timeline-defining properties are checked against a list of current timeline-defining properties in the graph, which is actually a list of keys for a dictionary mapping the properties to the most recent graph node sharing that property.[9] For every match, a correspondingly featurised edge is added between the new alert node and the matching node, and the new node replaces the previous one in the dictionary as head of the timeline for that property. We detail the algorithm with pseudocode in Algorithm 1.

Algorithm 1 Alert Graph Creation

procedure GENERATEALERTGRAPH(A, τ, ν, Δ)
    for A_i in A **do**
        $timelineProperties \leftarrow e(A_i)$
        $newNodeVector \leftarrow v(A_i)$
        addNode($alertGraph, newNodeVector, newNodeId = i$)
        for $(property, propertyType)$ in $timelineProperties$ **do**
            if $(property, propertyType) \in \tau'$ **then**
                $pred \leftarrow headOfTimelinesDict[(property, propertyType)]$
                addEdge($alertGraph, pred, newNodeId, edgeFeatures$)
                $headOfTimelinesDict[(property, propertyType)] \leftarrow newNodeId$
            else
                $headOfTimelinesDict[(property, propertyType)] \leftarrow newNodeId$
            end if
        end for
    end for
end procedure

3.2 Creating Graph-Based Alert Groups

The alert graph structure constructed in the previous section ties the alerts from a stream together, which we claim is a natural structure for further analysis. One way of using it when analysing an alert stream is to visualise an alert with its immediate graph neighbourhood, essentially the same as pre-performing all relevant pivots for the alert. However, we also believe that the alert graph structure provides this information robustly, which means that we can use the format for machine-assisted analysis methods.

---

[9] In an actual environment, there may be specific property values, like the IP address of a proxy server, that show up in so many alerts that they tie together systems for no good reason. In these cases, blacklisting specific values so that they do not create edges in the graph is a solution.

We use the term *global alert graph* for the graph containing all alerts. The global alert graph tends to grow very large in large environments. In many real-world cases, it will consist mainly of noise or false positives, simply because most logged events are non-malicious. We are interested in improving the understanding of single alerts in the graph represented by nodes through their surrounding context. If the timeline-defining properties are chosen correctly, this context corresponds to the graph neighbourhood around each alert. One natural machine-enhanced approach would be a node-classification method, which in a featurised graph utilises message-passing techniques to update the information in each node using the surrounding nodes [32].

Another approach is to see clusters of alerts in the graph as coherent groups having to do with the same incident, and consider the longer edges to be links between different events on the same system[10]. The underlying assumption is that when something suspicious happens in our systems, we have detectors that pick up traces of the activity that result in alerts spanning a relatively short time window. In this case, it can be more natural to consider the global alert graph as a structure from which smaller alert groups should be isolated (or cut off), by removing the longer edges representing links between different events on the same system. Looking at how analysts use properties to pivot between alerts, we are essentially asking how far back in time they would normally look along a hostname or an IP address.

The approach used in this paper, is to choose a delta cut-off time δ and remove, or never construct, any edge between alerts that have a chronological distance higher than δ. Since we are working with featurised edges, in which each edge contains at least one timeline defining property type, we can also pick a collection of deltas $\Delta = (\delta_1, ..., \delta_k)$ corresponding to the property types $\tau = \tau_1 \cup ... \cup \tau_k$, and then only keep an edge if it is of type τ_j and is shorter than δ_j. Given the choice Δ, we immediately go from a global, ever-growing alert graph G to *graph-based alert groups*[11]. Note that these groups resulting from removing certain edges retain their own graph structure as subgraphs of G. The hypothesis is that graph-based alert groups created with suitable timeline-defining properties τ and time deltas δ_j can capture single attack steps. In the following section, we will explore a graph learning approach to identifying the related attack step for a given graph-based alert group.

4 Matching Graph-Based Alert Groups

One of our primary motivations for grouping alerts is to be able to match our generated graph-based alert groups to similar historical graph-based alert groups. This means that the alert group can be contextualised with data present for the historic event, such as relevant CTI, how the incident was handled and any conclusions from the previous incident handling. This provides additional armoury

---

[10] Recall that we included the time-delta between two linked alerts as a feature of the edge, so talking about edge length is meaningful.

[11] Referred to as 'alert groups' throughout this paper for brevity.

for the analyst's toolbox. It is also a way of capturing patterns that keep repeating in the environment, or odd similarities that appear across systems over time. The alert groups we generate can be stored in a knowledge base – all of them or just the ones we deem important. Thus, deciding how to match against new groups is the next challenge.

Having turned our alert stream into alert groups with an underlying graph structure, the task of alert group matching amounts to comparing directed acyclic graphs with featurised nodes and edges. There is a rich literature of methods for doing this. Still, we have distinctive requirements for our graph matching: (1) the content of the alerts is likely to be the main information contained in an alert group, meaning that the node features should have a high weight; (2) noise arising from false positives needs to be taken into account, as well as some randomness in the chronology of the alerts, and therefore strict graph-comparison schemes that look for exact substructures are avoided; (3) alert group size is also expected to vary, even between good matches; (4) the edge information should contribute as it is also structured data. One promising *Graph Neural Network*(GNN) approach that satisfies these requirements is *Graph Matching Networks* (GMNs) [19], which we explore next.

4.1 The Graph Matching Network Approach

A GMN is a supervised graph neural network that learns the similarity of structured graph objects [19]. Given a pair of graphs, a function to compute a similarity score between them is learned. The model uses message passing within and between graphs to create vector space embeddings, employing a cross-graph attention mechanism to compute contextual matching vectors, enabling distance measurement in a shared vector space.

We utilise a GMN to learn a similarity measure between alert groups with the goal of correlating incoming (unknown) alert groups to previously seen (known) alert groups stored in a knowledge base. As this is a supervised learning technique, we create pairs of alert groups $< G_1, G_2 >$ from a training set, and label them with L as positive if they relate to the same attack step and negative if they relate to different attack steps or to false positives. This forms the tuple $< G_1, G_2, L >$. In addition to the trained model, a knowledge base of *known attack groups* is created, containing alert groups recorded from previous attacks. The alert groups in the knowledge base may include information to contextualise the new and unknown alert group. Such information could, for instance, be CTI or details about the phase of the attack.

During the inference phase, the goal is to identify whether an incoming alert group is similar to anything seen before. The alert group is compared with all alert groups in the knowledge base, one by one. The trained GMN measures distances, and if the distance is sufficiently short, the similarity score and related information from the known alert group are returned and can be used for further analysis. If the incoming group is not close to any known groups in the knowledge base, it is an indication that the group is irrelevant, unseen, or part of a novel type of behaviour. The strength of the cross-graph attention edges in a GMN indicates which nodes (between the two alert groups) that are deemed the most similar [19]. This provides an element of explainability that is considered essential when using AI in SOCs [9,22]. Next, we demonstrate both the generation of graph-based alert groups and the use of GMNs to match such groups.

5 Evaluation

Here, we provide experimental evidence for our graph-based approach to alert groups. We demonstrate and evaluate both the graph-based alert group creation and the subsequent graph correlation, thus addressing all three research questions from Sect. 1. The section consists of the following three parts:

1. *Dataset and experimental setup.* We first describe the dataset and the parameters for creating graph-based alert groups.
2. *Graph-based alert group creation.* We assess the quality of the graph creation technique by measuring the cluster purity and the silhouette score.
3. *Graph-based alert group correlation.* Finally, we evaluate the performance of the graph matching approach, by measuring the similarity to historical alert groups.

5.1 Dataset

We use the *AIT Log Data Set V2.0* [15] as our base system logs, as it contains varied log sources enabling different types of intrusion detection systems.

This dataset contains logs collected in a testbed representing a small enterprise with multiple attack steps. The dataset consists of eight repeated simulations with slight variations in both normal and malicious traffic. Crucially for our work, this dataset consists of a set of alerts generated from different intrusion detection systems, which in this case is: Suricata, Wazuh, AMiner [16] and Telosian [25]. This means the alerts are raised from both signature-based and anomaly-based IDSs. The resulting data set consists of 2,655,821 labelled alerts, with the distribution of alert labels shown in Table 1. The label "–" corresponds to false positive alerts. Most alerts are false positives, mirroring the challenges SOCs face today [1]. We also observe that the classes are very unbalanced. This is a natural consequence of different attack methods manifesting differently in the alerts. A directory scan (`dirb`) might request hundreds of thousands of endpoints, while remote code execution (`webshell_cmd`) might only be a few actions.

From the alerts, we create graph-based alert groups using the timeline-defining properties `username` and `IP`. As discussed in Sect. 3, different Δ are suitable for representing different attack steps. The Δ for the different attack steps are shown in Table 2.

5.2 Graph-Based Alert Group Evaluation

This first experiment aims to evaluate the creation of graph-based alert groups, addressing the first two research questions (RQ1 and RQ2). The metrics we

Table 1. Distribution of Alert Labels.

Attack Method	Wazuh	Suricata	AMiner	Telosian	Total
dirb	1,670,616	0	18,329	6944	1,695,889
–	595,604	233,523	9,444	66609	905,180
dnsteal	0	72,890	44	493	73,427
wpscan	27,288	0	27,491	146	54,922
service_scan	42	216	0	2	260
escalated_sudo_command	56	0	127	0	183
attacker_change_user	22	0	78	0	100
webshell_cmd	0	0	25	0	25
crack_passwords	0	0	11	0	11
dns_scan	0	0	9	0	9
online_cracking	0	6	0	0	6

Table 2. Time Δ for different attack steps

Attack Method	Username (seconds)	IP (seconds)
wpscan	0	3
service_scan	0	30
escalated_sudo_command	30	3
attacker_change_user	30	3
webshell_cmd	0	100

deemed relevant are *cluster purity* [26] and *silhouette score* [28]. The purity of an alert group is the proportion of alerts belonging to the true attack step. The silhouette score measures how well an alert group fits within its assigned cluster compared to all other clusters, and can be seen as a measure of the quality of the clustering. It is calculated by the following equation:

$$s(x_i) = \frac{b(x_i) - a(x_i)}{\max(a(x_i), b(x_i))} \quad (1)$$

where $a(x_i)$ the average distance to all other graphs in the same cluster (intra-cluster distance), and $b(x_i)$ is the average distance to graphs in the nearest different cluster (nearest-cluster distance).

It can thus indicate how recognisable alert groups with the same attack type are by measuring the cohesion within the same cluster and how distinguished they are from other attack groups by measuring their separation. Determining the silhouette score requires featurisation on the graph level, which is achieved by aggregating the features of the nodes in each graph. The distance is calculated using the Euclidean distance.

The graph-based alert aggregation method is run on all alerts in the data set for each scenario separately using the Δ outlined in Table 2. This method is compared to a purely time-based alert aggregation method[12], where alerts are combined if the time between them is shorter than the defined Δ. It is important to create good groups that capture actual attack steps, while the quality of groups that capture false positive alerts is pointless as they should be filtered out later. For this reason, we only analyse groups capturing actual attack steps. The results are shown in Table 3.

Table 3. Graph-based VS Time-based alert aggregation

Metric	Standard		Excluding dnsteal	
	Graph-based	Time-based	Graph-based	Time-based
Silhouette score	0.97385	0.90048	0.44622	0.06470
Purity	0.81632	0.30353	0.99850	0.95653

Looking at the first two columns, the silhouette score is very high for both methods, indicating clearly separated clusters, meaning that each group with the same attack type is clustered densely together. The graph-based method slightly outperforms a pure time-based aggregation. The purity of the graph-based method is high at 81.63%, indicating little noise, outperforming the time-based method.

Note that dnsteal has many times more groups than any other attack. This will have an extra large influence on the silhouette score. Therefore, it is also interesting to check the recognisability of groups excluding dnsteal; This is shown in the last two columns of Table 3. Here, the silhouette score indicates that the graph-based method's clustering abilities are solid. The time-based method created rather poorer groups that led to overlapping clusters, with overlap between graphs from different attack types. This makes it difficult to separate graphs using machine learning models. The purity of both methods is high, with the graph-based method consisting of nearly all the same attack types in each group.

Our initial experiment has shown that graph-based alert aggregation performs well in combining alerts from the same attack step while minimising noise, compared to a more straightforward purely time-based method. The alert groups are purer, recognisable, well-separated, and characteristic for each attack type. In contrast, the time-based method often contains more noise, combines more different attacks in a single group, and has more overlap between alert groups with different attack types. The alert groups show promise for use in machine learning models, since they mainly group alerts from the same attack steps while minimising the noise level.

---

[12] A published approach to alert aggregation [17].

5.3 Graph-Based Alert Group Matching Evaluation

Our second experiment aims to evaluate how accurately the GMN model can match an alert group (representing an attack step) to previously seen alert groups of the same attack step, while minimising matches with unrelated graphs. This experiment addresses the third research question (RQ3).

We create an encoding of each node as a vector of size 133. We wish to include as much information from the alerts as possible. All features are encoded except for IP and User as we wish to capture behavioural patterns, not identify specific users. We one-hot encode and multi-label encode the categorical features like rule_groups. Edges are encoded as a vector of size two, reflecting if the edge comes from an IP match, a user match or both. The distance function used is the dot product. The Adam optimiser [7] is used for optimising with a learning rate of 0.0001 to avoid overshooting.

One of the challenges for supervised machine learning in a real-world SOC environment is the scarcity of labelled data. This is made worse by the fact that most of the available data is benign or noise. However, it is reasonable to assume that an SOC stores details of handled incidents and associated alerts. Thus, this can be the source of a small number of high-quality manually labelled alerts. This is reflected in our dataset, as each attack step only has a few representative alert groups per simulation. On the other hand, unrelated alert groups are more widely available. In order to perform a meaningful evaluation of the technique, we do not try to classify attack labels with too few alerts, to avoid evaluating a graph-based approach on graphs with only one node. We also want to avoid attacks that manifest in massive graphs like dirb and dnsteal. These are scanning attacks that typically result in graphs with more than 10, 000 nodes where statistical methods can be sufficient for analysing them. We therefore focus on creating models for the following labels: attacker_change_user, escalated_sudo_command and wpscan.

The training set for each label consists of 80% of the relevant alert groups and a random selection of unrelated alert groups, both benign and other attack steps. The training stage consists of creating all possible pairs of the relevant alert groups for a given label <*attack, attack*> (positive pairs), along with the same number of pairs of different labels <*attack, benign*> or <*attack, different attack*> (negative pairs). We oversample the positive pairs to avoid the model favouring the negative pairs. The test set consists of the remaining 20% relevant alert groups representing the attack step, and all alert groups from one of the eight simulations representing unrelated groups[13]. The knowledge base consists of the relevant alert groups from the training set. This is similar to what would be done in a SOC, where the known previous incidents would be used first to train the GMN and secondly added to the knowledge base. We predict the distance between all alert groups in the knowledge base and all alert groups in the test set. This measures both how well the GMN correlates alert graphs that represent the same attack step, as well as how well the GMN

---

[13] This is the simulation called 'harrison' in [15].

does not correlate alert groups representing the attack step with unrelated alert groups.

A separate model is trained for each of the three attack steps: attacker_change_user, escalated_sudo_command and wpscan. The model is trained for 450 epochs, where each batch consists of two labelled pairs: one positive and one negative.

The columns for attacker_change_user and escalated_sudo_command in Table 4 show that both labels for the positive pairs have a mean predicted distance shorter than the negative pairs (-0.03 vs. -1.46 and -0.01 vs. -1.04). This indicates that the model learns to separate related and unrelated alert groups. In Fig. 2, we plot the alert groups predicted as the most similar to the ones in the knowledge base for escalated_sudo_command (left) and attacker_change_user (right). Here we see that the model is able to separate true positives with only a few false positives.

Table 4. Predicted distance for positive and negative alert group pairs

	Escalated Sudo Command		Attacker Change User		WPscan	
	Positive	Negative	Positive	Negative	Positive	Negative
Number of graphs	2	36681	2	36681	2	100
Mean distance	−0.03	−1.46	−0.01	−1.04	−1.73	−82401
Standard deviation	0.02	13.81	0.00	10.11	0.58	81456
Longest distance	−0.05	−1103.30	−0.01	−917.97	−2.31	−270081
Shortest distance	−0.00	−0.00	−0.00	−0.07	−1.15	−1828

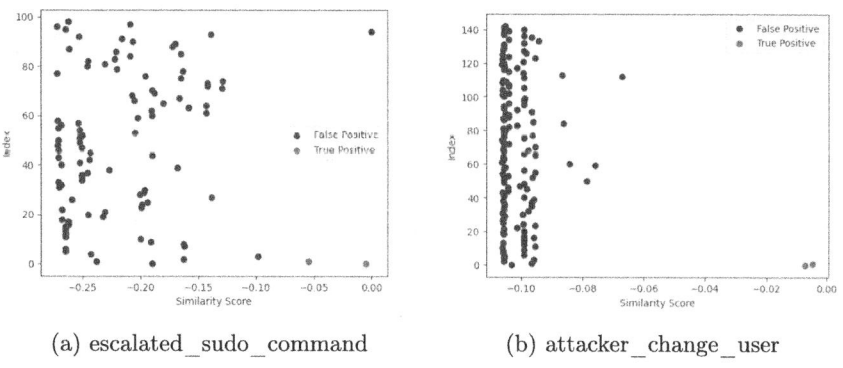

(a) escalated_sudo_command (b) attacker_change_user

Fig. 2. Predicted distances between all graphs in 'harrison' dataset and the alert groups in knowledge base for the two attacks.

Graphs from wpscan are much larger than the two other classes, and the resulting comparison is much slower. We therefore sample 100 graphs for the negative examples. In the wpscan columns of Table 4, we observe that the model is still able to separate alert groups representing wpscan from unrelated alert groups. However, issues with scalability become more apparent as comparisons are slow.

6 Discussion

Graph-based alert aggregation performs well in combining alerts related to the same attack step. Although it achieves a high cluster purity score, it cannot avoid all unrelated alerts. Achieving perfect purity requires knowing if an alert is a false positive, an exceedingly difficult challenge.

The graph matching approach shows promise in relating alert groups for attack types escalated_sudo_command and attacker_change_user. These are attacks that result in medium-sized graphs with the number of nodes between 15 and 100. When relating alert groups of type wpscan, scalability challenges become apparent due to the number of nodes in wpscan alert groups ranging from 1,400 to 13,300. The computational cost of GMNs is high as a separate comparison is done for each pair of alert groups. This means that the number of comparisons needed is $I * K$ where I is the number of incoming alert groups, and K is the number of known alert groups. Additionally, the comparison of two graphs has the computational cost of $O(|V1||V2|)$ where $|V_1|$ and $|V_2|$ are the number of nodes in the two graphs, respectively [19].

Future work should focus on mitigating this. One approach is to use a simpler *Graph Embedding Network* (GEN) [19], as it allows all alert groups to be embedded in the same space, but this comes at the cost of comparison quality. A hybrid approach, using GENs for coarse filtering followed by GMN for fine-grained matching on a smaller candidate set, could balance speed and accuracy. Furthermore, actively managing the content of the knowledge base by identifying representative *template graphs* for each attack step will reduce the number of comparisons. One interesting approach would be to search for a template graph using evolutionary algorithms [2], where the GMN distance function can be used as the fitness metric.

A central component of this approach to analysing alert groups is the knowledge base of previous alert groups. The capability of linking an alert group to past alert groups is only as good as the quality of what you are linking it to. Managing this knowledge base is therefore important. As attacks change over time, the knowledge base must be updated to reflect the changes. New variations of attacks should be added to the knowledge base, while obsolete attacks should be removed or at least deprioritised. Actively managing this can help mitigate concept drift [33]. The emergence of novel or unseen attacks will manifest as novel graph-based alert groups. Ideally, these groups should be identified and added to the knowledge base, with a model being be trained to detect them in an online learning fashion [4]. This is an interesting direction for future work. The knowledge base also serves as a resource for enrichment. By integrating relevant information into it prior to an incident, connections can be established instantly when it is most important.

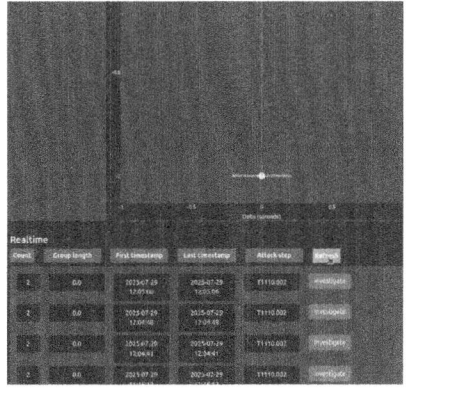
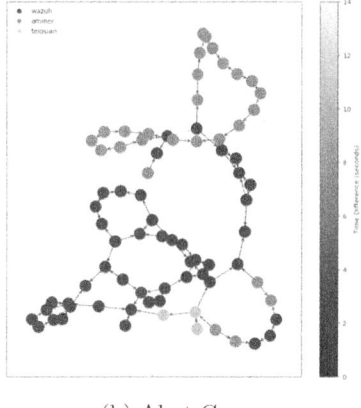

(a) Graphical User Interface (b) Alert Group

Fig. 3. Graphical Elements.

An minimal Graphical User Interface(GUI) was created to support analysis, as illustrated in Fig. 3. Transitioning from investigating alert graphs as opposed to single alerts is an interesting area for future research. Some information should be aggregated on a graph level, while other information should be kept on the alert level. Evaluating what constitutes a beneficial interface will requires a qualitative analysis in a SOC, similar to our previous work in [8].

7 Conclusion

We have addressed the challenge of understanding and contextualising security alerts within an SOC, which is a challenging task due to the large volume of alerts requiring rapid examination, correlation, and understanding.

We have presented an approach to correlate alerts in a structured way as *graph-based alert groups* based on *pivoting* around alert properties with the goal of capturing higher-level behavioural patterns. This data structure lays the foundation for a more in-depth analysis of incidents.

Building on this, we have employed a graph-based machine learning approach to correlate new graph-based alert groups with known ones (stored in a knowledge base). This enables analysts to leverage historical context to gain additional information. This knowledge base provides a good way of maintaining knowledge that can automatically be correlated with new alert groups.

Through experimentation, we have demonstrated that by carefully selecting timeline-defining properties and time cut-offs, it is possible to combine related alerts into a cohesive graph-based alert group corresponding to a specific attack step. The evaluation showed that our graph-based approach outperformed a simpler time-based approach in terms of group purity and recognisability. These experiments have provided promising results for our first (RQ1) and second (RQ2) research questions.

To demonstrate the usability for downstream machine learning tasks, we employed a Graph Matching Network (GMN) to correlate new alert groups with a knowledge base of historical incidents. Our experiments demonstrated that GMNs can successfully identify similarities between current and historical alert groups for attack types resulting in medium-sized graphs (10–100 nodes). However, performance in terms of comparison speed diminished with larger graphs. We have therefore provided positive results for our third research question (RQ3) for medium-sized graphs, with some limitations identified for large graphs.

To conclude, the two main contributions of this paper are: (1) a formal approach for constructing meaningful graph-based alert groups from raw alert streams; and (2) a demonstration of the capability of Graph Matching Networks for correlating these groups with historical incidents. This enables more abstract, behaviour-oriented analysis and automated contextualisation of alerts.

Acknowledgements. This work was partially funded by the European Union as part of the European Defence Fund (EDF) project AInception (GA No. 101103385). Views and opinions expressed are, however, those of the authors only and do not necessarily reflect those of the European Union (EU). The EU cannot be held responsible for them.

References

1. Alahmadi, B.A., Axon, L., Martinovic, I.: 99% false positives: a qualitative study of {SOC} analysts' perspectives on security alarms. In: 31st USENIX Security Symposium (USENIX Security 22), pp. 2783–2800 (2022)
2. Bäck, T., Schwefel, H.P.: An overview of evolutionary algorithms for parameter optimization. Evol. Comput. **1**(1), 1–23 (1993)
3. Bianco, D.: The pyramid of pain. Enterp. Detect. Response **112** (2013)
4. Carliner, S.: An overview of online learning. Human Resource Development (2004)
5. Maze, D., Haijun Zhai, S.L.: Behind the scenes: the ml approach for detecting advanced multistage attacks with sentinel fusion (2022). https://techcommunity.microsoft.com/blog/microsoftsentinelblog/behind-the-scenes-the-ml-approach-for-detecting-advanced-multistage-attacks-with/3239236. Accessed 25 May 2025
6. Davis, J.C.: (2024). https://www.msspalert.com/news/mssp-market-news-survey-shows-62-of-soc-alerts-are-ignored. Accessed 04 June 2025
7. Diederik, P., Kingma, J.B.: A method for stochastic optimization. arXiv preprint arXiv:1412.6980 (2014). **1412**(6)
8. Eriksson, H.S., Grov, G.: Towards xai in the soc – a user centric study of explainable alerts with shap and lime. In: 2022 IEEE International Conference on Big Data (Big Data), pp. 2595–2600 (2022). https://doi.org/10.1109/BigData55660.2022.10020248
9. Ntalampiras, S., Pascu, C., Barros Lourenco, M., Misuraca, G., Rossel, P.: Artificial intelligence and cybersecurity research – ENISA research and innovation Brief. European Union Agency for Cybersecurity (2023). European Union Agency for Cybersecurity, https://doi.org/10.2824/808362
10. Fleck, A.: Cybercrime expected to skyrocket in coming years (2024). https://www.statista.com/chart/28878/expected-cost-of-cybercrime-until-2027/. Accessed 23 May 2025

11. Fredj, O.B.: A realistic graph-based alert correlation system. Secur. Commun. Netw. **8**(15), 2477–2493 (2015)
12. Gelman, B., Taoufiq, S., Vörös, T., Berlin, K.: That escalated quickly: an ml framework for alert prioritization. arXiv preprint arXiv:2302.06648 (2023)
13. Google: Configure alert grouping. https://cloud.google.com/chronicle/docs/soar/investigate/working-with-alerts/alert-grouping-mechanism-admin. Accessed 02 June 2025
14. Jalalvand, F., Baruwal Chhetri, M., Nepal, S., Paris, C.: Alert prioritisation in security operations centres: a systematic survey on criteria and methods. ACM Comput. Surv. **57**(2), 1–36 (2024)
15. Landauer, M., Skopik, F., Frank, M., Hotwagner, W., Wurzenberger, M., Rauber, A.: Maintainable log datasets for evaluation of intrusion detection systems. IEEE Trans. Dependable Secure Comput. **20**(4), 3466–3482 (2022)
16. Landauer, M., Skopik, F., Wurzenberger, M.: Introducing a new alert data set for multi-step attack analysis. In: Proceedings of the 17th Cyber Security Experimentation and Test Workshop, pp. 41–53 (2024)
17. Landauer, M., Skopik, F., Wurzenberger, M., Rauber, A.: Dealing with security alert flooding: using machine learning for domain-independent alert aggregation. ACM Trans. Priv. Secur. **25**(3), 1–36 (2022)
18. Levin, Y.: Investigate incidents with microsoft sentinel (legacy) (2024). https://learn.microsoft.com/en-us/azure/sentinel/investigate-cases. Accessed 02 June 2025
19. Li, Y., Gu, C., Dullien, T., Vinyals, O., Kohli, P.: Graph matching networks for learning the similarity of graph structured objects. In: International Conference on Machine Learning, pp. 3835–3845. PMLR (2019)
20. Lin, T., Zhong, C., Yen, J., Liu, P.: Retrieval of relevant historical data triage operations in security operation centers. From Database to Cyber Security: Essays Dedicated to Sushil Jajodia on the Occasion of His 70th Birthday, pp. 227–243 (2018)
21. Liu, Y., Shu, X., Sun, Y., Jang, J., Mittal, P.: Rapid: real-time alert investigation with context-aware prioritization for efficient threat discovery. In: Proceedings of the 38th Annual Computer Security Applications Conference, pp. 827–840 (2022)
22. Miloslavskaya, N.: Analysis of siem systems and their usage in security operations and security intelligence centers. In: Samsonovich, A.V., Klimov, V.V. (eds.) BICA 2017. AISC, vol. 636, pp. 282–288. Springer, Cham (2018). https://doi.org/10.1007/978 3 319 63940 6_40
23. Nelson, A., Rekhi, S., Souppaya, M., Scarfone, K.: Incident response recommendations and considerations for cybersecurity risk management. NIST Special Publication (2025)
24. Norris, J.R.: Markov Chains. Cambridge university press, Cambridge (1998)
25. Olarra Maldonado, I.A., Meeuwissen, E., de Haan, P., van der Mei, R.: Telosian: reducing false positives in real-time cyber anomaly detection by fast adaptation to concept drift. In: Proceedings of the 11th International Conference on Information Systems Security and Privacy - Volume 2: ICISSP, pp. 84–97. INSTICC, SciTePress (2025). https://doi.org/10.5220/0013320500003899
26. Reddy, H.V., Agrawal, P., Raju, S.V.: Data labeling method based on cluster purity using relative rough entropy for categorical data clustering. In: 2013 International Conference on Advances in Computing, Communications and Informatics (ICACCI), pp. 500–506. IEEE (2013)

27. Sela, S.: Smartgrouping - precision ai-driven investigation (2024). https://www.paloaltonetworks.com/blog/security-operations/smartgrouping-precision-ai-driven-investigation/. Accessed 02 June 2025
28. Shutaywi, M., Kachouie, N.N.: Silhouette analysis for performance evaluation in machine learning with applications to clustering. Entropy **23**(6) (2021). https://doi.org/10.3390/e23060759
29. Tariq, S., Baruwal Chhetri, M., Nepal, S., Paris, C.: Alert fatigue in security operations centres: research challenges and opportunities. ACM Comput. Surv. **57**(9), 1–38 (2025)
30. Turcotte, M., Labrèche, F., Paquette, S.O.: Automated alert classification and triage (aact): an intelligent system for the prioritisation of cybersecurity alerts. arXiv preprint arXiv:2505.09843 (2025)
31. Vielberth, M., Böhm, F., Fichtinger, I., Pernul, G.: Security operations center: a systematic study and open challenges. IEEE Access **8**, 227756–227779 (2020)
32. Ward, I.R., Joyner, J., Lickfold, C., Guo, Y., Bennamoun, M.: A practical tutorial on graph neural networks. arXiv preprint arXiv:1912.11615 (2021)
33. Webb, G.I., Hyde, R., Cao, H., Nguyen, H.L., Petitjean, F.: Characterizing concept drift. Data Min. Knowl. Disc. **30**(4), 964–994 (2016). https://doi.org/10.1007/s10618-015-0448-4
34. Zhong, C., Yen, J., Liu, P., Erbacher, R.F.: Automate cybersecurity data triage by leveraging human analysts' cognitive process. In: 2016 IEEE 2nd International Conference on big data security on cloud (BigDataSecurity), IEEE International Conference on high performance and smart computing (HPSC), and IEEE International Conference on intelligent data and security (IDS), pp. 357–363. IEEE (2016)

HYPERSEC: An Extensible Hypervisor-Assisted Framework for Kernel Rootkit Detection

Lionel Hemmerlé[1], Guillaume Hiet[1], Frédéric Tronel[1](✉), Pierre Wilke[1], and Jean-Christophe Prévotet[2]

[1] CentraleSupélec, Inria, CNRS, University of Rennes, Rennes, France
{lionel.hemmerle,guillaume.hiet,frederic.tronel,
pierre.wilke}@centralesupelec.fr
[2] UnivRennes, INSA Rennes, CNRS, IETR-UMR 6164, Rennes, France
jean-christophe.prevotet@insa-rennes.fr

Abstract. Modern Endpoint Detection and Reaction (EDR) systems must remain reliable even when attackers acquire high privileges within the monitored operating system. Ideally, such systems should be protected from compromise, while maintaining deep visibility into the internal behavior of the target system. To meet this challenge, we aim to isolate the monitored system in a virtual machine (VM) and move the EDR logic into the hypervisor. We present HYPERSEC, a domain-specific language that allows the VM to safely delegate detection logic to the hypervisor by transmitting specialized monitoring programs. This design bridges the semantic gap by enabling the hypervisor to understand OS-level structures, while constraining accepted programs to protect the hypervisor against potential vulnerabilities. We evaluated our system against kernel rootkits that hide processes or elevate privileges and showed that HYPERSEC enables reliable detection of such threats. Our results indicate that the performance overhead remains acceptable, paving the way for broader adoption of hypervisor-based EDR with custom in-VM insight.

Keywords: Security · Hypervisor · Intrusion Detection Systems · Rootkit

1 Introduction

Modern Host-based Intrusion Detection Systems (HIDS), or more broadly Endpoint Detection and Response (EDR hereafter) systems, are essential components for detecting attacks directly within operating systems. These systems may operate as privileged user-space processes or kernel-space modules, relying on access to system internals to detect threats such as local privilege escalation.

If running inside the monitored operating systems, it has been shown that EDR can be disabled by attacker [41]. To strengthen security guarantees, recent research has explored out-of-guest monitoring approaches that isolate detection mechanisms from the system under surveillance. A prominent line of work relies on Virtual Machine Introspection (VMI), which allows a hypervisor to observe guest VM behavior without relying on its cooperation. Garfinkel and Rosenblum introduced this principle in their seminal paper [17]. Additionally, practical implementations like Samsung's Real-time Kernel Protection (RKP) [37] have shown how ARM-based systems can support such external monitoring.

However, deploying detection mechanisms outside the monitored system introduces a semantic gap, as the hypervisor does not natively understand OS-level abstractions (e.g., process lists or syscall tables). This semantic gap has been extensively studied in [13,16,20,42], and bridging it remains a fundamental challenge. Moreover, research has revealed that static monitoring or periodic checking introduces windows of opportunity for attackers. In particular, [21] demonstrated that attackers can manipulate address translation mechanisms to hide their activity from VMI-based tools. Similarly, [24] showed that event-triggered monitoring is necessary to handle mutable kernel objects that may be modified between periodic checks. These works stress the importance of dynamic and semantic-aware monitoring that reacts to actual system events.

To improve detection coverage while retaining strong isolation guarantees, we aim to design a system in which the monitored OS actively assists the hypervisor by conveying semantic information without exposing the hypervisor to compromise. Our goal is to react to VM events rather than rely on time-triggered polling, while allowing high-level detection logic to remain adaptable and verifiable.

We introduce HyperSec, a hypervisor-assisted monitoring architecture for ARM-based systems, which are increasingly used in embedded, server, and IoT deployments. HyperSec allows the monitored guest VM to provision event-triggered inspection programs to the hypervisor using a domain-specific introspection language. These programs are evaluated and safely executed by the hypervisor on relevant events (e.g., process creation), enabling precise kernel-state monitoring. Importantly, the hypervisor verifies the safety of HyperSec programs before loading them, and does not require persistent in-guest agents (only a transient boot-time module).

Our solution stands out from state-of-the-art work by proposing an approach that is sufficiently generic to detect a wide range of malicious behaviors at the kernel level while ensuring strong isolation properties for the monitor and performance comparable to existing approaches. Generality and extensibility are achieved through a dedicated introspection language, which is expressive enough to capture various forms of invariants on kernel data, including those legitimately modified. The use of this dedicated language ensures a balance between expressiveness and the verification of the safety of inspection programs. Finally, HyperSec benefits from architectural support such as ARM's virtualization extensions, and its deployment model aligns with emerging trusted computing bases, including Intel ME and AMD PSP architectures [35]. The contributions of this research can be summarized as follows:

- We design HyperSec, a language dedicated to the specification of security monitors inside a hypervisor.

- We implement a verifier for HYPERSEC programs running inside the XVisor [46] hypervisor.
- We implement three known and one new attacks that aim at hiding processes or elevating their privilege, as Linux kernel modules.
- We implement detection techniques against these attacks using HYPERSEC programs.
- We evaluate the performance and security of our approach using typical workloads.

The remainder of this article is organized as follows. First, Sect. 2 gives a high-level overview of our approach and Sect. 3 introduces several malicious techniques that we aim to detect with our solution. Section 4 presents the features of HYPERSEC, the proposed domain-specific language, and the associated security concerns. Section 5 reports on implementing HYPERSEC features on a Cortex-A53 ARM processor. Section 6 explains how we use HYPERSEC programs to detect all the rootkits described in Sect. 3. Section 7 describes the related work. Finally, Sect. 8 discusses the limitations of our approach and provides perspectives for future works. Section 9 concludes.

2 Threat Model and Approach

Threat Model. The OS kernel of VMs is assumed to be sane when it is first booted, so it can send valid information to the hypervisor. During that time, the integrity of the kernel can be protected using industry-grade security mechanisms like UEFI secure boot [40]. Once all the setup is done, the VM will send a specific signal to the hypervisor indicating not to accept any more information from the VM. After this, we suppose that the OS kernel of VMs can be compromised, and the hypervisor will not trust it anymore. Hence, we focus on detecting malware that can change the internal data structures of the kernel. We leave the task of detecting user-land malware to regular EDRs, which can themselves be protected by our system. Our hypervisor itself is assumed to be safe, and our goal is that our approach does not introduce vulnerabilities in the hypervisor.

Approach. To detect kernel rootkits, we introduce the HYPERSEC language. The VM to be protected will describe how intrusions should be detected by writing HYPERSEC programs, compile these programs into binary executables, and send them to the hypervisor. These programs contain all the information needed for the hypervisor to cross the semantic gap. More precisely, they allow to attach actions (update of the hypervisor view of the OS, raising alerts, monitoring new events, ...) to events (memory writes in specific kernel data structures, privileged register modifications, kernel function calls). The hypervisor will verify HYPERSEC programs, and run them upon detecting specific events.

Safely executing programs from untrusted sources, in a high-privilege context, is a problem that has already been addressed by EBPF [10], with proof-carrying code [30] or with Singularity [19], an OS that runs every process in ring 0 and relies on properties of its language to ensure the system's safety.

Our approach is analogous to the one used by EBPF inside the Linux kernel: EBPF is a language designed to trace events occurring in the kernel, from userspace. However, our approach differs from EBPF: the objective is not to provide the VM (the untrusted environment) with insight into the state of the hypervisor (the trusted environment) but rather the opposite: the hypervisor needs to get information about the state of the VM. Consequently, HYPERSEC programs can only read VM information, and send alerts to the hypervisor. We chose to design a new language instead of using directly EBPF because we wanted a simpler language, and only write a verifier in the hypervisor but no bytecode interpreter or JIT compiler. Furthermore, the implementation of EBPF in Linux would differ a lot from its implementation in an hypervisor. Our solution also has additional security constraints since an attacker may be able to manipulate our program's inputs (for example, the VM memory). Programs sent by the VM and executed by the hypervisor should not introduce vulnerabilities. In particular, they should not be able to access the whole hypervisor's memory. We develop these security aspects of HYPERSEC in Sect. 5.4.

3 Rootkits

In this section, we present rootkits targeting the Linux kernel (version 5.15.36). These rootkits are loaded either in the form of Linux kernel modules, or by exploiting vulnerabilities in the kernel, in the same vein as KOPYCAT [27].

We wrote five rootkits ($\mathbf{RK}_{ro}$, $\mathbf{RK}_{vfs}$, $\mathbf{RK}_{pid}$ and two variants of $\mathbf{RK}_{cred}$) and used two existing ones (Diamorphine [28] and Brokepkg [8]). $\mathbf{RK}_{cred}$ elevates a process' privileges, while the others aim to hide a process. To hide a process, a rootkit may delete or hide the directory corresponding to that process from the /proc filesystem. This can be achieved in a number of ways, as we will describe below. The techniques used in the rootkits $\mathbf{RK}_{ro}$, $\mathbf{RK}_{vfs}$, and $\mathbf{RK}_{cred}$ have already been described in [15,25,38]. However, to the best of our knowledge, $\mathbf{RK}_{pid}$, described below, has not been mentioned elsewhere.

In Rutkowska's classification [36], Type 1 malware modifies areas of code or data that are supposed to remain constant during the system's lifetime, while Type 2 malware alters data that evolves dynamically over time. Type 1 is easier to detect and mitigate since ensuring the read-only property is sufficient. Type 2 is more difficult to detect, since we cannot simply make data read-only. Instead, we must rely on invariants that usually have to be inferred from the knowledge of OS internals. Furthermore, although such invariants exist, they may be transiently violated by the OS code. For example, consider the invariant "all processes appear in a list": even in the absence of attacker, this invariant is broken when the kernel inserts a newly created process. So we cannot rely on simply checking regularly the consistency of this list. Rather, we must synchronize with the kernel code, to check the consistency at some critical points (e.g. after the creation or destruction of a process).

$\mathbf{RK}_{ro}$ changes only purely static data, and $\mathbf{RK}_{vfs}$ changes static data on a dynamic structure (e.g., a constant field in the inode structure). Those are Type

1 rootkits. $\mathbf{RK}_{pid}$ change structures that are dynamically allocated and deallocated by the kernel (pid structures), and $\mathbf{RK}_{cred}$ changes structures that can also be subject to legitimate changes (task_struct and cred structures), corresponding to Type 2 rootkits.

$\mathbf{RK}_{ro}$: **Modifying Read-Only Data.** A rootkit can hide a process by modifying the syscall table to intercept calls to getdents64 (*get directory entries*) and filter out some entries, e.g., the directories corresponding to the processes to hide. To implement such rootkits, we used Diamorphine [28], which directly tampers with the syscall table to make the kernel call its functions instead of the original ones, and Brokepkg [8], which uses the ftrace mechanism, that directly changes the kernel code to intercept function calls. Those two rootkits can then be used to hide a process. To detect this attack from the hypervisor, it is necessary to detect and prevent any write access to the syscall table.

$\mathbf{RK}_{vfs}$: **Modifying the Virtual File System Operations.** The Virtual File System (VFS) provides a uniform interface for supported filesystem types. It uses inode structures to represent files and directories and file_operations structures with function pointers for inode operations. $\mathbf{RK}_{vfs}$ modifies the pointer to the file_operations so that it points to an attacker-controlled structure, which filters entries of the /proc directory, as $\mathbf{RK}_{ro}$. This attack has been implemented in adore-ng [1] for AMD64; we re-implemented it for ARM64.

To detect this attack from the hypervisor, we need to detect writes to the structure file_operations used by the inode representing the directory /proc and to the inode's field pointing to that file_operations structure. Note that both the syscall table and the file_operations relative to the /proc filesystem are placed in read-only pages in the VM and are not expected to be modified during legitimate VM execution. However, some fields of the inode structure can be legitimately modified. This raises new challenges for detecting malicious writes on that structure, which will be solved in Sect. 5.1.

$\mathbf{RK}_{pid}$: **Tampering with pid *Structures*.** In the kernel, processes and threads are represented by task_struct structures. To keep track of the running processes, the kernel uses a radix-tree containing pid structures, which contain a field tasks that references to the corresponding task_struct. The /proc VFS iterates on this radix-tree to construct the list of running processes. Therefore, our third rootkit, $\mathbf{RK}_{pid}$, hides processes by tampering with the tasks field, pointing to the corresponding task_struct from the pid structure.

To detect this attack, it is necessary to build a shadow copy of the list of running processes, by tracking the execution of the kernel_clone and do_exit kernel functions.

$\mathbf{RK}_{cred}$: **Altering Credential Structures.** In each task_struct is a cred structure, which stores the various user identifiers (uid, euid, suid, fsuid) associated with the process. This structure is accessed for each operation that requires access control (e.g., open). The structure itself is supposed to be read-only, but the cred pointer in the task_struct can be modified, e.g. by the setuid syscall.

$\mathbf{RK}_{cred}$ changes the cred structure of an unprivileged process to elevate its privileges to the root user. We implemented $\mathbf{RK}_{cred}$ using two different methods: first with a kernel module that directly overwrites the credentials of the targeted process; second by exploiting a vulnerability in the BPF verifier [12], that allows arbitrary writes in the kernel memory.

To detect this attack, we need to distinguish legitimate changes by system calls of the setuid family, from illegitimate ones. We also need to verify that changes made by system calls are correct to ensure that an attacker does not use a system call and simultaneously rewrite the credentials to hide their attack from our detection system. This implies that we need a shadow copy in the hypervisor of the credentials of each process.

4 Language Specification

$$
\begin{aligned}
s \in \textbf{Symbol} &::= \$string \\
t \in \textbf{Type} &::= \texttt{u64} \mid \texttt{listener} \mid [\, t \,;\, u \,] \\
i \in \textbf{Instr} &::= e_1 \,[\, e_2 \,] = e_3 \,;\, \mid x \,:\, t = e \,;\, \\
&\mid \{\, i \,^* \,\} \mid f\,(\, e \,) \,;\, \\
&\mid \texttt{loop } n \,\{\, i \,^* \,\} \mid \texttt{return } e \,;\, \\
&\mid \texttt{if } e \texttt{ then } \{\, i_1^* \,\} \texttt{ else } \{\, i_2^* \,\} \\
&\mid \texttt{for } n \texttt{ in } m \,\{\, i \,^* \,\} \\
c \in \textbf{Cmd} &::= \texttt{map } m \,[\, t_1 \,] \rightarrow t_2 \\
&\mid \texttt{fun } f\,(\, \overrightarrow{x \,:\, t} \,) \rightarrow t_{ret} \,\{\, i \,^* \,\} \\
&\mid \texttt{exec } f \mid \texttt{last\_command}
\end{aligned}
$$

$$
\begin{aligned}
u &\in \textbf{Uint64} \\
x &\in \textbf{Var} ::= string \\
f &\in \textbf{Fun} ::= string \\
m &\in \textbf{MapId} ::= string \\
r &\in \textbf{Reg} ::= \texttt{pc} \mid \texttt{sp} \mid \texttt{SP\_EL0} \\
&\mid \texttt{x}_i \,(i \in [0; 31]) \\
e &\in \textbf{Expr} ::= m \mid u \mid \texttt{vm\_reg}\,(\, r \,) \\
&\mid e_1 \textit{ binop } e_2 \mid \textit{unop } e \\
&\mid e_1 \,[\, e_2 \,] \mid [\, e \,;\, u \,] \\
&\mid [\, e \,] \mid f\,(\, e \,) \mid s \mid x
\end{aligned}
$$

Fig. 1. Syntax of HyperSec.

The HyperSec language allows to bridge the semantic gap between a VM and the hypervisor, and to specify security properties to be enforced. The hypervisor executes HyperSec programs to react to events occurring inside the VM. We also introduce verifications when loading programs to ensure that these programs cannot cause vulnerabilities in the hypervisor. Examples of HyperSec programs are given in Fig. 2 and Fig. 3.

```
fun f_alert(l: listener) {
    alert();
}
fun protect_ro_data() {
    register_write($__start_rodata, $__end_rodata - $__start_rodata, f_alert);
    register_write($_stext, $_etext - $_stext, f_alert);
}
exec protect_ro_data
```

Fig. 2. A HyperSec program that detect writes on read-only section in the kernel.

```
map syscalls_per_pid[u64] -> u64
fun on_invoke_syscall(l: listener) {
  task_struct_ptr: u64 = vm_reg(SP_EL0);
  pid: u64 = vm_mem_4(task_struct_ptr + offset_of(task_struct, pid));
  counter: u64 = 1;
  if contains(syscalls_per_pid, pid) {
    counter = get(syscalls_per_pid, pid) + 1;
  }
  set(syscalls_per_pid, pid, counter);
}
fun init() {
  register_exec($invoke_syscall, on_invoke_syscall);
}
exec init
```

Fig. 3. A HYPERSEC program to count the number of syscalls per process.

The syntax of HYPERSEC is presented in Fig. 1. A program consists of a list of commands that are the messages sent by the VM to the hypervisor. These commands are: (1) map m [t_1] $\to t_2$, for the definition of a new map named m whose keys are of type t_1 and values of type t_2. Maps are key-value stores which are persistent between several invocations of the hypervisor; (2) fun f ($\overrightarrow{x : t}$) $\to t_{ret}$ { i * }, for the definition of a new function named f with arguments $\overrightarrow{x : t}$, returning a value of type t_{ret}, and whose body is i *; (3) exec f, for calling function f, previously defined. This command is typically used to initialize the monitor environment, and requires no argument; and (4) last_command, which indicates that the VM will stop sending programs.

The functions consist of instructions: array update, variable declaration and initialization, fixed count loops, loops over map entries, conditional statements, function calls, emission of alerts, and function returns.

Expressions may be unsigned 64-bit integers u, variables x, maps m, access to a register of the VM vm_reg(r), a kernel symbol s, binary or unary operations over expressions, a function call $f(e)$, array access $e_1[e_2]$, construction of an array by repeating u times an expression e: [e; u] or an array literal [$\overrightarrow{e}$]. Observable VM registers are the program counter pc, the stack pointer sp, the system register SP_EL0 and regular registers x_i (with i from 0 to 31).

The SP_EL0 register is made available to recover the identity of the process currently executing. Indeed, the Linux kernel updates this register with the address of the task_struct of the current process when the VM executes in kernel mode. This assumption is only valid if traps never occur directly from user mode to hypervisor mode. This should always be the case since we specifically target events from kernel space. The hypervisor checks any deviation from this behaviour and raises an alert if necessary.

We provide several built-in functions: (1) vm_mem_1, vm_mem_2, vm_mem_4, vm_mem_8 reads 1, 2, 4 or 8 bytes from the VM memory; (2) register_write and register_exec attach a handler to a write in a memory area and to the execution of a given function, respectively, and returns an opaque object identifying that handler; (3) unregister disables a previously defined handler; (4) get, set and reads and stores values in a map; (5) contains test if a key has an attributed value in a map; (6) **debug** prints a value; and (7) **alert** raises an alert when a rootkit is detected.

In HYPERSEC, kernel symbols are prefixed by a $ character and are replaced (at preprocessing time, using the /proc/kallsyms file) by the corresponding addresses before sending the program to the hypervisor. Field offsets within data structures are written offset_of(struct, field), and are compiled into actual offsets by reading the VM's debug information (BPF Type Format or BTF [7]) provided by recent Linux kernels. These primitives greatly help in bridging the semantic gap since address or structure offset can evolve between releases of the Linux kernel or depending on compilation options.

5 Language Implementation

Our implementation is based on XVisor [46], a small hypervisor that mainly targets ARM processors [31]. Our test setup is a Xilinx Zynq UltraScale+ ZCU104 development board, with a Cortex-A53 ARM processor, on which we run a VM with Linux (version 5.15.36) on top of XVisor. We extended XVisor with an execution environment and a verifier for compiled HYPERSEC programs. Our implementation largely differs from eBPF because our hypervisor does not include neither a JIT compiler nor a bytecode interpreter. It only verifies annotated binaries, using two simple passes over the instruction stream, making the process more tractable.

5.1 Intercepting Writes into Memory Locations

To intercept writes in memory, depending on the size of the memory area to be watched and its alignment, we rely either on page permissions of the second stage of the address translation mechanism (which is controlled by the hypervisor), or on hardware breakpoints.

Page Permissions. On ARM processors, virtual memory is configured by a set of page tables organized in a radix-tree structure. In a traditional setting, without any hypervisor, the translation of a virtual address is performed by splitting this address into several indexes and looking up the first index in the table whose address can be found in the system register TTBR1_EL1. This gives the address of the next-level page table to look up into, using the next index from the virtual address, and so on until the end of this lookup chain.

When a hypervisor is present, the address translation mechanism is split into two stages. The first stage translates VM virtual addresses into intermediate addresses. The second stage translates intermediate addresses into physical addresses, using a process similar to the first stage, starting from the page table whose address is given in the VTTBR_EL2 register.

The page tables corresponding to the first stage are controlled by the VM and, therefore, considered compromised, while the page tables corresponding to the second stage are controlled by the hypervisor and are considered safe.

To intercept writes in memory at a given virtual address, the hypervisor first translates this address into an intermediate address, using e.g. the at (for *Address Translate*) ARM instruction. For architectures such as x86 that do not have similar instruction [47], one can also translate the virtual address directly using the page tables. Then, we modify the page table entry in the second stage that corresponds to that memory area to make it read-only. Thus, any write access to that memory area will trigger a page fault exception in the hypervisor. The page fault handler will then determine, using the FAR_EL2 and ESR_EL2 registers that contain the address of the memory access and its size, respectiveley, whether the access is authorized. We give some details about the treatment of this exception in Sect. 5.3.

Mega Pages. To increase its performance, XVisor uses mega pages when mapping the VM memory to the physical memory. It thus exploits the possibility for page table level 2 to point directly to physical memory instead of a new page table. This reduces the number of steps needed to translate a virtual address. Consequently, since the data we want to protect are usually smaller than a mega page, we split those mega pages into 512 regular pages by creating the necessary level 3 page table to reduce the amount of data that may unnecessarily trigger exceptions in the hypervisor. Without this split, we would modify the permissions of the mega page and would trap every write access inside that mega page, incurring a larger overhead.

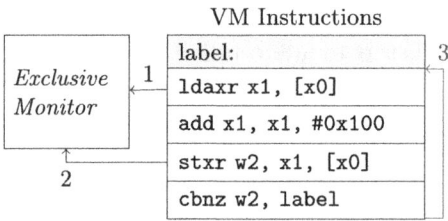

Fig. 4. Example of infinite loop caused by a memory trap in the hypervisor. The code comes from the compilation of the rwsem_acquire_read macro from the Linux kernel.

Atomic Instructions and Exclusive Monitor. In the course of implementing HYPERSEC, we encounter some difficulties related to atomic instructions and the way they are dealt with by ARM processors. This paragraph explains more thoroughly this difficulties and the way we solved them.

ARM v8.0 processors feature exclusive load and store instructions. ARM uses the load-linked/store-conditional semantics (also known as *ll/sc*) when the Large System Extensions extension [3] is not present. When an exclusive load is executed, the processor stores the address of that load in a component named exclusive monitor. Then, when an exclusive store is executed, the processor compares the address in the exclusive monitor with the one written at by the instruction. The memory write only occurs if the two addresses match. The store instruction will then write the status result of the store in an additional register. Furthermore, the exclusive monitor is emptied every time another write at the address stored in the exclusive monitor is made or when a CLREX (*CLeaR EXclusive*) or ERET (*Exception Return*) instruction is executed. Both instructions have this behavior to ensure that the exclusive monitor is emptied in case of a context switch to detect the loss of atomicity of execution for the instructions encompassed between the load and the store. Figure 4 shows an example of those instructions' usage from the rwsem_acquire_read macro [26] in the Linux kernel that can indeed turn into an infinite loop if it accesses an address monitored by the hypervisor. Without the proposed protection, the ldaxr instruction populates the exclusive monitor and reads at the address stored into x0 (1), then the stxr instruction compares its address to the one stored in the exclusive monitor (2) and performs the write since they are equal. If the exclusive monitor is emptied between the load and the store, the conditional jump executes again that block of code (3).

In the literature, multiple approaches have been proposed to address this problem: either by using other atomic instructions [14], a Transactional Hardware Memory extension [11], or by inferring the result of the exclusive store based on the previous instructions [23]. The first two approaches are not available to us because our processor does not feature these extensions, and the third is unacceptable since any instruction could be present between the ldxr and the stxr. We decided to fully emulate the exclusive monitor inside the hypervisor. When an exclusive write or an exclusive load targets an area protected by the hypervisor, the hypervisor will start to intercept both reads and writes on that area (by removing read and write permissions from the page). If the faulting instruction is an exclusive load or store, the hypervisor will emulate the instruction and store the targeted address in a memory structure we call a virtual exclusive monitor. Furthermore, when this virtual exclusive monitor is not empty, the hypervisor must intercept when the ERET instruction is called in the VM. Using the Fine-Grained Trap extension [2] of ARM, we could have generated an interrupt when ERET instructions are emitted [2]. Unfortunately, this extension is only available from version 8.6 of ARM processors, while we are targeting an ARM processor v8.0 (as it is frequently the case in embedded systems). Therefore, we decided to empty the virtual exclusive monitor when any interrupt occurs in the VM context. For that, we used the technique to intercept the execution of specific instructions described in Sect. 5.2 to intercept when the first instruction of every segment of the Interrupt Vector Table is executed. To reduce the overhead, we enable that interception only when the exclusive monitor is not empty.

Leveraging Hardware Watchpoints. Intercepting writes by modifying the address translation mechanism requires to protect a whole page (4096 bytes on this architecture): this incurs a large performance penalty onto the VM, especially when areas surrounding the protected one are frequently written to, and even worse when those writes use the exclusive operations described previously.

To improve the performance of our implementation, we leverage hardware watchpoints to detect writes whenever its size is 8 bytes or less, and one hardware watchpoint is available (only 4 are available for each core on our processor). The VM kernel can also use watchpoints. Therefore, we configure the hypervisor to trap VM accesses to these registers by setting the corresponding flag in MDCR_EL2 (*Monitor Debug Configuration Register*).

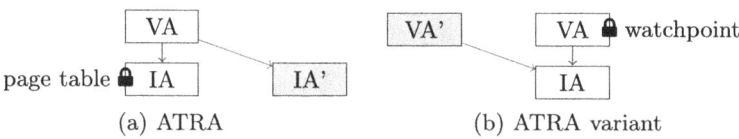

Fig. 5. Attacks against memory accesses interception.

Mitigating Evasion of the Memory Accesses Interception. If an attacker knows that we are intercepting memory writes, they could try to use the first step of the address translation mechanism, which is controlled by the VM, to avoid being detected. That technique is called Address Translation Redirection Attack (ATRA) [21]. To that end, they can use two different methods depending on the hook type used by the EDR.

If we use the second stage of the address translation mechanism to protect a given intermediate address (IA in Fig. 5a), a rootkit could copy this memory region somewhere else (at another intermediate address IA') and remap the original virtual address VA onto the new IA', thus evading the monitoring. This is one of the attacks presented by Jang et al. [21]. To detect and mitigate this attack, we enforce read-only permissions on page table entries used to translate each memory area we want to protect. Furthermore, we need to intercept writes to TTBR1_EL1, which contains the address of the first table used in stage one of the address translation process, to ensure that the intruder cannot change it. For that, we modified the TRM bit in the register HCR_EL2.

If watchpoints are used to monitor access to a given virtual address, rootkits can evade them using a variant of ATRA: they can map the same intermediate address to an unprotected virtual address as shown in Fig. 5b. To detect this attack, we use the hardware watchpoint to intercept both reads and writes to an address, and before every access, we compare the current value stored at the given address to a shadow copy stored in the hypervisor (updated after every access). If those two values differ, it means that an attacker used an ATRA-like technique to bypass our detection system.

5.2 Detecting the Execution of an Instruction

To trap the execution at a given address, we replace the targeted instruction with a hypercall, and remove the write permission on this memory region in the second stage of address translation to prevent an attacker from removing the hypercall. When the hypercall instruction is executed, the hypervisor restores the initial instruction, executes it in the VM, and replaces that instruction with the hypercall again.

5.3 Single Stepping Mode

Upon detection of a write or execution event, the hypervisor needs to temporarily remove protection so that exactly one instruction is executed in the VM. To do so, we use the debug extension of ARM processors to trigger software-step exceptions each time an instruction is executed in the VM. The configuration of this mechanism is done through the MDSCR_EL1 (*Monitor Debug System Control Register*), which can, by default, be accessed from kernel mode (EL1). We modify the MDCR_EL2 (*Monitor Debug Configuration Register*) register to prevent the VM from modifying the MDSCR_EL1 register, and so the generated step exceptions are handled in the hypervisor rather than in the OS kernel. Furthermore, we modify the PSTATE (*Processor State*) register to enable the software-step exceptions and disable other kernel mode interrupts. Without this last point, an attacker could trigger an kernel-level exception while the protection is lifted, and bypass our protection.

5.4 Hypervisor Verifications

The HYPERSEC programs that are supposed to protect the VM are sent by the VM itself. Therefore, we take some measures to ensure that these programs do not compromise the hypervisor and effectively protect the VM.

First, we restrict the ability of a VM to send commands to the hypervisor. We suppose the kernel is protected during its first boot, e.g. using Secure Boot. It can thus send its commands during this phase. When there are no more commands to be sent, the VM should send last_command to the hypervisor. Subsequent commands will be ignored by the hypervisor. This aims to prevent attackers who may compromise the VM from sending malicious programs.

The hypervisor verifies a number of properties when loading HYPERSEC programs, to ensure that they do not introduce vulnerabilities. Programs are sent together with annotations: each basic block of each function is annotated with preconditions, giving the type of registers and memory slots (in the stack or any memory area pointed by a register). When the type of a register is integer, additional bound and alignment information may be present. When it is a pointer type, information about the range of the pointed object is also provided.

Then, the hypervisor performs static analysis inside each basic block, to track the type information associated with registers and memory slots. With this analysis, the hypervisor can enforce that memory accesses are always aligned on

8-byte boundaries and within the bounds of the accessed objects. It also ensures that the type of the value read/written matches the type of the address accessed. This ensures that memory accesses are only allowed in the memory of the VM. Pointers themselves cannot be written to/read from memory.

Control flow is restricted to function calls and jumps to beginning of basic blocks inside the current function. Forward jumps are forbidden if they allow to enter a loop from anywhere else than its beginning. Backward jumps must target the beginning of a loop the current basic block is already in and only occurs if the iterator of that loop is decremented and different from zero. Loop iterators can only be modified this way. This ensures the termination of HYPERSEC programs.

Finally, when returning from a function, we ensure that callee-saved registers have been restored (including the stack pointer, the stack base and the link register), and if the function is expected to return a value, that the register x0 contains a value of the correct type.

If any instruction does not comply with the previous rules, the hypervisor rejects the program.

6 Rootkit Detection and Performance Evaluation

This section presents the various methods, using HYPERSEC programs, that we used to detect each rootkit and the overhead incurred by our EDR.

6.1 Detecting Rootkits Using HYPERSEC

RK_{ro} and RK_{vfs}. To detect those rootkits, we must detect writes to addresses that are constant in kernel virtual address space. This therefore does not incur overhead for legitimate usage. To detect attacks on the VFS, we also detect writes on the i_fop field of the inode corresponding to the /proc directory, which contains the address of the corresponding file_operations structure. Unlike the address of the file_operations used by /proc, the address of the corresponding inode is not exported in /proc/kallsyms and can vary between reboots, even when KASLR [9] is disabled. To find it, we use the address of the head of the super_blocks linked list.

RK_{pid}. To detect malicious modifications of pid structures, the hypervisor must maintain a shadow list of running processes. To do so, we first extract the initial running process list by iterating over the radix tree containing all the pid structures. Then, we detect newly created task_struct by hooking on the function on_wake_up_new_task and we detect process destruction by hooking on the do_exit function. The running process list and the addresses of the corresponding pid and task_struct structures are stored in a dedicated map.

The kernel calls proc_root_readdir to list the contents of the /proc directory. Consequently, we only need to verify that pid and task_struct are untampered with when that function is called. For that, at the beginning of the function call, the hypervisor iterates over all those structures to check that they correspond to the data saved earlier. Following this approach, we do not detect the initial tampering when the rootkit hides the process, but we detect it as soon as the kernel calls proc_root_readdir, which gives us better performance than detecting all writes to the task_struct and pid structures.

RK$_{cred}$. To detect changes in cred structures, we need to store a copy of the user and group identifiers of every process. Thus, we adapted the code that detects **RK**$_{pid}$ to store a copy of those identifiers when processes are created. Since some syscalls can legitimately change the credentials of a process (e.g. setuid or execve), we detect when these are called and update the hypervisor's copy of the credentials accordingly.

To detect syscalls, we track the execution of the invoke_syscall function, whose second argument is the syscall code, to compute the new credentials using the arguments of the syscall. To correctly compute the credentials after the execveat syscall, we also need to know the owner and group of the executed file. For that, we add a hook in a specific instruction of the bprm_execve function to get the inode structure representing the binary, which contains the user and group IDs of the file and the setuid and setgid flags.

We could detect the exiting of invoke_syscall by inserting a breakpoint at the address stored in the return address register (x30), but this greatly reduces the performance of our detection system. Instead, we check at the beginning of the next system call if the credentials have changed according to the rules of the last system call that has been made.

Even then, an attacker could modify the process credentials within the window between the hypervisor's initial and subsequent checks. This results in a Time Of Check vs. Time Of Use vulnerability. Indeed, the inode_permission function, which is used to check the process permission for various system calls (e.g., open or faccessat), will see the updated credentials that the hypervisor has not captured.

To protect against those attacks, we ensure that the corresponding fields of the cred and task_struct structure are not changed by the attacker while the kernel is using them. Since making those structures read-only adds a heavy overhead to the VM, we cannot protect them during the entire syscall. Instead, they are made read-only for the shortest time possible, only when the kernel uses them. Furthermore, since we only protect some fields of those structs, we use hardware watchpoints when available to detect writes on those fields. We implemented that protection for the inode_permission function. Before calling this function, we check that the credentials have not been changed, and we make them read-only during the function call.

6.2 Performance Evaluation

One initial metric of interest is the number of lines of code needed to detect each of the previously discussed rootkits. We need only 8 lines of code to detect **RK**$_{ro}$. We need 46 lines of code to detect **RK**$_{vfs}$. The most complex rootkit (**RK**$_{cred}$) requires 524 lines of code for its detection, which we believe remains modest.

Performance results are shown in Tables 1, 2, 3 and 4. The columns contain the execution time of our different benchmarks. The baseline corresponds to launching the VM in the hypervisor without any detection. Each line RK_i corresponds to activating protection against RK_i (Tables 1, 2, 3 and 4).

Table 1. Average overhead on the compilation time of binutils, the Mibench tests, and the time needed for 10 MQTT clients to send 10000 messages when detecting the different attacks.

	binutils	mibench overheads	MQTT
Baseline	147 m 42 s	–	223.2 s
RK_{ro}	148 m 53 s (1%)	0.4%	266.0 s (19.1%)
RK_{vfs}	148 m 16 s (0%)	0.0%	253.2 s (13.4%)
RK_{pid}	149 m 11 s (1%)	0.0%	268.8 s (20.4%)
RK_{cred}	218 m 52 s (48%)	20.4%	535.0 s (39.7%)

Table 2. Phoronix results for NGINX binary (overhead are in parentheses)

	NGINX (requests/s)				
Connexions	1	20	100	200	500
Baseline	300.0	248.5	284.7	205.5	100.6
RK_{ro}	279.3 (7.4%)	217.5 (14.2%)	263.3 (8.1%)	181.6 (13.2%)	94.7 (6.3%)
RK_{vfs}	286.6 (4.7%)	225.0 (10.4%)	262.4 (8.5%)	186.5 (10.2%)	96.7 (4.0%)
RK_{pid}	272.4 (10.1%)	216.6 (14.7%)	258.1 (10.3%)	188.8 (8.9%)	100.7 (−0.1%)
RK_{cred}	173.6 (72.8%)	144.7 (71.8%)	164.6 (72.9%)	120.5 (70.6%)	52.0 (93.6%)

We evaluated the overhead of our rootkit detection programs by compiling binutils [5] (once in each configuration) and using the MiBench [18] automotive, network, telecoms, and security benchmarks (except for the PGP test, which could not be compiled for our architecture) 250 times for each configuration. To evaluate the overheads in an embedded context, we also ran mosquitto MQTT server on the VM and launched 10 clients that sent 10000 messages each.

To emulate realistic uses, we also used some benchmarks from the Phoronix test suite [34]: 7Zip (compression and decompression), NGINX (1, 50, 100, 200 and 500 simultaneous connections), sqlite (with one thread), OPENSSL (RSA4096 sign and verify), and REDIS (get, lpop, sadd, and set with 50 connections).

For all tests except NGINX and MQTT, the overheads induced by the detection of RK_{ro}, RK_{vfs} and RK_{pid} are lower than 2%. For nginx and mqtt, the

Table 3. Phoronix results for OPENSSL, sqlite and 7Zip binaries (overhead are in parentheses).

	OPENSSL RSA4096		sqlite	7Zip (MIPS)	
	sign/s	verify/s	copy (s)	Compression	Decompression
Baseline	16.3	1088.8	128.4	979.0	1259.0
RK_{ro}	16.2 (0.6%)	1087.6 (0.1%)	130.9 (2.0%)	974.0 (0.5%)	1256.0 (0.2%)
RK_{vfs}	16.2 (0.6%)	1088.0 (0.1%)	128.8 (0.4%)	975.0 (0.4%)	1258.0 (0.1%)
RK_{pid}	16.2 (0.6%)	1087.0 (0.2%)	129.6 (1.0%)	974.0 (0.5%)	1256.0 (0.2%)
RK_{cred}	16.2 (0.6%)	1084.0 (0.4%)	183.8 (43.2%)	963.0 (1.7%)	1249.0 (0.8%)

Table 4. Phoronix results for REDIS database (overhead are in parentheses).

	REDIS, 50 simultaneous connexions (requests/s)			
	GET	LPOP	SADD	SET
Baseline	202873.5	205450.5	166348.9	144450.2
RK_{ro}	202334.6 (0.3%)	205716.0 (−0.1%)	166786.5 (−0.3%)	144003.5 (0.3%)
RK_{vfs}	204196.1 (−0.6%)	204408.5 (0.5%)	165393.2 (0.6%)	143335.7 (0.8%)
RK_{pid}	204848.8 (−1.0%)	207348.5 (−0.9%)	165712.3 (0.4%)	144130.8 (0.2%)
RK_{cred}	190246.5 (6.6%)	194639.0 (5.6%)	154435.9 (7.7%)	135891.3 (6.3%)

overheads can be up to 20.4% for those rootkits. We hypothesize that these services frequently interact with the kernel, and since the kernel code is now mapped in small pages instead of mega-pages, they induce more TLB cache misses.

The overhead incurred by the detection of RK_{cred} is 20.4% on average for the MiBench benchmark and 48% for the compilation of binutils. As expected, the benchmarks that frequently interact with the kernel exhibit a significant overhead (the most extreme cases are MQTT with an overhead of 39.7% and NGINX with an overhead of 93.6%). At the same time, those that mainly perform calculations are less affected (OPENSSL and 7zip have an overhead between 0.4% and 1.7%). Indeed, every system call, and especially those that interact with inodes and process credentials, involves permission checks. This overhead keeps the system usable for typical workloads and is acceptable for most security-critical applications.

7 Related Work

Various methods have been suggested for bridging the semantic gap. Garfinkel et al. [17] proposed developing a library for a specific version of the operating system that retrieves data from the VM memory. This approach is highly accurate but not very versatile, as the library needs to be rewritten for each new version of the operating system. Xiao et al. [45] use heuristics to increase versatility and work on multiple operating systems. However, they can only retrieve partial data, such as the names and process IDs of the running processes. Zhao et al. [16] propose a solution to reuse user-space programs as VM introspection tools, but their solution is vulnerable to direct kernel object manipulation from an attacker. Dolan-Gavit et al. [13] use a training phase to teach the intrusion detection system how to retrieve data. If the training process is incomplete, the VMI tool may fail to extract data from the VM memory. Westphal et al. [43] developed a domain-specific language that allows users to specify probes that are triggered on specific events inside a guest OS. However, their language can only describe a subset of data structures inside the Linux kernel. Adding new data structures would be possible, although this requires modifying the framework itself. On the contrary, our language is sufficiently expressive to handle any data structure used by a kernel (we are currently porting our approach to FreeBSD).

For our EDR to be compatible with multiple operating systems, we could use a paravirtualization technique [44] by modifying the VM to communicate with the hypervisor and provide information about its state. This would allow the VM to delegate certain security checks to the hypervisor [29] and send information to the hypervisor whenever specific events occur within the VM [32]. While this approach can help to protect the VM and provide detailed information to the hypervisor, it requires modifying the guest kernel code to enable communication between the VM and the hypervisor. Additionally, it could reduce the resilience of the EDR since an attacker could prevent the VM from communicating with the hypervisor.

An approach closely related to ours was proposed by Wei and Amit [42], but it has not been designed primarily for security purposes. Their equivalent of our programs can be sent at any time by the VM. This could allow a privileged attacker to turn off the security monitoring by sending malicious programs to the hypervisor. Additionally, they rely on hyperupcalls to react to events occurring in the hypervisor (such as memory reclaim or virtual processor preemption), whereas our solution detects events happening within a VM. Bitdefender [6] proposes a similar approach for x86. However, the semantic gap problem is not solved by the protected VM but is hardcoded in the introspection library, which is not flexible.

The detection of rootkits infecting OS kernels has been extensively studied in the literature. However, as highlighted by the recent study by Stühn et al. [39], the effective detection of these malware remains an open problem that requires specialized tools. In particular, few tools are available to detect rootkits on Linux, and their detection capabilities are limited. According to the authors, the most effective approach relies on memory snapshot analysis. However, while this method is relevant for post-mortem analysis, it is not robust against evasion when used for intrusion detection. Indeed, an attacker can erase their traces before the memory snapshot is taken. The approach we propose is event-based and does not suffer from this limitation.

Traditional signature-based detection methods are not resilient to evasion techniques and cannot detect new rootkits. Anomaly detection approaches appear more promising. Pham et al. propose analyzing side channels [33], but this method requires external hardware to measure electromagnetic emissions. Landauer et al. suggest analyzing the execution time of kernel functions [22]. However, observing these execution times relies on probes located within the OS kernel, which can be compromised by an attacker. In the evaluation of our approach, we developed monitoring programs to monitor the integrity of invariants on mutable kernel data. Baliga et al. emphasised the importance of monitoring such invariants for kernel rootkit detection, but their approach requires an external hardware device for the monitoring [4].

8 Limitations and Future Work

Reboots. First of all, detecting VM reboot is trivial within the hypervisor. We could easily add a new event to the language, so that programs can take into account VM reboot. They could for example, reset their internal state (maps) to reflect the fact that the VM has been restarted. A last problem is to retrieve the loading address of the kernel that can be randomized if KASLR [9] is enabled. We could hook into the `map_kernel` function that remap the kernel at random address to discover it dynamically and rebase all addresses accordingly.

Kernel Updates. Since kernel updates force the virtual machine to reboot, we propose to take advantage of this reboot to leverage on the possibility offered by (most) firmware to programmatically change the boot options of the next reboot so that the VM is not restarted immediately, but rather an isolated (and hence safe) *update* VM is started instead. This *update* VM will be minimalist to reduce its attack surface, and its unique goal will be to load the latest version of the HYPERSEC programs that correspond to the upgraded kernel. Finally, the *update* VM ends the whole process by rebooting and transferring control back to the upgraded VM.

Attack Mitigation. We are currently only *detecting* rootkits, but we could also mitigate some of them: attacks that only modify constant data like $\mathbf{RK}_{ro}$ and $\mathbf{RK}_{vfs}$ can be easily mitigated by discarding the incriminated memory writes. Rootkits that tamper with dynamic data ($\mathbf{RK}_{pid}$ and $\mathbf{RK}_{cred}$) are harder to mitigate since they can change existing data structures but they could also move those resources and update the references pointing to them. This makes it harder for the hypervisor to restore them without writing in incorrect places of the VM memory.

9 Conclusion

This paper presents HYPERSEC, a dedicated language for adaptive rootkit detection in virtual machines. HYPERSEC enables virtual machines to autonomously generate detection programs tailored to their specific configurations, enhancing adaptability and security. Our prototype was implemented on a ZCU104 platform featuring an ARM Cortex-A53 processor, selected to meet constraints from an ongoing research project[1] requirements. Despite this platform's modest virtualization performance compared to high-end Intel Xeon-based systems, our evaluation demonstrates the feasibility and potential of HYPERSEC for dynamic rootkit detection. All artifacts, including our XVisor extension, the rootkits we developed, and the detection scripts, are publicly available[2].

Acknowledgments. The work presented in this paper was realized in the frame of the TrustGW project number "ANR-21-CE39-0005", supported by a grant of the French National Research Agency (ANR) and by the "France 2030" government investment plan managed by the French National Research Agency, under the reference "ANR-22-PECY-0005".

Disclosure of Interests. The authors have no competing interests to declare that are relevant to the content of this article.

References

1. Linux rootkit adapted for 2.6 and 3.x (2024). https://github.com/yaoyumeng/adore-ng
2. Armv8-a architecture registers (2024). https://developer.arm.com/documentation/ddi0595/2020-12/AArch64-Registers/HFGITR-EL2--Hypervisor-Fine-Grained-Instruction-Trap-Register
3. Introduction to Large System Extensions (2024). https://learn.arm.com/learning-paths/servers-and-cloud-computing/lse/intro/
4. Baliga, A., Ganapathy, V., Iftode, L.: Detecting kernel-level rootkits using data structure invariants. IEEE Trans. Dependable Secur. Comput. 8(5), 670–684 (2011). https://doi.org/10.1109/TDSC.2010.38
5. Source code (2024). https://www.gnu.org/software/binutils/
6. Hypervisor memory introspection - specification (2023). https://hvmi.readthedocs.io/en/latest/index.html
7. Bpf type format (btf) — the linux kernel documentation (2024). https://docs.kernel.org/bpf/btf.html
8. Buzcti, J.: R3tr074/brokepkg: The lkm rootkit working in linux kernels 2.6.x/3.x/4.x/5.x (2024). https://github.com/R3tr074/brokepkg
9. Canella, C., Schwarz, M., Haubenwallner, M., Schwarzl, M., Gruss, D.: Kaslr: break it, fix it, repeat. In: Proceedings of the 15th ACM Asia Conference on Computer and Communications Security, pp. 481–493. ACM, New York, NY, USA (2020). https://doi.org/10.1145/3320269.3384747
10. Cilium: BPF and XDP Reference Guide (2022)
11. Cota, E.G., Bonzini, P., Bennée, A., Carloni, L.P.: Cross-isa machine emulation for multicores. In: 2017 IEEE/ACM International Symposium on Code Generation and Optimization (CGO), pp. 210–220. IEEE, Washington, D.C., USA (2017). https://doi.org/10.1109/CGO.2017.7863741

---

[1] https://trustgw.projects.labsticc.fr/.
[2] https://gitlab.inria.fr/SUSHI-public/hypersec.

12. Vulnerability details (2024). https://www.cvedetails.com/cve/CVE-2023-2163/
13. Dolan-Gavitt, B., Leek, T., Zhivich, M., Giffin, J., Lee, W.: Virtuoso: narrowing the semantic gap in virtual machine introspection. In: IEEE Symposium on Security and Privacy, pp. 297–312. IEEE, Washington, D.C., USA (2011). https://doi.org/10.1109/SP.2011.11
14. Exclusive monitors (2024). https://dynamorio.org/page_ldstex.html
15. Eitani, A.: Detecting drovorub's file operations hooking with tracee (2022). https://www.aquasec.com/blog/detect-drovorub-kernel-rootkit-attack-tracee/
16. Fu, Y., Lin, Z.: Space traveling across vm: automatically bridging the semantic gap in virtual machine introspection via online kernel data redirection. In: IEEE Symposium on Security and Privacy, pp. 586–600. IEEE, Washington, D.C., USA (2012). https://doi.org/10.1109/SP.2012.40
17. Garfinkel, T., Rosenblum, M.: A virtual machine introspection based architecture for intrusion detection. In: Proceedings of the Network and Distributed System Security Symposium, San Diego, California, USA, pp. 191–206. The Internet Society, 11710 Plaza America Drive, Suite 400, Reston, VA 20190, USA (2003)
18. Guthaus, M., Ringenberg, J., Ernst, D., Austin, T., Mudge, T., Brown, R.: Mibench: a free, commercially representative embedded benchmark suite. In: Proceedings of the Fourth Annual IEEE International Workshop on Workload Characterization, pp. 3–14. IEEE, Washington, D.C., USA (2001). https://doi.org/10.1109/WWC.2001.990739
19. Hunt, G.C., Larus, J.R.: Singularity: rethinking the software stack. ACM SIGOPS Oper. Syst. Rev. **41**(2), 37–49 (2007). https://doi.org/10.1145/1243418.1243424
20. Jain, B., Baig, M.B., Zhang, D., Porter, D.E., Sion, R.: Sok: introspections on trust and the semantic gap. In: 2014 IEEE Symposium on Security and Privacy, SP 2014, Berkeley, CA, USA, 18–21 May 2014, pp. 605–620. IEEE Computer Society, Washington, D.C., USA (2014). https://doi.org/10.1109/SP.2014.45
21. Jang, D., Lee, H., Kim, M., Kim, D., Kim, D., Kang, B.B.: Atra: address translation redirection attack against hardware-based external monitors. In: Proceedings of the 2014 ACM SIGSAC Conference on Computer and Communications Security, pp. 167–178. ACM, New York, NY, USA (2014). https://doi.org/10.1145/2660267.2660303
22. Landauer, M., Alton, L., Lindorfer, M., Skopik, F., Wurzenberger, M., Hotwagner, W.: Trace of the times: rootkit detection through temporal anomalies in kernel activity (2025). https://arxiv.org/abs/2503.02402
23. Lauterbach GmbH: Trace32: ARMv8-A/-R Debugger (2024). support for exclusive monitor, page 157
24. Lee, H., et al.: Ki-mon arm: a hardware-assisted event-triggered monitoring platform for mutable kernel object. IEEE Trans. Dependable Secure Comput. **16**(2), 287–300 (2017). https://doi.org/10.1109/TDSC.2017.2679710
25. Linux on-the-fly kernel patching without lkm (2001). http://phrack.org/issues/58/7.html
26. lockdep.h (2022). https://elixir.bootlin.com/linux/v5.15.36/source/include/linux/lockdep.h#L535
27. Matveychikov, I.V.: Kopycat - linux kernel module-less implant (backdoor) (2021). https://github.com/milabs/kopycat
28. Mello, V.R.: Diamorphine: lkm rootkit for linux kernels 2.6.x/3.x/4.x/5.x/6.x (x86/x86_64 and arm64) (2024). https://github.com/m0nad/Diamorphine
29. Morris, J., Salaün, M., Gopinath, T.: Linux virtualization based security (lvbs) (2023). https://lpc.events/event/17/contributions/1515/

30. Necula, G.C., Lee, P.: Safe kernel extensions without run-time checking. SIGOPS Oper. Syst. Rev. **30**(SI), 229–243 (1996). https://doi.org/10.1145/238721.238781
31. Patel, A., Daftedar, M., Shalan, M., El-Kharashi, M.W.: Embedded hypervisor xvisor: a comparative analysis. In: 2015 23rd Euromicro International Conference on Parallel, Distributed, and Network-Based Processing, pp. 682–691. IEEE, Washington, D.C., USA (2015). https://doi.org/10.1109/PDP.2015.108
32. Payne, B.D., Carbone, M., Sharif, M., Lee, W.: Lares: an architecture for secure active monitoring using virtualization. In: IEEE Symposium on Security and Privacy, pp. 233–247. IEEE, Washington, D.C., USA (2008). https://doi.org/10.1109/SP.2008.24
33. Pham, D.P., Marion, D., Heuser, A.: Ultra: ultimate rootkit detection over the air. In: Proceedings of the 25th International Symposium on Research in Attacks, Intrusions and Defenses, pp. 232–251. ACM, New York, NY, USA (2022). https://doi.org/10.1145/3545948.3545962
34. phoronix test suite (2019). https://www.phoronix-test-suite.com/
35. Ruan, X.: Boot with integrity, or don't boot. In: Platform Embedded Security Technology Revealed: Safeguarding the Future of Computing with Intel Embedded Security and Management Engine, chap. 6, pp. 143–163. Apress (2014). https://doi.org/10.1007/978-1-4302-6572-6_6
36. Rutkowska, J.: Introducing stealth malware taxonomy (2006)
37. Samsung: Real-time kernel protection (2024). https://docs.samsungknox.com/admin/fundamentals/whitepaper/core-platform-security/real-time-kernel-protection/
38. Linux rootkits part 3: A backdoor to root (2020). https://xcellerator.github.io/posts/linux_rootkits_03/
39. Stühn, J., Hilgert, J.N., Lambertz, M.: The hidden threat: analysis of linux rootkit techniques and limitations of current detection tools. Digital Threats **5**(3) (2024). https://doi.org/10.1145/3688808
40. UEFI Forum: Unified Extensible Firmware Interface Specification (2019). https://uefi.org/sites/default/files/resources/UEFI_Spec_2_8_final.pdf, version 2.8
41. Wavestone Cybersecurity and Digital Trust practice: EDRSandBlast (2022). https://github.com/wavestone-cdt/EDRSandblast
42. Wei, M., Amit, N.: Leveraging hyperupcalls to bridge the semantic gap: an application perspective. IEEE Data Eng. Bull. **42**(1), 22–35 (2019)
43. Westphal, F., Axelsson, S., Neuhaus, C., Polze, A.: Vmi-pl: a monitoring language for virtual platforms using virtual machine introspection. Digit. Investig. **11**, S85–S94 (2014). https://doi.org/10.1016/j.diin.2014.05.016, fourteenth Annual DFRWS Conference
44. Whitaker, A., Shaw, M., Gribble, S.D., et al.: Denali: lightweight virtual machines for distributed and networked applications. Technical report, University of Washington (2002)
45. Xiao, J., Lu, L., Wang, H., Zhu, X.: Hyperlink: virtual machine introspection and memory forensic analysis without kernel source code. In: International Conference on Autonomic Computing, pp. 127–136. IEEE, Washington, D.C., USA (2016). https://doi.org/10.1109/ICAC.2016.46
46. Xvisor hypervisor (2024). https://github.com/xvisor/xvisor
47. Zhao, S., Ding, X., Xu, W., Gu, D.: Seeing through the same lens: introspecting guest address space at native speed. In: 26th USENIX Security Symposium (USENIX Security 17), pp. 799–813. USENIX Association, Vancouver, BC (2017)

BOOTMARKER: UEFI Bootkit Defense via Control-Flow Verification

Jihoon Kwon[1], Junho Lee[2], MyeongYeol Lee[3], HyunA Seo[4], and Jinho Jung[5]([✉])

[1] Korea University, Seoul, South Korea
jimmyxyz@korea.ac.kr
[2] Mokpo National University, Muan, South Korea
b1ack3at.sec@gmail.com
[3] Chosun University, Gwangju, South Korea
dking11@chosun.kr
[4] Sungshin Women's University, Seoul, South Korea
20221102@sungshin.ac.kr
[5] Ministry of National Defense, Seoul, South Korea
jinho.jung@korea.kr

Abstract. Bootkits threaten the very foundation of system security. By exploiting vulnerabilities in firmware and bootloaders, these attacks gain persistent, stealthy control at the earliest stages of boot. Despite widespread adoption of UEFI Secure Boot and TPM-based measurements, limited visibility and complexity during early boot allow bootkits to evade detection. Ongoing discovery of critical firmware flaws enables privilege escalation and circumvention of core protections. Existing static verification methods cannot detect runtime modifications during early boot, highlighting the need for runtime-aware integrity monitoring. In this paper, we present BOOTMARKER, a runtime integrity monitoring framework built on a dual-layered architecture that combines Driver Execution Environment (DXE) and System Management Mode (SMM) instrumentation. BOOTMARKER dynamically enforces control-flow integrity in the bootloader and performs cryptographic validation of firmware components in real time. It detects and mitigates bootkit attacks as they occur during early execution. Our evaluation shows that BOOTMARKER reliably identifies diverse bootkit behaviors while imposing minimal performance overhead, making it practical for real-world deployment and significantly enhancing boot-time security.

1 Introduction

Bootkits undermine the foundation of modern system security. These stealthy malware variants target the earliest stages of the boot process, a critical vector often overlooked by conventional defenses. By operating beneath the operating system, bootkits can persist undetected, evade OS-level protections, and

---

J. Kwon and J. Lee—These authors contributed equally to this work.

compromise system integrity [62]. Despite the widespread adoption of Unified Extensible Firmware Interface (UEFI) Secure Boot [36,49] and Trusted Platform Module (TPM) based measurement frameworks [12], attackers continue to exploit vulnerabilities in firmware and bootloaders. Critical UEFI flaws are still discovered regularly [4,41,44,51], enabling privilege escalation, security bypass, and the erosion of hardware root-of-trust guarantees.

Researching and mitigating bootkit threats presents substantial technical and practical challenges. A key barrier is the limited availability of representative bootkit samples, which restricts thorough behavioral analysis and hinders the development of robust detection techniques. Additionally, the inherent complexity of firmware architectures makes monitoring difficult, particularly during early boot phases when system visibility is highly constrained. Conventional defenses rely heavily on static verification methods, which are insufficient for detecting runtime modifications that occur during the transition from firmware execution to OS initialization.

The technical complexity and low visibility of early-stage boot processes have historically diverted research focus toward more visible threats, such as ransomware and application-level malware. This gap has persisted, leaving few practical defenses capable of addressing advanced boot-time threats effectively. Existing academic and industrial solutions remain insufficiently robust against evolving bootkit techniques, which increasingly rely on subtle modifications and novel methods to bypass static, signature-based detection.

To address this critical security gap, we introduce BOOTMARKER, a runtime integrity monitoring framework based on a dual-component architecture. First, DXE-MON dynamically instruments key bootloader components, including the Windows Boot Manager and the Linux shim bootloader, to monitor and validate control-flow integrity during the transition from firmware to OS execution. This enables immediate detection and mitigation of runtime control-flow tampering attempts. Second, SMM-MON operates within System Management Mode (SMM) [47], providing a secure and isolated execution environment. It performs cryptographic validation of executables and essential configuration data, verifying the integrity of both DXE-MON operations and UEFI services at runtime. This dual-layer design significantly enhances detection capability against sophisticated attacks that could evade single-layer defenses.

Our evaluation of BOOTMARKER demonstrates its effectiveness in reliably identifying and mitigating diverse bootkit threats. The results show that our approach introduces negligible performance overhead during system boot, confirming its practicality for real-world deployment. These findings validate runtime integrity monitoring as a viable and critical component of boot-time security, capable of addressing threats that traditional methods fail to detect.

Our Contributions. Our primary contributions are summarized as follows:

1. **Bootkit Threat Analysis.** We analyze the core challenges in detecting and mitigating advanced bootkit attacks targeting firmware and early boot components.

2. **System Architecture.** We present BOOTMARKER, a runtime integrity monitoring framework that leverages coordinated DXE and SMM instrumentation to enhance detection during early boot stages.
3. **Dynamic Integrity Monitoring.** We introduce techniques for dynamic instrumentation and runtime verification, enabling continuous monitoring of critical boot components with minimal performance impact.
4. **Open Source for Future Research.** We will release BOOTMARKER as open source to support future research and promote collaboration within the security community.

2 Background

2.1 System Firmware Boot Process

System firmware initializes hardware and launches the operating system. Legacy Basic Input/Output System (BIOS) performs this role using the Power-On Self-Test (POST) and loads the bootloader from the Master Boot Record (MBR) [1]. However, BIOS operates in 16-bit real mode, which limits scalability and security. To address these limitations, UEFI replaces BIOS [7]. UEFI supports execution in 32-bit or higher address spaces and introduces a structured boot process. The process consists of SEC [59], PEI [58], DXE [57], and BDS [56] phases, which perform complete hardware initialization with modular architecture and flexible memory management [7,44] (Fig 1).

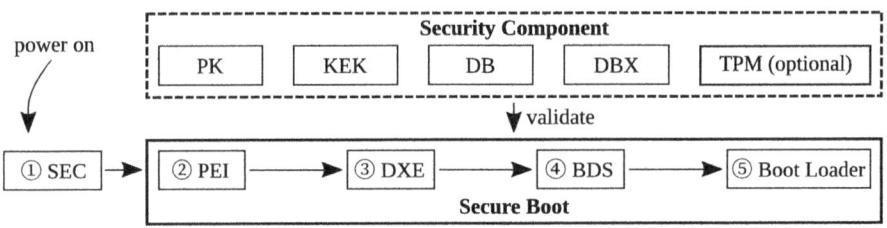

Fig. 1. Operating System Boot Process

UEFI Boot Process. The UEFI boot process consists of several sequential phases, each associated with different components, as illustrated in Figure 1. UEFI firmware begins booting in accordance with the Platform Initialization (PI) [60] specification, starting with the Security (SEC, ①) phase, which sets up temporary memory and establishes the root of trust.

The Pre-EFI Initialization (PEI, ②) phase follows, where the CPU cache acts as temporary memory until DRAM is initialized. Once memory is available, key hardware components are brought online. The Driver Execution Environment (DXE, ③) phase then loads drivers for the processor, chipset, and platform devices. During this phase, System Management Mode (SMM) is also initialized to handle power, thermal, and security events. Finally, the Boot Device Selection (BDS, ④) phase connects to boot devices and prepares for OS handoff. The UEFI boot process concludes when the OS loader calls the ExitBootServices function, which terminates UEFI boot services and transfers control to the operating system [53]. After this transition, most UEFI services become unavailable, and the system enters the runtime environment where only essential runtime services remain active.

UEFI supports integration with TPM [34] to enable comprehensive platform security [37]. The TPM provides measured boot capabilities by logging firmware measurements to Platform Configuration Registers (PCRs) to establish a hardware root of trust, while UEFI's built-in Secure Boot mechanism complements this by verifying digital signatures of boot components to prevent unauthorized code execution [15].

System Management Mode. SMM is a highly privileged execution mode in x86 processors that provides an isolated environment for handling system-wide functions independent of the operating system. Originally introduced by Intel for power management, SMM has evolved to address thermal control, hardware error handling, and security-critical operations. Operating at ring -2 privilege level, SMM code executes from a protected memory region called SMRAM [10], which becomes inaccessible to other system software during normal operation. Entry into SMM occurs when the processor receives a System Management Interrupt (SMI) [22], which suspends all other system activity until SMM code execution completes [9]. While SMM's elevated privileges make it valuable for implementing security features, they also create an attractive target for sophisticated attackers [61]. Modern systems implement protections such as System Management Range Registers (SMRR) [8] to prevent unauthorized access to SMRAM.

Secure Boot. To protect the early boot process from tampering, modern systems use Secure Boot to verify the integrity of each component through cryptographic signatures. During the UEFI boot sequence, the firmware checks the bootloader's signature against a hierarchical key management system. The Platform Key (PK) serves as the root of trust, while Key Exchange Keys (KEK) manage the signature databases. The signature database (DB) [26] contains trusted certificates and hashes, while the forbidden signature database (DBX) [26] holds revoked entries. This multi-layered key hierarchy ensures that only authorized entities can modify the trust relationships within the Secure Boot ecosystem. Boot continues only if validation succeeds. On Windows systems, UEFI verifies the Microsoft-signed Windows Boot Manager, which in turn verifies the kernel and subsequent drivers. For Linux, UEFI typically validates a Microsoft-signed Shim [46] bootloader, which then verifies GRand Unified Bootloader (GRUB) [13] or other loaders, followed by the Linux kernel. This layered verification chain defends against low-level threats such as bootkits and rootkits, ensuring that only trusted code runs before the operating system takes control.

UEFI Services. UEFI firmware provides three primary service tables that expose critical system functionality [39] to bootloaders and applications:

1. **Boot Services:** Boot Services are available during the pre-boot environment and include essential functions such as LoadImage() for loading executable images, StartImage() for transferring control to loaded images, SetTimer() for event scheduling, and memory management services. These services are fundamental to the boot process but become unavailable once ExitBootServices() is called.
2. **Runtime Services:** Runtime Services persist after OS handoff and provide ongoing firmware functionality including variable storage, time services, and system reset capabilities.
3. **DXE Services:** DXE Services are available during the Driver Execution Environment phase and offer platform-specific functionality for driver initialization and hardware configuration.

Since these service tables contain function pointers that control critical system operations, they represent high-value targets for bootkit attacks seeking to intercept or redirect system calls during the boot process.

2.2 Windows Boot Process

The Windows boot process consists of three primary stages: the Boot Manager, the OS Loader, and the NT Kernel. Each stage plays a critical role in establishing a trusted execution environment and enforcing integrity checks to defend against low-level threats such as bootkits.

Windows Boot Manager. The Windows Boot Manager, as bootmgfw.efi, selects the target operating system and prepares the environment for handoff. The Boot Manager is verified by UEFI Secure Boot before execution, and its measurements are recorded in the TPM to support measured boot. These mechanisms detect tampering and can restrict access to cryptographic material (*e.g.*, BitLocker keys [28]) if early boot integrity is compromised.

Windows OS Loader. winload.efi loads critical components into memory, including ntoskrnl.exe, hal.dll (hardware abstraction layer), and essential boot-time drivers. This phase enforces code signing policies [29] and includes protections such as Early Launch Anti-Malware (ELAM) [31] and Hypervisor Code Integrity (HVCI) [30]. If integrity checks fail, the system halts to prevent unauthorized code execution.

Windows NT OS Kernel. Once ntoskrnl.exe takes control, the system initializes core kernel structures, hardware interfaces, and system services. Security mechanisms such as Kernel Patch Protection (PatchGuard) [25] and Virtualization-Based Security (VBS) [27] ensure only verified code executes in kernel mode, defending against malware that attempt persistence during kernel initialization.

2.3 Linux Boot Process

The Linux boot process consists of four main stages: `Shim`, `GRUB`, the `Kernel`, and the `Init System`. Each stage securely transitions the system from firmware to user space with layered integrity verification and threat prevention mechanisms.

Shim Loader. Shim is a lightweight bootloader signed by Microsoft that enables Linux execution in UEFI Secure Boot environments. It establishes a chain of trust by verifying digital signatures of subsequent components like GRUB or the kernel. Shim integrates with the Machine Owner Key (MOK) [48] framework, allowing users to enroll custom keys for self-signed binaries while maintaining signature enforcement.

GRUB Bootloader. GRUB locates the installed OS, loads the initramfs, and transfers control to the Linux kernel. In Secure Boot setups, GRUB must be signed and verified by Shim. GRUB can enforce security policies through configuration files that restrict kernel parameters and disable insecure modes or debugging interfaces.

Linux Kernel Initialization. The kernel mounts the root filesystem and starts the first user-space process. It uses initramfs as a temporary root containing essential drivers and tools. Security features include mandatory module signature checks and lockdown modes [20] that disable debugging interfaces, limiting bootkit persistence mechanisms.

Init and Systemd. The init system (typically `systemd`) runs as PID 1 and manages user-space services and daemons. Systemd provides security mechanisms including service sandboxing, namespace isolation, and integration with Linux Security Modules such as SELinux [40] and AppArmor [2].

2.4 Bootkit Mechanism

Bootkits aim to disable or bypass kernel-integrity defenses before these mechanisms activate. Driver-signing policies and runtime protections, such as Windows PatchGuard and Samsung Knox RKP [38], prevent unsigned code from executing. To evade these checks, attackers increasingly target the pre-OS boot chain, where such defenses are not yet operational.

Legacy BIOS permitted disk-level tampering with the MBR and associated startup code [14]. UEFI Secure Boot improved code integrity through cryptographic verification. However, campaigns like LoJax exploit firmware vulnerabilities to undermine this trust model [11]. Once compromised, attackers hook UEFI services or execute malicious EFI applications. Early-stage bootkits such as MoonBounce [23] and CosmicStrand [16] inject malicious DXE drivers. Later-stage variants, including ESPecter [24] and BlackLotus [42], overwrite ESP boot files to execute payloads after the OS hand-off.

2.5 Related Work

Firmware-Level Threat Landscape. The bootkit threat landscape has evolved significantly from early BIOS-targeting malware that compromised Master Boot Records [17,43] to sophisticated UEFI-based attacks. Modern UEFI bootkits exploit firmware vulnerabilities and boot component weaknesses [3,62], with notable examples including LoJax—the first UEFI rootkit discovered in the wild—and BlackLotus, which demonstrates advanced Secure Boot bypass techniques.

Current detection approaches usually rely on offline analysis. BootStomp employs symbolic execution for vulnerability discovery in bootloader binaries [35], while BootKeeper focuses on configuration policy validation [6]. These methods excel at identifying potential weaknesses but lack the capability to monitor actual runtime behavior during boot execution.

Leveraging SMM for Security Enforcement. System Management Mode represents a privileged execution context isolated from the main processor operations. While SMI handler vulnerabilities have been documented as attack vectors for privilege escalation [61], and malicious SMM code can enable persistent rootkit installation [45], the isolation characteristics of SMM also present unique defensive opportunities.

Security researchers have explored SMM's protective potential through projects like BIOS Chronomancy, which performs periodic firmware integrity verification [5]. BootMarker extends this concept by establishing a cooperative monitoring relationship between DXE-phase instrumentation and SMM-based verification, enabling continuous integrity assessment throughout the boot process.

UEFI Security Mechanisms and Limitations. UEFI implements various security features including Secure Boot, SMM isolation, and SMRAM protection [18]. Detection tools like Chipsec [21] and UEFITool provide firmware analysis capabilities. However, these mechanisms primarily focus on preventing unauthorized code execution rather than detecting runtime tampering.

Memory forensics frameworks have been developed to detect function-pointer hooks and rogue UEFI modules [39], but operate post-compromise. BootMarker fills this gap by providing real-time detection during the critical firmware-to-OS transition, combining the benefits of static verification with dynamic runtime monitoring.

3 BootMarker Overview

In this section, we present BootMarker, a system for monitoring control-flow integrity during the UEFI boot process. BootMarker consists of two components: DXE-Mon (monitoring boot sequence during DXE execution) and SMM-Mon (protecting DXE-Mon from tampering in SMM). We implement

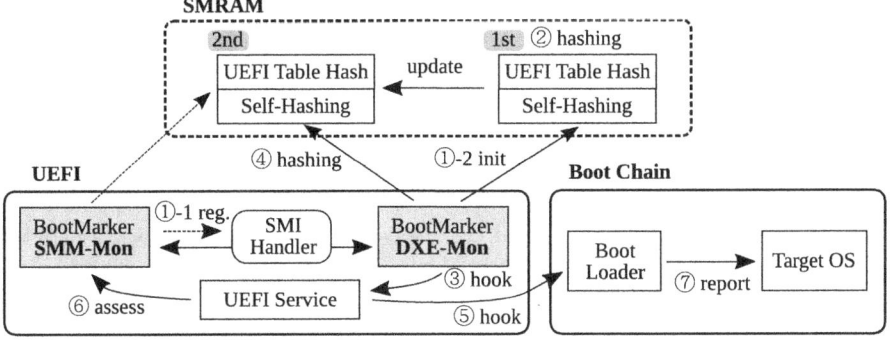

Fig. 2. BOOTMARKER Architecture and Runtime Workflow

BOOTMARKER in dual modes: as DXE/SMM drivers for virtual environments and as UEFI shell applications for physical hardware deployment, enabling evaluation across both virtual and physical platforms.

BOOTMARKER Deployment. BOOTMARKER deployment prioritizes early activation to maximize bootkit detection coverage. According to the UEFI Platform Initialization Specification [50], both SMM-MON and DXE-MON are configured with minimal dependencies, enabling them to load as soon as UEFI services become available [52]. Figure 2 illustrates the deployment process. SMM-MON initializes first, registering SMI handlers for secure communication (①-1), followed by DXE-MON loading to establish the complete monitoring framework (①-2). Early activation is critical for detecting bootkits during DXE or BDS phases, as BOOTMARKER must be operational before third-party drivers execute. Our threat model assumes SMM is the root of trust, remaining inaccessible to attackers.

Operational Workflow. During the boot process, BOOTMARKER verifies the integrity of the platform. First, BOOTMARKER computes hashes of critical UEFI tables and its own internal state. These hashes are generated twice: once during DXE initialization (②), and again at timed intervals later in the boot sequence (④). Second, DXE-MON monitors UEFI service routines and detects unauthorized control-flow caused by inline hooks (③). Third, DXE-MON intercepts bootloader execution to detect additional unauthorized control transfers (⑤). Then, SMM-MON evaluates boot integrity by verifying hash values within SMRAM (⑥). Finally, the bootloader writes a report to the target OS (⑦).

Threat Model. We consider a remote attacker who can install a bootkit by exploiting vulnerabilities in signed components, thereby bypassing UEFI Secure Boot [42]. Our assumptions are as follows. First, the monitoring components (DXE-MON and SMM-MON) load before any untrusted code thanks to early firmware integration. Second, SMM remains an isolated root of trust and is unreachable by the attacker. Third, BootMarker operates without prior knowledge of specific bootkit signatures, allowing it to detect both known and unknown variants. We evaluate BootMarker on Windows 24H2 and Ubuntu 24.04, and discuss possible evasion strategies in Section 7.

4 DXE-MON: Bootloader Integrity in DXE

DXE-MON is a UEFI driver that operates during the DXE phase to monitor bootloader integrity using cryptographic hashing and control-flow instrumentation. It generates hashes of critical code sections, instruments execution paths to detect anomalous behavior, and collaborates with SMM-MON to ensure comprehensive boot-time security.

[1] **Lifecycle Initialization and Baseline Establishment.** During initialization, DXE-MON hooks key UEFI services including LoadImage(), StartImage(), and ExitBootServices() to support continuous monitoring. It computes an initial SHA-256 hash of its own memory image and transmits this hash and an initial monotonic counter to SMM-MON to establish a secure baseline. In parallel, DXE-MON enumerates relevant UEFI services from Boot Services, Runtime Services, and DXE Services. It extracts their .text sections, computes a consolidated SHA-256 hash, and sends this hash and the corresponding pointer structure to SMM-MON. These baselines are essential for runtime integrity validation.

[2] **Continuous Integrity Monitoring.** DXE-MON performs integrity monitoring using both periodic self-checks and event-driven re-validations. For periodic monitoring, it registers a timer event using CreateEvent() and SetTimer(). At configured intervals, it recomputes its memory-image hash, increments the monotonic counter, and sends the updated hash-counter pair to SMM-MON. We set the timer interval to one second, balancing the performance-security tradeoff: shorter intervals increase boot-time overhead, while longer intervals may give attackers sufficient time to complete hook/unhook operations before detection. Event-driven checks occur on critical service events, specifically LoadImage() and StartImage(). Upon these events, DXE-MON re-scans the UEFI service tables, extracts updated .text sections, and computes a new SHA-256 hash. It transmits this hash and the current pointer structure to SMM-MON. This dual-layer validation using hash-based and pointer-level checks detects both code tampering and pointer redirection.

[3] **Bootloader Control-Flow Instrumentation.** To enforce control-flow integrity, DXE-MON instruments bootloader execution paths. It analyzes the bootloader's PE header to determine its type and select an appropriate instrumentation strategy. DXE-MON identifies control-transfer instructions, such as branches, calls, and returns, and replaces them with trap instructions like UD2 or INT1. Original opcodes are preserved for restoration at runtime. A custom exception handler, registered via the CPU Architecture Protocol, monitors triggered traps. Each control-transfer destination is validated against predefined trusted memory regions, including bootloader code, UEFI services, and protocol interfaces. Transfers to trusted regions proceed normally. Unauthorized control-flow transfers are logged with metadata for analysis.

4 Reporting and Monitoring Termination. At the OS handoff stage, DXE-MON uses its hooked `ExitBootServices()` to send a monitoring termination packet to SMM-MON. This packet signals the end of DXE-phase monitoring. DXE-MON then halts its instrumentation duties and delegates final log aggregation to SMM-MON. This handoff ensures a seamless transition from runtime monitoring to integrity attestation.

5 SMM-MON: SMM-Based Runtime Verification

SMM-MON operates in System Management Mode (SMM) and registers a custom System Management Interrupt (SMI) handler during initialization. This handler enables runtime integrity verification by processing integrity requests from DXE-MON. Upon receiving a request, SMM-MON compares the integrity data against baseline values securely stored in SMRAM. This design enables timely detection and response to boot-time anomalies.

1 Baseline Establishment. During boot initialization, SMM-MON establishes secure reference baselines that are essential for all subsequent integrity checks. It first waits to receive the memory-image hash from DXE-MON (see Figure 2 for component interactions). Upon receipt, it stores the hash securely in SMRAM. Because SMRAM is isolated from external access, this guarantees the baseline remains protected from tampering. In addition to the memory-image hash, SMM-MON receives a UEFI service-table hash from DXE-MON. This hash is computed by concatenating the code sections of Boot Services, Runtime Services, and DXE Services, and then applying SHA-256. SMM-MON stores both the resulting hash and the associated pointer structure securely in SMRAM. By maintaining these values in SMRAM, SMM-MON supports robust integrity validation through hash comparison and pointer-level verification. This tightly links baseline establishment to subsequent runtime checks.

2 Runtime Integrity Verification. Once baselines are established, SMM-MON performs runtime verification using both periodic and event-driven mechanisms. Throughout the boot sequence, DXE-MON sends updated memory-image hashes at regular intervals. SMM-MON compares each incoming hash against the baseline. A match confirms code integrity, while a mismatch suggests tampering and is logged for analysis. Event-driven verification is triggered by UEFI service calls, specifically `LoadImage()` and `StartImage()`. SMM-MON compares the current service-table hash with the baseline hash. If they match, the boot process continues. SMM-MON also performs pointer-level validation, comparing each pointer in the current service-table structure against those in SMRAM. Any discrepancy results in logging the function name and table offset for forensic use.

3 Replay-Attack Prevention and Secure Message Handling. To prevent replay attacks, BootMarker includes a monotonic counter in each integrity verification message sent to SMM-MON. The counter must increment with every transmission. SMM-MON verifies that the counter value increases and remains within valid bounds. If the check fails, the message is rejected. This mechanism blocks acceptance of stale or duplicated data. All failed validations are logged to support forensic analysis.

4 Final Integrity Assessment and Reporting. After Boot Services complete, SMM-MON receives a termination packet signaling the end of DXE-stage monitoring. It aggregates all verification results stored in SMRAM, including periodic checks, event-driven logs, and counter validations. SMM-MON then generates a final integrity assessment report. The report is stored in a volatile UEFI variable, which becomes immutable after `ExitBootServices()` is called. This ensures secure attestation of boot-time integrity [54].

6 Evaluation

In this section, we evaluate BOOTMARKER's performance and effectiveness in detecting Windows and Linux bootkits. Our experiments include the real sample (*e.g.,* BlackLotus [42]) and synthesized implementations where live samples are unavailable. We conduct evaluations on both bare metal and virtual machines, using custom UEFI firmware and a standalone UEFI shell application. The bare metal testbed uses a Lenovo IdeaPad 330-15ICH (i5-8300H, GTX1050, 8GB RAM) running Windows 11. Virtual environments run Windows 11 and Ubuntu 24.04.02 on QEMU with 4 CPU cores and 4GB RAM.

6.1 Implementation

BOOTMARKER consists of two collaborating UEFI components. They are implemented in C, with approximately 2,255 lines for the main component, 3,384 lines for DXE-MON, and 867 lines for SMM-MON. Together, these components monitor and protect the boot process. DXE-MON and SMM-MON operate during the DXE phase and execute in SMM, respectively. In this section, we describe the implementation details of both components.

Early Deployment Strategy. The DXE component of BOOTMARKER (*i.e.,*DXE-MON) is implemented as a standalone DXE driver with minimal dependencies. This ensures early loading in the boot process, before any third-party drivers, allowing immediate monitoring and protection of critical operations. To provide comprehensive coverage, DXE-MON hooks key UEFI services, including `LoadImage()`, `StartImage()`, and `ExitBootServices()`, by modifying their function pointers in the UEFI service tables. Original pointers are preserved to allow restoration when needed, ensuring normal system behavior. The SMM component (*i.e.,*SMM-MON) runs within the protected SMM environment. It communicates with DXE-MON using standardized UEFI protocols [55], supporting modularity and cross-platform compatibility. Together, these components coordinate to protect the boot process.

Control-Flow Instrumentation. For runtime monitoring, DXE-MON uses the Zydis disassembly engine [32] to identify all control-transfer instructions in the bootloader's code sections. We chose Zydis because it is a pure C engine with no external dependencies that reliably decodes x86/x86-64 instructions in milliseconds, minimizing boot-time overhead in UEFI/DXE contexts. After locating these instructions, DXE-MON replaces them with trap opcodes such as UD2 or INT1, which trigger arbitrary exceptions with minimal overhead. When an exception occurs, a custom handler checks if the control-transfer destination falls within predefined trusted regions. If an anomalous transfer is detected, the system logs the event for later analysis but allows execution to proceed. This design ensures effective monitoring while preserving system availability.

Integrity Verification Pipeline. DXE-MON periodically computes SHA-256 hashes of its memory image and transmits them, along with monotonic counters, to SMM-MON for validation. This mechanism ensures prompt detection of unauthorized changes to the DXE component. To verify the integrity of UEFI service tables, BOOTMARKER uses two complementary methods. First, it compares hashes of the concatenated.text sections to detect code modifications. Second, it performs pointer-level analysis to uncover function redirection attempts. All verification results are recorded in SMRAM. These records are compiled into a comprehensive integrity report, which is securely stored in a protected UEFI variable. We plan to release BOOTMARKER as open source after publication to support reproducibility and foster research in boot-time security (Table 1).

Table 1. BOOTMARKER Detection Results

Sample	OS	BootkitType	Detection Method	Result
① BlackLotus †	Windows	Bootloader replacement	Control-flow analysis	✓
② MoonBounce ‡	Windows	Inline code hooking	Hash validation	✓
③ CosmicStrand ‡	Windows	Function pointer hooking	Table integrity check	✓
④ Shim-Loader ‡	Linux	Shim boot loader hooking	Control-flow analysis	✓

†: Real-world bootkit, ‡: Synthesized bootkit

6.2 Bootkit Detection Evaluation

We evaluated BOOTMARKER with four bootkits spanning Windows and Linux:one real sample (BlackLotus) and three synthesized ones: MoonBounce, CosmicStrand,and a custom Linux kit recreated from leaked code.These kits cover bootloader replacement, inline hooks, pointer hijacking, and shim injection.The real sample tests detection on an authentic threat, while the synthetic DXE drivers, built from public analyses, retain key behaviors for reproducible experiments.

Table 1 summarizes BOOTMARKER's detection performance across all tested samples. The evaluation shows a 100% detection rate. Multiple detection mechanisms are typically triggered simultaneously, demonstrating BOOTMARKER's defense-in-depth design.

Windows-Based Bootkit Detection. We begin our evaluation with Windows-targeted threats, including one real-world bootkit and several synthesized attacks. These attacks demonstrate key methodologies observed in practice, such as UEFI service table manipulation and inline code hooks within the Windows OS loader. Such techniques are commonly used by Windows-focused bootkits [62] (Fig 3).

(a) Bootloader Replacement

```
[*] Boot Result: Failed!
[*] Load Image Info
[#] DevicePath: \EFI\Microsoft\Boot\bootmgfw.
     efi
 - ImageBase: 0x7C07E000
 - ImageSize: 0xCE000
[!] Boot Service Changed: Hdr.CRC32 (Offset:
     0x10)
[!] Boot Service Changed: Exit (Offset: 0x10)

[#] DevicePath: EFI\Microsoft\Boot\winload.
     efi
 - ImageBase: 0x10000000
 - ImageSize: 0x1E1000
[*] Searching UEFI OS Loader Hook
--------------------------------
[!] 1. Hook Found (Memory Operand)
--------------------------------
 - Location RIP: 0x100BDD60
 - BranchType: JMP (Unconditional)
 - Target Address Value: 0x7C2050FC
```

(b) Service Table Manipulation

```
[*] Boot Result: Failed!
[*] Load Image Info
[!] Boot Service Changed: Hdr.CRC32 (Offset:
     0x10)
[!] Boot Service Changed: HandleProtocol (
     Offset: 0x98)
[#] DevicePath: \EFI\Microsoft\Boot\bootmgfw.
     efi
 - ImageBase: 0x10000000
 - ImageSize: 0x1E1000
```

(c) Detection of Inline Hooking

```
[*] Boot Result: Failed!
[*] Load Image Info
[!] SERVICE INLINE HOOKING DETECTED!
[#] DevicePath: \EFI\Microsoft\Boot\bootmgfw.
     efi
 - ImageBase: 0x10000000
 - ImageSize: 0x1E1000
[*] Searching UEFI OS Loader Hook
```

Fig. 3. BOOTMARKER detection logs for three representative Windows UEFI bootkit techniques: (a) BlackLotus bootloader replacement, (b) CosmicStrand-style service table manipulation, and (c) MoonBounce-style inline hook on a Boot Services routine.

① **Bootloader Replacement Type:** BlackLotus [19] is a sophisticated UEFI bootkit that exploits CVE-2022-21894 to bypass Secure Boot protections [33]. It operates through bootloader replacement by deploying malicious files to the EFI System Partition (ESP). Specifically, it renames bootmgfw.efi to winload.efi to masquerade as a legitimate Windows loader component, while simultaneously placing malicious components in the EFI System Partition (ESP) directories. Finally, the bootkit maintains persistence by modifying boot configuration.

- **Detection:** BOOTMARKER detects the BlackLotus attack using multiple coordinated detection mechanisms, as shown in Figure 3-(a). First, it identifies a bootloader replacement pattern: the legitimate bootmgfw.efi is renamed and replaced by a malicious winload.efi, indicating tampering within the EFI System Partition. Next, it observes unauthorized modifications to the Boot Services Table, including a CRC32 mismatch at offset 0x10 and a modified Exit function pointer, pointing to low-level service manipulation. Finally, BOOTMARKER performs runtime control-flow analysis and flags a malicious in-memory hook at `RIP:0x100BDD60`, where an unconditional `JMP` redirects execution to a suspicious target address (i.e., `0x7C2050FC`). These findings confirm a multi-stage attack consistent with BlackLotus's behavior, demonstrating BOOTMARKER's ability to detect both structural corruption and runtime anomalies during early boot.

② **Function Pointer Hooking Type:** CosmicStrand [16] is a firmware-level implant that targets UEFI Boot Services by manipulating function pointers. We synthesize a DXE driver that replicates this methodology based on publicly available analyses. During the DXE phase, the malicious driver accesses the `EFI_SYSTEM_TABLE` to locate the Boot Services table. It overwrites the `HandleProtocol` function pointer with a malicious address to hijack control flow. To bypass basic integrity checks, the attack recalculates CRC32 checksums after modifying the service table.

- **Detection:** BOOTMARKER detects the pointer hooking attack via Boot Services Table integrity monitoring, as shown in Figure 3-(b). During the boot process, it observes unauthorized modifications to critical entries in the Boot Services Table. Specifically, BOOTMARKER flags a tampered CRC32 checksum at offset `0x10` and a modified `HandleProtocol` function pointer at offset `0x98`. These indicators reveal low-level manipulation of UEFI service routines. The alterations are detected before the OS loads, allowing BOOTMARKER to catch advanced bootkits that subvert firmware interfaces without modifying loaded binaries.

③ **Inline Code Modification Type:** This synthesized DXE driver demonstrates inline hooking of UEFI services, inspired by the MoonBounce [23] bootkit. The attack directly modifies executable code within UEFI Boot Services instead of altering function pointers. Our implementation targets the `AllocatePool` function, injecting a malicious jump to redirect execution to attacker-controlled code. Unlike pointer hooking, this method alters actual service code, making it more evasive against traditional table integrity checks.

- **Detection:** BOOTMARKER successfully detects the MoonBounce-style inline hooking attack using hash-based code integrity validation, as shown in Figure 3-(c). During the boot process, BOOTMARKER analyzes loaded images and performs integrity checks on critical UEFI service functions. The detection log shows that inline hooking is identified in `bootmgfw.efi`, despite no visible changes in the Boot Services Table structure. This indicates that malicious code was injected directly into the body of a service function, bypassing table-level indicators. By comparing computed hashes with known-good baselines, BOOTMARKER detects unauthorized modifications and flags them at runtime (Fig 4).

```
[*] Boot Result: Failed!
[*] Load Image Info
[#] DevicePath: \EFI\ubuntu\shimx64.efi
 - ImageBase: 0x7C09B000
 - ImageSize: 0x0D7000
[*] Searching UEFI OS Loader Hook
--------------------------------------------------
[!] 1. Hook Found
--------------------------------------------------
 - Location RIP: 0x7C0C8D19
 - BranchType: JMP (Unconditional)
 - Triggering Register: RAX
 - Register Value: 0x7DC8C2F3
```

Fig. 4. Detection analysis of custom Linux attack: BOOTMARKER identifies shim boot loader code modification and runtime control-flow manipulation

Linux-Based Attack Detection. We evaluate BOOTMARKER's cross-platform capabilities against Linux-targeted attack implementations. Due to the limited availability of in-the-wild Linux UEFI bootkits, we develop a custom DXE driver that targets Linux-specific boot components.

④ **Shim Boot Loader Hooking Type:** Our synthesized DXE driver demonstrates bootloader manipulation by targeting the Linux shim boot loader, which validates the Secure Boot chain. The attack performs inline hooking of the handle_image function using pattern matching (sigHandleImage) and installs a trampoline to redirect execution.

- **Detection:** BOOTMARKER successfully detects the custom Linux bootkit through runtime control-flow analysis, as shown in Figure 4. During execution, BOOTMARKER monitors the shim boot loader and logs the loading of the shimx64.efi image, including its base address and memory size. It then performs a dynamic scan for control-flow anomalies and detects a hook in the UEFI OS loader region. The hook is identified at instruction pointer RIP:0x7C0C8D19, where an unconditional JMP via the RAX register redirects execution to a non-standard address (i.e., 0x7DC8C2F3). This redirection indicates code injection or hijacking behavior, allowing the bootkit to alter normal control flow. These results confirm BOOTMARKER's ability to detect advanced control-flow manipulation during the early boot stage in Linux UEFI environments (Table 2).

Table 2. System Boot-Time Performance Overhead

System	Baseline Boot(s)	BootMarker(s)	Overhead(sec+/%)
Windows	10.1	13.4	+3.3 (33.0%)
Ubuntu	6.3	7.8	+1.5 (15.0%)

6.3 Performance Overhead

To evaluate the performance impact introduced by BOOTMARKER, we perform boot-time measurements on both Windows and Ubuntu systems, comparing baseline durations with those observed under active monitoring. Table 2 summarizes the average boot times recorded over ten consecutive trials for each configuration. This overhead primarily results from runtime components, including dynamic instrumentation, service table monitoring, and exception-handling mechanisms. While the observed overhead is substantial, it remains acceptable in security-sensitive environments where boot process integrity is critical. Performance impact may also vary across different hardware configurations and system specifications. These results show that BOOTMARKER maintains a practical balance between detection effectiveness and system performance (Table 3).

Table 3. BOOTMARKER Feature Comparison

Feature	BOOTMARKER	BootStomp [35]	BootKeeper [6]
Cross-Platform (Win/Linux)	✓	✗	✗
Runtime CF Verification	✓	✗	✗
Static UEFI Table Validation	✓	✓	✓
Exception-driven Analysis	✓	✗	✗
SMM-based Validation	✓	✗	✗

6.4 Comparison with Previous Approaches

Table 3 presents a comparative analysis of BOOTMARKER against two existing boot integrity verification frameworks: BootStomp [35] and BootKeeper [6]. The table highlights the distinguishing features of BOOTMARKER, particularly its runtime and platform-aware defenses against modern UEFI bootkits. First, BootStomp performs static analysis to detect vulnerabilities in UEFI firmware images by symbolically executing bootloader code. While useful for offline inspection, it lacks runtime detection and supports only Linux-based firmware environments. Second, BootKeeper analyzes UEFI bootloaders and configurations to identify policy violations, but it is also limited to static methods and does not support runtime enforcement or dynamic validation. In contrast, BOOTMARKER adopts a hybrid approach, combining static table validation with dynamic control-flow monitoring. This allows it to detect tampering and unauthorized behavior as it occurs during system execution. BOOTMARKER supports both Windows and Linux platforms, enhancing its deployment flexibility and real-world applicability.

Overall, the comparison shows that BOOTMARKER is the only framework among the three to provide a comprehensive, cross-platform solution with both static and runtime protections, exception-based detection, and SMM-backed enforcement. These capabilities enable BOOTMARKER to detect a broad range of stealthy and persistent bootkit behaviors often missed by traditional static tools.

7 Discussion and Limitations

Potential Evasion and Attack Surface. A key concern for any boot-level detection system like BOOTMARKER is whether a well-informed adversary could craft effective evasion strategies. BOOTMARKER activates in both the DXE and SMM phases, engaging very early in the boot process. To bypass its defenses, an attacker must gain control before BOOTMARKER initializes. However, early-stage compromise is highly constrained in practice. Code in the SEC and PEI phases is minimal, provides limited functionality, and exposes few opportunities for persistent or complex logic injection. Such early tampering risks destabilizing the boot process and is likely to be detected. In most realistic scenarios, evading BOOTMARKER before initialization would require physical access, hardware modification, or exploitation of rare vulnerabilities in early firmware stages, all beyond the reach of standard software-based threats.

BOOTMARKER also incorporates timer-based verification to detect inconsistencies during the boot flow. This introduces a potential for race conditions or time-of-check-to-time-of-use (TOCTOU) attacks. These risks can be mitigated through future extensions, including cryptographic timestamping, use of trusted platform modules (TPMs), or hardware-assisted continuous monitoring. Such enhancements would further increase BOOTMARKER's resilience against advanced timing-based evasion attempts.

Vendor Integration. Effective deployment of BOOTMARKER requires active collaboration with system vendors. Both SMM and DXE components must be integrated into system firmware, which may involve managing custom signing keys to maintain compatibility with Secure Boot policies. By embedding BOOTMARKER during firmware manufacturing, vendors can enable secure boot-time monitoring by default and establish a trusted channel for forwarding measurement results to the OS. This approach simplifies adoption for end users and preserves boot integrity across heterogeneous hardware platforms.

Detection Limitations After Boot. BOOTMARKER is designed to detect threats that occur during the boot process, prior to the operating system fully loading. It does not monitor or protect the system after the OS has initialized. As a result, if an attacker installs a rootkit or bootkit post-boot, BOOTMARKER cannot detect the compromise until the next system restart, when the boot sequence is monitored again. Additionally, the current SMM module operates in a largely passive role, running only on SMI events and lacking independent monitoring capabilities. This limitation highlights the need to deploy BOOTMARKER as part of a broader and layered defense strategy. Comprehensive protection requires combining boot-time detection with runtime monitoring solutions that continuously observe system behavior after the OS is active.

Challenges in Firmware Lifecycle Management. BOOTMARKER is tightly integrated into system firmware, making its maintenance and updates more complex than typical software. Firmware updates must be carefully tested to ensure compatibility with BOOTMARKER and to prevent stability or functional issues. This challenge is amplified when the base firmware and BOOTMARKER are developed or maintained by different vendors, each operating on independent release cycles. As a result, secure and reliable system maintenance requires close coordination, introducing significant overhead for both device vendors and system administrators, which greatly exceeds that of software-only solutions.

Limited Evaluation Scope. Our evaluation relies on a diverse set of synthesized bootkits to test BOOTMARKER across various attack types. However, these samples do not capture the full range of possible bootkit designs and strategies. Therefore, the demonstrated effectiveness of BOOTMARKER is bounded by the coverage and realism of the test cases used. Future work should expand the evaluation to include a broader set of threat models and bootkits that more accurately reflect real-world adversaries.

Limited Scope of Monitoring in Linux. BOOTMARKER monitors the Linux boot process by focusing on the shim boot loader, rather than extending into GRUB. This design choice is deliberate: shim offers a simpler and more consistent structure, making effective monitoring feasible with minimal overhead. By contrast, GRUB's plugin-based architecture and diverse configurations introduce significant complexity, making generalized monitoring more difficult and costly. To balance coverage and performance, BOOTMARKER prioritizes shim-stage monitoring as a practical and effective point of control.

8 Conclusion

Bootkits remain among the most challenging malware classes to defend against. They target firmware and pre-OS components that traditional security layers often overlook. Our work shows that monitoring at both the DXE and SMM levels can secure a significant portion of this attack surface. By detecting unauthorized tampering before the OS boots, BOOTMARKER prevents early-stage compromise. The integration of exception-driven analysis, self-hashing, and hardware-assisted validation offers a practical and effective approach to closing early boot security gaps. This layered, real-time architecture, reinforced by hardware-rooted trust, raises the bar for attackers and strengthens boot process integrity.

Acknowledgment. We thank the anonymous reviewers and our shepherd for their helpful feedback. This work was supported by the KITRI Best of the Best program.

References

1. Akbal, E., Yakut, Ö.F., Dogan, S., Tuncer, T., Ertam, F.: A digital forensics approach for lost secondary partition analysis using master boot record structured hard disk drives. Sakarya University J. Comput. Inf. Sci. (2021). https://doi.org/10.35377/saucis...1022600
2. AppArmor project: apparmor: Linux kernel security module (2024). https://apparmor.net/
3. Bashun, V., Sergeev, A., Minchenkov, V., Yakovlev, A.: Too young to be secure: analysis of UEFI threats and vulnerabilities. In: Proceedings of the 13th Conference of Open Innovations Association FRUCT (FRUCT 2013) (2013)
4. binarly: Logofail exploited to deploy bootkitty, the first uefi bootkit for linux (2024). https://www.binarly.io/blog/logofail-exploited-to-deploy-bootkitty-the-first-uefi-bootkit-for-linux
5. Butterworth, J., Kallenberg, C., Kovah, X., Herzog, A.: Bios chronomancy: fixing the core root of trust for measurement. In: Proceedings of the 2013 ACM SIGSAC conference on Computer and Communications Security, pp. 25–36 (2013)
6. Chevalier, R., et al.: Bootkeeper: validating software integrity properties on boot firmware images. In: Proceedings of the 9th ACM Conference on Data and Application Security and Privacy (CODASPY). pp. 315–325. ACM, Dallas, TX, USA (2019). https://doi.org/10.1145/3292006.3300026
7. Cooper, D., Polk, W., Regenscheid, A., Souppaya, M., et al.: Bios protection guidelines. NIST Special Publication (2011)
8. Corporation, I.: Intel®64 and IA-32 architectures software developer's manual (2013). https://www.intel.com/content/www/us/en/content-details/782158/. Combined Volumes 1-4
9. Duflot, L., Etiemble, D., Grumelard, O.: Using CPU system management mode to circumvent operating system security functions. CanSecWest/core06 (2006)
10. Duflot, L., Levillain, O., Morin, B., Grumelard, O.: Getting into the smram: smm reloaded. In: CanSecWest Conference (2009)
11. ESET Research: Lojax: first uefi rootkit found in the wild, courtesy of the sednit group. Tech. rep., ESET (2018). https://www.welivesecurity.com/2018/09/27/lojax-first-uefi-rootkit-found-in-the-wild/
12. Ezirim, K., Khoo, W., Koumantaris, G., Law, R., Perera, I.M.: Trusted platform module–a survey. Graduate Center City Univ. New York **11** (2012)
13. GNU: Gnu grub 2 manual (2023). https://www.gnu.org/software/grub/manual/grub/grub.html
14. Grill, B., Bacs, A., Platzer, C., Bos, H.: "nice boots!"–a large-scale analysis of bootkits and new ways to stop them. In: Proceedings of the 12th DIMVA Conference (DIMVA 2015) (2015). https://doi.org/10.1007/978-3-319-20550-2_2
15. Hosseinzadeh, S., Sequeiros, B., Inácio, P.R., Leppänen, V.: Recent trends in applying TPM to cloud computing. Secur. Priv. (2020). https://doi.org/10.1002/spy2.93
16. Kaspersky Lab GReAT Team: cosmicstrand: the discovery of a sophisticated UEFI firmware rootkit. Securelist (Kaspersky Lab) (2022). https://securelist.com/cosmicstrand-uefi-firmware-rootkit/106973/
17. Kumar, N., Kumar, V.: Vbootkit 2.0-attacking windows 7 via boot sectors. In: Proceedings of the 7th Hack in the Box Security Conference (HITBSecConf 2009) (2009)

18. Kuzminykh, I., Yevdokymenko, M.: Analysis of security of rootkit detection methods. In: Proceedings of the 1st IEEE International Conference on Advanced Trends in Information Theory (ATIT 2019) (2019)
19. ldpreload: Blacklotus uefi bootkit github repository (2023). https://github.com/ldpreload/BlackLotus. GitHub repository
20. Linux Kernel Documentation: kernel lockdown (2024). https://man7.org/linux/man-pages/man7/kernel_lockdown.7.html
21. Loucaides, J., Bulygin, Y.: Platform security assessment with chipsec. In: Proceedings of the 17th CanSecWest Conference (CanSecWest 2014) (2014)
22. Mannthey, K.: System management interrupt free hardware. In: Presentation slides: Linux Plumbers Conference, Portland, OR, USA (2009)
23. Mark Lechtik,Vasily Berdnikov,Denis Legezo,Ilya Borisov: Moonbounce: the dark side of uefi firmware (2022). https://securelist.com/moonbounce-the-dark-side-of-uefi-firmware/105468/
24. Martin Smolár,Anton Cherepanov: UEFI threats moving to the ESP: Introducing especter bootkit (2021). https://www.welivesecurity.com/2021/10/05/uefi-threats-moving-esp-introducing-especter-bootkit/
25. Microsoft: kernel patch protection (2017). https://learn.microsoft.com/en-us/previous-versions/windows/hardware/design/dn613955(v=vs.85)?redirectedfrom=MSDN
26. Microsoft: windows secure boot key creation and management guidance (2022). https://learn.microsoft.com/en-us/windows-hardware/manufacture/desktop/windows-secure-boot-key-creation-and-management-guidance?view=windows-11
27. Microsoft: Virtualization-based security (vbs) (2023). https://learn.microsoft.com/en-us/windows-hardware/design/device-experiences/oem-vbs
28. Microsoft: Bitlocker overview (2024). https://learn.microsoft.com/en-us/windows/security/operating-system-security/data-protection/bitlocker/
29. Microsoft: driver signing policy (2024). https://learn.microsoft.com/en-us/windows-hardware/drivers/install/kernel-mode-code-signing-policy--windows-vista-and-later-
30. Microsoft: hypervisor-protected code integrity (hvci) (2024). https://learn.microsoft.com/en-us/windows-hardware/drivers/bringup/device-guard-and-credential-guard
31. Microsoft: overview of early launch antimalware (2024). https://learn.microsoft.com/en-us/windows-hardware/drivers/install/early-launch-antimalware
32. Nar, M., Kakisim, A.G., Yavuz, M.N., Soğukpinar, İ.: Analysis and comparison of disassemblers for opcode based malware analysis. In: 2019 4th International Conference on Computer Science and Engineering (UBMK) (2019). https://doi.org/10.1109/UBMK.2019.8907153
33. NIST: Cve-2022-21894: Secure boot security feature bypass vulnerability (2022). https://nvd.nist.gov/vuln/detail/CVE-2022-21894
34. Osborn, J.D., Challener, D.C.: Trusted platform module evolution. Johns Hopkins APL Technical Digest (Applied Physics Laboratory) (2013)
35. Redini, N., et al.: Bootstomp: on the security of bootloaders in mobile devices. In: 26th USENIX Security Symposium (USENIX Security) (2017)
36. Research, E.: Eset research discovers uefi secure boot bypass vulnerability (2025). https://www.eset.com/us/about/newsroom/press-releases/eset-research-discovers-uefi-secure-boot-bypass-vulnerability/?srsltid=AfmBOoqPDNlhAy9r53NIxbveKLUslmypMvcn_lkJoXdNi0A4nee6jqGF
37. Rossow, T.: Tpm 2.0, uefi and their impact on security and users' freedom (2013)

38. Samsung Knox: real-time kernel protection (2025). https://docs.samsungknox.com/admin/fundamentals/whitepaper/samsung-knox-mobile-security/system-security/real-time-kernel-protection/
39. Segal, K.S., Gorelik, H.C., Brodt, O., Elbahar, Y., Elovici, Y., Shabtai, A.: Uefi memory forensics: a framework for uefi threat analysis. arXiv preprint arXiv:2501.16962 (2025). https://doi.org/10.48550/arXiv.2501.16962
40. SELinux Project: Selinux: security-enhanced linux (2017). https://selinuxproject.org/page/Main_Page
41. Shafiuzzaman, M., Desai, A., Sarker, L., Bultan, T.: Uefi vulnerability signature generation using static and symbolic analysis. arXiv preprint arXiv:2407.07166 (2024). DOIurlhttps://doi.org/10.48550/arXiv.2407.07166
42. Smolár, M.: Blacklotus uefi windows bootkit (2023). https://www.welivesecurity.com/2023/03/01/blacklotus-uefi-bootkit-myth-confirmed/
43. Soeder, D., Permeh, R.: eeye bootroot. BlackHat USA (2005)
44. Surve, P.P., Brodt, O., Yampolskiy, M., Elovici, Y., Shabtai, A.: Sok: security below the os–a security analysis of uefi. arXiv preprint arXiv:2311.03809 (2023). DOIurlhttps://doi.org/10.48550/arXiv.2311.03809
45. Szaknis, M., Szczypiorski, K.: The design of the simple SMM rootkit. In: Proceedings of the 9th International Conference on Wireless Communication and Sensor Networks (ICWCSN 2022) (2022)
46. Team, R.H.B.: Shim: A first-stage uefi bootloader (2024). https://github.com/rhboot/shim/blob/main/README.md
47. TianoCore: Memory protection in SMM (2020). https://tianocore-docs.github.io/ATBB-Memory_Protection_in_UEFI_BIOS/draft/memory-protection-in-SMM.html
48. Tianocore: Machine owner key (MOK) (2021). https://tianocore-docs.github.io/Understanding_UEFI_Secure_Boot_Chain/draft/additional_secure_boot_chain_implementations/machine_owner_key_mok.html
49. Tianocore: Uefi secure boot (2021). https://tianocore-docs.github.io/Understanding_UEFI_Secure_Boot_Chain/draft/secure_boot_chain_in_uefi/uefi_secure_boot.html
50. TianoCore: Platform initialization (2024). https://tianocore-docs.github.io/edk2-UefiDriverWritersGuide/draft/3_foundation/315_platform_initialization/README.15.html
51. UEFI Forum: About uefi forum. https://uefi.org/about
52. UEFI forum: Dxe dispatcher. https://uefi.org/specs/PI/1.8/V2_DXE_Dispatcher.html
53. UEFI forum: Services—boot services. https://uefi.org/specs/UEFI/2.10/07_Services_Boot_Services.html
54. UEFI forum: Services—runtime services. https://uefi.org/specs/UEFI/2.10/08_Services_Runtime_Services.html
55. UEFI forum: Uefi protocols. https://uefi.org/specs/PI/1.8/V4_UEFI_Protocols.html#efi-mm-communication-protocol-communicate
56. UEFI Forum: Boot manager. https://uefi.org/specs/PI/1.8/V2_Boot_Manager.html (2022)
57. UEFI Forum: Driver execution environment (dxe) phase (2022). https://uefi.org/specs/PI/1.8/V2_Overview.html
58. UEFI Forum: Pre-efi initialization overview (2022). https://ucfi.org/specs/PI/1.8A/V1_Overview.html#pre-efi-initialization-pei-phase
59. UEFI Forum: Security (sec) phase information (2022). https://uefi.org/specs/PI/1.8/V1_Security_SEC_Phase_Information.html

60. UEFI forum: Uefi platform initialization specification (2024). https://ucfi.org/specs/PI/1.9/
61. Yin, J., et al.: Finding SMM privilege-escalation vulnerabilities in Uefi firmware with protocol-centric static analysis. In: Proceedings of the 43rd IEEE Symposium on Security and Privacy (SP 2022), pp. 2629–2646 (2022). https://doi.org/10.1109/SP46214.2022.9833723
62. Zhou, Y., Peng, G., Li, Z., Liu, S.: A survey on the evolution of bootkits attack and defense techniques. China Communications (2024). https://doi.org/10.23919/JCC.ja.2022-0409

Ali2Vul: Binary Vulnerability Dataset Expansion via Cross-Modal Alignment

Xinyu Bai, Yisen Wang$^{(\boxtimes)}$, Jiajun Du, Chen Liang, Siyuan Liang, and Zirui Jiang

Information Engineering University, Zhengzhou 450000, HN, China
851067568@qq.com

Abstract. In the context of software supply chain security and IoT device firmware analysis, binary vulnerability detection faces dual challenges of detection efficiency and coverage due to scarce annotated binary data. Although the open-source ecosystem has accumulated vast amounts of source-level vulnerability data, direct migration to binary vulnerability detection inevitably encounters a semantic gap caused by cross-modal representation differences such as compiler optimizations and symbol stripping. To address data scarcity in binary vulnerability detection and bridge the semantic gap in cross-modal matching with source code, this paper proposes a hierarchical semantic fusion framework for binary-source alignment. Through heterogeneous modal semantic bridging and hierarchical attention mechanisms, our approach significantly enhances cross-modal matching precision and scalability between binary and source code, achieving 94.3% accuracy. Furthermore, we introduce a vulnerability detection task-driven transfer framework that maps source-level vulnerability patterns to binary code feature space via cross-modal alignment. Leveraging dimensional expansion within the model's knowledge space enables exponential scaling of usable data for binary vulnerability detection, thereby transcending data scarcity constraints. We collected 400 CVEs from 8 real-world vulnerable projects, achieving 80.3% detection accuracy. This research establishes an effective technical pathway for expanding usable data resources in automated binary vulnerability detection.

Keywords: Binary Vulnerability Detection · Cross-Modal Alignment · Code Representation

1 Introduction

Against the increasingly severe threats to software supply chain security, automated vulnerability detection has become a critical defense line for cybersecurity. Current mainstream commercial software is predominantly distributed as closed-source binaries, making vulnerability detection in binary code the primary battleground for offensive and defensive operations. However, traditional binary vulnerability detection methods face severe data scarcity challenges: while numerous closed-source software products exist in the market, acquiring and annotating binary vulnerability samples heavily relies on manual reverse engineering analysis by security experts, where precise binary vulnerability data requires human annotation of millions of instructions. How to rapidly expand binary vulnerability datasets and advance practical applications of binary vulnerability detection remains a pressing challenge.

Binary vulnerability detection has advanced with the development of deep learning (BinAbsInspector [1], VulHawk [2]). However, limited by scarce annotated data, its detection accuracy and generalization capabilities remain difficult to break through. Meanwhile, source code vulnerability datasets show explosive growth under expanding open-source scenarios. The essential semantic correlation between source and binary code creates inherent connections between source and binary vulnerability data. Yet source code presents logical structures and developer intent through high-level languages, while binary code loses symbolic information after compilation optimization, creating modal differences between them. This makes source vulnerability samples difficult to directly transfer to binary scenarios, forming a "data silo" effect. Although Bin2Source [3] has made matching attempts, its effectiveness remains unsatisfactory. Therefore, existing vulnerability detection research universally faces two-dimensional fragmentation: First, source and binary vulnerability detection datasets differ significantly - open-source vulnerability databases NVD and SARD contain millions of source samples, while the recently released CveBinarySheet [4] dataset covers only 1,033 CVE entries with associated binary samples; Second, although essential semantic correlations exist between source and binary, the semantic fracture in their vulnerability feature spaces causes difficult knowledge transfer.

The continuous advancement of cross-modal learning offers new solutions to this challenge. Some works(CodeCMR [5], XLIR [6]) employ deep learning models to map source code and binaries into a shared semantic space, enabling cross-modal similarity computation and automated learning of semantic relationships between source and binary code. However, most efforts still focus on generic program analysis, having not yet fully explored their targeted applications in real-world vulnerability detection scenarios.

To address these challenges, this paper proposes a deep alignment-based binary-source feature mapping framework: It leverages locally deployed large language models to generate natural language explanations that bridge the semantic gap across heterogeneous modalities. These explanations are jointly processed with code structural features and constant anchor encodings to form unified multi-granular representations. Subsequently, a Hierarchical Attention Alignment Network reconciles cross-modal discrepancies, ultimately achieving source-binary alignment. We adapted this alignment model to vulnerability detection tasks, substituting massive source code vulnerability data samples for scarce binary samples, thereby mitigating the data scarcity problem inherent to traditional binary vulnerability detection scenarios. Our principal contributions are as follows:

- Leveraging the locally deployed DeepSeek-R1-70B model, we establish a dual-channel natural language explanation system for source and binary code, extracting their universal semantic features.

- Within the alignment network architecture, we propose a hierarchical attention mechanism to progressively fuse multi-granular semantic features. This ensures effective cross-tier transmission of critical information, prevents feature submergence, and enhances noise robustness.
- We transfer the proposed cross-modal alignment architecture to vulnerability detection. This approach capitalizes on the vast scale of source code vulnerability datasets to efficiently and rapidly scale binary vulnerability detection datasets.
- Evaluated on public benchmarks, experimental results demonstrate that our alignment framework achieves 94.3% accuracy. Testing in real-world vulnerability datasets confirms our method rapidly and effectively detects binary vulnerabilities, attaining an 80.3% recall rate.

2 Related Work

2.1 Binary Vulnerability Detection

In the field of binary vulnerability detection, technological evolution demonstrates a multi-layered transition from static rules to intelligent analysis: Early methods relying on pattern matching gradually evolved into deep learning-integrated detection systems. Among these, BVDetector [7] achieves fine-grained vulnerability pattern learning through program slicing and BiGRU models; VulSeeker [8] innovatively constructs Labeled Semantic Flow Graphs (LSFG) to model cross-platform function similarity; while BinXray [9] pioneers patch signature analysis, enabling source-free vulnerability localization by comparing vulnerable functions with their patched versions. Collectively, these works form a multidimensional technical system covering fine-grained detection, cross-platform matching, firmware adaptation, and patch verification.

Despite continuous breakthroughs in detection accuracy and applicability scope, the scarcity of training data remains a fundamental constraint on the generalization capabilities of detection models. However, observed through advances in cross-modal techniques, we can leverage vast source-level vulnerability repositories to project semantic knowledge onto binary code, promising to overcome binary data scarcity challenges.

2.2 Cross-Modal Learning

Cross-modal learning has undergone a paradigmatic shift from behavior-driven to data-driven approaches, gradually evolving into a technical system centered on representation alignment and knowledge transfer: Early works like DeViSE [10] established foundational semantic mapping by aligning images and textual labels in cross-modal embedding spaces. CLIP [11] further validated the universal potential of cross-modal pretraining through large-scale image-text contrastive learning, enabling open-world zero-shot recognition. ALBEF [12] innovatively introduced momentum distillation to achieve unimodal semantic alignment before feature fusion, effectively mitigating noisy data interference. Meanwhile, Capture [13] introduced adversarial reprogramming to code analysis, successfully transferring visual models to vulnerability detection tasks through AST-to-image structural sequence transformation.

These works progressively construct a generalizable, extensible cross-modal intelligence paradigm through continuous innovations in multi-granular alignment, multimodal scaling, and multi-task adaptation. The explosive advancement of cross-modal learning provides new insights for source-binary code matching.

2.3 Binary-Source Matching

The binary-source matching task presents significant challenges due to the substantial discrepancies between source and binary code. Early binary-source alignment approaches focused on lexical feature extraction combined with traditional matching algorithms (Hungarian algorithm [14], graph isomorphism detection [15]). These methods were limited by shallow semantic representation capabilities and manual dependency, struggling to accommodate code transformations induced by compiler optimizations. To address this, BinPro [16] pioneered a machine learning and static analysis fusion paradigm. By predicting compiler optimization behaviors and integrating cross-platform features, it constructed a bipartite graph matching model. CodeCMR [5] further leveraged deep neural networks to capture structural features of source ASTs and binary CFGs, achieving function-level semantic embedding alignment. Meanwhile, CLAP [17], inspired by CLIP's foundational concepts, innovatively introduced natural language as a cross-modal bridge between source and binary code. By fine-tuning encoders to map binary code into source explanation NLP spaces, it established a semantics-driven alignment paradigm.

These works have achieved significant progress in cross-modal source-binary matching, yet improvement space remains: First, insufficient semantic modeling depth – either focusing solely on structural and lexical features while neglecting deep semantics, or extracting only universal semantic representations while ignoring structural properties; Second, coarse-grained cross-modal interaction – most approaches employ feature concatenation or shallow contrastive learning without establishing fine-grained cross-modal attention mechanisms, resulting in inadequate robustness against complex optimizations; Third, open-source large models will substantially reduce the cost and time required for implementing natural language explanations as semantic bridges.

3 Methodology

This study proposes a dual-stream architecture-based cross-modal function-level alignment framework (see Fig. 1). Through heterogeneous feature disentanglement and hierarchical semantic fusion, it accomplishes deep semantic matching between source code and binary programs. Figure 1 illustrates the architectural framework of our approach, which adopts a dual-stream cross-modal alignment architecture comprising multi-granular feature extractors and a hierarchical alignment network.

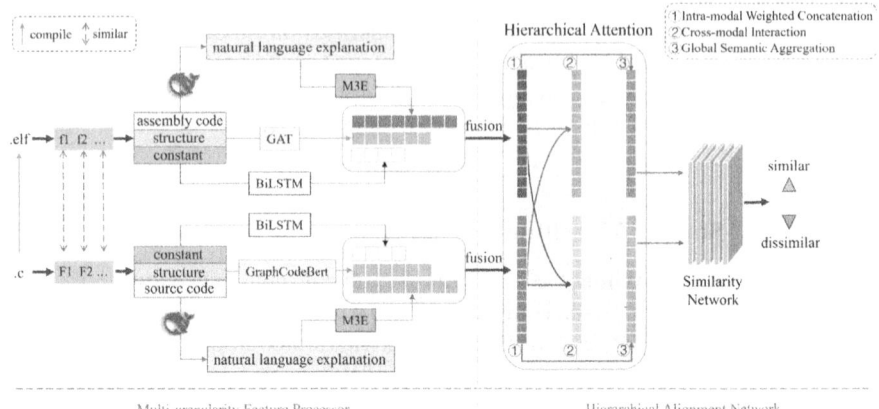

Fig. 1. The overall architecture of the cross-modal alignment network comprises two main components: a multi-granularity feature processor and a hierarchical alignment network.

This framework adopts a dual-path parallel processing mechanism to extract multi-granular information from source and binary modalities: semantic information (natural language explanations), structural features (AST and data flow for source; CFG for binary), and constant semantics (integers and strings), then leverages pretrained domain-expert networks to generate multi-granular specificity embeddings.

For cross-modal feature space heterogeneity, we design a hierarchical attention alignment mechanism. It employs Intra-Modal Feature-Weighted Concatenation, Cross-Domain Gated Interaction, and Global Semantic Aggregation in a three-stage progressive fusion strategy to dynamically capture deep correlation patterns between source and binary. Ultimately, we leverage similarity metrics in joint representation space to build robust cross-modal matching classifiers, achieving function-level source-binary alignment.

Our framework, through multi-granular feature extraction and hierarchical alignment networks, while avoiding early feature confusion, effectively enhances semantic alignment accuracy for heterogeneous code representations.

3.1 Formal Problem Formulation

This study establishes a cross-modal similarity relationship between source code and binary code at the function granularity, grounded in program semantic equivalence theory. Following jTrans's [18] definition of functions in binary programs, we assert that a source function and a set of ordered binary instructions (functions) compiled from it are equivalent, thus similar.

Similarity. For source code functions $\mathcal{S} = \{s_1, \ldots, s_n\}$ and compiled binary functions $\mathcal{B} = \{b_1, \ldots, b_m\}$, define a similarity relation: if $s \in \mathcal{S}$ and $b \in \mathcal{B}$ correspond to the same high-level language function and its compilation result, then they form a positive sample pair $(s, b) \in \mathcal{P}$; otherwise, they form a negative sample pair $(s, b) \in \mathcal{N}$.

Alignment. We define the alignment task as finding a mapping function $\mathcal{F} : (s, b) \to [0, 1]$ such that:

$$\mathcal{F}(s,b) = \begin{cases} \sigma\left(f_{\text{align}}\left(\phi_{\text{src}}(s), \phi_{\text{bin}}(b)\right)\right) \to 1 & \text{if } (s,b) \in \mathcal{P} \\ \sigma\left(f_{\text{align}}\left(\phi_{\text{src}}(s), \phi_{\text{bin}}(b)\right)\right) \to 0 & \text{if } (s,b) \in \mathcal{N} \end{cases}$$

The output probability represents *cross-modal alignment confidence*, where: ϕ_{src} and ϕ_{bin} are independent feature encoders, f_{align} denotes the alignment network, $\sigma(\cdot)$ is the sigmoid activation function.

3.2 Feature Selection Mechanism

In cross-modal code alignment tasks, the quality of feature representation directly influences the model's ability to capture semantic consistency across heterogeneous modalities; traditional methods often fall into the "modality gap" dilemma, primarily manifested as: (1) heterogeneous syntactic structures inducing topological feature mismatch; (2) semantic noise introduced by compiler optimizations disrupting constant consistency; (3) abstract-level disparities causing intent representation fragmentation; to overcome these limitations, this paper proposes a triple joint representation system: first, high-level semantic bridging is constructed through dual-channel natural language explanations, overcoming semantic fragmentation caused by syntactic differences; second, hierarchical structure mapping based on control-flow topology achieves cross-modal equivalent transformation of program logic; third, a constant-aware anchor-assisted alignment mechanism enhances model robustness against compilation perturbations; these three feature dimensions exhibit complementary enhancement in spatial topology, semantic abstraction, and data entity levels, collectively forming a complete solution space for cross-modal alignment.

Natural Language Explanation. To address the cross-modal semantic gap, this study innovatively leverages locally deployed large language models (LLMs) to construct a dual-channel natural language explanation framework, establishing a semantic bridge through natural language information to achieve explainable cross-modal alignment.

Prior research CLAP (Code-Language Alignment Pretraining) attempted to leverage natural language explanations as bridges for source-binary alignment. However, it relies on GPT-4 API for initial explanation data accumulation, then trains a shadow model of GPT-4 by fine-tuning LLaMA [19]; crucially, it only generates explanations for the source code side, embedding binaries into the natural language space through an adapted encoder. Deepseek's [20] open-sourcing facilitated this work—we utilize Deepseek-R1-70B to build a localized code comprehension engine for explanation generation, significantly improving cost-efficiency compared to CLAP's cloud API dependency and shadow model training.

Addressing CLAP's unilateral limitation (source-only processing), we employ IDA [21] for assembly-enhanced binary processing and specifically generate natural language explanations for assembly code. This bidirectional explanation framework bridges cross-modal semantic gaps, substantially fulfilling precision requirements for cross-modal alignment.

For both source and binary channels, we deploy domain-adapted prompts to maximize LLM code comprehension (Fig. 2):

- Binary Reverse Engineering Channel: Register state tracking templates standardize semantic annotation of input/output registers. Using a "First-Then-Finally" causal-ordered instruction flow deconstruction paradigm, we guide LLMs to accurately parse assembly-level control transfer patterns.
- Source Analysis Channel: Function signature deduction templates enforce "parameter type → return type → functional summary" progressive parsing paths, with a technical term preservation mechanism mandating verbatim retention of domain terms.

```
template = """As an ARM reverse engineering expert,
strictly generate natural language descriptions
according to the following template:
This function receives input via registers [r0]-
[purpose], [r1]-[purpose] and returns [rX]-[purpose].
Its core functionality is [functional summary]. The
implementation logic first [key step 1], subsequently
[key step 2], and finally [key step 3]."""

prompt = """Analyze the ARM32 assembly function
and strictly extract the following elements:
1. Input registers, return register and their purposes
2. Use technical documentation style in English
3. Maintain paragraph coherence without bullet points
4. Core functional summary
5. Key steps phased as "Initially - Subsequently -
Ultimately"
6. No fabrication
7. Output only a single paragraph
"""
```

```
template = """As a C language expert, strictly
generate a natural language description according to
the following template:
This function receives [parameter list] and returns
[return type]. Its core functionality is [functional
summary]. The implementation logic first [key step 1],
subsequently [key step 2], and finally [key step 3]."""

prompt = """Analyze the following C function and
generate a technical description with requirements:
1. Identify function signature (parameter types, return
type)
2. Use technical documentation style in English
3. Maintain paragraph coherence without bullet points
4. Preserve original English technical terms
5. No fabrication
6. Output only a single paragraph
"""
```

Fig. 2. A prompt template for natural language explanation of source code and binaries. Primarily for explaining the holistic functional semantics.

Program Structural Topology. The structural characteristics of programs reflect the organizational logic and execution flow of code, serving as vital bridges connecting source and binary representations. Despite numerous transformations introduced during compilation, fundamental control flows and critical structural relationships are typically preserved. The core program logic—including control flow branching decisions, loop nesting hierarchies, and function call layers—remains explicitly represented in binary through basic block partitioning and jump instructions. For instance: Source-level conditional branches may be reconstructed as indirect jumps or conditional flag checks post-compilation optimization, yet the mutual exclusivity and execution order of branch paths can still be precisely mapped via control-flow graph (CFG) topology. Code obfuscation techniques can obscure symbol tables or variable readability but rarely disrupt the incoming/outgoing edge distribution patterns of critical nodes in original CFGs. This inherent robustness against syntactic interference establishes structural topology as a stable semantic carrier bridging source and binary code. Although source functions and compiled binaries differ significantly in form, their high-level logic features—such as function call trees and loop nesting depth—maintain cross-modal consistency, providing an abstract structural framework decoupled from implementation details for matching tasks.

Cross-Modal Constant Anchor Points. In cross-modal code representation alignment tasks, constants—such as hardcoded integers and string literals—are selected as cross-modal anchor points due to their compilation invariance and semantic stability. Constants provide high-confidence correlation cues between source and binary. Despite being coarse-grained features [5], constants exhibit unique anti-perturbation properties during compilation. For example: Magic numbers in cryptographic algorithms invariably appear with identical values in binaries. Source constants directly map to literal operands in binary, remaining valid regardless of compiler optimization levels or instruction set architecture changes. This stability originates from logical immutability: even when applying obfuscation techniques like control-flow flattening or function inlining, constant values persist as underlying operands.

3.3 Multi-Granularity Feature Processor
Data Preprocessing.

Function Partitioning. Source code and its compiled binaries are considered semantically similar. Leveraging the BinKit open-source dataset, which provides source projects and their corresponding compiled binaries, we perform function-level partitioning: source functions and binary functions from the same project sharing identical names form positive similarity pairs. A unified naming convention based on project and function names is applied to all partitioned source and binary functions.

Multi-Granularity Feature Extraction. For the source code modality: locally deployed DeepSeek parses code semantics to generate natural language descrip-

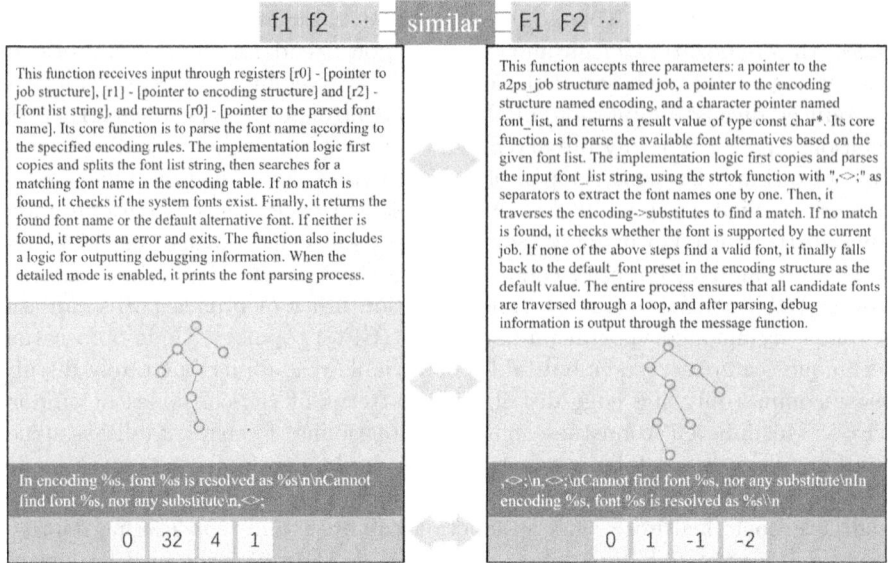

Fig. 3. Features are extracted from both source code and binaries across three dimensions: natural language explanations, structural patterns, and constant values. These three-dimensional features effectively capture the deep semantics of functions.

tions; combines with Joern [22] for AST structural feature extraction; precisely extracts constant strings and integers using regex and Clang.For the binary modality: IDA Pro-derived disassembly code is fed into LLMs for explanation generation; leverages Angr [23] to extract CFG control-flow features; by writing IDA Pro scripts to extract integer constants and string literals. All six-category cross-modal features (see Fig. 3) undergo standardized storage with function names as discriminative labels, thereby establishing a multidimensional data foundation for alignment tasks.

Feature Embedding. To effectively fuse multi-source heterogeneous information, this study devised domain-expert embedding strategies specifically designed for cross-modal features. For natural language explanations of source and binary code, the M3E model [24] is uniformly employed for embedding representations. Each text segment is independently fed into the model, with the [CLS] token vector extracted as the final semantic representation. Trained on a large-scale Chinese sentence-pair dataset (>22 million samples), the M3E model surpasses OpenAI's text-embedding-ada-002 model in text classification and retrieval tasks, ultimately generating 768-dimensional semantic vectors. For binary control-flow graphs (CFGs), a custom three-layer graph attention network (GAT) processes topological properties. Basic block nodes are initialized with feature vectors, and multi-head attention (8 heads) aggregates neighbor node information. Node importance ranking algorithms extract subgraph-level representations, yielding

256-dimensional feature vectors. Abstract syntax trees (ASTs) of source code are converted into graph structures incorporating sibling and parent-child relationships, then embedded via the GraphCodeBERT model [25]. This model utilizes a data flow-enhanced Transformer architecture, pretrained using masked prediction tasks on node traversal paths. Graph pooling layers aggregate information to produce 256-dimensional vectors representing syntactic structures. For numerical constants and string literals across architectures, a bidirectional LSTM encoder constructs context-sensitive embeddings. Input sequences employ byte-level encoding: the forward LSTM captures syntactic constraint patterns, while the backward LSTM models calling-context dependencies. Integers and strings are finally embedded into unified 128-dimensional vectors.

3.4 Hierarchical Alignment Network

To address the multidimensional heterogeneous gaps in syntactic information, control-flow structures, and low-level representations between source and binary modalities, we propose a hierarchical attention mechanism for fusing source and binary embedding vectors. This achieves adaptive fusion of source-binary embeddings through multi-granular cross-modal alignment.

The tripartite features (from multi-granular feature extractors) of both source and binary sides enter the hierarchical attention layer. This layer employs a three-stage gated attention network: First, feature dependencies are computed via multi-head attention (8 heads), enabling intra-modal feature fusion (① in Fig. 1); subsequently, cross-modal feature interaction is achieved in the cross-attention layer (② in Fig. 1); finally, multi-source features (① and ② in Fig. 1) are integrated through a dynamic gating mechanism.

The first intra-modal fusion layer integrates multi-granular features. The second layer is the source-binary feature interaction layer, which introduces cross-modal features into the unimodal vectors. Using the source features as *Query* and binary features as *Key/Value* (or vice versa), it outputs the cross-attention augmented feature representations:

$$C_{\text{src}\to\text{bin}} = \text{MultiHead}(h_{\text{src}}, h_{\text{bin}}, h_{\text{bin}}) \quad (1)$$

where Multi-Head Attention enhances feature diversity by independently computing attention per head and concatenating results:

$$\text{head}_i = \text{Attention}\left(QW_Q^{(i)}, KW_K^{(i)}, VW_V^{(i)}\right) \quad (2)$$

The third layer dynamically fuses information, adaptively balancing self-features and cross-modal interaction information:

$$h_{\text{final}} = g \cdot h_{\text{self}} + (1-g) \cdot h_{\text{cross}} \quad (3)$$

The Deep Similarity Network receives feature vectors from the source and binary sides, output by the hierarchical attention module. It computes the cross-modal alignment score through multi-dimensional interaction modeling and non-linear semantic fusion. Three fundamental interaction operators are designed to construct interaction features, capturing complementary relationships by computing difference, similarity, and product interactions:

$$\text{Difference:} \quad \Delta = |\mathbf{h}_{\text{src}} - \mathbf{h}_{\text{bin}}| \quad (4)$$
$$\text{Similarity:} \quad S = \mathbf{h}_{\text{src}} \cdot \mathbf{h}_{\text{bin}} \quad (5)$$
$$\text{Product:} \quad P = \mathbf{h}_{\text{src}} \odot \mathbf{h}_{\text{bin}} \quad (6)$$

where $\odot$ denotes the Hadamard product. The original features and interaction features are then concatenated to form a high-dimensional joint representation. This design simultaneously preserves the *interpretability* of original features and *discriminative power* of interaction features. A multilayer perceptron (MLP) models higher-order nonlinear relationships, ultimately computing the alignment probability (similarity score between 0-1) via the sigmoid function.

3.5 Vulnerability Detection Transfer

To address dataset scarcity in binary vulnerability detection, we innovatively leverage source-binary alignment to map binary vulnerabilities to source vulnerabilities (Fig. 4). Simply put: given a binary function, using our alignment model to iteratively evaluate against a pre-constructed source vulnerability database determines: whether the binary contains vulnerabilities and which specific vulnerabilities exist. The presence of vulnerabilities is confirmed when the binary function aligns with source functions containing documented vulnerabilities.

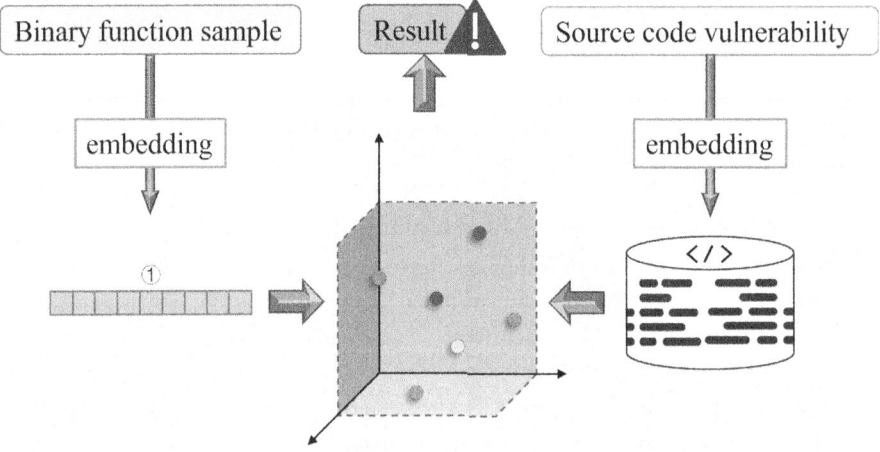

Fig. 4. Vulnerability detection workflow. Expanding binary vulnerability datasets by applying the model to vulnerability detection tasks.

We collected publicly disclosed CVE vulnerabilities and associated vulnerability types (CWE-IDs) from 8 projects: ffmpeg, libav, libtiff, linux, openssl, qemu, tcpdump, and xen across different versions. After data cleansing that removed duplicate vulnerabilities based on CVE-IDs and function names, we obtained 400 unique vulnerability functions and related information, including stack overflows, heap overflows, format string vulnerabilities, memory leaks, and other types.

For the openssl project specifically, we collected source code and binaries from four versions (0.9.8, 1.0.1, 1.1.0, and 1.1.1) spanning 60 CVEs from 2006 to 2021 (only the source vulnerability database was pre-constructed, while binary vulnerabilities were used for validation in subsequent experiments). The Table 4 of the APPENDIX shows a partial vulnerability list example for these four openssl versions.

Leveraging the multi-granular feature extractor, we embed source code functions to obtain three feature vectors of vulnerable functions. By freezing the weights of the hierarchical attention module and invoking the first weighted concatenation layer (denoted as ① in Fig. 1), we derive the feature embedding vector of source code vulnerabilities. We then utilize FAISS to construct an efficient index supporting large-scale vector similarity search, thereby building a scalable vulnerability knowledge base.

4 Experimental Evaluation

4.1 Experimental Setup

Environment and Hardware Configuration. Our experimental environment operates on Ubuntu 22.04, powered by an Intel® Xeon® Platinum 8558P CPU with 8× NVIDIA A100-SXM4-80GB GPUs, locally deploying the DeepSeekR1-70B large language model.

Datasets. Based on the BinKit2.0 public dataset, we establish <source code, binary> matching pairs through project name plus function name partitioning. Positive examples are same-name function pairs within identical projects, while negative examples include differently-named function pairs within the same project and cross-project function pairs. Finally, our dataset contains 49,016 training pairs, 9,992 validation pairs, and 9,784 test pairs.

The constructed vulnerability detection dataset comprises binary functions extracted from vulnerabilities in 8 real-world software projects, covering 52 vulnerability types from public CVEs (including Buffer Overflow, Integer Overflow, Use-After-Free, etc.). It contains 3,440 binary function samples (400 vulnerable samples), all annotated with CVE-ID, vulnerable function name, and CWE-ID. Compilation used ARM architecture with O0/O1/O2/O3 optimization levels via GCC and Clang compilers.

Baseline Models. We select the following two cutting-edge methods as baseline models for comparative experiments:

CodeCMR: This method proposes an end-to-end cross-modal retrieval network CodeCMR for function-level binary-source code matching.

CLAP: This approach proposes a method for learning transferable binary code representations through natural language supervision, using contrastive learning to align assembly code with corresponding natural language explanations.

4.2 Experiment

To systematically validate the effectiveness and innovativeness of our model, this study designs a multi-dimensional experimental framework based on mainstream academic benchmarks for binary cross-modal detection. The experimental section encompasses: ablation studies to deconstruct the contribution of key model components; comparative experiments for horizontal performance benchmarking; and vulnerability detection experiments to verify the efficacy of the alignment model in vulnerability identification tasks. To assess the model's practical applicability, we document the associated time costs in the Appendix.

Model Component Effectiveness Validation. To verify the effectiveness of multimodal feature fusion and hierarchical attention mechanisms, we design the following ablation studies: Feature ablation: Sequentially remove semantic Explanation, structural, and constant feature components. Architecture ablation: Replace the hierarchical attention module with direct concatenation.

Table 1. Ablation study outcomes. The "w/o [Component]" indicates configurations where the specified component was removed from the model.

Ablation Setting	Accuracy	Precision	Recall	F1-score
w/o Semantic Explanation	0.8266	0.6062	0.8742	0.7159
w/o Structural Features	0.9222	0.8469	0.8410	0.8439
w/o Constant Features	0.9205	0.8039	0.9019	0.8501
w/o Attention Module	0.9297	0.8776	0.8352	0.8559
Full Model	0.9433	0.8553	0.9305	0.8913

The experimental results (Table 1) indicate that the full model demonstrates optimal comprehensive performance in the cross-modal alignment task, with its accuracy (0.9433), recall (0.9305), and F1-score (0.8913) significantly outperforming all ablation conditions, validating the efficacy of multi-component collaborative design.

Specifically: (1) The absence of the large language model module causes a precipitous performance drop, demonstrating that deep semantic understanding is crucial for suppressing false positives. The core value of the semantic explanation component lies in constructing a semantic space for heterogeneous feature alignment. It maps binaries and source code onto a unified conceptual level, effectively distinguishing between superficially similar but functionally divergent code patterns. (2) The absence of structural features triggers a

9.52% recall decline, revealing its critical role in capturing the intrinsic essence of program behavior. A typical case is the recognition of semantic equivalence between a whileloop and its functionally equivalent gotoimplementation at the structural level. Modeling structural representations of both binaries and source code enables resilience against superficial variations induced by compiler optimizations. (3) Specific magic numbers can differentiate test code from malicious backdoors. Cryptographic constants identify algorithm families. This numerical semantic analysis compensates for the limitations of structural abstraction. Experiments show removing this component caused precision to drop by 5.99%, which proves integrating constants effectively mitigates misjudgments. (4) The essence of the attention module is dynamic feature weighting. Its absence caused a 10.27% recall drop, confirming its effectiveness in dynamically focusing on critical alignment regions via the three-layer attention architecture. Notably, precision increasedby 2.6% when attention was absent, indicating the model shifted towards a conservative strategy âĂŞ reducing false positives at the cost of missed detections.

Baseline Model Comparison Experiments. For comparative experiments, we selected CodeCMR—which directly performs source-to-binary alignment—and CLAP—which leverages Natural Language Explanations of source code as semantic anchors to train binary encoding models. Regarding CodeCMR, since its model is not open-source and its public dataset lacks original assembly code, adaptation to our framework was infeasible. We thus used its reported binary-to-source metric for comparison. We ensured fairness by adopting the public BinKit dataset, an industry-standard benchmark. Relative to CodeCMR's dataset, both cover:X64 and ARM architectures, GCC and Clang compilers, O0 and O3 optimizations, while maintaining equivalent dataset scale and experimental objectives. For CLAP, we utilized its open-sourced CLAP-ASM model to embed binary data, computed cosine similarity for scoring, and performed ranking based on scores. Evaluation metrics were Recall@1, Recall@10, and MRR. The experimental results in the Table 2 demonstrate our model's superiority over the baselines in cross-modal scenarios:

Table 2. Performance benchmarking in retrieval tasks. "-" indicates empty entries.

Model	Recall@1 (%)	Recall@10 (%)	MRR
CodeCMR	87.3	97.5	-
CLAP	81.9	93.7	0.824
Our Model	89.7	98.3	0.912

Compared to CodeCMR, our model achieves a 2.4% improvement in Recall@1. This gain is primarily attributed to the introduced Natural Language Explanation features, which bridge binaries and source code at a more unified abstraction level. Additionally, the Hierarchical Attention Architecture partially mitigates semantic deviation issues caused by varying compilation settings. Compared to CLAP, our model demonstrates superior performance. Analysis suggests that while using natural language explanations as semantic anchors enhances the model's zero-shot generalization capability, relying solely on natural language representations sacrifices certain structural information inherent to functions. Undoubtedly, CLAP exhibits robust zero-shot generalization. However, for precise code matching, explicit alignment achieved through end-to-end learning may prove more effective than CLAP's approach leveraging implicit linguistic supervision.

Vulnerability Detection Experiments. To verify the effectiveness of the alignment model for binary vulnerability dataset expansion, we designed vulnerability detection experiments. Using our constructed source vulnerability database as the benchmark and binary functions as input, we tested the model's cross-modal vulnerability matching performance. The overall vulnerability detection performance (average values) is presented in Table 3:

Table 3. Vulnerability detection performance evaluation. Results were tested at both function-level granularity.

Granularity	Accuracy(%)	Precision(%)	Recall(%)	F1(%)
Function-level	0.872	0.786	0.803	0.794

Specifically, detection performance varies significantly across different CWE vulnerability types as shown in Fig. 5.

Key analytical findings are as follows: Vulnerabilities such as stack overflows and format string vulnerabilities—which rely on specific function call patterns or data structures—demonstrate stable semantic alignment between binary representations and source code. The model effectively captures instruction-level and function-level co-occurrence features through hierarchical attention. Conversely, vulnerabilities like memory leaks and race conditions exhibit high semantic dependency on code context or runtime states. Compilation optimizations may eliminate critical variables or alter instruction sequences, preventing the model from recovering complete logic from static binaries. Deep analysis of false positives revealed primary causes: The alignment model erroneously associated secure binary functions (snprintf) with dangerous source functions (sprintf) in the vulnerability database; Memory-leak vulnerabilities suffered mismatches because optimization inlined or deleted resource-release code.

Experiments confirm that vulnerability detection based on source-binary alignment achieves superior performance for structurally distinct vulnerabilities but requires improvement for dynamic or optimization-sensitive vulnerabilities.

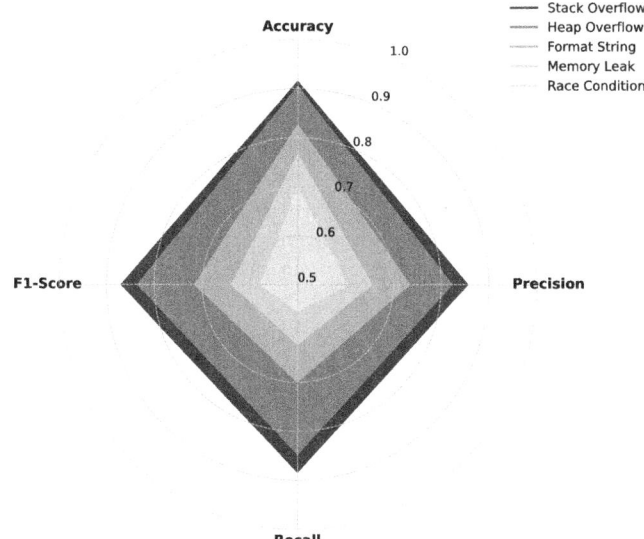

Fig. 5. When applied to vulnerability detection, the model exhibits differential sensitivity across distinct vulnerability classes.

5 Conclusion

This research addresses the core challenge of binary vulnerability detection in software supply chain security. Targeting existing techniques limited by the scarcity of binary vulnerability data and the cross-modal semantic gap, we propose a deep-alignment-based framework for cross-modal vulnerability knowledge transfer. Innovatively integrating natural language explanation generation with hierarchical attention mechanisms, we establish a function-level cross-modal feature alignment model that effectively resolves semantic drift in heterogeneous code representations. By constructing the source-binary semantic mapping space, we have achieved knowledge transfer from massive source code vulnerability data to binary detection tasks, effectively alleviating the data scarcity problem faced in traditional binary vulnerability detection tasks. Experiments show our method achieves 92.3% accuracy in cross-modal matching tasks, with 80.3% detection rate on real-world binary vulnerability datasets. This validates the transferability of the source code vulnerability database to binary detection, providing a new paradigm for overcoming the scarcity of binary vulnerability data, and represents an initial exploration of expanding the available data in the field of binary vulnerability detection.

APPENDIX

Table 4. Vulnerability Dataset Samples with Binary Associations (openssl)

CVE-ID	Function	Version	CWE-ID	Binary
CVE-2006-2937	tasn_dec:asn1_d2i_ex_primitive	0.9.8	CWE-399	tasn_dec.o
CVE-2008-0891	t1_lib:ssl_parse_clienthello_tlsext	0.9.8	CWE-189	t1_lib.o
CVE-2010-0433	kssl:kssl_ctx_show	0.9.8	CWE-20	kssl.o
CVE-2011-4576	s3_enc:ssl3_enc	0.9.8	CWE-310	s3_enc.o
CVE-2012-2333	d1_enc:dtls1_enc	0.9.8	CWE-189	d1_enc.o
CVE-2014-3569	s23_srvr:ssl23_get_client_hello	0.9.8	CWE-476	s23_srvr.o
CVE-2015-0205	s3_srvr:ssl3_get_cert_verify	0.9.8	CWE-310	s3_srvr.o
CVE-2015-0207	d1_lib:dtls1_listen	0.9.8	CWE-476	d1_lib.o
CVE-2015-0286	a_type:ASN1_TYPE_cmp	0.9.8	CWE-17	a_type.o
CVE-2015-0288	x509_req:*X509_to_X509_REQ	0.9.8	CWE-476	x509_req.o
CVE-2015-1793	x509_vfy:X509_verify_cert	1.0.1	CWE-254	x509_vfy.o
CVE-2015-1794	bn_mont:BN_MONT_CTX_set	1.0.1	CWE-189	bn_mont.o
CVE-2016-0701	dh_check:DH_check	1.0.1	CWE-200	dh_check.o
CVE-2016-0705	dsa_ameth:	1.0.1	CWE-415	dsa_ameth.o
CVE-2016-0797	bn_print:BN_hex2bn+BN_dec2bn	1.0.1	CWE-190	bn_print.o
CVE-2016-2105	encode:EVP_EncodeUpdate	1.0.1	CWE-190	encode.o
CVE-2016-2178	dsa_ossl:	1.0.1	CWE-203	dsa_ossl.o
CVE-2016-2182	bn_print:*BN_bn2dec	1.1.0	CWE-787	bn_print.o
CVE-2016-6304	t1_lib:ssl_scan_clienthello_tlsext	1.1.0	CWE-401	t1_lib.o
CVE-2016-7053	tasn_dec:asn1_item_embed_d2i	1.1.0	CWE-476	tasn_dec.o
CVE-2017-3733	ssl3_record:ssl3_get_record	1.1.0	CWE-20	ssl3_record.o
CVE-2018-0732	dh_key:generate_key	1.1.0	CWE-320	dh_key.o
CVE-2018-0734	dsa_ossl:	1.1.0	CWE-327	dsa_ossl.o
CVE-2018-0735	ec_mult:ec_scalar_mul_ladder	1.1.0	CWE-327	ec_mult.o
CVE-2019-1543	e_chacha20_poly1305:chacha20_poly1305_ctrl	1.1.0	CWE-327	e_chacha20_poly1305.o
CVE-2020-1967	t1_lib:tls1_check_sig_alg	1.1.1	CWE-476	t1_lib.o
CVE-2021-23840	evp_enc:evp_EncryptDecryptUpdate+EVP_DecryptUpdate	1.1.1	CWE-190	evp_enc.o
CVE-2021-23841	x509_cmp:X509_issuer_and_serial_hash	1.1.1	CWE-476	x509_cmp.o
CVE-2021-3449	extensions:init_sig_algs	1.1.1	CWE-476	extensions.o
CVE-2021-3712	ec_asn1:*EC_GROUP_new_from_ecparameters	1.1.1	CWE-125	ec_asn1.o

To validate the model's detection capability using real-world vulnerable binaries, we identified affected libssl package versions from Ubuntu security notices for OpenSSL CVEs (source vulnerability functions were pre-stored in our vulnerability database). By analyzing binary distributions of packages containing the

CVE-2015-0288 vulnerability, we successfully detected the vulnerable function X509_to_X509_REQ within the top-10 similarity-ranked function matches.

To specifically measure the runtime overhead of this method in practical execution and assess the feasibility and efficiency of its real-world application, we tested 2,446 functions extracted from eight projects in the BinKit dataset. The evaluation was divided into the time consumed during the embedding phase (experimental results shown in Fig. 6) and the time consumed during the detection phase (experimental results presented in Table 5). For each project function, embeddings are generated from three aspects: textual, structural, and constant-

Table 5. Model detection time evaluation. The metrics include Loading Time(LT), Retrieval Time(RT), Average Query Latency(AQL), Query Throughput(QT), and total Execution Time(ET), where the total Execution Time of the "total projects" encompasses the model loading time.

Project	LT(s)	RT(s)	AQL(ms)	QT(qps)	total ET(s)
a2ps-4.14_a2ps	0.58	64.83	70.93	14.10	65.41
gdbm-1.23_gdbmtool	0.22	19.78	63.80	15.67	20.00
hello-2.12.1_hello	0.06	5.98	65.68	15.23	6.04
bool-0.2.2_bool	0.03	3.54	62.18	16.08	3.57
datamash-1.8_datamash	0.19	21.40	69.25	14.44	21.59
which-2.21_which	0.02	2.37	76.57	13.06	2.39
readline-8.2_libreadline.so.8.2	0.46	49.73	69.94	14.30	50.19
time-1.9_time	0.01	1.58	68.81	14.53	1.59
total projects	1.57	169.22	69.18	14.45	171.03

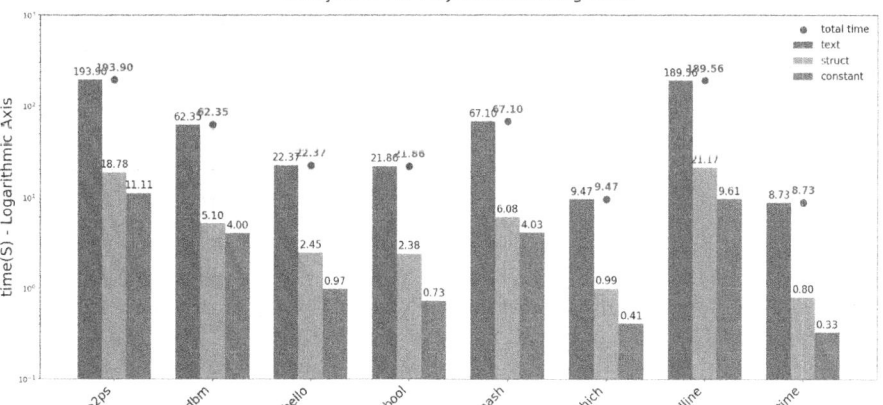

Fig. 6. Embedding Time Evaluation. project names appear in abbreviated form.

based. The embedding consumption time is dictated by the longest duration among these three parallel embedding processes.

It is important to note that source code data is preprocessed and vector embeddings are saved in advance to enable offline caching and avoid real-time computational overhead; thus, this processing time is not included in the model runtime. The actual data inputs available for the model architecture are the preprocessed three-dimensional features: natural language descriptions, CFG structures, and constants. The time required for function partitioning and preprocessing of the target binary file depends on the complexity of the file parsing itself, which is independent of the model architecture and belongs to the offline phase; thus, it is also excluded from the runtime calculation.

References

1. Jiang, L., et al.: Binaryai: binary software composition analysis via intelligent binary source code matching (2024). arXiv:2401.11161
2. Luo, Z., et al.: Cross-architecture vulnerability detection with entropy-based binary code search. In NDSS, Vulhawk (2023)
3. Aslanyan, H., Movsisyan, H., Arutunian, M., Sargsyan, S.: Bin2source: matching binary to source code. In: 2021 Ivannikov Ispras Open Conference (ISPRAS), pp. 3–7 (2021)
4. Chen, L.: Cvebinarysheet: a comprehensive pre-built binaries database for IOT vulnerability analysis. arXiv preprint arXiv:2501.08840 (2025)
5. Yu, Z., Zheng, W., Wang, J., Tang, Q., Nie, S., Wu, S.: Codecmr: cross-modal retrieval for function-level binary source code matching. In: Proceedings of the 34th International Conference on Neural Information Processing Systems, NIPS 2020, Curran Associates Inc, Red Hook (2020)
6. Gui, Y., et al.: Cross-language binary-source code matching with intermediate representations. In: 2022 IEEE International Conference on Software Analysis, Evolution and Reengineering (SANER), pp. 601–612 (2022)
7. Tian, J., Xing, W., Li, Z.: Bvdetector: a program slice-based binary code vulnerability intelligent detection system. Inf. Softw. Technol. **123**, 106289 (2020)
8. Gao, J., Yang, X., Fu, Y., Jiang, Y., Sun, J.: Vulseeker: a semantic learning based vulnerability seeker for cross-platform binary. In: 2018 33rd IEEE/ACM International Conference on Automated Software Engineering (ASE), pp. 896–899 (2018)
9. Xu, Y., Xu, Z., Chen, B., Song, F., Liu, Y., Liu,T.: Patch based vulnerability matching for binary programs. In: Proceedings of the 29th ACM SIGSOFT International Symposium on Software Testing and Analysis, ISSTA 2020, page 376–387. Association for Computing Machinery, New York (2020)
10. Frome, A., et al.: Devise: a deep visual-semantic embedding model. In: Proceedings of the 27th International Conference on Neural Information Processing Systems - Volume 2, NIPS 2013, pp. 2121–2129. Curran Associates Inc, Red Hook (2013)
11. Radford, A., et al.: Learning transferable visual models from natural language supervision. In: International Conference on Machine Learning, pp. 8748–8763. PMLR (2021)
12. Li, J., Selvaraju, R.R., Gotmare, A.D., Joty, S., Xiong, C., Hoi, S.C.H.: Align before fuse: vision and language representation learning with momentum distillation. In: Proceedings of the 35th International Conference on Neural Information Processing Systems, NIPS 2021, Curran Associates Inc, Red Hook, NY, USA, (2021)

13. Tian, Z., Qiu, R., Teng, Y., Sun, J., Chen, Y., Chen, L.: Towards cost-efficient vulnerability detection with cross-modal adversarial reprogramming. J. Syst. Softw. **223**, 112365 (2025)
14. Munkres, J.: Algorithms for the assignment and transportation problems. J. Soc. Ind. Appl. Math. **5**(1), 32–38 (1957)
15. Xu, K., Hu, W., Leskovec, J., Jegelka, S.: How powerful are graph neural networks? (2019). arXiv:1810.00826
16. Miyani, D., Huang, Z., Lie, D.: Binpro: a tool for binary source code provenance (2017). arXiv:1711.00830
17. Wang, H., et al.: Clap: learning transferable binary code representations with natural language supervision. In: Proceedings of the 33rd ACM SIGSOFT International Symposium on Software Testing and Analysis, ISSTA 2024, pp. 503–515. Association for Computing Machinery, New York (2024)
18. Wang, H., et al.: Jtrans: jump-aware transformer for binary code similarity detection. In: Proceedings of the 31st ACM SIGSOFT International Symposium on Software Testing and Analysis, pp. 1–13 (2022)
19. Touvron, H., Lavril, T., Izacard, G.,et al.: Llama: open and efficient foundation language models (2023). arXiv:2302.13971
20. DeepSeek-AI, Guo, G., Yang, D., Zhang, H., et al.: Deepseek-r1: incentivizing reasoning capability in LLMs via reinforcement learning (2025). arXiv:2501.12948
21. Hex-Rays. IDA Pro: Interactive disassembler and debugger. Product webpage (2024). https://hex-rays.com/ida-pro. Accessed 10 June 2025
22. joernio. Joern: Open-source code analysis platform. GitHub repository (2023). https://github.com/joernio/joern
23. Shellphish, The Computer Security Lab at UC Santa Barbara, SEFCOM at Arizona State University, and Rhelmot. angr: A powerful and user-friendly binary analysis platform. GitHub repository (2024). https://github.com/angr/angr
24. Chen, J., Xiao, S., Zhang, P., Luo, K., Lian, D., Liu, Z.: Bge m3-embedding: multi-lingual, multi-functionality, multi-granularity text embeddings through self-knowledge distillation (2024). arXiv:2402.03216
25. Guo, D., Ren, S., Lu, S., et al.: Graphcodebert: pre-training code representations with data flow (2021). arXiv:2009.08366

Access Control and Privacy

CryptNyx: Password-Hardened Encryption with Strong Anonymity Guarantees

Tassos Dimitriou[✉] [iD] and Shahad Alshaher

Department of Computer Engineering, Kuwait University, Kuwait, Kuwait
`tassos.dimitriou@ieee.org, s.alshaher@ku.edu.kw`

Abstract. In this work, we introduce CryptNyx, a Password Hardening (PH) framework that enhances the security of stored password records through collaboration between the authentication server and an external server, also known as rater. PH mitigates *offline* password brute force attacks on stolen databases by involving the rater in the password verification process, enabling it to impose limits on password decryption attempts. However, this means that the remote server can track user login requests, raising concerns about potential compromises to user privacy. Consequently, achieving effective rate-limiting while preserving user anonymity has remained an unresolved challenge.

CryptNyx ensures anonymity *without* sacrificing rate-limiting. Essentially, the user pseudonym, which allows the rater to track login requests, can be refreshed any number of times in a controlled but unlinkable manner, offering complete anonymity while still mitigating offline guessing attempts. Furthermore, CryptNyx allows for password-hardened encryption capabilities, which enable users to securely encrypt sensitive data using their strengthened password records. Additional features include an "Opt-out" protocol that facilitates client withdrawal, and an "Anonymous Opt-in" protocol designed for efficient batch registration.

Experimental results demonstrate the effectiveness and practicality of our approach, highlighting the balance between user privacy, security, and system functionality.

Keywords: Password-hardened encryption · Anonymity · Obliviousness · Forward security · Verifiability · Offline password guessing attacks

1 Introduction

Password-based authentication is widely used to authorize users into accessing online services that store sensitive user data—such as credit card details, critical documents, and photos—requiring user authorization to protect user privacy and security. The traditional method of implementing password-based authentication is commonly referred to as Salted Password Hashing; a random salt is added to the password before hashing and the resulting string is stored in the server's database, helping prevent password leakage, brute-force, and rainbow table attacks [19]. However, despite these protections, the growing incidents of credential database breaches reveal its limitations. With enough computational power, attackers can perform an *offline* brute-force attack on stolen salted hashes to recover the passwords and impersonate users. Major companies like Yahoo, Adobe, and Canva have suffered from the consequences of such breaches [24][1].

Password Hardening. To prevent offline brute-force attacks against password databases, Password Hardening (PH) was introduced [8,14,15]. PH involves the collaboration of an additional remote server (besides the authentication server) to harden stored password records. It applies a Pseudo Random Function (PRF), such as HMAC, using a secret known only to the remote server to generate a "hardened" password record. During user registration, the hardened password record can only be constructed through the *collaboration* of both servers. Likewise, the login process requires both servers to validate a candidate password. Additionally, the remote server enforces *rate-limiting* on the number of password record decryption attempts. If an attacker compromises the authentication server and steals the password database, they must verify guesses *online* with the remote server. This is further mitigated by the rate-limiting measures, which restrict the number of online attempts and enhance security. Thus, an attacker must compromise both servers to successfully mount a brute-force attack.

Facebook was among the first to adopt PH [17], relying on a remote server to apply HMAC using a secret known only to that server. The result is stored by Facebook's authentication server database. This design distributes critical information: the password hashes reside on the authentication server, while the secret remains in the remote server. As a result, compromising a single server is inefficient to perform an offline brute-force attack. However, Facebook's design lacks a mechanism for secret rotation. If the remote server is breached, the only way to update the secret is to delete the entire password database and re-register users, which is cumbersome and risky. Additionally, Facebook's design is vulnerable to online guessing attacks: an attacker with the password database can repeatedly prompt the remote server until the correct password is found.

Everspaugh et al. [8] proposed Pythia to formalize the notion of PH and address these gaps. Pythia inherits Facebook's design with additional advantages. Its novelty lies in the proposed cryptographic primitive called verifiable partially oblivious PRF (PO-PRF). As opposed to conventional OPRFs [9] and their verifiable variants V-OPRFs [12], this primitive enables revealing only a specific portion (e.g., a pseudonym) of the message being hardened, while keeping other sensitive information (e.g., the password) hidden from the remote server (for more information, see [6]). As a result, the remote server can prevent online guessing by *limiting* login attempts per user without learning the

---

[1] "Crypt" is a reference to the procedure employed in traditional password systems to securely hash and store passwords. "Nyx" is regarded as one of the primordial deities in Greek mythology, emerging from Chaos and embodying the essence of darkness. CryptNyx denotes a robust and innovative approach to harden user passwords.

password. Pythia also supports bulk key rotation that enables updating the key without re-encrypting the entire password database. Since then, many distinct PH schemes were proposed inheriting Pythia's features while introducing unique advantages [4,10,14,15,25].

Motivation and Challenges. Maintaining user anonymity is a critical aspect of security. This concept has various formal definitions in academic literature and encompasses different levels and forms of anonymity. For instance, pseudonymity involves the use of an alias in place of a user's true identity, while unlinkability ensures that multiple actions by a user cannot be connected to one another [20]. In the context of authentication with PH, user anonymity is defined against the public, including the remote server enforcing rate-limiting (referred to as "rater") and eavesdroppers, but not the authentication server itself (referred to as "client"). This is because the latter is obliged to obtain the user identity for purposes like account recovery, billing, etc. Achieving user anonymity from the rater, however, is essential for preventing tracking, mitigating targeted attacks, and safeguarding user privacy. This area remains an open research direction, as highlighted by Lai et al. [14], who emphasized the need of ensuring user anonymity *while* implementing rate-limiting in PH. This is both crucial and contradictory, as the rater needs to link user login requests to limit password decryption attempts and prevent online guessing. Consequently, it gains knowledge about the login history of all users and potentially compromises their privacy.

A contribution towards addressing this issue is a scheme called Anonymous Password Hardened-Encryption (APHE) [10]. APHE leverages trusted execution environments (called Enclaves) provided by Intel's Software Guard Extensions (SGX) [11,16]. The authors propose dividing time into short intervals called epochs; rate-limiting is ensured within any epoch such that the remote server still traces login requests back to the user. However, user anonymity is only guaranteed across different epochs, whose durations are the same for all users. Additionally, APHE heavily relies on Intel's SGX for its Secure Enclave features, resulting in a lack of cross-platform compatibility and limiting its use to Intel-based systems. Moreover, these systems are vulnerable to attacks, as demonstrated in [18].

Despite advancements in PH schemes, a significant gap still exists: there is currently no scheme that *simultaneously* achieves message encryption, user anonymity without sacrificing rate-limiting, and support for both client deregistration from rater (opt-out)[2] and anonymous batch registration to a new rater (opt-in), all while ensuring cross-platform compatibility.

Contributions. In response to this need, we propose **CryptNyx**, a framework that builds upon and extends previous research to ensure user anonymity without

---

[2] The opt-out capability (originally proposed in [13]) allows a client to withdraw from a rater, for instance, to revert to traditional password storage like salted hashing or to migrate to a different rate-limiting service.

compromising rate limiting. Our anonymity guarantee is defined on a per-user basis: the rater can link a user's login requests and enforce rate-limits up to a configurable threshold of successful authentications. This threshold can be adjusted based on *user-specific* preferences (e.g., some prioritize privacy more than others) or according to the application's anonymity and privacy requirements. Once the threshold is met, CryptNyx breaks the connection to previous requests, effectively preventing the rater from associating future logins with past activity. Additionally, setting the threshold to 1 facilitates a pseudonym refresh after each login, ensuring *complete* unlinkability of pseudonyms. This approach prevents the rater from linking long-term behavior to a single identity, thereby offering strong anonymity while supporting rate-limiting.

Our contributions can be summarized as follows:

1. We propose a cryptographic anonymization mechanism that enforces per-user anonymity by unlinking login requests after a specified threshold of successful authentications is reached. Anonymity is achieved asynchronously through an "Anonymize" protocol, executed individually per user.
2. We incorporate "Key rotation" to enable offline updates of all user records. Additionally, we consider an "Opt-out" protocol that allows clients to withdraw from a rater as well as an anonymous "Opt-in" protocol for private, batch registration of existing users to a new rater.
3. Following prior designs, we incorporate password-based message encryption into the hardened records to enable secure storage of sensitive data.
4. Finally, we analyze security and conduct extensive experiments to evaluate the practicality and performance of CryptNyx, demonstrating its viability for deployment in authentication systems.

Organization. The next section reviews related work on PH. Section 3 introduces the system overview, high-level functionality, security goals, and assumptions underlying CryptNyx. Section 4 provides a comprehensive description of CryptNyx's operations. A security analysis and experimental evaluation of CryptNyx are presented in Sect. 5. Finally, Sect. 6 concludes this work and outlines directions for future research.

2 Related Work

Facebook was among the first to adopt PH, utilizing a remote server for HMAC-based password security [17]. The HMAC is applied to passwords using a secret known only to the remote server. This concept was formalized later by Everspaugh et al. as a PH service called Pythia [8], which strengthens and expands Facebook's construction through preventing online guessing attacks while preserving the privacy of the record sent to the remote server. It also proposes a new feature: batch key update without user intervention.

Subsequent advances led to more efficient schemes like PO-COM [21] and Phoenix [15], the latter being a state-of-the-art PH solution during that time. But until then, the functionality of PH schemes was limited to the hardening (and validation) of one special message which is the password. Specifically, PH was used to validate a candidate password against a hardened record, whereas the functionality of message encryption and decryption was not supported. A year after Phoenix, a scheme called Password-Hardened Encryption (PHE) [14] was proposed supporting the aforementioned property. In particular, the scheme provides encryption and decryption of a message besides the password, making the scheme useful for applications that require both authentication and data encryption. However, Baecker et al. in [2] identified a weakness in PHE that enables an offline brute-force attack on password records, and proposed a mitigation strategy.

A threshold variant of PHE was proposed in [4], to increase the availability of the PH service and mitigate single point of failure. When one remote server is unreachable due to a failure, encryption and decryption can still be performed through an alternative remote server. A TLS-based PH scheme was proposed in [7], and PH scheme with "opt-out" feature was proposed in [13]. The withdrawal feature is necessary in case the client seeks to revert to the traditional method of storing password hashes, i.e. without utilizing an external encryption secret from a rater, or wishes to register to a different rater.

Anonymous PHE (APHE) [10] is a scheme that preserves user anonymity by ensuring untraceability from the rater between short time intervals (regarded as epochs). APHE introduces a trade-off between rate-limiting and anonymity between these intervals. For example, if an epoch is set to one day, all user logins within that day can be linked and traced back to the user, while rate-limiting is preserved. Once a new epoch starts, subsequent logins cannot be linked with ones in past epochs. Consequently, the rate-limiting counter is restarted in every new epoch. However, APHE uses Secure Enclaves in Software Guard Extensions (SGX), built into Intel processors, hence this method relies heavily on specialized hardware which might create a vulnerability due to potential exploits in the underlying architecture [18]. Furthermore, epochs are uniform across all users and cannot be customized. More importantly, if the duration of an epoch is too short, the ability to rate-limit is lost. Our work overcomes these limitations by achieving full anonymity across updates, on a per-user basis, utilizing solely cryptographic means.

Other protocols provide similar security guarantees to PH but lack some of its essential features. For instance, Password Protected Secret Sharing (PPSS) [3] and Distributed Password Verification (DPV) [5] do not support per-user rate-limiting and are difficult to adopt for this purpose. Anonymous tokens with public metadata [1,22] focus on unlinkability but lack built-in support for password verification. In general, PH research is based on the concept of partially oblivious PRFs which are application motivated [22,23]; these PRFs enable a server to effectively manage and enforce a rate limit on the number of requests made by a client, based on a specific public component of the input (for more, the reader is referred to [6]). However, to fully realize the potential of PH, additional properties are required to ensure its effectiveness and robustness.

A summary of the key properties achieved by our protocol and a comparison with the most relevant works is shown in Table 1.

Table 1. Comparison with existing protocols

Properties	Pythia [8]	PHE [14]	APHE [10]	PW-Hero [13]	CryptNyx
Password Hardening	✓	−[1]	✓	✓	✓
Encryption	−	✓	✓	−	✓
Key-rotation	✓	✓	✓	✓	✓
Anonymity	−	−	◇[2]	−	✓
Opt-out	−[3]	−[3]	−	✓	✓
Batch opt-in	−[3]	✓	−	−	✓

✓: Provided ◇: Partially provided −: Not provided
[1]Scheme falls prey to offline password guessing attack as shown in [2].
[2]Relies on specialized hardware, which may limit compatibility and introduce additional vulnerabilities. Epoch durations are the same for all users and must be sufficiently long; otherwise, rate-limiting is lost.
[3]Although not mentioned, it can be incorporated into the scheme with minimal modifications.

3 CryptNyx Overview

For the remainder of this paper, we will denote the authentication server as "client" (as it is considered a client to the remote PH server), and the remote server providing PH services while ensuring rate-limiting as "rater". In our model, we identify three key participants: *users* U, the *client* C, and the *rater* R (Fig. 1). The user seeks to securely access her online resources using her password. The client's role is to facilitate secure access by verifying the provided password against the password record stored in its database. Moreover, the client is responsible for safeguarding the records against offline brute-force attacks. To achieve this, the client registers with a rater that offers PH and rate-limiting services. The rater provides external encryption and decryption services for password records using its own secret. Furthermore, it aims to mitigate online guessing attacks by monitoring the login attempts of each user.

3.1 Security and Functionality Goals

To ensure maximum anonymity, it is crucial to prevent the rater from linking any login request to previous ones submitted by the same user. This can be accomplished by employing a one-time value (referred to as a "rater pseudonym") for every login request. Although this method provides a strong level of anonymity, it introduces challenges for implementing rate-limiting. In particular, the rater needs to link login requests tied to a pseudonym to effectively apply rate-limiting measures and thwart online guessing attacks on passwords. Consequently, a trade-off between preserving user anonymity and enforcing rate-limiting seems to be unavoidable.

In this work, we propose a method for rate-limiting that safeguards user privacy. Specifically, the rater pseudonym can be refreshed after any number of successful logins – potentially even after just one! This approach enables asynchronous anonymization for users, eliminating the need for batch processing. As a result, our method ensures *complete unlinkability* with only a slight increase in cryptographic operations.

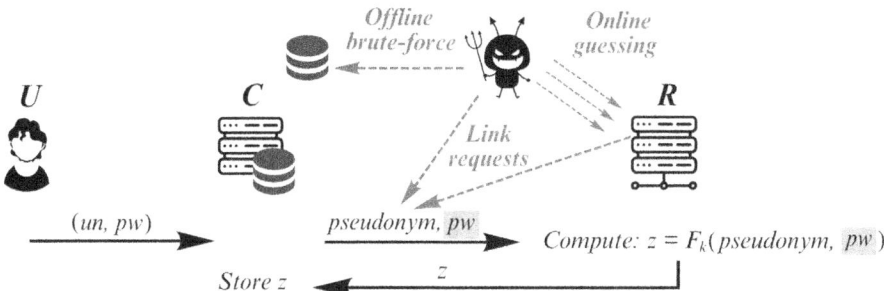

Fig. 1. General workflow of PH. The PRF z is computed by R on blinded password pw (shaded) using its secret k, and stored by C. An adversary can mount offline brute-force attacks on a stolen database if PH is not used or attempt online guessing attacks by interacting with R. A malicious rater can undermine the privacy of U by attempting to correlate different authentication requests through the observation of the transmitted pseudonym value.

CryptNyx incorporates the basic security properties of PH systems and extends them to support our user anonymity goal. Below, we outline the high-level security properties:

– *Message Hiding*: This property protects against offline password guessing attacks by adversaries who compromise the client. Specifically, an adversary who observes a PRF record F_k generated for a known distribution of passwords (potentially just two) should be unable to determine which password was used, even with access to the client's key, by *guessing* the password. Furthermore, any such guesses must go through rate-limiting measures, allowing only online attempts.
– *Partial Obliviousness*: While the rater learns the pseudonym value, it must learn nothing about the user's password or secret message. This ensures that sensitive values are kept private even if the rater is compromised. It also promotes organizational acceptance of subscribing to PRF services provided by third parties. This property relates to the concept of a *partial oblivious* PRF [8] that allows the secure computation of a PRF $F_k(t, m)$ on rater key

k in which only a portion of the input is revealed (the pseudonym t) while the rest remains hidden from the rater.
- *Forward Security*: Rotating the keys of the client and the rater results in total removal of the previous key(s) and their corresponding update tokens. The key rotation also acts as a cryptographic erasure of all PRF records encrypted with the old key(s).
- *Pseudonym Unlinkability*: This property ensures that once a user undergoes anonymization, their new pseudonym cannot be linked to their previous one by the rater—it must be cryptographically concealed from the rater during the jointly executed anonymization process. Consequently, login requests after anonymization appear unlikable to those prior to it. This property should hold regardless of the user's login frequency and should correspond to the number of successful logins before anonymization, which is set by the client to match their service requirements. Additionally, anonymization must be asynchronous–each user can be anonymized independently without requiring batch processing.

CryptNyx includes functionalities expected by all PH schemes such as:

- *Rate-Limiting*: The rater must be able to limit each user's login attempts via the pseudonym value, preventing offline password guessing by requiring client interaction.
- *Verifiability*: The client must be able to verify the PRF values returned by the rater to ensure correct subsequent executions, i.e. logins.
- *Key Rotation*: The authenticated client can request a key change. After verifying the client, the rater provides an update token for the client to update *all* PRF records *without* requiring the users to be online.

We further extend the list of functionalities as follows:

- *Encryption*: As in [10,14], the client can use the hardened password record to securely encrypt a user's secret (e.g., a symmetric key K for subsequent user data encryption), ensuring it can only be decrypted with the correct password.
- *Opt-out*: The client must be able to withdraw from the PRF service, allowing migration or reversion to unhardened records. This action requires prior authentication by the rater to prevent misuse.
- *Batch Opt-in*: A client must be able to batch-register all users to a new rater without requiring them to be online to re-enter their passwords, avoiding the need to generate hardened records individually.

We assume that the adversary can compromise either the client or the rater, but not both at the same time. Our primary focus is on preventing offline password brute-force attacks, which occur when a compromised client steals the password database. While such a client could attempt to interact with users to learn their passwords, this strategy significantly increases the likelihood of detection. Therefore, we do not classify this user interaction as an attack. Instead, we concentrate on protecting against the more insidious threat of offline guessing attacks. Finally, we assume the existence of a secure channel between the client and the rater (e.g., through TLS), which is also a common assumption in other password hardening schemes [8,10,14,15].

3.2 Definition of CryptNyx

Below, we present the key operations of CryptNyx. For the sake of simplicity, we do not enumerate every possible input that these algorithms may require. More details can be found in Sect. 4. The system includes a client C, users U, rater R, and the following operations:

- Setup(1^λ): On input security parameter λ, this algorithm outputs bilinear-group parameters $params \leftarrow (\mathbb{G}_1, \mathbb{G}_2, \mathbb{G}_T, g_1, g_2)$.
- RaterKeyGen($params$): Generates the key material for the rater. For each client identifier w, it samples $k_w \in \mathbb{Z}_p$, stores it in a table indexed by w, and gives $Y_w = g^{k_w}$ to the client, where g is a generator of $\mathbb{G}_1$.
- ClientKeyGen($params$): Generates the key material for the client. It samples a secret $k_c \in \mathbb{Z}_p$, for use in record hardening and encryption.
- RegisterUser(U): When a user registers to the client for an account with a chosen password m_U, the client initializes a fresh pseudonym t_U and a symmetric key K, which is used to encrypt user data. Using oblivious PRF evaluation with the rater, they generate $z_U = F_{k_w}(t_U, m_U)$ for rate-limiting logins and $v_U = G_{k_w}(t_U, m_U, K)$ to conceal the user key K. The tuple $\langle U, t_U, z_U, v_U \rangle$ is then stored in the client's database.
- VerifyUser(U): On input $\langle U, t_U, z_U, v_U \rangle$ and a candidate password m'_U, the client and rater recompute $z'_U = F_{k_w}(t_U, m'_U)$ and check $z'_U \stackrel{?}{=} z_U$. Regardless of success, the rate-limit counter for t_U is incremented. If $z'_U = z_U$, the rater returns a mask to enable the client to recover K from the record v_U.
- AnonymizeUser(U): When login counter reaches a threshold, the client assigns the user a fresh pseudonym t_U^* via an oblivious refresh with the rater, replacing $\langle U, t_U, z_U, v_U \rangle$ by $\langle U, t_U^*, z_U^*, v_U^* \rangle$. Throughout this process, the new pseudonym t_U^* is never revealed to R, thus breaking the link with previous user logins.
- RotateKeys(): After authentication, the client requests an update token α by the rater and both sides update $k'_c = \alpha k_c$ and $k'_w = \alpha k_w$. As a result, the client re-encrypts all records (z_U, v_U) under the new keys without requiring users to be online.
- Opt-out(): The authenticated client retrieves k_w from the rater and reverts every hardened record to its baseline (unhardened) form.
- Opt-in(): The client registers all existing users with a new rater R in a single batch. It blinds all password records (z_U) and sends them to the rater. The rater samples a fresh k_w, returns new PRF outputs and masks, then the client uses the masks to compute z_U and stores the new records $\langle U, t_U, z_U, v_U \rangle$ without any user interaction.

3.3 Security Definitions

CryptNyx incorporates many of the security properties provided by Pythia and similar protocols. Due to space constraints, however, we provide formal definition only for the user pseudonym unlinkability property, which presents a significant innovation and is not addressed in previous works. Thus, we focus on a malicious rater acting as the adversary, whose objective is to link pseudonyms before and after anonymization. The definition of *Unlinkability* (Unl) and the relevant oracles are given in the sequel. Analysis of the remaining properties can be found in Sect. 5.1, where the game structure is described but *not* detailed due to space restrictions. Adversary $\mathcal{A}$ has access to the following oracles:

- SysS(R): A call to this procedure enables $\mathcal{A}$ to initiate the system setup process and produce the system parameter params along with a public key for R, who is under the control of $\mathcal{A}$.
- RegU(U): A call to this procedure enables $\mathcal{A}$ to generate a new user U through an RegisterUser call executed between R and C. Upon successful termination, $\mathcal{A}$ will acquire any resulting transaction data.
- VfyU(U): A call to this procedure enables $\mathcal{A}$ to interact with an existing user U through a VerifyUser call executed between R and C. Upon successful termination, $\mathcal{A}$ will acquire any resulting transaction data.
- CorR(R): A call to this procedure allows $\mathcal{A}$ corrupt an honest rater R and obtain R's secret keys.
- AnonU(t): A call to this procedure allows $\mathcal{A}$ to run the Anonymize protocol with an honest C, and current pseudonym t. Upon successful termination, $\mathcal{A}$ will acquire any resulting transaction data, while a new pseudonym will be associated with U.
- Challenge($\mathcal{U}_0, \mathcal{U}_1$): A call to this procedure allows $\mathcal{A}$ to initiate an Anonymize protocol by suggesting two honest users U_0 and U_1. The RegU queries for these two users are executed, and the Anonymize protocol is run for both users, hence obtaining new pseudonyms for them. Then a final Vfy call is executed for user U_b, for random $b \in \{0, 1\}$, between C and $\mathcal{A}$, where $\mathcal{A}$ acts as the rater R. The goal of $\mathcal{A}$ is to determine which of the two users is being verified.

Unlinkability (Definition 1) is ensured through the game shown in Fig. 2. The goal is to prevent the adversary from linking users to their pseudonyms under the assumption that all actions are controlled by $\mathcal{A}$. Initially, the adversary registers multiple users and interacts with a client C through the VfyU, and AnonU protocols. Following this learning phase, $\mathcal{A}$ enters a Challenge phase with two users U_0 and U_1, chosen by $\mathcal{A}$. Both users are anonymized and then a user U_b from the chosen pair, determined by a random bit b unknown to $\mathcal{A}$, is selected to be verified. Ultimately, $\mathcal{A}$ outputs a value b'. The scheme ensures unlinkability if the adversary cannot determine b from transactional data with probability significantly better than $1/2$.

Experiment $\text{Exp}_{\mathcal{A}}^{\text{Unl}}(\lambda)$:
$b \leftarrow \mathcal{A}^{\text{SysS, RegU, VfyU, CorR, AnonU, Challenge}}(1^\lambda)$

The experiment returns 1 iff $\mathcal{A}$ passes the following phases:

- *Setup phase*: $(pk_\mathcal{R}) \leftarrow \mathcal{A}^{\text{SysS}}(1^\lambda)$
- *Learning phase*: $\text{transRecord} \leftarrow \mathcal{A}^{\text{SysS, RegU, VfyU, CorR, AnonU, Challenge}}()$
- *Challenge phase*: $\text{transRecord}(U_b) \leftarrow \mathcal{A}^{\text{Challenge}}(U_0, U_1)$

Finally, $\mathcal{A}$ outputs $U_{b'}$ that is equal to U_b.

Fig. 2. Pseudonym unlinkability experiment.

Definition 1. (Unlinkability) *A password hardening system achieves pseudonym unlinkability if, for any probabilistic polynomial-time adversary $\mathcal{A}$ in the experiment of Fig. 2, the advantage of $\mathcal{A}$ is defined by*

$$\text{Adv}_{\mathcal{A}}^{\text{Priv}}(\lambda) := Pr[\text{Exp}_{\mathcal{A}}^{\text{Priv}}(\lambda) = 1] = 1/2 + \epsilon,$$

where ϵ is negligible in λ.

It is implicitly assumed that $\mathcal{A}$ lacks any access to the internal memory of users or the client. Otherwise, it could easily win the game described above. As stated in Sect. 3.1, all transfers are made through anonymous communication channels so that users are not identified by their IP addresses or other metadata.

4 CryptNyxDescription

Denote by $\mathbb{G}_1$, $\mathbb{G}_2$, and $\mathbb{G}_T$ be groups of prime order p with a valid bilinear pairing defined as $e : \mathbb{G}_1 \times \mathbb{G}_2 \to \mathbb{G}_T$. Hence, for the generators $g_1 \in \mathbb{G}_1$ and $g_2 \in \mathbb{G}_2$ there exists a generator $g_T \in \mathbb{G}_T$ such that the following formula $e(g_1^\alpha, g_2^\beta) = g_T^{\alpha\beta}$ applies for all $\alpha, \beta \in \mathbb{Z}_p$. Furthermore, let $H_1, H_3 : \{0,1\}^* \to \mathbb{G}_1$ and $H_2 : \{0,1\}^* \to \mathbb{G}_2$ be three hash functions modeled as random oracles.

4.1 User Registration

When a user U registers to a client C (which can be a web cloud service, social media service, etc.), two new PRF records z_U, v_U are constructed, containing her chosen password m_U and a pseudonym t_U (which is a randomly generated salt). z_U is used to verify U in subsequent logins, whereas v_U encrypts her secret message or a symmetric key K_U encrypting all her data. The records are computed jointly by C and R as shown in Fig. 3.

First, C initializes a pseudonym t_U and a symmetric key K_U for U (which may also be user-chosen). The pseudonym must be unique for every user, as it serves as a user identifier to R to enforce rate-limiting. To ensure confidentiality, it is necessary to conceal the password m_U from R. To achieve this, C initializes

Client C	**Rater** R
$(t_U, m_U, k_c, K_U, Y = g^{k_w})$	(k_w)

$r \xleftarrow{\$} \mathbb{Z}_p$		
$x \leftarrow H_2(m_U)^r$	$\xrightarrow{w, t_U, x}$	Initialize a counter to rate-limit on t_U
		$z'_U \leftarrow e(H_1(t_U), x)^{k_w}$
		$h \leftarrow e(H_3(t_U), x)^{k_w}$
Verify π. If ok, proceed	$\xleftarrow{z'_U, h, \pi}$	$\pi \leftarrow ZKP(DL(Y) = DL(z'_U) = DL(h))$
$z_U \leftarrow z'^{1/r}_U$		
$v_U \leftarrow h^{1/r} \cdot H_3(t_U, m_U)^{k_c} \cdot K_U^{k_c}$		
Store $\langle U, t_U, z_U, v_U \rangle$		

Fig. 3. User registration with client C.

Client C	**Rater** R
$(m'_U, k_c, Y = g^{k_w})$	(k_w)

Retrieve $\langle U, t_U, z_U, v_U \rangle$		
$r_0 \xleftarrow{\$} \mathbb{Z}_p$		
$x_0 \leftarrow H_2(m'_U)^{r_0}$	$\xrightarrow{w, t_U, x_0, z_U^{r_0}}$	Retrieve rate-limit counter c_U on t_U
		Proceed if $c_U < Limit$, else abort
		$z'_U \leftarrow e(H_1(t_U), x_0)^{k_w}$
		If $z'_U \neq z_U^{r_0}$, increase c_U. Notify C and abort
		$c_U \leftarrow 0$ $\triangleright$ reset rate-limit counter
		$h \leftarrow e(H_3(t_U), x_0)^{k_w}$
Verify π. If ok, proceed	$\xleftarrow{h, \pi}$	$\pi \leftarrow ZKP(DL(Y) = DL(h))$
$\triangleright$ Recover user key		
$t \leftarrow v_U / H_3(t_U, m'_U)^{k_c}$		
$K_U \leftarrow (t/h^{1/r_0})^{1/k_c}$		

Fig. 4. User verification.

a random exponent $r \in \mathbb{Z}_p$ and blinds m_U as $x = H_2(m_U)^r$. To construct the PRF record, C sends its identifier w, user's pseudonym t_U and her blinded password x to R. It is important to note that only m_U was blinded from R. This is necessary because R needs to identify U using their pseudonym t_U value in order to implement rate-limiting for subsequent login attempts.

Subsequently, R retrieves k_w and computes the PRF record through $z'_U = e(H_1(t_U), H_2(m_U)^r)^{k_w} = e(H_1(t_U), H_2(m_U))^{k_w r}$ and the mask $h = e(H_3(t_U), H_2(m_U)^r)^{k_w}$. Then, it returns h and z'_U along with a ZK proof of knowledge of k_w.[3] C unblinds z'_U by raising it to $1/r$ to obtain z_U and computes $v_U = h^{1/r} \cdot H_3(t_U, m_U)^{k_c} \cdot K_U^{k_c}$. Then both r and h are safely discarded and the new entry $\langle U, t_U, z_U, v_U \rangle$ is stored in C's database.

---

[3] The rater proves knowledge of k_w used in the construction of z'_U and h as well as in the public key $Y = g^{k_w}$. This is straightforward and omitted.

4.2 User Verification

This protocol is jointly executed between C and R to verify a registered user U during login. The user U provides her password m'_U to access her encrypted data. It is important to note that this password may not necessarily be her correct chosen password due to a typo or a potential online guessing attack. If verification is successful, the encryption key K_U can be recovered to unlock user data as shown in Fig. 4.

Client C retrieves $\langle U, t_U, z_U, v_U \rangle$ and sends $t_U, x_0, z_U^{r_0}$, where $x_0 = H_2(m'_U)^{r_0}$ and z_U is the password record, both blinded with a new random value r_0. First, R performs rate-limiting on t_U. If the number of login attempts is not exceeded, R computes the PRF record from the provided password as $z'_U = e(H_1(t_U), x_0)^{k_w}$ and validates it by checking whether $z'_U =^? z_U^{r_0}$. Matching values indicate that U provided a correct password and incorrect, otherwise.

If verification is successful, R computes the mask $h = e(H_3(t_U), x_0)^{k_w}$ and returns it with a ZK proof of knowledge of k_w; otherwise, it returns an error message indicating an incorrect user password and increments the rater counter for t_U. To recover the user's key, C first computes $t = v_U / H_3(t_U, m'_U)^{k_c}$. Once h is received, the key K_U can be recovered as $K_U = (t/h^{1/r_0})^{1/k_c}$, where k_c is the secret key of C. Upon successful login, C increments the successful logins counter of U, which once reaches its predefined maximum, the anonymization process of U is triggered.

Client C	Rater R
$(m'_U, k_c, Y = g^{k_w}, t_U^*)$	(k_w)
Retrieve $\langle U, t_U, z_U, v_U \rangle$	
$r_0, r_1, r_2 \xleftarrow{\$} Z_p^3$	
$x_0 \leftarrow H_2(m'_U)^{r_0}$	
$x_1 \leftarrow H_1(t_U^*)^{r_1}$ $\xrightarrow{w, t_U, x_0, x_1, x_2, z_U^{r_0}}$	Rate-limit t_U as in Verification
$x_2 \leftarrow H_3(t_U^*)^{r_2}$	$z'_U \leftarrow e(H_1(t_U), x_0)^{k_w}$
	If $z'_U \neq z_U^{r_0}$, signify error and abort
	$c_U \leftarrow 0$ ▷ reset rate-limit counter
	$\tilde{z}_U \leftarrow e(x_1, x_0)^{k_w}$
Verify π. If ok, proceed $\xleftarrow{h, h', \tilde{z}_U, \pi}$	$h \leftarrow e(H_3(t_U), x_0)^{k_w}$, $h' \leftarrow e(x_2, x_0)^{k_w}$
▷ Update U's record	$\pi \leftarrow \text{ZKP}(DL(Y) = DL(h) = DL(h') = DL(\tilde{z}_U))$
$z_U^* = \tilde{z}_U^{1/r_0 r_1}$	
$t = v_U \cdot h'^{(1/r_0 r_2)} / h^{1/r_0}$	
$v_U^* = t \cdot H_3(t_U^*, m'_U)^{k_c} / H_3(t_U, m'_U)^{k_c}$	
Store $\langle U, t_U^*, z_U^*, v_U^* \rangle$	

Fig. 5. User anonymization protocol.

4.3 Anonymize

This protocol is executed for each user once they reach a predefined number of successful logins. It refreshes the user's old rater pseudonym to ensure unlinkability from the rater's perspective. As a result, the rater will not be able to associate logins linked to the new pseudonym with those linked to the old pseudonym for any user. Moreover, this protocol allows for independent anonymization of users in an asynchronous manner. Active users who log in more frequently will be anonymized more often than less active or inactive users, thereby preserving the anonymity of all. The end result, is a refreshed record of a user U, containing the new rater pseudonym as shown in Fig. 5.

In more details, the protocol is initiated by C to anonymize a user U once she reaches the maximum number of successful logins[4]. The process is analogous to VerifyUser(U) with an extra step to refresh t_U to a new value t_U^* without rater R learning the new value. Let $\langle U, t_U, z_U, v_U \rangle$ be the current record of U in the client C and r_0, r_1, r_2 new random values. Besides sending $w, t_U, x_0 = H_2(m'_U)^{r_0}, z_U^{r_0}$ to R, the client C also sends $x_1 = H_1(t_U^*)^{r_1}$ and $x_2 = H_3(t_U^*)^{r_2}$, where t_U^* is the new pseudonym blinded with r_1 and r_2, respectively.

First, R performs rate-limiting on t_U. If number of login attempts is acceptable, R computes $z'_U = e(H_1(t_U), x_0)^{k_w}$ and validates it by checking whether $z'_U \stackrel{?}{=} z_U^{r_0}$. If the test succeeds, it uses the new blinded pseudonym to compute $\tilde{z}_U = e(x_1, x_0)^{k_w}$, which is a new blinded PRF record of U, together with $h = e(H_3(t_U), x_0)^{k_w}$ and $h' = e(x_2, x_0)^{k_w}$. Then, R sends the three values along with a ZK proof of knowledge of k_w to C. Upon validating the proof, C unblinds $\tilde{z}_U$ by raising it to $(1/r_0 r_1)$ to obtain z_U^*. Next, C recovers the user's key as described in the verification protocol (Fig. 4). Finally, C updates v_U by unblinding h'—raising it to $1/r_0 r_2$—then computing $v_U^* = v_U \cdot (h'^{(1/r_0 r_2)}/h^{1/r_0})$. $(H_3(t_U^*), m'_U)^{k_g}/H_3(t_U, m'_U)^{k_c})$. The new user record becomes $\langle U, t_U^*, z_U^*, v_U^* \rangle$.

4.4 Key Rotation

This protocol is executed when a client C (or the rater) requests to update the keys k_w and k_c to new ones $k'_w = \alpha k_w$ and $k'_c = \alpha k_c$. This update is essential in the event of a detected compromise or can be implemented as a proactive security measure to enhance overall system security.

In particular, client C, identified to R by w, initiates the key reset operation by sending a signed request to R. Due to the critical nature of this operation, R

---

[4] A concern here is that the rater might learn to associate certain pseudonyms that consistently disappear when a threshold is met. However, this issue can be effectively mitigated by assigning *multiple* pseudonyms to users. Hence, establishing thresholds for these pseudonyms can significantly enhance the overall anonymity set. Additionally, setting the threshold to 1 facilitates a pseudonym refresh after *each* login, ensuring *complete* unlinkability of pseudonyms. This strategy further reduces the risk of diminished anonymity, as it prevents the rater from making associations between pseudonyms.

requires C to authenticate itself before issuing the update token. This authentication can be performed by a special re-key message $\text{Sig}_C(\text{"Rekey"})$, which is signed by the client and is used to initiate the whole process.

Once C is successfully authenticated, R generates a random integer α and transmits it over a secure channel to C. The client can then use α to update all records z_U, v_U as follows: $z_U^\alpha = e(H_1(t_U), H_2(m_U))^{\alpha k_w} = e(H_1(t_U), H_2(m_U))^{k'_w}$ and $v_U^\alpha = e(H_3(t_U), H_2(m_U))^{\alpha k_w} \cdot H_3(t_U, m_U)^{\alpha k_c} \cdot K_U^{\alpha k_c} = e(H_3(t_U), H_2(m_U))^{k'_w} \cdot H_3(t_U, m_U)^{k'_c} \cdot K_U^{k'_c}$. This effectively updates the keys of rater and client to k'_w and k'_c, respectively, without requiring any user involvement.

4.5 Opt-Out and Opt-in

The Opt-out protocol allows the client C to revert the users' hardened password records to their baseline form. This means that the records will no longer be encrypted under the external secret of the rater R. This process is accomplished in a single exchange, which significantly simplifies the procedure. More importantly, it eliminates the need for costly and risky re-registration or active participation from users, thereby ensuring a smoother transition. Opt-out works by having the rater R release the key k_w to C, who, upon validation, uses it to revert the records z_U, v_U for all users U to traditional salted hashes.

Once the client C has opted out from the rater R, it can proceed to register all existing users with a new rater R' using the Opt-in protocol. This subsequent batch registration process is designed to be efficient and secure, allowing the client to maintain user anonymity while facilitating a seamless transition to the new rater. The Opt-in protocol operates by having the client C send blinded values to the new rater R', which then hardens each record using a newly initialized key k_w. Thus, Opt-in ensures that existing users can be re-registered offline in a manner that protects their privacy, thereby reinforcing the integrity of the system.

Due to space restrictions, the full description of these protocols will be provided in an extended version of the paper.

5 Analysis

5.1 Security of CryptNyx

In what follows we present a number of theorems demonstrating that CryptNyx satisfies obliviousness, hiding, verifiability, forward security, and unlinkability. The proofs are presented in manner consistent with earlier works on PH [8,14,15], however, with details omitted due to space restrictions. Recall that we assume that an adversary will not compromise both the client and the server simultaneously; if this were to occur, any PH protocol would be rendered insecure. Additionally, we assume that the client involved during verification and anonymization cannot be malicious unless explicitly stated otherwise.

Theorem 1. (Partial Obliviousness). *Suppose the Discrete Log assumption holds and the hash functions are modeled as random oracles. Then CryptNyx is partially oblivious.*

Proof (sketch). This property protects against a malicious rater who intends to learn the password m from a user's record, while allowing it to learn the pseudonym to enforce the rate-limiting. Obliviousness can be proved by arguing that the rater cannot distinguish whether the password used during registration or verification is m_0 or m_1. In the relevant game, the adversary is allowed to create a user U and select two passwords m_0, m_1. These passwords are then given to a challenger, who randomly selects a bit $b \in \{0, 1\}$ and sets the user password to m_b. Then it creates the necessary records through an interaction between the client and the rater. The adversary's goal is to correctly guess b.

However, among the values transmitted between client and rater only $H_2(m_b)^r$ depends on the password, where r is a random nonce. Hence the adversary needs to distinguish between $H_2(m_0)^r$ and $H_2(m_1)^r$, which is impossible without knowledge of r (essentially this is equivalent to the Discrete Log problem). Since this problem is hard, the adversary's chances of success are negligible.

Theorem 2. (Hiding). *Suppose the Discrete Log assumption holds and the hash functions are modeled as random oracles. Then CryptNyx is hiding.*

Proof (sketch). This property protects against an attacker who compromises the client—gaining access to its keys and all user records—and intends to extract a user's password m_U or secret key K_U, from one of the records.

First, notice that extracting the user password from the PRF record $z_U = e(H_1(t_U), H_2(m_U))^{k_w}$ requires the recovery of rater key k_w in order to perform an offline dictionary attack on m_U. However, this task is equivalent to solving the Discrete Logarithm problem, which is considered infeasible. Second, recovering the key K_U from the value $v_U = h \cdot H_3(t_U, m_U)^{k_c} \cdot K_U^{k_c}$ requires knowledge of the mask $h = e(H_3(t_U), H_2(m_U))^{k_w}$, which has been safely deleted during registration. Thus, the probability of the attacker recovering the password m_U and key K_U is equivalent to guessing h, which is again negligible.

Theorem 3. (Forward Security) *Suppose CryptNyx is hiding and the Discrete Log assumption holds. Then CryptNyx is forward secure.*

Proof (sketch). The key rotation protocol protects against an attacker who steals all user records and intends to extract a user's password pw from one of the records. It functions as cryptographic erasure of all previous keys and user records encrypted with those keys, rendering them useless to an attacker even if they have already been stolen. Thus, the old secret keys must not provide any advantage to an adversary attempting to extract information from an updated record. This is essential as it ensures that even if an adversary has access to outdated keys, they cannot leverage that access to compromise the integrity of the new records.

To establish forward security, we demonstrate that the verification records updated through the key rotation protocol are indistinguishable to freshly generated records. Let $z_U = e_0^{k_w}$ denote an old record, where e_0 is a shorthand for $e(H_1(t_U), H_2(m_u))$. After rotation, the record becomes $z'_u = e_0^{\alpha k_w}$, or equivalently $z'_u = (e_0^\alpha)^{k_w} = e_0'^{k_w}$, for random α and $e'_0 = e_0^\alpha$. Thus, in the context of the security game, and owing to the hardness of the Discrete Log problem, an adversary cannot distinguish between the records $\langle k_w, e_0, e_0^{k_w} \rangle$ and $\langle k_w, e'_0, e_0'^{k_w} \rangle$ with probability better than random guessing. The same applies to the record v_U and the client key k_c since the protocol is hiding.

Theorem 4. (Verifiability). *Given that the proof system is Sound and Zero-Knowledge, CryptNyx satisfies the verifiability property.*

Proof (sketch). This property protects against a malicious rater replying to client requests with incorrect values. The client can verify all returned values before processing them. Security thus depends on the soundness of the Zero-Knowledge proofs employed in the protocol. A malicious rater cannot convince the client into accepting a wrong record, without demonstrating a valid proof of knowledge. Specifically, the rater has to prove knowledge of the secret key k_w used in the construction of the record z_U and the computation of the mask h. The requirement for the rater to provide such proof ensures that the client can independently verify the correctness of the computations involved. Moreover, the soundness property of Zero-Knowledge proofs ensures that if the rater claims to have knowledge of k_w and fails to do so, the probability of the client being convinced of a false statement is negligible. Thus, if an adversary exists that can generate proofs for contradictory statements in the protocol, this adversary can be leveraged to undermine the soundness of the ZK proof systems.

Theorem 5. (Unlinkability). *Given that the Discrete Logarithm problem is hard, and the proof system is Zero-Knowledge, CryptNyx satisfies the unlinkability property.*

Proof (sketch). This property protects against a rater who intends to link the pseudonyms t_U and t_U^* after executing the anonymize protocol for some user U. During the unlinkability game, an adversarial rater $\mathcal{A}$ might engage in the protocol operations with two users U_0 and U_1. At some point, the challenger picks a random bit b and calls the anonymize protocol for user U_b. The goal of the adversary is to find b with probability better than random guessing (recall Definition 1). Below, we explain why this is not possible.

We consider the following cases under which $\mathcal{A}$ might be able to win the unlinkability game. In the first case, the adversary extracts $H_2(m_{U_b})$ from $H_2(m_{U_b})^{r_0}$ transmitted during anonymization. Doing the same for the values transmitted during verification, it can compare $H_2(m_{U_b})$ against $H_2(m_{U_0})$ or $H_2(m_{U_1})$, hence distinguish between U_0 and U_1. However, this is infeasible due to the hardness of the Discrete Logarithm problem. In the second case, the adversary recovers the new pseudonym $t_{U_b}^*$ from the value $H_1(t_{U_b}^*)^{r_1}$ transmitted by the client in the second phase of the anonymization protocol. Knowing

Table 2. Rater requests per second for different methods on a single core. Operations in [15] are termed enroll/validate, whereas in [14], they are designated as encrypt/decrypt.

System	Operation	Rater Throughput
Pythia [8]	register/verify	136.3
Phoenix [15]	register	1580.97
	verify	370.61
PHE [14]	register	570.21
	verify	567.35
CryptNyx	register	79.21
	verify	73.81
	anonymize	44.47

the pseudonym value, can help in linking this value to the previous one, thus de-anonymizing the user among verification requests. However, this is again infeasible due to the hardness of the Discrete Log. In the third case, the adversary extracts the secret key k_w from the proofs posted during registration or verification/anonymization, thus recovering the nonces t_U, t_U^*. However, this is infeasible due to the ZK property of the NIZK proof system.

5.2 Experimental Evaluation

In our experiments, we evaluate our solution within the context of a PHE web service. We independently benchmark the cryptographic operations in CryptNyx and other methods, namely Pythia [8], Phoenix [15], and PHE [14], to estimate the overall cost of each protocol. To ensure our simulations closely reflect real-word web server behavior, we assume an `https` connection with `keep-alive`, as in [14]. This configuration maintains persistent connections, minimizing latency and emulating the rapid response times of modern web servers, i.e. raters managing concurrent client requests. We include benchmarked network delays based on this assumed configuration. All simulations and benchmarks were implemented in Python 3.8.10, and conducted in a virtual machine running Ubuntu 20.04, allocated four CPU cores. The host system is equipped with Intel Core i7 (1.80 GHz) processor and 16 GB of RAM.

Rater Throughput. We evaluated the rater's processing capacity by measuring the number of requests it can handle per second for each method. The simulations were executed on a single core, and the measurements were averaged over 200 trials. The findings, presented in Table 2 indicate that CryptNyx achieves rater throughput about half that of Pythia, due to the additional bilinear pairing computation required for encryption. However, in settings where encryption is not needed, the throughput effectively doubles approaching Pythia's performance. Overall, the reduced performance represents an acceptable trade-off for preserving anonymity, especially given that CryptNyx also incorporates encryption and decryption in addition to Pythia's features.

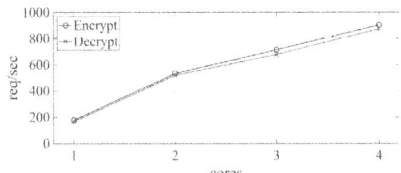

Fig. 6. PHE client throughput in req/s.

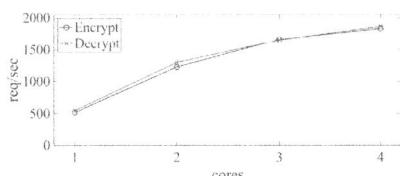

Fig. 7. PHE rater throughput in req/s.

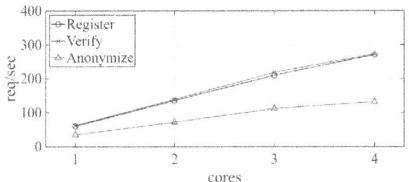

Fig. 8. CryptNyx client throughput in req/s.

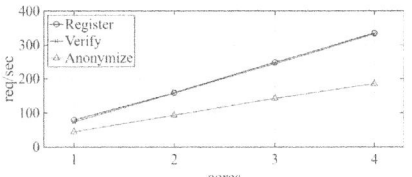

Fig. 9. CryptNyx rater throughput in req/s.

Client Throughput. We also measured the client throughput in both CryptNyx and PHE, averaging the results over 200 trials. PHE was chosen for this comparison as it is the only cryptographic PH scheme that supports encryption and decryption, despite the recent vulnerabilities discovered in [2]. By analyzing the throughput of both the client and the rater, we can estimate the latency a user experiences after entering her password, prior to verification and data decryption. Given that the client side computations are more than those on the rater side, it is expected that the client throughput will be lower than that of the rater. This expectation is confirmed by the experimental results, as illustrated in Figs. 6 and 8 for PHE and CryptNyx, respectively.

Scalability. We evaluated the client and rater throughput of the main protocols of CryptNyx and PHE across varying CPU core configurations —1, 2, 3 and 4 cores— to compare the scalability and assess the impact of parallel processing on performance. The obtained results reveal that the throughput of CryptNyx grows linearly with the number of CPU cores. Notably, when utilizing 4-5 CPU cores, CryptNyx approaches the efficiency of PHE operating on a single core as demonstrated in Figs. 6, 7 for PHE, and 8, 9 for CryptNyx. This shows that the overhead associated with the use of pairings is minimal when weighed against the significant benefits of providing both user anonymity and effective rate-limiting.

6 Conclusions

In this work, we proposed CryptNyx, a password hardened encryption (PHE) service that retains all properties of existing PH schemes, while introducing a critical missing property: unlinkability against the external PH server, referred to as the "rater". This property prevents the rater from tracking the users' login activity, thereby safeguarding user privacy. Achieving unlinkability in PH schemes is inherently challenging, as it appears to conflict with the fundamental requirement of per-user rate-limiting—an open problem also highlighted by Lai et al. [14].

CryptNyx resolves this tension by achieving full unlinkability without compromising rate-limiting. Unlike prior work, which offers only partial unlinkability and requires costly batch anonymization, our scheme supports per-user anonymization once a configurable threshold of successful authentications is reached. Moreover, CryptNyx relies purely on cryptographic primitives, ensuring broader compatibility and resilience against hardware-based vulnerabilities. CryptNyx also incorporates additional practical features: opt-out, which enables a client to efficiently withdraw from a PH service, and batch opt-in, which allows the registration of all existing users to a new PH service in a single exchange.

In terms of security, CryptNyx satisfies the security guarantees inherited from prior PH schemes, while providing anonymity through unlinkability of pseudonyms. Finally, comparative experimental evaluation across multiple PH schemes further demonstrate the practicality and scalability of our approach. As part of future work, we plan to focus on eliminating the need for pairings, thereby optimizing CryptNyx for efficient scaling in high-traffic web applications. Furthermore, we aim to address metadata-related privacy leaks—such as login timing patterns and frequency—which continue to undermine anonymity in existing online systems.

Acknowledgments. The authors would like to thank the anonymous reviewers for their constructive feedback, which helped improve the readability of the paper. This work was supported and funded by Kuwait University Research Grant No. EO03/25.

References

1. Amjad, G., Yeo, K., Yung, M.: RSA blind signatures with public metadata. Cryptology ePrint Archive (2023)
2. Baecker, R., Gerhart, P., Schröder, D.: Password-hardened encryption revisited. Cryptology ePrint Archive (2025)
3. Bagherzandi, A., Jarecki, S., Saxena, N., Lu, Y.: Password-protected secret sharing. In: Proceedings of the 18th ACM Conference on Computer and Communications Security, pp. 433–444 (2011)
4. Brost, J., Egger, C., Lai, R.W., Schmid, F., Schröder, D., Zoppelt, M.: Threshold password-hardened encryption services. In: Proceedings of the 2020 ACM SIGSAC Conference on Computer and Communications Security, pp. 409–424 (2020)
5. Camenisch, J., Lehmann, A., Neven, G.: Optimal distributed password verification. In: Proceedings of the 22nd ACM SIGSAC Conference on Computer and Communications Security, pp. 182–194 (2015)
6. Casacuberta, S., Hesse, J., Lehmann, A.: SoK: oblivious pseudorandom functions. In: 2022 IEEE 7th European Symposium on Security and Privacy (EuroS&P), pp. 625–646. IEEE (2022)
7. Diomedous, C., Athanasopoulos, E.: Practical password hardening based on TLS. In: Perdisci, R., Maurice, C., Giacinto, G., Almgren, M. (eds.) DIMVA 2019. LNCS, vol. 11543, pp. 441–460. Springer, Cham (2019). https://doi.org/10.1007/978-3-030-22038-9_21

8. Everspaugh, A., Chaterjee, R., Scott, S., Juels, A., Ristenpart, T.: The pythia PRF service. In: 24th USENIX Security Symposium (USENIX Security 15), pp. 547–562 (2015)
9. Freedman, M.J., Ishai, Y., Pinkas, B., Reingold, O.: Keyword search and oblivious pseudorandom functions. In: Kilian, J. (ed.) TCC 2005. LNCS, vol. 3378, pp. 303–324. Springer, Heidelberg (2005). https://doi.org/10.1007/978-3-540-30576-7_17
10. Ha, G., Jia, C., Ge, X., Yuan, J., Chen, H., Li, M.: Efficient and anonymous password-hardened encryption services. Inf. Sci. **653**, 119771 (2024)
11. Intel Corporation: Intel® Software Guard Extensions Programming Reference, Rev. 2. Intel Corporation (2014). https://www.intel.com/content/dam/develop/external/us/en/documents/329298-002-629101.pdf
12. Jarecki, S., Kiayias, A., Krawczyk, H.: Round-optimal password-protected secret sharing and t-PAKE in the password-only model. In: Advances in Cryptology–ASIACRYPT, pp. 233–253. Springer (2014)
13. Jia, C., Wu, S., Wang, D.: Reliable password hardening service with opt-out. In: 2022 41st International Symposium on Reliable Distributed Systems (SRDS), pp. 250–261. IEEE (2022)
14. Lai, R.W., Egger, C., Reinert, M., Chow, S.S., Maffei, M., Schröder, D.: Simple password-hardened encryption services. In: 27th USENIX Security Symposium (USENIX Security 18), pp. 1405–1421 (2018)
15. Lai, R.W., Egger, C., Schröder, D., Chow, S.S.: Phoenix: rebirth of a cryptographic password-hardening service. In: 26th USENIX Security Symposium (USENIX Security 17), pp. 899–916 (2017)
16. McKeen, F., et al.: Innovative instructions and software model for isolated execution. Hasp@ isca **10**(1) (2013)
17. Muffet, A.: Facebook: password hashing and authentication. Presentation at Real World Crypto (2015)
18. Nilsson, A., Bideh, P.N., Brorsson, J.: A survey of published attacks on intel SGX. arXiv preprint arXiv:2006.13598 (2020)
19. Oechslin, P.: Making a faster cryptanalytic time-memory trade-off. In: Boneh, D. (ed.) CRYPTO 2003. LNCS, vol. 2729, pp. 617–630. Springer, Heidelberg (2003). https://doi.org/10.1007/978-3-540-45146-4_36
20. Pfitzmann, A., Hansen, M.: A terminology for talking about privacy by data minimization: anonymity, unlinkability, undetectability, unobservability, pseudonymity, and identity management (2010)
21. Schneider, J., Fleischhacker, N., Schröder, D., Backes, M.: Efficient cryptographic password hardening services from partially oblivious commitments. In: Proceedings of the 2016 ACM CCS, pp. 1192–1203 (2016)
22. Silde, T., Strand, M.: Anonymous tokens with public metadata and applications to private contact tracing. In: International Conference on Financial Cryptography and Data Security, pp. 179–199. Springer (2022)
23. Tyagi, N., Celi, S., Ristenpart, T., Sullivan, N., Tessaro, S., Wood, C.A.: A fast and simple partially oblivious PRF, with applications. In: Annual International Conference on the Theory and Applications of Cryptographic Techniques, pp. 674–705. Springer (2022)
24. Wikipedia: List of data breaches — Wikipedia, The Free Encyclopedia (2016). https://en.wikipedia.org/wiki/List_of_data_breaches#List_of_data_breaches_involving_companies, Accessed 2 Nov 2024
25. Wu, S., Wang, D.: Universally composable and reliable password hardening services. Cryptology ePrint Archive (2024)

Efficient Dynamic Group Signatures with Forward Security

Amin Mohammadali(✉) and Riham AlTawy

University of Victoria, Victoria, BC, Canada
{aminmohammadali,raltawy}@uvic.ca

Abstract. In dynamic group signature schemes (GSS), forward security ensures that newly joined members cannot generate valid signatures for past time periods. Additionally, non-frameability prevents even privileged entities, such as the group manager or key issuer, from falsely attributing signatures to honest users. Most GSS either lack non-frameability or face significant efficiency challenges when updating signing keys to ensure forward security. In this paper, we introduce a forward-secure dynamic group signature scheme that guarantees non-frameability. We also present an alternative scheme that, while lacking non-frameability, offers higher efficiency compared to existing schemes with comparable security. For both protocols, we propose efficient revocation mechanisms that allow an authority to revoke users without requiring re-registering existing users. Additionally, we propose a technique that enables the verification process of both protocols to be performed in batches. We prove the security of our schemes, ensuring the standard dynamic GSS security notions; anonymity, traceability and non-frameability (second scheme). Experimental results demonstrate that our schemes are competitive in both computational and communication efficiency when compared to existing literature.

Keywords: Dynamic Group Signature · Forward Security · Non-framability · Revocation

1 Introduction

Group Signature Schemes (GSS) were first introduced by Chaum and van Heyst in 1991 [13] and has since gained substantial attention from the cryptographic community as well as various stakeholders, specifically, those concerned with user privacy in the digital world. In a GSS, each signer (a.k.a member) has a secret signing key to generate signatures that can be verified using the group's public key. A valid group signature authenticates the signer's membership in the group while ensuring their anonymity. However, in the event of misbehavior, an authorized entity known as Group Manager (GM) can identify the signer. Furthermore, a trusted entity has the power to revoke a user's membership such that the remaining members can continue the group signing process [3,

13,31,36]. Group signatures, have found extensive applications across multiple domains such as electronic voting systems [30], blockchains [1,36], anonymous authentication [15,25], access control systems [40], and vehicle communication systems [22,38].

Group signatures are classified as static or dynamic. In static groups, a trusted entity known as key issuer assigns unique signing keys to a static number of users, requiring complete trust in the issuer and limiting the scalability of the scheme [6]. On the other hand, in dynamic groups, users participate in generating their own keys using an interactive *Join* procedure with the issuer which reduces the trust assumptions about the key issuer and extends the flexibility of the scheme [6,23]. Bellare et al. have defined anonymity, traceability and non-framability and have shown that they are required security notions for dynamic GSS [7]. Moreover, they have proven that these three requirements imply other notions such as unforgeability, unlinkability, exculpability, and collusion resistance. Anonymity ensures that a signature does not reveal the signer's identity within the group and prevents linking multiple signatures to the same signer. Traceability ensures that an adversary cannot generate a signature that either prevents the GM from identifying its signer or causes the GM to mistakenly attribute it to an honest member. Non-framability on the other hand guarantees that no entity, even the group manager and key issuer, can falsely generate a signature and convince a judge that it is generated by an honest user.

Key challenges in dynamic schemes include forward security, preventing new users from signing past messages[6], and revocation, ensuring revoked users cannot sign while preserving the validity of other members' signatures. Group signature revocation processes generally fall into two main categories. The first approach involves maintaining a revocation list that records information about excluded members [11,28]. The second method focuses on updating the secret information of remaining members to prevent the revoked user from participating in future signing [37,39]. These distinct strategies offer different trade-offs in terms of efficiency and security in managing group membership. In existing schemes that support revocation [3,10], revoked users are effectively prevented from participating in the signature generation process. However, when new users join the group, they can still generate valid signatures for events that occurred prior to their enrollment. To add forward security, existing approaches typically require all group members to participate in a new join procedure to obtain updated public and private keys. This process imposes substantial computational and communication overhead, rendering it impractical for large-scale systems. To date, there have been proposed a wide range of schemes that do not guarantee efficient forward security [2,9,10,12,16,18,19,24,26,32,36]. We aim to design an efficient forward secure group signature scheme that ensures standard security properties while achieving high efficiency across all procedures, including signature generation, verification, tracing, and revocation.

Related Works. Boneh et al. introduced the BBS scheme which prevents even the key issuer from generating a signature on behalf of a valid user [10]. Subsequently, Boneh et al. proposed a variant with verifier-Local revocation, reducing communication overhead but increasing computational costs, as verification time grew with the number of revoked users [11]. They suggested a modification to achieve constant-time verification at the expense of slightly reduced anonymity. Ferrara et al. extended BBS by integrating batch verification, but this significantly increased signature size, making it less suitable for constrained environments [19]. Bichsel et al. explored an alternative to BBS but introduced higher computational costs for both signing and verification [9]. Delerablee et al. developed a GSS scheme with stronger security model (CCA-anonymity instead of CPA) and slightly reduced signature size compared to BBS but increased computational overhead [17]. Similarly, Libert et al. proposed a GSS that ensures anonymity but suffers from high computational costs in both signer and verifier sides [26]. Bichsel et al. introduced the Sign-Randomize-Prove (SRP) paradigm, significantly improving the signature size but imposing high computational costs for identity opening and revocation. Specifically, verification required checking an equation for each revoked user, making it impractical for large groups [9]. Pointcheval and Sanders later extended SRP but lacked a revocation mechanism, further limiting its scalability [32]. Derler et al. proposed a group signature scheme, but it remained inefficient in the opening phase and incurred high computational and communication costs [18]. Clarisse et al. improved SRP-based schemes, achieving competitive efficiency but failed to support revocation and efficient opening process [16]. Kim et al. extended the PointchevalSanders (PS) scheme to support batch verification. However, their approach lacked a revocation mechanism [24]. Libert et al. [27] proposed a forward-secure group signature scheme; however, their definition of forward security deviates from that of Bellare et al. [6]. In Libert et al.'s model, the private key is periodically updated, and even if a key is compromised, it cannot be used to derive keys from earlier time periods. In contrast, Bellare et al.'s definition strengthens this notion by additionally requiring that an adversary, even after compromising the current key, must not be able to forge valid signatures for any *past* time periods. Building on these concepts, Ling et al. [29] proposed a forward-secure group signature scheme based on a lattice-based cryptosystem. However, it suffers from substantial communication overhead.

Our Contribution. This paper presents two practical dynamic group signature schemes (GSSs) that address forward security, non-frameability, and computational and communication efficiency. Our schemes ensure efficiency in signature generation, opening, and revocation. We propose two protocols: the first, denoted as DGSS, prioritizes efficiency but does not maintain non-frameability, while the second, denoted as xDGSS, guarantees non-frameability with a slight increase in communication and computation overhead. Additionally, we introduce a batch verification technique that enhances the efficiency of both schemes. We provide a comprehensive security analysis, proving that our protocols satisfy anonymity, traceability, and non-frameability (for xDGSS). Finally, we implement the cryptographic operations of our schemes and, using experimental measurements, compare their performance and security with other related works.

2 Preliminaries

In what follows, we briefly introduce the cryptographic primitives that are used in the design of our schemes. We also detail the generic description of dynamic group signature schemes and the associated security requirements.

2.1 Bilinear Pairing

Let a bilinear group be denoted by $\{q, \mathbb{G}_1, \mathbb{G}_2, \mathbb{G}_T, e, g_1, g_2\}$ where $\mathbb{G}_1, \mathbb{G}_2$ and $\mathbb{G}_T$ are groups of prime order q, e is a bilinear map such that $e : \mathbb{G}_1 \times \mathbb{G}_2 \longrightarrow \mathbb{G}_T$. g_1 and g_2 are generators of $\mathbb{G}_1$ and $\mathbb{G}_2$, respectively. Let φ denote a computable isomorphism from $\mathbb{G}_2$ to $\mathbb{G}_1$, with $\varphi(g_2) = g_1$. We assume that the φ is one-way (easy to compute $\mathbb{G}_1 = \varphi(\mathbb{G}_2)$, and hard to compute $\mathbb{G}_2$ from $\mathbb{G}_1$.

2.2 Complexity Assumptions

In what follows, we introduce the complexity assumptions used in the proposed group signature.

Definition 1. *(Computational Diffie-Hellman Problem (CDH)[34]): Given $g \in \mathbb{G}$, $X = g^x$ and $Y = g^y$, for unknowns x and y chosen at random from $\mathbb{Z}_q^*$, find Z such that $Z = g^{xy}$.*

Definition 2. *(Strong Diffie-Hellman (SDH) problem [10]): Let $\mathbb{G}_1$ and $\mathbb{G}_2$ be two cyclic groups of prime order p. Given generators $g_1 \in \mathbb{G}_1$, $g_2 \in \mathbb{G}_2$ and $(g_1, g_2, g_2^x, g_2^{x^2}, \ldots, g_2^{x^q})$ for a randomly chosen $x \in \mathbb{Z}_p^*$, the Strong Diffie-Hellman (SDH) assumption states that no probabilistic polynomial-time adversary $\mathcal{A}$ can compute a pair $(g_1^{1/(x+c)}, c)$, where $c \in \mathbb{Z}_p^*$, with non-negligible probability.*

2.3 Dynamic Group Signature Schemes

A dynamic GSS consists of a tuple of seven probabilistic polynomial-time (PPT) algorithms: KeyGen, Join, Sign, Verify, Open, Judge, and Update.

In the *KeyGen* algorithm, given a security parameter λ, a key generator produces the issuer's secret key(s) isk, the group public key(s) gpk, and the GM/opener's secret key(s) ok. Secret keys are securely delivered to their respective owners, and gpk is published. A user u_i engages in the interactive *Join* algorithm with the issuer to obtain a secret signing key sk_i, after which the issuer stores the user's registration information reg_i in the registration list $Rlist$. Using sk_i, a member signs a message $M \in \{0,1\}^*$ via the *Sign* algorithm to produce a group signature σ. Anyone can run the *Verify* algorithm with gpk, M, and σ to check validity, returning 1 if valid, and 0 otherwise. The GM executes the *Open* algorithm using ok, M, σ, and $Rlist$ to identify the signer, returning the identity or $\perp$ if no match is found. The *Judge* algorithm allows anyone to verify the correctness of the GM's output, taking M, σ, gpk, and the revealed identity as input, and returning 1 if valid, or 0 otherwise. Finally, the key issuer updates the public keys to ensure that a new member cannot generate a valid signature using the previous public key, while existing members can continue signing with the updated keys.

GSS Security Notions. Bellare et al. [7] established three essential requirements for a dynamic group signature scheme: anonymity, traceability, and non-framability. They showed that these three requirements guarantee all the necessary GSS requirements defined in the literature, including unlinkability, unforgeability, collusion resistance [4], strong exculpability [10], and framing resistance [14]. We briefly explain these properties and refer the reader to the original paper [7] for details. Moreover, we formally define the notion of forward security in dynamic group signatures, based on the framework presented in Bellare et al. [6].

Anonymity. This requirement ensures that no adversary can identify the signer or link signatures to the same signer. The anonymity model for dynamic GSSs allows adversaries to collude with a malicious key issuer, while the GM is assumed to be honest [7]. In this model, an adversary $\mathcal{A}$ queries the anonymity challenger with two uncorrupted identities (i_0^*, i_1^*) and a message m^*. The challenger responds with a signature σ_b^* under i_b^* for a randomly chosen bit $b \in \{0,1\}$. If $\mathcal{A}$ can distinguish which identity was used, it successfully breaks anonymity by returning $b' = b$. Note that the (m^*, σ^*) tuple is restricted from being queried to the open oracle. The adversary can leverage an oracle to obtain secret keys for all users except i_0^* and i_1^*.

Traceability. This requirement ensures that an adversary cannot generate a valid signature that prevents the *Open* algorithm from identifying the actual signer. Additionally, it guarantees that if the *Open* algorithm identifies the signer, the *Judge* algorithm must successfully verify this identity. In this model, the adversary gains access to the GM's key by compromising it, while GM remains an honest entity. The adversary also obtains the secret values of all users except the target user it intends to attack. The adversary $\mathcal{A}$ is allowed to query the sign oracle with messages of its choice and receives a valid signature σ. $\mathcal{A}$ is also allowed to query the open oracle with the signatures and receive valid identifier i. $\mathcal{A}$ succeeds if it outputs a valid σ^* for a message m^* such that m^* has not been queried before and the *Open* algorithm fails to output an identifier of a valid member or it outputs an identifier of an honest member which the *Judge* algorithm fails to verify.

Non-frameability: Non-frameability ensures that an adversary cannot produce a valid signature σ^*, m^* and i^* that convinces the *Judge* algorithm that an honest user created it. The adversary is extremely powerful as it can fully corrupt both the GM/opener and key issuer, obtaining their secret keys. In this model, the adversary $\mathcal{A}$ outputs a message m^*, a signature σ^*, and an identity i^*. $\mathcal{A}$ succeeds if σ^* is a valid signature for m^*, i^* is an honest user, and the *Judge* algorithm accepts that i^* created σ^*. This must occur without the adversary querying the signing oracle with i^* and m^* or obtaining i^*'s signing key.

Forward Security: Intuitively, a forward-secure group signature scheme ensures that a member cannot generate valid signatures for any previous time period in which they were not a group member [6]. An alternative definition proposed in [35] interprets forward security as the inability of an adversary to efficiently recover past keys from the current one. However, this notion is insufficient, as it does not fully capture the practical security requirements. In a more rigorous model, the adversary, who may be a legitimate group member, is given the current secret key of the targeted signer, as well as the current and previous keys of all other group members. The adversary is considered successful if it can forge a valid signature by the target signer for a document or message corresponding to an earlier time period, i.e., the signature is valid under a group public key that was valid during that previous time period.

3 The Proposed Dynamic Group Signature Schemes

We propose two protocols. The first scheme, DGSS, prioritizes efficiency at the cost of non-framability. The second protocol, xDGSS, ensures non-framability with a slight increase in computational and communication overhead.

3.1 Design Rationale and Technical Contribution

Our scheme builds upon the efficient BBS group signature scheme by Boneh et al. [10], but introduces several key modifications to achieve forward security and non-frameability simultaneously, batch verification, CCA-anonymity, and reduced computational and communication overhead. The original BBS scheme relies on a malleable linear encryption scheme to provide anonymity, which makes it vulnerable to chosen-ciphertext attacks (i.e., it cannot achieve CCA-anonymity). To address this, we replace the linear encryption with an ElGamal encryption augmented by an additional signature element to ensure that tampering with ciphertexts can be detected. This modification allows us to achieve CCA-anonymity while also reducing both computational and communication costs. To support both forward security and non-frameability simultaneously, we introduce an updatable parameter into the user's credentials and public parameters so that newly joined users are unable to produce valid signatures for previously issued messages. This is because those messages are verifiable only under an expired public parameter. Finally, we propose a batch verification technique that aggregates pairing-based verification equations in our group signature scheme, enabling more efficient signature validation across multiple signatures.

3.2 First Protocol: DGSS

Let $DGSS = \{KeyGen, Join, Sign, Verify, Open, Judge, Update\}$ be our group signature scheme. In the following, we give the details of each procedure.

KeyGen. In this phase, a key generator generates public and private parameters of the scheme. Firstly, it creates $\{\mathbb{G}_1, \mathbb{G}_2, \mathbb{G}_T, q, e, g_1, g_2\}$ as the public parameter of the scheme where $g_1 \in \mathbb{G}_1$, $g_2 \in \mathbb{G}_2$ ($\varphi(g_2) = g_1$) are two random generators. Subsequently, it generates a random value $z \in \mathbb{Z}_q$ as opening key (ok) and computes $h = g_1^z \in \mathbb{G}_1$. Additionally, it creates three secret values, $b, \beta,$ and α as issuer keys (ik) and computes the public parameters $Y = g_1^{b\beta} \in \mathbb{G}_1$ and $w = g_2^{\alpha} \in \mathbb{G}_2$. Finally, the key generator securely send z and b, β, α to GM and key issuer, respectively. Furthermore, it selects a hash function $H : \{0,1\} \longrightarrow \mathbb{Z}_q$ and publishes the group public key of scheme as $gpk = \{g_1, g_2, h, Y, w, q, e, \mathbb{G}_1, \mathbb{G}_2, H(.)\}$.

Join. Whenever a user requests to join the group (assuming the request is valid), the key issuer generates a unique random value $a_i \in \mathbb{Z}_q$, computes $A_i = g_1^{\frac{b}{a_i}}$ and $x_i = \beta a_i + \alpha$, and securely transmits these values (x_i, A_i) to the user. Additionally, the key issuer records the pair (a_i, A_i) in the registration list as a valid user entry. The registration list is maintained in the form $Rlist = \{(a_1, A_1), (a_2, A_2), \ldots, (a_i, A_i)\}$.

Sign. To sign a message M, the signer performs the following steps:

1. The signer first generates a random value $k \in \mathbb{Z}_q$ and computes $T_1 = g_2^k$, $T_2 = A_i h^k$ and $T_3 = A_i^k$.
2. Then, the signer generates two random values r_k and r_e and evaluates $R_1 = g_2^{r_k}$ and $R_2 = e(A_i, g_2)^{r_e}$.
3. To prove the knowledge of $x_i = \beta a_i + \alpha$, A_i and k, the signer computes $c = H(M, T_1, T_2, T_3, R_1, R_2)$, $s_k = r_k + ck$ and $s_e = r_e + ckx_i$. Finally, the signer sends $\sigma_i = \{T_1, T_2, T_3, c, s_k, s_e\}$ as the signature to the verifier.

Verify. In order to verify a signature σ_i, a verifier performs the following:

1. The verifier computes $\tilde{R}_1 = g_2^{s_k} T_1^{-c}$ and $\tilde{R}_2 = e(T_2, g_2)^{s_e} e(Y^{-c} h^{-s_e}, T_1) e(T_3^{-c}, w)$.
2. Then, it computes $c' = H(M, T_1, T_2, T_3, \tilde{R}_1, \tilde{R}_2)$ and compares c' with c. If they are equals, the signature is valid, otherwise verification does not pass.

Open. This algorithm is run by GM and is used to trace a signature back to its signer. It takes as input a group public key $gpk = \{g_1, g_2, h, Y, w, e, \mathbb{G}_1, \mathbb{G}_2, H(.)\}$ and the corresponding GM private tracing key z, together with a message M and a signature $\sigma_i = (T_1, T_2, T_3, c, s_k, s_e)$. Then, it extracts the identity A_i of the signer. In order to reveal A_i, the GM (opener) firstly verifies that σ_i is a valid signature on M. then, it recovers the identity as $A_i \longleftarrow \frac{T_2}{\varphi(T_1)^z}$, then checks $e(A_i, T_1) \stackrel{?}{=} e(T_3, g_2)$. If so, it outputs A_i as the identity of signer, otherwise, it aborts. The open procedure requires isomorphism φ to reveal A_i. Computing the isomorphism takes roughly the same time as an exponentiation in the corresponding group (using fast computations of the trace map) [11].

Judge. Any entity can invoke the *Judge* algorithm to verify the opener's disclosure. This algorithm takes three inputs: a message M, a valid signature σ_i on M, and the A_i revealed by the opener. *Judge* first verifies the validity of the signature σ_i. If the signature is valid, the *Judge* algorithm then validates the opening process by checking $e(A_i, g_2) \cdot e(h, T_1) \stackrel{?}{=} e(T_2, g_2)$. If successful, it outputs 1 otherwise it outputs 0.

Update. In the proposed protocol, each group member holds a secret key tuple (x_i, A_i), and the scheme's public parameters include $Y = g_1^{b\beta}$ and $w = g_2^\alpha$. To ensure forward security, we update the issuer's secret parameter b periodically, and accordingly, the group public parameters are also updated. The steps performed by the key issuer are as follows:

1. The key issuer broadcasts $l \in \mathbb{Z}_p$, $\delta = g_1^{\frac{b}{l}}$, and $\varkappa = \beta l - \alpha$ to all users where l is a random value.
2. Each user can then update their secret key component as $A_{i_{new}} = (\delta \cdot A_{i_{old}})^{\frac{1}{x_i + \varkappa}}$.
3. The key issuer publishes $Y_{new} = g_1^{b'\beta}$ as new public parameters where $b' = \frac{b}{\beta l}$.

Revocation. Our scheme enables the revocation of user membership without affecting the signing capability of other users.

1. The key issuer generates a random value $l \in \mathbb{Z}_p$ and computes $\delta = g_1^{\frac{b}{l}}$, $\varkappa = \beta l - \alpha$. To revoke a user with secret keys $x_i = \beta a_i + \alpha$ and A_i, the issuer broadcasts the values δ, $\varkappa$, x_i, and $A_i' = g_1^{\frac{b'}{a_i}}$ to all users, where $b' = \frac{b}{\beta l}$.
2. Upon receiving these transmissions, users update their secret identifiers by $A_{k_{new}} = (\frac{A_i'}{(\delta \cdot A_{k_{old}})^{\frac{1}{x_i + \varkappa}}})^{\frac{1}{(x_k - x_i)}}$ where $k \neq i$. Note that the revoked user is not able to update its $A_{i_{new}}$ because the new exponent is invalid.
3. Finally, the key issuer updates g_1 to $\hat{g}_1 = g_1^{\frac{1}{\beta a_i}}$ and publishes $Y_{new} = \hat{g}_1^{\beta b'}$ as a new public verification parameter.

In order to revoke user A_i, the key issuer first updates the user's credential from A_i to A_i' using the values δ and $\varkappa$. This step is necessary because, without updating A_i and publishing it, an adversary could link signatures previously generated by the revoked user. Specifically, the adversary could check whether $e(T_2, g_2) \stackrel{?}{=} e(A_i, g_2) \cdot e(h, T_1)$ holds for given values T_1 and T_2.

Note that we assume that an online or blockchain-based service is available to store the values $(\delta, \varkappa, x_i, A_i')$, which users must check regularly to update their keys. Otherwise, their signatures are not verifiable.

3.3 Second Protocol: xDGSS

In xDGSS, we build on DGSS to present a dynamic group signature scheme that ensures non-frameability. Instead of simply assigning user i the private key $A_i = g_1^{\frac{b}{a_i}}$, $x_i = \beta a_i + \alpha$, the user and key issuer engage in an interactive protocol such that key issuer is not able to know the user's secret signing. Note that *Open* and *Judge* algorithms are the same as in DGSS.

KeyGen. In addition to public values produced in previous protocol, the key generator adds two extra public values as $h_1 \in \mathbb{G}_1$ and $Y_1 = h_1^{b\beta} \in \mathbb{G}_1$.

Join: User i generates a random number $y_i \in \mathbb{Z}_q$, computes $L_i = h_1^{-y_i}$ and sends L_i to the key issuer via secure channel. The key issuer then generates a random number a_i and evaluates $A_i = (g_1 L_i)^{\frac{b}{a_i}} = (g_1 h_1^{-y_i})^{\frac{b}{a_i}}$ and sends the pair $(A_i, x_i = \beta a_i + \alpha)$ to the user.

Sign. The signing procedure in the second protocol follows the same steps as in the first, with the following modifications. The value R_2 is updated to $R_2 = e(A_i, g_2)^{r_e} \cdot e(Y_1, g_2)^{kr_{y_i}}$, and an additional response value $s_y = r_y + cy_i$ is computed, where r_y is a newly chosen random value. The final signature consists of $T_1, T_2, T_3, c, s_k, s_e, s_y$.

Verify. The verification process is the same as in the first protocol, except that $\tilde{R}_2$ is computed as $\tilde{R}_2 = e(T_2^{s_e}, g_2) \cdot e(h^{-s_e} Y^{-c} Y_1^{s_y}, T_1) \cdot e(T_3^{-c}, w)$. The signature is accepted if $c' = c$, and rejected otherwise.

Update. Similar to DGSS, the key issuer periodically updates the public parameters and helps users refresh their secret keys. In addition to the steps in the original scheme, the issuer now also broadcasts $\gamma = h_1^{\frac{b}{\tau}}$ and publishes an extra public value $Y_{1_{\text{new}}} = h_1^{b'\beta}$. Each user updates their secret key component as $A_{i_{\text{new}}} = (\delta \cdot \gamma^{y_i} \cdot A_{i_{\text{old}}})^{\frac{1}{x_i + \varkappa}}$.

This ensures that new members, whose keys align with the updated parameters $Y_{\text{new}} = g_1^{b'\beta}$ and $Y_{1_{\text{new}}} = h_1^{b'\beta}$, cannot forge valid signatures for messages verified under the previous public keys $Y = g_1^{b\beta}$ and $Y_1 = h_1^{b\beta}$.

Revocation. Similar to the first revocation phase, the key issuer broadcasts $x_i = \beta a_i + \alpha$ of the revoked user. Additionally, the issuer sends $s = h_1^{-\frac{b}{a_i}}$ and $s' = g_1^{\frac{b}{a_i}}$. Each remaining user computes $X = s' \cdot s^{y_k}$ and updates their secret key as $A_{k_{\text{new}}} = \left(\frac{X}{A_{k_{\text{old}}}}\right)^{\frac{1}{x_k - x_i}}$ for $k \neq i$. Since the revoked user cannot compute a valid exponent due to division by zero, it loses the ability to generate updated credentials. The key issuer then updates the public keys: g_1 and h_1 are changed to $\hat{g}_1 = g_1^{\frac{1}{\beta a_i}}$, $\hat{h}_1 = h_1^{\frac{1}{\beta a_i}}$, and publishes the new verification parameters $Y_{\text{new}} = \hat{g}_1^{\beta b}$ and $Y_{1_{\text{new}}} = \hat{h}_1^{\beta b}$.

3.4 Batch Verification

To improve efficiency in applications verifying multiple group signatures, we modify our protocol to support batch verification, minimizing costly pairing operations on the verifier side. Instead of computing R_2, the signer computes $T_4 = A_i^{r_e}$ and includes it in the hash: $c = H(M, T_1, T_2, T_3, T_4, R_1)$. The final signature σ includes $T_1, T_2, T_3, T_4, c, s_k, s_e, s_y$. On the verifier's side, the verification process involves computing $\tilde{R}_1$ and $c' = H(M, T_1, T_2, T_3, T_4, \tilde{R}_1)$. The verifier first checks $c \stackrel{?}{=} c'$ for each received signature and then verifies the following equalition:

$$e(\prod_{i=1}^{t} T_{4_i}, g_2) e(h, \prod_{i=1}^{t} T_{1_i}^{s_{e_i}}) e(Y, \prod_{i=1}^{t} T_{1_i}^{c_i}) e(\prod_{i=1}^{t} T_{3_i}^{c_i}, w) \stackrel{?}{=} e(\prod_{i=1}^{t} T_{2_i}^{s_{e_i}}, g_2) \quad (1)$$

If both equalities hold, the verifier confirms the validity of the signer.

For a group signature scheme with non-frameability, a similar approach can be applied. In this case, the signers compute $T_4 = A_i^{r_e} g_2^{r_{y_i}}$ and Eq. 1 is modified to:

$$e(\prod_{i=1}^{t} T_{4_i}, g_2) e(h, \prod_{i=1}^{t} T_{1_i}^{s_{e_i}}) e(Y, \prod_{i=1}^{t} T_{1_i}^{c_i}) e(Y_1, \prod_{i=1}^{t} T_1^{-s_{y_i}}) e(\prod_{i=1}^{t} T_{3_i}^{c_i}, w) \stackrel{?}{=} e(\prod_{i=1}^{t} T_{2_i}^{s_{e_i}}, g_2)$$

The soundness of the NIZK proof in the DGSS scheme with batch verification is provided in Appendix A. For the xDGSS scheme, the soundness analysis remains identical to that of DGSS.

3.5 Zero Knowledge Proof of the Protocol

Our DGSS is built on a zero-knowledge proof (ZKP) by which the signer convinces the verifier that it possesses valid values x_i and A_i such that $e(A_i, g_2^{x_i} w^{-1}) = e(Y, g_2)$ and that A_i is encrypted using public key h in T_1 and T_2 and the secret value k. A secure ZKP should ensure *completeness* which implies that if the statement is true, an honest signer can convince a verifier of that fact. It should also ensure *soundness* which means that if the statement is false, no cheating signer can convince the verifier that it is true, except with some small probability. ZKPs achieves *zero-knowledge* which implies that after verification, the verifier learns nothing about the witness other than the fact that the verification is true [8,21]. In the protocols, we apply the Fiat-Shamir heuristic [20] to convert an interactive zero-knowledge scheme into a non-interactive one. For the purpose of our proof, we assume the protocol is non-interactive.

In the following, we explain how DGSS satisfies the zero-knowledge properties, while the proof for the xDGSS scheme follows straightforwardly.

Lemma 1 *The NIZK in the DGSS protocol is complete.*

Proof. If the signer is an honest prover possessing a valid pair (x_i, A_i), then they can generate a valid signature $\sigma_i = (T_1, T_2, T_3, c, s_k, s_e)$. Upon receiving the signature, the verifier computes $\tilde{R}_1$ and $\tilde{R}_2$. If the signature is valid, these values satisfy $\tilde{R}_1 = R_1$ and $\tilde{R}_2 = R_2$. Consequently, the verifier accepts $c = c'$.

Lemma 2 *There exists an extractor for the NIZK in DGSS protocol.*

Proof. We assume an interactive ZKP where c is a challenge sent by the verifier after the prover sends the values T_1, T_2, T_3, R_1, R_2 to the verifier. Assume a scenario where an extractor can rewind a prover in the protocol to just before the prover receives a challenge c. In the initial step of the protocol, the prover sends T_1, T_2, T_3 along with R_1, R_2. When faced with the challenge c, the prover responds with s_k and s_e. For a different challenge $c' \neq c$, the prover responds with s'_k and s'_e. Hence, the following two verification equations hold for each set of values.

$$g_2^{s_k} \stackrel{?}{=} R_1 T_1^c$$

$$e(T_2, g_2)^{s_e} \stackrel{?}{=} R_2 e(h^{s_e} Y^c, T_1) e(T_3^c, w)$$

Therefore,

$$g_2^{s_k} = R_1 T_1^c, g_2^{s'_k} = R_1 T_1^{c'} \qquad (2)$$
$$e(T_2, g_2)^{s_e} = R_2 e(h^{s_e} Y^c, T_1) e(T_3^c, w),$$
$$e(T_2, g_2)^{s'_e} = R_2 e(h^{s'_e} Y^{c'}, T_1) e(T_3^{c'}, w) \qquad (3)$$

We define three new parameters such that $\Delta c = c - c', \Delta s_k = s_k - s'_k$ and $\Delta s_e = s_e - s'_e$.

By dividing the two instances of Eq. 2 (one instance using c and the other using c'), we obtain $g_2^{\Delta s_k} = T_1^{\Delta c}$ meaning that $T_1 = g_2^{\frac{\Delta s_k}{\Delta c}}$. Therefore, we reveal the value of k as $k = \frac{\Delta s_k}{\Delta c}$. Similarly, the value k can be obtained from the equations $s_k = r_k + ck$ and $s'_k = r_k + c'k$. By subtracting the equations, we get $\Delta s_k = \Delta c \cdot k$, which leads to $k = \frac{\Delta s_k}{\Delta c}$.

On the other hand, by dividing the two instance of Eq. 3, the following holds.

$$e(A_i, g_2)^{\frac{\Delta s_e}{\Delta c}} = e(Y, T_1) e(T_3, w)$$

Therefore, $kx_i = \frac{\Delta s_e}{\Delta c}$. In addition, we have $k = \frac{\Delta s_k}{\Delta c}$, therefore $x_i = \frac{\Delta s_e}{\Delta s_k}$. Similarly, the value x_i can be computed from the equations $s_e = r_e + cx_i k$ and $s'_e = r_e + c'x_i k$. By subtracting the equations, we get $\Delta s_e = \Delta c k x_i$, which leads to $x_i = \frac{\Delta s_e}{\Delta s_k}$.

Finally, one can obtain A_i from $T_2 = A_i h^k$. Hence, an extractor exists for (x_i, A_i, k), therefore the ZKP is sound.

Lemma 3 *Transcripts of the DGSS protocol can be simulated.*

Proof. : We describe a simulator that outputs transcripts of the protocol. The simulator begins by picking $A \in \mathbb{G}_1$ and $k \in \mathbb{Z}_q$. It sets $T_1 = g_2^k$, $T_2 = Ah^k$, and $T_3 = A^k$. Since the verifier does not know the private key of the ElGamal encryption, it cannot recognize T_1, T_2 and T_3 are generated via invalid A. Now, the simulator computes other values without knowing A_i, x_i, k and constructs the transcript perfectly, following the standard simulation of a Schnorr proof of knowledge [33]. The simulator chooses a challenge $c \in \mathbb{Z}_q$ and values s_k, s_e. It computes R_1, R_2 as follows:

$$R_1 = g_2^{s_k} T_1^{-c}, \ R_2 = e(T_2, g_2)^{s_e} e(Y^{-c} h^{s_e}, T_1) e(T_3, w)^{-c}$$

The simulator outputs the transcript $(T_1, T_2, T_3, R_1, R_2, c, s_k, s_e)$. This transcript is verifiable since $\tilde{R}_1$ and $\tilde{R}_2$ are computed in the same manner. Moreover, it is indistinguishable from the transcripts generated by the protocol.

4 Security Analysis

In this section, we demonstrate that our DGSS scheme satisfies the security requirements of anonymity, traceability and forward secrecy. Additionally, we show that xDGSS also satisfies non-frameability. Since the traceability, anonymity and forward secrecy properties of xDGSS are similar to those of the DGSS scheme, we leave their verification to the reader.

Theorem 1. *If the CDH problem is intractable in G_1, then the group signature scheme is anonymous.*

Proof. Given an anonymity adversary $\mathcal{A}$ that takes as input the public parameters of the group signature, then queries its challenger with i_0 and i_1, corresponding to identifiers A_0 and A_1, and receives a group signature σ_b by i_b where b is a secret random bit. $\mathcal{A}$ wins if it returns bit $b' = b$, i.e., recognizes the identifier of the signer (A_b). We will show how to use this adversary to create an adversary $\mathcal{B}$ to solve the CDH.

The CDH challenger randomly generates $x, p \in \mathbb{Z}_q$ and computes $X = g_1^x$ and $P = g_1^p$. They are given to $\mathcal{B}$, and $\mathcal{B}$ is required to output the value $Z = g_1^{x \cdot p}$. $\mathcal{B}$ simulates xDGSS to $\mathcal{A}$, it sets $h = X$ and $g_2 = P^{\frac{1}{\theta}}$ where θ is randomly selected such that $P^{\frac{1}{\theta}} \in \mathbb{G}_2$. $\mathcal{B}$ then computes $w = P^\alpha$ and $Y = g_1^{f\theta}$ where f and α are security parameter of group signature and are selected randomly from $\mathbb{Z}_p$. Finally, it sends the public values $(g_1, g_2 = P^{\frac{1}{\theta}}, h = X, Y = g_1^{f\theta}, w = P^\alpha)$ along with the users' private keys (except target users) $\{(A_i = g_1^{\frac{f}{a_i}}, x_i = \theta(\beta a_i + \alpha))\}_{i=1}^n$ to $\mathcal{A}$ which queries its anonymity challenge by providing i_0, i_1 and the message to be signed M. $\mathcal{B}$ selects one of users $b \in \{0, 1\}$ randomly, generates a random value $s \in \mathbb{G}_1$ and calculates the signature to pass to $\mathcal{A}$ as follows:

$$T_1 = P \in \mathbb{G}_2, T_2 = sh^\theta, T_3 = s^{\frac{\beta a_b + \alpha}{\alpha \theta}} g_1^{-\frac{f\beta}{\alpha}}, R_1 = P^{r_k}, R_2 = e(s, g_2)^{r_c},$$
$$c = H(M, T_1, T_2, T_3, R_1, R_2), s_k = \theta(r_k + c), s_e = r_e + c(\beta a_b + \alpha)$$

When $\mathcal{A}$ sends back b' as its response, if $b \neq b'$, the adversary $\mathcal{B}$ aborts, otherwise, by dividing T_2 by A_b, the algorithm $\mathcal{B}$ computes the value h^p. This follows from the assumption that T_2 is of the form $A_h h^p$; indeed, since $sh^\theta = A_b h^p$, it implies that $\mathcal{B}$ successfully recovers h^p. Consequently, $\mathcal{B}$ can compute $Z = g_1^{xp}$. However, this contradicts the assumed hardness of the Computational Diffie-Hellman (CDH) problem. Therefore, such an adversary $\mathcal{B}$ cannot exist, which in turn implies that the adversary $\mathcal{A}$ cannot exist either.

Theorem 2. *The proposed group signature scheme is traceable under SDH assumption.*

Proof. Suppose $\mathcal{A}$ breaks the traceability of the group signature scheme. We show how to construct an adversary $\mathcal{B}$ that breaks the intractability of the SDH assumption.

$\mathcal{B}$ is challenged with an $n+1$-SDH instance $\{g, \tilde{g}, \tilde{g}^\theta, \tilde{g}^{\theta^2}, \ldots, \tilde{g}^{\theta^{n+1}}\}$. It simulates the DGSS protocol to $\mathcal{A}$ by randomly choosing $b, \beta \leftarrow \mathbb{Z}_q$ and $a_i \leftarrow \mathbb{Z}_q$

for $i = 1, \ldots, n$. It defines $g_2 = \tilde{g}^{\prod_{i=1}^{n}(\beta a_i + \theta)} = \tilde{g}^{\sum_{i=1}^{n}(\nu_i \theta^i)}$, and $g_1 = \varphi(g_2)$. For each user, the adversary $\mathcal{B}$ computes a pair of signing keys as $x_i = \beta a_i$ and $A_i = g^{b \prod_{j=1, j \neq i}^{n}(\beta a_j + \theta)}$. The point is that a_i is uniquely used across all join protocol executions. This ensures that A_i and x_i are also unique.

$\mathcal{B}$ considers $\alpha = -\theta$, which is unknown, and computes w as $g_2 = \tilde{g}^{-\theta \prod_{i=1}^{n}(\beta a_i + \theta)} = \tilde{g}^{\sum_{i=1}^{n}(\zeta_i \theta^i)}$.

$\mathcal{B}$ computes the public value Y as follows:

$$Y = \varphi\left(\tilde{g}^{b \prod_{i=1}^{n}(\beta a_i + \theta)}\right) = g^{b \prod_{i=1}^{n}(\beta a_i + \theta)}. \tag{4}$$

It then picks a random value $z \in \mathbb{Z}_q$ and computes $h = g_1^z \in \mathbb{G}_1$. $\mathcal{B}$ initializes $\mathcal{A}$ by providing it with the group public key (g_1, g_2, h, w, Y) and the secret opening key z.

The $\mathcal{A}$ outputs a forged group signature $\sigma^* = (T_1^*, T_2^*, T_3^*, c^*, s_k^*, s_e^*)$ on a message M^*.

There are two types of traceability adversaries; a valid signature that the opener fails to identify its signer (*Type I*) or a valid signature that is traced back to an honest user via the open and judge algorithms (*Type II*).

Type I. If the adversary $\mathcal{A}$ generates a signature σ^*, $\mathcal{B}$ can calculate A_i^* using the opening key ok and can also compute $x_i^* = \beta a_{i^*} + \alpha$ using extractor $\mathcal{E}$. Consequently, $\mathcal{B}$ can compute $(A_i^*)^{(b\beta)^{-1}} = \left(g_1^{\frac{b}{a_i^*}}\right)^{(b\beta)^{-1}} = g_1^{\frac{1}{x_i^* + \theta}}$. On the other hand, observe that $g_1^{\frac{1}{x_i^* + \theta}} = \varphi(g_2)^{\frac{1}{x_i^* + \theta}} = \varphi(\tilde{g}^{f(\theta)})^{\frac{1}{x_i^* + \theta}} = g^{\frac{f(\theta)}{x_i^* + \theta}}$, where $f(\theta) = \prod_{i=1}^{n}(\beta a_i + \theta)$. It is clear that $f(\theta)$ can be expressed as $f(\theta) = \sum_{i=0}^{n} \eta_i \theta^i$, with $\eta_i \in \mathbb{Z}_q$. Using polynomial long division, we can write $f(\theta) = g(\theta)(x_i^* + \theta) + k$, where $g(\theta) = \sum_{i=1}^{n-1} \eta_i \theta^i$ and $k \in \mathbb{Z}_q$ is the remainder. Therefore,

$$g_1^{\frac{1}{x_i^* + \theta}} = g^{\frac{k}{x_i^* + \theta} + g(\theta)} = g^{\frac{k}{x_i^* + \theta} + \sum_{i=1}^{n-1} \eta_i \theta^i}.$$

Thus, the adversary $\mathcal{B}$ can compute $g^{\frac{1}{x_i^* + \theta}}$ using $(g_1^{\frac{1}{x_i^* + \theta}} \cdot \prod_{i=1}^{n-1} g^{(\theta^i)^{-\eta_i}})^{k^{-1}}$ because it knows the coefficients of $f(\theta)$.

Finally, it sends $(g^{\frac{1}{x_i^* + \theta}}, x_i^*)$ to its challenger as a solution for the SDH problem.

Type II. In this case, the adversary $\mathcal{A}$ generates a signature such that the GM traces it back to an honest member with identifier A_j. In addition, the returned value from GM, A_j, passes the *Judge* algorithm, which implies $e(A_j, g_2) \cdot e(h, T_1) = e(A^*, g_2)e(h^k, g_2)$.

It then means that $e(A_j, g_2) = e(h^k, g_2)$ (or $e(A^*, g_2) = e(h, T_1)$) for some $A^* \neq A_j$, then $A_j = h^k$. In that case, the $\mathcal{B}$ can compute $g_1^{\frac{1}{x_j + \theta}}$ via $\varphi(T_1^{z(b\beta)^{-1}})$. Consequently, $\mathcal{B}$ can solve the SDH problem such as the previous case. Since the SDH problem is hard, $\mathcal{B}$ does not exist and therefore, $\mathcal{A}$ cannot exist.

Theorem 3. *Assuming that the zero-knowledge proof is simulatable and extractable, xDGSS group signature is non-frameable under the discrete logarithm problem.*

Proof (sketch). Let $Y = g_1^y$ be an instance of the discrete logarithm (DL) problem, and let $\mathcal{S}$ and $\mathcal{E}$ be the zero-knowledge simulator and the knowledge extractor, respectively. The proof idea is that the DL adversary $\mathcal{B}$ assumes the unknown $y_i = \log_{g_1} Y$ as a signing key of the framing target user i^*. When $\mathcal{A}$ succeeds in forging a signature with respect to y_i, $\mathcal{B}$ can solve the DL problem (using $\mathcal{E}$). In this game, the adversary $\mathcal{A}$ can act as the key issuer during the join phase and generate a secret key x_i and a credential A_i in response to a join request. $\mathcal{B}$ randomly generates $g_1, g_2, \alpha, \beta, b, z$ and computes $w = g_2^\alpha, Y = g_1^{b\beta}$. Finally, $\mathcal{B}$ transfers issuer keys, opener key and public parameters to $\mathcal{A}$ which is allowed to request signing keys of any identity i as follows:

- If $i \neq i^*$, $\mathcal{B}$ generates y_i and computes $L_i = g_1^{-y_i}$ and sends to $\mathcal{A}$ which sends back partial secret parameters (x_i, A_i) to $\mathcal{B}$ using the join procedure.
- If $i = i^*$, $\mathcal{B}$ sets $L_{i^*} = Y$ and sends it to $\mathcal{A}$ which sends back $(x_i, A_i = (g_1 X)^{\frac{b}{a_{i^*}}})$. $\mathcal{B}$ then stores whole secret parameters as (y_i, x_i, A_i) if $i \neq i^*$; otherwise $(\bot, x_{i^*}, A_{i^*})$.

To respond to signing queries using identity i and a message M, if $i \neq i^*$, $\mathcal{B}$ is able to generate a group signature on any message, because $\mathcal{B}$ has the corresponding signing key. On the other hand, if $i = i^*$, $\mathcal{B}$ can produce a signature using the stored partial secret credentials and the NIZK simulator $\mathcal{S}$. The resulting signature σ is then given to $\mathcal{A}$.

At the end, $\mathcal{A}$ returns $M^*, \sigma^* = (T_1^*, T_2^*, T_3^*, c^*, s_k^*, s_e^*, s_y^*)$ and A_i that passes Judge algorithm. This indicates that since $L = Y$, the exponent $y = \log_{g_1} X$ is a NIZK witness. In that case, $\mathcal{B}$ can obtain y using extractor $\mathcal{E}$, which is the solution of the DL problem. Since the DL problem is hard, $\mathcal{B}$ does not exist and therefore, $\mathcal{A}$ cannot exist.

Theorem 4. *The proposed group signature scheme is forward secure under SDH assumption.*

Proof. (sketch) Suppose an adversary $\mathcal{A}$ breaks the forward secrecy of the group signature scheme by producing a valid signature $\sigma^* = (T_1^*, T_2^*, T_3^*, c^*, s_k^*, s_e^*)$ that verifies under the old group public key $Y_{\text{old}} = g_1^{b\beta}$, despite not possessing the secret key corresponding to the previous user public key $A_i = g_1^{\frac{b}{a_i}}$. We use $\mathcal{A}$ to construct an adversary $\mathcal{B}$ that solves the $(n+1)$-SDH problem.

Given an $(n+1)$-SDH instance $\{g, \tilde{g}, \tilde{g}^\theta, \tilde{g}^{\theta^2}, \ldots, \tilde{g}^{\theta^{n+1}}\}$, $\mathcal{B}$ simulates the DGSS protocol for $\mathcal{A}$ by choosing $b, b', \beta \leftarrow \mathbb{Z}_q$ and $a_i \leftarrow \mathbb{Z}_q$ for $i = 1, \ldots, n$. It sets $g_2 = \tilde{g}^{\prod_{i=1}^n (\beta a_i + \theta)} = \tilde{g}^{\sum_{i=1}^n \nu_i \theta^i}$ and $g_1 = \varphi(g_2)$. For each user, $\mathcal{B}$ computes $x_i = \beta a_i$ and $A_i = g^{b' \prod_{j=1, j \neq i}^n (\beta a_j + \theta)}$. Each a_i is unique, ensuring unique x_i and A_i. Letting $\alpha = -\theta$ (unknown to $\mathcal{B}$), it defines $g_2 = \tilde{g}^{-\theta \prod_{i=1}^n (\beta a_i + \theta)} = \tilde{g}^{\sum_{i=1}^{n+1} \zeta_i \theta^i}$, and computes $Y_{\text{old}} = g^{b \prod_{i=1}^n (\beta a_i + \theta)}$ and $Y_{\text{new}} = g^{b' \prod_{i=1}^n (\beta a_i + \theta)}$. $\mathcal{A}$ outputs a forged group signature $\sigma^* = (T_1^*, T_2^*, T_3^*, c^*, s_k^*, s_e^*)$ on message M^* verified by Y_{old}. Using the opening key ok, $\mathcal{B}$ extracts A_i^* and $x_i = \beta a_i + \alpha$, then computes $(A_i^*)^{(b\beta)^{-1}} = g_1^{1/(x_i^* + \theta)}$, which gives $g^{1/(x_i^* + \theta)}$ as described in Theorem 2. Thus, $\mathcal{B}$ solves the SDH problem. Since SDH is assumed hard, $\mathcal{B}$ cannot exist, and therefore, neither can $\mathcal{A}$.

5 Performance and Comparison

In this section, we compare our protocol with others in terms of security properties. Additionally, we implement the basic cryptographic operations of the protocol, measure their execution time and compare our protocol with other schemes in terms of computational cost, communication overhead, and signature size.

5.1 Security and Feature Comparison

In this subsection, we compare group signature schemes based on their security properties and functionalities. Table 1 summarizes key features across schemes, identified by authors (e.g., BBS for Boneh, Boyen, and Shacham [10]). Notations used are clarified below.

For anonymity, CCA2-anonymity (CCA2) is the strongest, allowing both opening and signing key queries, except on the challenge pair. CPA-anonymity (CPA) [10] disallows opening queries, while CCA-anonymity (CCA) forbids signing key queries [18].

Two related notions, non-frameability and strong exculpability (SE), differ slightly: non-frameability prevents any entity, including the issuer, from forging signatures accepted by both the opening and judging algorithms; SE only ensures that no valid signature can be forged on behalf of a user. Since non-frameability implies SE, we use SE for broader comparison.

Some schemes suffer from inefficient opening algorithms with $\mathcal{O}(n)$ complexity, unsuitable for large groups. Efficient schemes support constant-time opening $\mathcal{O}(1)$. Batch verification is also critical, allowing the verifier to process multiple signatures with a single algorithm run, reducing load in centralized systems.

Forward security prevents new members from signing past messages. Our scheme enables efficient key updates by broadcasting just two values, avoiding full re-enrollment. Revocation is another essential property, allowing removal of compromised users. Schemes supporting both revocation and forward security offer stronger guarantees.

In Table 1, we compare protocols on key properties. Only a few, such as BBS^2 [17], LMP [26], CS [16], DS [18], ACJT [2], and our scheme, provide CCA2-anonymity. Among them, DP [17], ACJT [2], and our scheme also support practical revocation and efficient opening.

While several protocols support SE, batch verification is less common, only KLA [24] and CL [12] provide it. However, these lack efficient key update mechanisms. Our scheme uniquely combines forward security with efficient key updates, a feature absent in prior work. We analyze the computational costs of these properties in the next subsection.

5.2 Computation and Communication Performance

To evaluate our schemes in comparison with other related protocols, we group the analysis based on shared properties. Therefore, the efficiency of our work

Table 1. Security and property comparison between different schemes. BV: Batch Verification. SE: Strong Exculpability (non-frameability). EFS: Efficient Forward Security. ▽: This scheme does not have revocation protocol, but it has a revocation list.

Scheme	Anonymity	Revocation	Opening	BV	SE	EFS
BBS [10]	CPA	✓	$\mathcal{O}(1)$	✗	✗	✓
BBS^+ [10]	CPA	✗	$\mathcal{O}(1)$	✗	✓	✗
BS [11]	CPA	▽	$\mathcal{O}(1)$	✗	✗	✗
$FGHP$ [19]	CCA2	✗	$\mathcal{O}(1)$	✓	✗	✗
LMP [26]	CCA2	✗	$\mathcal{O}(1)$	✗	✗	✗
PS [32]	CCA	✗	$\mathcal{O}(n)$	✓	✗	✗
DS [18]	CCA2	✗	$\mathcal{O}(n)$	✗	✗	✗
CS [16]	CCA2	✗	$\mathcal{O}(n)$	✗	✗	✗
BBS^{++} [9]	CPA	✗	$\mathcal{O}(1)$	✗	✓	✗
$BSNS$ [9]	CCA	▽	$\mathcal{O}(n)$	✗	✓	✗
CL [12]	CCA	✗	$\mathcal{O}(n)$	✓	✓	✗
DP [17]	CCA2	✓	$\mathcal{O}(1)$	✗	✓	✗
$ACJT$ [2]	CCA2	✓	$\mathcal{O}(1)$	✗	✓	✗
$SKHS$ [36]	CPA	✓	$\mathcal{O}(1)$	✗	✓	✗
KLA [24]	CCA	✗	$\mathcal{O}(n)$	✓	✓	✗
Our DGSS	CCA2	✓	$\mathcal{O}(1)$	✓	✗	✓
Our xDGSS	CCA2	✓	$\mathcal{O}(1)$	✓	✓	✓

is assessed in two distinct classes; schemes with strong exculpability and those without strong exculpability.

To compute the communication and computation overheads, we adopt the Barreto-Naehrig (BN254) curve over $\mathbb{F}_p$ where p is a 254-bit prime number [5]. For computational evaluation, we focus exclusively on expensive operations, specifically exponentiation in $\mathbb{G}_T$, scalar multiplication in $\mathbb{G}_1$ and $\mathbb{G}_2$, and pairing operations.

To evaluate computational performance across various scenarios, we conducted measurements on a laptop equipped with a Core i7 CPU (2.6 GHz) and 8 GB of RAM. The results indicate that a single exponentiation operation in $\mathbb{G}_T$, denoted by E_T, requires approximately 0.14 ms. Additionally, scalar multiplication in $\mathbb{G}_1$ and $\mathbb{G}_2$ take around 0.76 ms. A pairing operation, represented by P, requires approximately 4.45 ms. These times are calculated by averaging the execution duration of each operation over 100,000 runs.

Schemes Without Strong Exculpability. In DGSS, which does not provide non-frameability, the signer outputs a signature $(T_1, T_2, T_3, c, s_k, s_e)$, totaling 192 bytes assuming a 32-byte hash function. Table 2 compares group signature schemes without strong exculpability in terms of communication and computation. While CS [16] and PS [32] offer smaller signature sizes than DGSS, they lack efficient opening and revocation mechanisms, and require re-running the join phase to update signing keys for forward security. Among comparable schemes, DGSS achieves the best communication efficiency.

In terms of signer-side computation, DGSS is more efficient than most schemes, with the exception of PS [32], which lacks comparable security guarantees. On the verifier side, BBS [10], PS [32], and FGHP [19] exhibit better performance than DGSS. However, only PS supports batch verification, whereas DGSS includes this feature, making it more suitable for scalable applications.

Table 2. Comparison of group signature without strong exculpability

Schemes	Signature size (Bytes)	Signer (ms)	Verifier(ms)
BBS [10]	$3\mathbb{G}_1 + 6\mathbb{Z}_q$ (288)	$9M + 3E_T$ (7.26)	$10M + 3E_T + P$ (12.47)
BS [11]	$2\mathbb{G}_1 + 5\mathbb{Z}_q$ (224)	$10M + 2P$ (16.5)	$10M + 3P$ (20.95)
$FGHP$ [19]	$3\mathbb{G}_1 + 6\mathbb{Z}_q + \mathbb{G}_T$ (672)	$9M + 3E_T$ (7.26)	$10M + 3E_T + P$ (12.47)
LMP [26]	$7\mathbb{G}_1 + 3\mathbb{Z}_q$ (320)	$13M + 2E_T + 4P$ (27.96)	$15M + 4P$ (29.2)
PS [32]	$2\mathbb{G}_1 + 2\mathbb{Z}_q$ (128)	$2M + E_T$ (1.66)	$3M + 3P$ (15.63)
DS [18]	$4\mathbb{G}_2 + 3\mathbb{G}_1 + 3\mathbb{Z}_q$ (320)	$11M$ (8.36)	$6M + 5P$ (26.81)
CS [16]	$\mathbb{G}_2 + 4\mathbb{G}_1$ (160)	$6M$ (4.56)	$M + 5P$ (23.01)
Our DGSS	$2\mathbb{G}_1 + \mathbb{G}_2 + 3\mathbb{Z}_q$ (192)	$4M + E_T$ (3.18)	$6M + 3P$ (17.91)

Schemes with Strong Exculpability. xDGSS ensures non-frameability by including one additional element (s_y) in the signature compared to DGSS, increasing the total size by 32 bytes to 224 bytes. It also requires one extra point multiplication on both the signer and verifier sides. As shown in Table 3, the schemes in [9] and [24] achieve lower communication costs than xDGSS. However, both suffer from expensive opening phases for large groups, as the group manager must perform exhaustive searches to identify the signer. Moreover, the scheme in [24] lacks revocation support, and [9] incurs significant overhead during revocation. In contrast, xDGSS enables efficient key updates by broadcasting only two values, avoiding the need to re-initiate the join phase for all users.

xDGSS also demonstrates strong signer-side efficiency, outperforming most existing schemes except [9], which lacks comparable features. This makes xDGSS particularly suitable for resource-constrained environments such as IoT applications. On the verifier side, schemes like BBS [10], BBS[3] [9], CL [12], BSNS [9], ACJT [2], and KLA [24] offer lower computational costs. However, batch verification, a critical feature for scalability, is only supported by xDGSS and CL [12]. For a fair comparison, we assume ACJT [2] operates over $\mathbb{Z}_q$ with a 2048-bit prime to match the 127-bit security level.

Table 3. Comparison of group signature without strong exculpability

Schemes	Signature size (Bytes)	Signer (ms)	Verifier (ms)
BBS^+ [10]	$3\mathbb{G}_1 + 7\mathbb{Z}_q$ (320)	$9M + 4E_T$ (7.4)	$10M + 4E_T + P$ (12.61)
BBS^{++} [9]	$4\mathbb{G}_1 + 5\mathbb{Z}_q$ (288)	$11M + 5E_T$ (9.06)	$15M + 2P$ (20.3)
$BSNS$ [9]	$3\mathbb{G}_1 + 2\mathbb{Z}_q$ (160)	$3M + E_T$ (2.42)	$3M + 4P$ (20.08)
CL [12]	$7\mathbb{G}_1 + 4\mathbb{Z}_q$ (352)	$13M + 2E_T$ (10.16)	$11M + 4P$ (26.16)
DP [17]	$4\mathbb{G}_1 + 5\mathbb{Z}_q$ (288)	$7M + 4E_T$ (5.88)	$12M + 2P$ (18.02)
$ACJT$ [2]	$3\mathbb{G}_1 + 4\mathbb{Z}_q$ (1792)	$12E_T$ (1.68)	$11E_T$ (1.54)
$SKHS$ [36]	$6\mathbb{G}_1 + 6\mathbb{Z}_q$ (384)	$15M + 6P$ (38.1)	$7M + 6P$ (32.02)
KLA [24]	$3\mathbb{G}_1 + 2Z_p$ (160)	$4M$ (3.04)	$2M + 3P$ (14.87)
Our xDGSS	$2\mathbb{G}_1 + \mathbb{G}_2 + 4\mathbb{Z}_q$ (224)	$4M + 2E_T$ (3.32)	$7M + 3P$ (18.67)

6 Conclusion

We proposed two forward-secure dynamic group signature schemes that balance efficiency and security. The first scheme, DGSS, prioritizes efficiency but does not ensure non-frameability, while the second scheme, xDGSS, provides non-frameability with minimal additional computational and communication cost. Both schemes introduce an efficient revocation mechanism and a batch verification technique that reduces verification overhead. Our key update mechanism allows for forward security without requiring all users to rejoin the group, overcoming a major limitation in existing solutions. Through security analysis, we demonstrated that our schemes satisfy key security properties, including anonymity, traceability, and non-frameability (for the second scheme). Performance evaluations indicate that our protocols are compatitive compared to existing group signature schemes, particularly in signature generation and batch verification.

A Soundness Proof of NIZK in Batch Verification Mode

Lemma 4 *There exists an extractor for the NIZK in DGSS protocol in batch verification mode.*

Proof. Consider the soundness game defined in the extractability proof of Lemma 2. W.L.O.G, we assume we have two signatures from two users, u_1 and u_2, to be verified in batch. For valid signatures, the following three equations hold:

$$g_2^{s_{k_1}} = R_{1_1} \cdot T_{1_1}^c \tag{5}$$

$$g_2^{s_{k_2}} = R_{1_2} \cdot T_{1_2}^c \tag{6}$$

$$e(T_{4_1}T_{4_2}, g_2) \cdot e(h, T_{1_1}^{s_{c_1}} T_{1_2}^{s_{c_2}}) \cdot e(Y, T_{1_1}^c T_{1_2}^c) \cdot e(T_{3_1}^c T_{3_2}^c, w) = e(T_{2_1}^{s_{c_1}} T_{2_2}^{s_{c_2}}, g_2) \tag{7}$$

Equations (5) and (6) are verification equations for u_1, and u_2, respectively, while Eq. (7) is the pairing batch verification equation for the two users. Assume we have two transcripts with challenges c and c', and the corresponding set of responses from u_1 and u_2, $s_{k_1}, s_{e_1}, s_{k_2}, s_{e_2}$ and $s'_{k_1}, s'_{e_1}, s'_{k_2}, s'_{e_2}$. Define the differences $\Delta c = c - c'$, $\Delta s_{k_1} = s_{k_1} - s'_{k_1}$, $\Delta s_{e_1} = s_{e_1} - s'_{e_1}$ and $\Delta s_{k_2} = s_{k_2} - s'_{k_2}$, $\Delta s_{e_2} = s_{e_2} - s'_{e_2}$. By dividing the two instances of Eq. 5 for u_1, we obtain $g_2^{\Delta s_{k_1}} = T_{1_1}^{\Delta c}$ which implies $T_{1_1} = g_2^{\frac{\Delta s_{k_1}}{\Delta c}}$. Hence, we extract the value $k_1 = \frac{\Delta s_{k_1}}{\Delta c}$. For u_2, we similarly obtain $k_2 = \frac{\Delta s_{k_2}}{\Delta c}$ from Eq. 6. By dividing the two instanses of Eq. 7:

$$\frac{e(h, T_{1_1}^{s_{e_1}} T_{1_2}^{s_{e_2}}) \cdot e(Y, T_{1_1}^{c} T_{1_2}^{c}) \cdot e(T_{3_1}^{c} T_{3_2}^{c}, w)}{e(h, T_{1_1}^{s'_{e_1}} T_{1_2}^{s'_{e_2}}) \cdot e(Y, T_{1_1}^{c'} T_{1_2}^{c'}) \cdot e(T_{3_1}^{c'} T_{3_2}^{c'}, w)} = \frac{e(T_{2_1}^{s_{e_1}} T_{2_2}^{s_{e_2}}, g_2)}{e(T_{2_1}^{s'_{e_1}} T_{2_2}^{s'_{e_2}}, g_2)},$$

we obtain $e(h, T_{1_1}^{\frac{\Delta s_{e_1}}{\Delta c}} T_{1_2}^{\frac{\Delta s_{e_2}}{\Delta c}}) \cdot e(Y, T_{1_1} T_{1_2}) \cdot e(T_{3_1} T_{3_2}, w) = e(T_{2_1}^{\frac{\Delta s_{e_1}}{\Delta c}} T_{2_2}^{\frac{\Delta s_{e_2}}{\Delta c}}, g_2)$ which implies that if $k_1 x_1 = \frac{\Delta s_{e_1}}{\Delta c}$ and $k_2 x_2 = \frac{\Delta s_{e_2}}{\Delta c}$, the equation holds. Therefore, given the extracted k_1 and k_2, one can compute $x_1 = \frac{\Delta s_{e_1}}{\Delta s_{k_1}}$ and $x_2 = \frac{\Delta s_{e_2}}{\Delta s_{k_2}}$.

Finally, since $T_{2_1} = A_1 \cdot h^{k_1}$ and $T_{2_2} = A_2 \cdot h^{k_2}$, and both k_1, k_2 and x_1, x_2 are extracted, one can extract the value of A_1 for u_1 and A_2 for u_2. Therefore, an extractor exists for the tuple (x_1, A_1, k_1) and (x_2, A_2, k_2), which implies that the zero-knowledge proof is sound.

References

1. AlTawy, R., Gong, G.: Mesh: a supply chain solution with locally private blockchain transactions, pp. 149–169 (2019)
2. Ateniese, G., Camenisch, J., Joye, M., Tsudik, G.: A practical and provably secure coalition-resistant group signature scheme. In: Bellare, M. (ed.) Advances in Cryptology — CRYPTO 2000, pp. 255–270. Springer, Berlin (2000)
3. Ateniese, G., Song, D., Tsudik, G.: Quasi-efficient revocation of group signatures. In: Blaze, M. (ed.) Financial Cryptography, pp. 183–197. Springer, Berlin (2003)
4. Ateniese, G., Tsudik, G.: Some open issues and new directions in group signatures. In: Franklin, M. (ed.) Financial Cryptography, pp. 196–211. Springer, Berlin (1999)
5. Barreto, P.S.L.M., Naehrig, M.: Pairing-friendly elliptic curves of prime order. In: Preneel, B., Tavares, S. (eds.) Selected Areas in Cryptography, pp. 319–331. Springer, Berlin (2006)
6. Bellare, M., Micciancio, D., Warinschi, B.: Foundations of group signatures: Formal definitions, simplified requirements, and a construction based on general assumptions. In: Biham, E. (ed.) Advances in Cryptology – EUROCRYPT 2003, pp. 614–629. Springer, Berlin (2003)
7. Bellare, M., Shi, H., Zhang, C.: Foundations of group signatures: the case of dynamic groups. In: Menezes, A. (ed.) Topics in Cryptology - CT-RSA 2005, pp. 136–153. Springer, Berlin (2005)
8. Bernhard, D., Pereira, O., Warinschi, B.: How not to prove yourself: pitfalls of the Fiat-Shamir heuristic and applications to Helios. In: Wang, X., Sako, K. (eds.) Advances in Cryptology - ASIACRYPT 2012, pp. 626–643. Springer, Berlin (2012)

9. Bichsel, P., Camenisch, J., Neven, G., Smart, N.P., Warinschi, B.: Get shorty via group signatures without encryption. In: Garay, J.A., De Prisco, R. (eds.) Security and Cryptography for Networks, pp. 381–398. Springer, Berlin (2010)
10. Boneh, D., Boyen, X., Shacham, H.: Short group signatures. In: Franklin, M. (ed.) Advances in Cryptology - CRYPTO 2004, pp. 41–55. Springer, Berlin (2004)
11. Boneh, D., Shacham, H.: Group signatures with verifier-local revocation. In: Proceedings of the 11th ACM Conference on Computer and Communications Security, CCS '04, pp. 168–177. Association for Computing Machinery, New York (2004)
12. Camenisch, J., Lysyanskaya, A.: Signature schemes and anonymous credentials from bilinear maps. In: Franklin, M. (ed.) Advances in Cryptology - CRYPTO 2004, pp. 56–72. Springer, Berlin (2004)
13. Chaum, D., Heyst, E.: Group signatures. In: Davies, D.W. (ed.) Advances in Cryptology – EUROCRYPT '91, pp. 257–265. Springer, Berlin (1991)
14. Chen, L., Pedersen, T.P.: New group signature schemes. In: De Santis, A. (ed.) Advances in Cryptology – EUROCRYPT'94, pp. 171–181. Springer, Berlin (1995)
15. Chen, S., Chen, J.: Lattice-based group signatures with forward security for anonymous authentication. Heliyon **9**(4), e14917 (2023)
16. Clarisse, R., Sanders, O.: Group signature without random oracles from randomizable signatures. In: Nguyen, K., Wu, W., Lam, K.Y., Wang, H. (eds.) Provable and Practical Security, pp. 3–23. Springer International Publishing, Cham (2020)
17. Delerablée, C., Pointcheval, D.: Dynamic fully anonymous short group signatures. In: Nguyen, P.Q. (ed.) Progress in Cryptology - VIETCRYPT 2006, pp. 193–210. Springer, Berlin (2006)
18. Derler, D., Slamanig, D.: Highly-efficient fully-anonymous dynamic group signatures. In: ASIACCS '18, pp. 551–565. Association for Computing Machinery, New York (2018)
19. Ferrara, A.L., Green, M., Hohenberger, S., Pedersen, M.Ø.: Practical short signature batch verification. In: Fischlin, M. (ed.) Topics in Cryptology - CT-RSA 2009, pp. 309–324. Springer, Berlin (2009)
20. Fiat, A., Shamir, A.: How to prove yourself: practical solutions to identification and signature problems. In: Odlyzko, A.M. (ed.) Advances in Cryptology – CRYPTO' 86, pp. 186–194. Springer, Berlin (1987)
21. Groth, J.: Simulation-sound NIZK proofs for a practical language and constant size group signatures. In: Lai, X., Chen, K. (eds.) Advances in Cryptology - ASIACRYPT 2006, pp. 444–459. Springer, Berlin (2006)
22. Guo, J., Baugh, J.P., Wang, S.: A group signature based secure and privacy-preserving vehicular communication framework. In: 2007 Mobile Networking for Vehicular Environments, pp. 103–108 (2007)
23. Kiayias, A., Yung, M.: Group signatures with efficient concurrent join. In: Cramer, R. (ed.) Advances in Cryptology - EUROCRYPT 2005, pp. 198–214. Springer, Berlin (2005)
24. Kim, H., Lee, Y., Abdalla, M., Park, J.H.: Practical dynamic group signature with efficient concurrent joins and batch verifications. J. Inf. Secur. Appl. **63**, 103003 (2021)
25. Lee, Y.K., Han, S.W., Lee, S.J., Chung, B.H., Lee, D.G.: Anonymous authentication system using group signature. In: 2009 International Conference on Complex, Intelligent and Software Intensive Systems, pp. 1235–1239 (2009)
26. Libert, B., Mouhartem, F., Peters, T., Yung, M.: Practical "signatures with efficient protocols" from simple assumptions. In: Proceedings of the 11th ACM on Asia Conference on Computer and Communications Security, ASIA CCS '16, pp. 511–522. Association for Computing Machinery, New York (2016)

27. Libert, B., Yung, M.: Dynamic fully forward-secure group signatures. In: Proceedings of the 5th ACM Symposium on Information, Computer and Communications Security, ASIACCS '10, pp. 70–81. Association for Computing Machinery, New York (2010)
28. Lin, C., He, D., Kumar, N., Huang, X., Vijayakumar, P., Choo, K.K.R.: Homechain: a blockchain-based secure mutual authentication system for smart homes. IEEE Internet Things J. **7**(2), 818–829 (2020)
29. Ling, S., Nguyen, K., Wang, H., Xu, Y.: Forward-secure group signatures from lattices. In: Ding, J., Steinwandt, R. (eds.) Post-Quantum Cryptography, pp. 44–64. Springer International Publishing, Cham (2019)
30. Malina, L., Smrz, J., Hajny, J., Vrba, K.: Secure electronic voting based on group signatures. In: 2015 38th International Conference on Telecommunications and Signal Processing (TSP), pp. 6–10 (2015)
31. Perera, M., Nakamura, T., Hashimoto, M., Yokoyama, H., Cheng, C., Sakurai, K.: A survey on group signatures and ring signatures: traceability vs. anonymity. Cryptography **6**(1) (2022). publisher Copyright: 2022 by the authors. Licensee MDPI, Basel, Switzerland
32. Pointcheval, D., Sanders, O.: Short randomizable signatures. In: Sako, K. (ed.) Topics in Cryptology - CT-RSA 2016, pp. 111–126. Springer International Publishing, Cham (2016)
33. Schnorr, C.P.: Efficient signature generation by smart cards. J. Cryptol. **4**(3), 161–174 (1991)
34. Smart, N.P.: Cryptography Made Simple, 1st edn. Springer Publishing Company, Incorporated (2015)
35. Song, D.X.: Practical forward secure group signature schemes. In: Proceedings of the 8th ACM Conference on Computer and Communications Security, CCS '01, pp. 225–234. Association for Computing Machinery, New York (2001)
36. Song, H.J., Kim, T., Hwang, Y.W., Seo, D., Lee, I.Y.: A study on dynamic group signature scheme with threshold traceability for blockchain. High-Confidence Comput. **4**(2), 100163 (2024)
37. Su, Q., Zhang, R., Xue, R., Sun, Y.: An efficient traceable and anonymous authentication scheme for permissioned blockchain. In: Miller, J., Stroulia, E., Lee, K., Zhang, L.J. (eds.) Web Services - ICWS 2019, pp. 110–125. Springer International Publishing, Cham (2019)
38. Sun, X., Lin, X., Ho, P.H.: Secure vehicular communications based on group signature and id-based signature scheme. In: 2007 IEEE International Conference on Communications, pp. 1539–1545 (2007)
39. Tian, H., Luo, P., Su, Y.: A group signature based digital currency system. In: Zheng, Z., Dai, H.N., Tang, M., Chen, X. (eds.) Blockchain and Trustworthy Systems, pp. 3–14. Springer Singapore, Singapore (2020)
40. Zheng, H., Zhao, Z., Zhang, X.: Access control based on group signatures in cloud service. In: 2012 IEEE International Conference on Computer Science and Automation Engineering (CSAE), vol. 2, pp. 316–320 (2012)

Zero Trust Continuous Authentication Models and Automated Policy Formulation

Nikhill Vombatkere and Philip W. L. Fong[✉]

University of Calgary, Alberta, Canada
{nikhill.vombatkere,pwlfong}@ucalgary.ca

Abstract. Continuous authentication helps mitigate the risk of session hijacking, insider attack, and privilege abuse. Applying zero trust principles, this paper proposes a family of four formally specified access control models to account for the use of continuous authentication to monitor user access patterns in user-facing software applications, each model providing increasingly expressive user modeling capabilities. We name these models Zero Trust Continuous Authentication (ZTCA). Deploying a ZTCA model requires the authoring of policies. To ease the challenge of developing ZTCA policies, we studied the problem of automatically generating ZTCA policies from declarative usability and security requirements. We devised a novel SAT encoding for the automated policy formulation problem, so that policy formulation can be performed by state-of-the-art SAT solvers. Empirical experiments demonstrate that our novel encoding approach runs significantly faster than a competing encoding approach previously published in the literature.

Keywords: Access control · Zero trust principles · Continuous authentication · Automated policy formulation · NP-hardness · SAT encoding

1 Introduction

Granting resource access to the wrong people is risky. Such risks persist even in systems equipped with well-designed access control models. Traditional authentication and authorization mechanisms are insufficient against threats such as session hijacking [21], insider attacks [19], and privilege abuse, where legitimate credentials and authorization tokens are compromised or misused after initial authentication and authorization. Continuous authentication emerges as a promising protection mechanism to address these evolving security challenges by maintaining ongoing verification throughout user sessions, taking into account real-time behavioral and contextual information.

In this work, we propose a formally specified access control model, *Zero Trust Continuous Authentication (ZTCA)*, that employs continuous authentication to regulate user access to resources. A novelty is that the model design is based on zero trust (ZT) principles [22, Sect. 2.1]. Recent work on

ZT-inspired access control focuses either on the network level [2,3,17,18] or on the interaction between Internet-of-Things devices [1]. On the contrary, we apply ZT principles to user-facing applications.

1. **No implicit trust.** Traditional network protection relies on the idea of implicit trust zones: Hosts within the network perimeter are trusted. The ZT philosophy treats every access as originating from an untrusted origin. This prevents the "lateral movement" of compromized actors. When applied to user-facing applications, this philosophy implies that even after a subject has been authorized into a protection domain, we must still defend against the possibility of session hijacking, and reauthentication and reauthorization could be triggered even within the same user session.
2. **Least privilege.** A fundamental ZT principle is to make authorization as granular as possible. In user-facing applications, this means not only minimizing the set of granted resources, but designing the access control model to account for the users' usual access patterns and workflows. When user behavior deviates from these expected patterns, it signals potential risk that requires immediate mitigation. Such a design significantly reduces the impact of session hijacking, insider attacks, and privilege abuse.
3. **Continuous verification.** A key ZT principle requires that all actors be continuously monitored and their trust levels dynamically reassessed. Detected risks should trigger mitigating responses. In this work, when a user deviates from the expected access pattern, an authentication challenge will be issued to that user. Only when the offending user satisfies the challenge will the access request be granted.

When one attempts to encode least privilege in an access control policy, a persistent challenge is what we call the *Least Privilege Granularity Dilemma*. First, statically identifying the least set of privilege used by a program is an undecidable problem (easy reduction from the Halting Problem). Second, manually specifying the precise behavioural pattern of a system requires intense human efforts. Even though least privilege is desirable, there does not appear to be a straightforward way to capture that notion in a policy. In previous work on ZT access control, researchers address this dilemma by either providing tool-support for policy development [18] or employing Machine Learning to mine policies from data [17]. In this work, we explore the feasibility of *automated policy formulation*, in which the policy engineer specifies both *usability and security constraints*, and a tool then constructs a ZTCA policy that balances both usability and security. A usability constraint specifies that a frequently occurring use case shall not trigger more than a certain number of authentication challenges. A security constraint demands that resources enabling a known attack chain shall be protected by a certain number of authentication challenges. We believe it is easier to incrementally write down security and usability constraints than to develop a full-blown ZTCA policy from scratch, as the policy engineer usually has some intuitive ideas of the common use cases and attack chains.

We claim the following contributions.

(1) We propose a formal model of ZTCA based on the notion of application-level segmentation (Sect. 2). We use this model to study the problem of automated policy formulation while balancing usability and security: i.e., computing a segmentation of application resources that satisfies some high-level usability and security requirements. We name this problem the Resource Grouping Problem (RGP), which we demonstrate to be NP-complete.
(2) In Sect. 3, the segmentation model is generalized to a family of four ZTCA models: (i) segmentation, (ii) risk level, (iii) neighbourhood, and (iv) workflow. We show that automated policy formulation remains intractable (NP-hard or coNP-hard) in each of the models.
(3) Even though RGP is NP-complete, in practice we still desire to automate the development of segmentation policies. We propose to reduce RGP to SAT and employ off-the-shelf SAT solvers to solve RGP instances. To that end, we devised a novel SAT-encoding known as the equivalence-based encoding (Sect. 4).
(4) We empirically evaluated our SAT encoding, and found our equivalence-based encoding to perform more efficiently than the mapping-based encoding approach of Zhang and Fong [23] (Sect. 5).

2 A First ZTCA Model: Segmentation

System Overview. We envision a user-facing system equipped with a ***static*** access control model (e.g., RBAC, ABAC, ReBAC, etc.). Once authenticated, a user, say Alice, is granted permissions by the static model to access certain ***resources***, examples of which include application endpoints, server port ranges, DNS namespaces, cloud storage buckets, Kafka topics, etc. Let $\mathcal{R}$ be the set of all resources for which Alice has been granted permissions. In other words, $\mathcal{R}$ is the ***protection domain*** to which Alice is placed. In a traditional access control scheme, Alice would have unrestricted access to every resource in $\mathcal{R}$. It is different in our ZTCA scheme, due to the ZT principle of *"no implicit trust"* (Sect. 1). Specifically, we layer a ***dynamic*** authorization mechanism, a ***ZTCA model***, on top of the static model. Based on continuous evaluation of risk, Alice's access requests are not automatically granted even when she has the right permissions. What constitutes a risky access is defined in a ***ZTCA policy***. More specifically, a ZTCA policy is a means to realize the ZT principle of *"least privilege"* (Sect. 1): the policy specifies certain expected behavior patterns of the user (details to be given below). When an access request of Alice is deemed risky because it deviates from the policy's expectation, the ZTCA model issues an ***authentication challenge*** to Alice. The authentication challenge may be a multi-factor authentication (MFA) or a step-up authentication involving, for example, hardware tokens or active liveness detection [12], or it may be a proof of location. Only when Alice authenticates successfully will the access request be granted. Depending on risk severity, subsequent authentication challenges could be different even within a user session. This risk-triggered injection of authentication challenges is analogous to the prescription of obligations in risk-based access control [9,20], and is our means of realizing the ZT principle of *"continuous verification"* (Sect. 1). This two-layer authorization architecture can be easily implemented in a Policy Enforcement Point such as the Zero Trust Exchange of Zscaler [24]. This system architecture is assumed in the rest of this paper.

A Segmentation Model. We introduce a first formal model of ZTCA. The model is called **ZTCA-RST**; the meaning of the suffix RST will become clear in the next section. In this model, a policy is a grouping of resources into "segments". Intuitively, a segment is a collection of resources that are expected to be accessed together for an application-level use case. When the user crosses a segment boundary and requests to access a resource belonging to a different segment than the one she has been accessing, the ZTCA layer will consider this an unexpected and thus risky event, and respond with an authentication challenge. For example, say Alice is a university employee working with an enterprise software (e.g., PeopleSoft). Suppose application features can be roughly classified into three types: grading, research accounting, and payroll. The web pages corresponding to each feature class are assigned to its own application segment. Alice frequently accesses the grades administration system. When she does that, no extra authentication challenges will be issued to her as all the resources related to grading resides in the same segment. When Alice moves beyond that segment and requests access to features belonging to a different segment (e.g., research accounting), she is required to prove her identity by MFA. In short, when a user attempts to access the resources of a segment for the first time, an authentication challenge is issued. Segments are therefore *dynamic* protection domains with finer granularity than those protection domains of the *static* access control model. For the sake of terminological generality, we call a segmentation a grouping, and call a segment a group within that grouping.

Definition 1. *Suppose $\mathcal{R}$ is a finite set of resources representing a static protection domain to which a user is placed. A* **grouping** *of $\mathcal{R}$ is a partition of $\mathcal{R}$ into a family $G = \{G_1, G_2, \ldots, G_m\}$ of disjoint subsets of $\mathcal{R}$, such that $\mathcal{R} = G_1 \uplus G_2 \uplus \cdots \uplus G_m$. Each subset G_i is called a* **group**.

Policy Requirement Specification. We want to devise a ZTCA-RST policy (i.e., a grouping) that balances security and usability. We do not believe that there is a single metric that every policy (i.e., segmentation) must optimize. Instead, based on one's understanding of the application's usage, one may want to ensure that common use cases are not clobbered by frequent authentication challenges, while a risky constellation of resources shall be protected by an adequate number of authentication challenges. We envision that such requirements of policy development are specified as usability and security constraints.

Definition 2. *Suppose $\mathcal{R}$ is a finite set of resources, and $G = \{G_1, G_2, \ldots, G_m\}$ is a grouping of $\mathcal{R}$.*

- *A* **usability constraint** *is a pair $(S, \leq b)$, where $S \subseteq \mathcal{R}$ and b is a positive integer. G* **satisfies** *$(S, \leq b)$ iff S intersects with at most b groups in G.*

– A **security constraint** is a pair $(S, \geq b)$, where $S \subseteq \mathcal{R}$ and b is a positive integer. G **satisfies** $(S, \geq b)$ iff S intersects with at least b groups in G.

Intuitively, a usability constraint represents a use case. S is a set of resources that a user typically accesses together to complete a recurring task. The desire is to streamline accesses, so that no more than b authentication challenges are issued to the user. On the contrary, a security constraint represents a security concern. The set S represents a risky constellation of resources: e.g., simultaneously obtaining access to all the resources in S may enable a bad actor to exploit a known attack vector. Consequently, we demand any user who gains access to all members of S to be challenged with at least b authentications. The riskier the set S is, the larger b will be.

Automating Policy Formulation. It is desirable to automate the formulation of ZTCA-RST policies, so that the requirements of policy development are specified as usability and security constraints, and an appropriate grouping that satisfies all constraints are computed automatically. The following decision problem captures this computational task:

Problem: *The Resource Grouping Problem (RGP)*[1]
Instance: A finite set $\mathcal{R}$ of resources, a finite set UC of usability constraints, and a finite set SC of security constraints.
Question: Does there exist a grouping G of $\mathcal{R}$ that satisfies every constraint in UC and SC?

It turns out that RGP is computationally intractable.

Theorem 1. *RGP is NP-complete.*

Even though RGP is NP-complete, we devised efficient SAT encodings for it (Sect. 4) so that we can employ an off-the-shelf SAT solver for automating ZTCA policy formulation (Sect. 5).

3 A Family of ZTCA Models

A ZTCA policy informs the enforcement mechanism on when an authentication challenge shall be issued. In our first model, a ZTCA policy is a grouping of resources. The purpose is to balance usability and security: Once the user has accessed a resource from a group, further access to resources from the same group will not trigger authentication. In this section, we generalize the notion of a ZTCA policy. We want to express authorization rules of the following form:

> If the user is trusted to access resource u, then she is trusted to access resource v without triggering an authentication challenge.

---

[1] Later on, we will call this decision problem GRGP-RST to differentiate it from other variations of the problem.

Without the rule above, accessing v after u is considered risky, and an authentication is triggered. This rule can be summarized as an edge (u, v) in a directed graph. This so called "lateral movement graph" specifies which lateral movements of the user are expected and thus considered trusted (and which are risky). By introducing different trust propagation axioms (e.g., reflexivity, symmetry, and transitivity) to constrain the shape of that directed graph, we can specialize the general model in different ways, resulting a family of distinct ZTCA models, each having a different way of expressing expected user behavior.

3.1 Notation and Terminology

We begin with fixing our notation and terminology. Consult standard textbooks for more details [7,10].

Directed Graphs. A vertex u in directed graph G is a **source vertex** iff its in-degree is zero. A **sink vertex** is one for which the out-degree is zero. Given a directed graph G and a subset $S \subseteq V(G)$ of vertices, the **subgraph of G induced by S**, denoted by $G[S]$, has S as its vertex set and $E(G) \cap (S \times S)$ as its edge set. A directed graph G is **strongly connected** iff there is a directed path from u to v and another from v to u for every pair of distinct vertices $u, v \in V(G)$. A **strongly connected component (SCC)** of a directed graph G is a maximal subgraph of G that remains strongly connected. The **component graph** $G^{SCC} = (V^{SCC}, E^{SCC})$ of a directed graph G is defined as follows: The members of V^{SCC} are the SCCs of G; $(C, D) \in E^{SCC}$ iff there is a directed edge $(u, v) \in E(G)$ such that $u \in C$ and $v \in D$. Component graphs are acyclic [10, Sect. 22.5]. A directed graph is **complete** iff (a) there is a loop at every vertex and (b) both directed edges (u, v) and (v, u) exist for every pair of distinct vertices u and v.

Undirected Graphs. Suppose G is a directed graph such that $E(G)$ is a symmetric relation. Then we write G^I for the **undirected graph interpretation of** G, which is obtained by (a) eliminating the loops, and (b) turning each pair of directed edges (u, v) and (v, u) into an undirected edge uv. An undirected graph is **connected** iff there is an undirected path between u and v for every pair of distinct vertices u and v. A **connected component** of an undirected graph H is a maximal subgraph of H that is connected.

3.2 Generalized ZTCA

We formulate a generalized ZTCA model below, so that the segmentation model of Sect. 2 is but a specialization.

Policies. When a user interacts with a ZTCA system, the user's activities can be represented as a sequence of requests to access resources. Such a trace is called a user session.

Definition 3 (User Session). *Given a set $\mathcal{R}$ of resources, a* **user session** *is a sequence from $\mathcal{R}^*$.*

A ZTCA system mediates the accesses to the resources. Specifically, the ZTCA enforcement mechanism issues authentication challenges to the user when the access is considered "risky." A ZTCA policy specifies when such an authentication challenge is required.

Definition 4 (Policy). *Given a set $\mathcal{R}$ of resources, a **policy** G for $\mathcal{R}$ is a directed graph where $V(G) = \mathcal{R}$.*

Intuitively, the vertices of the directed graph G represent the resources in $\mathcal{R}$. The directed edges in G specifies what resources the user may access without additional authentication based on what she has already accessed in the past. We formalize below the semantics of a policy. Specifically, we specify two different semantics: the strict semantics and the liberal semantics. In the ***strict semantics***, if the user has just accessed resource u, and now proceeds to access resource v, then an authentication challenge will be issued to the user if the edge (u, v) is not in G. In addition, the first access request in a user session always triggers an authentication challenge

Definition 5 (Strict Semantics). *Suppose G is a policy for resource set $\mathcal{R}$, and $\tau = v_1 v_2 \cdots v_n \in \mathcal{R}^*$ is a user session. The number of authentication challenges issued to the user under the strict semantics, denoted $auth_s(\tau, G)$, is $1 + |\{i \mid 1 \leq i < n, (v_i, v_{i+1}) \notin E(G)\}|$.*

Under the strict semantics, a policy G can be seen as an automaton, with resources as states and directed edges as transitions. When the user accesses resources by following a directed path in G, no authentication challenge will be issued (except for the first access, which always triggers an authentication). Deviation from sanctioned transitions causes the user to have to authenticate again.

In the ***liberal semantics***, a request to access resource v requires an authentication challenge only if the user has never accessed a resource u for which $(u, v) \in E(G)$. In other words, once a resource u has been accessed, every resource v for which $(u, v) \in E(G)$ can be accessed without additional reauthentication. (Again, the first access request always triggers an authentication challenge.)

Definition 6 (Liberal Semantics). *Suppose G is a policy for resource set $\mathcal{R}$, and $\tau = v_1 \cdot v_2 \cdots v_n \in \mathcal{R}^*$ is a user session. The number of authentication challenges issued to the user under the liberal semantics, denoted $auth_l(\tau, G)$, is $|\{i \mid 1 \leq i \leq n, \neg \exists j < i . (v_j, v_i) \in E(G)\}|$.*

Under the liberal semantics, a ZTCA policy is **monotonic** in the following sense: Suppose user session τ is a prefix of user session π. If requesting to access resource v immediately after τ does not require an authentication challenge, then requesting v immediately after π does not either. In other words, accessing more resources never reduces accessibility. Conversely, if requesting v immediately after π triggers an authentication, then requesting v immediately after τ will trigger authentication as well. The strict semantics, on the contrary, is not monotonic. Monotonicity is a desirable property of an access control model, as it streamlines formal reasoning. With monotonicity, ZTCA becomes a form of access control based on shallow execution history [14]: what is accessible next is a function of the *set* of previous accesses. **In the rest of this paper, we focus on the liberal semantics.**

Automated Policy Formulation. As in Sect. 2, we aspire to specify the requirements of policy development in declarative terms, and then compute a policy that satisfies all such objectives. Again, we use a usability constraint to specify a use case and a security constraint to articulate a security concern. Generalized constraints maintain the same syntax as before, but their semantics is now expanded to work with user sessions.

Definition 7 (Constraint). *Suppose $\mathcal{R}$ is a set of resources, $S \subseteq \mathcal{R}$ is a subset of resources, b is a positive number, and G is a policy for $\mathcal{R}$.*

- *The pair $(S, \geq b)$ is a* **security constraint***, while the pair $(S, \leq b)$ is a* **usability constraint***.*
- *A user session $\tau \in S^*$ satisfies $(S, \geq b)$ iff $auth_l(\tau, G[S]) \geq b$; and τ satisfies $(S, \leq b)$ iff $auth_l(\tau, G[S]) \leq b$.*
- *A user session $\tau \in S^*$ is* **full-fledged** *for S iff every resource in S appears at least once in τ. We write $full(S)$ to denote the set of all full-fledged user sessions for S.*
- *G satisfies $(S, \geq b)$ iff every $\tau \in full(S)$ satisfies $(S, \geq b)$. G satisfies $(S, \leq b)$ iff every $\tau \in full(S)$ satisfies $(S, \leq b)$.*

Here is the decision form of the policy formulation problem.

Problem: *Generalized RGP (GRGP)*
Instance: A finite set $\mathcal{R}$ of resources, a finite set UC of usability constraints, and a finite set SC of security constraints.
Question: Does there exists a ZTCA policy G (i.e., a directed graph) such that G satisfies every constraint in UC and SC?

In the following, we will examine various specialization of the ZTCA model, by imposing different restrictions over the topology of the directed graph that is a ZTCA policy. Such restrictions lead to nontrivial subproblems of GRGP.

Reflexive Policies. A policy G captures a binary relation (i.e., $E(G)$) defined over the resources (i.e., $V(G)$). Consequently, we will speak of G as if we are describing a binary relation.

Definition 8. *A policy G for resource set $\mathcal{R}$ is respectively* **reflexive, symmetric***, or* **transitive** *iff $E(G)$ is a reflexive, symmetric, or transitive binary relation.*

Reflexivity, symmetry, and transitivity are examples of ***trust propagation axioms***, each prescribing how trust relationships can be inferred. For example, symmetry says: "If the user is trusted to access v after she has accessed u, then she is trusted to access u after having accessed v." We consider reflexivity first.

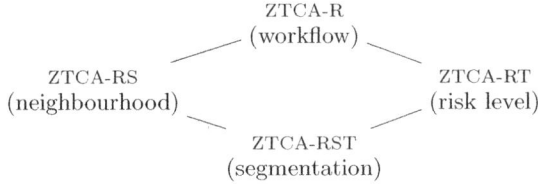

Fig. 1. A family of ZTCA models.

Suppose a policy G is *not* reflexive. Suppose further that an access to a resource u has triggered an authentication challenge. There are now two cases. First, $(u, u) \in E(G)$, and thus gaining access to u enables the user to access u for a second time without triggering authentication. Second, $(u, u) \notin E(G)$, and thus the user still requires an authentication next time u is accessed. We believe the second case is a violation of the **Principle of Privilege Attentuation (POPA)** [13, p. 372], which states that: "A subject may not give rights it does not possess to another" [6, p. 43]. Imposing reflexivity prevents this problem. **In the following, we consider only reflexive policies.** With a reflexive policy G, once a resource v has been accessed for the first time, future requests to access v will never trigger an authentication challenge. Under this design, there is no need to consider all full-fledged user sessions when we determine if a constraint $(S, \text{op}\, b)$ is satisfied by a policy. It suffices to consider only the *permutations* of S. We make this observation formal in the following.

Definition 9. *Given finite resource set $\mathcal{R}$, suppose $\tau \in \mathcal{R}^*$ is a user session and $S \subseteq \mathcal{R}$ is a subset of resources.*

- *unique(τ) is the subsequence of τ obtained by keeping only the first occurrence of every resource from $\mathcal{R}$.*
- *perm(S) is the subset of S^* made up of permutations of S.*

For example, $unique(aabacb) = abc$ and $unique(bcbcabca) = bca$. Also, $perm(\{a, b, c\}) = \{abc, acb, bac, bca, cab, cba\}$. Note that $perm(S) \subseteq full(S)$.

Corollary 1. *Suppose G is a reflexive policy for resource set $\mathcal{R}$, $S \subseteq \mathcal{R}$, $\tau \in S^*$, $\text{op} \in \{\leq, \geq\}$, and b is a positive integer. Then the following statements hold:*

1. $auth_l(\tau, G) = auth_l(unique(\tau), G)$.
2. G satisfies $(S, \text{op}\, b)$ iff every $\tau \in perm(S)$ satisfies $(S, \text{op}\, b)$.

In the following, we study a family of four ZTCA models (Fig. 1). Each model is obtained by restricting the general ZTCA model to use only reflexive policies and then optionally demand that the policies be symmetric and/or transitive. We name the resulting ZTCA models ZTCA-*xxx*, where *xxx* is a string indicating the trust propagation axioms we impose on the underlying policies. For example, ZTCA-RST is the ZTCA model obtained by demanding the policies to be reflexive (R), symmetric (S), and transitive (T), while ZTCA-RT is the

ZTCA model restricted to reflexive (R) and transitive (T) policies. The policy formulation problem GRGP is restricted accordingly. For example, the policy formulation problem for the ZTCA-RT model is designated GRGP-RT, which is a restriction of GRGP to consider only reflexive and transitive policies.

3.3 ZTCA-RST: Segmentation

In our first model, ZTCA-RST, policies are reflexive, symmetric, and transitive, meaning that $E(G)$ is an equivalence relation. Every equivalence class coincides with an SCC of G. Each such SCC is a complete subgraph, and no two SCCs are connected by any edge. Once the user has accessed a resource within an equivalence class, subsequent requests to access other resources from the same equivalence class will not trigger an authentication challenge. The number of authentication challenges triggered by a user session τ is thus the number of equivalence classes that intersect with τ.

It is not hard to recognize that this specialization of ZTCA is essentially the same as the segmentation model defined in Sect. 2, so that an equivalence class plays the same role as a group (aka segment). The policy formulation problem of this model, GRGP-RST, is GRGP restricted to reflexive, symmetric, and transitive policies. Theorem 1 asserts that this decision problem is NP-complete.

3.4 ZTCA-RT: Risk Level

Policies in our second model, ZTCA-RT, are reflexive and transitive (but not necessarily symmetric). This model is a generalization of ZTCA-RST. ZTCA-RT allows one to express policies that are more liberal than those in ZTCA-RST. More specifically, ZTCA-RT can be used for expressing **risk levels**. Each risk level is like a group (equivalence class) in ZTCA-RST: i.e., once the user has gained access to one resource in a risk level, future requests to access resources belonging to the same level will not trigger an authentication challenge. In addition, the risk levels form a partial ordering. If the user has secured access to a resource from a riskier level, then future requests to access resources belonging to a less risky level will not require an authentication challenge. Moving from less risky levels to riskier levels, or between incomparable levels, requires authentication. We explain in the following how reflexivity and transitivity give rise to this notion of risk levels.

Let G be a reflexive and transitive directed graph. Consider an SCC C of G. For every pair of vertices u and v in C, there is a directed path from u to v and another directed path from v to u. By transitivity, both directed edges (u,v) and (v,u) exist. This means every SCC is a complete subgraph. Such a complete subgraph defines a risk level. A user session will trigger at most one authentication challenge for each risk level. Not only that, if there is a directed path in the component graph of G from one SCC C to another SCC D, then by transitivity, there is a directed edge (u,v) from every $u \in C$ to every $v \in D$. Consequently, once a resource from a more risky level C has been accessed, no authentication challenge is needed to access a resource from a less risky level.

In the segmentation model (ZTCA-RST) of Sect. 2 and Sect. 3.3, we assumed that groups are disjoint. What if we desire to have "intersecting groups"? By this we mean there are two groups G_1 and G_2 of resources such that each of G_1 and G_2 is commonly accessed together, but $G_1 \cap G_2$ is a non-empty set. This can be modelled in the ZTAC-RT model by defining three risk levels: $L_1 = G_1 \setminus G_2$, $L_2 = G_2 \setminus G_1$, and $L_3 = G_1 \cap G_2$. We make L_1 and L_2 riskier than L_3, while L_1 and L_2 are incomparable. Suppose resources of only one of G_1 and G_2 are accessed in a single session. If the first accessed resource belongs to L_1 or L_2, then only one authentication challenge will be triggered. Otherwise, the first accessed resource belongs to L_3. The system cannot discern whether the user intends to work with G_1 or G_2, so the secure thing to do is to issue an additional authentication challenge when a resource from L_1 or L_2 is accessed later. This is the secure way to realize "intersecting groups."

We now assess the complexity of GRGP-RT, the subproblem of GRGP obtained by considering only reflexive and transitive policies. We first observe that verifying if a constraint is satisfied can be done in polynomial time, and then assert that GRGP-RT is NP-complete.

Proposition 1. *Suppose G is a reflexive and transitive policy for resource set $\mathcal{R}$, and $S \subseteq \mathcal{R}$ is a resource subset.*

1. *The minimum value of $auth_l(\tau, G)$, where $\tau \in perm(S)$, is the number of source vertices in the component graph of $G[S]$.*
2. *The maximum value of $auth_l(\tau, G)$, where $\tau \in perm(S)$, is the number of SCCs in $G[S]$.*

Theorem 2. *GRGP-RT is NP-complete.*

3.5 ZTCA-RS: Neighbourhood

A ZTCA-RS policy G is both reflexive and symmetric, but not necessarily transitive. Such a policy has an unambiguous interpretation as an undirected graph G^I. A resource v can be accessed authentication-free only if one of its neighbours u has already been accessed. To "separate" two resources u and v, there are now two strategies. The first is to put them into two distinct connected components of G^I. Then accessing one after another always triggers an authentication challenge. The second, milder form of separation is to put them in the same connected component of G^I, but separate them by a distance of $d(u, v)$. The user will then have to access $d(u, v) - 1$ other resources along a shortest path between u and v before v can be accessed without triggering an authentication challenge.

The following result implies that checking if a usability constraint is satisfied is a coNP-complete problem [15, Sect. 7.1], but the satisfaction of a security constraint can be verified in polynomial time.

Proposition 2. *Suppose G is a reflexive and symmetric policy for resource set $\mathcal{R}$, $S \subseteq \mathcal{R}$, and b is a positive number.*

1. G satisfies usability constraint $(S, \leq b)$ iff $G[S]^I$ does not contain an independent set of size $b + 1$.
2. G satisfies security constraint $(S, \geq b)$ iff $G[S]^I$ contains at least b connected components.

Since verifying the satisfaction of a usability constraint is already coNP-hard, GRGP-RS itself is coNP-hard, but no harder than Σ_2^p. It is not known whether GRGP-RS is Σ_2^p-complete.[2]

Theorem 3. *GRGP-RS is in Σ_2^p and is coNP-hard.*

3.6 ZTCA-R: Workflow

The ZTCA-R model is a generalization of both ZTCA-RS and ZTCA-RT. A ZTCA-R policy is reflexive, but it may or may not be symmetric or transitive. To avoid authentication challenges, the user will access resources by tracing directed paths in the policy. Therefore, a ZTCA-R policy can be used for expressing workflows. More specifically, the resources specific to a workflow step can be grouped into a clique, and then directed edges connecting cliques express ordering of steps within the workflow. Policy formulation in ZTCA-R is coNP-hard. Whether GRGP-R is Σ_2^p-complete is an open problem.

Theorem 4. *GRGP-R is in Σ_2^p and is coNP-hard.*

4 An Efficient SAT Encoding for RGP

Even though the RGP (Sect. 2) and its GRGP variants (Sect. 3) are intractable, we still want to automate the formulation of ZTCA policies. We propose to reduce RGP instances to SAT instances, and employ state-of-the-art SAT solvers to compute a ZTCA-RST policy from a given set of usability and security constraints. An important contribution of this work is an efficient SAT encoding for RGP, which we dub the ***equivalence-based encoding***. This encoding approach models a partition of a set as an equivalence relation defined over the set members. Each part corresponds to an equivalence class. The equivalence-based encoding searches for a way to partition an underlying set ($\mathcal{R}$) such that certain requirements are satisfied (usability and security constraints).

Notations. For non-negative integer x, we write $[x]$ to denote the set $\{1, 2, \ldots, x\}$. Specifically, $[0] = \emptyset$. In addition, we assume that an RGP instance is represented in the following way:

- Let $n = |\mathcal{R}|$. The resources are identified by the indices $1, 2, \ldots, n$. We use variables i, j, and k to refer to resources. In other words, $i, j, k \in [n]$.
- There are m constraints: $(S_1, \mathrm{op}_1 b_1), (S_2, \mathrm{op}_2 b_2), \ldots, (S_m, \mathrm{op}_m b_m)$, where each op_i is either $\leq$ or $\geq$. We use the variable r for identifying constraints. Thus $r \in [m]$.

---
[2] Background on Σ_2^p and the polynomial hierarchy can be found in [15, Sect. 7.2].

Boolean Variables:
For every pair $i, j \in [n]$ such that $i < j$:
$x_{i,j}$ asserts that resources i and j are equivalent.
For every $r \in [m]$, for every $p \in [\ell_r]$:
$y_{r,p}$ asserts that i_p^r is inequivalent to $i_1^r, i_2^r, \ldots, i_{p-1}^r$.

Clauses:
For every triple $i, j, k \in [n]$ such that $i < j < k$:
$((\neg x_{i,j} \vee \neg x_{j,k} \vee x_{i,k}) \wedge$
$(\neg x_{i,j} \vee x_{j,k} \vee \neg x_{i,k}) \wedge$
$(x_{i,j} \vee \neg x_{j,k} \vee \neg x_{i,k}))$ (1) The equivalence relation is transitive.

For every $r \in [m]$:
$(y_{r,1})$ (2) No other member of S_p precedes i_1^p.

For every $r \in [m]$, for every $p \in [\ell_r]$ such that $p > 1$:
$\left(\left(\bigvee_{q=1}^{p-1} x_{i_q^r, i_p^r} \right) \vee y_{r,p} \right)$ (3) If i_p^r is inequivalent to every i_q^r, for $q < p$, then $y_{r,p}$ is true.

For every $r \in [m]$, for every $p, q \in [\ell_r]$ such that $p > 1$ and $q < p$:
$(\neg x_{i_q^r, i_p^r} \vee \neg y_{r,p})$ (4) If i_p^r is equivalent to some i_q^r, where $q < p$, then $y_{r,p}$ is false.

For every $r \in [m]$:
$\left(\sum_{p=1}^{\ell_r} y_{r,p} \leq b_r \right)$ if op_r is $\leq$ (5) S_r intersects with at most b_r groups.

$\left(\sum_{p=1}^{\ell_r} y_{r,p} \geq b_r \right)$ if op_r is $\geq$ (6) S_r intersects with at least b_r groups.

Fig. 2. Equivalence-based encoding of RGP.

- For the constraint with index r, let $\ell_r = |S_r|$. We also write S_r as $\{i_1^r, i_2^r, \ldots, i_{\ell_r}^r\}$, where $i_1^r < i_2^r < \cdots < i_{\ell_r}^r$. We use the variables p and q for indices of the members of S_r, as in i_p^r and i_q^r. Therefore, $p, q \in [\ell_r]$.

Encoding. The equivalence-based encoding for RGP is summarized in Fig. 2. This encoding models an equivalence relation between resources. Specifically, every equivalence class corresponds to a group. The encoding formulated in terms of two types of boolean variables. Firstly, the variable $x_{i,j}$ indicates that resource i and resource j belong to the same group. In order words, they are equivalent. We define $x_{i,j}$ only when $i < j$. For example, $x_{3,7}$ is defined, but $x_{3,3}$ and $x_{7,3}$ are not. The reason is that the clauses of this encoding do not need to check whether i is equivalent to j unless $i < j$. Thus we have $\binom{n}{2} = \frac{n(n-1)}{2}$ such variables. Secondly, the variable $y_{r,p}$ (for $r \in [m]$ and $p \in [\ell_r]$) asserts that the member i_p^r of S_r is inequivalent to every other members preceeding it in S_p (i.e., inequivalent to each of $i_1^r, i_2^r, \ldots, i_{p-1}^r$). As such, $y_{r,p}$ signals that S_r intersects with a new group that is not represented by $i_1^r, i_2^r, \ldots, i_{p-1}^r$. Therefore, the number of groups that S_r intersects with can be obtained by the pseudo-boolean sum $\sum_{p=1}^{\ell_r} y_{r,p}$. Lastly, there are altogether $\sum_{r=1}^{m} \ell_r = \sum_{r=1}^{m} |S_r|$ many variables of the form $y_{r,p}$. In summary, the number of boolean variables in this encoding is quadratic to the size of $\mathcal{R}$ and linear to the total size of the usability and security constraints.

Here is an exposition of the clauses in Fig. 2. Firstly, clause (1) essentially captures the transitivity of the equivalence relation. The reader may wonder why reflexivity and symmetry are not encoded. That is because we only work with $x_{i,j}$ for which $i < j$. Therefore reflexivity and symmetry do not need to be explicitly spelled out. Secondly, clauses (2), (3), and (4) enforce the intended semantics of $y_{r,p}$. Clause (3) ensures that if i_p^r is inequivalent to its preceeding elements in S_r, then $y_{r,p}$ is set to true. Clause (4) encodes the converse. Clause (2) takes care of the special case when $p = 1$. Thirdly, cardinality constraints (5) and (6) enforce the semantics of the usability and security constraints. Recall that the number of groups that intersect with S_r can be obtained by the sum $\sum_{p=1}^{\ell_r} y_{r,p}$. If constraint r is a usability constraint (meaning op_r is $\leq$), then we require that the sum adds up to at most b_r. If constraint r is a security constraint (op_r is $\geq$), then the sum shall add up to at least b_r.

5 Experiments

This section presents an experiment in which we compare the relative performance of the two SAT encodings for RGP. The first is called the ***mapping-based encoding***, which was originally proposed by Zhang and Fong for domain-based policy mining [23]. This encoding approach models grouping by a mapping, and it comes with sophisticated symmetry-breaking optimization. We mimic their encoding approach to obtain a SAT encoding for RGP. Space limit does not permit us to report the details of this encoding. We use the mnemonic MAP to refer to the mapping-based encoding of RGP. The second encoding is the equivalence-based encoding of Sect. 4, which we denote by the mnemonic EQV. We measured the efficiency and scalability of these encodings using an off-the-shelf SAT solver (PySAT [16]). The results of this experiment will contribute to understanding which encoding approach performs better under various parameter configurations, ultimately informing future work on automated policy formulation, policy mining, and policy analysis problems.[3]

Experiment Setup. The experiment was performed on one node of the Advanced Research Computing (ARC) high-performance computing cluster at the University of Calgary. The node has 80 Intel Xeon Gold 6148 @ 2.40GHz CPUs and runs Rocky Linux 8.8 (Green Obsidian) with 3000GB memory. The experiment involved single-node jobs, with 40 CPUs and 500GB memory being allocated to each job. The CaDiCaL solver (CaDiCaL195) [4,5] was employed for solving SAT instances. The implementation was provided by the PySAT library [16].

Experiment Design. We benchmarked the performance of MAP and EQV by creating a benchmark suite consisting of a collection of RGP instances. The

---

[3] The Python codebase for the implementation of the experiment, including the two SAT encodings, can be found at https://github.com/NVombat/zeetee.

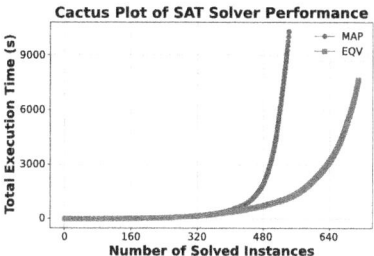

	# Variables	# Clauses	Total Clause Length
MAP	63,176.5	41,202,700.0	82,542,730.0
EQV	143,867.4	80,676,190.0	242,006,800.0

(a) Average size of SAT instances. (b) Cactus plot for the results.

Fig. 3. SAT instance size statistics and cactus plot for the experiment results.

following parameters were systematically varied to explore the performance of the two encodings under different conditions: (a) the number of resources (n), (b) constraint percentages (CP), which is the number of constraints expressed as a ratio to n, and (c) constraint size (CS), which is the size of the set S in a constraint $(S, \text{op } b)$.

For each $n \in \{100, 200, 300, ..., 800\}$, $CP \in \{20, 40, 60, 80, 100\}$ and $CS \in \{10, 15, 20\}$, we applied the algorithm in Appendix A to generate 6 RGP instances, resulting in a total of 720 RGP instances as our benchmark suite. We then applied MAP and EQV in turn to encode the RGP instances as SAT instances. In the case of MAP, we supplied $t = \sqrt{n}$ as an upper bound on the number of groups. (Fig. 3a reports the average size of the SAT instances.) The SAT instances are then solved by the SAT solver. We set a timeout limit of 6 min: i.e., we terminated the solving of an instance by an encoding when that instance could not be solved by that encoding within the timeout limit. When an instance could be solved by an encoding within the timeout limit, we measured the execution time.

Results. Fig. 3b visualizes the results in a ***cactus plot***, which is now the standard way by which the SAT community depicts experimental results [8]. The X-axis represents the number of solved instances, and the Y-axis represents the total execution time (in seconds) to solve those instances.

More specifically, suppose an encoding solved N of the 720 RGP instances. We sorted the execution time of the N instances: $t_1 \leq t_2 \leq \cdots \leq t_N$. Then we computed $T_i = t_1 + t_2 + \cdots + t_i$. Lastly, we plotted (i, T_i), for $1 \leq i \leq N$, to depict the performance of that encoding. In other words, a point (i, T_i) in the cactus plot indicates that the encoding in question was able to solve i instances within T_i seconds. We repeated this for each encoding to obtain Fig. 3b.

These are the takeaways from the results:

1. **EQV is the more efficient encoding.** EQV produces SAT instances that are not only faster to solve but more instances can be solved within a set time period.

2. **EQV takes longer to generate SAT instances from the RGP instances.** This can be explained by EQV having a larger instance size than MAP (Fig. 3a).

6 Related Work

A number of works have been published for realizing zero trust principles at the network level [2,3,17,18]. To realize Least Privilege, NetViews presents to each host a limited "view" of the network consisting of only a subset of existing hosts and services [2]. Views are specified via NGAC policies and enforced by Software-Defined Network (SDN) technology. Users and resources in the NGAC policy are mapped to IP addresses. MSNetViews extends the above work to account for enterprise networks that span geographically distributed sites [3]. NEUTRON is a network-level access control policy development framework for supporting zero trust principles [18]. It provides a tool-supported pipeline for authoring policies that regulate network traffic: specifying interaction needs via a graph-based policy formalism, checking compliance between policies and constraints, compilation of policies to device-specific enforcement rules, testing, and pushing enforcement rules to devices. The work is later extended to employ Machine Learning to automate the authoring of policies [17].

Zero trust principles are considered in novel contexts other than network traffic regulation. ZeroDNS combines DNS queries with authorization requests in a Zero Trust Architecture, thereby reducing Time-to-First-Byte [11]. ZTA-IoT is a Zero Trust Architecture for Internet of Things (IoT) systems [1]. The focus is on protecting devices as well as information stored in or generated by these devices against access by users or other devices. This is achieved by a formally specified usage control model that supports continuous authorization with dynamic attribute updates.

Compared to the above works, ZTCA is distinctive in that it realizes ZT principles in a user-facing application rather than at the network or device level. While tool support and Machine Learning are employed in [17,18] to address the Least Privilege Granularity Dilemma, our approach compiles declarative usability and security requirements to ZTCA policies. Our ZTCA models are comparable to risk-based access control [9,20], in which obligations are triggered when the requested access is assessed to be risky. A novelty of our ZTCA models lies in assessing risk based on how the user's access pattern deviates from the expectation of the ZTCA policy. Our ZTCA models are also comparable to execution monitoring based on shallow execution history [14]. Our novelty lies in expressing authorization rules using a directed graph rather than an automaton, and studying trust propagation axioms such as reflexivity, symmetry, and transitivity.

Recently, Zhang and Fong reduced Domain-Based Policy Mining to MaxSAT [23]. We dub their encoding approach "mapping-based encoding." Their approach incorporates sophisticated optimization techniques, such as the breaking of permutation and combination symmetry. An important contribution of our work is the invention of the equivalence-based encoding, which outperforms the highly-optimized mapping-based encoding. This opens up the possibility of speeding up other SAT/MaxSAT-based policy analysis and policy mining tasks.

7 Conclusion and Future Work

We proposed a family of four ZTCA models, of which the classical segmentation model is a member. We studied the problem of automatically computing a ZTCA policy from a set of declaratively specified usability and security requirements. The problem turns out to be computationally hard in all four models. We invented an efficient SAT encoding, known as equivalence-based encoding, for solving the policy formulation problem, and empirically demonstrated that this novel encoding outperforms the mapping-based encoding of Zhang and Fong.

We plan to pursue several future research directions. (1) We plan to compile high-level description of user cases and workflows to usability and security constraints. (2) We plan to study other aspects of user monitoring, including contextual information and evolution of trustworthiness. (3) We plan to apply the equivalence-encoding approach to other policy mining and policy analysis problems.

Acknowledgement. This work is supported in part by the Natural Sciences and Engineering Research Council of Canada under the Discovery Grant RGPIN-2020-05238.

A Algorithm for Generating a Random RGP Instance

High-level Algorithm. Given n, CP, and CS, we generated an RGP instance using the following steps: (1) Create a set $\mathcal{R}$ of n resources. (2) Generate a random number k between 2 and $\sqrt{n}$, and then generate a random partition G of $\mathcal{R}$ into into k groups. (3) Compute the number of constraints to generate: $M = n \times CP\%$. For example, if $CP = 20$, then $M = n \times 0.2$. (4) Apply Subroutine A (see below) repeatedly to generate M satisfiable constraints. (5) With probability 0.5, use Subroutine B (see below) to generate constraints that render this RGP instance unsatisfiable.

Subroutine A: Generating a Satisfiable Constraint. The following steps were employed to generate a satisfiable constraint of the form $(S, \text{op } b)$: (1) Generate S by randomly sampling CS resources from $\mathcal{R}$. (2) Randomly choose op to be "$\leq$" (i.e., usability) or "$\geq$" (i.e., security) with equal probability. (3) Let dg be the number of distinct groups from G that S intersects with. (4) If op is "$\leq$", then set b to $dg + 1$; otherwise set b to $dg - 1$.

Subroutine B: Generating Unsatisfiable Constraints. We used the follow steps to generate unsatisfiable constraints: (1) Randomly generate an integer g in between 2 and k (the total number of groups in G). (2) Randomly sample g groups from the existing k groups, and randomly select one resource from each of the chosen g groups. Let these resources be $v_1, v_2, \ldots, v_g$. (3) Generate a security constraint $(\{v_i, v_j\}, \geq 2)$ for every pair of distinct i and j, so that $1 \leq i < j \leq g$. These security constraints demand each of the g resources to be assigned to a distinct group. (4) Generate a usability constraint $(\{v_1, v_2, \ldots, v_g\}, \leq g - 1)$. This usability constraint demands the g resources to be assigned to fewer than g groups. The usability and security constraints cannot be satisfied simultaneously.

B Proofs

Proof of Theorem 1.

RGP is in NP. A nondeterministic decision procedure can first guess a grouping G and then verify in polynomial time that every constraint is satisfied.

RGP is NP-hard. We present a reduction from graph 3-colorability [15, GT4] to RGP. Given a 3-colorability instance (i.e., an undirected graph) H, we construct an RGP instance $(\mathcal{R}, UC, SC)$ as follows. First, we set $\mathcal{R} = V(H)$. Second, we formulate security constraints $SC = \{(\{u, v\}, \geq 2) \mid uv \in E(G)\}$. In English, for every edge uv in H, a constraint is imposed to ensure that u and v belong to two distinct groups. Third, UC contains only one usability constraint, $(\mathcal{R}, \leq 3)$. Thus, no more than three groups are allowed. □

Proof of Proposition 1. We prove the two statements in turn.

Statement 1. Let m be the number of source vertices in the component graph of $G[S]$. Consider a permutation τ of S. Consider further an SCC C in $G[S]$ that is a source vertex in the component graph of $G[S]$. The first time when a resource v from C is accessed in τ, an authentication challenge is triggered, because C is a source vertex in the component graph of $G[S]$ and thus there is no resource u appearing before v in τ such that (u, v) is an edge of $G[S]$. Consequently, we know that $auth_l(\tau, G) \geq m$ no matter which τ we choose.

We argue that there is a permutation τ of S such that $auth_l(\tau, G) = m$. Let $C_1, C_2, \ldots, C_m$ be the source vertices of $G[S]$'s component graph, and $v_1, v_2, \ldots, v_m$ be vertices taken from each of $C_1, C_2, \ldots, C_m$. We run a Depth-First Search (DFS) over $G[S]$, with $v_1, v_2, \ldots, v_m$ as the tree roots of the DFS forest [10, Sect. 22.3]. Construct τ by listing the members of S in ascending order of discovery time. Only $v_1, v_2, \ldots v_m$ will trigger authentication challenges.

Statement 2. Let M be the number of SCCs in $G[S]$. Once a resource from an SCC C of $G[S]$ has been accessed in a user session, further access to resources within C will not trigger an authentication challenge. Therefore, the total number of authentication challenges for a user session from $perm(S)$ is at most M.

We argue that there is a permutation τ of S for which $auth_l(\tau, G) = M$. Suppose $\langle C_1, C_2, \ldots, C_M \rangle$ is a topological sort [10, Sect. 22.4] of the vertices in the component graph of $G[S]$. Recall that each C_i is an SCC of $G[S]$. Now we construct τ by listing the resources in C_M first, then those in C_{M-1} next, so on and so forth, and lastly the resources in C_1. Let v_i be the first resource in C_i to be accessed in τ. When v_i is accessed, no resource u for which (u, v_i)

is an edge has been accessed yet. Thus, authentication challenges are triggered exactly when a vertex of an SCC is accessed for the first time. □

Proof of Theorem 2.

Membership in NP. We describe a nondeterministic algorithm for deciding GRGP-RT. Such an algorithm guesses a reflexive and transitive directed graph G with resources as vertices. The algorithm checks if G satisfies a security constraint $(S, \geq b)$ by testing if the component graph of $G[S]$ has at least b source vertices (by Statement 1 of Proposition 1). This is a polynomial-time operation. The algorithm checks if G satisfies a usability constraint $(S, \leq b)$ by verifying that $G[S]$ has no more than b SCCs (by Statement 2 of Proposition 1). This, again, can be performed in polynomial time.

NP-hardness. As in the proof of Theorem 1, we reduce Graph 3-Colorability [15, GT4] to our problem. Given a 3-colorability instance, that is, an undirected graph H, we construct a GRGP-RT instance $(\mathcal{R}, UC, SC)$ in three steps. The first two steps are identical to those of the proof of Theorem 1, while the third step deviates from before. First, set $\mathcal{R} = V(H)$. Second, add the security constraint $(\{u, v\}, \geq 2)$ to SC whenever $uv \in E(H)$. Third, add $(\mathcal{R}, \leq 3)$ and $(\mathcal{R}, \geq 3)$ to UC and SC respectively.

Suppose policy G satisfies both $(\mathcal{R}, \leq 3)$ and $(\mathcal{R}, \geq 3)$. The usability constraint ensures that G has at most 3 SCCs (Statement 2 of Proposition 1). The security constraint guarantees that at least 3 SCCs of G are source vertices in G's component graph (by Statement 1 of Proposition 1). This implies G has 3 SCCs that are not connected to one another by any directed edge. In other words, the resources are partitioned into 3 equivalence classes. □

Proof of Proposition 2. We prove the two statements in turn.

Statement 1. Let τ be a permutation of S. Let k be $auth_l(\tau, G)$. Let $v_1, v_2, \ldots, v_k$ be the resources in τ that trigger authentication challenges, ordered in their order of occurrence. Then there is no directed edge (v_i, v_j) for $1 \leq i < j \leq k$. Since G is symmetric, there is also no directed edge (v_j, v_i) for $1 \leq i < j \leq k$. Thus the set $\{v_1, v_2, \ldots, v_k\}$ is an independent set of $G[S]^I$. If G satisfies $(S, \leq b)$, then the above independent set cannot have a size greater than b.

Statement 2. Suppose $C_1, C_2, \ldots, C_k$ are the connected components of $G[S]^I$. Consider a permutation τ of S. An authentication challenge is always triggered whenever a vertex v_i from C_i appears in τ for the first time. We can also construct τ in such a way that requests other than $v_1, v_2, \ldots, v_k$ do not trigger any authentication challenge. Specifically, perform a DFS on $G[S]$, using $v_1, v_2, \ldots, v_k$ as roots of the DFS forest. Then construct τ to list the resources of S in ascending order of discovery times. In conclusion, $(S, \geq b)$ is satisfied iff $G[S]^I$ has at least b connected components. □

Proof of Theorem 3.

Membership in Σ_2^p. GRGP-RS can be decided in polynomial time by a nondeterministic algorithm with access to an oracle for deciding Independent Set [15,

GT20]. This algorithm guesses a reflexive and symmetric directed graph, and then checks the satisfaction of constraints. By Proposition 2, the satisfaction of a usability constraint can be verified by querying the Independent Set oracle, while a security constraint can be checked in polynomial time.

CoNP-hardness. We reduce the complement of Independent Set to ZTCA-RS. Let (H, k) be an instance of Independent Set, where H is an undirected graph and k is a positive integer greater than 1. We construct a ZTCA-RS instance $(\mathcal{R}, UC, SC)$ in three steps. First, set $\mathcal{R}$ to $V(H)$. Second, add $(\{u, v\}, \leq 1)$ to UC if $uv \in E(H)$, and add $(\{u, v\}, \geq 2)$ to SC otherwise. (Policy G satisfies the above constraints iff G^I is isomorphic to H.) Third, add the usability constraint $(\mathcal{R}, \leq k - 1)$ to UC. (By Proposition 2, a policy G that satisfies this usability constraint does not have an independent set of size k.) □

Proof of Theorem 4. The proof of Theorem 3 can be adopted unchanged here. We note two points about reusing the reduction of Theorem 3. First, while ZTCA-R policies need not be symmetric, any ZTCA-R policy satisfying the constraints generated by the reduction of Theorem 3 will be symmetric. To see this, note that the reduction imposes constraints of the form $(\{u, v\}, \geq 2)$ and $(\{u, v\}, \leq 1)$. The former ensures that u and v are not connected by any directed edge, and the latter ensures that u and v are connected by directed edges in both directions. Such a directed graph has an unambiguous interpretation as an undirected graph. Second, because of the first point, Proposition 2 holds for the ZTCA-R policy satisfying the constraints generated by the reduction of Theorem 3. □

References

1. Ameer, S., Praharaj, L., Sandhu, R., Bhatt, S., Gupta, M.: ZTA-IoT: a novel architecture for zero-trust in IoT systems and an ensuing usage control model. ACM Trans. Priv. Secur. **27**(3) (2024)
2. Anjum, I., et al.: Removing the reliance on perimeters for security using network views. In: Proceedings of the 27th ACM on Symposium on Access Control Models and Technologies, SACMAT '22, pp. 151–162 (2022)
3. Anjum, I., et al.: MSNetViews: geographically distributed management of enterprise network security policy. In: Proceedings of the 28th ACM Symposium on Access Control Models and Technologies, SACMAT '23, pp. 121–132 (2023)
4. Biere, A.: CaDiCaL SAT solver (2024). https://github.com/arminbiere/cadical. Accessed 11 Dec 2024
5. Biere, A., Faller, T., Fazekas, K., Fleury, M., Froleyks, N., Pollitt, F.: CaDiCaL 2.0. In: Computer Aided Verification - 36th International Conference (Part I). LNCS, vol. 14681, pp. 133–152. Springer (2024)
6. Bishop, M.: Computer Security. Addison Wesley (2002)
7. Bondy, J.A., Murty, U.S.R.: Graph Theory with Applications. North-Holland (1976)
8. Brain, M., Davenport, J.H., Griggio, A.: Benchmarking solvers, SAT-style. In: SC²@ ISSAC (2017)
9. Chen, L., Crampton, J.: Risk-aware role-based access control. In: Security and Trust Management, pp. 140–156. Springer (2012)

10. Cormen, T.H., Leiserson, C.E., Rivest, R.L., Stein, C.: Introduction to Algorithms, 3rd edn. MIT Press (2009)
11. Csikor, L., Ramachandran, S., Lakshminarayanan, A.: ZeroDNS: towards better zero trust security using DNS. In: Proceedings of the 38th Annual Computer Security Applications Conference, ACSAC '22, pp. 699–713 (2022)
12. Cybersecurity and Privacy Standards Committee of the IEEE Computer Society: IEEE Standard for Biometric Liveness Detection. IEEE Std 2790-2020 (2020)
13. Denning, P.J.: Fault tolerant operating systems. ACM Comput. Surv. **8**(4), 359–389 (1976)
14. Fong, P.W.: Access control by tracking shallow execution history. In: Proceedings of the 2004 IEEE Symposium on Security and Privacy, pp. 43–55 (2004)
15. Garey, M.R., Johnson, D.S.: Computers and Intractability: A Guide to the Theory of NP-Completeness. Freeman, W. H (1979)
16. Ignatiev, A., Morgado, A., Marques-Silva, J.: PySAT: a Python toolkit for prototyping with SAT oracles. In: International Conference on Theory and Applications of Satisfiability Testing, pp. 428–437. Springer (2018)
17. Katsis, C., Bertino, E.: ZT-SDN: an ML-powered zero-trust architecture for software-defined networks. ACM Trans. Priv. Secur. **28**(2) (2025)
18. Katsis, C., Cicala, F., Thomsen, D., Ringo, N., Bertino, E.: NEUTRON: a graph-based pipeline for zero-trust network architectures. In: Proceedings of the Twelfth ACM Conference on Data and Application Security and Privacy, CODASPY '22, pp. 167–178 (2022)
19. Khan, S., Kabanov, I., Hua, Y., Madnick, S.: A systematic analysis of the capital one data breach: critical lessons learned. ACM Trans. Priv. Secur. **26**(1) (2022)
20. Ni, Q., Bertino, E., Lobo, J.: Risk-based access control systems built on fuzzy inferences. In: Proceedings of the 5th ACM Symposium on Information, Computer and Communications Security, ASIACCS '10, pp. 250–260 (2010)
21. Prentosito, A., Skoczen, M., Kahrs, L., Bhunia, S.: Case study on a session hijacking attack: the 2021 CVS health data breach. In: Mobile Web and Intelligent Information Systems, pp. 93–105 (2022)
22. Rose, S., Borchert, O., Mitchell, S., Connelly, S.: Zero trust architecture. NIST SP 800-207, National Institute of Standards and Technology (2020)
23. Zhang, S., Fong, P.W.L.: Mining domain-based policies. In: Proceedings of the Fourteenth ACM Conference on Data and Application Security and Privacy, CODASPY '24, pp. 403–414 (2024)
24. Zscalar: Zscalar help portal (2024). https://help.zscaler.com/

Smart Contracts and Blockchain Security

Jakiro: A Cross-Modal Contrastive Learning Framework for Detecting Vulnerabilities in Smart Contracts

Zixuan Niu[1,2], Xiaofeng Li[1,2], He Zhao[1,2(✉)], Tong Zhou[2,3(✉)], and Haotian Cheng[1,2]

[1] University of Science and Technology of China, Hefei, China
[2] Hefei Institutes of Physical Science, Chinese Academy of Sciences, Hefei, China
{zxniu,xfli,hzhao,tzhou,htcheng}@hfcas.ac.cn
[3] Anhui ZhongKeJingGe Technology Co., Ltd., Hefei, China

Abstract. With the rapid development of blockchain technology, vulnerabilities in smart contracts have become a major threat to asset security. Traditional rule-based detection methods, although interpretable, often suffer from high false positive rates and limited scalability. Despite recent progress, deep learning methods are often limited to unimodal approaches and lack the capability for fine-grained analysis. Our analysis of 14 common vulnerabilities revealed that function-level granularity strikes the optimal balance between detection accuracy and efficiency. Building on this observation, we propose the Jakiro method, which improves detection accuracy by integrating the semantic information from control flow graphs (CFGs) and source code using cross-modal contrastive learning. Experiments conducted on a dataset of more than 38,000 real-world contracts demonstrate that Jakiro surpasses the majority of the 10 baseline methods across three tasks: reentry, integer overflow, and transaction order dependency, achieving average improvements of 6.49%, 2.66%, and 4.62% in precision, recall, and F1 score, respectively.

Keywords: software security · vulnerabilities · blockchain

1 Introduction

Blockchain, due to its decentralization and privacy features, has emerged as a transformative technology in financial systems and computer networks. As a core component of blockchain technology, smart contracts have been extensively applied in domains such as decentralized finance (DeFi) and NFT trading. By August 9, 2024, over 51.1 million smart contracts had been deployed, with the peak daily deployment on the BNB smart chain surpassing 1.75 million. While the automated execution feature of smart contracts significantly enhances transaction efficiency, it also introduces critical security vulnerabilities. For instance:

Blockchain's decentralization and privacy features have made it a transformative technology for financial systems and computer networks. Smart contracts, a core blockchain component, are widely used in decentralized finance (DeFi) and NFT trading. By August 9, 2024, over 51.1 million smart contracts were deployed, with BNB Smart Chain peaking at 1.75 million daily deployments. While smart contracts enhance transaction efficiency through automation, they introduce significant security vulnerabilities, as evidenced by:

- **February 3, 2023:** Orion Protocol's smart contracts on ETH [1] and BNB Smart Chain [2] were exploited, causing $3 million in losses.
- **March 13, 2023:** Euler Finance's lending project on Ethereum was attacked, resulting in $200 million in losses [8].
- **October 7, 2023:** Stars Arena on Avalanche suffered a reentrancy attack, losing $2.9 million.
- **August 1, 2024:** Convergence Finance was attacked, with 58 million CVG tokens minted and sold, worth $210,000.

These incidents highlight security challenges in smart contracts, hindering blockchain ecosystem growth. Early rule-based methods [6,14,16,20,21], such as symbolic execution and AST analysis, effectively detect known vulnerabilities but struggle with novel ones, high false positives, and scalability. Deep learning-based approaches [4,5,11,13,27] have gained attention for vulnerability detection but often focus on single-modal features (e.g., source code), neglecting multi-modal data like Control Flow Graphs (CFGs) and bytecode, which limits performance in complex tasks. Current methods also rely on contract-level data, overlooking finer-grained analysis.

We propose a function-granularity multi-modal contrastive learning approach to improve deep learning-based vulnerability detection. Function-level analysis is prioritized, as vulnerabilities (e.g., in `withdraw` functions for reentrancy) are often localized. Compared to contract-level data, function-level granularity offers more precise vulnerability feature representation.

Using the ScrawID dataset [24] with 9,253 Ethereum contract addresses, we extracted 38,404 non-system contracts covering reentrancy, integer overflow, and transaction order dependence vulnerabilities. Experiments show our approach, Jakiro, outperforms state-of-the-art methods like Clear [4], improving F1-score by 4.62

- **A novel function-level multi-modal contrastive learning framework**, integrating source code and CFGs to capture cross-modal associations for improved vulnerability detection.
- **Extensive experiments** on the ScrawID dataset with over 38,000 contracts, demonstrating superior performance for three vulnerability types (RE, IO, TD).
- **A reproducible, open-source implementation** at https://github.com/SylvanasW1ndrunner/Jakiro-SCVD-tool.

2 Related Work

2.1 Smart Contract Vulneranbility Detection

The earliest tools for smart contract vulnerability detection adopted a **rule-based approach**, which relies on predefined patterns to identify potential risks. For instance, Oyente [14], one of the pioneering tools in this domain, employs symbolic execution to detect vulnerabilities by analyzing Ethereum's state and bytecode. Mythril [16], a static analysis framework, is specifically tailored to uncover prevalent vulnerability patterns in smart contracts. Slither, on the other hand, translates smart contracts into an intermediate representation called SlithIR [6], which not only facilitates the detection of vulnerabilities but also offers suggestions for code optimization. Similarly, Smartcheck [20], a scalable static analysis tool, converts Solidity source code into an XML-based intermediate representation and utilizes XPath queries for identifying vulnerabilities.

At the same time, a growing body of research efforts has explored the application of **deep learning** techniques to smart contract vulnerability detection, owing to their ability to automatically learn complex patterns from data. For instance, Safesc [23] is the first framework leveraging deep learning for this purpose. It employs Long Short-Term Memory (LSTM) networks to extract features from Ethereum opcodes, enabling effective vulnerability detection. Ton-Ton Hsien-De Huang et al. [11]. Transformed bytecode into colored images and utilized **Convolutional Neural Network (CNN)** for classification tasks. Similarly, Wesley Joon-Wie Tann et al. [13] adopted **Recurrent Neural Networks (RNN)** to identify vulnerabilities in smart contracts. Yuan Zhuang et al. proposed the **TMP** [27] method, which extracts key functions from contracts and converts them into control flow graphs (CFGs) for vulnerability detection. Wanqing Jie et al. demonstrated competitive performance by performing decision fusion across three modalities: CFG, source code, and bytecode [5]. Furthermore, Clear [4] is the first framework to introduce contrastive learning into deep learning-based vulnerability detection, achieving state-of-the-art results in this domain.

2.2 Contrastive Learning

Contrastive learning has emerged as a widely adopted paradigm in representation learning, particularly in scenarios with limited labeled data. Its core principle lies in aligning semantically similar samples while separating dissimilar ones in the feature space. Initially, this approach gained substantial attention in computer vision tasks, such as instance discrimination [15], and has since been extended to various domains, including natural language processing (NLP) [26] and graph representation learning [25]. Techniques such as SimCLR [3] and MoCo [9] have demonstrated the effectiveness of contrastive pretraining, significantly improving the performance of downstream tasks, including classification and clustering. Notably, in some cases, these methods achieve results comparable to or even

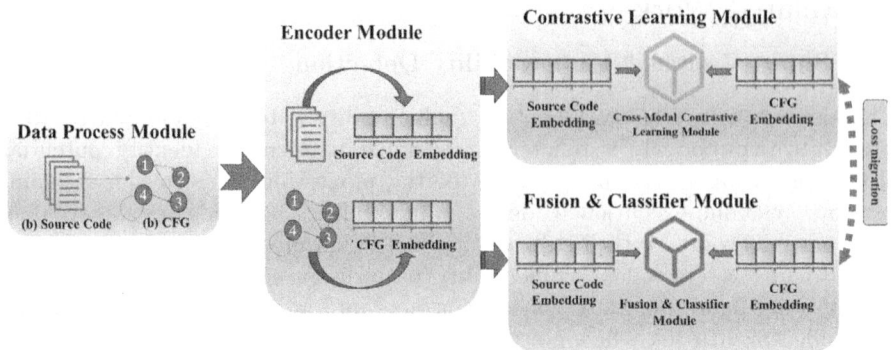

Fig. 1. Overview of Architecture Modules

surpassing their supervised counterparts. The success of contrastive learning highlights its potential applicability in diverse fields, including smart contract vulnerability detection.

Cross-Modal Contrastive Learning. extends the contrastive framework to cross-modal scenarios, where information is encoded across multiple modalities, such as text, images, or graph structures. By aligning representations across different modalities, cross-modal contrastive learning integrates complementary information, proving particularly effective for tasks that require integrating heterogeneous data sources. Recent advancements, including CLIP [19] and ALIGN [12], have demonstrated the scalability and robustness of cross-modal contrastive methods, particularly in visual-language tasks. These methods employ dual encoders to project different modalities into a shared latent space, facilitating semantic alignment across modalities through a contrastive objective function designed to minimize the modality gap.

In the domain of smart contract vulnerability detection, **cross-modal contrastive learning** holds great potential. This is largely due to the multimodal nature of smart contract code, which encompasses source code, bytecode, and control flow graphs (CFG), among other modalities. By effectively integrating diverse representations across these modalities, cross-modal contrastive learning enables the detection of vulnerabilities at various granularities. Furthermore, its minimized reliance on labeled data makes it a practical and efficient approach for smart contract vulnerability detection, particularly in scenarios where annotated datasets are scarce.

In our study, we propose a **cross-modal contrastive learning** method, as illustrated in Fig. 1, to explore the relationship between smart contract source code and its control flow graph (CFG). This method leverages Transformer [22] modules to map one modality to another in the embedding space and employs cosine similarity between the generated and original embeddings as the loss function to improve classification accuracy. Furthermore, Jakiro enables the contrastive learning module to leverage unsupervised data during the training process, leading to significant improvements in the performance of smart contract vulnerability detection tasks.

3 Methodology

3.1 Overview

In the task of detecting vulnerabilities by integrating multimodal fusion learning with cross-modal contrastive learning, we utilize **source code** and **control flow graphs** CFGs as the primary modalities. The key challenges we aim to address are outlined as follows:

1. **Selection of Data Granularity:** Smart contract vulnerabilities exhibit significant diversity, ranging from issues caused by individual statements to those arising within functions or from cross-function and cross-contract interactions. Consequently, determining the appropriate granularity for data selection plays a crucial role. Different granularities entail varying feature dimensions and levels of complexity in feature extraction. For instance, selecting a contract-level dataset preserves more cross-function call information within the contract but may include irrelevant components, such as abstract functions limited to definitions, making it less effective in identifying statement-level vulnerabilities. Conversely, a function-level dataset excludes many irrelevant abstract functions but may lose critical function relationships involving internal calls within the contract.
2. **Cross-Modal Contrastive Learning:** One of the key challenges in designing cross-modal contrastive learning frameworks lies in formulating subtasks that effectively align the representations of different modalities within a shared embedding space. These subtasks must not only facilitate alignment but also improve the performance of downstream tasks.
3. **Modality Fusion and Classification:** Extending the cross-modal contrastive learning framework, an additional challenge involves the effective integration of source code and CFG representations for vulnerability classification. This necessitates the design of a fusion strategy to effectively integrate these two modalities, while jointly optimizing the contrastive learning and classification objectives via backpropagation within the model.

To address these issues, we propose a novel detection framework, **Jakiro**, as illustrated in Fig. 2. The framework performs vulnerability detection through the following steps:

1. **Data Processing:** We set the detection granularity to the **function level**. Functions are extracted from the smart contract code to form the source code modality. The source code is then transformed into control flow graphs (CFGs), representing the second modality. To ensure the reliability and relevance of the dataset, we filter out abstract functions and redundant data entries, refining the dataset to enhance downstream processing and analysis.

2. **Data Embedding:** For both the source code and CFG datasets, distinct models are employed to generate embeddings for each modality, preparing the data for subsequent stages of the framework.
3. **Cross-Modal Contrastive Learning:** We design an **embedding-level subtask** for cross-modal contrastive learning. Using embeddings generated from both modalities, a Transformer module is employed to map one modality to the other at the embedding level. The cosine similarity between the generated representations and the original embeddings is calculated, and a **cross-modal loss** is derived based on this similarity.
4. **Vulnerability Classification:** The embeddings generated from both the source code and CFGs are integrated using a decision-level fusion mechanism. This approach leverages the complementary features of both modalities to improve the precision and robustness of vulnerability detection.

3.2 Data Process

Table 1. Vulnerabilities and Their Occurrence Levels

Vulnerability Type	Statement Level	Function Level	Contract Level
Reentrancy	-	✓	✓
Integer Overflow	v	✓	-
Access Control	-	✓	✓
Time Dependency	-	✓	✓
Unchecked Input	✓	✓	-
Uninitialized Variables	✓	✓	-
Unsafe Calls	✓	✓	-
Unauthorized Access	-	✓	✓
Short Address Attack	✓	-	-
Denial of Service (DoS)	-	✓	✓
Gas Limit Issues	-	✓	✓
Transaction Order Dependence	-	✓	✓
Race Condition	-	✓	✓
Fallback Function	✓	✓	-

Choose Granularity. We investigated 14 common types of smart contract vulnerabilities [17,18] and analyzed their manifestations within various contracts. To gain deeper insights into how vulnerabilities manifest across different granularities, we define the following three levels:

- **Statement-level:** Vulnerabilities that arise from a single statement.
- **Function-level:** Vulnerabilities that occur within a specific function, often due to logic errors in the function's implementation or due to external interactions.

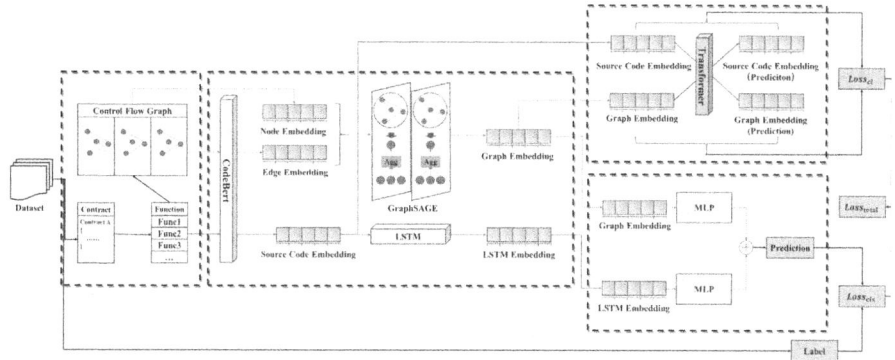

Fig. 2. Architecture of Jakiro

– **Contract-level:** Vulnerabilities that occur at the interaction and structural level of the entire contract, involving the cooperation of multiple functions.

Table 1 summarizes the potential occurrence levels of these 14 vulnerabilities. Our analysis reveals that 13 vulnerabilities occur at the function level, 6 at the statement level, and 9 at the contract level. Notably, contract-level vulnerabilities often stem from function-level errors that cascade during the calling process, resulting in new vulnerabilities. Addressing these function-level issues can typically resolve contract-level vulnerabilities.

Thus, addressing function-level vulnerabilities is identified as a primary focus. Moreover, the smaller size of function-level samples facilitates the detection of statement-level vulnerabilities.

Based on former analysis, we chose function-level granularity for our dataset due to its ability to address both function-specific vulnerabilities and statement-level issues, while avoiding the complexities associated with contract-level interactions.

Function and CFG Extraction. To obtain function-level representations, we employed **Slither**, a static analysis tool for smart contracts, to extract individual functions from the code. Each function's execution logic was represented using its corresponding **control flow graph (CFG)**. The overall process is illustrated in Figure ??.

This process yielded function-level source code and corresponding CFG data, resulting in **379,190** entries. After removing abstract functions and duplicate functions, we finalized a dataset comprising **105,364** entries. Specifically, the dataset contains the following:

– 2,455 entries with **Reentrancy vulnerabilities**,
– 8,990 entries with **Integer Overflow vulnerabilities**,
– 4,436 entries with **Timestamp Ordering vulnerabilities**, and
– 89,483 entries labeled as **secure functions**.

3.3 Source Code and CFG Representation

In Jakiro, the input data comprises two modalities: source code and control flow graphs (CFGs). The source code (x_s) is extracted from smart contract functions, while the CFGs (x_g) are generated during a pre-processing phase. Each CFG x_g is represented as $G = (V, E)$, where:

- $V = \{v_1, v_2, \ldots, v_n\}$ denotes the set of nodes.
- E denotes the set of edges, classified into three categories:
  1. $e_{ij} = 0$: unconditional edges,
  2. $e_{ij} = 1$: edges corresponding to True conditions in decision statements,
  3. $e_{ij} = 2$: edges corresponding to False conditions in decision statements.

This dual-modality input ensures that both the functional semantics of the source code and the structural properties of the contract logic are comprehensively represented.

3.4 Feature Embedding

Feature embedding transforms the input data into a shared latent space suitable for downstream tasks. Different embedding strategies are applied to source code and CFGs, leveraging pretrained models to ensure robust and informative representations.

Source Code Embedding. We utilize CodeBert [7] to extract sequence embeddings from the source code:

- **Sequence Embedding ($\mathbf{Z}_s = \{\mathbf{z}_1, \mathbf{z}_2, \ldots, \mathbf{z}_m\}$):** Token-level embeddings representing the full sequence of the source code, where m denotes the number of tokens in the sequence.

Control Flow Graph Embedding. CFG embeddings are constructed through a combination of CodeBert and GraphSAGE, the former aims to generate node feature, the latter will aggregate node and edge into graph feature:

- Each node $v_i \in V$ is mapped to a node embedding $\mathbf{h}_i \in \mathbb{R}^d$ using CodeBert, which captures the semantic features of the node.
- GraphSAGE is applied to aggregate features across the graph and compute a graph-level embedding:

$$\mathbf{z}_g = \text{GraphSAGE}(G) \in \mathbb{R}^d.$$

3.5 Cross-Modal Contrastive Learning

To ensure alignment between the representations from the two modalities, we employ a Cross-modal contrastive learning mechanism. This mechanism facilitates the projection of source code and CFG embeddings into a shared latent space.

Cross-Modal Embedding Generation. A Transformer module ($f_{\text{Transformer}}$) is used to generate cross-modal embeddings, enabling mutual translation between the two modalities. Specifically:

$$\mathbf{z}_g^{\text{pred}} = f_{\text{Transformer}}(\mathbf{Z}_s), \tag{1}$$

$$\mathbf{z}_s^{\text{pred}} = f_{\text{Transformer}}(\mathbf{z}_g). \tag{2}$$

Here:

- $\mathbf{Z}_s = \{\mathbf{z}_1, \mathbf{z}_2, \ldots, \mathbf{z}_m\}$ represents the sequence embedding of the source code.
- $\mathbf{z}_g$ denotes the graph-level embedding of the CFG.
- $\mathbf{z}_g^{\text{pred}}$ is the graph embedding predicted from the source code sequence embedding.
- $\mathbf{z}_s^{\text{pred}}$ is the source code embedding predicted from the graph embedding.

Cosine Similarity. The alignment between the original embeddings and the predicted embeddings is measured using cosine similarity:

$$\text{Sim}(\mathbf{a}, \mathbf{b}) = \frac{\mathbf{a} \cdot \mathbf{b}}{\|\mathbf{a}\|\|\mathbf{b}\|}.$$

The cosine similarity scores for each modality are defined as:

$$\text{Sim}_s = \text{Sim}(\mathbf{z}_s, \mathbf{z}_s^{\text{pred}}), \tag{3}$$

$$\text{Sim}_g = \text{Sim}(\mathbf{z}_g, \mathbf{z}_g^{\text{pred}}). \tag{4}$$

Contrastive Loss. The contrastive loss encourages alignment in the shared latent space by minimizing the discrepancy between the two modalities:

$$\mathcal{L}_{\text{CL}} = 1 - \frac{1}{2}\left(\text{Sim}_s + \text{Sim}_g\right).$$

3.6 Fusion and Classification

The fusion and classification module integrates the embeddings from both modalities to predict vulnerabilities.

LSTM [10] *Embedding Generation* The sequence embedding $\mathbf{Z}_s = \{\mathbf{z}_1, \mathbf{z}_2, \ldots, \mathbf{z}_m\}$ is passed through an LSTM network to generate an LSTM embedding ($\mathbf{z}_{\text{LSTM}}$):

$$\mathbf{z}_{\text{LSTM}} = \text{LSTM}(\mathbf{Z}_s),$$

where $\mathbf{z}_{\text{LSTM}} \in \mathbb{R}^d$ captures the temporal dependencies and contextual information from the sequence embedding.

Single-Modal Predictions. Each modality independently generates predictions:

$$y_s = \sigma(\text{MLP}_s(\mathbf{z}_{\text{LSTM}})), \tag{5}$$

$$y_g = \sigma(\text{MLP}_g(\mathbf{z}_g)), \tag{6}$$

where σ is the sigmoid activation function that outputs probabilities.

Fusion Mechanism. The final prediction is calculated through a weighted voting mechanism:

$$y_{\text{final}} = \alpha \cdot y_s + (1 - \alpha) \cdot y_g,$$

where $\alpha \in [0, 1]$ is a hyperparameter controlling the contribution of each modality.

Classification Loss. The classification loss is defined using binary cross-entropy (BCE):

$$\mathcal{L}_{\text{CLS}} = -\frac{1}{N} \sum_{i=1}^{N} \left[y_i \log y_{\text{final}}^{(i)} + (1 - y_i) \log(1 - y_{\text{final}}^{(i)}) \right],$$

where y_i represents the ground truth label, and $y_{\text{final}}^{(i)}$ is the predicted probability.

3.7 Overall Objective

The final objective function combines the contrastive loss and classification loss:

$$\mathcal{L}_{\text{total}} = \lambda_{\text{CL}} \cdot \mathcal{L}_{\text{CL}} + \lambda_{\text{CLS}} \cdot \mathcal{L}_{\text{CLS}}.$$

Here, λ_{CL} and λ_{CLS} are hyperparameters that balance the contributions of the two losses.

4 Experimental Setup

To evaluate the performance of our proposed framework, we designed experiments to address the following research questions (RQs):

- **RQ1**: Can Jakiro achieve better performance in detecting multiple types of vulnerabilities?
- **RQ2**: Does the integration of the cross-modal contrastive learning module improve detection accuracy?
- **RQ3**: How does the choice of detection granularity (e.g. function-level, or contract-level) affect vulnerability detection performance?

4.1 Dataset

We selected the publicly available smart contract vulnerability dataset, **ScrawID**. This dataset contains 9,253 real-world Ethereum contract addresses, each comprising multiple contracts. From these, we extracted 38,404 non-system contracts. Among them, 2,414 contracts exhibit reentrancy vulnerabilities (RE), 8,568 have integer overflow vulnerabilities (IO), and 4,302 are affected by transaction-ordering dependence vulnerabilities (TD).ScrawID uses detection tools to label smart contracts. It contains the results of detection tools.

Table 2. Comparison of Smart Contract Vulnerability Detection Methods (n/a means that the dataset does not include the detection results of this tool)

Method	RE				IO				TD				Avg			
	Acc(%)	P(%)	R(%)	F(%)	Acc(%)	P(%)	R(%)	F(%)	Acc(%)	P(%)	R(%)	F(%)	Acc(%)	P(%)	R(%)	F(%)
Mythril	75.74	56.15	98.98	71.66	59.50	48.96	73.82	58.87	53.36	31.88	32.91	32.39	62.87	45.66	68.57	54.31
Osiris	59.98	41.92	39.93	40.90	64.30	52.61	91.58	66.83	n/a	n/a	n/a	n/a	64.30	52.61	91.58	66.83
Oyente	69.64	65.00	4.41	8.25	44.20	41.29	99.83	58.42	66.61	68.00	3.06	5.85	60.15	58.10	35.77	24.17
Slither	62.82	45.43	99.32	62.34	n/a	n/a	n/a	n/a	52.32	37.62	61.51	46.69	57.57	41.53	80.42	54.52
Smartcheck	n/a	n/a	n/a	n/a	59.44	27.27	1.98	3.70	n/a	n/a	n/a	n/a	59.44	27.27	1.98	3.70
CNN-vanilla	73.69	63.50	80.50	71.00	77.36	73.79	67.31	70.40	75.03	78.18	52.15	62.57	75.36	71.82	66.65	67.99
RNN-vanilla	67.22	56.50	78.42	65.68	75.78	67.74	73.16	70.35	67.77	88.13	22.47	35.81	70.26	70.79	58.01	57.28
GCN-vanilla	64.15	71.55	17.22	27.76	72.38	75.88	45.38	56.79	74.38	79.10	48.89	60.43	70.30	75.51	37.16	48.32
TMP	79.84	75.34	30.43	43.45	76.10	73.51	61.19	66.79	81.66	81.64	40.51	37.49	79.20	76.83	44.04	49.21
Clear	90.06	85.33	96.17	90.42	82.87	80.18	90.18	84.89	90.54	87.97	95.94	91.78	87.82	84.49	93.83	89.03
Jakiro	93.96	89.56	96.13	92.73	93.81	89.38	95.94	92.54	96.48	94.02	97.41	95.69	94.75	90.98	96.49	93.65

At the contract level, we identified 2,414 contracts with RE vulnerabilities, 8,568 with IO vulnerabilities, and 4,302 with TD vulnerabilities. At the function level, these correspond to 2,455 functions with RE vulnerabilities, 8,990 with IO vulnerabilities, and 4,436 with TD vulnerabilities, reflecting a finer granularity of analysis.

To address class imbalance during training, we randomly selected secure data at a ratio of 1.5:1 relative to the vulnerable data. For the experiments, we randomly split the dataset into 80% for training and 20% for testing.

The selection of the above three types of vulnerabilities is motivated by two main reasons. First, these vulnerabilities account for a significant proportion of the economic losses caused by contract vulnerabilities in Ethereum. Second, they are widely studied in prior research, making them representative for comparison and analysis.

Reentrancy (RE). occurs when a contract calls an external contract, which recursively invokes the original contract before the initial execution is completed. This can lead to unexpected behaviors, such as withdrawing more funds than intended. **Integer Overflow (IO)** arises when a numerical value exceeds the maximum limit of a variable's data type. This typically occurs during arithmetic operations, leading to calculation errors or vulnerabilities. **Transaction-ordering dependence (TD)** happens when the outcome of a transaction is influenced by the order of transaction execution. Attackers may exploit this to manipulate contract behavior, causing financial losses or other unintended consequences. Examples of code illustrating these three types of vulnerabilities are provided in Fig. 3.

To address class imbalance, we ensured that the number of non-vulnerable functions in the dataset is 1.5 times that of vulnerable functions. The dataset was randomly split into 80% for training and 20% for testing. **Notably**, contracts with vulnerabilities were labeled as 1, while those without vulnerabilities were labeled as 0 (Fig 4).

```
function withdrawBalance() public {
    uint amountToWithdraw = userBalances[msg.sender];
    (bool success, ) = msg.sender.call.value(amountToWithdraw)("");
    require(success);
    userBalances[msg.sender] = 0;
}
```

Reentrancy(RE): Invoke Call before altering value

```
function deposit(uint256 amount) public {
    balance += amount;
}
```

Integer Overflow(IO): Probably interger overflow

```
function withdraw(uint256 amount) public {
    require(balances[msg.sender] >= amount, "Insufficient balance");
    balances[msg.sender] -= amount;
    payable(msg.sender).transfer(amount);
}

function transfer(address to, uint256 amount) public {
    require(balances[msg.sender] >= amount, "Insufficient balance");
    balances[msg.sender] -= amount;
    balances[to] += amount;
}
```

Time-ordering Dependence(**TD**): Result depends on the ordering of ***Withdraw*** and ***Transfer***

Fig. 3. Three common vulnerabilities

4.2 Baselines

To ensure a robust comparison, we evaluated Jakiro against both static analysis tools and neural network-based methods commonly used in smart contract vulnerability detection.

First, we included four widely used **static analysis tools**: **Mythril**, **Oyente**, **Osiris**, and **Slither**. These tools rely on rule-based detection mechanisms to identify vulnerabilities in smart contracts. Although these tools have been widely adopted in the field, previous research has demonstrated their limitations in detection accuracy when compared to deep learning-based methods. Nevertheless, they remain essential baselines for evaluating Jakiro's performance, providing insights into the strengths and weaknesses of rule-based approaches.

Moreover, we selected five representative **neural network-based models** as baselines for comparison. These models span a variety of architectures, each tailored for specific data representations: **CNN (Convolutional Neural Networks)**: Capable of extracting local patterns and features, CNNs are particularly effective for structured data representation such as code fragments.

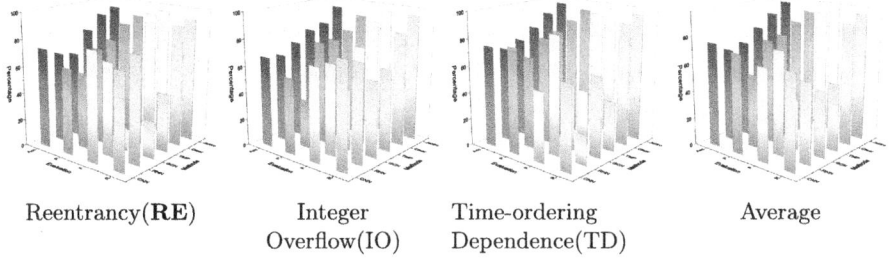

Reentrancy(**RE**)   Integer Overflow(**IO**)   Time-ordering Dependence(**TD**)   Average

Fig. 4. Deep Learning Methods Visualization

RNN (Recurrent Neural Networks): Designed for sequential data, RNNs are well-suited for processing code token sequences. **GCN (Graph Convolutional Networks)**: Specialized for graph-structured data, such as control flow graphs. **TMP (temporal message propagation)**: This graph-based model is specifically designed to capture both temporal and structural relationships. It has been widely recognized as an effective approach for CFG representation. **Clear**: An advanced framework that leverages contrastive learning techniques on source code to enhance detection performance.Except Clear, we use CodeBert as the encoder to generate embedding, which is the input of the models.

For all baselines, we adopted a contract-level granularity for vulnerability detection, consistent with the configurations in their original implementations.

4.3 Evaluation Metrics

We utilized standard metrics to evaluate the performance of Jakiro and baselines, including:

- **F1-Score**: The harmonic mean of precision and recall, indicating the balance between these two measures. It is calculated as $F1 = \frac{2 \cdot \text{Precision} \cdot \text{Recall}}{\text{Precision} + \text{Recall}}$.

- **Accuracy**: The proportion of correctly classified samples over the total number of samples. It is expressed as $Accuracy = \frac{TP+TN}{TP+TN+FP+FN}$, where TP, TN, FP, and FN represent the true positives, true negatives, false positives, and false negatives, respectively.

- **Recall**: The proportion of correctly identified vulnerabilities to the total number of actual vulnerabilities, representing the model's sensitivity in detecting vulnerabilities. It is expressed as $Recall = \frac{TP}{TP+FN}$.

- **Precision**: The proportion of correctly identified vulnerabilities to the total number of reported vulnerabilities, representing the model's specificity in avoiding false alarms. It is expressed as $Precision = \frac{TP}{TP+FP}$.

These metrics collectively offer a comprehensive framework for evaluating model performance. They measure both the predictive accuracy and the robustness of the models under various conditions. However, in the context of smart

Table 3. The results of the ablation test

Method	RE				IO				TD				Avg			
	Acc(%)	P(%)	R(%)	F(%)	Acc(%)	P(%)	R(%)	F(%)	Acc(%)	P(%)	R(%)	F(%)	Acc(%)	P(%)	R(%)	F(%)
Jakiro - No CL	85.16	83.81	78.00	80.80	86.74	87.42	78.09	82.49	94.23	93.58	91.89	92.73	88.71	88.27	82.66	85.34
Jakiro	93.96	89.56	96.13	92.73	93.81	89.38	95.94	92.54	96.48	94.02	97.41	95.69	94.75	90.98	96.49	93.65

Table 4. Base Methods on different granularity

Method	RE				IO				TD				Avg			
	Acc(%)	P(%)	R(%)	F(%)	Acc(%)	P(%)	R(%)	F(%)	Acc(%)	P(%)	R(%)	F(%)	Acc(%)	P(%)	R(%)	F(%)
CNN-SC	73.69	63.50	80.50	71.00	77.36	73.79	67.31	70.40	75.03	78.18	52.15	62.57	75.36	71.82	66.65	67.99
RNN-SC	67.22	56.50	78.42	65.68	75.78	67.74	73.16	70.35	67.77	88.13	22.47	35.81	70.26	70.79	58.01	57.28
GCN-SC	64.15	71.55	17.22	27.76	72.38	75.88	45.38	56.79	74.38	79.10	48.89	60.43	70.30	75.51	37.16	48.32
CNN-FUNC	82.97	79.87	76.78	78.30	86.67	82.96	83.93	83.44	92.52	89.85	91.67	90.75	87.38	84.26	84.12	84.16
RNN-FUNC	79.95	68.48	92.46	78.68	84.25	89.10	69.08	77.82	90.27	84.29	93.02	88.44	84.82	80.62	84.85	81.64
GCN-FUNC	76.20	73.98	62.53	67.77	83.16	76.22	84.15	79.99	87.66	84.49	84.68	84.59	82.34	78.23	77.12	77.45

contract vulnerability detection, the relative importance of these metrics can vary depending on the specific application scenario.

Note: Misclassifying a vulnerable instance as non-vulnerable (**false negative, FN**) can lead to more severe consequences. Therefore, in our experimental setup, we prioritize achieving a **higher recall rate**, as vulnerable code is labeled as positive. This ensures that the model is more sensitive to detecting vulnerabilities, minimizing the risk of false negatives. Conversely, if the labeling were reversed (i.e., labeling vulnerable code as negative), the focus would shift towards achieving a **higher precision**, emphasizing the avoidance of false positives.

4.4 Details

During the experiments, the input dimension of our Transformer module was set to 512, and a six-layer attention module with eight attention heads was used. The learning rate was set to 1×10^{-3}, and the AdamW optimizer was employed for optimization. The batch size was set to 32. During the loss fusion phase, the parameter λ_{CLS} for $\mathcal{L}_{\text{CLS}}$ was set to 1, while the parameter λ_{CL} for $\mathcal{L}_{\text{CL}}$ was set to $\frac{current\ epoch}{epoches}$. This approach introduced contrastive learning loss as the classification task gradually converged. The number of training epochs was set to 40, and early stopping was configured with a patience of 3.

The hardware resources used for the experiments included an Nvidia RTX 4090 GPU with 24 GB of video memory. The software environment was based on PyTorch running on the Windows 11 operating system.

5 Results

RQ1: Efficiency of Jakiro
Table 2 demonstrate that the Jakiro model exhibits significant performance advantages in smart contract vulnerability detection tasks, particularly in comparison with the primary baseline, Clear. Jakiro outperforms Clear in most evaluation metrics (accuracy, precision, recall, and F1 score), achieving an average

accuracy of 94.75%, precision of 90.98%, recall of 96.49%, and F1 score of 93.65%. In contrast, Clear achieves an average accuracy of 87.82%, precision of 84.49%, recall of 93.83%, and F1 score of 89.03%. Although Clear achieves recall rates close to Jakiro in certain tasks (e.g., 96.17% for RE and 90.18% for IO), its lower precision and F1 score indicate room for improvement in reducing false positives.

Specifically, in the three tasks of RE (Reentrancy), IO (Integer Overflow), and TD (Time Dependency), Jakiro consistently outperforms Clear:

- **RE Task:** Jakiro achieves accuracy, precision, and F1 scores of 93.96%, 89.56%, and 92.73%, respectively, all higher than Clear's 90.06%, 85.33%, and 90.42%.
- **IO Task:** Jakiro achieves an F1 score of 92.54%, significantly higher than Clear's 84.89%. Although Clear's recall (90.18%) is close to Jakiro's (95.94%), its precision (80.18%) is notably lower than Jakiro's (89.38%).
- **TD Task:** Jakiro achieves recall and F1 scores of 97.41% and 95.69%, respectively, compared to Clear's 95.94% and 91.78%, demonstrating Jakiro's superior capability in capturing complex time dependency vulnerabilities.

Furthermore, compared to traditional deep learning models (e.g., CNN, RNN, and GCN) and vulnerability detection tools (e.g., Mythril, Slither, and Osiris), Clear performs relatively well overall, particularly in RE and TD tasks, where it achieves high recall rates (96.17% and 95.94%, respectively). However, Clear's main limitation lies in its lower precision, which results in F1 scores that fall short of Jakiro's. In contrast, Jakiro not only leads in recall but also effectively balances precision and recall, thereby achieving superior F1 scores across all tasks.

RQ2: Efficiency of Cross-Modal Contrastive Learning

To further validate the effectiveness of the Jakiro model, we conducted an ablation study by removing a key component (denoted as "Jakiro - No CL") and evaluating its impact on performance. As shown in Table 3, the complete Jakiro model significantly outperforms the ablated version across all metrics, highlighting the importance of the removed component.

The complete Jakiro model achieves an average accuracy of 94.75% and an F1 score of 93.65%, compared to 88.71% and 85.34% for Jakiro - No CL, representing improvements of 6.04% and 8.31%, respectively. For the RE, IO, and TD tasks, Jakiro consistently demonstrates superior performance, with F1 score improvements of 11.93%, 10.05%, and 2.96%, respectively. These results indicate that the removed component plays a critical role in enhancing Jakiro's ability to detect vulnerabilities across different tasks.

In conclusion, the ablation study confirms that the complete Jakiro model benefits significantly from the inclusion of the removed component, leading to better generalization and more robust performance in smart contract vulnerability detection.

RQ3: Efficiency of Different Granularity

From the Table 4, we observe significant differences in model performance between contract-level (SC) and function-level (FUNC) granularity. The analysis is detailed as follows.

Firstly, at the contract-level (SC), all three models (CNN-SC, RNN-SC, and GCN-SC) exhibit suboptimal performance, with GCN-SC particularly failing to meet our expectations. Specifically, GCN-SC achieves only 20.82% and 34.61% F1 scores on the RE and TD tasks, respectively, which is significantly lower than the other models. We attribute this to the graph structure generation method. In this study, we directly utilized the Slither tool to generate the graph structure without further optimization or simplification, leading to GCN's inability to fully leverage the graph information. However, at the function-level (FUNC), GCN's performance improves significantly, achieving F1 scores of 79.99% and 84.59% on the IO and TD tasks, respectively. This improvement highlights the importance of granularity selection. Compared to investing substantial effort in data optimization and preprocessing, selecting an appropriate granularity, such as function-level, can more easily enhance model performance.

Secondly, the results demonstrate that function-level modeling outperforms contract-level modeling in overall performance. All models achieve significantly better results at the function-level. For instance, CNN-FUNC achieves F1 scores of 78.30%, 83.44%, and 90.75% on the RE, IO, and TD tasks, respectively, which are far superior to CNN-SC's performance. Notably, CNN-FUNC's outstanding performance is beyond our expectations. We believe this is due to the more concentrated and clear semantic information at the function-level, which aligns well with CNN's ability to extract local features. Similarly, RNN-FUNC also performs exceptionally well at the function-level, achieving an F1 score of 88.44% on the TD task, further validating the advantages of function-level granularity in feature modeling.

In summary, the results show that function-level modeling significantly improves model performance, while contract-level granularity, due to its dispersed and complex information, makes it challenging for models to capture effective features. Additionally, the direct use of Slither-generated graph structures without optimization limits GCN's performance, but GCN shows significant improvement at the function-level. This indicates that granularity selection can easily enhance model performance without relying on complex data preprocessing. Future work can further explore how to combine granularity selection with data optimization to improve overall model performance.

6 Conclusion

As a critical carrier of the blockchain economy, the security of smart contracts cannot be overlooked. To address issues such as missed detections and high data annotation costs in existing smart contract vulnerability detection methods, we integrated cross-modal concepts into the fundamental ideas of contrastive learning. This enables deep learning models to establish connections between different modalities, thereby improving the detection of vulnerabilities in smart contracts. Our proposed Jakiro model outperformed existing state-of-the-art detection methods on a dataset containing over 8,000 Ethereum contract addresses and more than 38,000 non-system contracts. Furthermore, we investigated the impact of different data granularities on the model's detection performance, exploring the influence of varying data granularities on vulnerability detection from a data perspective.

Acknowledgement. We sincerely thank the anonymous reviewers for their insightful feedback on this work. This research was supported, in part, by the Science, Technology, and Innovation Key Challenge Program of Anhui Province under Grant No. 202423k09020016.

References

1. Buterin, V., et al.: Ethereum White Paper GitHub Rep. **1**, 22–23 (2013)
2. Chain, B.: Bnb chain (2025). https://www.bnbchain.org. Accessed: 2025-01-07
3. Chen, T., Kornblith, S., Norouzi, M., Hinton, G.: A simple framework for contrastive learning of visual representations (2020). https://arxiv.org/abs/2002.05709
4. Chen, Y., Sun, Z., Gong, Z., Hao, D.: Improving smart contract security with contrastive learning-based vulnerability detection. In: Proceedings of the IEEE/ACM 46th International Conference on Software Engineering, pp. 1–11 (2024)
5. Deng, W., Wei, H., Huang, T., Cao, C., Peng, Y., Hu, X.: Smart contract vulnerability detection based on deep learning and multimodal decision fusion. Sensors **23**(16), 7246 (2023)
6. Feist, J., Grieco, G., Groce, A.: Slither: a static analysis framework for smart contracts. In: 2019 IEEE/ACM 2nd International Workshop on Emerging Trends in Software Engineering for Blockchain (WETSEB), pp. 8–15. IEEE (2019)
7. Feng, Z., et al.: Codebert: a pre-trained model for programming and natural languages (2020). https://arxiv.org/abs/2002.08155
8. Finance, E.: Euler finance (2025). https://www.euler.finance/. Accessed: 2025-01-07
9. He, K., Fan, H., Wu, Y., Xie, S., Girshick, R.: Momentum contrast for unsupervised visual representation learning (2020). https://arxiv.org/abs/1911.05722
10. Hochreiter, S., Schmidhuber, J.: Long short-term memory. Neural Comput. **9**(8), 1735–1780 (1997)
11. Hwang, S.J., Choi, S.H., Shin, J., Choi, Y.H.: Codenet: code-targeted convolutional neural network architecture for smart contract vulnerability detection. IEEE Access **10**, 32595–32607 (2022)
12. Jia, C., et al.: Scaling up visual and vision-language representation learning with noisy text supervision (2021). https://arxiv.org/abs/2102.05918
13. Lutz, O., et al.: Escort: Ethereum smart contracts vulnerability detection using deep neural network and transfer learning. arXiv preprint arXiv:2103.12607 (2021)
14. Luu, L., Chu, D.H., Olickel, H., Saxena, P., Hobor, A.: Making smart contracts smarter. In: Proceedings of the 2016 ACM SIGSAC Conference on Computer and Communications Security, pp. 254–269 (2016)

15. Morgado, P., Vasconcelos, N., Misra, I.: Audio-visual instance discrimination with cross-modal agreement. In: Proceedings of the IEEE/CVF Conference on Computer Vision and Pattern Recognition, pp. 12475–12486 (2021)
16. Mueller, B.: A framework for bug hunting on the ethereum blockchain. ConsenSys/mythril (2017)
17. Praitheeshan, P., Pan, L., Yu, J., Liu, J., Doss, R.: Security analysis methods on Ethereum smart contract vulnerabilities: a survey. arXiv preprint arXiv:1908.08605 (2019)
18. Qian, P., Liu, Z., He, Q., Huang, B., Tian, D., Wang, X.: Smart contract vulnerability detection technique: a survey. arXiv preprint arXiv:2209.05872 (2022)
19. Radford, A., et al.: Learning transferable visual models from natural language supervision (2021). https://arxiv.org/abs/2103.00020
20. Tikhomirov, S., Voskresenskaya, E., Ivanitskiy, I., Takhaviev, R., Marchenko, E., Alexandrov, Y.: Smartcheck: static analysis of ethereum smart contracts. In: Proceedings of the 1st International Workshop on Emerging Trends in Software Engineering for Blockchain, pp. 9–16 (2018)
21. Torres, C.F., Schütte, J., State, R.: Osiris: Hunting for integer bugs in Ethereum smart contracts. In: Proceedings of the 34th Annual Computer Security Applications Conference, pp. 664–676 (2018)
22. Vaswani, A., et al.: Attention is all you need (2023). https://arxiv.org/abs/1706.03762
23. Wang, X., He, J., Xie, Z., Zhao, G., Cheung, S.: Contractguard: defend Ethereum smart contracts with embedded intrusion detection. IEEE Trans. Serv. Comput. pp. 1–1 (2019). https://doi.org/10.1109/tsc.2019.2949561
24. Yashavant, C.S., Kumar, S., Karkare, A.: Scrawld: a dataset of real world Ethereum smart contracts labelled with vulnerabilities (2022). https://arxiv.org/abs/2202.11409
25. You, Y., Chen, T., Sui, Y., Chen, T., Wang, Z., Shen, Y.: Graph contrastive learning with augmentations. Adv. Neural. Inf. Process. Syst. **33**, 5812–5823 (2020)
26. Zhang, R., Ji, Y., Zhang, Y., Passonneau, R.J.: Contrastive data and learning for natural language processing. In: Proceedings of the 2022 Conference of the North American Chapter of the Association for Computational Linguistics: Human Language Technologies: Tutorial Abstracts, pp. 39–47 (2022)
27. Zhuang, Y., Liu, Z., Qian, P., Liu, Q., Wang, X., He, Q.: Smart contract vulnerability detection using graph neural networks. In: Proceedings of the Twenty-Ninth International Conference on International Joint Conferences on Artificial Intelligence, pp. 3283–3290 (2021)

BLOCKLENS: Detecting Malicious Transactions in Ethereum Using LLM Techniques

Chi Feng(✉) and Lei Fan

Shanghai Jiao Tong University, Shanghai 200240, China
{gdpeaceminusone,fanlei}@sjtu.edu.cn

Abstract. This paper presents BLOCKLENS, a supervised, trace-level framework for detecting malicious Ethereum transactions using large language models (LLMs). Unlike prior approaches limited to static features or storage-level abstractions, BLOCKLENS processes complete execution traces, capturing opcode sequences, memory information, gas usage, and call structures to accurately represent the runtime behavior of each transaction. This framework harnesses the exceptional reasoning capabilities of LLMs for long input sequences and is fine-tuned on transaction data. We design a tokenization strategy aligned with Ethereum Virtual Machine (EVM) semantics, mapping execution traces into interpretable tokens. Each transaction captures its complete execution trace through simulated execution and is then sliced into overlapping chunks using a sliding window, allowing for long-range context modeling within memory constraints. During inference, the model outputs both a binary decision and a probability score indicating the likelihood of malicious behavior. We implement the framework based on LLaMA 3.2-1B backbone and fine-tune the model using Low-Rank Adaptation (LoRA). We evaluate it on a curated dataset containing both real-world attacks and normal DeFi transactions. BLOCKLENS outperforms representative baselines, achieving higher F1 scores and recall at top-k thresholds than representative baselines. Additionally, BLOCKLENS offers interpretable chunk-level outputs by localizing suspicious trace segments that enhance explainability, facilitating rapid forensic analysis and actionable decision-making in security-critical environments.

Keywords: Ethereum · Malicious Transaction Detection · Large Language Models

1 Introduction

1.1 Background

Ethereum [4], as a representative blockchain platform, has rapidly emerged as the cornerstone infrastructure for decentralized applications (DApps) due to its native support for smart contracts and highly programmable nature. Its versatile transaction model encompasses a diverse range of operations, including asset transfers, smart contract invocations, non-fungible token (NFT) transactions, and decentralized finance (DeFi) activities. To date, the Ethereum network has processed more than 2.6 billion transactions, representing a cumulative monetary value exceeding trillions of dollars.

However, alongside this growth, Ethereum's rapid ecosystem expansion has exposed security vulnerabilities. Malicious transactions exploiting smart contract vulnerabilities, such as reentrancy attacks, front-running attacks, and price manipulation attacks, have become increasingly frequent. Such incidents not only result in substantial financial losses for users but also threaten the stability and credibility of the blockchain network. According to recent statistics from Etherscan, over 405 security incidents have targeted decentralized finance (DeFi) protocols operating on the Ethereum platform, leading to financial losses of approximately $3.8 billion. One prominent example is the reentrancy attack on the DAO smart contract in April 2016, leading to the theft of $3.6 million [2].

Timely identification of malicious transactions is critical for enabling attack forensics, mitigating financial damage, and maintaining user confidence in the integrity of blockchain systems. Accurate detection allows researchers to analyze attack mechanisms and processes. For example, when smart contract vulnerabilities are reported with sufficient detail, researchers can trace suspicious transactions to reconstruct the corresponding call graph and interaction pathways, thereby understanding attackers' methodologies and identifying potential attack vectors. Also, detection mechanisms enable protocols to swiftly trigger emergency actions, such as suspending compromised smart contracts or issuing timely alerts, thus mitigating further financial damages and maintaining protocol stability and liquidity. For instance, prompt detection of front-running [6] or price manipulation attacks allows protocols to protect user funds proactively.

1.2 Related Works

Existing research on detecting malicious transactions within Ethereum can be categorized into three main methodologies: classical machine learning (ML) methods, rule systems, and large language model (LLM) approaches.

Classical ML-based methods have been widely adopted in blockchain malicious detection. For example, the Doc2Vec method introduced by Le and Mikolov [13] represents blockchain transactions as a collection of words and employs distributed word embeddings to generate vectorized transaction representations. These vectors are then analyzed using Gaussian Mixture Models (GMM) to estimate the likelihood of a transaction being malicious [19]. Although this probabilistic approach is capable of capturing malicious behaviors based on distributional deviations, its limitation lies in the inherent treatment of transactions as unordered word sets. This approach fails to capture contextual relationships, which are essential in distinguishing differences between normal and malicious transactions. As a result, Doc2Vec-based methods struggle with detecting attacks characterized by specific contextual conditions.

Rule-based methods, combined with ML techniques, have also been proposed to detect malicious behaviors by modeling transaction patterns or heuristic properties. For instance, LSTM-based methods can learn normal transaction patterns and identify malicious behaviors based on deviations from the learned patterns [1]. Moreover, heuristic approaches use simplistic assumptions, such as identifying malicious behaviors by input sequence length under the assumption that malicious transactions are generally longer than normal ones [16]. Although these approaches can quickly identify well-understood malicious patterns, their primary drawback is their lack of adaptability and robustness in detecting new or evolving attacks. As malicious behaviors become increasingly sophisticated, relying solely on static, predefined rules significantly diminishes detection efficacy. Consequently, their utility diminishes significantly in real-world environments where attacks vary widely in complexity, length, and execution patterns.

Recently, LLM-based methods have gained attention due to their semantic modeling capabilities. BlockGPT [9] employs a GPT-like causal transformer model trained on quantities of normal transaction data. It aims to detect malicious behaviors by measuring the conditional likelihood of each token within transaction sequences. While BlockGPT integrates dynamic execution information, it limits its analysis to persistent storage read-write operations, explicitly avoiding opcode trace analysis due to computational complexity concerns. Furthermore, due to its causal design, BlockGPT inherently relies solely on prior tokens to predict subsequent tokens. This sequential, causal prediction approach diminishes its sensitivity in detecting malicious transactions, as blockchain transaction sequences do not follow a natural generative order akin to language.

Another representative LLM-based method, BlockFound [20] leverages a BERT-based Masked Language Modeling (MLM) approach to learn normal transaction patterns. Despite effectively capturing bidirectional contextual information, BlockFound notably neglects the dynamic execution context, particularly opcode-level transaction details. This omission restricts the model's capability to capture hidden attack behaviors embedded within execution traces. Consequently, BlockFound's performance suffers when faced with malicious transactions that differ subtly in execution rather than in textual representations alone.

Also, several recent studies have explored generative LLMs for modeling execution sequences. EarlyMalDetect [12] leverages an autoregressive transformer to analyze early-stage API call sequences during program execution, enabling the detection of malicious behavior before it fully manifests. TRACED [8] introduces execution-aware pre-training for source code by incorporating dynamic runtime traces alongside static code, significantly improving downstream tasks such as execution path prediction and vulnerability detection. These works collectively highlight that generative modeling of execution traces, whether system calls, virtual machine instructions, or runtime program states, provides a paradigm for detecting malicious behaviors in structured environments, and motivates our application of this approach to Ethereum transaction opcode traces.

1.3 Our Contributions

In this paper, we propose BLOCKLENS, the first detection framework to fully input Ethereum execution-level opcodes into LLMs, enabling reasoning over complete EVM traces that include gas usage, call depth, and control flow.

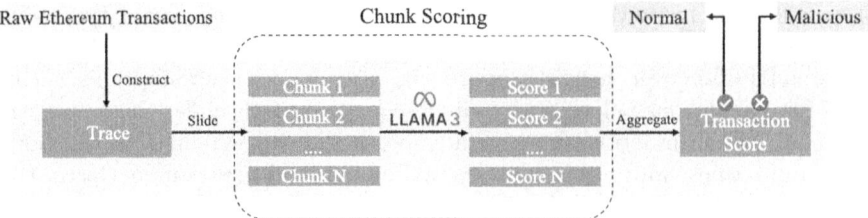

Fig. 1. Overview of BLOCKLENS Detection Framework.

Unlike traditional rule-based or heuristic-driven approaches, which detect attacks through pattern matching or static vulnerability analysis, we construct a transaction-level detection pipeline using dynamic execution traces, which capture runtime behaviors such as opcode sequences, gas usage, and control flow, providing richer semantics than static features.

To effectively analyze the complexity of transaction data, we integrate recent advancements in Large Language Models into our detection framework. LLMs are particularly suited to detection due to their contextual modeling capabilities gained through extensive pre-training on large-scale datasets. Unlike conventional ML methods, which typically truncate lengthy context sequences abruptly, thereby losing critical contextual information, we can utilize a chunk scoring mechanism that preserves more comprehensive context information. This strategy improves the model's ability to interpret complex and lengthy transaction traces. We also propose an aggregation strategy to convert chunk-level scores into transaction-level predictions, demonstrating that LLMs can effectively distinguish malicious behaviors even in long, multi-step transactions.

Based on this method in Fig. 1, we systematically leverage historical attack data to train an LLM model capable of recognizing diverse malicious transaction patterns, which can explicitly learn characteristics from various known attacks and integrate internal contract execution details.

2 Preliminaries

2.1 Large Language Models (LLMs)

Built upon the transformer architecture [18], Large Language Models (LLMs) process input sequences through stacked self-attention and feedforward layers, enabling them to capture long-range dependencies and complex token interactions. LLMs are typically pre-trained on large-scale corpora using self-supervised learning objectives. Common pretraining strategies include masked language modeling (MLM), as employed in BERT [7], and next-token prediction, as used in autoregressive models like GPT [3]. Pretraining enables LLMs to learn generalizable representations that can be transferred to various downstream applications. While initially designed for natural language, LLMs have been successfully adapted to domains with structured or symbolic data, such as programming languages [15], scientific formulas [14]. Their ability to understand structured sequential patterns makes them promising tools for analyzing program-like execution traces in areas such as smart contract transactions or runtime behaviors.

2.2 Generative Decoder-Only Models

A major class of LLMs is the *decoder-only* or *generative* language model, which predicts sequences in a left-to-right, autoregressive manner. Compared to bidirectional models, generative LLMs naturally preserve temporal order and can model the probabilistic structure of an execution trace as it unfolds. This autoregressive nature is particularly beneficial in domains where the execution context is directional or causally dependent, such as bytecode interpretation, program simulation, or blockchain transaction modeling, where each step logically follows the previous. Such models are trained to generate the next token given prior context. Well-known examples include GPT [3], PaLM [5], and LLAMA [17].

2.3 Blockchain

Blockchain is a distributed ledger technology characterized by decentralization, immutability, and transparency. Structurally, a blockchain is composed of sequential blocks, each containing a cryptographic hash that links it to the preceding block, thereby forming an immutable chain. Each block includes a set of validated transactions, timestamps, and consensus-related metadata.

Among various blockchain platforms, Ethereum, introduced in 2015, stands out as the most prominent environment. It extends the original concept by integrating the EVM, a Turing-complete virtual machine, which enables general-purpose computation on-chain. Transactions are fundamental operations within Ethereum, representing requests from accounts to modify the blockchain state. Ethereum transactions primarily include asset transfers, smart contract executions, and interactions within decentralized applications.

3 Methodology

3.1 Problem Definition

We address the problem of identifying malicious transactions through a learned model, using both statistical transaction features (e.g., transaction hashes, values, addresses) and dynamic opcode-level execution sequences (VMtrace).

Threat Model. We assume an adversarial threat model primarily focused on malicious transactions that exploit vulnerabilities or logic flaws in smart contracts within the Ethereum blockchain ecosystem.

An attacker may build transactions specifically designed to trigger known or unknown vulnerabilities. He can interact directly with deployed smart contracts by crafting specially designed transactions containing abnormal opcode sequences or unusual execution paths. He might intentionally obfuscate the characteristics of malicious transactions to evade traditional static detection mechanisms. Therefore, he can achieve malicious objectives such as asset theft, market manipulation, or disrupting contract execution.

Detection Model. Given a set of transactions T, each transaction $t \in T$ can be represented by its associated statistical features and dynamic execution trace. The primary objective is to determine whether a given transaction t belongs to the set of anomalous transactions $A \subset T$. To accomplish this, we define a binary decision function $f : T \to \{0,1\}$, which classifies transaction t based on the model's predicted probability of malicious, denoted as $P(\text{abnormal} \mid t)$:

$$f(t) = \begin{cases} 1, & \text{if } P(\text{abnormal} \mid t) \geq \tau \\ 0, & \text{otherwise} \end{cases} \quad (1)$$

where:

- T denotes the complete transaction set under consideration;
- $P(\text{abnormal} \mid t)$ represents the model's probabilistic prediction of transaction t being malicious;
- τ is a decision threshold to balance precision and recall in the detection task.

A transaction t is classified as malicious if $f(t) = 1$; otherwise, it is normal.

3.2 Technique Overview

To effectively detect malicious behaviors in Ethereum transactions, we propose a four-stage framework that transforms raw execution data into structured inputs suitable for large language model (LLM)-based analysis. The overall architecture consists of the following components as illustrated in Fig. 2.

Trace Construction. We first extract and simplify multiple layers of Ethereum execution traces–including call traces, opcode traces, and VM traces—into a unified, structured format. This step involves operand extraction, depth annotation, gas cost tagging, and hierarchical call flattening, culminating in a linearized and semantically enriched sequence representation.

Trace Tokenization. We construct a custom tokenizer tailored for Ethereum semantics, incorporating dedicated vocabularies for opcodes, addresses, function signatures, numerical operands, and gas values. To enhance generalization and reduce sparsity, all numerical and gas-related tokens are quantized using multi-level bucketing strategies.

Trace Embedding. Tokenized traces are mapped into integer sequences and padded or split using a sliding window to conform to fixed-length input constraints. Additional structures, such as attention masks and sequence boundary markers, are added to support masked modeling and classification tasks.

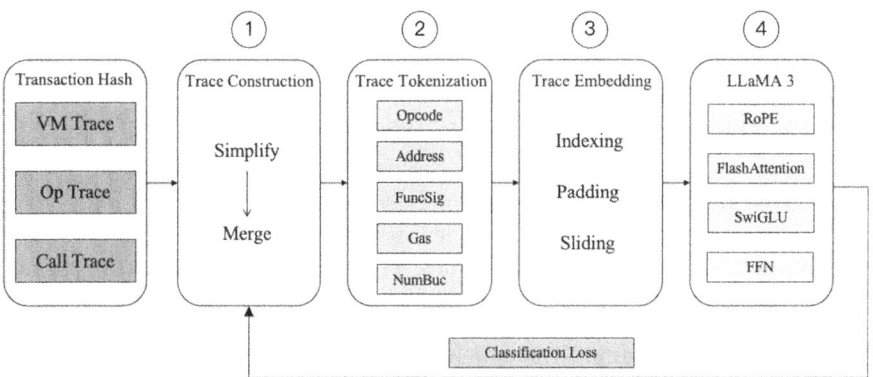

Fig. 2. System pipeline for malicious transaction detection. Starting from trace construction (①), we simplify and merge multiple trace types, tokenize the structured sequence (②), embed the result into a fixed-length vector input (③), and feed it into a fine-tuned LLaMA 3 model (④) for classification. A loop with supervised loss propagates gradients to guide learning.

Model Fine-Tuning. We employ LLaMA 3, a decoder-only Transformer architecture, as the core detection engine. The model is fine-tuned on labeled Ethereum traces using a supervised classification objective. Its architectural features—including FlashAttention v2, SwiGLU activation, and rotary positional embeddings—enable efficient handling of long-range dependencies in execution sequences. To further improve adaptability, our design supports low-rank adaptation (LoRA) modules and gas-aware token fusion.

3.3 Technique Details

Due to space limitations, we have left the complete technical details in the appendix. Here, we introduce only a few key technologies.

Trace Construction. For each collected transaction (both normal and malicious), we retrieved three distinct execution-level traces from the blockchain: Call trace, op trace, and VM trace.

- **CallTrace**: captures high-level statistical metadata for each transaction, such as the addresses of senders and recipients, transferred amounts, and smart contract calls. Each call trace entry documents an interaction, including the call type, input and output data, and any nested internal calls.
- **OpTrace**: captures the precise opcode execution sequence. It includes opcode types, gas details, and stack contents at each execution step.
- **VMTrace**: provides an operational view of opcode-level execution within the EVM. It records the state changes during execution, particularly memory operations, stack manipulations, and interactions with persistent storage.

These traces are cleaned, simplified, and hierarchically merged to produce a unified representation. The resulting trace is formatted as a linearized sequence of opcodes and arguments, suitable for downstream language modeling. Details, examples, and formatting rules refer to Appendix A.

Trace Tokenization. To support effective modeling, we construct a structured vocabulary encompassing opcodes, Ethereum addresses, function signatures, numerical operands, and gas values. These tokens are designed to preserve EVM semantics while reducing redundancy and improving interpretability.

- **Address Vocabulary:** Ethereum addresses are normalized to a fixed 20-byte hexadecimal format by padding truncated values and validating operand patterns. We extract candidate addresses from both call trace fields and opcode operands. The final address vocabulary contains 12,980 unique entries.
- **Function Signature Vocabulary:** Function selectors are derived from the first 8 hexadecimal characters of the calldata `input` field. To standardize them, we trim excessive leading zeros and pad short selectors when necessary. A total of 8,437 unique function signatures are included in the vocabulary.
- **Numerical Value Bucketing:** Operands not identified as addresses or signatures are treated as numerical values. These are converted from hexadecimal to normalized decimal, then discretized into a two-level scheme of buckets and blocks. The number of buckets serves as an adjustable hyperparameter. Empirically, 90 buckets and 100 blocks yield good performance.
- **Gas Value Bucketing:** Opcode-level gas costs are log-transformed and bucketed to capture computational characteristics. We tune the bucket resolution using entropy-based selection and represent each gas value with a symbolic token (e.g., `[GAS_x]`). Each gas value g is mapped to a discrete bucket index b using the following transformation:

$$b = \min\left(\lfloor \log(g+1) \cdot c \rfloor, b_{\max}\right) \quad (2)$$

where c is a scaling constant that controls bucket resolution, and $b_{\max}$ denotes the maximum allowable bucket index to prevent outlier explosion. To select an appropriate logarithmic base for bucketing, we empirically evaluate the entropy of bucket distributions under different bases. The base yielding the highest entropy is chosen to be the representation of gas costs.

The vocabulary consists of special tokens (10), EVM opcodes (149), function signatures (8,437), addresses (12,980), numerical buckets (90), blocks (100), and gas values (300). Compared to general-purpose tokenizers (e.g., BPE), our custom tokenizer can leverage domain knowledge to preserve EVM semantics, reduce vocabulary size and sequence length by avoiding sub-token fragmentation, and enable interpretable token-to-behavior mapping, beneficial for analysis.

Trace Embedding. To align with the domain-specific vocabulary described above, we map each token in the trace into a structured integer sequence. The tokenizer is implemented as a deterministic mapping function tokenizer : $\mathcal{V} \to \mathbb{Z}^+$, where $\mathcal{V}$ denotes the constructed vocabulary and each token is assigned a unique integer ID. The tokenization process consists of three primary stages:

- **Vocabulary Indexing:** All elements in the final vocabulary are indexed sequentially. Special tokens are assigned reserved positions (e.g., PAD = 0, UNK = 1), followed by opcodes, function selectors, addresses, numeric bucket-block combinations, and gas numbers.
- **Trace Parsing:** The tokenizer identifies instruction types.
- **Token Mapping:** Tokens are mapped to their corresponding indices. If a token is not found in $\mathcal{V}$, it is assigned to the UNK token.

All tokenized traces are processed to a fixed sequence length. Short traces are right-padded with the PAD token, while long traces are truncated or split using a sliding window strategy. Special tokens such as [START], [CONTINUE], and [END] are also added to indicate sequence boundaries during pretraining.

Model Fine-Tuning. In this work, we adopt LLAMA 3 [10], an open-source large language model released by Meta AI, as the backbone for malicious transaction detection. LLAMA 3 supports input sequences up to 4096 tokens, making it well-suited for long and complex transaction traces observed in Ethereum.

Given the variable length of traces, we implement a sliding window chunk-level mechanism to divide each trace into overlapping segments of fixed size. For long transactions, the window slides with a stride to preserve contextual continuity. We also conduct zero-shot experiments without fine-tuning, as detailed in Appendix B.

We fine-tune LLAMA 3 using supervised learning on labeled transactions from our curated dataset. The model is trained to minimize cross-entropy loss over the prediction probability $P(\text{abnormal}|t)$ for each input trace t:

$$\mathcal{L} = -y \cdot \log P(\text{abnormal}|t) - (1-y) \cdot \log(1 - P(\text{abnormal}|t))$$

where $y \in \{0, 1\}$ is the ground-truth label. The objective of fine-tuning is to adjust the pre-trained model weights so that the attention layers and embedding mechanisms specialize in recognizing malicious patterns in transaction traces.

4 Experimental Setup

4.1 Dataset

To evaluate our proposed detection framework, we construct a labeled dataset, including both normal and malicious Ethereum transactions. We collect all transactions by running a full Ethereum node locally, which allows direct access to raw data, including transaction traces and execution metadata.

We deploy the local node on a high-performance workstation equipped with a 12th Gen Intel(R) Core i9-12900KF processor (24 cores), an NVIDIA RTX

4080 SUPER GPU with 16 GB of memory, 64 GB of DDR4 RAM, and an 8 TB NVMe SSD. The system runs on Ubuntu 20.04.06 LTS.

Our dataset contains 240 malicious and around 3,000 normal transactions sampled across one year. The data is split using a random seed into 70% training, 10% validation, and 20% testing. We train our model on the labeled dataset.

Normal Transactions. To ensure the diversity of transaction behaviors, we sample normal transactions from user interactions with a set of widely used Ethereum-based decentralized finance (DeFi) applications. These applications include token exchanges, lending protocols, liquidity pools, and other financial primitives deployed across the Ethereum mainnet.

The sampling process spans over one year and follows a weekly strategy:

- For each week, we randomly select two Ethereum block numbers.
- For each selected block, all contained transaction hashes are retrieved.
- Using these hashes, we extract full transaction details and trace data directly from the local full node.

After initial collection, we perform manual curation to remove failed transactions or transactions unrelated to target DeFi applications. This cleaning step ensures the representativeness and relevance of normal samples while minimizing noise from spam or protocol-internal system calls. The resulting normal dataset comprises thousands of diverse and valid transaction records.

Malicious Transactions. We collect malicious transactions from public repositories such as DeFiHackLabs, De.Fi, and Slowmist, which document well-known attacks on Ethereum DeFi protocols. Specifically, we extract 240 confirmed malicious transaction hashes that correspond to real-world exploits, including reentrancy attacks, flash loan-based arbitrage, price manipulation, and oracle abuse.

Trace Extraction For each malicious or normal transaction, we obtain three types of execution traces from the local Ethereum node:

- `Call Trace`: records the high-level contract invocation sequence;
- `Op Trace`: captures opcode-level EVM execution data and gas usage;
- `VM Trace`: contains detailed stack and memory operations during runtime.

All collected traces are processed according to the methodology described in Sect. 3.3, including trace simplification, trace merging, and trace tokenization. Appendix A will introduce the trace extraction demo.

4.2 Baselines

To comprehensively evaluate the effectiveness of our proposed LLaMA-based transaction malicious detection model, we compare it with two representative baselines from large language model (LLM)-based approaches.

BlockFound [20]: BlockFound utilizes masked language modeling (MLM) to identify patterns in normal transactions. It is based on the BERT architecture (300M parameters, hidden size 768, 12 layers, 12 attention heads), and trained using MLM over normal transactions. During inference, each transaction is partially masked, and the reconstruction error is computed as a malicious score. BlockFound benefits from bidirectional attention, allowing it to capture both past and future contextual information. However, it does not incorporate execution-level information, such as opcodes or call traces, limiting its capability in detecting subtle behavior-based malicious activity.

BlockGPT [9]: BlockGPT adopts a GPT-style causal transformer trained to predict the next token in a transaction trace. The underlying assumption is that malicious transactions deviate from the learned distribution of normal patterns. For each transaction, it computes the sum of conditional likelihoods of all tokens, treating a lower total likelihood as a higher malicious potential. Unlike BlockFound, BlockGPT only attends to previous tokens and does not consider future context. Moreover, it processes traces derived from persistent storage read/write operations only, without fine-grained opcode or call data, which could overlook necessary attack signatures. As no official code is available, we contacted the authors and implemented BlockGPT under their guidance.

4.3 Fine-Tuning Model

We adopt the publicly released Meta-Llama-3.2-1B model [10] as the backbone for our malicious detection task. Compared to larger-scale LLMs, the 1 billion parameter variant offers a more efficient trade-off between inference cost and representation power. It supports a maximum context length of 4096 tokens, making it well-suited for modeling long transaction traces.

To ensure memory efficiency, we avoid loading the entire in-memory dataset. Instead, each transaction is sliced using a sliding window of 2048 tokens and a stride of 1024 tokens. Each chunk is framed by [START] and [END] tokens.

We utilize the Huggingface Trainer API for supervised fine-tuning of the model. The tokenizer is initialized from a custom vocabulary, and model parameters are loaded from the Meta-provided pre-trained checkpoint.

To reduce the memory footprint and accelerate training, we adopt Low-Rank Adaptation (LoRA) [11] for parameter-efficient fine-tuning. We inject trainable, rank-decomposed matrices into attention and projection layers while keeping the original model weights frozen. In our configuration, we set the LoRA rank to 8 and the scaling factor `lora_alpha` to 16. This lightweight adaptation mechanism significantly reduces the number of trainable parameters, enabling efficient fine-tuning even on consumer-grade GPUs without sacrificing detection performance.

5 Evaluation and Discussion

5.1 Quantitative Evaluation

Performance Comparison Across Different Models. To assess the effectiveness of our proposed modeling approach, we compare its performance with four representative baselines in the blockchain malicious transaction detection:

- **BlockGPT** [9]: A GPT-style autoregressive transformer that takes persistent storage access traces as input and outputs a score of token-level log-likelihood. Malicious transactions are identified by lower sequence likelihood.
- **BlockFound** [20]: A BERT-based masked language model trained on normal transactions. During inference, it measures reconstruction error of masked tokens in opcode-level sequences to assign malicious scores.
- **GMM + Doc2Vec** [13]: A classical machine learning method where transactions are embedded using Doc2Vec to produce fixed-length vector representations, and a Gaussian Mixture Model (GMM) estimates the likelihood of each sample belonging to the distribution of normal transactions.
- **Rule-based (length)** [16]: A simple heuristic method that classifies transactions based on the total length of their sequences, under the assumption that malicious transactions tend to be longer.
- **BLOCKLENS**: A supervised classification model based on LLAMA3 interleaves opcodes into a unified input sequence. The model outputs both a continuous probability score representing the likelihood of malicious behavior and a binary prediction indicating whether the transaction is malicious or normal.

And all models are evaluated on the same test set using a *ranking-based* approach. Each transaction receives a predicted malicious score, and transactions are sorted in descending order of score. We then compute evaluation metrics based on the top-k% most suspicious transactions, which simulates real-world alert systems where only the highest-risk samples are reviewed manually.

Table 1 and 2 present the False Positive Rate (FPR), Precision, Recall, and F1-score at various detection thresholds (Top-5%, 10%, 15%, and 20%).

Table 1. Performance comparison at Top-5% and Top-10% thresholds.

Model	Top 5%				Top 10%			
	FPR	Precision	Recall	F1	FPR	Precision	Recall	F1
BLOCKGPT	1.43%	73.33%	45.83%	56.41%	4.46%	58.33%	72.92%	64.81%
BLOCKFOUND	1.07%	80.00%	50.00%	61.54%	4.29%	60.00%	75.00%	66.67%
GMM + Doc2Vec	2.14%	60.00%	37.50%	46.15%	6.79%	36.67%	45.83%	40.70%
Rule-based (length)	1.61%	70.00%	43.75%	53.65%	6.07%	43.33%	54.17%	48.11%
Our BLOCKLENS	0.89%	83.33%	52.08%	63.93%	3.75%	65.00%	81.25%	72.28%

Table 2. Performance comparison at Top-15% and Top-20% thresholds.

Model	Top 15%				Top 20%			
	FPR	Precision	Recall	F1	FPR	Precision	Recall	F1
BlockGPT	9.82%	39.56%	75.00%	51.80%	17.35%	32.23%	82.12%	33.46%
BlockFound	9.46%	41.76%	79.17%	54.68%	14.29%	33.88%	85.42%	48.52%
GMM + Doc2Vec	11.25%	30.77%	58.33%	40.33%	15.71%	27.27%	68.75%	39.00%
Rule-based (length)	10.54%	35.16%	66.67%	46.25%	15.18%	29.75%	75%	42.46%
Our BlockLens	8.92%	45.05%	85.42%	58.92%	13.75%	36.36%	91.67%	52.00%

Across all thresholds, our BlockLens consistently demonstrates strong recall performance, which is essential in security applications where missing malicious cases can be far more costly than raising a few false alarms.

At the Top-5% threshold, BlockLens achieves a recall of **52.08%**, surpassing both BlockGPT (45.83%) and BlockFound (50.00%), while maintaining a substantial precision of 83.33%.

At the Top-10% threshold, recall of BlockLens improves to **81.25%**, outperforming BlockGPT (72.92%) and BlockFound (75.00%).

At the Top-15% threshold, BlockLens reaches a recall of **85.42%**, exceeding BlockGPT (75.00%) and BlockFound (79.17%). While precision drops to 45.05%, the F1 score remains competitive, indicating a well-balanced trade-off.

At the Top-20% threshold, BlockLens attains the highest recall of **91.67%**, outperforming both BlockGPT (82.12%) and BlockFound (85.42%). This performance demonstrates the model's robustness in identifying nearly all malicious transactions when a broader detection margin is acceptable.

We further examine how varying the score threshold affects detection performance. As shown in Table 3, lower thresholds (10âĂŞ20) yield perfect recall (100.00%) but suffer from extremely high false positive rates (up to 92.68%). In contrast, higher thresholds (80-90) lead to excellent precision (up to 100.00%) but miss a large portion of malicious samples, with recall dropping below 40%.

At intermediate thresholds (50-70), the model achieves a more favorable trade-off. For instance, at threshold 70, we observe a recall of 81.25% and a precision of 57.35%, resulting in the highest F1-score (67.14%). This setting strikes a balance between false alarms and detection effectiveness, making it suitable for real-world deployment.

To further illustrate the trade-off between precision and recall under varying malicious score thresholds, we plot a precisionâĂŞrecall (PR) curve using empirical data points from our threshold tuning experiments. As shown in Fig. 3, each black point corresponds to a specific threshold setting, while the blue curve represents a polynomial regression fit that models the precisionâĂŞrecall relationship.

This curve demonstrates the inverse relationship between recall and precision—higher recall rates often come at the cost of reduced precision. The regression fit provides a smooth estimate of this trend, enabling more effective threshold selection strategies and improved interpretability in real-world deployments.

Table 3. Performance at different malicious score thresholds.

Thres	FPR	Precision	Recall	F1-score
10	92.68%	8.46%	100.00%	15.61%
20	86.78%	8.99%	100.00%	16.50%
30	58.39%	12.57%	97.92%	22.33%
40	40.18%	16.97%	95.83%	28.92%
50	27.32%	22.34%	91.67%	35.99%
60	11.07%	40.38%	87.50%	55.33%
70	5.18%	57.35%	81.25%	67.14%
80	0.53%	85.71%	37.50%	52.00%
90	0.00%	100.00%	16.67%	28.57%

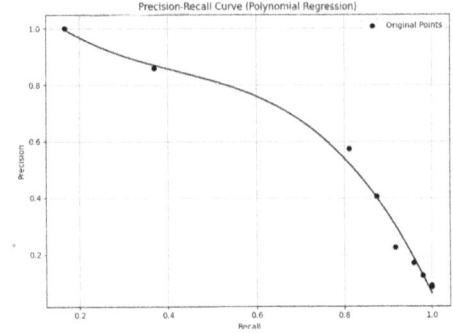

Fig. 3. Precision-Recall curve fitted over threshold-tuned data points.

5.2 Qualitative Evaluation

Case Studies of Correctly and Incorrectly Classified Transactions. To better understand the model's decision-making process and evaluate its strengths and limitations, we present several case studies. These examples cover both successful and failed predictions.

Correctly Classified Malicious Transaction. One case involves a transaction exploiting a DELEGATECALL vulnerability. The opcode trace includes a sequence of CALLER, SLOAD, DELEGATECALL, and JUMPI instructions, with unusually high gas usage clustered around memory manipulation. Our model correctly identified this segment with a high score (>95), emphasizing the contribution of both control-flow patterns and gas cost peaks.

Correctly Classified normal Transaction. Another example is a common ERC-20 token transfer, which utilizes standard opcodes such as CALLVALUE, TRANSFER, and RETURN, resulting in low and steady gas consumption. The model assigned a low score (<5), correctly identifying it as normal.

False Positive: Normal Transaction Misclassified as Malicious. In some cases, complex but legitimate smart contract patterns—such as multi-signature wallet operations or DeFi position adjustments—are mistakenly flagged as high-risk. For instance, a transaction with nested SWAP and DUP instructions, along with multiple storage writes, appeared structurally similar to attack patterns. Despite being legitimate, it received a high score, showing the model's over-sensitivity to intricate opcode compositions.

False Negative: Malicious Transaction Missed. A particularly challenging false negative case involved a long transaction with over 2000 chunks. While a few chunks exhibited high scores (>90) with suspicious use of some opcodes, the remaining chunks were normal. When aggregated using mean-based scoring, the overall transaction score fell below the detection threshold.

5.3 Ablation Study in Impact of Opcode and Gas

Unlike prior works that often rely solely on high-level transaction metadata or simplified traces, BLOCKLENS directly operates on execution sequences composed of low-level opcode tokens and aligned gas cost.

To evaluate the contribution of each component, we perform an ablation study by selectively removing gas or specific opcodes from the input sequence. Results are shown in Table 4.

Table 4. Ablation study: effect of gas embedding and opcode removal on detection performance.

Model Variant	Top-10%			Top-15%		
	FPR	Precision	Recall	FPR	Precision	Recall
BLOCKLENS	3.75%	65.00%	81.25%	8.92%	45.05%	85.42%
w/o Gas	4.29%	60.00%	75.00%	9.11%	43.96%	83.33%
w/o POP	3.93%	48.33%	60.42%	10.36%	36.26%	68.75%
w/o JUMP	6.61%	38.33%	47.92%	11.07%	31.89%	60.42%

We observe that removing key opcodes such as POP or JUMP results in a substantial drop in both precision and recall. In particular, removing JUMP severely impairs detection at Top-10%, highlighting the critical role of opcode semantics.

Moreover, removing gas embedding leads to consistent performance degradation, particularly in terms of precision. This confirms that gas usage patterns provide meaningful signals for distinguishing malicious behaviors.

Model Interpretability. To enhance interpretability and support actionable security analysis, we integrate a local outlier detection strategy into our framework. We exploit the natural alignment between sliding-window chunk-level and token-level granularity in LLMs. Each transaction is divided into multiple overlapping segments (*chunks*) via a sliding window, and each chunk is independently passed through the model to produce a local malicious score.

These local scores can be aggregated using simple strategies such as *max*, *mean*, or *voting* to produce a final transaction-level decision. They also offer a natural mechanism for explainability: individual high-risk chunks highlight specific regions of the trace that contribute most to the malicious prediction.

This approach is efficient for detecting localized attacks, such as flash loan exploits or price manipulation, where the malicious behavior is confined to a short segment within a long and otherwise normal transaction. In these weak-signal scenarios, global averaging may dilute malicious signals, whereas chunk-level prediction preserves sensitivity to local patterns.

Moreover, from an engineering standpoint, this chunk decomposition provides direct answers to a common practical question in blockchain security: *"Why is this transaction considered malicious?"* By inspecting which chunks receive high malicious scores, e.g., token ranges [0, 2048], [8192, 10240], security analysts can pinpoint specific operations (such as a suspicious CALL or SSTORE) that contributed to the model's decision.

This localized interpretability enhances model transparency and supports downstream tasks such as automatic alert prioritization, rule extraction, or transaction-level mitigation strategies.

5.4 Ablation Study in Effectiveness of Fine-Tuning

To evaluate the necessity of task-specific fine-tuning, we compare our model with some LLM baselines under zero-shot inference. We want to answer a question: *Can a sufficiently large, general-purpose LLM detect malicious transactions without any fine-tuning?* We conduct experiments using the following models:

- **LLaMA 3.2-1B (base)**: a non-instruction-tuned model. We use structured prompts to guide the model to produce meaningful anomaly scores.
- **LLaMA 3.1-8B-Instruct**: an instruction-tuned version of LLaMA 3 that supports chat-style interactions and better prompt following.
- **GPT-4o (OpenAI)**: a state-of-the-art LLM accessed via API for evaluating practical zero-shot inference with strong general reasoning capabilities.

Since most transaction traces are too long to fit into a single model input, we adopt a sliding window strategy to segment each trace into chunks. Each chunk is independently scored, and results are aggregated using max, mean, or majority voting. Each prompt follows this format:

> **Prompt and Example**
>
> You are an expert blockchain security analyst tasked with evaluating a blockchain transaction for potential anomalous or malicious behavior.
> The following input is a transaction execution trace, including opcodes, operands, gas usage, addresses, and function signatures. Analyze the opcode sequence and execution trace provided. Identify if the opcode pattern matches known vulnerability or attack signatures (e.g., Reentrancy, Delegatecall exploits, Infinite loops, or unusual control flows).
> Below is chunk {chunk_id} of a transaction. Provide your assessment logically. Assign an anomaly score ranging from 0 to 100, where:0 means completely normal, 100 means highly malicious. Clearly articulate the reasoning behind your assessment, structured logically.
> Format your answer like this:
> "Score: <number>"A numerical anomaly score between 0 and 100.
> "Reason: <short explanation>step-by-step explaining the analysis."
> In addition, we provide few-shot examples such as:
> Code: CALLCODE DELEGATECALL SLOAD......
> Score: 70. Reason: Use of delegatecall with external input suggests reentrancy risk.

We also tested instruction-following models, including LLaMA 3.1-8B-Instruct and GPT-4o, by prompting them via a chat-style interface. Despite their advanced reasoning capabilities, both models exhibited similar over-sensitivity, frequently misjudging normal segments. Nearly all sequences received high scores (70â Ş90) with explanations referencing generic features like JUMP, SWAP/DUP usage, or memory manipulation, even in completely normal transactions.

Zero-shot performance exhibited two major weaknesses. First, the models lacked domain knowledge. Despite detailed prompts and examples, they had not been trained on transaction data and were unable to distinguish between normal and malicious behaviors. Second, the models showed a tendency to overgeneralize, often misclassifying long transactions as malicious based on surface-level features, while missing deeper semantic cues. Due to the absence of instruction tuning, they frequently failed to follow the format.

5.5 Scalability and Deployment Considerations

Real-Time Feasibility of LLAMA-Based Fraud Detection. To assess the practicality of deploying our model in real-world blockchain monitoring systems, we evaluate the end-to-end latency of our detection pipeline.

Upon receiving a transaction hash, the system immediately queries an EVM simulation backend to retrieve execution traces (op trace, VM trace, call trace). Our preprocessing pipeline, including trace simplification, tokenization, and chunking, is efficient and completes within milliseconds per transaction.

We benchmark our LLAMA-based detector on a single NVIDIA RTX 4080 SUPER GPU (16 GB memory). The prediction time for a single 2048-token chunk is approximately **0.27 s**, including embedding lookup, attention computation, classification, and decompilation for high-risk samples.

Given that most transactions can be processed in 1-4 chunks, we achieve near-real-time throughput, making it feasible to integrate into on-chain monitoring pipelines for high-frequency, high-stakes scenarios such as DeFi protocols.

Memory and Latency Constraints for Transaction Monitoring. To evaluate the feasibility of deploying models for real-time Ethereum transaction monitoring, we conduct a series of system-level measurements, including inference latency and GPU memory usage under varying input and batch sizes. The experiments are conducted on a single NVIDIA RTX 4080 SUPER (16 GB) card.

Table 5. Latency(sec) and Memory Usage(MB) under Different Chunk Lengths

Chunk Length	Latency	Memory Usage
512	0.0168	4017.35
1024	0.0289	4300.61
1536	0.0416	4714.87
2048	0.0564	5259.13
4096	0.1177	8635.18

Latency vs. Chunk Length. The inference latency increases approximately linearly with the input token length, as shown in Table 5. This is expected due to the quadratic complexity of attention operations in Transformer models.

Memory Usage vs. Chunk Length. Table 5 illustrates how GPU memory usage grows with input length. For large-scale monitoring, selecting appropriate chunk lengths is crucial to prevent Out-of-Memory (OOM) errors.

6 Conclusion

In this paper, we present BLOCKLENS, a novel LLM-based framework for detecting malicious transactions on the Ethereum blockchain. Our method introduces a new tokenization strategy that integrates opcode semantics and execution costs into a unified flattened modeling input. By fine-tuning a decoder-only LLaMA 3.2-1B model with Low-Rank Adaptation (LoRA), we enable efficient classification over long and complex transaction traces. Through evaluation against established baselines, our approach demonstrates strong recall and precision.

Furthermore, the chunk-level prediction architecture not only improves detection granularity but also enhances interpretability, allowing security analysts to localize and inspect specific segments contributing to malicious scores. Our results underscore the value of opcode-level modeling and domain-specific token engineering in transaction-level malicious detection.

Acknowledgment. We thank the contributors of open-source Ethereum datasets that supported our data collection and preprocessing. We also acknowledge the maintainers of the Meta LLaMA model [17] and the Huggingface ecosystem for enabling efficient model fine-tuning. We further appreciate the availability of the BLOCKFOUND [20] open-source codebase, which greatly supported our development.

Appendix A: Trace Extraction Demo

Trace Cleaning

There are three execution-level traces from the blockchain: Call trace, op trace, and VM trace.

```
"Call Trace":[
{"from":"0x838b...8270","gas":"0x1835a","gasUsed":"0x2591","to":"0xcf2a...10f2","input":"0
    x69d48074","output":"0x0000...a6972cde3b","type":"STATICCALL"}, ...]

"Op Trace":[
        {"pc":0,"op":"PUSH1","gas":35577,"gasCost":3,"depth":1,"stack":[]}, ...]

"VM Trace":[
     {"cost":3,"ex":{"mem":null,"push":["0x80"],"store":null,"used":116472},"pc":0,"sub
    ":{},"op":"PUSH1","idx":"327-0"}, ...]
```

Trace Simplification

Op Trace Simplification. We begin by sorting all op trace entries by their program counter values to ensure temporal consistency. Operand extraction is guided by opcode semantics: POP retrieves the top stack value (i.e., the last element), JUMPI captures two parameters—counter and condition—from the top two elements, and JUMP uses only the top element as the counter. Arithmetic and logical operations such as ADD, MUL, SUB, DIV, MOD, EXP, AND, EQ, LT, and GT consume the top two stack elements, while three-operand instructions like ADDMOD and MULMOD use the top three. Single-operand opcodes, including NOT, ISZERO, CALLDATALOAD, SLOAD, and TLOAD, retain only the top element. For all other opcodes, operand extraction is deferred to the trace merging phase. Additionally, we annotate each opcode with its corresponding execution gas cost (gasCost), as gas patterns are useful, such as a malicious trace may contain unusually expensive instructions like a high-cost CALL, or repetitive low-cost operations such as SLOAD.

```
{"pc": 882, "op": "GAS", "depth": 1, "gasCost": 2}
{"pc": 883, "op": "CALL", "depth": 1, "gasCost": 5180926}
{"pc": 0, "op": "PUSH1", "depth": 2, "gasCost": 3}
{"pc": 2, "op": "PUSH1", "depth": 2, "gasCost": 3}
```

Virtual Machine Trace Simplification. Each trace entry is simplified to contain pc, op, stack manipulation (push) and persistent storage interactions (store).

To represent hierarchical contract calls, we annotate each opcode with a call depth, initialized to 1. The depth is incremented whenever encountering opcodes indicating nested calls (CALL, STATICCALL, DELEGATECALL, CREATE, or CREATE2). Within each nested call structure (sub), the depth increments accordingly, clearly preserving the hierarchical execution context. Once a nested call concludes, depth returns to the previous level. The final simplified format is:

```
{"ex":{"mem":[],"push":["0x504f39"],"store":[]},"pc":882,"sub":[],"op":"GAS","depth":1}
{"ex":{"mem":[],"push":["0x1"],"store":[]},"pc":883,"sub":[],"op":"CALL","depth":1}
{"ex":{"mem":[],"push":["0x80"],"store":[]},"pc":0,"sub":[],"op":"PUSH1","depth":2}
{"ex":{"mem":[],"push":["0x40"],"store":[]},"pc":2,"sub":[],"op":"PUSH1","depth":2}
```

Call Trace Simplification. We simplify it by flattening nested call structures into a sequential list. Each nested call is annotated with an execution depth, which is initialized to 1. For each level of nested calls, the depth increments by 1.

```
{"from": "0x81..", "to": "0x97..", "input": "0x63..", "type": "CALL", "depth": 0}
{"from": "0x97..", "to": "0xc1..", "input": "0x42..", "type": "CALL", "depth": 1}
{"from": "0xc1..", "to": "0x66..","input": "0x47..", "type": "DELEGATECALL", "depth": 2}
```

Trace Merging

Merge Op Trace and VM Trace. The merging process follows several heuristic rules to enrich opcode semantics with runtime information. For PUSH and DUP, we extract operand values from the VM trace's push field and record them as value. For arithmetic and logical operations such as ADD, EQ, and LT, only the computation result from the push field is retained as result. In the case of SWAP, we record the first and last stack elements from the VM trace push as value1 and value2 respectively. For CALLDATALOAD, both the offset (from the op trace) and the corresponding data value (data[i]) are stored. Opcodes that access blockchain state, such as CALLER, BALANCE, or GAS, have their associated address or numeric values extracted from the `push` field. Memory operations like `MSTORE` and `MLOAD` include values and memory offsets retrieved from `mem.data` and `mem.off`, with long hexadecimal strings simplified when possible. For storage operations such as `SSTORE` and `TSTORE`, both the `key` and `value` fields from the `store` field are preserved. All other opcodes are left in their original form without further augmentation. The result is as follows:

```
{"pc": 882, "op": "GAS", "depth": 1, "value": "0x504f39"}
{"pc": 883, "op": "CALL", "depth": 1}
{"pc": 0, "op": "PUSH1", "depth": 2, "value": "0x80"}
{"pc": 2, "op": "PUSH1", "depth": 2, "value": "0x40"}
```

Merge with Call Trace. To integrate high-level contract call semantics, we further align the merged_trace_1 with the flattened call trace to be the merged_trace_2. Each call-related opcode (`CALL`, `STATICCALL`, etc.) is matched sequentially with entries in call trace based on both opcode type and depth.

Format into Final Trace. To prepare the final trace format for model input, we remove structural metadata such as `pc` and `depth`. Field names are stripped, leaving only raw opcodes and operands arranged sequentially as plain text. For JUMPDEST instructions, we retain the original `pc` value as a label, e.g., JUMPDEST 0x38, to preserve jump targets. In arithmetic and logical operations, only the computation `result` is kept to reduce redundancy. For external calls, the `input` field is truncated to its first 10 bytes, corresponding to the function selector. In contrast, for contract creation instructions like `CREATE` and `CREATE2`, the `input` field is discarded entirely.

And the final trace ready for subsequent processing is presented below:

```
"transaction_id": "12345",
"input": "START FROM 0x81.. TO 0x97.. INs 0x63.. VALUE 0x0 OPTRACESTART .. POP 0x0 GAS 0
    x504f39 CALL 0x97.. 0xc1.. 0x42.. 0x0 PUSH1 0x80 PUSH1 0x40 MSTORE 0x80 64 .. END",
"label": "1"
```

References

1. Aldaham, T., Hamdi, H.: Enhancing digital financial security with LSTM and blockchain technology. Int. J. Adv. Comput. Sci. Appl. **15**(8) (2024)
2. Atzei, N., Bartoletti, M., Cimoli, T.: A survey of attacks on ethereum smart contracts (sok). In: International Conference on Principles of Security and Trust, pp. 164–186. Springer (2017)
3. Brown, T., Mann, B., Ryder, N.: Language models are few-shot learners. In: Larochelle, H., Ranzato, M., Hadsell, R., Balcan, M., Lin, H. (eds.) Advances in Neural Information Processing Systems. vol. 33, pp. 1877–1901. Curran Associates, Inc. (2020). https://proceedings.neurips.cc/paper_files/paper/2020/file/1457c0d6bfcb4967418bfb8ac142f64a-Paper.pdf
4. Buterin, V.: Ethereum white paper: a next generation smart contract & decentralized application platform (2013). https://github.com/ethereum/wiki/wiki/White-Paper
5. Chowdhery, A., Narang, S., Devlin, J.: J. Mach. Learn. Res. **24**(1) (2023)

6. Daian, P., Goldfeder, S., Kell, T., Li, Y., Zhao, X., Bentov, I., Breidenbach, L., Juels, A.: Flash boys 2.0: frontrunning, transaction reordering, and consensus instability in decentralized exchanges. arXiv preprint arXiv:1904.05234 (2019)
7. Devlin, J., Chang, M.W., Lee, K., Toutanova, K.: BERT: pre-training of deep bidirectional transformers for language understanding. In: Burstein, J., Doran, C., Solorio, T. (eds.) Proceedings of the 2019 Conference of the North American Chapter of the Association for Computational Linguistics: Human Language Technologies, Volume 1 (Long and Short Papers), pp. 4171–4186. Association for Computational Linguistics, Minneapolis, Minnesota (2019). https://doi.org/10.18653/v1/N19-1423
8. Ding, Y., Steenhoek, B., Pei, K., Kaiser, G., Le, W., Ray, B.: Traced: execution-aware pre-training for source code. In: Proceedings of the IEEE/ACM 46th International Conference on Software Engineering. ICSE '24, Association for Computing Machinery, New York, NY, USA (2024). https://doi.org/10.1145/3597503.3608140
9. Gai, Y., Zhou, L., Qin, K.: Blockchain large language models (2023). https://arxiv.org/abs/2304.12749
10. Grattafiori, A., Dubey, A., Jauhri, A.: The llama 3 herd of models (2024). https://arxiv.org/abs/2407.21783
11. Hu, E.J., Shen, Y.: Lora: low-rank adaptation of large language models (2021)
12. Ince, P., Luo, X., Yu, J., Liu, J.K., Du, X.: Detect llama - finding vulnerabilities in smart contracts using large language models. In: Information Security and Privacy: 29th Australasian Conference, ACISP 2024, Sydney, NSW, Australia, July 15–17, 2024, Proceedings, Part III, pp. 424–443. Springer-Verlag, Berlin, Heidelberg (2024). https://doi.org/10.1007/978-981-97-5101-3_23
13. Le, Q., Mikolov, T.: Distributed representations of sentences and documents. In: Proceedings of the 31st International Conference on International Conference on Machine Learning, vol. 32, pp. II–1188–II–1196. ICML'14, JMLR.org (2014)
14. Lu, S., Guo, D., Ren, S.: Codexglue: a machine learning benchmark dataset for code understanding and generation (2021). https://arxiv.org/abs/2102.04664
15. Mark Chen, J.T., Jun., H.: Evaluating large language models trained on code. ArXiv **abs/2107.03374** (2021). https://api.semanticscholar.org/CorpusID:235755472
16. Risse, N., Böhme, M.: Top score on the wrong exam: on benchmarking in machine learning for vulnerability detection (2024). https://arxiv.org/abs/2408.12986
17. Touvron, H., Lavril, T., Izacard, G.: Llama: Open and efficient foundation language models. CoRR **abs/2302.13971** (2023). http://dblp.uni-trier.de/db/journals/corr/corr2302.html#abs-2302-13971
18. Vaswani, A., Shazeer, N., Parmar, N.: Attention is all you need. In: Guyon, I., Luxburg, U.V., Bengio, S., Wallach, H., Fergus, R., Vishwanathan, S., Garnett, R. (eds.) Advances in Neural Information Processing Systems. vol. 30. Curran Associates, Inc. (2017). https://proceedings.neurips.cc/paper_files/paper/2017/file/3f5ee243547dee91fbd053c1c4a845aa-Paper.pdf
19. Yang, L., Dong, X., Xing, S.: An abnormal transaction detection mechanim on bitcoin. In: 2019 International Conference on Networking and Network Applications (NaNA), pp. 452–457 (2019). https://doi.org/10.1109/NaNA.2019.00083
20. Yu, J., Wu, X., Liu, H.: Blockfound: customized blockchain foundation model for anomaly detection (2024). https://arxiv.org/abs/2410.04039

Author Index

A
Alnahawi, Nouri 107
Alshaher, Shahad 497
AlTawy, Riham 518

B
Bai, Xinyu 474
Barbier, Morgan 323
Belousova, Anastasiia 216

C
Cai, Dongshu 24
Chen, Bingyuan 239
Chen, Chi 258
Chen, Tieming 239
Chen, Yincen 3
Cheng, Haotian 563
Cheng, Jinghui 69
Conti, Mauro 216

D
Deng, Robert H. 131
Dimitriou, Tassos 497
Du, Jiajun 474

E
Eckert, Claudia 388
Eckhoff, Magnus Wiik 411
Eian, Martin 411

F
Fan, Lei 581
Feng, Chi 581
Flydal, Peter Marius 411
Fong, Philip W. L. 539
Fujio, Masakazu 303

G
Grov, Gudmund 411

H
Haidar, Calvin Abou 152
Halvorsen, Jonas 411
Han, Chansu 367
Han, Dongchi 24
Hasan, Raiful 279
Heinemann, Andreas 107, 175
Hemmerlé, Lionel 431
Henrich, Johanna 107
Hiet, Guillaume 431
Huang, Xiaofei 258

I
Islam, Tariqul 279

J
Jeon, Sohyun 152
Jiang, Qingyan 239
Jiang, Zirui 474
Jung, Jinho 452

K
Khan, Shahriar Rahman 279
Kwon, Jihoon 452

L
Le Bars, Jean-Marie 323
Lee, Junho 452
Lee, MyeongYeol 452
Li, Xiaofeng 563
Li, Yinglong 239
Liang, Chen 474
Liang, Siyuan 474
Liu, Gang 347

Liu, Hongbo 24
Liu, Senlin 24
Lu, Xianhui 24
Lv, Yin 3

M
Ma, Hao 196
Ma, Kensei 367
Majbour, Sara 323
Marchiori, Francesco 216
Mavroeidis, Vasileios 411
Mohammadali, Amin 518

N
Naito, Yusuke 45
Nakamura, Wataru 303
Niu, Zixuan 563
Norouzian, Mohammad Reza 388

O
Ouyang, Ciyan 196

P
Peters, Siem 411
Prévotet, Jean-Christophe 431

S
Sasaki, Yu 45
Schmitt, Nicolai 107, 175
Seo, HyunA 452
Shen, Yanbing 347
Song, Ling 3
Song, Wei 196
Sugawara, Takeshi 45
Sun, Hao 347
Suzuki, Yusei 303

T
Takahashi, Kenta 303
Takahashi, Takeshi 367
Takeuchi, Jun'ichi 367
Tanaka, Akira 367
Tang, Guofeng 131
Tibouchi, Mehdi 152
Tronel, Frédéric 431

V
Vombatkere, Nikhill 539

W
Wang, Chengdong 89
Wang, Jiacheng 347
Wang, Yisen 474
Wang, Zhidong 196
Weng, Jian 131
Wilke, Pierre 431
Wu, Pengfei 131

X
Xie, Da 196
Xu, Haitao 347
Xue, Haiyang 131

Y
Yang, Guomin 131
Yang, Lin 89
Yao, Lisha 131
Yu, Bo 89

Z
Zeitschner, Jannik 175
Zeng, Fanping 69
Zhang, Fan 347
Zhang, Zhongxin 3
Zhao, He 563
Zhou, Tong 563
Zhu, Xiaojie 258

Made in the USA
Monee, IL
03 May 2026

49438662R00341